Lecture Notes in Computer Science

Lecture Notes in Bioinformatics 16678

The series Lecture Notes in Bioinformatics (LNBI) was established in 2003 as a topical subseries of LNCS devoted to bioinformatics and computational biology.

The series publishes state-of-the-art research results at a high level. As with the LNCS mother series, the mission of the series is to serve the international R & D community by providing an invaluable service, mainly focused on the publication of conference and workshop proceedings and postproceedings.

Pedro T. Monteiro
Editor

Computational Methods in Systems Biology

24th International Conference, CMSB 2026
Lisbon, Portugal, July 24–25, 2026
Proceedings

Springer

Editor
Pedro T. Monteiro
INESC-ID/IST – University of Lisbon
Lisbon, Portugal

ISSN 0302-9743 ISSN 1611-3349 (electronic)
Lecture Notes in Bioinformatics
ISBN 978-3-032-30869-6 ISBN 978-3-032-30870-2 (eBook)
https://doi.org/10.1007/978-3-032-30870-2

LNCS Sublibrary: SL8 – Bioinformatics

This Springer imprint is published by the registered company Springer Nature Switzerland AG
The registered company address is: Gewerbestrasse 11, 6330 Cham, Switzerland

Preface

This volume contains the regular and tool papers presented at the 24rd International Conference on Computational Methods in Systems Biology (CMSB 2026), held on July 25-25, 2026, in Lisbon, Portugal. The conference website can be found at https://arsr.inesc-id.pt/cmsb2026/.

The CMSB annual conference series was initiated in 2003. The previous editions of the conference were held in Rovereto, Italy (2003), Paris, France (2004, 2011), Edinburgh, UK (2005, 2007), Trento, Italy (2006, 2010), Rostock, Germany (2008), Bologna, Italy (2009), London, UK (2012), Klosterneuburg, Austria (2013), Manchester, UK (2014), Nantes, France (2015), Cambridge, UK (2016), Darmstadt, Germany (2017), Brno, Czech Republic (2018), Trieste, Italy (2019), Konstanz, Germany (2020, online), Bordeaux, France (2021, hybrid), Bucharest, Romania (2022), Luxembourg City, Luxembourg (2023), Pisa, Italy (2024), and Lyon, France (2025). The website for the conference series is at https://cmsb.sciencesconf.org/.

CMSB brings together researchers from across the biological, computational, mathematical, and physical sciences who are interested in the modelling, simulation, analysis, inference, design, and control of biological systems. It covers the broad field of computational methods and tools in systems and synthetic biology and their applications. Topics of interest to the conference include, but are not limited to: formalisms for modelling biological processes; methods and tools for biological system analysis, modelling, and simulation; frameworks for model verification, validation, analysis, and simulation of biological systems; automated parameter and model inference; machine learning and data analytics in biology and biomedicine; data-driven model learning and scientific discovery; high-performance methods for computational systems biology; model integration and biological databases; data-based approaches for systems and synthetic biology; optimality and control of biological systems; design, analysis, and verification methods for synthetic biology; methods for biomolecular computing and engineered molecular devices; multi-scale modelling, multi-agent simulation and analysis methods; and modelling, analysis, and control of microbial communities.

CMSB 2026 received 43 regular and tool paper submissions that were sent for reviews. 14 were accepted at first-round review and 3 were accepted after revision and second review. Each paper was reviewed by three program committee members, 2 in rare cases. From the 17 accepted papers, 2 were shorter tool papers evaluated for the quality of the tool itself and its usability and documentation, in addition to the scientific contribution of the communication. The papers that were not accepted for publication but whose topic was relevant for the conference were invited for poster presentation.

We had two invited talks at CMSB 2026 given by Anna Niarakis (University of Toulouse, France), and Miguel Rocha (University of Minho, Portugal). The abstracts of their talks are included in the front matter of this volume. The regular and tool papers presented at CMSB 2026 follow, organized in four sections: Boolean and qualitative networks, rule-based and stochastic models, causal inference and multi-omics integration, and constraint-based modelling and molecular computation.

The CMSB 2026 conference was co-located with FLoC 2026, benefiting from the large and diverse audience interested in mathematical logic, formal methods, automated reasoning, and their applications. The Federated Logic Conference (FLoC) 2026, https://www.floc26.org/, is organized every four years, uniting the ten leading international conferences focused on mathematical logic, as well as dozens of dedicated workshops.

We would like to first thank all the members of the Program Committee and our reviewers for their thoughtful and diligent work. We also thank the FLoC main organizers for their support with the local organization of all conferences and workshops. Finally, we would like to thank Springer Nature for their sponsoring of the best paper and best student paper awards.

May 2026 Pedro T. Monteiro

Organization

Program Committee Chair

Pedro T. Monteiro	INESC-ID/IST - University of Lisbon, Portugal

Steering Committee

Luca Cardelli	University of Oxford, UK
François Fages	INRIA Saclay, France
Monika Heiner	Brandenburg TU Cottbus-Senftenberg, Germany
Satoru Miyano	University of Tokyo, Japan
Ion Petre	University of Turku, Finland
Gordon Plotkin	University of Edinburgh, UK
Corrado Priami	University of Pisa, Italy
Carolyn Talcott	SRI International, USA
Mirco Tribastone	IMT Lucca, Italy
Adelinde Uhrmacher	University of Rostock, Germany

Plus Guest Members

Eugenio Cinquemani	INRIA Grenoble Rhône-Alpes, France
Roberta Gori	University of Pisa, Italy
Pedro T. Monteiro	INESC-ID/IST - University of Lisbon, Portugal
Joachim Niehren	INRIA Lille, France
Jun Pang	University of Luxembourg, Luxembourg
Loïc Paulevé	CNRS, LaBRI, France
Sabine Pérès	University of Lyon 1, France

Program Committee

Pedro T. Monteiro (Chair)	INESC-ID/IST - University of Lisbon, Portugal
David Doty	University of California, Davis, USA
Dong-Yup Lee	Sungkyunkwan University, South Korea
Andrzej Mizera	University of Warsaw, Poland
Ashutosh Gupta	Indian Institute of Technology Bombay, India
Paolo Milazzo	University of Pisa, Italy

Corrado Priami	University of Pisa, Italy
Jérôme Feret	Inria Paris, France
Adelinde Uhrmacher	University of Rostock, Germany
Anna Niarakis	University of Toulouse, France
François Fages	Inria Saclay, France
Tatsuya Akutsu	University of Kyoto, Japan
Albin Salazar	University of Konstanz, Germany
David Šafránek	Masaryk University, Czechia
Ina Koch	Goethe University Frankfurt, Germany
Sabine Peres	University of Lyon 1, France
Tatjana Petrov	University of Trieste, Italy
Hillel Kugler	Bar-Ilan University, Israel
Max Tschaikowski	Aalborg University, Denmark
Ion Petre	University of Turku, Finland
Linda Brodo	University of Sassari, Italy
Jun Pang	University of Luxembourg, Luxembourg
Joachim Niehren	Inria Lille, France
Monica Heiner	Brandenburg University of Technology Cottbus-Senftenberg, Germany
Loïc Paulevé	CNRS/LaBRI, Bordeaux, France
Verena Wolf	Saarland University, Germany
Eugenio Cinquemani	Inria Grenoble Rhône-Alpes, France

Additional Reviewers

Mina Latifi
Ondrej Kuzlik
Virgile Andreani
Sylvain Soliman
Alexandre Tan-Lhernould
Joschka Gross

Keynote Speakers

Embedding Intracellular Logic into Agent-Based Models of Cellular Systems

Anna Niarakis

Molecular, Cellular and Developmental Biology Unit (MCD), Centre for Integrative Biology (CBI), University of Toulouse, UPS, CNRS, Toulouse, France
anna.niaraki@utoulouse.fr

Abstract. Developing digital twins for complex human diseases requires computational frameworks that bridge molecular regulation, cellular decision-making, and tissue-level dynamics [1]. Agent-based models (ABMs) are well suited to capture spatially resolved immune cell interactions [2], while Boolean networks can offer a mechanistic description of intracellular signalling and cell fate control [3]. Recent advances in logic-based modelling of rheumatoid arthritis have shed light on how qualitative regulatory logic can be applied to study the mechanisms governing phenotypic outputs, such as cell activation, differentiation, apoptosis, and inflammation-driven cytokine production [4–6]. Complementary ABM approaches have also been developed to simulate immune cell dynamics in inflammatory and rheumatoid arthritis [7, 8]. Building on these foundations, we introduce a generic framework for coupling Boolean networks with ABMs. We explicitly define coupling maps, time-scale separation, and scheduling semantics to enable the coherent embedding of intracellular Boolean dynamics within heterogeneous agent populations. This architecture supports feedback between molecular/cellular and tissue levels and can serve as a building block for hybrid immune digital twins that integrate mechanistic knowledge, spatial dynamics, and patient-specific data. Multi-omics data — including single-cell and spatial transcriptomics — and prior biological knowledge can be used to parametrise and calibrate the coupled multiscale models, enabling the identification of novel therapeutic targets, drug repurposing opportunities, and the prediction of patient-specific treatment responses.

Keywords: Boolean networks · Agent-based models · Digital Twins · Autoimmune diseases

Acknowledgments. The framework was developed in collaboration with Van-Giang Trinh, Samuel Pastva, and Georgios Argyris. Anna Niarakis is supported by the PEPR Digital Health grant for the project DigiTREAT (2026-2030).

References

1. Niarakis, A., et al.: Immune digital twins for complex human pathologies: applications, limitations, and Challenges. NPJ Syst. Biol. Appl. **10**(1), 141 (2024)
2. Bayani, A., Dunster, J.L., Crofts, J.L., Nelson, M.R.: Spatial considerations in the resolution of inflammation: elucidating leukocyte inter actions via an experimentally-calibrated agent-based model. PLOS Comput. Biol. **16**(11), e1008413 (2020)
3. Hemedan, A. A., Niarakis, A., Schneider, R., Ostaszewski, M.: Boolean modelling as a logic-based dynamic approach in systems medicine. Comput. Struct. Biotechnol. J. **20**, 3161–3172 (2022)
4. Zerrouk, N., Augé, F., Niarakis, A.: Building a modular and multi cellular virtual twin of the synovial joint in rheumatoid arthritis. NPJ Digit. Med. **7**, 379 (2024)
5. Zerrouk, N., Alcraft, R., Hall, B.A., Augé, F., Niarakis, A.: Large-scale computational modelling of the M1 and M2 synovial macrophages in rheumatoid arthritis. NPJ Syst. Biol. Appl. **10**(1), 10 (2024)
6. Singh, V., Naldi, A., Soliman, S., Niarakis, A.: A large-scale Boolean model of the rheumatoid arthritis fibroblast-like synoviocytes predicts drug synergies in the arthritic joint. Npj Syst. Biol. Appl. **9**, 33 (2023)
7. McBride, D.A., Wang, J.S., Johnson, W.T., Bottini, N., Shah, N.J.: ABCD of IA: a multi-scale agent-based model of T cell activation in inflammatory arthritis. Biomater. Sci. **12**(8), 2041–2056 (2024)
8. Ricort, N., Niarakis, A.: ABRAAM: Agent-Based RheumAtoid Arthritis Model for personalised therapy. JOBIM 2025 (2025). Poster

An Ecosystem of Tools and Applications of Constraint-Based Modeling: From Model Reconstruction, Prediction and Optimization to AI Integration

Miguel Rocha[1,2]

[1] Centre of Biological Engineering, University of Minho, Braga, Portugal
mrocha@di.uminho.pt
[2] LabbelslAssociate Laboratory, University of Minho, Braga, Guimarães, Portugal

Abstract. In this lecture, I will perform a walk through a number of distinct computational tools for constraint-based modeling (CBM) developed in our group that encompass genome annotation, model reconstruction and validation, phenotype prediction, strain optimization, and integration of omics data with models, including merlin, OptFlux, MewPy, Troppo, COBAMP, and others. I will also address the recent integration of Artificial Intelligence-based tools, based on Large Language Models (LLMs), for the improved explainability of CBM models and their simulations, integrating with LLMs and semantically enabled knowledge graphs. I will go through different applications of those methods and tools, ranging from metabolic engineering to human health (cancer, neurodegenerative and infectious diseases), and plant sciences, using metabolic models of organisms as diverse as bacteria, fungi, algae, woody plants, fish, and humans, many developed with our collaboration.

Keywords: Constraint-based models · Metabolic modeling · AI synergies with systems biology · Metabolic model reconstruction · Open-source software

Contents

Boolean and Qualitative Networks

Source-Target Control of Boolean Networks with Minimal Edge Perturbations

Gustavo Magaña-López[1(✉)], Andrzej Mizera[2,3], and Jun Pang[1]

[1] Department of Computer Science, University of Luxembourg, 4364 Esch-sur-Alzette, Luxembourg
{gustavo.maganalopez,jun.pang}@uni.lu

[2] Faculty of Mathematics, Informatics and Mechanics, University of Warsaw, 02-097 Warsaw, Poland
amizera@mimuw.edu.pl

[3] IDEAS Research Institute, 00-060 Warsaw, Poland

Abstract. In this work, we study the source-target control problem of Boolean networks, which has important applications for cellular reprogramming. More specifically, we want to perturb the input Boolean network such that it leaves a predetermined source attractor to eventually find itself in the target attractor. We use edge perturbations, which modify the update functions of a Boolean network without necessarily setting them to constants. This work improves an existing method in which edge perturbations are used to eliminate all but the target attractor. Both approaches are based on Thomas' first rule: the existence of at least one positive cycle in the interaction graph of a dynamical system is a necessary condition for the existence of multiple steady states. Thus, if all positive cycles are removed, the resulting dynamical system has a single steady state. This requires removing a subset of edges so that at least one edge of every cycle in the graph is perturbed: the feedback edge set. Information on the source and target attractors allows reducing the number of relevant feedback edge sets and, subsequently, candidate perturbations. We propose a carefully designed strategy that combines exhaustive search and a heuristic inspired by Simulated Annealing to effectively reduce the number of required perturbations with respect to the feedback edge set. We evaluate our method on a wide array of Boolean networks from the literature to demonstrate its efficacy and efficiency.

Keywords: Boolean Networks · Source-target Control · Edgetic Perturbations · Simulated Annealing

1 Introduction

All around the world, diseases such as cancers, dementias, and diabetes are leading causes of death [23]. They are difficult to treat because of their complex nature in which multiple molecular processes are disrupted. To analyse disease

P. T. Monteiro (Ed.): CMSB 2026, LNBI 16678, pp. 3–18, 2027.
https://doi.org/10.1007/978-3-032-30870-2_1

mechanisms and propose therapeutic strategies, mathematical models such as Boolean networks (BNs) are used. BNs represent the activity of biological entities as active or inactive. This allows for reasoning about causal relationships between entities without having to estimate kinetic parameters or regulation thresholds. BNs are discrete dynamical systems that evolve until they reach stable states known as attractors from which the dynamics cannot escape. Healthy and diseased phenotypes can be mapped to BNs' attractors. Cellular reprogramming (CR) is a way to achieve conversion from an initial cell type to a cell type of interest [26]. In this work, we address the CR problem formulated as driving the dynamics of an input BN from an attractor (source) to another attractor (target) by modifying some parameters of the BN.

Classical CR procedures are performed with specific combinations of transcription factors (TFs) that deactivate or activate particular genes. These interventions are known as *node perturbations.* In a BN, a node perturbation corresponds to setting the local function of the perturbed node to a constant (either 1 or 0). However, not all mutations in living cells lead to complete loss of function or constituent activation of a given gene. Instead, they change the way two molecular species interact within the cell. These are known as *edge perturbations*, and give rise to diverse phenomena. For instance, single amino-acid substitutions can affect specific binding sites in a protein. This may result in partially functional proteins whose affinity for one substrate has changed drastically but remains the same for another substrate. Similarly, mutations in TF binding sites can lead to a loss of a regulatory edge to a specific target gene. Thus, a mutation causing a molecular defect to a protein may lead to a distinct perturbation of an interaction in a cellular network. Such perturbations of interactions in cellular networks can subsequently give rise to distinct phenomena [25]: (i) a single gene can be associated with multiple disorders: *allelic heterogeneity* or *pleiotropy*; (ii) a single disorder can be caused by mutations in any one of several genes: *locus heterogeneity*; (iii) only a subset of individuals carrying a mutation are affected by the disease: *incomplete penetrance*; and (iv) not all individuals with a given mutation are affected equally: *variable expressivity.* To account for such phenomena, node-perturbation models are insufficient and novel predictive models of genotype-phenotype relationships are required. Towards this end, the conceptual model of 'edgetic perturbations' was proposed [3,25],

Previous examples show that the effects of edge perturbations are more specific than those of node perturbations. Thus, edge perturbations may offer a more fine grained control over a BN's dynamics, minimising side effects while remaining effective control strategies for CR. Unfortunately, the problem of edge-perturbation control is even harder than the node-perturbation control, as the number of edges in a network can be quadratic in the number of nodes. Few works addressing CR via edge perturbations of a BN model are available.

CR has various formulations, each corresponding to a specific instance of the problem. These formulations vary with regard to the perturbations' temporal modality (instantaneous, temporary, permanent) and application (simultaneous, sequential) [2,8,9,19,19–21]. Additionally, the scope of CR may be global or restricted to a given initial condition. Further constraints can be added, such as reprogramming between fixed points, cyclic attractors, restricted to the unperturbed BN's attractors, etc. In this work, we focus solely on source-target reprogramming without any restriction on the type of source and target attractors. In molecular biology, this is referred to as direct cell reprogramming, where fate conversion between different types of somatic cells is achieved without passing through a pluripotent intermediate state. It finds applications in disease modelling, cell replacement therapy, regenerative medicine, and immunotherapy [1]. To address the source-target CR problem (STCR), we use permanent, simultaneous edge perturbations.

STCR only needs to guarantee reachability from one given attractor (source) to one desired attractor (target). Furthermore, the source attractor provides valuable information that can be used to narrow down the set of candidate perturbations. Hence, STCR may require perturbing fewer nodes than strategies that must work from any possible initial state. However, STCR still requires enumerating reachable attractors from the source after the perturbation. Enumerating reachable attractors from an initial configuration is a *PSPACE*−complete problem under the (a)synchronous update modes. To overcome this limitation, we employ the Most Permissive update mode whose attractors are the BN's minimal trap spaces. Computing minimal trap spaces is at most in *coNP* for locally monotone BNs, and in $coNP^{coNP}$ for non-locally monotone BNs. This offers a considerable drop in computational complexity while ensuring consistency with underlying quantitative models [14,15].

2 Preliminaries

2.1 Concepts for Boolean Networks

Boolean network (BN) over nodes $\{1,\dots,n\}$ is a function that maps binary vectors of dimension n to themselves $f : \mathbb{B}^n \to \mathbb{B}^n$, where $\mathbb{B} \triangleq \{0,1\}$ is the Boolean domain. It is made up of n local functions $f_i, i \in \{1,\dots,n\}$. Hence, f_j is the local function of component j. The evaluation of a local function determines the next state of the given component. See Fig. 1 for an example.

Configuration is a Boolean vector $\mathbf{x} \in \mathbb{B}^n$ which specifies a Boolean state for each component $x_i \in \mathbf{x}, i \in \{1,\dots,n\}$. Two configurations are different if and only if they differ at least one coordinate. The set of components on which two configurations differ is defined by Eq. 1. For example, $\mathbf{x} = 01100$ and $\mathbf{y} = 01111$ yield $\Delta(\mathbf{x},\mathbf{y}) = \{4,5\}$.

$$\Delta(\mathbf{x},\mathbf{y}) = \{i \in \{1,\cdots,n\} \mid x_i \neq y_i\} \tag{1}$$

Influence graph of a BN f is a directed signed graph, noted $G(f)$, whose vertices are the nodes of the BN. $G(f)$ captures the dependencies of Boolean functions. Formally, $j \xrightarrow{+} i \in G(f) \iff \exists \mathbf{x},\mathbf{y} \in \mathbb{B}^n : f_i(\mathbf{x}) < f_i(\mathbf{y}) \wedge \Delta(\mathbf{x},\mathbf{y}) = \{j\} \wedge \mathbf{x}_j < \mathbf{y}_j$. Analogously, $j \xrightarrow{-} i \in G(f) \iff \exists \mathbf{x},\mathbf{y} \in \mathbb{B}^n : f_i(\mathbf{x}) >$

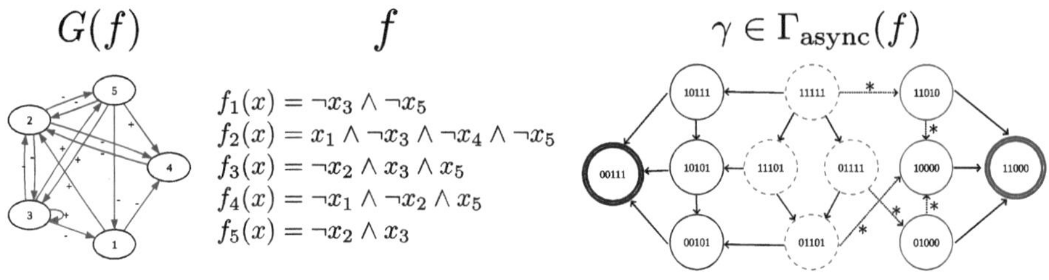

Fig. 1. Left: Influence graph; **Centre:** Boolean network; **Right:** (partial) transition graph, showing a subset of all configurations and transitions. Nodes with double countours represent fixed points of f: $\text{fp}_1 = 00111$ (leftmost), and $\text{fp}_2 = 11000$ (rightmost).

$f_i(\mathbf{y}) \wedge \Delta(\mathbf{x}, \mathbf{y}) = \{j\} \wedge \mathbf{x}_j < \mathbf{y}_j$. Note that it is possible to have both edges $j \xrightarrow{+} i$ and $j \xrightarrow{-} i$ in the same influence graph.

Cycles are closed paths in a directed graph where no vertex appears twice. Two cycles are distinct $c_1 \neq c_2$ if they are not cyclic permutations of each other. Cycles can be grouped into two types: negative $\mathcal{C}^-$ when they contain an odd number of inhibitory edges $j \xrightarrow{-} i$, and positive $\mathcal{C}^+$ when this number is even.

Update Mode and Transition Graph. An *update mode* μ is defined by elementary transition relations $\rightarrow_\mu$ amongst the set of configurations $\mathbb{B}^n$. For a given BN f, we write $\mathbf{x} \rightarrow_\mu \mathbf{y}$ to denote that a BN f can take the system from $\mathbf{x}$ to $\mathbf{y}$ in one transition in update mode μ. In the asynchronous update mode $\rightarrow_{\text{async}}$ one and only one local function is applied, generating up to n different transitions per configuration. Given a BN f and an update mode μ, $\Gamma_\mu(f)$ is the *transition graph* whose nodes are the states $\mathbb{B}^n$ and the directed edges are μ's transitions.

Reachability. We write $\mathbf{x} \rightarrow_\mu^* \mathbf{y}$ (read $\mathbf{x}$ *reaches* $\mathbf{y}$) to indicate that there exists a path from $\mathbf{x}$ to $\mathbf{y}$ in $\Gamma_\mu(f)$.

$$\mathbf{x} \rightarrow_\mu^* \mathbf{y} \iff (\mathbf{x} = \mathbf{y}) \vee (\mathbf{x} \rightarrow_\mu \mathbf{y}) \vee \left(\exists \mathbf{z} : \mathbf{x} \rightarrow \mathbf{z} \wedge \mathbf{z} \rightarrow_\mu^* \mathbf{y}\right) \tag{2}$$

Attractors represent the dynamical system's possible asymptotic behaviours. An attractor A_μ is a strongly connected terminal component of the state-transition graph $\Gamma_\mu(f)$ meaning that: (1) $\forall \mathbf{x}, \mathbf{y} \in A_\mu, \mathbf{x} \neq \mathbf{y} \implies \mathbf{x} \rightarrow_\mu^* \mathbf{y}$ and (2) $\forall \mathbf{x} \in A, \exists \mathbf{z} \in \mathbb{B}^n : \mathbf{x} \rightarrow_\mu^* \mathbf{z} \implies \mathbf{z} \in A$. If an attractor contains a single configuration, it is called a *fixed point*, otherwise it is a *cyclic attractor*. We write $\mathcal{A}_\mu(f) = \{A_\mu^1, \cdots, A_\mu^{\leq 2^n}\}$ to denote the set of attractors of the BN f. The subset $\mathcal{A}_\mu(f, \mathbf{x}) \subseteq \mathcal{A}_\mu(f)$ denotes attractors reachable from $\mathbf{x}$, and $\mathcal{A}_\mu(f, b) \subseteq \mathcal{A}_\mu(f)$ the same from any configuration in a set $b = \{\mathbf{x}, ..., \mathbf{y}\}$.

Most Permissive Semantics are a dynamical interpretation of BNs, where a component can exist in 4 states $\mathbb{P} \triangleq \{0, \nearrow, \searrow, 1\}$. Given a BN f, $\forall \mathbf{x}, \mathbf{y}\ \mathbf{x} \rightarrow_{\text{MP}} \mathbf{y}$ if and only if $\exists i \in \{1, \cdots, n\} : \Delta(\mathbf{x}, \mathbf{y}) = i$ and y_i is given by Eq. 4. The function

$\eta(\mathbf{x})$ of Eq. 3 gives all possible Boolean interpretations $\mathbf{z}$ of a MP configuration $\mathbf{x}$.

$$\eta(\mathbf{x}) = \{\mathbf{z} \in \mathbb{B}^n \mid \forall i \in \{1, \cdots, n\}, \mathbf{x}_i \in \mathbb{B} \implies \mathbf{z}_i = \mathbf{x}_i\} \tag{3}$$

$$y_i = \begin{cases} \nearrow & \text{if } \mathbf{x}_i \neq 1 \wedge \exists \mathbf{z} \in \eta(\mathbf{x}) : f_i(\mathbf{z}) = 1 \\ 1 & \text{if } \mathbf{x}_i = \nearrow \\ \searrow & \text{if } \mathbf{x}_i \neq 0 \wedge \exists \mathbf{z} \in \eta(\mathbf{x}) : f_i(\mathbf{z}) = 0 \\ 0 & \text{if } \mathbf{x}_i = \searrow \end{cases} \tag{4}$$

Trap spaces are sub-hypercubes of $\mathbb{B}^n$ closed by f such that for any vertex $\mathbf{x}$ of the trap space, $f(\mathbf{x})$ is also one of its vertices. In a trap space some dimensions can be fixed to singular values, and others left free. For example, the states on the left in Fig. 1 $B = \{10111, 10101, 00101, 00111\}$. Alternatively, this trap space can be written $B = {*}01{*}1$ where components $\{2, 3, 5\}$ are fixed and $\{1, 4\}$ are free. A trap space is called minimal when it contains no other trap spaces. Any minimal trap space necessarily encloses at least one attractor of any update mode [10]. Finally, minimal trap spaces are exactly the attractors of the most permissive MP update mode which has lower computational complexity than the popular (a)synchronous update modes [14]. In the rest of the article, we focus on the Most Permissive attractors of the BN (its minimal trap spaces).

Canalisation is formally defined in Eq. 5 for any Boolean function $g : \mathbb{B}^n \to \mathbb{B}$. An example is the inhibitor dominant rule where any single active inhibitor suffices to have the output be 0, regardless of the state of all activators.

$$\exists i \in \{1, \cdots, n\} \;\wedge\; \exists b, c \in \mathbb{B} \;\wedge\; \forall x \in \mathbb{B}^n \;:\; x_i = b \implies g(x) = c \tag{5}$$

2.2 Edge Perturbations

Unlike node perturbations, edge perturbations modify the local function(s) of some component(s) without necessarily making them constant functions. Formally, a perturbation p is a map that associates an edge with a Boolean value as defined in Eq. 6.

$$p = \{(j \xrightarrow{\sigma} i) \mapsto b : (j \xrightarrow{\sigma} i) \in G(f) \wedge \sigma \in \{-, +\} \wedge b \in \mathbb{B}\} \tag{6}$$

This means that from the target gene's perspective, the source of the edge will always be seen as either true or false. The source gene will keep its update function unchanged, and other genes will continue to see its unaltered state dictated by its local function. The effect of perturbing an edge will depend on both the perturbation value and the target gene's local function: it can either simplify it or make it constant. For example, the perturbation $p = \{(3 \xrightarrow{+} 5) \mapsto 1\}$ applied to the BN of Fig. 1 will change 5's local function from $f_5(x) = \neg x_2 \wedge x_3$ to $f_5/p(x) = \neg x_2 \wedge 1$, thus $f_5/p(x) = \neg x_2$.

Algorithm 1. Generic Simulated Annealing

Select X_1 at random, set T_1.
for $i \in [1, N]$ **do**
  Compute $E(X_i)$
  Sample a neighbouring design vector X_{i+1}.
  Compute $E(X_{i+1})$
  $\Delta_E \leftarrow E(X_{i+1}) - E(X_i)$
  $p_{accept} \leftarrow \min(1, \exp\{-\Delta/T_i\})$
  if $p_{accept} \geq u \sim \mathcal{U}[0,1]$ **then**
    $X_i \leftarrow X_{i+1}$
  $T_{i+1} \leftarrow CS(T_i)$

2.3 The Source-Target Control Problem

The original formulation of this control problem was proposed in [13] with instantaneous node perturbations. In this work, we adapt it for permanent edge perturbations. Given a BN f, a source attractor $s \in \mathcal{A}_{\text{MP}}(f)$ and a target attractor $t \in \mathcal{A}_{\text{MP}}(f)$, compute a set of simultaneous and permanent edge perturbations p such that the following conditions hold: (i) The source is not an attractor of the perturbed BN $s \notin \mathcal{A}_{\text{MP}}(f/p)$. (ii) Only the target attractor is reachable from the source $\mathcal{A}_{\text{MP}}(f/p, s) = \{t\}$.

2.4 Simulated Annealing

Simulated Annealing (SA) [6] is a combinatorial optimisation heuristic inspired by statistical mechanics. It imitates the cooling process by which a set of atoms reaches a state of minimum energy. In the physical system, each atomic arrangement corresponds to an energy level. In the optimisation problem, each configuration has an associated objective function value. SA is defined in terms of the design vector X, system energy E and temperature T, cooling schedule CS, and number of steps N. As shown in Algorithm 1, SA follows a Metropolis-Hastings sampling scheme coupled with iterative cooling in the search for optimal solutions (having minimal energy). SA's backbone is straightforward to implement, but its success relies on proper neighbour sampling X_{i+1}. Neighbour sampling is problem dependent and often requires domain specific knowledge. The neighbour sampling scheme should satisfy the *detailed balance* condition given by Eq. 7. This is a sufficient condition for the existence of a stationary distribution $\pi(X)$, for a fixed temperature T.

$$P(X_i \rightarrow X_{i+1})\pi(X_i) = P(X_{i+1} \rightarrow X_i)\pi(X_{i+1}) \tag{7}$$

In addition to the existence of a stationary distribution $\exists\pi(X)$, we want it to be unique $\exists!\pi(X)$ which requires the underlying Markov chain to be ergodic. Ergodicity requires that every state must (i) be aperiodic and (ii) positive recurrent. Aperiodic means that the system does not return to the same state at fixed intervals. Positive recurrent means that the same state is always revisited after a finite number of steps.

2.5 An Existing Method

Target control with permanent edge perturbations was addressed in [24]. Target control requires that the selected perturbation always drives the system from any initial state to a desired target attractor. Their method is based on structural conditions for multistability: (i) Thomas' first rule, if the influence graph of a BN has no positive cycles, then the BN has at most one attractor $\mathcal{C}^+(G(f)) = \emptyset \implies \exists! A_{\text{async}}(f)$ [16,22]. (ii) The positive cycle responsible for the presence of two disjoint trap spaces A and B only contains nodes in which they are different, i.e. $\Delta(\mathbf{x}, \mathbf{y}), \mathbf{x} \in A \wedge \mathbf{y} \in B$ [17]. Thus, the method proposed in [24] focuses on removing all relevant cycles to the emergence of multiple attractors $\mathcal{C}^+(\Delta(\mathbf{x}, \mathbf{y})) \subset \mathcal{C}^+(G(f))$. They start by computing $\Delta(\mathbf{x}, \mathbf{y})$ and subsequently removing all relevant positive cycles. This requires perturbing at least one edge of every cycle in $\mathcal{C}^+(\Delta(\mathbf{x}, \mathbf{y}))$. This set of edges is known as the Feedback Edge Set (fes). A fes is said to be minimal if there is no smaller set of edges such that their removal renders the graph acyclic. Because there may be multiple minimal fes, FES denotes the set of all minimal fes. The method of [24] is a sound solution to the target control problem, but it has two important limitations that our method improves upon: (i) Perturbing the fes may translate to a prohibitively large number of perturbations. (ii) Verifying that a perturbation is a solution to the control problem requires recomputing all the BN's attractors (under the asynchronous semantics) which hinders its scalability.

3 Our Approach

This work aims to provide minimal perturbations to solve the source-target cellular reprogramming problem (STCR). Given a source minimal trap space s and a target minimal trap space t (attractors in MP semantics), recall the positive cycle responsible for their presence only contains nodes in which they are different, i.e. $\Delta(\mathbf{x}, \mathbf{y}), \mathbf{x} \in s \wedge \mathbf{y} \in t$ [17]. It follows that STCR may not necessarily require the removal of all positive cycles but only of a subset (possibly a single cycle) $c^\star \in \mathcal{C}^+(\Delta(\mathbf{x}, \mathbf{y}))$. This means that STCR may be achievable by removing a strict subset of any given minimal fes. The set of possible perturbations is given by Eq. 8, where $FES(\Delta(\mathbf{x}, \mathbf{y}))$ is the set of all minimal fes over the nodes on which s differs from t and $\mathcal{P}(fes)$ denotes the power set (the set of all subsets) of its argument fes.

$$\Omega = \bigcup_{fes \in FES(\mathcal{C}^+(\Delta(\mathbf{x}, \mathbf{y})))} \mathcal{P}(fes) \tag{8}$$

Our approach consists of the following steps: (i) select the nodes on which the source and target differ $\Delta(s, t)$, (ii) enumerate all the relevant positive cycles $\mathcal{C}^+(\Delta(s, t))$, (iii) compute the size of the minimal fes, (iv) enumerate all minimal fes to build Ω, (v) search for a minimal perturbation in Ω. Steps (ii) to (iv) are performed using Answer-Set Programming [4]. In some cases, Ω may be small enough to be explored exhaustively (or up to a fixed computational

Algorithm 2. Perturbation strategy

t target attractor (minimal trap space) $t = \{i \mapsto b : i \in \{1, \cdots, n\} \wedge b \in \mathbb{B} \cup \{*\}\}$.
f Boolean network.
$pe \in \Omega$ Selected Edges to perturb (in exhaustive or Annealing-like search).
$sm = \{+ \mapsto 1, - \mapsto 0\}$ sign map.
isCanalising$(\cdots)$ checks $\exists i$ of Eq. 5.
CanalisingValue$(\cdots)$ returns b of Eq. 5.
function TargetedEdgePerturbations(f, pe, t)
    $f/p \leftarrow$ copy(f)
    for (regulator, targetGene, sign) $\in pe$ **do**
        if isCanalising($f_{\text{targetGene}}$, regulator) $\wedge$ t[targetGene] $= *$ **then**
            $cv \leftarrow$ CanalisngValue($f_{\text{targetGene}}$, regulator)
            $f/p_{\text{targetGene}} \leftarrow$ substitute($f_{\text{targetGene}}$, regulator, $1 - cv$)
        else
            if sm[sign] $= t$[regulator] **then**
                $f/p_{\text{targetGene}} \leftarrow$ substitute($f_{\text{targetGene}}$, regulator, 1)
            else
                $f/p_{\text{targetGene}} \leftarrow$ substitute($f_{\text{targetGene}}$, regulator, 0)
    return f/p

budget). In such cases, we follow an *exhaustive search* scheme where we start with the smallest subsets ($|p| = 1$) and gradually increase until one of two conditions is met: (i) a solution is found, (ii) the specified computational budget has been depleted (fixed number of iterations or maximum subset size to consider). These conditions are independently checked, and the execution is stopped when either of them is verified. The first condition means stopping and returning the first successful perturbation. This guarantees the minimality of the solution: if there was a smaller successful perturbation in Ω, we would have encountered it first and stopped the execution. Thus, the exhaustive search continues as long as no successful perturbation is found and the computational budget is not depleted. The default computational budget is the maximal size of a strict subset: $\max(|p|) = |fes| - 1$, because allowing $\max(|p|) = |fes|$ would include the baseline method [24]. We propose a heuristic method inspired by simulated annealing that finds solutions for cases where an exhaustive search would be intractable.

3.1 Perturbation Strategy

Edge perturbations are defined by Eq. 6 in Sect. 2.2 as a map that modifies local functions by substituting specific regulators for constants. However, the choice of constants depends on the desired outcome: Algorithm 2 defines our strategy in terms of the input BN and the target attractor. Perturbation values are selected monotonically to facilitate the emergence of the target attractor. When the target gene for the candidate edge is free in the target attractor, the edge is perturbed with the complementary of the regulators' canalising value to prevent fixing the target gene to a constant value.

Algorithm 3. Efficient source-target reprogramming checker

s source attractor.
t target attractor.
f Boolean network.
p Edge perturbation.
function CHECKONLYTARGETREACHABLE(f/p, s, t)
    $i \leftarrow 0$
    success $\leftarrow 0$
    for $a \in \mathcal{A}_{\mathrm{MP}}(f/p, s)$ **do**
        $i \leftarrow i + 1$
        if $i > 1$ **then**
            success $\leftarrow 0$
            return success
        else if $a = t$ **then**
            success $\leftarrow 1$
    return success

3.2 Solution Verification

In addition to the minimality of solutions, we propose an efficient approach to verify whether a given perturbation p is a solution to an STCR instance. Our verification approach is shown in Algorithm 3. Rather than exhaustively enumerating the perturbed BN's reachable attractors from the source ($\mathcal{A}_{\mathrm{MP}}(f/p, s)$ which may be numerous), we enumerate at most two. The Algorithm 3 is a form of early rejection that stops the enumeration of attractors upon failure. When the considered perturbation is successful or $|\mathcal{A}_{\mathrm{MP}}(f/p, s)|$ is small, this offers little improvement. However, Algorithm 3 offers improvements that are proportional to $|\mathcal{A}_{\mathrm{MP}}(f/p, s)|$, irrespective of the order in which the attractors are enumerated.

3.3 Annealing-Like Heuristic for Minimal Perturbation Search

A perturbation of optimal size $p^\star \in \mathrm{fes} \; : \; |p^\star| < |\mathrm{fes}|$ may exist, but the naive search may fail to find it within the fixed computational budget. To tackle this limitation in a tractable manner, we propose a strategy based on SA specially tailored to search for perturbations of minimal size. As explained in Sect. 2.4, SA requires (i) properly defining the system's total energy E and (ii) building a neighbour sampler to generate new candidates $X_{i+1} \sim \mathcal{N}_{eigh}(X_i)$. Our annealing-like approach is presented in Algorithm 5. This section first explains all the building blocks that set its foundation.

System Energy is defined by Eq. 9, which accounts for the perturbation size $|p|$ and $\mathrm{SAT}_E(p)$, a relaxation of the source-target reprogramming problem described in Sect. 2.3. $\mathrm{SAT}_E(p)$ accounts for the number of components on which the f/p's attractors reachable from s differ from the target attractor t. This number is averaged across all attractors reachable from the original f's source

Algorithm 4. Hierarchical neighbour sampling

$fes_0 \sim \mathcal{U}\{FES\}$
$p_0 \sim \mathcal{U}\{p \subseteq fes_0 : |p| = k\}$
if not IsStronglyConnected(G_{JM}) **then**
    $m^+_{min} := min\{\ jm_{i,j} : jm_{i,j} \in JM \setminus \{0\}\}$
    for $jm_{i,j} \in JM : jm_{i,j} = 0$ **do**
        $jm_{i,j} \leftarrow m^+_{min}$
function SampleNeighbour(fes_i, k, JM)
    $\omega \leftarrow JM[fes_i, :]$
    $\tilde{\omega} \leftarrow \frac{\omega}{\sum \omega}$
    $fes_{i+1} \sim \mathrm{Cat}(\tilde{\omega})$
    $p_{i+1} \sim \mathcal{U}\{p \subseteq fes_{i+1} : |p| = k\}$
    return fes_{i+1}, p_{i+1}

attractor s by f/p, denoted $\mathcal{A}(f/p, s)$. This ensures having comparable energies, across any number of attractors $|\mathcal{A}(f/p, s)|$. The relaxation produces a smoother energy landscape which facilitates the convergence of our annealing-like heuristic. The original problem is solved if and only if Eq. 10 equals zero.

$$E(p) = |p| \ + \ \mathrm{SAT}_E(p) \tag{9}$$

$$\mathrm{SAT}_E(p) = \frac{1}{n \times |\mathcal{A}(f/p, s)|} \sum_{a \in \mathcal{A}(f/p,s)} \sum_{i=1}^{n} I\{a(i) \neq t(i)\} \tag{10}$$

The Neighbour Sampler must account for similarity between sampled perturbations and be communicating, meaning that from every sampled perturbation it must be able to reach any other perturbation in a finite number of steps. To explore Ω, we use a hierarchical neighbour sampler. We define a neighbourhood in terms of pairwise fes-to-fes similarities, which we measure using the Jaccard Index presented in Eq. 11. We store all pairwise comparisons in a Jaccard similarity matrix JM, used by Algorithm 4.

$$J(A, B) = \frac{|A \cap B|}{|A \cup B|} \tag{11}$$

Note that it is possible to have fully disjoint candidates for minimal fes, which makes Eq. 11 zero. In principle, this does not pose a problem as long as JM is irreducible, or equivalently, its associated graph G_{JM} is strongly connected. $G_{JM} = (N, E)$ is defined by a set of nodes N (the candidates $fes \in FES$) and a set of oriented edges $E \subseteq N \times N$. We write $i \to j$ to indicate $(i, j) \in E$, if and only if $JM[i, j] > 0$ (whenever $|\ fes_i \cap fes_j| \geq 1$). To ensure that SA can explore the entire search space, G_{JM} must be strongly connected. If G_{JM} is not strongly connected, we replace all zero entries with the smallest non-zero value in JM. This modification is not minimal, but ensures the irreducibility of JM.

As shown in Algorithm 4, we first sample a fes_{i+1} with probabilities proportional to fes_i. Subsequently, we sample a subset of size k which is the proposed perturbation p_{i+1}. By biasing these probabilities, we propose perturbations that are more likely to have elements in common ($p_{i+1} \cap p_i \neq \emptyset$ is unlikely) than what would arise from uniform sampling.

Theorem 1. *Algorithm 5 satisfies detailed balance for fixed k.*

Proof. Algorithm 5 uses the Metropolis acceptance criterion which satisfies detailed balance for symmetric proposals (see line 10 of Algorithm 1). First, decompose the transition probability of Eq. 7 into the product of proposal Q and acceptance A probabilities: $P(X_i \rightarrow X_{i+1}) = Q(X_i \rightarrow X_{i+1})A(X_i \rightarrow X_{i+1})$. Where $A(X_i \rightarrow X_{i+1})$ is dictated by lines 14 and 20 of Algorithm 5, which in turn are equivalent to lines 7 and 8 of Algorithm 1 (Metropolis acceptance criterion). Per Algorithm 4, a proposal can be decomposed into sampling a fes, and then sampling a perturbation of fixed size from the selected fes. This gives $Q(X_i \rightarrow X_{i+1}) = Q(fes_i \rightarrow fes_{i+1})Q(X_{i+1} \sim fes_{i+1})$. Because the latter is done with uniform probability, it is symmetric for all subsets of size k. To prove Theorem 1, we only need to show the symmetry of fes sampling, which is not uniform. Because Eq. 11 is defined over sets, we have $J(fes_i, fes_{i+1}) = J(fes_{i+1}, fes_i)\ \forall fes_i, fes_{i+1}$. This means that the matrices JM and $\tilde{JM}$ are symmetric. From this we have $Q(fes_i \rightarrow fes_{i+1}) = Q(fes_{i+1} \rightarrow fes_i)$. Thus, the proposal function is symmetric.

Theorem 2. *Algorithm 5 creates an ergodic Markov chain for fixed k.*

Proof. Proving ergodicity requires showing that the Markov chain is positive recurrent and aperiodic. As for Theorem 1's proof, we concentrate on the proposal probabilities $Q(X_i \rightarrow X_{i+1}) = Q(fes_i \rightarrow fes_{i+1})Q(X_{i+1} \sim fes_{i+1})$. Given a fixed subset size, edges are sampled with equal probability. Given that any subset can be sampled, for a fixed fes_i the Markov chain is positive recurrent. Because the same subset can be sampled twice in a row, the Markov chain is aperiodic. The proof of ergodicity now requires proving the proposals $Q(fes_i \rightarrow fes_{i+1})$ are ergodic. Note that $Q(fes_i \rightarrow fes_{i+1})$ is given by the right stochastic matrix $\tilde{JM}$ (lines 8-10 of Algorithm 4). Due to the correction of lines 3-6 in Algorithm 4, JM is irreducible and so is $\tilde{JM}$. This has two implications: First, the chain is positive recurrent because we can transition from any fes_i to any fes_j in a finite number of steps. Second, all states have the same period, which means that we simply need to find the period of a single state. Whenever a state has a self loop i.e. $Q(fes_i \rightarrow fes_{i+1}) > 0$ for $fes_i = fes_{i+1}$, its period is 1, meaning that it is aperiodic. From Eq. 11 we have $JM_{i,i} = 1 \implies \tilde{JM} > 0$. It follows that all states have period 1. Recapitulating: because JM and $\tilde{JM}$ are irreducible, the Markov chain is positive recurrent. Given the presence of self loops and the irreducibility of $\tilde{JM}$, all states of the Markov chain are aperiodic. These are the two requirements for ergodicity.

Algorithm 5. Perturbation size minimisation via Annealing-like search

α cooling parameter.
T_0 initial temperature.
N is the given budget.
$fes_0 \sim \mathcal{U}\{FES\}$
$p_0 \sim \mathcal{U}\{p \subseteq fes_0 : |p| = 1\}$
$\mathrm{SAT}_{E_{p_0}} \leftarrow \mathrm{SAT}_E(p_0)$ given by Eq. 10.
$E_{p_0} \leftarrow E(p_0)$ given by Eq. 9.
for $i \in 1 \cdots N$ **do**
  $k \leftarrow \max(1, \lfloor \frac{i}{N} \rfloor)$
  $\mathrm{proposal}_i \leftarrow \textsc{SampleNeighbour}(fes_i,\, k,\, JM)$
  $\mathrm{SAT}_{E_{proposal_i}} \leftarrow \mathrm{SAT}_E(\mathrm{proposal}_i)$.
  $E_{\mathrm{proposal}_i} \leftarrow |\mathrm{proposal}_i| + \mathrm{SAT}_{E_{proposal_i}}$
  $\Delta E \leftarrow E_{\mathrm{proposal}_i} - E_{p_{i-1}}$
  if $\mathrm{SAT}_{E_{proposal_i}} \leq \mathrm{SAT}_{E_{p_{i-1}}}$ **then**
    $p_i \leftarrow \mathrm{proposal}_i$
    $E_{p_{i-1}} \leftarrow E_{\mathrm{proposal}_i}$
    $\mathrm{SAT}_{E_{p_i}} \leftarrow \mathrm{SAT}_{E_{proposal_i}}$
    if $0 = \mathrm{SAT}_{E_{proposal_i}}$ **then**
      return p_i
  else if $exp\{\frac{-\Delta E}{T_i}\} >= r \sim \mathcal{U}(0, 1)$ **then**
    $p_i \leftarrow \mathrm{proposal}_i$
  else
    $p_i \leftarrow p_{i-1}$
  $T_i \leftarrow \alpha \times T_{i-1}$

4 Performance Evaluation

To assess our method, we used the Biodivine Boolean Models (BBM) Benchmark Dataset [12]. BBM is a comprehensive open-source collection of more than 230 real-world Boolean network models used in systems biology compiled from databases such as GINsim [11], CellCollective [5], and BioModels [7]. We filtered out translations from multi-valued models in order to focus exclusively on Boolean network models. We obtained 215 different BNs, 24 having no input nodes. Because input nodes represent the environment rather than the cell state per se, it is important that these are fixed upstream of any reprogramming problem. We sampled up to 5 different random valuations of the input nodes per model in order to avoid potential biases induced by manually setting them to arbitrary values. When accounting for all the possible instantiations of the input nodes, we obtained a total of 900 BN/input node valuation instances. We subsequently used MPBN [14,18] to filter out any models that (i) had only one attractor or (ii) had more than 10 attractors. The former (479 instances) were excluded because they are ineligible for our formulation of the source-target control problem. The latter (94 instances) were excluded because the number of pairwise permutations could have been intractable within the fixed time frame.

Table 1. Distribution of successes across methods (for a single Annealing-like run).

FES	Exhaustive	Annealing-like	counts	percentage	cumulative
True	True	True	2647	58.90	58.90
	False	True	1340	29.82	88.72
False	False	False	417	9.28	98.00
		True	39	0.87	98.87
True	False	False	37	0.82	99.69
False	True	True	10	0.22	99.91
True	True	False	4	0.09	100
False	True	False	0	0.00	100

Having set all the model-environment instances, we enumerated all the attractors for each instance. We generate all size 2 permutations to construct triplets (f, s, t) where f is the Boolean network, s and t are the source and target attractors, respectively. These constitute the test-bed on which we applied both the exhaustive search presented at the beginning of Sect. 3 and the annealing-like heuristic of Sect. 3.3. We apply the method of [24] to provide a baseline (perturbing the whole fes). For exhaustive search, we define the computational budget as the maximum subset size to be explored $\min(5, |fes| - 1)$. Note that the computational budget is a hyper-parameter our method. We store all successful perturbations, specifying the method employed as well as the (f, s, t) triplet.

Table 1 summarises the distribution of successes across different approaches. The three columns on the left represent different methods: FES is the baseline, followed by Exhaustive and Annealing-like, our proposed methods. The rows summarise the number of cases, indicating whether each method could find (True) or not (False) a perturbation for the given (f, s, t) triplet. The columns on the right include the number of instances (counts), the fraction of the total instances that the given row comprises (percentage), and the cumulative percentage. Recapitulating Table 1, the exhaustive scheme solved 2661 (59.21%) instances, our annealing-like heuristic 4036 (89.80%), and the baseline *FES* 4028 (89.63%). There were 1379 (30.68%) cases solved by the annealing-like heuristic but not by the exhaustive search.

Because we aim to solve the STCR problem with a minimal number of edge perturbations, it is important to analyse the sizes of the solutions obtained with our methods. Figure 2 summarises the improvements in terms of the number of required perturbations. Overall, the results are quite encouraging: We get up to 20-fold reductions in the number of necessary perturbations with both our methods, with regard to the baseline (perturbing the whole fes [24]). The instances in Fig. 2 are distributed in a column-like fashion. The first column shows all 551 instances where perturbing a single edge sufficed, accounting for 13% of all solved instances. The bottom facet of Fig. 2 stops at subsets of size 5 because that is the fixed computational budget for the exhaustive search scheme. We assessed the

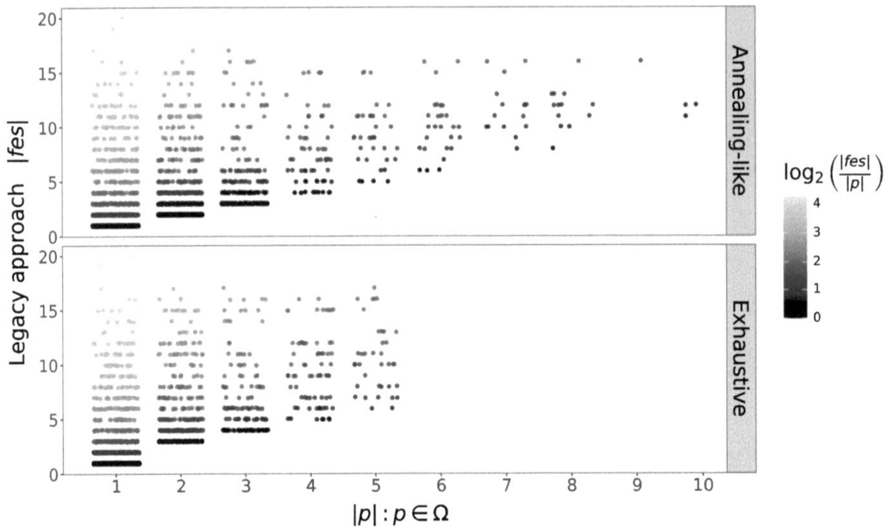

Fig. 2. Reduction in the size of required perturbations per STCR instance. Each dot is a unique (f, s, t) triplet. Small random noise has been applied on the x axis, so that overlapping points become visible.

convergence of the annealing-like scheme by performing 100 independent runs on each BN and then comparing the solution sizes (number of perturbed edges) to those obtained with exhaustive search. A perturbation found by annealing-like search was considered minimal if it required perturbing the same number of edges than the solution found with exhaustive search, otherwise it was considered non-minimal. Thus, the minimality of solutions perturbing 6 or more edges was not assessed. Across all replicates, the annealing-like scheme found minimal solutions for $64.72 \pm 0.11\%$ (mean $\pm$ standard deviation) of solved instances. 92.61% of non-minimal solutions found by annealing-like search perturbed only 1 edge more than the minimal solution found by exhaustive search. The 100 independent experiments performed on each BN using the annealing-like heuristic exhibited similar runtimes. The median runtime per BN (considering all permutations of source-target attractors) was about a minute and 75% of BNs were analysed in less than 8 min. Maximum runtime for a single experiment, across all experiments, was 3 h and 58 min. All experiments ran on 2 GHz CPUs with 256 GBs of RAM with one job scheduled per BN and a timeout of 4 h.

5 Discussion and Conclusion

In this work, we have addressed the source-target control problem of Boolean networks, which has important applications in cellular reprogramming. To the best of our knowledge, this is the first work that applies edge perturbations for reprogramming under Most Permissive semantics. Furthermore, this work provides both an exact exhaustive exploration scheme and a heuristic method to find minimal perturbation sets. Extensive experiments on a test-bed of biological Boolean networks show the efficiency, efficacy, and scalability of our method. Future work includes other variations of the BN control problem (such as sequential reprogramming and non-permanent edge perturbations), as well as a dedicated biological case study.

Acknowledgements. This work was supported by the Luxembourg National Research Fund (FNR) under the grant agreement INTER/NCN/24/18732364/EdgeCR and by the National Science Centre, Poland under the OPUS call in the Weave programme, grant number 2023/51/I/ST6/02864. The experiments were carried out using the HPC facilities of the University of Luxembourg—see https://hpc.uni.lu.

Code Availability. Our method has been implemented as a Python package.The source code can be found at github.com/edge-CR/mepst.

Disclosure of Interests. The authors have no competing interests to declare that are relevant to the content of this article.

References

1. Ahlenius, H.: Past, present, and future of direct cell reprogramming. Cell. Reprogram. **24**(5), 205–211 (2022). https://doi.org/10.1089/cell.2022.0110
2. Baudin, A., Paul, S., Su, C., Pang, J.: Controlling large Boolean networks with single-step perturbations. Bioinformatics **35**(14), 558–567 (2019)
3. Charloteaux, B., Zhong, Q., Dreze, M., Cusick, M.E., Hill, D.E., Vidal, M.: Protein–protein interactions and networks: forward and reverse Edgetics. In: Castrillo, J.I., Oliver, S.G. (eds.) Yeast Systems Biology, pp. 197–213. Humana Press, c/o Springer Science+Business Media (2011)
4. Gebser, M., Kaminski, R., Kaufmann, B., Schaub, T.: Multi-shot asp solving with clingo. Theory Pract. Logic Program. **19**(1), 27–82 (2019). https://doi.org/10.1017/S1471068418000054
5. Helikar, T., et al.: The cell collective: toward an open and collaborative approach to systems biology. BMC Syst. Biol. **6**(1), 96 (2012). https://doi.org/10.1186/1752-0509-6-96
6. Kirkpatrick, S., Gelatt, C.D., Vecchi, M.P.: Optimization by simulated annealing. Science **220**(4598), 671–680 (1983). https://doi.org/10.1126/science.220.4598.671
7. Le Novere, N.: Biomodels database: a free, centralized database of curated, published, quantitative kinetic models of biochemical and cellular systems. Nucleic Acids Res. **34**(90001), D689–D691 (2006). https://doi.org/10.1093/nar/gkj092
8. Mandon, H., Su, C., Haar, S., Pang, J., Paulevé, L.: Sequential reprogramming of Boolean networks made practical. In: Bortolussi, L., Sanguinetti, G. (eds.) CMSB 2019. LNCS, vol. 11773, pp. 3–19. Springer, Cham (2019). https://doi.org/10.1007/978-3-030-31304-3_1
9. Mandon, H., Su, C., Pang, J., Paul, S., Haar, S., Paulevé, L.: Algorithms for the sequential reprogramming of Boolean networks. IEEE/ACM Trans. Comput. Biol. Bioinf. **16**(5), 1610–1619 (2019)

10. Moon, K., Lee, K., Paulevé, L.: Computational complexity of minimal trap spaces in Boolean networks. SIAM J. Discret. Math. **38**(4), 2691–2708 (2024). https://doi.org/10.1137/23M1553248
11. Naldi, A., Hernandez, C., Abou-Jaoudé, W., Monteiro, P.T., Chaouiya, C., Thieffry, D.: Logical modeling and analysis of cellular regulatory networks with GINsim 3.0. Front. Physiol. **9** (2018). https://doi.org/10.3389/fphys.2018.00646
12. Pastva, S., Šafránek, D., Beneš, N., Brim, L., Henzinger, T.: Repository of logically consistent real-world Boolean network models. bioRxiv (2023). https://doi.org/10.1101/2023.06.12.544361
13. Paul, S., Su, C., Pang, J., Mizera, A.: An efficient approach towards the source-target control of Boolean networks. IEEE/ACM Trans. Comput. Biol. Bioinformatics **17**(6), 1932–1945 (2020)
14. Paulevé, L., Kolčák, J., Chatain, T., Haar, S.: Reconciling qualitative, abstract, and scalable modeling of biological networks. Nat. Commun. **11**(1) (2020). https://doi.org/10.1038/s41467-020-18112-5
15. Paulevé, L., Sené, S.: Boolean networks and their dynamics: the impact of updates. Syst. Biol. Model. Anal., 173–250 (2022). https://doi.org/10.1002/9781119716600.ch6
16. Remy, E., Ruet, P., Thieffry, D.: Graphic requirements for multistability and attractive cycles in a Boolean dynamical framework. Adv. Appl. Math. **41**(3), 335–350 (2008). https://doi.org/10.1016/j.aam.2007.11.003
17. Richard, A., Comet, J.P.: Necessary conditions for multistationarity in discrete dynamical systems. Discret. Appl. Math. **155**(18), 2403–2413 (2007). https://doi.org/10.1016/j.dam.2007.04.019
18. Roncalli, T., Paulevé, L.: Variable-depth simulation of most permissive Boolean networks. In: Proceedings of 20th International Conference on Computational Methods in Systems Biology. Lecture Notes in Computer Science, vol. 13447, pp. 138–157. Springer (2022)
19. Su, C., Pang, J.: Sequential temporary and permanent control of Boolean networks. In: Abate, A., Petrov, T., Wolf, V. (eds.) CMSB 2020. LNCS, vol. 12314, pp. 234–251. Springer, Cham (2020). https://doi.org/10.1007/978-3-030-60327-4_13
20. Su, C., Paul, S., Pang, J.: Controlling large Boolean networks with temporary and permanent perturbations. In: ter Beek, M.H., McIver, A., Oliveira, J.N. (eds.) FM 2019. LNCS, vol. 11800, pp. 707–724. Springer, Cham (2019). https://doi.org/10.1007/978-3-030-30942-8_41
21. Su, C., Pang, J.: A dynamics-based approach for the target control of Boolean networks. In: Proc. 11th ACM Conference on Bioinformatics, Computational Biology, and Health Informatics, pp. 1–8. ACM Press (2020)
22. Thomas, R.: On the relation between the logical structure of systems and their ability to generate multiple steady states or sustained oscillations. In: Numerical Methods in the Study of Critical Phenomena, pp. 180–193. Springer (1981)
23. World Health Organization: The top 10 causes of death (2020). https://www.who.int/news-room/fact-sheets/detail/the-top-10-causes-of-death. Accessed 08 Apr 2026
24. Zeyen, O., Pang, J.: Target control of Boolean networks with permanent Edgetic perturbations. In: Proceedings of 61st IEEE Conference on Decision and Control, pp. 4236–4243 (2022). https://doi.org/10.1109/CDC51059.2022.9992790
25. Zhong, Q., et al.: Edgetic perturbation models of human inherited disorders. Mol. Syst. Biol. **5**, 312 (2009)
26. Zhu, F., Nie, G.: Cell reprogramming: methods, mechanisms and applications. Cell Regeneration **14**(1), 12 (2025)

Modulation-Reaction Networks

Leo Lobski[1] and Yoàv Montacute[2](✉)

[1] University College London, London, UK
leo.lobski.21@ucl.ac.uk
[2] National Institute of Informatics, Tokyo, Japan
montacute@nii.ac.jp

Abstract. Biochemical systems involve both the flow of matter, in which entities transform into one another via reactions, and the flow of information, in which entities regulate which reactions may occur. Boolean networks capture the latter; reaction networks capture the former. Yet no unified qualitative formalism treats regulated reactions as its principal objects of study, despite their prominence in standards such as the Systems Biology Graphical Notation Process Description (SBGN-PD) language. We introduce modulation-reaction networks (MR-networks), a mathematical framework in which entities modulate reactions through activations and inhibitions, and study their synchronous Boolean semantics. To reason about MR-networks we develop Modulation-Reaction Logic (MRL), a hybrid modal μ-calculus whose modalities reason about the structure of the network and whose fixed-point operators capture temporal evolution of the computation. We establish a collection of validities, including a complete characterisation of the one-step update rule, and demonstrate the expressive power of MRL by formalising properties of biological interest such as reachability, sustained production, and presence of attractors. We show that MRL admits model-checking via an evaluation game, and introduce a bisimulation relation for MR-networks, which is proved to be invariant for all MRL-formulas. As a step towards a biologically more realistic computational model, we sketch the asynchronous semantics of MR-networks, and outline how the developments for the synchronous case transfer to the study of the asynchronous one.

Keywords: Boolean network · Reaction network · SBGN-PD · MR-network · Modal logic · μ-calculus · Model checking

1 Introduction

Boolean networks are a widely used and studied model for regulatory networks in biology and related sciences [5,14,17,23,24,26]. A Boolean network features a *regulatory graph* [1], which consists of a set of vertices that represent the entities (e.g. genes) which regulate each other via two kinds of edges: *activations* and

L. Lobski and Y. Montacute—Both authors contributed equally to this work.

P. T. Monteiro (Ed.): CMSB 2026, LNBI 16678, pp. 19–37, 2027.
https://doi.org/10.1007/978-3-032-30870-2_2

inhibitions. We give an example of a regulatory graph in Fig. 1(A). The *state* of a Boolean network is simply an assignment of Boolean truth values to each vertex of the regulatory graph. The interpretation is that an entity (e.g. signal, molecule or a phenotype) is either present (active) or absent (inactive). A model of computation provides the rules that are used to transition from one state to another: this takes the form of a Boolean function for each node, together with conditions under which the truth value of the state is updated by applying the function. We note that in the usual presentation, the Boolean functions are taken to be part of the data of the Boolean network, rather than part of the semantics. We choose to view them as part of the semantics, while the syntax is provided by the regulatory graph. This allows interpreting the regulatory graphs under other dynamics, including quantitative ones. A Boolean network can be thought to represent the *logical* or *information* flow between the entities: instead of capturing transformations between entities, it tells how they activate or inhibit each other.

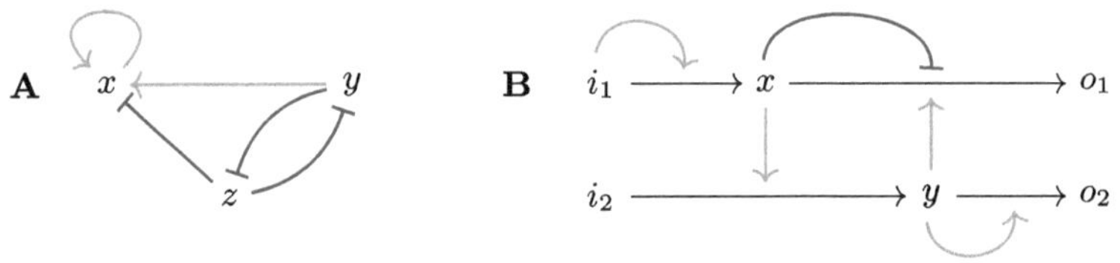

Fig. 1. **A**: An example of a regulatory graph taken from [10, Fig. 1]. **B**: An example MR-network, whose structure is taken from [25, Fig. 9].

Reaction networks, on the other hand, represent transformations between entities, by describing how reactants transform into products [12,15]. At the bare minimum, a reaction network consists of a graph, whose edge indicates a reaction between chemical or biological entities. A reaction network, therefore, represents *matter* or *entity* flow. Depending on the level of abstraction, a reaction network may include enough information to describe a dynamical system, or it may be purely qualitative, describing *possibilities* of transformations rather than rates of change. Qualitative networks can capture essential features of interest by abstracting away the details, thereby reducing computational complexity. Since we are interested in combining reaction networks with Boolean networks, we mostly focus on qualitative semantics. A well-studied qualitative semantics of reaction networks is given by the Boolean semantics of BIOCHAM [6,7], where, akin to Boolean networks, the state of a network is represented by an assignment of Boolean truth values, but crucially to both all the entities *and* all the reactions. The interpretation is that each entity is either present or absent, and that each reaction is either *active* or *inactive*. The transitions of BIOCHAM take place asynchronously, resulting in nondeterministic semantics.

Any modelling of biochemical processes involves a mix of regulatory and process-like behaviour, and hence a mix of information and matter flow. This is accounted for in the approaches to chemical reaction networks including inhibitors as part of reaction data [11,12]. For example, the diagram in Fig. 2 represents modulation of nicotinic receptor opening by nicotine. Similarly, Fig. 1(B) depicts a system where x activates the production of y and inhibits its own degradation, while y activates the degradation of x. Systems Biology Graphical Notation (SBGN) is a graphical notational standard for representing biological processes, featuring three levels of description, of which Process Description (SBGN-PD) captures both matter flow in the form of the *process nodes* and information flow in the form of the *modulations*. Figure 2 shows an example of a (rather simple) SBGN-PD diagram. The feature distinguishing SBGN-PD diagrams from both Boolean and reaction networks is that, instead of directly regulating other entities, the entities regulate the processes (via the modulations). This can be thought of as a refinement of a Boolean network: instead of describing the regulation relations between the entities, the precise mechanism via which the regulation happens is included [1,11].

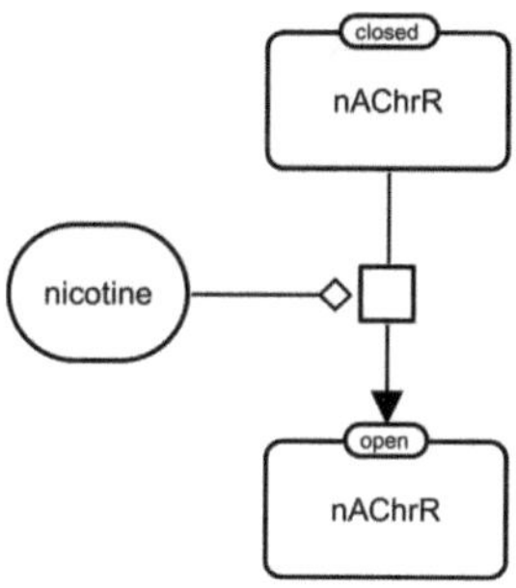

Fig. 2. An example of an SBGN-PD diagram with one process and one modulation, taken from [19, Fig. 2.42].

In this work, taking inspiration from SBGN-PD, we introduce *modulation-reaction networks* (MR-networks) as formal mathematical models of regulated reactions. While here we consider only two kinds of regulations, *activation* and *inhibition*, we expect this framework to generalise to MR-networks with more diverse regulatory components, ultimately yielding a mathematical theory of all the modulations allowed in SBGN-PD and more broadly in biological modelling.

As in reaction networks, we represent the matter flow as a graph. The graph, however, varies with time, as the edges can appear and disappear as they are being activated or inhibited by the entities, much like in Boolean networks. Figure 1(B) shows an example of an MR-network. We study Boolean synchronous semantics for the MR-networks in detail, and give an overview of asynchronous BIOCHAM style semantics and of discrete qualitative semantics. In order to reason with MR-networks, we introduce a formal language and a logic **MRL** that is sound with respect to the computational semantics. From the logical point of view, we treat MR-networks as a sequence of labelled transition systems: the modalities control which transitions affect the truth value of a formula. We identify formulas that capture biologically interesting properties of the MR-networks. While the developments of this paper mostly pertain to the synchronous update rule introduced in Sect. 2, we emphasise that the formulas of **MRL** can be interpreted over the asynchronous semantics outlined in Sect. 6. This, in particular, applies to the formulas describing biologically relevant network properties of Sect. 4. Asynchronous semantics is more interesting from the biological point of view: it is more realistic to assume that the transitions occur locally in their own time rather than following a global clock. The precise validities and network properties under the asynchronous semantics are the subject of a forthcoming paper.

Structure of the Paper. In Sect. 2, we define MR-networks and their synchronous semantics. Section 3 introduces the logic of MR-networks **MRL** and establishes some validities. In Sect. 4, we further study the formulas of **MRL** and the network properties they correspond to, with particular emphasis on biologically relevant properties. Section 5 introduces evaluation games and the bisimulation relation for MR-networks: the former is used for model-checking, the latter is used to obtain inexpressibility results. In Sect. 6, we give a translation from MR-networks to Boolean networks, and discuss alternative semantics, including the asynchronous semantics. Section 7 concludes and outlines directions for future work.

2 MR-Networks

We introduce our main objects of study.

Definition 1 (MR-network). *An* MR-network $(V, R, M^{\to}, M^{\dashv})$ *consists of a finite set* V *of* vertices, *a binary relation* $R \subseteq V \times V$ *whose pairs are called* reactions, *and binary relations* $M^{\to}, M^{\dashv} \subseteq V \times R$ *whose pairs are called* modulations.

We will often write uRv to denote $(u, v) \in R$. If uRv, we say that u is the *source* and v is the *target* of the reaction. If $wM^{\to}r$, we say that the vertex w *activates* the reaction r, and if $wM^{\dashv}r$, we say that w *inhibits* r. In both cases, we say that w *modulates* r.

Example 1. On the right, we draw the MR-network with $V = \{x, y, z\}$, $R = \{(x, y)\}$, $M^{\to} = \{(z, (x, y))\}$ and $M^{\dashv} = \varnothing$. It formalises the SBGN-PD diagram of Fig. 2, once the modulation is interpreted as activation.

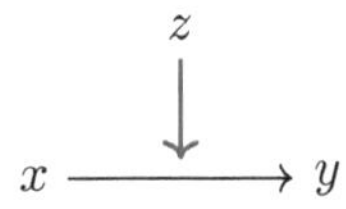

Next, we define the synchronous update rule of MR-networks, which will be the semantics studied for the majority of the paper; alternative semantics are discussed in Sect. 6. We write $\mathbb{Z}_2 = \{0, 1\}$ for the integers modulo 2.

Definition 2 (Valuation and state). *Let* $(V, R, M^{\to}, M^{\dashv})$ *be an MR-network. A* valuation *is a function* $f : V \to \mathbb{Z}_2$. *A* state *is a pair* (f, g) *of a valuation* f *and a function* $g : R \to \mathbb{Z}_2$.

Given a valuation $f : V \to \mathbb{Z}_2$, it induces the function $g : R \to \mathbb{Z}_2$ as follows:

$$g(u,v) := f(u) \wedge \bigvee_{w \in V : M^{\to}(w,(u,v))} f(w) \wedge \bigwedge_{w \in V : M^{\dashv}(w,(u,v))} \neg f(w). \tag{1}$$

Given a state (f, g), it induces a valuation $f' : V \to \mathbb{Z}_2$ as follows:

$$f'(u) := f(u) \vee \bigvee_{w \in V : (w,u) \in R} g(w,u). \tag{2}$$

A *transition* is a pair of states, written as $(f, g) \longrightarrow (f', g')$ such that f' is the valuation induced by (f, g), and g' is the function induced by f'.

Definition 3 (Computation). *Let $(V, R, M^{\to}, M^{\dashv})$ be an MR-network, and let $f_0 : V \to \mathbb{Z}_2$ be a valuation. The* computation *starting from f_0 is the sequence of states $\{(f_i, g_i)\}_{i \in \mathbb{N}}$ such that (f_0, g_0) is the state extending f_0, and for each $i \in \mathbb{N}$, the pair $(f_i, g_i) \longrightarrow (f_{i+1}, g_{i+1})$ is the state transition induced by (f_i, g_i).*

Example 2. Consider the MR-network obtained from Example 1 by making y an inhibitor of the reaction, i.e. $M^{\dashv} = \{(y, (x, y))\}$. With the initial valuation $x, z \mapsto 1$ and $y \mapsto 0$, we obtain the computation below. Note that the reaction (x, y) is inactive in the fixed-point, so that the production of y is not sustained.

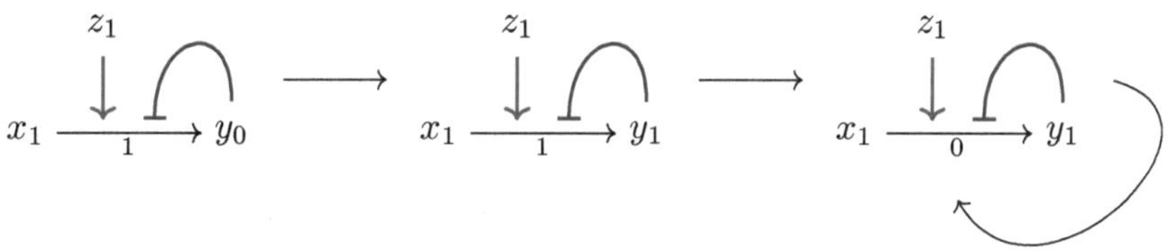

3 Formal Language

We define the formal language of *Modulation-Reaction Logic* (**MRL**). The syntax of **MRL** is defined recursively as follows:

$$\varphi ::= 0 \mid 1 \mid \neg\varphi \mid \varphi \wedge \psi \mid \Diamond^{+}\varphi \mid \Diamond^{-}\varphi \mid X\varphi \mid \mu p.\varphi \mid i \mid @_i\varphi,$$

where $i \in \mathbf{Nom}$; the set **Nom** is a finite set whose members are called *nominals*. In $\mu p.\varphi$, we require that p occurs only positively in φ (i.e. under an even number of negations). We define the Boolean operations $\vee, \to$ and $\leftrightarrow$ in the usual way; we define $\top := 0 \vee 1$ and $\bot := 0 \wedge 1$; we define the duals $\Box^{(\cdot)} := \neg \Diamond^{(\cdot)} \neg$, where $(\cdot) \in \{+, -\}$, and $\nu p.\varphi := \neg \mu p. \neg \varphi[\neg p/p]$. We further abbreviate $F\varphi := \mu p.(\varphi \vee Xp)$ and $G\varphi := \neg F \neg \varphi$.

The constants 0 and 1 test the current activation value of a vertex. The connectives $\neg$ and $\wedge$ are Boolean. The *network modalities* express movement on the graph: $\Diamond^{+}\varphi$ (resp. $\Diamond^{-}\varphi$) holds at a vertex if some successor (resp. predecessor) along an active reaction satisfies φ. The *computation modalities* express movement on the temporal axis: $X\varphi$ holds if φ holds at the next computation step. The derived modalities $F\varphi$ and $G\varphi$ hold if φ holds at some (resp. every) future step. The *fixed-point operator* $\mu p.\varphi$ denotes the least property p satisfying φ; its dual $\nu p.\varphi$ denotes the greatest such property. The *hybrid operators* allow reference to specific vertices: a nominal i holds at x iff x is the vertex named i, and $@_i\varphi$ asserts that φ holds at the vertex named i.

Semantics. By an *MR-model* we mean a pair $(\mathcal{M}, f_0)$ of an MR-network $\mathcal{M}$ and a valuation f_0. An MR-model thus induces a sequence of states $\{(f_i, g_i)\}_{i\in\mathbb{N}}$, and hence a sequence of MR-models $\{\mathcal{M}_i\}_{i\in\mathbb{N}}$ defined by $\mathcal{M}_i := (\mathcal{M}, f_i)$.

The fixed-point operator $\mu p.\varphi$ binds the variable p; evaluating φ during the fixed-point computation requires interpreting p as a set of vertex-time pairs that changes at each approximation stage. To handle this, satisfaction is defined relative to an *assignment* $\sigma : \mathbf{Var} \to \mathcal{P}(V \times \mathbb{N})$, which maps each propositional variable to the set of pairs (x, i) at which it is considered true. We write $\sigma[p \mapsto S]$ for the assignment that maps p to S and agrees with σ otherwise.

In the clauses in Table 1, we assume a fixed MR-model $(\mathcal{M}, f_0)$ and an assignment σ; we refer to the whole chain of induced models $\mathcal{M}_i$ and states (f_i, g_i). Given $x \in V$ we define the satisfaction relation $\vDash_\sigma$ recursively in Table 1. For the fixed-point modality, we note that the positivity condition on p ensures that $\Phi_\sigma^{\varphi,p}$ is monotone, so the least fixed-point exists by the Knaster-Tarski theorem. On finite MR-networks with monotone activation, the valuation $\{f_i\}_{i\in\mathbb{N}}$ stabilises: the fixed-point is therefore reached in finitely many iterations of $\Phi_\sigma^{\varphi,p}$ and is thus computable. A formula with no free propositional variables is called a *sentence*; for sentences, the satisfaction relation does not depend on σ, and we write simply $\mathcal{M}_i, x \vDash \varphi$.

Table 1. Satisfaction of **MRL** formulas.

Network modalities

$\mathcal{M}_i, x \vDash_\sigma j \iff f_i(x) = j, for j \in \mathbb{Z}_2$

$\mathcal{M}_i, x \vDash_\sigma p \iff (x, i) \in \sigma(p)$

$\mathcal{M}_i, x \vDash_\sigma \neg\varphi \iff \mathcal{M}_i, x \nvDash_\sigma \varphi$

$\mathcal{M}_i, x \vDash_\sigma \varphi \wedge \psi \iff \mathcal{M}_i, x \vDash_\sigma \varphi$ and $\mathcal{M}_i, x \vDash_\sigma \psi$

$\mathcal{M}_i, x \vDash_\sigma \Diamond^{+}\varphi \iff \exists y \in V$ s.t. $xRy, g_i(x, y) = 1$ and $\mathcal{M}_i, y \vDash_\sigma \varphi$

$\mathcal{M}_i, x \vDash_\sigma \Diamond^{-}\varphi \iff \exists y \in V$ s.t. $yRx, g_i(y, x) = 1$ and $\mathcal{M}_i, y \vDash_\sigma \varphi$

Computation modalities

$\mathcal{M}_i, x \vDash_\sigma X\varphi \iff \mathcal{M}_{i+1}, x \vDash_\sigma \varphi$

$\mathcal{M}_i, x \vDash_\sigma F\varphi \iff \mathcal{M}_\ell, x \vDash_\sigma \varphi$ for some $\ell \geq i$

Fixed-point modality

$\mathcal{M}_i, x \vDash_\sigma \mu p.\varphi \iff (x, i) \in \bigcap \{S \subseteq V \times \mathbb{N} : \Phi_\sigma^{\varphi,p}(S) \subseteq S\}$,

where $\Phi_\sigma^{\varphi,p}(S) = \{(x', i') \in V \times \mathbb{N} : \mathcal{M}_{i'}, x' \vDash_{\sigma[p\mapsto S]} \varphi\}$

Hybrid modalities

$\mathcal{M}_i, x \vDash_\sigma y \iff x = y$

$\mathcal{M}_i, x \vDash_\sigma @_y\varphi \iff \mathcal{M}_i, y \vDash_\sigma \varphi$

An MR-model $(\mathcal{M}, f_0)$ *models* a sentence $\varphi \in \mathbf{MRL}$ at time i, written $\mathcal{M}_i \vDash \varphi$, if for all $x \in V$ we have $\mathcal{M}_i, x \vDash \varphi$. A sentence φ is *valid in* an MR-network $\mathcal{M}$ if for all valuations f_0 we have $\mathcal{M}_0 \vDash \varphi$. A sentence φ is *valid* if it is valid in all

MR-networks. We write $\mathcal{M} \vDash \varphi$ for validity in $\mathcal{M}$, and $\vDash\varphi$ for validity. We write $\varphi \equiv \psi$ for logical equivalence, i.e. iff $\varphi \leftrightarrow \psi$ is valid.

Proposition 1. *The following formulas are valid:*

(i) $1 \to X1$ *(ii)* $X1 \leftrightarrow (1 \vee \Diamond^{-}\top)$ *(iii)* $FG1 \vee G0$ *(iv)* $\neg \Diamond^{-}0$
(v) $\Diamond^{+}\top \to 1$ *(vi)* $\mu p.(1 \vee \Diamond^{+}Fp) \leftrightarrow 1$ *(vii)* $\mu p.(0 \vee \Diamond^{-}Fp) \leftrightarrow 0$.

Remark 1. As a corollary of (i) , $1 \to G1$ follows by induction. Validities (iv) and (v) demonstrate the asymmetry between $\Diamond^{+}$ and $\Diamond^{-}$: an active reaction requires an active source, but may target an inactive vertex. Note that $\neg\Diamond^{+}0$ is not valid. This asymmetry has no analogue in standard modal logic. Validity (ii) is a complete formal characterisation of the MR-network update rule. The disjuncts in (iii) are mutually exclusive. Validity (vi) expresses that temporal reachability of 'active' collapses to 'currently active': since the source of any forward reaction must itself be active, the signal cannot originate from an inactive vertex. The backward case (vii) is analogous: any vertex reached along backward reactions was necessarily active at an earlier time and hence remains active. Note that our logic also includes the standard validities of hybrid logic (see e.g. [3]).

In Sect. 6, we outline how to interpret the syntax of **MRL** under the asynchronous update rule for MR-networks.

4 Expressivity

We demonstrate the expressive power of **MRL** by formalising several properties of central importance in systems biology. For each, we discuss its biological motivation, give a precise **MRL**-formalisation, and note any subtleties. We note that all the formulas in this section are readily interpreted under the asynchronous semantics introduced in Sect. 6 – hence capturing corresponding properties in a biologically more realistic scenario – while the propositions and the examples are specific to the synchronous semantics studied here.

Throughout, we assume a fixed MR-network $\mathcal{M} = (V, R, M^{\to}, M^{\dashv})$.

Property 1 (Producibility). Given finite sets of nominals X and Y, we define the formula "Y is producible from X" as

$$\mathsf{Prod}(X,Y) := \left(\bigwedge_{x \in X} @_x 1 \right) \to \left(\bigwedge_{y \in Y} @_y F1 \right).$$

The formula $\mathsf{Prod}(X,Y)$ captures the situation in which initial activity of vertices X guarantees that vertices Y eventually become active. In chemical terms, this expresses the fact that an entity in Y is necessarily among the products of X, if the system is allowed to interact long enough. We identify an MR-network condition sufficient for producibility.

Definition 4 (Feedback closure). *Let $\mathcal{M}$ be an MR-network, and let $X \subseteq V$ be a subset of vertices. We define the* feedback closure *of X as the subset $\overline{X} \subseteq V$ recursively constructed as follows. Base case: $X \subseteq \overline{X}$. Recursive case: for every R-path $(x_0, \ldots, x_n)$ satisfying*

- *$x_0 \in \overline{X}$,*
- *for every $i = 1, \ldots, n$, there is an activation $zM^{\rightarrow}(x_{i-1}, x_i)$ such that either $z \in \overline{X}$ or $z = x_j$ for some $j \leq i - 1$,*
- *if $zM^{\multimap}(x_{i-1}, x_i)$ is an inhibition for some reaction in the path, then $z = x_j$ for some $j \geq i$,*

we stipulate that $x_n \in \overline{X}$.

Proposition 2. *Let $\mathcal{M}$ be an MR-network with $X, Y \subseteq V$ such that $Y \subseteq \overline{X}$. Then $\mathcal{M} \vDash \mathsf{Prod}(X, Y)$.*

The simplest non-trivial instance of feedback closure is a path from x to y whose every reaction is activated by some vertex occurring before the reaction, and the only inhibitions come from vertices occurring after the reaction. We note that such paths exhibiting feedback inhibition have been studied by Savageau [21] in the context of the power law approximation.

Example 3. We give an example of a path with feedback inhibition on the right. The feedback closure of $\{x\}$ is $\{x, y\}$, and we have $\mathcal{M} \vDash \mathsf{Prod}(x, y)$ and $\mathcal{M} \nvDash \mathsf{Prod}(x, x_1)$.

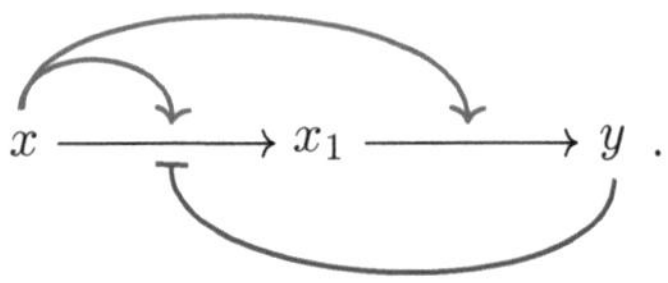

If we think of a subset X as the biochemical entities that are initially present, finding the largest set Y such that $\mathsf{Prod}(X, Y)$ is valid corresponds to *reaction prediction*, or exploring the full product space. Proposition 2 implies that the feedback closure $\overline{X}$ gives a particularly well-behaved subset of the product space, which is computable using Definition 4: one starts with X, and iteratively adds all vertices reachable by paths that satisfy the specified conditions. The full product space is significantly more complicated to compute.

The opposite question to reaction prediction is that of *(retro)synthesis* or *production*: given a subset Y, can we find a (disjoint) subset X such that $\mathsf{Prod}(X, Y)$? This has a much higher computational complexity than reaction prediction, as it is quantified over all subsets of an MR-network, thus scaling exponentially with the size of the network. In practice, the question of production, of course, also involves the design of the network.

The notion of producibility discussed above is a rather weak one: it merely records whether an entity is produced *at least once* during the computation. **MRL** can also capture a stronger notion.

Property 2 (Sustained production). Given a nominal y, we define the formula of *sustained production* of y as $\mathsf{Sust}(y) := @_y \, FG \, \Diamond^{-} 1$. *Sustained producibility* on sets X and Y is then defined analogously to producibility (Property 1):

$$\mathsf{SustProd}(X,Y) := \left(\bigwedge_{x\in X} @_x 1\right) \to \left(\bigwedge_{y\in Y} \mathsf{Sust}(y)\right).$$

The formula $\mathsf{Sust}(y)$ says that y can be kept in a state where it is continuously receiving active input. Validity (i) $(1 \to X1)$ implies that once a vertex becomes active it remains active. So the property of sustained production is not about the vertex value, but about whether the incoming reactions remain active.

In Example 3, we saw that y is producible from x; however, $\mathsf{SustProd}(x,y)$ fails to be valid, as under the valuation $(x \mapsto 1, x_1 \mapsto 0, y \mapsto 1)$ neither reaction will ever activate, so that there are no incoming active reactions to y. On the other hand, the formula $\mathsf{SustProd}(\{x,x_1\},y)$ is valid.

Property 3 (Reachability). Given two nominals x and y, we define the formula "y is reachable from x" as

$$\mathsf{Reach}(x,y) := @_x\, \mu p.\, (y \vee F\, \Diamond^+ p)\,.$$

The formula $\mathsf{Reach}(x,y)$ is satisfied in $\mathcal{M}_i$ if and only if either $x = y$ or there is an R-path $(x = x_0, \ldots, x_n = y)$ and a sequence of time instances $i_1, \ldots, i_n$ satisfying $i \le i_1 \le \cdots \le i_n$ and $g_{i_j}(x_{j-1}, x_j) = 1$ for all $j = 1, \ldots, n$. Thus, $\mathsf{Reach}(x,y)$ generalises the usual notion of reachability within a graph (i.e. the reflexive and transitive closure of the edge relation), while taking into account the fact that reactions can be absent or present. In Example 2 we have $\mathcal{M}_0 \vDash \mathsf{Reach}(x,y)$ but $\mathcal{M}_2 \nvDash \mathsf{Reach}(x,y)$, as the reaction (x,y) will never reactivate. In Example 3, $\mathsf{Reach}(x,y)$ is satisfied if and only if x is initially present and y is initially absent; this suggests a more general link between reachability and producibility.

Proposition 3. *$\mathcal{M} \vDash \mathsf{Prod}(x,y)$ implies $\mathcal{M}_0 \vDash \mathsf{Reach}(x,y)$ with the valuation f_0 defined by $x \mapsto 1$ and $z \mapsto 0$ for $z \ne x$.*

Note that the converse is not true, as there might be inactive inhibitions that prevent producibility. Thus, reachability can be thought of as a refined notion of producibility: it demands that all the reactions between x and y are activated in order, so that there is a material flow from x to y.

The logic **MRL** is able to detect temporal cycles and loops in MR-networks, which we capture in the following two properties.

Property 4 (Cycle). Given a nominal x, we define the formula for "x lies on a cycle" as

$$\mathsf{Cycle}(x) := @_x\, F\, \Diamond^+ (\mu p.\, (x \vee F\, \Diamond^+ p))\,.$$

Property 5 (Infinite forward path). Given a nominal x, we define the formula for "x admits an infinite forward path" as

$$\mathsf{InfFwd}(x) := @_x\, \nu p.\, (F\, \Diamond^+ p)\,.$$

Note that $\mathsf{Cycle}(x)$ is not equivalent to $\mathsf{Reach}(x, x)$, as the latter is valid (x is always reachable from itself), whereas the former is satisfied if there is an R-path from x to itself whose all reactions are activated in order. We, moreover, note that since all of our models are finite, satisfiability of $\mathsf{InfFwd}(x)$ implies presence of a cycle, though x need not lie on it:

Proposition 4. *$\mathcal{M}_i \vDash \mathsf{InfFwd}(x)$ implies there is a $y \in V$ such that $\mathcal{M}_i \vDash \mathsf{Reach}(x, y) \wedge \mathsf{Cycle}(y)$.*

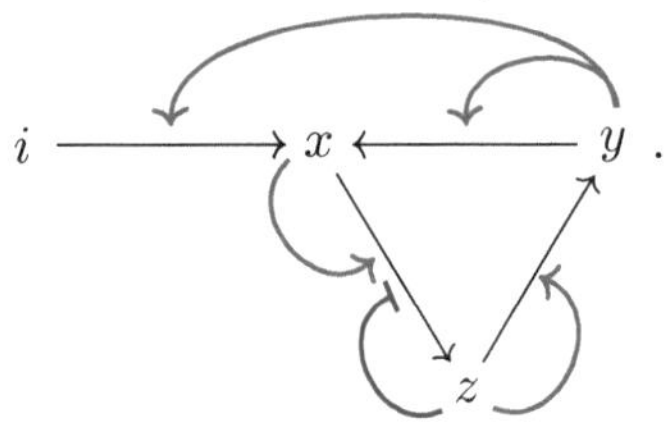

Example 4. We give an example showing that the converse of Proposition 4 fails. Consider the catalytic cycle on the right with the initial valuation $i, y \mapsto 1$ and 0 otherwise. We note that $\mathcal{M}_0 \vDash \mathsf{Reach}(i, x) \wedge \mathsf{Cycle}(x)$, but $\mathcal{M}_0 \nvDash \mathsf{InfFwd}(i)$, as the reaction (x, z) can be activated exactly once. In the network without the inhibition, we would indeed have that $\mathsf{InfFwd}(i)$ is satisfied.

The presence of cycles becomes more interesting under semantics where vertices can deactivate, such as the asynchronous semantics of Sect. 6.

We list further properties expressible in **MRL** in the table below, partially inspired by the properties in [7]:

MRL formula	Meaning
$@_x\, \mu p.\,(z \vee F\,\Diamond^+ p) \wedge @_z\, \mu q.\,(y \vee F\,\Diamond^+ q)$	y is reachable from x via z
$\mu p.\,(\varphi \vee (\psi \wedge Xp))$	ψ holds until φ holds (weak until)
$\mu p.\,(@_x 1 \vee (\neg(@_y 1) \wedge Xp))$	x is producible without producing y
$@_x\,(1 \to \nu p.\,(1 \wedge Xp))$	x is a steady state
$@_x\,(1 \to G1)$	x is a permanent state
$\bigwedge_{a\in A} @_a\, G\, \Box^+ (\bigvee_{a'\in A} a')$	A is a sink set
$\bigwedge_{b\in B} @_b\, \mu p.\,(\bigvee_{a\in A} a \vee (F\,\Diamond^+ p \wedge \Box^+ p))$	B flows into A

The properties expressing steady and permanent states are meaningful only in a semantics where vertices can deactivate, as under current semantics they are validities.

The last two properties can be used to define *attractors*. Let us write $\mathsf{Sink}(A)$ for "A is a sink set" and $\mathsf{Flow}(B, A)$ for "B flows into A". $\mathsf{Sink}(A)$ is satisfied if there are no outgoing active reactions from A – once matter flows into A, it is trapped in A. In Example 3, the formulas $\mathsf{Sink}(y)$ and $\mathsf{Sink}(x_1, y)$ are evidently valid; less evidently, the formula $XX\mathsf{Sink}(x)$ is also valid. $\mathsf{Flow}(B, A)$ is satisfied if from every vertex in B some vertex in A is reachable, and all paths that start from B end up in A.

Property 6 (Attractors). For sets of nominals A and B, we define the formula "A is a preattractor of B" as $\mathsf{PreAttr}(A, B) := \mathsf{Sink}(A) \wedge \mathsf{Flow}(B, A)$. We then define "$A$ is the attractor of B" as

$$\mathsf{Attr}(A, B) := \mathsf{PreAttr}(A, B) \bigwedge_{A' \subsetneq A} \neg \mathsf{PreAttr}(A', B).$$

The attractor of B is thus the minimal sink set A into which B flows: every proper subset of A is either not a sink set or B does not flow into it. In Example 4, we have $\mathcal{M}_0 \vDash \mathsf{Flow}(V, z)$, but z cannot be a (pre)attractor as it is not a sink. Instead, we have $\mathcal{M}_0 \vDash \mathsf{Attr}(\{x, y, z\}, V)$ and $\mathcal{M}_2 \vDash \mathsf{Attr}(x, V)$.

5 Evaluation Games and Bisimulation

Here we characterise satisfiability of **MRL**-formulas in MR-models in two alternative ways: *evaluation games* give an algorithm for model-checking, while invariance under *bisimulation* is used to obtain inexpressibility results.

5.1 Evaluation Games

The Tarski-style semantics of Sect. 3 defines truth via set-theoretic fixed-points. The evaluation game provides an equivalent game-theoretic characterisation in which truth is witnessed by a concrete strategy. Existence of a winning strategy (Theorem 1) gives an algorithm to determine whether a property is satisfied in an MR-network, thus giving a complexity bound for model-checking (Corollary 1). To demonstrate that a vertex satisfies a formula, Verifier must exhibit the relevant neighbours, choose the right future time steps, and unfold fixed-points until an atom is reached. In MR-networks, this has a direct biological consequence: a play of the game traces a signal propagation path through the network across time, constrained at each step by active reactions.

Every formula of **MRL** can be brought into *negation normal form* (NNF) by pushing negations inward using De Morgan duality, the dual modalities defined in Sect. 3, the self-duality $\neg X\varphi \equiv X \neg \varphi$ (since the temporal successor is deterministic), and the atom dualities $\neg 0 \equiv 1$, $\neg 1 \equiv 0$. For example, the NNF of $\neg \Diamond^{+} \neg 0$ is $\Box^{+}0$, and the NNF of $\neg F(1 \wedge \Diamond^{+}0)$ is $G(0 \vee \Box^{+}1)$. We assume throughout this subsection that formulas are in NNF.

Let φ be an **MRL** sentence in NNF. The *evaluation game* $\mathcal{E}(\varphi, \mathcal{M}_i, x)$ is played between two players, **Verifier** ($\exists$) and **Falsifier** ($\forall$), starting from position $(\varphi, (x, i))$. A *position* is a pair $(\psi, (y, j))$ with $\psi \in \mathrm{cl}(\varphi)$ and $(y, j) \in V \times \mathbb{N}$, where $\mathrm{cl}(\varphi)$ denotes the *closure* of φ, i.e. the set of subformulas of φ, closed under unfolding of fixed-point variables.

Moves and Winning Condition. From a position $(\psi, (y, j))$ the game proceeds according to the outermost connective of ψ as depicted in Table 2.

If the active player at a $\Diamond^{(\cdot)}$ or $\Box^{(\cdot)}$ position has no legal move (i.e. no active edge in the required direction), that player loses immediately. A play at an atom $a \in \{0, 1\}$ terminates: $\exists$ wins if $f_j(y) = a$; $\forall$ wins otherwise. Similarly, at a nominal a (resp. $\neg a$), $\exists$ wins if $y{=}a$ (resp. $y{\neq}a$). A play may be infinite if it passes through fixed-point positions $\mu p.\psi$ or $\nu p.\psi$ infinitely often. To each fixed-point subformula $\sigma p.\psi$ of φ (where $\sigma \in \{\mu, \nu\}$) we assign a *priority* $\Omega(\sigma p.\psi) \in \mathbb{N}$, such that:

1. $\Omega(\mu p.\psi)$ is odd and $\Omega(\nu p.\psi)$ is even;
2. if $\sigma_1 p_1.\psi_1$ is a proper subformula of $\sigma_2 p_2.\psi_2$, then $\Omega(\sigma_1 p_1.\psi_1) > \Omega(\sigma_2 p_2.\psi_2)$.

Table 2. Table of moves

Position	Move	Next position
$(\psi_1 \vee \psi_2,\ (y,j))$	$\exists$ picks $k \in \{1,2\}$	$(\psi_k,(y,j))$
$(\psi_1 \wedge \psi_2,\ (y,j))$	$\forall$ picks $k \in \{1,2\}$	$(\psi_k,(y,j))$
$(\Diamond^{+}\psi,\ (y,j))$	$\exists$ picks z s.t. $yRz,\ g_j(y,z)=1$	$(\psi,(z,j))$
$(\Box^{+}\psi,\ (y,j))$	$\forall$ picks z s.t. $yRz,\ g_j(y,z)=1$	$(\psi,(z,j))$
$(\Diamond^{-}\psi,\ (y,j))$	$\exists$ picks z s.t. $zRy,\ g_j(z,y)=1$	$(\psi,(z,j))$
$(\Box^{-}\psi,\ (y,j))$	$\forall$ picks z s.t. $zRy,\ g_j(z,y)=1$	$(\psi,(z,j))$
$(X\psi,\ (y,j))$	—	$(\psi,(y,j+1))$
$(F\psi,\ (y,j))$	$\exists$ picks $\ell \geq j$	$(\psi,(y,\ell))$
$(G\psi,\ (y,j))$	$\forall$ picks $\ell \geq j$	$(\psi,(y,\ell))$
$(@_a\psi,\ (y,j))$	—	$(\psi,(a,j))$
$(\mu p.\psi,\ (y,j))$	—	$(\psi,(y,j))$
$(\nu p.\psi,\ (y,j))$	—	$(\psi,(y,j))$
$(p,\ (y,j))$ for p bound by σ	—	$(\sigma p.\psi,(y,j))$

An infinite play is won by $\exists$ if and only if the highest priority visited infinitely often is *even*. Thus, infinite looping through a ν-variable is favourable to $\exists$ (the property persists), while infinite looping through a μ-variable is favourable to $\forall$ (the least fixed-point is never witnessed).

Example 5. Consider the MR-network of Example 3 with the initial valuation $x \mapsto 1,\ x_1 \mapsto 0,\ y \mapsto 0$. We demonstrate the evaluation game on $\mathsf{Reach}(x,y) = @_x\mu p.(y \vee F \Diamond^{+} p)$. The game tree is depicted on the right. Note that all moves in this game are verifier moves.

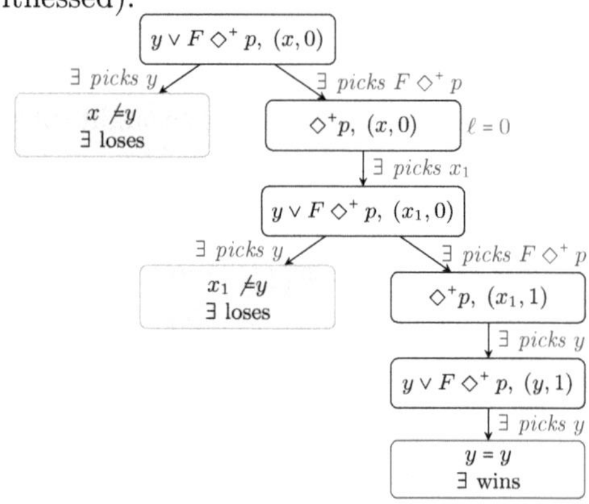

Theorem 1 (Adequacy). *Let φ be an* **MRL** *sentence in NNF. Then*

$$\mathcal{M}_i, x \vDash \varphi \iff \exists \text{ has a winning strategy in } \mathcal{E}(\varphi, \mathcal{M}_i, x).$$

Corollary 1 (Model-checking complexity). *For finite MR-networks, model-checking* **MRL** *reduces to solving a parity game and is hence decidable in* **NP** $\cap$ **coNP**. *More concretely, checking $\mathcal{M}_i, x \vDash \varphi$ can be done in time $O(|V|^d \cdot |\varphi|^d)$ where d is the alternation depth of φ.*

5.2 Bisimulation

Bisimulation is a relation between two MR-models whose existence guarantees that related vertices satisfy the same **MRL** sentences.

Definition 5 (Bisimulation). *Let* $(\mathcal{M}, f_0)$ *and* $(\mathcal{N}, f_0')$ *be MR-models with vertex sets* V *and* W*, edge relations* R *and* S*, and induced state sequences* $(f_i, g_i)_{i\in\mathbb{N}}$ *and* $(f_i', h_i)_{i\in\mathbb{N}}$*, respectively. An* MRL-bisimulation *is a relation* $Z \subseteq (V \times \mathbb{N}) \times (W \times \mathbb{N})$ *satisfying the following conditions whenever* $(v,k)\ Z\ (w,\ell)$*:*

(1) $f_k(v) = f_\ell'(w)$.
(2) $(v, k+1)\ Z\ (w, \ell+1)$.
(3) $(a^{\mathcal{M}}, k)\ Z\ (a^{\mathcal{N}}, \ell)$*, for each nominal* $a \in \mathbf{Nom}$.
(4) ***($\Diamond^+$-forth)*** *If* vRv' *and* $g_k(v,v') = 1$*, then there exists* $w' \in W$ *with* wSw'*,* $h_\ell(w,w') = 1$*, and* $(v',k)\ Z\ (w',\ell)$.
(5) ***($\Diamond^+$-back)*** *If* wSw' *and* $h_\ell(w,w') = 1$*, then there exists* $v' \in V$ *with* vRv'*,* $g_k(v,v') = 1$*, and* $(v',k)\ Z\ (w',\ell)$.
(6) ***($\Diamond^-$-forth)*** *If* $v'Rv$ *and* $g_k(v',v) = 1$*, then there exists* $w' \in W$ *with* $w'Sw$*,* $h_\ell(w',w) = 1$*, and* $(v',k)\ Z\ (w',\ell)$.
(7) ***($\Diamond^-$-back)*** *If* $w'Sw$ *and* $h_\ell(w',w) = 1$*, then there exists* $v' \in V$ *with* $v'Rv$*,* $g_k(v',v) = 1$*, and* $(v',k)\ Z\ (w',\ell)$.

We write $(\mathcal{M}_k, v) \backsim (\mathcal{N}_\ell, w)$ *if there exists an MRL-bisimulation* Z *such that* $(v,k)\ Z\ (w,\ell)$.

Theorem 2 (Bisimulation invariance). *If* $(\mathcal{M}_k, v) \backsim (\mathcal{N}_\ell, w)$*, then for every* **MRL** *sentence* φ *we have* $\mathcal{M}_k, v \models \varphi \iff \mathcal{N}_\ell, w \models \varphi$.

The properties defined in Sect. 4 demonstrate that **MRL** can detect the *existence* of active paths, cycles, and temporal reachability. Here we use bisimulation invariance to show that **MRL** cannot distinguish the *number* of active reactions incident to a vertex.

Proposition 5. *There is no* **MRL** *sentence* φ *such that for all MR-models* $(\mathcal{M}, f_0)$ *one has* $\mathcal{M}_i, x \models \varphi \iff \left|\{y \in V : yRx, g_i(y,x) = 1\}\right| = 2$.

A second source of indistinguishability is structural: two MR-networks with distinct modulation structures but identical induced dynamics $(f_i, g_i)_{i\in\mathbb{N}}$ satisfy the same **MRL** sentences at every vertex and time, as the satisfaction relation depends only on f_i and g_i. Thus, **MRL** is blind both to multiplicities of active reactions and to the particular modulation mechanism.

6 Other Models of Computation

Here we briefly discuss how MR-networks and their synchronous semantics connect to other models of computation. We do this by encoding MR-networks as Boolean networks, as well as by describing two possibilities for more elaborate semantics: *asynchronous Boolean semantics*, resulting in a nondeterministic computation, and *discrete quantitative dynamics*, which is deterministic.

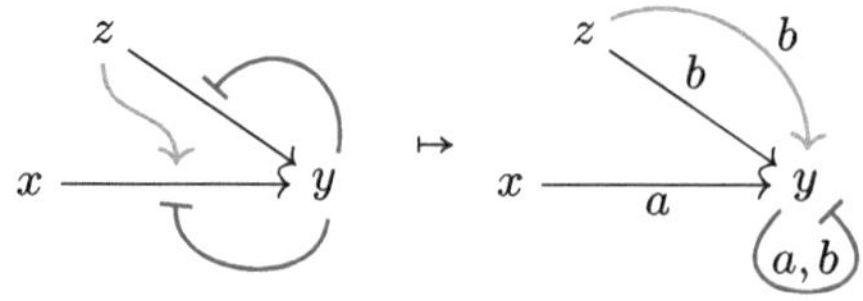

Fig. 3. An encoding of an MR-network as a Boolean network.

Translation to Boolean Networks. Every MR-network can be encoded as a regulatory graph with the same vertices and three binary relations: *reaction*, *activation* and *inhibition* relations, as well as a label for each edge in the graph. We give an example translation from an MR-network to the corresponding regulatory graph in Fig. 3. The translation thus assigns a unique label to each reaction, and shifts the target of a modulation to the target of the reaction it modulates, while adding the label of the reaction to the set of labels of the modulation. In the resulting regulatory graph, each modulation is, therefore, labelled with a non-empty subset of the reaction labels. The Boolean update function for a vertex v is then defined analogously to MR-networks: v activates if and only if v is already active, or there is a reaction (u, v) with label a such that u is active, there is at least one activation with label a and no inhibitions with label a. While this translation is a faithful representation of MR-networks (in the sense of being an injective map from MR-networks to Boolean networks), the conceptual intuition of reactions appearing and disappearing as the computation proceeds is lost. For example, while it is still possible to define the semantics of the reachability modalities $\Diamond^+$ and $\Diamond^-$, the definitions become rather cumbersome. Moreover, the translation is tied to the synchronous semantics: e.g. the asynchronous semantics we shall discuss next is not equivalent to the usual asynchronous update scheme of Boolean networks, as (in)activity of a reaction is part of a state, and can thus be updated without any of the vertices being updated. Nonetheless, we find it important to point out the existence of such translation, as it can help with implementation as well as with establishing connections to well-understood models of computation, such as Petri nets [1].

Asynchronous Boolean Semantics. The asynchronous Boolean semantics is given as follows, which is a restricted version of the semantics introduced in [18]:

- a reaction can go from inactive to active if its source is active, at least one of its activators is active, and none of its inhibitors are active (that is, precisely when the update condition (1) is satisfied),
- a reaction can go from active to inactive if the activation condition above is no longer satisfied, or if its target is active,
- a vertex can go from inactive to active if there is at least one active incoming reaction (that is, precisely when the update condition (2) is satisfied),
- a vertex can go from active to inactive if there is an active outgoing reaction.

The logic **MRL** can be interpreted over the asynchronous semantics: the assignment function now takes the form $\sigma : \mathbf{Var} \to \mathcal{P}(V \times (V \sqcup R)^*)$, i.e. a proposition is interpreted as a pair of a vertex and a finite sequence of vertices and reactions. The set of such sequences $(V \sqcup R)^*$ plays the role of time: each vertex and reaction in the sequence attempts to change its state according to the rules above. The next step modality X now becomes a *one-step possibility modality*: $X\varphi$ holds if and only if there exists a single vertex or a reaction such that φ holds once the update is applied. Similarly, $F\varphi$ holds if there is a sequence in $(V \sqcup R)^*$ such that φ holds once all updates are applied. We also need to change the notion of a model to include the initial state (rather than merely the initial valuation), as the state is no longer uniquely determined by the valuation. After these modifications, the **MRL** formulas are interpreted as in Sect. 3. The set of validities is, of course, now distinct, although we note that the modalities F and G can still be obtained via fixed-point operators as before.

Discrete Quantitative Dynamics. The state of discrete quantitative dynamics is given by assigning a nonnegative integer to each vertex and each reaction. The interpretation for vertices is (discretised) concentration of a given entity, while for reactions the integer n tells the flow rate (cf. [2]). At each step, each reaction attempts to transport n units from its source to its target. We additionally assume that each reaction and each modulation is labelled by a positive real number, which represents the strength of the modulation and global reaction rate. In order to have interesting behaviour, we consider *open* MR-networks, whose vertices come with specified subsets of *inputs* and *outputs*. The input and the output sets are assumed to be disjoint, the inputs are assumed to have no incoming reactions, and the outputs are assumed to have no outgoing reactions. The input and output vertices correspond to the *empty set* notation of SBGN-PD for sources and sinks. Semantically, to each input we assign a function $\omega \to \mathbb{N}$, i.e. a *stream* of nonnegative integers, specifying the influx of new matter at each time step. Correspondingly, the update rule for vertices induces a stream for each output. Hence an open MR-network can be thought of as a function $(\mathbb{N}^\omega)^n \to (\mathbb{N}^\omega)^m$, where n is the number of inputs and m is the number of outputs, giving an interesting connection to the theory of *signal flow graphs* [4,20,22]. Let us denote the labelling function for reactions and modulations by $\ell : R \sqcup M^{\rightarrow} \sqcup M^{\dashv} \to \mathbb{R}_+$. Given an initial valuation $f_0 : V \setminus I \to \mathbb{N}$ on the non-input vertices and a stream $s_v : \omega \to \mathbb{N}$ for each input vertex $v \in I$, we first extend the valuation to the initial state $f_0 : V \to \mathbb{N}$ by defining $f_0(v) := s_v(0)$ on the input vertices $v \in I$. The one-step update rule $f_i \mapsto f_{i+1}$ is then given as follows:

- for each reaction r, the *potential flow* is given by

$$\mathsf{PF}_i(r) := \left\lfloor \ell(r) \cdot \left(\sum_{(v,r)\in M^{\rightarrow}} \ell(v,r) \cdot f_i(v) - \sum_{(v,r)\in M^{\dashv}} \ell(v,r) \cdot f_i(v) \right) \right\rfloor$$

  if the difference between the sums is nonnegative, and by $\mathsf{PF}_i(r) := 0$ otherwise,

- for each vertex v, the *potential outflow* is given by

$$\mathsf{POF}_i(v) := \sum_{(v,u)\in R} \mathsf{PF}_i(v,u);$$

if $\mathsf{POF}_i(v) \leq f_i(v)$, then for each outgoing reaction the *realised flow* is given by its potential flow: $\mathsf{RF}_i(v,u) := \mathsf{PF}_i(v,u)$; if $\mathsf{POF}_i(v) > f_i(v)$, then for each outgoing reaction the realised flow is a fraction of the current state weighted by its potential flow: $\mathsf{RF}_i(v,u) := \left\lfloor \frac{\mathsf{PF}_i(v,u)}{\mathsf{POF}_i(v)} \cdot f_i(v) \right\rfloor$,
- for a non-input and non-output vertex $v \in V \setminus (I \cup O)$, the updated state is given by

$$f_{i+1}(v) := f_i(v) - \sum_{(v,u)\in R} \mathsf{RF}_i(v,u) + \sum_{(u,v)\in R} \mathsf{RF}_i(u,v);$$

for an input vertex $v \in I$, the updated state is given as above, except that the last sum is replaced by the stream value $s_v(i+1)$; for an output vertex $v \in O$, the updated state is simply given by the last sum above, i.e. by the sum of all the realised flows into it.

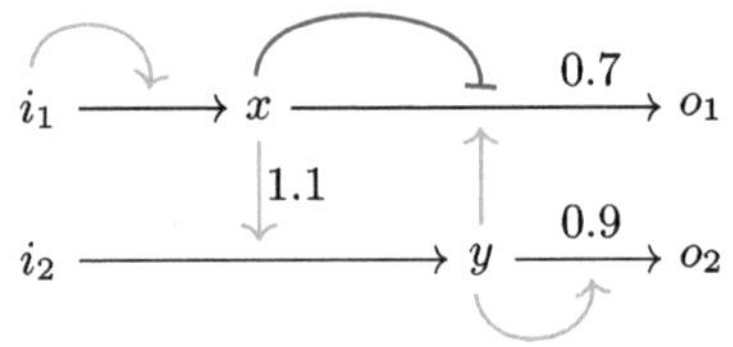

Fig. 4. An open MR-network with labels.

Consider the open MR-network with labels in Fig. 4, which is the network from Fig. 1(B) with added labels. We adopt the convention that an unlabelled edge stands for label 1, i.e. an unweighted reaction or modulation. The input vertices are $\{i_1, i_2\}$ and the output vertices are $\{o_1, o_2\}$. Let us define the initial valuation on the non-input vertices as $f_0(x)$=100, $f_0(y)$=300 and $f_0(o_1)$=$f_0(o_2)$=0, and the streams $s_1(n) := \left\lfloor \frac{100}{n+1} \right\rfloor$ and $s_2(n) :=$150 corresponding to the input vertices i_1 and i_2. The structure of the network implies that the stream s_1 is increasing the entities x, so that we keep increasing x by a decreasing amount, until after time $n = 100$ there is no new inflow of x. The stream s_2 is so chosen in order to have an essentially unlimited supply, so that the only factor on which the production of entities y depends is the number of entities x. We plot the values of entities x and y for the first 130 steps of the computation in Fig. 5. We observe damped oscillatory behaviour that reaches a fixed-point once the input from i_1 stops, which is exactly the behaviour of the continuous time dynamical system obtained for this network by Voit [25].

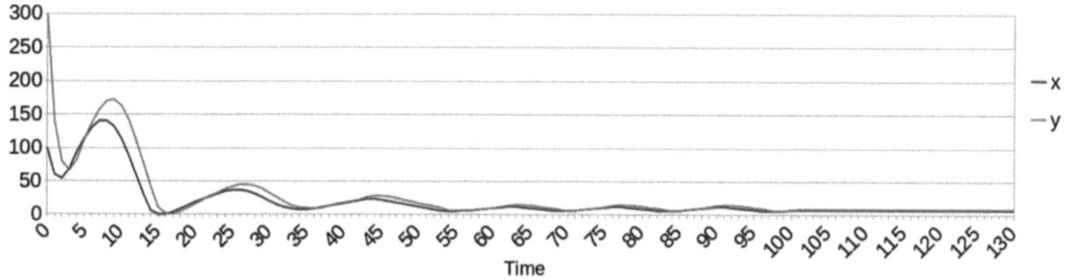

Fig. 5. An example computation of an open labelled MR-network.

7 Conclusion and Future Work

We have introduced MR-networks, their synchronous computation, as well as their logic **MRL**. Three perspectives on the satisfiability of **MRL**-formulas allow formulating *expressibility*, *model-checking* and *inexpressibility* of biological properties in **MRL** with respect to the synchronous semantics. Our usage of the fixed-point modalities streamlines and unifies many properties studied in the literature on a case-by-case basis. While the synchronous update rule is inadequate for most biological applications, we believe that the modular approach taken here – separating networks, computation, formal language and its interpretation – lays the groundwork for more general study of MR-networks and their use in applications. For example, the properties in Sect. 4 can be readily interpreted in the asynchronous semantics described in Sect. 6: what changes are the precise details of models and networks captured by a formula – the overarching biological concept remains the same. In a forthcoming article, we will extend all the developments here – expressibility, model-checking and inexpressibility – to the asynchronous semantics.

Beyond the Boolean case, we have described a quantitative discrete semantics in Sect. 6. An interesting future development would be to give a logic for this semantics. The atomic case would need to be extended to capture the concentration being above (or below) a given threshold, while the other properties of **MRL** would be expected to carry over to the quantitative case.

In order to represent realistic reactions with multiple reactants and products (usually represented using multisets [12,15]), one has to extend MR-networks from graphs to hypergraphs: the relation R would no longer be binary, but would specify a set of sources and a set of targets [2]. Another step closer to a more complete description of biochemical processes will be accounting for other kinds of modulations present in SBGN-PD [19].

In the direction of quantitative semantics, it would be interesting to define composition of open MR-networks, following e.g. the approach of [9] for SBGN-PD diagrams. This would provide a systematic way of building larger MR-networks from smaller ones.

Lastly, for comparing different semantics, it is important to connect MR-networks to model reduction and abstract interpretation techniques [8,11,13,16].

Acknowledgments. Yoàv Montacute is supported by ACT-X, Grant No. JPMJAX24CR, JST, Japan; and by ASPIRE, Grant No. JPMJAP2301, JST, Japan. Leo Lobski is partially supported by ARIA Safeguarded AI programme, UK.

Disclosure of Interests. The authors have no competing interests to declare that are relevant to the content of this article.

References

1. Aduddell, R., Fairbanks, J., Kumar, A., Ocal, P.S., Patterson, E., Shapiro, B.T.: A compositional account of motifs, mechanisms, and dynamics in biochemical regulatory networks. Compositionality **6** (2024). https://doi.org/10.32408/compositionality-6-2
2. Andersen, J.L., Flamm, C., Merkle, D., Stadler, P.F.: Chemical transformation motifs - modelling pathways as integer hyperflows. IEEE/ACM Trans. Comput. Biol. Bioinform. **16**(2), 510–523 (2019). https://doi.org/10.1109/TCBB.2017.2781724
3. Areces, C., ten Cate, B.: Hybrid logics. In: Blackburn, P., van Benthem, J.F.A.K., Wolter, F. (eds.) Handbook of Modal Logic. Studies in Logic and Practical Reasoning, pp. 821–868. North-Holland (2007). https://doi.org/10.1016/S1570-2464(07)80017-6
4. Bonchi, F., Sobociński, P., Zanasi, F.: A Survey of Compositional Signal Flow Theory, pp. 29–56. Springer, Cham (2021). https://doi.org/10.1007/978-3-030-81701-5_2
5. Bornholdt, S.: Boolean network models of cellular regulation: prospects and limitations. J. Roy. Soc. Interface **5**(suppl_1), S85–S94 (2008). https://doi.org/10.1098/rsif.2008.0132.focus
6. Calzone, L., Fages, F., Soliman, S.: Biocham: an environment for modeling biological systems and formalizing experimental knowledge. Bioinformatics **22**(14), 1805–1807 (2006). https://doi.org/10.1093/bioinformatics/btl172
7. Chabrier-Rivier, N., Fages, F., Soliman, S.: The biochemical abstract machine BIOCHAM. In: Danos, V., Schachter, V. (eds.) CMSB 2004. LNCS, vol. 3082, pp. 172–191. Springer, Heidelberg (2005). https://doi.org/10.1007/978-3-540-25974-9_14
8. Chaouiya, C., Feret, J., Tenera Roxo, P.: On model reductions of boolean networks. In: Fages, F., Pérès, S. (eds.) Computational Methods in Systems Biology, pp. 42–60. Springer, Cham (2026). https://doi.org/10.1007/978-3-032-01436-8_3
9. Chaudhuri, A., Köhl, R., Wolkenhauer, O.: A mathematical framework to study organising principles in graphical representations of biochemical processes (2026). https://doi.org/10.48550/arXiv.2410.18024
10. Cury, J.E.R., Tenera Roxo, P., Manquinho, V., Chaouiya, C., Monteiro, P.T.: Computation of immediate neighbours of monotone boolean functions. In: Fages, F., Pérès, S. (eds.) Computational Methods in Systems Biology, pp. 3–22. Springer (2026). https://doi.org/10.1007/978-3-032-01436-8_1
11. Fages, F., Martinez, T., Rosenblueth, D.A., Soliman, S.: Influence networks compared with reaction networks: semantics, expressivity and attractors. IEEE/ACM Trans. Comput. Biol. Bioinform. **15**(4), 1138–1151 (2018). https://doi.org/10.1109/TCBB.2018.2805686

12. Fages, F., Gay, S., Soliman, S.: Inferring reaction systems from ordinary differential equations. Theor. Comput. Sci. **599**, 64–78 (2015). https://doi.org/10.1016/j.tcs.2014.07.032
13. Fages, F., Soliman, S.: Abstract interpretation and types for systems biology. Theoret. Comput. Sci. **403**(1), 52–70 (2008). https://doi.org/10.1016/j.tcs.2008.04.024
14. Kauffman, S.: Metabolic stability and epigenesis in randomly constructed genetic nets. J. Theor. Biol. **22**(3), 437–467 (1969). https://doi.org/10.1016/0022-5193(69)90015-0
15. Niehren, J., Vaginay, A., Versari, C.: Abstract simulation of reaction networks via boolean networks. In: Petre, I., Păun, A. (eds.) Computational Methods in Systems Biology, pp. 21–40. Springer, Cham (2022). https://doi.org/10.1007/978-3-031-15034-0_2
16. Paulevé, L., Magnin, M., Roux, O.: Static analysis of biological regulatory networks dynamics using abstract interpretation. Math. Struct. Comput. Sci. **22**(4), 651–685 (2012). https://doi.org/10.1017/S0960129511000739
17. Paulevé, L., Sené, S.: Boolean Networks and Their Dynamics: The Impact of Updates, chap. 6, pp. 173–250. Wiley (2022). https://doi.org/10.1002/9781119716600.ch6
18. Rougny, A., Froidevaux, C., Calzone, L., Paulevé, L.: Qualitative dynamics semantics for sbgn process description. BMC Syst. Biol. **10**(1), 42 (2016). https://doi.org/10.1186/s12918-016-0285-0
19. Rougny, A., et al.: Systems biology graphical notation: process description language level 1 version 2.0. J. Integr. Bioinform. **16**(2), 20190022 (2019). https://doi.org/10.1515/jib-2019-0022
20. Rutten, J.J.: A tutorial on coinductive stream calculus and signal flow graphs. Theor. Comput. Sci. **343**(3), 443–481 (2005). https://doi.org/10.1016/j.tcs.2005.06.019
21. Savageau, M.A.: The behavior of intact biochemical control systems. In: Horecker, B.L., Stadtman, E.R. (eds.) Current Topics in Cellular Regulation, vol. 6, pp. 63–130. Academic Press (1972). https://doi.org/10.1016/B978-0-12-152806-5.50010-2
22. Shannon, C.E.: The Theory and Design of Linear Differential Equation Machines. Report to National Defense Research Council, January, 1942, pp. 514–559. Wiley-IEEE Press (1942). https://doi.org/10.1109/9780470544242.ch33
23. Thieffry, D., Romero, D.: The modularity of biological regulatory networks. Biosystems **50**(1), 49–59 (1999). https://doi.org/10.1016/S0303-2647(98)00087-2
24. Thomas, R.: Boolean formalization of genetic control circuits. J. Theor. Biol. **42**(3), 563–585 (1973). https://doi.org/10.1016/0022-5193(73)90247-6
25. Voit, E.O.: Biochemical systems theory: a review. Int. Sch. Res. Not. **2013**(1), 897658 (2013). https://doi.org/10.1155/2013/897658
26. Wang, R.S., Saadatpour, A., Albert, R.: Boolean modeling in systems biology: an overview of methodology and applications. Phys. Biol. **9**(5), 055001 (2012). https://doi.org/10.1088/1478-3975/9/5/055001

Inference of Qualitative Models from Steady-State Data via Weighted MaxSMT

Ondřej Huvar, Nikola Beneš, Martin Jonáš, David Šafránek(✉), and Samuel Pastva

Masaryk University, Brno, Czechia
{xhuvar,xbenes3,xjonas,xsafran,xpastva}@fi.muni.cz

Abstract. Qualitative models provide crucial instruments for modelling complex biological systems. While advances in automated reasoning and symbolic encodings have enabled rigorous inference of these models from data, the process remains highly fragile. First, biological measurement errors inevitably propagate into formal model specifications. Second, when a specification becomes unsatisfiable, distinguishing between fundamental design flaws and minor technical errors is notoriously difficult. This uncertainty often leads to under-specification, as it is unclear which observations are still "safe" to incorporate. To overcome these challenges, we introduce a robust inference method based on weighted MaxSMT. By encoding uncertain biological observations as weighted soft constraints, our approach enables the solver to identify a model best reflecting the observations, even with some conflicting constraints. Our method allows for Boolean and multi-valued variable domains, alongside observations derived from discretisation (level constraints) and differential expression (ordering constraints). We show our approach can be used to successfully infer neural cell differentiation models from prior-knowledge networks with approximately 200–1,300 genes using ordering constraints on all included genes.

1 Introduction

Qualitative (logic-based) models of regulatory networks, such as Boolean Networks (BNs) [18] or Thomas Networks (TNs) [30], represent an abstract yet mechanistic framework for studying the non-linear dynamics emerging from influences (regulations) among the system's components. Qualitative models have proven useful for modelling many processes in living cells, including gene regulation and protein activities in signal transduction. Every qualitative model consists of variables, each associated with an update function governing its dynamics based on the current state and the effect of incoming regulations. The goal of qualitative model inference is to reconstruct a particular model from experimental observations and other prior knowledge. Inference of models that reproduce experimental observations, satisfy desired structural and dynamic properties, and reflect the expert knowledge remains a challenge.

P. T. Monteiro (Ed.): CMSB 2026, LNBI 16678, pp. 38–55, 2027.
https://doi.org/10.1007/978-3-032-30870-2_3

Existing inference methods for qualitative models mostly focus on BNs and require the data to be preprocessed by a suitable binarisation (discretisation) technique. These inference methods can be broadly divided into two classes. The first consists of heuristic optimisation-based approaches that employ score-driven procedures to identify one or several high-scoring candidate models, without strong guarantees on completeness or optimality. These approaches, recently reviewed in [24], include methods based on genetic programming [11], best-fit extensions [19], or mutual information [1]. The second class consists of exact approaches that utilise formal methods [3, 8, 32, 34] to compute candidate models that are guaranteed to be consistent with the model specification. However, the current exact methods are poorly suited for noisy experimental data and critically suffer from scalability issues. In general, the outcome of most methods in both families strongly depends on the settings of the data discretisation procedure.

In [17], we tackled the inference problem of qualitative models by using Satisfiability Modulo Theories (SMT). The unknown update functions are encoded directly as uninterpreted functions subject to additional constraints derived from fixed-point observations and the prior knowledge of the influence graph.

In this paper, we utilise the optimisation techniques developed within SMT (specifically, weighted MaxSMT [5, 26]) to overcome the problems of existing inference methods mentioned above. Our inference problem is set up for Multi-Valued Networks (MVNs) where each variable has a finite discrete domain [23, 25] (i.e., MVNs cover TNs as well as BNs). The input to the inference procedure is: (i) the influence graph associated with "regulation constraints" (monotonicity and essentiality) expressing prior knowledge about the effects of specific influences; (ii) the "observation constraints", asserting the existence of several data-informed fixed-point states (biological steady states). Although BN and MVN models admit several alternative semantics representing their concurrent dynamics, the concrete choice of the update scheme becomes immaterial when the focus is restricted to steady states. Consequently, our approach is semantics-agnostic.

Constraints of our inference problem can be prescribed as *hard* (required) or *soft* (not necessarily required to be satisfied). Hard constraints must be satisfied by every admissible model. Soft constraints are associated with weights and provide a natural mechanism for representing uncertainty in biological knowledge and observations. The weights reflect the strength (or reliability) of the corresponding experimental evidence, and the objective is to identify candidate models that maximise the total weight of the satisfied soft constraints. Hence, unlike purely satisfiability-based formulations, we do not require all observations to be jointly satisfiable. Instead, we compute a model that best explains the imprecise steady-state observations, while also adhering to all prescribed hard regulation constraints.

Our contribution proceeds as follows. First, we introduce the constraint-based inference problem for MVNs. Second, we provide the SMT encoding of the inference problem, defining the regulation and observation constraints, including their weighting and the objective function construction. Third, we describe the workflow for translating prior knowledge and experimental observations into a set of weighted constraints. Finally, we demonstrate the applicability of the method on an extensive set of inference problem instances targeting differentiation of neural tissue cells in the mouse cerebral cortex using an scRNA-seq expression dataset. Influence graphs of the inferred MVNs represent large gene regulatory networks (from 200 to $\geq$ 1,300 genes) explaining the processes behind cell differentiation. Steady states correspond to phenotypes representing individual cell types. The results are supported by a reproducible artefact.

Related Work. To the best of our knowledge, the existing tools for exact inference do not employ optimisation to overcome uncertainty in data. Moreover, most of the existing tools focus on Boolean models only. The only other line of methods we are aware of that employs SMT encoding of the inference problem is based on RE:IN [32,34]. It utilises satisfiability without optimisation. The constraints are syntactically restricted to a limited subset of update functions *without* uninterpreted functions (employing a finite library of biologically motivated regulation conditions). In [33], SMT-based frameworks such as REIL generalise this line of work to broader classes of partially specified discrete dynamical systems with finite-domain variables. BoNesis [7,8] and Caspo [14] rely on Answer Set Programming (ASP) with exhaustive Disjunctive Normal Form (DNF) encodings. Finally, AEON [3,4] presents a symbolic approach employing Binary Decision Diagrams (BDDs) to exhaustively represent the update function space.

2 Preliminaries

We first present the formalism of multi-valued networks. We then provide a brief overview of satisfiability modulo theories and their optimisation extension.

2.1 Multi-valued Networks

Definition 1 (Multi-valued network). *A* multi-valued network (MVN) *is a triple* $\mathcal{M} = (V, D, F)$, *such that*

- $V = \{v_1, \ldots, v_n\}$ *is an indexed set of* network variables.
- $D = \{D_1, \ldots, D_n\}$ *is an indexed set of* variable domains; *each* D_i *is either Boolean* ($D_i = \{0, 1\}$) *or a finite integer interval (e.g.,* $D_i = \{0, \ldots, 5\}$*).*
- $F = \{F_1, \ldots, F_n\}$ *is an indexed set of* update functions. *Each variable* v_i *is equipped with an* update function $F_i \colon \prod_{j=1}^{n} D_j \to D_i$.

If all the variable domains are Boolean, $\mathcal{M}$ *is called a* Boolean network *(BN).*

A *system state* $x \in \prod_{j=1}^{n} D_j$ is a mapping that assigns each network variable v_i a value $x[i] \in D_i$. A state x is a *fixed-point state* if $F_i(x) = x[i]$ for all $1 \leq i \leq n$.

Each update function F_i typically depends only on a subset of variables $dep(F_i) \subseteq V$. These variables $v_j \in dep(F_i)$ are called *essential inputs of* F_i or *regulators of* v_i. Furthermore, the regulators may exhibit different *monotonicities.* A regulator v_j is called an *activator (inhibitor)* of v_i if F_i is positively (resp. negatively) monotone with respect to v_j. Some regulators may also have non-monotone effects, i.e., they are neither positively nor negatively monotone.

2.2 Satisfiability Modulo Theories and Optimisation

Given a first-order formula φ over a given logical theory $\mathcal{T}$, the goal of *Satisfiability Modulo Theories* (SMT) [2] is to decide whether there is a model of the theory $\mathcal{T}$ that satisfies φ. SMT solvers implement efficient decision procedures for various theories. In this paper, we consider the theory of *linear integer arithmetic with uninterpreted functions* (UFLIA), where the formulas consist of integer variables, integer constants (such as 2 or -42), the addition function $+$, and the relational operators $\bowtie \in \{=, \neq, \leq, \geq, <, >\}$. Additionally, formulas can contain *uninterpreted function symbols* (such as f, g, ...). The model of such a formula φ over UFLIA is an assignment of integers to the free variables in φ and of functions to the uninterpreted function symbols such that the assignment satisfies φ.

The SMT problem can be extended with optimisation, resulting in a problem known as *Optimisation Modulo Theories* (OMT) [26]. In OMT, the problem is for the given formula φ over the theory $\mathcal{T}$ and an objective function *obj* to find a model μ of φ with a maximal (or dually, minimal) value of $obj(\mu)$. The technique can be extended to multiple objective functions obj_1, ..., obj_k; the goal is then to find a model that *lexicographically* maximises the value of the tuple $(obj_1(\mu), obj_2(\mu), \ldots, obj_k(\mu))$.

A special case of OMT, which is supported by several existing solvers [5, 26], is *weighted MaxSMT*. In weighted MaxSMT, the input is a set of formulas C_h, called *hard constraints*, and a set of formulas C_s, called *soft constraints*. Each soft constraint $c \in C_s$ has an assigned non-negative *weight* $w(c)$. The goal of weighted MaxSMT is then to find an assignment μ that *satisfies all the hard constraints* and that maximises the sum of weights of the satisfied soft constraints $score(C_s, \mu) = \sum\{w(c) \mid c \in C_s, \mu \text{ satisfies } c\}$. As an example, consider the hard constraints $C_h = \{x + y = z,\ y \geq 10\}$ and the soft constraints $C_s = \{x \geq 0,\ z \leq 0,\ x + z \geq 40\}$ with weights 8, 3, and 6, respectively. An optimal solution is $\mu(x) = 20$, $\mu(y) = 10$, $\mu(z) = 30$, which has the score $8 + 6 = 14$. The problem can be naturally extended to several priority classes $C_s^1, C_s^2, \ldots, C_s^k$ of soft constraints. The goal is then to maximise the value of the tuple $(score(C_s^1, \mu), score(C_s^2, \mu), \ldots, score(C_s^k, \mu))$ lexicographically. Intuitively, the hard constraints must be satisfied, and the score achieved by the satisfied constraints from C_s^i is more important than the score of each C_s^j with $j > i$.

Notably, most of the existing solvers for weighted MaxSMT implement *anytime algorithms*, i.e., during the computation, they produce solutions with increasingly better scores. If they are stopped early, they still output a valid solution to the hard constraints, albeit possibly not a maximal one.

3 Weighted MVN Inference Problem

This section defines the main problem addressed in our paper: *the weighted MVN inference problem*. Its input is the *inference specification* consisting of (a) regulation constraints derived from a prior-knowledge influence graph (incorporating monotonicity and essentiality) that restrict the structure of the inferred model, and (b) fixed-point observation constraints that restrict the model's dynamics. The fixed-point specification can come from noisy or otherwise uncertain observations, and can thus be treated either as hard or as soft constraints with assigned weights, depending on our confidence in these observations. The goal is to find an MVN that satisfies all the hard constraints and maximises the sum of the weights of the satisfied observations.

Regulation Constraints. The general structure of the model is determined by a directed *influence graph* $\mathcal{I} = (V, E)$, where nodes $V = \{v_1, \ldots, v_n\}$ are the network variables and edges $E \subseteq V \times V$ represent potential *regulations* (i.e., v_i can regulate v_j only if $(v_i, v_j) \in E$). For each variable $v_i \in V$, we prescribe an associated domain D_i (Boolean or multi-valued). Finally, some of the regulations are constrained to be essential or have a specific monotonicity.

A regulation $(v_i, v_j) \in E$ is *essential* if the regulator v_i has an observable influence on the target v_j. Regulations without an essentiality constraint are optional and are not required to influence the target's update function at all. A regulation can also be assigned a *monotonicity*, forcing the regulator to act as either an activator or an inhibitor.

The *regulation constraints* are prescribed by a pair of functions (Ess, Mon) with signatures $Ess\colon E \to \{ess, any\}$ (ess for essential regulations, any for unspecified essentiality) and $Mon\colon E \to \{act, inh, any\}$ (act for activations, inh for inhibitions, and any for unspecified monotonicity).

Definition 2 (Regulation constraints consistency). *Let $\mathcal{I} = (V, E)$ be an influence graph and $\mathcal{M} = (V, D, F)$ an MVN over the same n variables. An update function $F_i \in F$ is* consistent *with $\mathcal{I}$ if $dep(F_i) \subseteq \{v_j \mid (v_j, v_i) \in E\}$.*

Furthermore, let (Ess, Mon) be regulation constraints on E. A function $F_i \in F$ is consistent with (Ess, Mon) if all $(v_j, v_i) \in E$ satisfy:

- *if $Ess(v_j, v_i) = ess$, then $v_j \in dep(F_i)$,*
- *if $Mon(v_j, v_i) = act$, then F_i is positively monotone with respect to v_j, and*
- *if $Mon(v_j, v_i) = inh$, then F_i is negatively monotone with respect to v_j.*

Observation Constraints. Moreover, the model is required to exhibit the prescribed *fixed points*, with specific *observation constraints* placed on the values of network variables in these states. Each of the m required fixed-point states is specified as a vector s^j of *state variables* $(s^j_1, \ldots, s^j_n)$, where s^j_i represents the value of v_i in the fixed-point state s^j. An additional Boolean parameter $distinct \in \{0, 1\}$ specifies whether the fixed-point states are constrained to be pairwise distinct.

The admissible values of the fixed-point state variables are restricted by a set of observation constraints $\mathcal{C}$. Each $c \in \mathcal{C}$ is defined by a relational operator $\bowtie \in \{=, \neq, \geq, \leq, >, <\}$ comparing either two state variables $(s^j_i \bowtie s^{j'}_{i'})$, or a state variable and an integer constant $(s^j_i \bowtie k)$. Each $c \in \mathcal{C}$ has a weight assigned by a *weighting function* $w\colon \mathcal{C} \to \mathbb{Q} \cup \{hard\}$. All c with $w(c) = hard$ are *hard* constraints that must always be satisfied, while the others are considered *soft*.

Since observation constraints may qualitatively differ in their importance, they are divided into $l+1$ disjoint categories (levels) $\{\mathcal{C}_{hard}, \mathcal{C}_1, \ldots, \mathcal{C}_l\}$, creating a partition of $\mathcal{C}$. While $\mathcal{C}_{hard}$ represents the hard constraints, the remaining sets $\mathcal{C}_1, \ldots, \mathcal{C}_l$ contain soft constraints whose qualitative importance decreases with larger l. The motivation for such a partitioning is explained in Sect. 5.

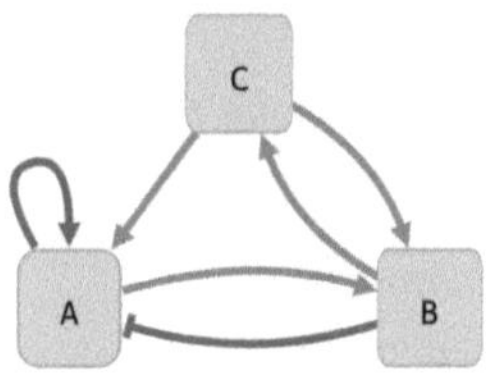

$D_A = \{0, 1\}$
$D_B = \{0, 1, 2\}$
$D_C = \{0, 1, 2\}$

(a) Influence graph

Scenario I

Fixed points: (s_A^1, s_B^1, s_C^1), (s_A^2, s_B^2, s_C^2)

value	s_A^1	s_B^1	s_C^1	s_A^2	s_B^2	s_C^2
0	**0.74**	0.07	**0.53**	0.07	**0.57**	0.20
1	0.26	0.11	0.28	**0.93**	0.22	**0.61**
2	—	**0.82**	0.19	—	0.21	0.19

(b) Inference specification I

Scenario II

Fixed points: (s_A^1, s_B^1, s_C^1), (s_A^2, s_B^2, s_C^2), (s_A^3, s_B^3, s_C^3)

$\bowtie$	$s_B^1 \bowtie s_B^2$	$s_C^1 \bowtie s_C^2$	$s_B^2 \bowtie s_B^3$	$s_C^2 \bowtie s_C^3$
$<$	0.05	**0.52**	0.04	**0.45**
$=$	0.34	0.40	0.31	0.44
$>$	**0.61**	0.08	**0.65**	0.11

Hard constraints: $s_A^1 = s_A^2 = s_A^3 = 1$

(c) Inference specification II

Fig. 1. (a) An influence graph of a three-variable MVN with regulation constraints. The grey arrow (the self-loop over A) denotes a regulation with no assigned monotonicity; the red arrow (from B to A) denotes an inhibition; the remaining green arrows represent activations. All regulations are essential. The monotonicity and essentiality constraints have to be satisfied by all feasible solutions. (b) An example of observation constraints in the form of equality with constants (e.g., discretised activity levels). There are two fixed points, with 16 soft constraints succinctly represented in a table together with their weights: $s_A^1 = 0$ with weight 0.74, $s_B^1 = 1$ with weight 0.11, etc. The maximal weights are depicted in boldface. (c) An example of observation constraints formulated as a comparison between fixed-point state values (e.g., differential expression). There are three fixed points, with the hard constraints that the value of A is 1 in all of them. There are 12 soft constraints represented in the table: $s_B^1 < s_B^2$ with weight 0.05, etc. (Color figure online)

Example 1. Two example scenarios (I and II) of the inference specification are given in Fig. 1, both sharing the same influence graph and domains (Fig. 1a). For better clarity, we use the names A, B, C for variables instead of v_1, v_2, v_3. The influence graph has six regulations, all of which are essential. The monotonicity of the self-regulation on A is unconstrained, the regulation (B, A) is an inhibition, and all the remaining regulations are activations. The domain of A is Boolean, while the domains of B and C are three-valued.

In Scenario I (Fig. 1b), the specification requires two fixed points. Here, every constraint is given as an equality with an integer, and the table shows the constraints' weights, i.e., $s_A^1 = 0$ with the weight of 0.74, etc. For simplicity, the constraints are all assigned the same level of importance.

In Scenario II (Fig. 1c), the specification requires three fixed points. Three hard constraints state that the value of A is 1 in each fixed point. Soft constraints are equalities and inequalities over pairs of state variables, i.e., $s_B^1 < s_B^2$ with the weight of 0.05, $s_B^1 = s_B^2$ with the weight of 0.34, etc. Again, all the soft constraints are given the same level of importance.

Definition 3 (Weighted MVN Inference Problem). *Let n be the number of variables and m the number of fixed points. Additionally,*

- *let $D = \{D_1, \ldots, D_n\}$ be an indexed set of variable domains,*
- *let $\mathcal{I} = (V, E)$ be a network influence graph over n variables,*
- *let (Ess, Mon) be the regulation constraints on E,*
- *let $S = \{s_i^j \mid 1 \le i \le n, 1 \le j \le m\}$ be the state variables of the m fixed points, with $distinct \in \{0, 1\}$ being the distinctness parameter, and*
- *let $\mathcal{C} = \mathcal{C}_{hard} \cup \mathcal{C}_1 \cup \ldots \cup \mathcal{C}_l$ be a set of observation constraints partitioned into $l + 1$ levels, with w as their weighting function.*

A feasible solution *of the MVN inference problem is a pair $(\mathcal{F}, \mathcal{S})$ consisting of an indexed set of functions $\mathcal{F} = \{F_1, \ldots, F_n\}$ and a function $\mathcal{S}$ mapping each s_i^j to a value from D_i, such that:*

- *$\mathcal{M} = (V, D, \mathcal{F})$ is a valid multi-valued network,*
- *each function $F_i \in \mathcal{F}$ is consistent with $\mathcal{I}$ and with constraints (Ess, Mon),*
- *for each $1 \le j \le m$, $(\mathcal{S}(s_1^j), \ldots, \mathcal{S}(s_n^j))$ is a fixed-point state of $\mathcal{M}$, all of which must be pairwise distinct if $distinct = 1$, and*
- *all constraints $c \in \mathcal{C}_{hard}$ are satisfied by the assignment $\mathcal{S}$.*

We write $\mathcal{S} \models c$ to denote that the assignment $\mathcal{S}$ satisfies the constraint $c \in \mathcal{C}$. For each level k, the k-level weight of a feasible solution is given as

$$w_k(\mathcal{S}) = \sum \{w(c) \mid c \in \mathcal{C}_k, \mathcal{S} \models c\}.$$

The weight *of a feasible solution is then defined as an l-tuple $(w_1(\mathcal{S}), \ldots, w_l(\mathcal{S}))$. A feasible solution is* optimal *if its weight is a lexicographic maximum of the weights of all feasible solutions.*

Example 2. We now continue with the examples from Fig. 1. In Scenario I, there are no feasible solutions that satisfy all the maximally-weighted constraints (i.e., constraints with the highest user confidence; depicted by boldface in Fig. 1b), since having (0, 2, 0) as a fixed point is impossible due to the essentiality and monotonicity constraints. An optimal solution instead assigns the values (0, 2, 1) and (1, 2, 1) to the fixed-point states. The weight of this solution is 3.59. The corresponding update functions are described in Appendix A of [16]. Note that although the fixed point (1, 0, 1) would also be allowed by the essentiality and monotonicity requirements, it cannot appear together with a fixed point (0, 2, 1), and all other solutions including (1, 0, 1) have a worse weight. Also note that there are, in fact, many optimal solutions (with different choices of update functions), but they all agree on the two fixed-point states listed here.

In Scenario II, there are again no feasible solutions that satisfy all the maximally weighted constraints. If we do not constrain the fixed points to be pairwise distinct, there are many optimal solutions leading to a variety of fixed-point states. However, all share the property that the first and the second fixed point are the same. One such possibility is (1, 2, 2), (1, 2, 2), and (1, 1, 1), with the weight of 1.50. Adding the distinctness constraint, we get an optimal solution with the fixed points (1, 2, 2), (1, 1, 1), and (1, 0, 0) and the weight of 1.45. This suggests an issue with the observations on which the constraints are based. For example, if each fixed point is meant to represent a dedicated cell type, the best explanation of the data that the model can provide instead suggests that the first and second cell type are in fact the same.

4 Encoding Weighted MVN Inference in MaxSMT

We now show that the problem of weighted MVN inference naturally maps to MaxSMT over linear integer arithmetic with uninterpreted functions. To encode the model specification, we construct SMT formulas for regulation monotonicity and fixed-point constraints by the approach introduced in our previous work [17]. Subsequently, we add the observation constraints with the desired weights. The optimal models of the resulting formula directly correspond to solutions to the inference problem.

First, an uninterpreted function f_i is declared for each v_i to represent its update function. The arity of each f_i corresponds to the in-degree of v_i in the influence graph (only the variable's regulators can influence the output of its update function), and the function domain matches the regulators. In addition, all state variables s_i^j are treated as variables in the SMT formulas.

The following SMT formulas are then constructed and asserted to impose constraints on the uninterpreted functions and state variables, obtaining an interpretation that corresponds to an optimal solution to the MVN inference.

Regulation Essentiality. A requirement of regulation $(v_i, v_j) \in E$ being essential naturally translates to a constraint requiring that the input of the function f_j corresponding to v_i is essential. Assuming without loss of generality that v_i is the first of k regulators for v_j, we encode the essentiality as the hard constraint $\eta_{i,j}$ defined in Eq. 1.

$$\eta_{i,j} \equiv \exists a, b, e_2, \ldots, e_k.\, f_j(a, e_2, \ldots, e_k) \neq f_j(b, e_2, \ldots, e_k) \quad (1)$$

Regulation Monotonicity. The monotonicity of a regulation $(v_i, v_j) \in E$ also naturally translates into a hard constraint requiring the function f_j to be monotone with respect to its input corresponding to v_i. Following the approach proposed in [28] and evaluated in [17], the monotonicity of any function g (of arity k)

can be enforced via the formula template ψ_g defined in Eq. 2. Here, $\mathcal{P}_g$ and $\mathcal{N}_g$ denote the sets of positively and negatively monotone input indices, respectively, while $\mathcal{R}_g$ denotes the set of remaining (non-monotone) input indices. These sets can be easily derived from the monotonicity specification *Mon*. We use $\overline{x}$ as a shorthand for $x_1, \ldots, x_k$ (same for $\overline{y}$). Using this template, the monotonicity of each update function f_i can be ensured by constructing its corresponding ψ_{f_i}. Furthermore, to avoid universal quantifiers in each ψ_{f_i}, we use the quantifier instantiation approach introduced in [28], which, as shown in [17], significantly improves solver performance on practical problem instances.

$$\forall \overline{x}, \overline{y}. \left(\left(\bigwedge_{i \in \mathcal{P}_g} x_i \leq y_i \right) \wedge \left(\bigwedge_{i \in \mathcal{N}_g} y_i \leq x_i \right) \wedge \left(\bigwedge_{i \in \mathcal{R}_g} x_i = y_i \right) \right) \Rightarrow g(\overline{x}) \leq g(\overline{y}) \quad (2)$$

Fixed-Point States. For each fixed-point state s in the specification, we enforce that $(s_1, \ldots, s_n)$ is indeed a fixed point by asserting the hard-constraint formula σ_s constructed according to the template in Eq. 3, where $r_1^i, \ldots, r_k^i$ denote the indices of the k regulators of v_i. If required, we can additionally ensure that all these fixed-point states are pairwise distinct by asserting the hard constraint $\delta_{s,t} \equiv \bigvee_{1 \leq i \leq n} s_i \neq t_i$ for each pair of fixed-point states $s \neq t$.

$$\sigma_s \equiv \bigwedge_{1 \leq i \leq n} s_i = f_i(s_{r_1^i}, \ldots, s_{r_k^i}) \quad (3)$$

Observation Constraints. As observation constraints consist of comparisons between state variables and constants, they naturally translate to the SMT representation. Each $c \in \mathcal{C}_{hard}$ is asserted as a hard constraint. For each level $1 \leq i \leq l$, each $c \in \mathcal{C}_i$ is asserted as a soft constraint with weight $w(c)$ and priority level i.

Finally, for each variable or uninterpreted function with a multi-valued domain, we also introduce a hard constraint asserting its domain bounds. For Boolean variables, the encoding uses propositional variables instead of bounded integers. The values of propositional variables are naturally ordered by *false* < *true*, which can be expressed in propositional logic as an implication.

5 Data-Informed Steady-State Constraints

The method presented in Sects. 3 and 4 is general: it accommodates any combination of essentiality, monotonicity, and *weighted* observation constraints. Ultimately, it is up to the modeller to select constraints that best reflect the biological reality. However, a practical MVN inference method should also provide guidance on how to construct these constraints. As such, we next discuss various approaches to deriving constraints from biological data and prior knowledge.

To ground the discussion in a specific modelling scenario, assume that the influence graph represents a gene regulatory network, and the fixed points correspond to different cell-type phenotypes. For each cell type, we have a collection

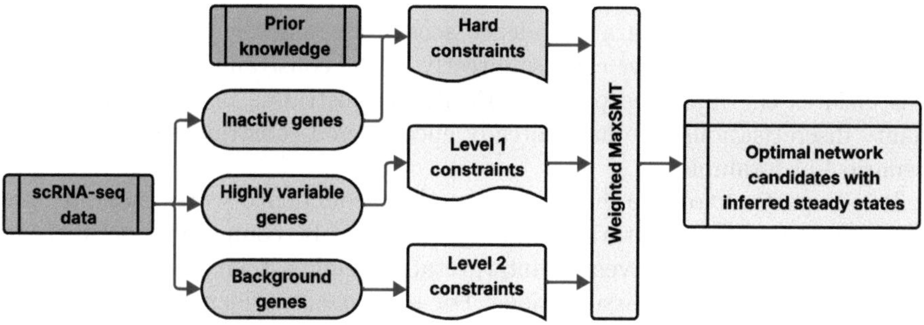

Fig. 2. An overview of the data-informed workflow for MVN inference used for evaluation in this paper. Other applications of our weighted MaxSMT approach are free to introduce their own dedicated strategies for deriving constraints from biological observations.

of scRNA-seq expression data. The inferred model provides a plausible explanation for the differences in gene expression observed across these cell types. The specific approach we propose for this scenario is also illustrated in Fig. 2.

Prior-Knowledge Constraints. A realistic modelling scenario (e.g., [13]) is often subject to prior-knowledge assumptions that are believed to be true but are supported indirectly—such as through literature or curated databases—rather than by direct, quantifiable observations. For example, we may wish to incorporate cell-type marker genes compiled through a literature search, or to ensure the existence of a cell-type phenotype present in a pre-existing model.

Prior-knowledge constraints generally belong to the $\mathcal{C}_{hard}$ level of observation constraints, as we expect them to be satisfied by any valid model. Nevertheless, if the prior knowledge proves to be contradictory, we can instead introduce them as soft constraints within a dedicated level $\mathcal{C}_1$ using equal weights (e.g., $w(c) = 1$ for each $c \in \mathcal{C}_1$). This maximises the number of satisfied prior-knowledge constraints, allowing us to further reconsider the unsatisfied ones.

Level-Based Observation Constraints. Constraints on the biological steady states typically appear as *binarised* or otherwise *discretised* observations [7,15,34]. These discrete observations are derived from real-world measurements, such as bulk [6] or single-cell RNA [15] gene expression, or other observation techniques (e.g., Western blots [27], proteomics [21]). These are then processed by a chosen discretisation tool, such as `scBoolSeq` [20] or `BiTrinA` [22]. Various ad hoc discretisation strategies or portfolios of tools are often employed as well [7,15].

In our framework, each discretised measurement results in an observation constraint $s_i^j = k$ (with $k \in D_i$). Some measurements are so reliable that we may introduce them as hard constraints. For example, we assert that $s_i^j = 0$ is a hard constraint for each gene i that is never expressed within cell type j (*inactive genes* in Fig. 2). Nevertheless, most discretised observations are subject to some uncertainty, meaning we should treat them as soft constraints. Discretisation methods typically provide a confidence score reflecting the quality of the discretisation result, which we can use directly as the constraint weight $w(s_i^j = k)$. This ensures the inference process prioritises constraints obtained from high-quality discretisations. We have already encountered constraints of this type in Scenario I of Example 1.

It is important to note, however, that these confidence scores may not have a clear statistical interpretation, and they may not be comparable between different tools or datasets. Even for interpretable weights, their interpretation can be subject to additional assumptions. For example, considering the constraint $s_i^j = 1$ with weight ξ, we could interpret ξ as the estimated probability that the expression of gene i in cell type j exceeds a specific threshold θ. However, this interpretation relies on an implicit assumption that the chosen θ accurately captures a qualitative switch in the underlying behaviour of gene i. Two discretisation methods may not agree on the same threshold, making their weights incomparable. Consequently, we do not recommend mixing constraint weights from diverse sources within one level $\mathcal{C}_i$ of observation constraints without careful consideration.

Ordering-Based Constraints. To eliminate reliance on assumed discretisation thresholds, we can consider constraints based on ordering. For a gene i and a pair of steady states s^a and s^b, we introduce three mutually exclusive soft constraints: $s_i^a < s_i^b$, $s_i^a = s_i^b$, and $s_i^a > s_i^b$. The weights assigned to these soft constraints reflect our confidence in the ordering of the corresponding values. Depending on the nature of our measurements, we can again use different tools to derive these constraint weights. For example, given RNA expression data, we can use the results of differential expression analysis [29] as the basis for suitable weights. We have already encountered constraints of this type in Scenario II of Example 1.

As a concrete use case, let ξ be the estimated probability that the expression of gene i in cell type a is lower than in cell type b. Then, we set $w(s_i^a < s_i^b) = \xi$, $w(s_i^a = s_i^b) = 1$, and $w(s_i^a > s_i^b) = 1 - \xi$. Compared to level-based constraints, this approach is more cautious: it reflects the ordering between the respective observations, but it does not require that a *quantitative* difference in gene expression also results in a *qualitative* difference within the inferred model. This is because the $s_i^a = s_i^b$ constraint is always the optimal choice, forcing the solver to introduce qualitative differences only in situations where they are required by other, higher-priority constraints (e.g., distinctness of fixed points, prior-knowledge, monotonicity, essentiality). In the absence of higher-priority constraints, an optimal model simply consists of constant update functions.

As an alternative, we also propose the weight assignment $w(s_i^a < s_i^b) = \xi^2$, $w(s_i^a = s_i^b) = 2\xi(1-\xi)$, and $w(s_i^a > s_i^b) = (1-\xi)^2$. Here, equality is only optimal if the estimated probability falls within the interval $(\frac{1}{3}, \frac{2}{3})$. This is conceptually similar to level-based discretisation, as it assumes that a quantitative change in gene expression should also result in a different discrete level. However, compared to the level-based approach, this formulation is more flexible in the case of multi-valued models: instead of fixed levels established by the discretisation tool, the solver can select a level assignment that optimises both the quantitative changes in gene expression and other dynamical properties of the model. In other words, beyond absolute gene expression, the solver can consider additional factors, such as the qualitative effect of the gene on its downstream regulation targets.

Priority of Ordering-Based Constraints. In our tested workflow, we propose the following approach to using ordering-based constraints: For genes assumed to be significant contributors to the observed cell-type phenotypes, we use the second approach and place the constraints into the $\mathcal{C}_1$ level. These should primarily be known marker genes, but can also include other selected genes with highly variable expression (*highly variable genes* in Fig. 2). Meanwhile, in the absence of further evidence or assumptions, we use the first, more cautious approach and place these constraints in the $\mathcal{C}_2$ level (*background genes* in Fig. 2). In other words, we require that the inferred model primarily explains the differences in gene expression that we associate with the cell-type phenotypes, with a secondary requirement that any other genes included in the model follow the ordering derived from their RNA-seq expression. However, we should note that this approach still depends on the user's choice of phenotype-determining genes, the criteria for which are the responsibility of the model authors. We view this as a somewhat unavoidable aspect of qualitative modelling, where part of the model design is to determine which qualitative differences are to be explained by the model.

6 Experiments

To evaluate our method, we perform a thorough investigation of its capabilities on 502 benchmark instances derived from a realistic modelling scenario based on scRNA-seq data and a prior-knowledge gene regulatory network. All code, data, and computed results are available as a Zenodo archive.[1]

Implementation. Our MaxSMT encoding is implemented in a Rust-based open-source tool available on GitHub.[2] As input, the tool accepts an influence graph in the `.aeon` format [4], with additional annotations describing the number of fixed points as well as the hard and soft constraints to be applied during model inference. The tool then constructs the SMT query as proposed in Sect. 4 and delegates the optimisation to the Z3 SMT solver [9].

6.1 Test Instances

To prepare a challenging environment for our method, we have constructed a collection of large-scale inference problems, following the workflow outlined in Sect. 5 and Fig. 2. However, we emphasise that in this paper, we focus on evaluating the technical aspects of the inference method, rather than on the biological validation of the models inferred during the evaluation.

[1] https://doi.org/10.5281/zenodo.19508672.
[2] https://github.com/sybila/biodivine-algo-smt-inference.

Table 1. Summary of the tested inference instances. Instances are grouped by the number of included cell types. For each group, the table lists the total number of test instances, along with the ranges of genes, regulations, and soft constraints within that group. The final two columns report the number of instances where an optimal solution was successfully found within a six-hour time limit for either the first soft constraint level ($\mathcal{C}_1$) or for both levels simultaneously ($\mathcal{C}_1, \mathcal{C}_2$). Bold values indicate that 100% of the instances within that group were solved to optimality.

Cell Types	Instances	Genes	Regulations	Soft Constraints	Fully Solved	
					$\mathcal{C}_1$	$(\mathcal{C}_1, \mathcal{C}_2)$
2	36	183–612	882–2,434	362–869	**36**	**36**
3	84	211–865	1,037–3,182	1,255–4,326	**84**	**84**
4	126	280–1,004	1,269–3,666	3,278–10,676	**126**	89
5	126	349–1,136	1,526–4,080	6,743–20,672	**126**	28
6	84	409–1,225	1,728–4,316	11,847–34,158	**84**	8
7	36	524–1,275	2,027–4,480	21,110–50,249	32	0
8	9	955–1,307	3,445–4,599	51,108–69,238	2	0
9	1	1,326	4,664	90,964	0	0

Modelling Scenario. As the basis for our test instances, we consider neural differentiation in the mouse cerebral cortex, as mapped by the single-cell RNA atlas from [10] and a prior-knowledge gene regulatory network available in the Omnipath database [31]. Here, we briefly describe the process used to create the inference constraints from these inputs. Additional technical details are given in Appendix B of [16] and the reproducibility artefact. After initial filtering, we select nine cell types that correspond to various fully differentiated neural cells to act as phenotypes. We then consider all 502 possible unique combinations of two or more cell types when constructing individual test instances.

For each test instance, we first construct a prior-knowledge network. We exclude any genes that are not covered by Omnipath and any genes that are inactive in all considered cell types. Consequently, the size of the influence graph is different for each test instance, as each cell type introduces different active genes with available prior-knowledge regulations. Overall, the influence graph size ranges from 183 to 1,326 genes and from 882 to 4,664 regulations. Additional information about the test instances is available in Table 1. We primarily report results for Boolean domains, as Boolean model inference is more common in literature. In Appendix C of [16], we also compare the runtime with multi-valued instances where the gene domain size is the number of its outgoing regulations. Overall, we find that using multi-valued domains does introduce a non-trivial, order-of-magnitude slowdown, but is still tractable for many test instances in our benchmark. Furthermore, our test represents a worst-case scenario; in practical applications, variable domains are often much smaller.

Constraint Preparation. First, if a gene is not expressed in a specific cell type at all, we introduce this observation as a hard constraint. Then, to derive the ordering-based constraints, we train an `scvi-tools` [12] statistical model on the scRNA-seq data, assuming a zero-inflated negative binomial distribution of gene expression. In other words, the true expression of each gene is modelled using a negative binomial distribution that is subject to stochastic dropout, explaining the observed zero-inflation in lowly expressed genes (see also Appendix B of [16]). We then use this learned distribution to estimate for each gene i the probability ξ that its expression is lower in cell type a compared to cell type b. Finally, for each pair of cell types, we identify candidate marker genes as those where the difference in expression is not only highly likely ($\xi > 0.8$), but also substantial in magnitude (at least 80% of the gene's maximal expression across all cell types). As discussed in Sect. 5, we use the second type of weight assignment (prioritising inequalities) for the identified marker genes to construct soft constraints $\mathcal{C}_1$, and the first type of weight assignment (prioritising equalities) for the remaining active genes to construct $\mathcal{C}_2$. This yields a complete inference problem specification.

6.2 Evaluation Results

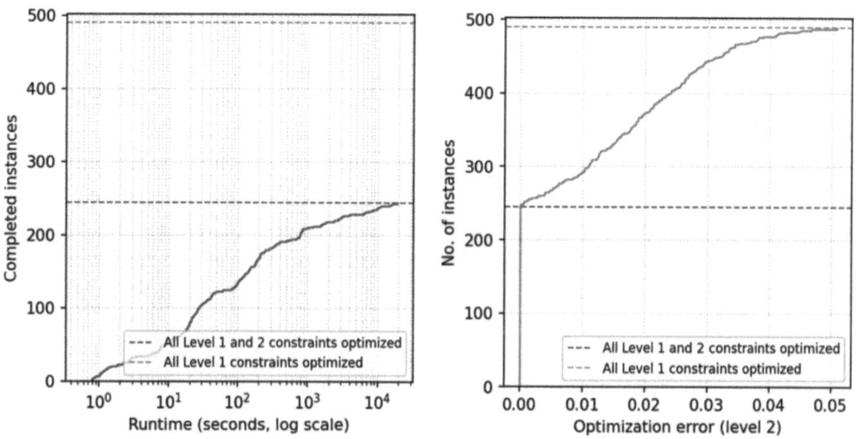

Fig. 3. Cumulative plots showing the performance of our method on the tested benchmark instances. Left: The 245/502 instances where an optimal solution was found within the 6h timeout. The plot shows the number of instances (y-axis) completed within a certain time (x-axis; logarithmic). Right: The 490/502 instances where an optimal solution for $\mathcal{C}_1$ constraints was found within the 6h timeout. The plot shows the number of instances (y-axis) with a less than or equal relative optimisation error in $\mathcal{C}_2$ constraints (x-axis). The relative optimisation error is the size of the confidence interval produced by the MaxSMT solver relative to the sum of constraint weights in $\mathcal{C}_2$.

The experiments were conducted with a six-hour timeout on a Ryzen 9900X3D CPU with 128GB RAM, running up to 10 instances in parallel. We rely on the fact that in the absence of an optimal solution, the solver still reports the best solution discovered before the timeout and bounds on the optimal weight within the first unsolved level of constraints. In Table 1, we report the number of instances where (a) the solver successfully optimised constraint level $\mathcal{C}_1$; (b) the solver successfully optimised both $\mathcal{C}_1$ and $\mathcal{C}_2$, producing a fully optimal solution. Here, we see that fully optimal solutions are found in instances with up to 6 cell types, and optimal solutions w.r.t. $\mathcal{C}_1$ are found for up to 8 cell types.

In Fig. 3 (left), we summarise the runtime of 245 problem instances that were fully solved. Meanwhile, for the 490 instances where at least $\mathcal{C}_1$ was fully optimised, we report the normalised optimisation error in Fig. 3 (right). This error is computed as the size of the interval that must contain all optimal solutions, which is reported by the solver, relative to the sum of constraint weights in $\mathcal{C}_2$. Overall, we see that for all 490 instances, the solver found a solution within 5 % of the total weight. Detailed visualisation with respect to inference problem size and comparison with multi-valued results is then given in Appendix C of [16]. Overall, we show that our method can handle even very large instances ($\geq$1,200 genes, 35,000 constraints), and in the absence of an optimal solution, provides results that are close to optimal (within 5% of the total weight).

7 Discussion

In this work, we present a novel method for Boolean and multi-valued network inference from uncertain experimental data based on weighted MaxSMT. The novelty of the approach lies in the fact that it (a) takes into account the grade of uncertainty in the experimental observations, encoding it using rational weights, and (b) allows us to express more general comparison constraints instead of just relying on a binarisation (or discretisation) method to preprocess the data.

Experimental results show that the method is applicable to real-world data and scales well to deal with a large number of network variables. Moreover, our approach admits an *anytime* implementation, provided the SMT optimiser supports it. Hence, even for larger instances, the computation can be stopped at any time while still returning a feasible solution together with a bound on its suboptimality, i.e., how close its weight is to the optimal one.

Note that we currently only use a specific fragment of the possibilities offered by the SMT encoding. In the future, we plan to include objective functions that allow, e.g., minimising the number of regulations, minimising the domain size (while maintaining the optimal weight), and other forms of optimisation. We also plan to tackle complex long-term behaviour phenomena, such as trap spaces.

Moreover, we plan to provide a more efficient enumeration of the resulting models. Currently, enumeration is possible by instructing the underlying SMT solver to avoid the previously generated solutions and then calling the procedure again. In this way, we get the candidate models one by one. A more efficient approach, planned for the future, would produce candidate models in larger batches, e.g., by describing them in terms of partially-specified functions.

A theoretical limitation of our approach is that we cannot require the model to have *exactly* the prescribed number of fixed points. Encoding this would require alternating quantifiers, which makes the problem significantly harder to solve.

Acknowledgements. Supported by the MUNI/JS/1954/2025 project of Masaryk University and the GA26-21507S project of the Czech Science Foundation.

Competing Interests. The authors have no competing interests to declare.

References

1. Barman, S., Kwon, Y.K.: A novel mutual information-based Boolean network inference method from time-series gene expression data. PLoS ONE **12**(2), e0171097 (2017)
2. Barrett, C.W., Sebastiani, R., Seshia, S.A., Tinelli, C.: Satisfiability modulo theories. In: Biere, A., Heule, M., van Maaren, H., Walsh, T. (eds.) Handbook of Satisfiability, 2nd edn, pp. 1267–1329. Frontiers in Artificial Intelligence and Applications, IOS Press (2021)
3. Beneš, N., Brim, L., Huvar, O., Pastva, S., Šafránek, D.: Boolean network sketches: a unifying framework for logical model inference. Bioinformatics **39**(4), btad158 (2023)
4. Beneš, N., Brim, L., Huvar, O., Pastva, S., Šafránek, D., Šmijáková, E.: AEON.py: python library for attractor analysis in asynchronous Boolean networks. Bioinformatics **38**(21), 4978–4980 (2022)
5. Bjørner, N., Phan, A.-D., Fleckenstein, L.: νZ - an optimizing SMT solver. In: Baier, C., Tinelli, C. (eds.) TACAS 2015. LNCS, vol. 9035, pp. 194–199. Springer, Heidelberg (2015). https://doi.org/10.1007/978-3-662-46681-0_14
6. Chagas, M.D.S., Trindade dos Santos, M., Argollo de Menezes, M., da Silva, F.A.B.: Boolean model of the gene regulatory network of Pseudomonas aeruginosa CCBH4851. Front. Microbiol. **14**, 1274740 (2023)
7. Chevalier, S., et al.: Data-driven inference of Boolean networks from transcriptomes to predict cellular differentiation and reprogramming. NPJ Syst. Biol. Appl. **11**(1), 105 (2025)
8. Chevalier, S., Boyenval, D., Magaña-López, G., Roncalli, T., Vaginay, A., Paulevé, L.: BoNesis: a python-based declarative environment for the verification, reprogramming, and synthesis of most permissive Boolean networks. In: International Conference on Computational Methods in Systems Biology, pp. 71–79. Springer (2024)
9. De Moura, L., Bjørner, N.: Z3: an efficient SMT solver. In: International Conference on Tools and Algorithms for the Construction and Analysis of Systems, pp. 337–340. Springer (2008)
10. Di Bella, D.J., et al.: Molecular logic of cellular diversification in the mouse cerebral cortex. Nature **595**(7868), 554–559 (2021)
11. Gao, S., Sun, C., Xiang, C., Qin, K., Lee, T.H.: Learning asynchronous Boolean networks from single-cell data using multiobjective cooperative genetic programming. IEEE Trans. Cybern. **52**(5), 2916–2930 (2020)
12. Gayoso, A., et al.: A Python library for probabilistic analysis of single-cell omics data. Nat. Biotechnol. **40**(2), 163–166 (2022)

13. Greene, G., Zonfa, I., Ravasz Regan, E.: A Boolean network model of hypoxia, mechanosensing and TGF-β signaling captures the role of phenotypic plasticity and mutations in tumor metastasis. PLoS Comput. Biol. **21**(4), e1012735 (2025)
14. Guziolowski, C., et al.: Exhaustively characterizing feasible logic models of a signaling network using answer set programming. Bioinformatics **29**(18), 2320–2326 (2013)
15. Hérault, L., Poplineau, M., Duprez, E., Remy, É.: A novel Boolean network inference strategy to model early hematopoiesis aging. Comput. Struct. Biotechnol. J. **21**, 21–33 (2023)
16. Huvar, O., Beneš, N., Jonáš, M., Šafránek, D., Pastva, S.: Inference of qualitative models from steady-state data via Weighted MaxSMT (2026). https://arxiv.org/abs/2605.07433
17. Huvar, O., Jonáš, M., Pastva, S.: SMT with uninterpreted functions and monotonicity constraints in systems biology. In: The 29th International Conference on Theory and Applications of Satisfiability Testing, SAT 2026, July 20-23, Lisbon, Portugal (2026, to appear)
18. Kauffman, S.: Homeostasis and differentiation in random genetic control networks. Nature **224**(5215), 177–178 (1969)
19. Lähdesmäki, H., Shmulevich, I., Yli-Harja, O.: On learning gene regulatory networks under the Boolean network model. Mach. Learn. **52**(1), 147–167 (2003)
20. Magaña-López, G., Calzone, L., Zinovyev, A., Paulevé, L.: scBoolSeq: linking scRNA-seq statistics and Boolean dynamics. PLoS Comput. Biol. **20**(7), 1–25 (2024)
21. Mayer, G., Marcus, K., Eisenacher, M., Kohl, M.: Boolean modeling techniques for protein co-expression networks in systems medicine. Expert Rev. Proteomics **13**(6), 555–569 (2016)
22. Müssel, C., Schmid, F., Blätte, T.J., Hopfensitz, M., Lausser, L., Kestler, H.A.: BiTrinA–multiscale binarization and trinarization with quality analysis. Bioinformatics **32**(3), 465–468 (2016)
23. Naldi, A., et al.: Logical modelling of regulatory networks with GINsim 2.3. Biosystems **97**(2), 134–139 (2009)
24. Pušnik, Ž., Mraz, M., Zimic, N., Moškon, M.: Review and assessment of Boolean approaches for inference of gene regulatory networks. Heliyon **8**(8) (2022)
25. Schaub, M.A., Henzinger, T.A., Fisher, J.: Qualitative networks: a symbolic approach to analyze biological signaling networks. BMC Syst. Biol. **1**(1), 4 (2007)
26. Sebastiani, R., Trentin, P.: OptiMathSAT: a tool for optimization modulo theories. J. Autom. Reason. **64**(3), 423–460 (2020)
27. Singh, A., Nascimento, J.M., Kowar, S., Busch, H., Boerries, M.: Boolean approach to signalling pathway modelling in HGF-induced keratinocyte migration. Bioinformatics **28**(18), i495–i501 (2012)
28. Sofronie-Stokkermans, V., Ihlemann, C.: Automated reasoning in some local extensions of ordered structures. In: 37th International Symposium on Multiple-Valued Logic (ISMVL 2007), p. 1. IEEE (2007)
29. Soneson, C., Delorenzi, M.: A comparison of methods for differential expression analysis of RNA-seq data. BMC Bioinform. **14**(1), 91 (2013)
30. Thomas, R.: Regulatory networks seen as asynchronous automata: a logical description. J. Theor. Biol. **153**(1), 1–23 (1991)
31. Türei, D., et al.: OmniPath: integrated knowledgebase for multi-omics analysis. Nucleic Acids Res. **54**(D1), D652–D660 (2025)

32. Yordanov, B., Dunn, S.J., Gravill, C., Arora, H., Kugler, H., Wintersteiger, C.M.: The reasoning engine: a satisfiability modulo theories-based framework for reasoning about discrete biological models. J. Comput. Biol. **30**(9), 1046–1058 (2023)
33. Yordanov, B., Dunn, S.J., Gravill, C., Kugler, H., Wintersteiger, C.M.: An SMT-based framework for reasoning about discrete biological models. In: International Symposium on Bioinformatics Research and Applications, pp. 114–125. Springer (2022)
34. Yordanov, B., Dunn, S.J., Kugler, H., Smith, A., Martello, G., Emmott, S.: A method to identify and analyze biological programs through automated reasoning. NPJ Syst. Biol. Appl. **2**(1), 16010 (2016)

pyModRev: A Python Tool for Model Revision of Boolean Networks

Pedro T. Monteiro[1] and Filipe Gouveia[2](✉)

[1] INESC-ID, Department of Computer Science and Engineering, Instituto Superior Técnico, Universidade de Lisboa, Lisbon, Portugal
pedro.tiago.monteiro@tecnico.ulisboa.pt

[2] LASIGE, Department of Informatics, Faculdade de Ciências, Universidade de Lisboa, Lisbon, Portugal
jfgouveia@ciencias.ulisboa.pt

Abstract. Biological regulatory networks can be represented by computational models, which allow the study and analysis of biological behaviours, therefore providing a better understanding of a given biological process. However, as new information is acquired, biological models may need to be revised in order to also account for this new information. Current model revision tools are scarce and often lack the flexibility to integrate with broader analysis workflows. Here, we present pyModRev, an enhanced iteration of the model revision tool ModRev, capable of verifying the consistency of Boolean regulatory models, and finding minimal repairs in case of inconsistency. pyModRev supports model validation against both steady state observations as well as time-series data, being able to consider different update schemes simultaneously. pyModRev supports different model formats, and is available as a Python package in PyPI, for easy integration with other model analysis tools, significantly improving accessibility and utility for the logical modelling community.

Keywords: Model Revision · Logical Models · Biological Regulatory Networks

1 Introduction

Biological regulatory networks can be represented by computational models, which are of great interest in Systems Biology [14]. These computational models allow the study and analysis of biological behaviours, therefore providing a better understanding of a given biological process. However, as new experimental data become available, these computational models may become inconsistent, *i.e.*, they may not be able to reproduce the new information acquired. In this case, models need to be revised [8, 10].

Repairing an inconsistent model is a hard problem, due to the inherent combinatorial nature associated with all the possible changes that can be made to render a model consistent. Additionally, model revision tools are scarce and

P. T. Monteiro (Ed.): CMSB 2026, LNBI 16678, pp. 56–70, 2027.
https://doi.org/10.1007/978-3-032-30870-2_4

often lack the flexibility to integrate with broader analysis workflows. In this work, we present pyModRev, an enhanced iteration of the model revision tool ModRev [9], addressing many of its limitations.

Given a Boolean model and a set of experimental observations, pyModRev determines whether the model explains the observational data. If inconsistencies are found, it identifies minimal repair operations to fix the model, and generates the corresponding revised model files. The tool supports model validation (and repair) against both steady state observations and time-series data, considering different update schemes: synchronous, asynchronous, and complete (also known as general asynchronous). Furthermore, pyModRev is able to validate (and repair) a model considering several simultaneously observational data with different update schemes, which was a limitation of ModRev addressed in this work. Furthermore, pyModRev can now also consider an observation specifying that a given state cannot be a steady state, repair the model such that the state is no longer steady.

pyModRev is open-source[1] and is openly available as a Python package[2]. Moreover, it supports different model formats, such as ModRev's ASP-based description [9], BoolNet format [17], and GINsim format [18], as well as different observation formats: ASP-based description and tabular formats. Due to its availability as a Python package and its modular implementation, pyModRev can integrate easily with other model analysis tools, significantly improving accessibility and utility for the logical modeling community.

The paper is organised as follows. Section 2 presents the background and related work. The pyModRev tool is presented in Sect. 3. Evaluation is described in Sect. 4. We conclude and discuss future work in Sect. 5. Appendix A presents a tutorial and a user manual of the tool. A case study is presented in Appendix B.

2 Preliminaries

Biological regulatory networks describe complex biological processes. A regulatory network is composed of a set of biological compounds and corresponding interactions. Different formalisms are used to build computational models of such networks [5,14,22,23]. Here, we consider the Boolean logical formalism [23].

A Boolean logical model is defined by: a set of nodes, representing biological compounds; a set of edges, representing interactions between compounds; and a set of regulatory functions, one for each node (compound). Each node has a Boolean variable associated with it, representing whether the corresponding compound is present (1, TRUE) or absent (0, FALSE). Edges have a sign associated, representing positive (activations) or negative (inhibitions) interactions between compounds (nodes). The value of a node can change over time, depending on the value of its regulators, *i.e.*, nodes with an incoming edge, and the corresponding regulatory function. In this work, we consider all regulators to be

[1] https://github.com/ptgm/pymodrev/.
[2] https://pypi.org/project/pymodrev/.

essential and without a dual role, thus regulatory functions are considered to be monotone non-degenerate Boolean functions [3,4].

2.1 Related Work

In systems biology, when modeling a regulatory network, several works focus on the inference of the computational model given a set of experimental observations and some prior knowledge [2,11,12,20,21]. In this work, we focus on the revision process, where we start with a fully instantiated model and a set of observations, and the goal is to assess whether the model can reproduce the given observations, and if not, repair the model.

Current model revision tools are scarce and often lack the flexibility to integrate with broader analysis workflows. Some approaches to model revision consider different formalisms, such as the Sign Consistency Model formalism, with less expressiveness in regulatory function when compared to the logical formalism [6,22]. Other approaches have a limitation in the repair operations that can be performed, the definition of the regulatory functions, and the supported dynamic behaviours [16].

ModRev [9] is a model revision tool capable of repairing inconsistent Boolean models, considering steady-state and time-series observations under synchronous and asynchronous update schemes. When a model is inconsistent with a given set of observations, ModRev finds a minimal set of repair operations to render the model consistent, considering: changing regulatory functions; changing the sign of the edges (change between activations and inhibitions); adding new edges (new interactions between biological compounds); and removing existing edges (removing interactions). However, ModRev has some limitations that hinder its adoption from the wider community, such has: being developed in C++ with non-easy to install bindings; model and observation formats limited to Answer Set Programming (ASP) direct encodings; an architecture not suitable to accommodate alternative update schemes; among others.

3 pyModRev

pyModRev is an enhanced iteration of the model revision tool ModRev [9], re-written in Python, minimizing external dependencies, and capable of addressing most of the previous tool limitations. It focus on improving usability, accessibility, easiness of integration with other model analysis tools, and utility for the systems biology community.

Our tool implements the revision method previously used by ModRev [8, 9]. Given a Boolean logical model and a set of experimental observations, it assesses whether the model is consistent using an ASP-based approach. In case of inconsistency, it finds minimal sets of repair operations to render the model consistent. Four repair operations are considered: change a regulatory function; change the sign of an edge (type of interaction); remove an edge (a regulator); and add an edge (a regulator).

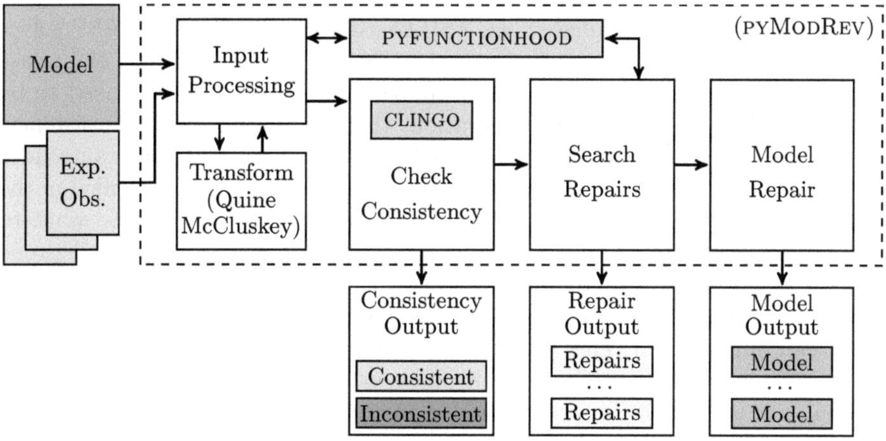

Fig. 1. PYMODREV workflow.

In Fig. 1, we present an overall workflow of PYMODREV, highlighting some of the new features. In order to improve usability and provide an easier way to integrate with other model analysis tools, PYMODREV supports different model formats, supporting not only the original ASP-based format used in MODREV (`.lp`), but also the BoolNet format (`.bnet`) [17], and GINsim format (`.ginml`/`.zginml`) [18]. Observational data can be given using the original ASP-based format (`.lp`), or using well-known tabular formats (`.csv`, `.xls`, `.xlsx`). For easy integration with other tools or workflows, such as the CoLoMoTo Notebook [19], different output formats for the information produced by our tool are supported: compact format (easily parsable), JSON format (more verbose but structured), and human-readable. Note that revised models produced as output maintain the format provided in the original model to be revised.

Like in MODREV, regulatory functions are monotone non-degenerated Boolean functions, represented in Canonical Disjunctive Normal Form (CDNF) [3,4]. To support different model formats, considering that functions in BoolNet and GINsim are defined as strings representing the Boolean formula, we use the Quine-McCluskey algorithm [15] to transform into CDNF, before using it in `pyfunctionhood`. Note that GINsim models relying on parameters for function specification, instead of a function string, are currently not supported.

In PYMODREV, the model revision process is now divided into three consecutive phases: consistency check, repair search, and model repair. The previous tool (MODREV) supported only consistency check and repair search, and without a clear separation between them. Here, we introduce the last phase, model repair, to actually apply identified minimal repairs to the original model and generate all the corresponding model files. We also separate each phase to allow stopping the process at any phase, getting the corresponding output information.

The consistency check phase is an ASP-based approach using the ASP solver `clingo`[3] [7]. It produces as output whether the model is consistent, or in case of inconsistency, the information regarding the minimal nodes that need to be repaired, and the experimental observations that originated such inconsistency. The repair search phase searches for possible repair operations that can render the model consistent, given the possible reasons of inconsistency identified in the previous phase. When considering changing a regulatory function, we want to change it for the closest consistent function considering the family of monotone Boolean functions, since it reduces the changes on the dynamic behaviour [3]. For that, we use `pyfunctionhood`[4], a library to compute immediate neighbours of Boolean functions [4]. This Python library is a corrected version of a previous one (used by ModRev). This search phase can produce as output the set of minimal repairs found. The newly added model repair phase produces all the models (in the desired format) that result from applying the minimal repair operations found to render the original model consistent. Note that multiple minimal sets of repairs can be found in the search phase, thus several consistent models can be produced.

In our tool, we support different types of observations: steady-state and time-series. For time-series observations, we support synchronous, asynchronous, and complete (also known as general asynchronous) update schemes. The observations provided can be fully instantiated observations, in which all state values are defined, or they can have missing values, *i.e.*, observations where some values were not observed. In case of missing values, our tool assumes they can have any value (0/1), considering all combinations to assess consistency. Note that if an observation has only an initial and final state, with missing values in all the states in between, the tool will consider all possible state transitions, being equivalent to check the reachability between two states. Enhancing the capabilities of previous work, our tool now supports the definition of not steady states, meaning that the model cannot have them as part of its steady states. If it does, our tool will repair the model so that these states are no longer steady. Furthermore, our tool can now confront a model with several observational data simultaneously, from different types and update schemes.

In pyModRev, we changed the handling of different update schemes used in ModRev to a more modular implementation. The intention for this effort was to easily associate a possibly different update scheme with each observation, in order to assess the model consistency simultaneously on all observations. Also, this paves the way to easily extend our tool with future update schemes, such as the Most Permissive update scheme [2].

4 Evaluation

To assess the correctness of pyModRev, we considered the dataset of corrupted model files created by Gouveia [8]. This dataset considers a set of 5 Boolean mod-

[3] https://pypi.org/project/clingo/.

[4] https://pypi.org/project/pyfunctionhood/.

els, and applies four types of corruptions: change in regulatory function, change in the edge sign, remove a regulator, and add a regulator. For each model, 24 combinations of these corruptions were applied, and for each combination, 100 corrupted instances were generated. As steady-state observations, the original steady-states of the 5 Boolean models were considered. For dynamical observations, synchronous and asynchronous simulations of 3, 5, 10, 15 and 20 time-steps were also generated.

pyModRev was capable of repairing most models under a time limit of 3600 s. Also, all proposed repairs were consistent with the observations and were similar to the repairs proposed by ModRev, showing the correctness of the model revision approach implemented in our tool.

Additionally, to illustrate the easiness of use of pyModRev to the logical modelling community, in Appendix B we reproduce the study in [1], where ModRev was used to proposed revisions to the Boolean model on the early differentiation of hematopoietic stem cells, proposed by Héraut et al. [13], in order to recover desired reachabilities with the asynchronous update scheme.

5 Conclusion and Future Work

In this work, we present pyModRev, an enhanced iteration of the model revision tool ModRev [9], that assesses whether a Boolean logical model of a biological regulatory network is consistent with a set of experimental observations. We show the correctness of pyModRev with respect to ModRev, and its usability and utility by providing it as Python package in PyPI. Nevertheless, we intend to improve pyModRev in several aspects.

Currently, for time-series observations, the exact number of time steps must be provided to the tool, making the search incremental. We intend to relax this constraint to fully support reachability properties without knowing the number of time-steps in between (partial) states.

Also, we already refactored the handling of the update schemes in pyModRev to easily extend to new update schemes. As future work, we plan to include support for reachability properties using the Most Permissive update scheme [2].

We included three different output formats, notably the JSON format, with the aim to include pyModRev within the CoLoMoTo Notebook [19] for easier integration with other analysis pipelines, already used by the community.

Acknowledgments. This work was supported by national funds through FCT, Fundação para a Ciência e a Tecnologia, under projects UID/50021/2025 (DOI: 10.54499/UID/50021/2025), UID/00408/2025 (DOI: 10.54499/UID/00408/2025), FCT TENURE program 2023.15441.TENURE.044/CP00003/CT00033, FCT-Mobility investment 11/C06-i06/2024 (FCT/Mobility/1419033983/2024-25), and by OSCARS project, funded by the European Commission's Horizon Europe Research and Innovation Programme under grant agreement No. 101129751.

Disclosure of Interests. The authors have no competing interests to declare.

A Tutorial/User Manual

pyModRev is a Python reimplementation of ModRev for automated: i) consistency checking of Boolean logical models against experimental observations, ii) computation of minimal repair operations using Answer Set Programming (ASP) and the `clingo` solver, and iii) automatic production of the corresponding repaired models.

The tool supports multiple model formats (`.lp`, `.bnet`, `.ginml`/`.zginml`) for input and output, and multiple observation formats (`.lp`, `.csv`, `.xls`, `.xlsx`).

A.1 Preparation

Installation. You can install it from source (inside the repository directory), having previously git cloned or downloaded the project:

```
pip install .
```

or install the latest release directly from PyPI:

```
pip install pymodrev
```

Command Line Usage. Using the command line, pass the `-h` option to list all possible parameters:

```
pymodrev -h
usage: cli.py [-h] -m MODEL -obs OBS [UPDATER ...] -t {c,r,m}
              [--exhaustive-search] [-s {1,2,3,4}] [-f {c,j,h}]
              [--fixed-nodes FIXED_NODES [FIXED_NODES ...]]
              [--fixed-edges FIXED_EDGES [FIXED_EDGES ...]] [-d]


options:
  -h, --help            show this help message and exit
  -m, --model MODEL     Input model file
  -obs, --observations OBS [UPDATER ...]
                List of observation files and updater pairs.
                Each observation *must* be followed by its updater type.
                Example: -obs obs1.lp async obs2.lp sync
                Or: -obs obs1.lp async -obs obs2.lp sync
  -t, --task {c,r,m}    Specify the task to perform (default=r):
                            c - check for consistency
                            r - get repairs
                            m - get repaired models
  --exhaustive-search   Force exhaustive search of function
                repair operations (default=false)
  -s, --solutions {1,2,3,4}
                All solutions are optimal w.r.t. number of nodes needing
                repairs. But a solution may be sub-optimal w.r.t. number
                of repair operations.
                    1 - Show only the first ASP optimal solution, which
```

```
                        may be sup-optimal in terms of repairs (fastest)
                      2 - Show only the first ASP&repairs optimal solution
                      3 - Show all optimal solutions (default)
                      4 - Show all optimal solutions, including sub-optimal
                          repairs (slowest)
  -f, --format {c,j,h}  Specify output format (default=h):
                              c - compact format
                              j - json format
                              h - human-readable format
  --fixed-nodes FIXED_NODES [FIXED_NODES ...]
                        List of nodes ids not to repair.
                        Example: --fixed-nodes A B C
  --fixed-edges FIXED_EDGES [FIXED_EDGES ...]
                        List of edges ids not to repair.
                        Example: --fixed-edges A,B C;D E:F
  -d, --debug           Enable debug mode
```

Observation File Formats. pyModRev supports observations written as ASP facts (`.lp`) using ModRev's format [9], or in a tabular format (`.csv`/`.xls`/`.xlsx`). Additionally, it steady-state vs. time-series have slightly different formats to account for an explicit mention of time.

- **Steady-state:** first header field empty, first column is the profile identifier.

```
,node1,node2,node3
p1,0,1,0
p2,1,1,1
...
```

- **Time-series:** two empty header fields, where first column is the profile identifier, second column is time.

```
,,node1,node2,node3
p1,0,0,1,1
p1,1,1, ,0
p1,2,*,0,0
...
```

Missing values (empty fields, `*`, `N/A`, `NaN`, `-`) are skipped so that no constraint is generated for that node/time point, and pyModRev can produce repairs instantiated with either value.

A.2 Command Line Usage

Checking Consistency of a Model. To check if a model is consistent with a set of observations, a user can use the following command:

```
pymodrev -m examples/boolean_cell_cycle/03/model.bnet \
  -obs examples/boolean_cell_cycle/03/steady.csv steady -t c
This model is inconsistent!
  node(s) needing repair: "p27", "rb", "cdc20", "cycd"
  present in profile(s): "p1"
```

In this case, it is indicated that the model has four nodes inconsistent in the specific profile, that should be repaired. If the model is consistent, the tool will report that no repair is needed.

Computing Minimal Repair Operations. To compute the minimal repairs on these four nodes, a user can change the `-t` parameter to ask for a `r`epair task:

```
pymodrev -m examples/boolean_cell_cycle/03/model.bnet \
  -obs examples/boolean_cell_cycle/03/state.csv steady -t r
### Found solution with 4 repair operations.
Inconsistent node p27.
Repair #1:
Change function of p27 to: (!cycb && !cyce) ||
                             (cyca && !cycb && cycd && !p27)
Inconsistent node rb.
Repair #1:
Change function of rb to: (!cycb && cycd && cyce) ||
                            (!cycb && cycd && !p27) ||
                            (!cycb && !cyca)
Inconsistent node cdc20.
Repair #1:
Flip sign of edge (cycb,cdc20) to: positive
Inconsistent node cycd.
Repair #1:
Flip sign of edge (cycd,cycd) to: positive
```

Notice that to repair this model, one must apply repairs on four different nodes. And on each node there is a single possible repair. In this case, two nodes need to change its function, and the other two only the sign of the regulatory influence.

There are cases where more than one repair per model node is possible, such as the following example using a toy model and asking for sub-optimal repairs. Here, we can also observe cases where a repair is composed of multiple changes, e.g. the regulatory sign and regulatory function.

```
pymodrev -m examples/toy/00/model.bnet \
  -obs examples/toy/00/sync.csv sync -t r -s 4
(Sub-Optimal Solution)
### Found solution with 4 repair operations.
```

```
Inconsistent node v1.
Repair #1:
Change function of v1 to: (v3) || (!v2)
Flip sign of edge (v2,v1) to: negative
Repair #2:
Change function of v1 to: (!v3) || (v2)
Flip sign of edge (v3,v1) to: negative
Inconsistent node v2.
Repair #1:
Change function of v2 to: (v3 && v1)
Flip sign of edge (v3,v2) to: positive
Repair #2:
Change function of v2 to: (!v3 && !v1)
Flip sign of edge (v1,v2) to: negative
### Found solution with 3 repair operations.
Inconsistent node v1.
Repair #1:
Change function of v1 to: (v3) || (!v2)
Flip sign of edge (v2,v1) to: negative
Inconsistent node v2.
Repair #1:
Change function of v2 to: (!v3 && v1)
(Sub-Optimal Solution)
### Found solution with 4 repair operations.
Inconsistent node v1.
Repair #1:
Change function of v1 to: (!v3) || (v2)
Flip sign of edge (v3,v1) to: negative
Inconsistent node v2.
Repair #1:
Change function of v2 to: (v3 && v1)
Flip sign of edge (v3,v2) to: positive
```

Generating Repaired Models. A user can manually edit its model using the suggested repairs, or it can use pyModRev to automatically generate the repaired models files. For this, it suffices to change the `-t` parameter to ask for repaired models. In the optimal solution of the Boolean cell cycle case, since there was only one possible repair per model node, there is a single generated model containing all the repairs.

```
pymodrev -m examples/boolean_cell_cycle/03/model.bnet \
  -obs examples/boolean_cell_cycle/03/steady.lp steady -t m
Repaired model: examples/boolean_cell_cycle/03/model_1.bnet
```

Using the toy example, and asking for sub-optimal repairs, we can see that six repaired models are generated, considering the number of solutions, and the combination of repairs within the model nodes in each solution.

```
pymodrev -m examples/toy/00/model.bnet \
  -obs examples/toy/00/sync.csv syncupdater -t m -s 4
Repaired model: examples/toy/00/model_1.bnet
Repaired model: examples/toy/00/model_2.bnet
Repaired model: examples/toy/00/model_3.bnet
Repaired model: examples/toy/00/model_4.bnet
Repaired model: examples/toy/00/model_5.bnet
Repaired model: examples/toy/00/model_6.bnet
```

B Case Study

Héraut et al. [13] proposed a workflow to build a Boolean model on the early differentiation of hematopoietic stem cells (HSCs), combining gene regulatory network inference methods, single-cell transcriptomic data defining cell (steady) states, and dynamical constraints between cell states. The resulting model (see Fig. 2) was capable of generating 5 cell (steady) states: lymphoid (pLymph), neutrophils and mastocytes (pNeuMast), erythrocytes (pEr), megakaryocytes (pMk), and an inactive state (zeros). It was also capable of generating reachabilities under MP update scheme between some identified cell states and these cell steady states. Nevertheless, some of these reachabilities were not possible under the asynchronous update scheme.

In [1], the authors utilised ModRev to propose revisions to the original model[5], to recover these missing asynchronous reachabilities. Here, we illustrate how pyModRev can easily be used to recover these asynchronous reachabilities.

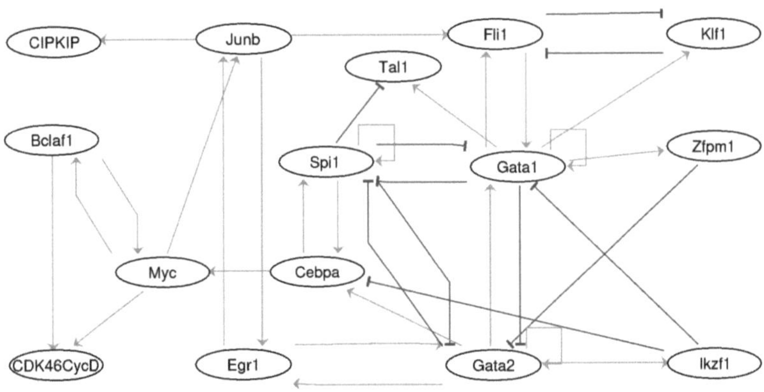

Fig. 2. Boolean model of the early differentiation of Hematopoietic Stem Cells (HCS).

[5] https://ginsim.github.io/models/2023-early-differentiation-hematopoietic-stem-cells/.

We start by defining a tabular `.xlsx` file with the 5 cell (steady) states:

```
,Egr1,Junb,Bclaf1,Myc,Fli1,Gata2,Spi1,Cebpa,Gata1,Klf1,Tal1,\
Ikzf1,Zfpm1,CDK46CycD,CIPKIP
Zero,0,0,0,0,0,0,0,0,0,0,0,0,0,0,0
pEr,0,0,0,0,0,0,0,0,1,1,1,0,1,0,0
pNeuMast,0,0,0,0,0,0,1,1,0,0,0,0,0,0,0
pLymph,0,0,0,0,0,1,1,0,0,0,0,1,0,0,0
pMk,0,0,0,0,1,0,0,0,1,0,1,0,1,0,0
```

We then check for the consistency of the model against this observation tabular file, which is expected, using the following command with task parameter `-t c`:

```
pymodrev -m hsc.zginml -obs hsc_steadystates.xlsx steady -t c
This model is consistent!
```

B.1 Reachability: iHSC to pLymph

In [1] the authors started by verifying the reachability between iHSC and pLymph. We define this reachability property from state iHSC to state pLymph, with five time steps, in a tabular `.xlsx` file as follows, where "iHSC2pLymph" is the name of the observation profile:

```
,,Egr1,Junb,Bclaf1,Myc,Fli1,Gata2,Spi1,Cebpa,Gata1,Klf1,Tal1,\
Ikzf1,Zfpm1,CDK46CycD,CIPKIP
iHSC2pLymph,0,0,0,1,0,1,1,0,0,0,0,1,0,0,0,0
iHSC2pLymph,5,0,0,0,0,0,1,1,0,0,0,0,1,0,0,0
```

We then check for the consistency of the model against this reachability, and observe that there is a node, in this case "Spi1", that needs to be repaired.

```
pymodrev -m hsc.zginml -obs hsc_steadystates.xlsx steady \
  -obs hsc_iHSC_2_pLymph.xlsx async -t c
This model is inconsistent!
  node(s) needing repair: "Spi1"
  present in profile(s): "iHSC2pLymph"
```

To ask for the specific repairs to make the model consistent with both observations, we change the task parameter `-t r`, and the solutions parameter `-s 1` (considering sub-optimal repairs - the fastest). One repair with two changes must be applied to node "Spi1":

```
pymodrev -m hsc.zginml -obs hsc_steadystates.xlsx steady \
  -obs hsc_iHSC_2_pLymph.xlsx async -t r -s 1
### Found solution with 2 repair operations.
  Inconsistent node Spi1.
Repair #1:
   Change function of Spi1 to: (!Gata1 && Gata2) || \
              (!Gata1 && Spi1) || (!Gata1 && Cebpa)
   Flip sign of edge (Gata2,Spi1) to: positive
```

To generate the repaired model file, we change the task parameter to `-t m`:

```
pymodrev -m hsc.zginml -obs hsc_steadystates.xlsx steady \
  -obs hsc_iHSC_2_pLymph.xlsx async -t m -s 1
Repaired model: hsc_1.zginml
```

This repaired model file `hsc_1.zginml` should be consistent with the observations, which can be confirmed with the following command:

```
pymodrev -m hsc_1.zginml -obs hsc_steadystates.xlsx steady \
  -obs hsc_iHSC_2_pLymph.xlsx async -t c
This model is consistent!
```

B.2 Reachability: qHSC to pLymph

Considering this new model, the authors in [1] then verified the additional reachability from state qHSC towards pLymph. We define this reachability property in a tabular `.xlsx` file as follows, where "qHSC2pLymph" is the name of the observation profile (note the missing value on node "zfpm1"):

```
,,Egr1,Junb,Bclaf1,Myc,Fli1,Gata2,Spi1,Cebpa,Gata1,Klf1,Tal1,\
Ikzf1,Zfpm1,CDK46CycD,CIPKIP
qHSC2pLymph,0,1,1,0,1,1,1,0,0,0,0,1,0,,1,1
qHSC2pLymph,9,0,0,0,0,0,1,1,0,0,0,0,1,0,0,0
```

To ask for the specific repairs to make this `hsc_1.zginml` model consistent with both the steady states and the "qHSc2pLymph" observation, we run the following command with the task parameter `-t r`, and the solutions parameter `-s 1` (considering sub-optimal repairs - the fastest). In this case, there is only one minimal repair to be applied to node "Junb":

```
pymodrev -m hsc_1.zginml -obs hsc_steadystates.xlsx steady \
  -obs hsc_iHSC_2_pLymph.xlsx async
  -obs hsc_qHSC_2_pLymph.xlsx async -t r -s 1
### Found solution with 1 repair operations.
  Inconsistent node Junb.
    Repair #1:
   Change function of Junb to: (Myc && Egr1)
```

We generate the repaired model file, changing the task parameter to `-t m`:

```
pymodrev -m hsc_1.zginml -obs hsc_steadystates.xlsx steady \
  -obs hsc_iHSC_2_pLymph.xlsx async
  -obs hsc_qHSC_2_pLymph.xlsx async -t m -s 1
Repaired model: hsc_1_1.zginml
```

References

1. Chaouiya, C., Monteiro, P.T., Remy, E.: Logical modelling, some recent methodological advances illustrated. In: Cellular Automata and Discrete Complex Systems, pp. 3–22. Springer (2024)
2. Chevalier, S., Boyenval, D., Magaña López, G., Roncalli, T., Vaginay, A., Paulevé, L.: BoNesis: a python-based declarative environment for the verification, reprogramming, and synthesis of most permissive boolean networks. In: 22th International Conference on Computational Methods in Systems Biology (CMSB). LNCS. Springer (2024)
3. Cury, J.E., Monteiro, P.T., Chaouiya, C.: Partial Order on the set of Boolean Regulatory Functions. arXiv preprint arXiv:1901.07623 (2019)
4. Cury, J.E.R., Tenera Roxo, P., Manquinho, V., Chaouiya, C., Monteiro, P.T.: Computation of immediate neighbours of monotone boolean functions. In: Computational Methods in Systems Biology, pp. 3–22. Springer (2025)
5. De Jong, H.: Modeling and simulation of genetic regulatory systems: a literature review. J. Comput. Biol. **9**(1), 67–103 (2002)
6. Gebser, M., et al.: Repair and prediction (under inconsistency) in large biological networks with answer set programming. In: Lin, F., Sattler, U., Truszczynski, M. (eds.) Principles of Knowledge Representation and Reasoning: Proceedings of the Twelfth International Conference, KR 2010. AAAI Press (2010)
7. Gebser, M., Kaminski, R., Kaufmann, B., Schaub, T.: Multi-shot ASP solving with clingo. Theory Pract. Logic Program. **19**(1), 27–82 (2018)
8. Gouveia, F.: Model revision of Boolean logical models of biological regulatory networks. Ph.D. thesis, Instituto Superior Técnico, Universidade de Lisboa (2021)
9. Gouveia, F., Lynce, I., Monteiro, P.T.: ModRev - model revision tool for boolean logical models of biological regulatory networks. In: Computational Methods in Systems Biology, pp. 339–348. Springer (2020)
10. Gouveia, F., Lynce, I., Monteiro, P.T.: Revision of boolean models of regulatory networks using stable state observations. J. Comput. Biol. **27**(2), 144–155 (2020)
11. Guziolowski, C., et al.: Exhaustively characterizing feasible logic models of a signaling network using answer set programming. Bioinformatics **29**(18), 2320–2326 (2013)
12. Huvar, O., Beneš, N., Brim, L., Pastva, S., Šafránek, D.: Sketchbook: logical model inference from boolean network sketches. Bioinform. Adv. **6**(1) (2026)
13. Hérault, L., Poplineau, M., Remy, E., Duprez, E.: Single cell transcriptomics to understand HSC heterogeneity and its evolution upon aging. Cells **11** (2022)
14. Karlebach, G., Shamir, R.: Modelling and analysis of gene regulatory networks. Nat. Rev. Mol. Cell Biol. **9**(10), 770 (2008)
15. McCluskey, E.J.: Minimization of boolean functions. Bell Syst. Tech. J. **35**(6), 1417–1444 (1956)
16. Merhej, E., Schockaert, S., Cock, M.D.: Repairing inconsistent answer set programs using rules of thumb: a gene regulatory networks case study. Int. J. Approx. Reason. **83**, 243–264 (2017)
17. Muessel, C., Hopfensitz, M., Kestler, H.A.: Boolnet - an R package for generation, reconstruction and analysis of boolean networks. Bioinformatics **26**(10), 1378–1380 (2010)
18. Naldi, A., Hernandez, C., Abou-Jaoudé, W., Monteiro, P.T., Chaouiya, C., Thieffry, D.: Logical modeling and analysis of cellular regulatory networks with GINsim 3.0. Front. Physiol. **9** (2018)

19. Naldi, A., et al.: Cooperative development of logical modelling standards and tools with CoLoMoTo. Bioinformatics **31**(7), 1154–1159 (2015)
20. Ostrowski, M., Paulevé, L., Schaub, T., Siegel, A., Guziolowski, C.: Boolean network identification from perturbation time series data combining dynamics abstraction and logic programming. Biosystems **149**, 139–153 (2016)
21. Schaub, T., Siegel, A., Videla, S.: Reasoning on the response of logical signaling networks with ASP. In: Logical Modeling of Biological Systems, pp. 49–92. Wiley (2014)
22. Siegel, A., Radulescu, O., Le Borgne, M., Veber, P., Ouy, J., Lagarrigue, S.: Qualitative analysis of the relation between DNA microarray data and behavioral models of regulation networks. Biosystems **84**(2), 153–174 (2006)
23. Thomas, R.: Boolean formalization of genetic control circuits. J. Theor. Biol. **42**(3), 563–585 (1973)

Rule-Based and Stochastic Models

Statistical Model Checking for Rule-Based Models in the Kappa Language

Albin Salazar[3,4], Jérôme Feret[2], and Tatjana Petrov[1,3,5](✉)

[1] Università degli Studi di Trieste, Trieste, Italy
tatjana.petrov@units.it
[2] DI ENS, École Normale Supérieure, PSL, CNRS, INRIA, Paris, France
[3] Centre for the Advanced Study of Collective Behaviour, Konstanz, Germany
[4] University of Konstanz, Konstanz, Germany
[5] Max Planck Institute of Animal Behavior, Radolfzell, Germany

Abstract. Kappa is a graph-rewriting language originally developed for modeling molecular interactions in cellular processes. A key feature of Kappa models is that, inspired by organic chemistry, interaction rules operate on patterns i.e., partially specified molecular species, thus allowing compact descriptions of otherwise large or even infinite models.

In this paper, we propose and implement a framework for statistical model checking for stochastic Kappa models against properties written in bounded linear temporal logic (BLTL). A key feature of our approach is that temporal properties operate over Kappa patterns, making the specification language native to Kappa and avoiding the expensive—and sometimes theoretically impossible—translation of the model into an equivalent chemical reaction network with a finite number of species. Concretely, given a Kappa model and a property, we first instrument the model by introducing additional variables and observables that track the truth value of each atomic proposition. For each simulated trace, the BLTL formula satisfaction is evaluated using an offline monitoring procedure. Finally, the satisfaction probability is statistically estimated from repeated model simulations.

The proposed model checking framework enables a systematic exploration of behavioral properties of Kappa models, that is computationally efficient while able to capture stochastic and finite size effects with any predefined desired accuracy/precision. As such, it can serve in applications for e.g. model selection, property-driven parameter exploration, or robustness analysis. The framework is illustrated on representative case studies from systems biology and swarm robotics.

Keywords: Statistical model checking · stochastic systems · rule-based modelling · formal methods

1 Introduction

Chemical reaction networks (CRNs) are a modelling formalism that compactly describes non-linear and stochastic behaviours of a system of diverse entities. It

P. T. Monteiro (Ed.): CMSB 2026, LNBI 16678, pp. 73–103, 2027.
https://doi.org/10.1007/978-3-032-30870-2_5

is used in numerous application domains, including biology, ecology and swarm robotics. However, CRNs require the explicit enumeration of all possible species and reactions, which becomes intractable in complex systems.

Rule-based frameworks generalize CRNs by representing interacting agents as site-graphs. Originally developed to simulate molecular interactions in cells, these frameworks use graph-rewriting rules to model complex reaction systems. The existing implementations of rule-based framework, such as Kappa [7] and BioNetGen [19], each offers a wide-range toolbox to investigate rule-based models, including a stochastic simulation engine, mean-field analysis, static analysis and causal analysis. A major advantage for a modeler using a rule-based model is the "*don't care, don't write*" policy: rules operate over *patterns*, partially defined species. Writing rules over patterns allows not only to alleviate the burden of enumerating the list of all possible species in a system, but also to significantly reduce the dimension of mean-field and stochastic analyses of rule-based models, through automated reduction procedures with static analysis [15–17,26]. Despite these advantages, formal analysis of rule-based models remains challenging. In particular, existing approaches to model checking often rely on translating rule-based models into equivalent CRNs, which can be computationally expensive, and is in some cases infeasible due to the potentially unbounded state space.

In this work, we propose a method for statistical model checking of rule-based models written in Kappa, against properties written in bounded linear temporal logic (BLTL). Our approach operates natively within the rule-based modeling paradigm: the temporal formula can contain atomic propositions which can be any Kappa expression over pattern occurrences. Moreover, our model checking procedure does not require translating the rule-based model into a CRN.

Our key idea is to use the *intervention* feature in Kappa to encode the satisfaction of atomic propositions over time. With such approach, the temporal formula can contain atomic propositions which can be a Kappa expression over occurrences of a *pattern*, partially defined species that are native to Kappa. As such, it is not limited to occurrences of single, fully defined species, but it can refer to any algebraic conditions over Kappa pattern occurrences. Moreover, such expressions can be combined with Boolean operations. Given a Kappa model and a BLTL property, we first instrument the model by introducing additional variables, observables and interventions that track the truth value of atomic propositions. Then, for each trace generated by the KaSim tool [7], the formula satisfaction is evaluated using an offline monitoring procedure. Finally, as is standard in statistical model checking (SMC) [24], we analyse batches of stochastic simulations of the corresponding continuous-time Markov chain (CTMC) in order to estimate probability of property satisfaction with desired statistical guarantees.

Following the network free approach [12,29], our approach never requires the unfolding of the set of Kappa rules into a reaction network, which would have been untractable for large models of protein-protein interaction networks. Whereas our work focuses on Kappa, it can be adapted straightforwardly to languages such as BNGL [2], or mød [1].

We demonstrate our proposed method over a number of case studies. The first case study involves a system with a polymerizing agent. With this simple case study, we demonstrate that our approach on a system that would otherwise not be amenable to SMC procedures if translated into a CRN. Here, we also highlight the ability to monitor properties over patterns (rather than fully defined species). The second case study focus on long-lived transient dynamics in a single cell genetic system. This system offers an approach to assess bistable behaviors which can emerge given the order of classes of transcription factors regulating this aforementioned system. Finally, third case study concerns consensus dynamics, a scenario commonly studied in the swarm robotics community, where robots must collectively align on a decision despite the presence of disruptive agents. This example showcases the generality of our methodology; in particular, we demonstrate its ability to handle nested temporal operators.

Contributions. The main contributions of this work are:

- A SMC framework for stochastic rule-based models written in Kappa;
- A native specification approach where BLTL atomic propositions are defined over Kappa patterns, enabling expressive and flexible property definitions;
- A model instrumentation technique based on Kappa interventions for tracking temporal properties during simulation;
- An implementation and evaluation on representative case studies from systems biology and swarm robotics.

1.1 Related Works

Our work is closely related to early efforts on SMC for rule-based models, in particular the BioLab framework [10], which introduced SMC techniques for models specified in BioNetGen. Subsequent work [31] extended these ideas and demonstrated their applicability on a variety of case studies expressed in the BioNetGen language.

While these approaches share the goal of enabling statistical verification of stochastic rule-based systems, they differ from our work in several important aspects. First, our framework supports a more expressive class of BLTL properties, where atomic propositions can be arbitrary combinations of Boolean and algebraic constraints over *pattern counts*. This allows properties to refer directly to partially specified species, rather than relying on fully specified states or auxiliary variables. Second, we exploit the Kappa intervention mechanism to dynamically track the truth values of atomic propositions during simulation, resulting in a hybrid monitoring strategy that combines online tracking of state properties with offline evaluation of time-bounded temporal operators.

Another line of related work focuses on querying and analysing execution traces of rule-based models. For instance, [23] introduces a trace query language for specifying temporal properties over individual agents. Our approach is complementary, as it focuses on population-level properties and supports probabilistic verification of temporal specifications.

Parameter synthesis and calibration techniques for rule-based models have also been studied. In [30], the authors use probabilistic computation tree logic (PCTL) in combination with the PRISM model checker [22] to calibrate model parameters. However, this requires abstracting pattern-based representations into a finite system of state variables compatible with PRISM, which may reduce the expressiveness and structural clarity of the original rule-based model. In contrast, our framework operates directly on Kappa patterns, preserving the native modelling abstraction and enabling more expressive specifications.

Finally, calibration approaches such as [3] also rely on network-free simulation of Kappa models to estimate parameters of stochastic systems. These methods are complementary to our work, as they focus on parameter inference rather than temporal property verification.

1.2 Motivating Case Study

We first introduce Kappa language informally, through an example of unbounded polumerization. For a formal introduction to Kappa, we refer the interested reader to [11].

(a) A Kappa agent monomer.

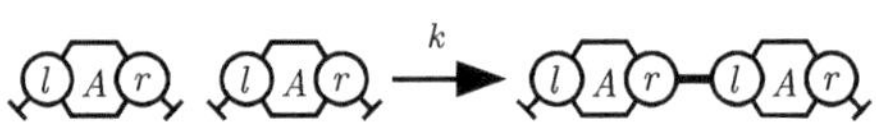

(b) A rule depicting a binding event between two monomers with free sites.

Fig. 1. A model of unbounded asymmetric polymerization.

Example 1 (unbounded, asymmetric polymerization [6]). Agents of type A can bind and create polymers (linear or cyclic) of any length through binding sites x (right) and y (left). Each of A's sites can be free or bound to a compatible site of another agent. An example of a monomer in Kappa is given in Fig. 1a. Therefore, the molecular species formed by such model would be monomers (agent A free on both sites), dimers (with a single bond or with two bonds when we refer to it as'ring'), trimers (with two bonds or a ring with three bonds), etc. A classical CRN model would require an enumeration of all polymers that can be formed, and an enumeration of all possible (un)binding events. For simplicity, we here assume that there are no unbinding events.

In Kappa, a free monomer of agent of type A would be represented by a string

$$A(x\,[.]\,,y\,[.]\,),$$

while a dimer between two agents of type A would be represented by a string

$$A(x\,[.]\,, y\,[1]\,),\ A(x\,[1]\,, y\,[.]\,),$$

where 1 uniquely identifies the bond between site y of one agent of type A and the site x of the other agent of type A.

Kappa *pattern* allows to omit parts of agent's interface. For instance, we can compactly represent any species that is free at site x by a string $A(x\,[.]\,)$, without being concrete as to whether the site y of an agent is free, bound to a polymer of four agents, or bound to a polymer of one thousand agents. The entire polymerization model is then captured by a single Kappa rule:

$$'bind\_A' \quad A(x\,[.]\,), A(y\,[.]\,) \rightarrow A(x\,[1]\,), A(y\,[1]\,) \quad @ \ k_1 \tag{1}$$

The left-hand side (LHS) depicts two patterns, which are *partially* defined species, $A(x\,[.]\,)$ and $A(y\,[.]\,)$. The full stop "." in the brackets after the site name indicates that the site is free to bind to another agent. As the second site of involved agents is not mentioned, the binding occurs independently of whether the other site is bound or not. The right-hand side (RHS) of this rule depicts the binding (labeled by the integer 1). The rule occurs at rate k_1. An example of this rule is depicted in Fig. 1b.

For comparison, for initially 100 free agents, a CRN model would enumerate 200 species (100 linear chains and 100 rings), and 2600 reactions (explicitly enumerating the binding reaction between any two chains with a free site x and y respectively, as well as the potential closing of chains into rings). In general, for initially n agents, a CRN would count $2n$ species and $O(n^2)$ reactions, while the rule-based model has a single agent and single rule, independently of the initial population size.

As in CRNs, the dynamics of Kappa models follow a CTMC, where each state represents a Kappa mixture. A Kappa mixture is a site-graph representing a mixture of fully defined species, and it is equivalent to a multiset of species in a CRN. A rule can be activated whenever the site-graph representing the mixture of patterns at the LHS of the rule *embeds* into the current Kappa mixture. The propensity functions of Kappa rules are computed following the mass-action principle [12]: the propensity is directly proportional to the number of site-graph embeddings of the LHS of the Kappa rule to the Kappa mixture. In our experiments, we will use the KaSim tool [7] to generate stochastic simulations for our case studies. Internally, KaSim is an engine for running forward stochastic (Gillespie) simulations over Kappa mixtures [12]. Accordingly, this engine outputs stochastic trajectories carrying a finite number of state changes (also termed *jumps* in a Markov process) of Kappa mixtures realized over a rule set.

In Sect. 2 we introduce two major ingredients motivating our SMC framework: (i) a minimal Kappa syntax and its corresponding semantics, and (ii) a BLTL framework lifted over these Kappa constructs. To reiterate, a primary objective along this avenue is to make such Kappa objects amenable to SMC procedures. Accordingly, in Sect. 3 we will revisit our model of polymerization to lift our proposed BLTL framework, and additionally discuss three more complex case studies. We conclude in Sect. 4

$$
\begin{array}{rll}
E & ::= \epsilon \mid a, E & \text{(expression)} \\
a & ::= A(\sigma) & \text{(agent)} \\
\sigma & ::= \epsilon \mid s, \sigma & \text{(interface)} \\
s & ::= n\iota\lambda & \text{(site)} \\
\iota & ::= \epsilon \mid \{\omega\} & \text{(internal state)} \\
\lambda & ::= \epsilon \mid [.] \mid [l] & \text{(binding state)}
\end{array}
\qquad
\begin{array}{rll}
A & ::= \mathrm{A} \in \mathcal{A} & \text{(agent type)} \\
 & & \\
n & ::= \mathrm{n} \in \mathcal{S} & \text{(site name)} \\
\omega & ::= \mathrm{w} \in \mathbb{I} & \text{(internal state)} \\
l & ::= \mathrm{i} \in \mathbb{N} & \text{(bond label)}
\end{array}
$$

Fig. 2. Syntax for agents.

2 Methods

2.1 Kappa Syntax

In this section, we define a minimal syntax for the Kappa rule-based modelling framework in order to motivate our SMC procedure.

Definition 1 (Signature). *A Kappa signature is a tuple $(\mathcal{A}, \mathcal{S}, \mathbb{I}, \Sigma)$ such that:*

1. *$\mathcal{A}$ is a finite set of agent types;*
2. *$\mathcal{S}$ is a finite set of sites;*
3. *$\mathbb{I}$ is a finite set of strings;*
4. *Σ is a mapping from agent types to a set of sites.*

In Definition 1, a Kappa signature has four components that pave the type of objects that we would like to assess throughout this report. Here, the first component of a signature, Item 1, is a set of agent types which correspond to labels given to, for example, a chemical species or a robot. The second component, Item 2, gives the interaction points between agent types. Component three, Item 3, is a set of strings $\mathbb{I}$, which depict the potential internal states that the sites in $\mathcal{S}$ can bare. Finally, Item 4 is a set of functions Σ that maps each agent type to its associated set of sites.

The syntax of expressions is given in Fig. 2. Expressions are sequences of agents. Each agent $A(\sigma)$ is given by an agent type A and interface σ that expresses potential sites. Each site s may carry an internal state and a binding state. The internal state is a string w that can encode a level of energy (such as a phosphorylation state) and the binding state is a bond label l. The absence of an internal/binding state is denoted by the symbol ϵ, which is usually omitted. The binding state '.' denotes the free sites, whereas the bound sites share a common binding label. The symbol ϵ also stands for the end of site and agent sequences. It is omitted also when used this way.

Accordingly, we now define the Kappa object central to our report: patterns.

Definition 2 (Patterns). *A Kappa pattern E is an expression E such that:*

1. *for every interface σ, each site appears at most once in the interface;*
2. *each site name that occurs in the interface of the agent A occurs in $\Sigma(A)$;*
3. *each binding label in E if present occurs exactly twice.*

The set of Kappa patterns is denoted $\mathcal{O}$.

In Definition 2, Items 1 and 2 ensure that each agent signature occurring in a pattern are well-formed. Additionally, Item 3 ensures that every binding site is either free (when it carries no binding label) or bound to exactly one other site (the one with the other occurrence of its binding label).

Finally, we can define relations between pairs of modifiable patterns that occur with a given rule rate, which we refer to as Kappa rules.

Definition 3 (Kappa rules). *A Kappa rule is given by a pair* $((E_l, E_r), k) \in (\mathcal{O} \times \mathcal{O}) \times \mathbb{R}$. *A rule can be written as* $E_l \xrightarrow{k} E_r$*, such that it has to be possible to obtain* E_r *from* E_l *in the following way (the order matters):*

1. *creation: some agents each with their full interfaces with free and specified internal states are added;*
2. *unbinding: some binding types are removed;*
3. *deletion: some agents are removed;*
4. *modification: some non-empty internal states are replaced with other non-empty internal states;*
5. *binding: some free sites are bounded pairwise.*

The set of Kappa rules is denoted by $\mathcal{K}$.

In Definition 3, a Kappa rule is composed of two components. The first component is a pair of patterns (E_l, E_r) such that E_l is the LHS pattern that participates in this rule, while E_r is the RHS pattern that details the instructions that occurred in the rule. The rate k is the rate constant of this rule. Applying a Kappa rule transforms agents and interfaces of the LHS pattern component, and the types of transformations that can occur is described now. The constraints in Definition 3 ensure a proper matching of the LHS pattern to the right-hand side one.

2.2 Stochastic Semantics of Kappa

The stochastic semantics of Kappa is obtained by applying stochastically the Kappa rules to rewrite the state of the system. A rule can be applied to a pattern when an occurrence of the left-hand side of this rule is identified in the corresponding pattern. The result of the rule application is then obtained by replacing the corresponding occurrence to an occurrence of the right-hand side of the rule. The detailed description of the operational semantics of Kappa is omitted for the sake of conciseness. Formal definitions of these elements can be found in Appendix A.

For our purpose, it is enough to know that a model is a collection of Kappa rules, and that it induces a CTMC: from any state being a Kappa mixture (site graph where all agents have complete interface given), each applicable rule will be triggered at a time following the exponential law of parameter equal to the rate of the corresponding Kappa rule. A single stochastic trace will be referred to as a map from real time to a Kappa mixture $\tau : [0, \infty] \mapsto \mathcal{O}$. The Kappa simulator samples the traces of this CTMC. Its efficiency relies on several features. Firstly, it operate directly on Kappa expressions without having to unfold the set of Kappa rule into a reaction network [12]. Secondly, it updates dynamically the set of potential rule applications after each rule application thanks to a dedicated data-structure that take benefit of potential sharing between patterns [5].

2.3 Bounded Linear Time Logic

In this work, we focus on bounded linear temporal logic (BLTL). State formulae in BLTL follow the grammar:

$$\varphi ::= True \mid a \in AP \mid \neg\varphi \mid \varphi \bigtriangleup \varphi \mid \varphi \bigtriangleup \Psi \mid \mathcal{P}_{\underline{\bigtriangleup} p}(\Psi), \tag{2}$$

$\bigtriangleup \in \{\wedge, \vee\}$, $\mathcal{P}$ is the classical probability operator, $\underline{\bigtriangleup}$ is an element in the set $\{=, \leq, \geq, >, <\}$, and $p \in [0,1]$ is a threshold value. When the threshold p is not prescribed beforehand, then we write ? indicating that this probability value is to be computed. AP is the set of atomic propositions, which we formally define now.

Definition 4. *Let $\mathcal{AL}$ be a set of algebraic expressions over Kappa pattern occurrences (syntax of which is given in Appendix, Fig. 12) An atomic proposition is a triple $(\eta, \underline{\square}, \eta') \in \mathcal{AL} \times \{>, \geq, <, \leq\} \times \mathcal{AL}$, which can also be written as $\eta \,\underline{\square}\, \eta'$. A reaction mixture (state variable) visited at time t, $\tau(t) \in \mathcal{O}$, satisfies an atomic proposition if the evaluation of the respective algebraic expressions in state $\tau(t)$ are related by standard interpretation of relation $\underline{\square}$. We denote the set of atomic propositions AP.*

For example, in the polymerization example, AP can be represented by the expression $(|A(x[.], y[.])|, \geq, 4)$, which is evaluated to `True` if and only if the number of free monomers in the state is not smaller than constant 4. The rich expressiveness of algebraic expressions allows us to also query a state variable of form e.g. $|A(x[.])|, \leq, 2 \cdot |A(y[.])|$, which is `True` if and only if the total number of A agents free at site x is at least 2 times larger than the total number of agents A free at site y.[1]

The grammar for the path operator is:

$$\Psi ::= \varphi_1 \mathbf{U}^{[t_1,t_2]} \varphi_2, \tag{3}$$

with the *until* operator defined in the usual way. The *finally* operator and the *globally* operator can be derived: $\mathbf{F}^{[t_1,t_2]}\varphi = True\ \mathbf{U}^{[t_1,t_2]}\varphi$, and $\mathbf{G}^{[t_1,t_2]}\varphi = \neg\mathbf{F}^{[t_1,t_2]}\neg\varphi$. [25].

2.4 Kappa Interventions

Before introducing our framework for SMC on stochastic Kappa models wrt. BLTL properties, we introduce Kappa interventions. The intervention feature in

[1] *Remark.* For practical reasons, in our implementation, each $a \equiv (\eta, \underline{\square}, \eta') \in AP$ is first translated to a single algebraic expression $(\eta - \eta')$.

Kappa provides a strategy for scheduling perturbations or tracking the quantities of patterns over the course of a simulation [7]. In particular, we use the intervention feature to track whether a prescribed atomic proposition is satisfied during the course of a stochastic simulation. That is, we encode in each intervention atomic proposition(s) to track if the number of patterns of a given agent satisfy some BLTL state property of interest. In Kappa, interventions are declared using the following syntax:

$$\%mod: \varphi\ do\ \$UPDATE\ \ v \in \mathbb{V}\ \ r \in \mathbb{R};\ \ repeat\ \varphi'. \tag{4}$$

The grammar for interventions can be found in the Appendix. In Eq. 4, '$\%mod$' is the declaration for an intervention in Kappa. During the course of a stochastic simulation, interventions are applied only when a condition is satisfied, which in itself is triggered by a rule event (*jumps* in the underlying Markov process). Importantly, φ, φ' are each a BLTL state formula (which may or may not be equal; see Eq. 2) over patterns, and *do* $\$UPDATE$ allows a user to update *during a simulation* the variable v (which may be pattern occurrences, a Boolean variable, etc.) to a value $r \in \mathbb{R}$ if the state formula φ is satisfied. This intervention will repeat itself for as long as φ' remains $True$, indicated after the semicolon in Eq. 4.

2.5 Statistical Model Checking

The SMC procedure is shown in Fig. 3, Algorithm 1. Given a Kappa model M and a BLTL property φ, we first extract the atomic propositions appearing in φ. We instrument the model by introducing additional variables, observables, and interventions that track the truth value of each atomic proposition. Notice that encoding Boolean conditions over inequalities on pattern counts is *not* possible with only additional variables and observables, i.e. interventions are necessary for this step. The simulator then produces execution traces containing both the model variables and the truth values of the atomic propositions which constitute the given BLTL formula.

For each simulated trace, the BLTL formula is evaluated using an offline monitoring procedure, shown in Fig. 3 (Algorithm 2 and Algorithm 3). The procedure for modifying the model wrt. a list of atomic propositions is given in Fig. 3 (Algorithm 4). The probability that the model satisfies the property is estimated by treating the formula satisfaction at time 0 as Bernoulli random variable, as usual in SMC [24]. To ensure that the estimation error does not exceed a user-specified tolerance ε with confidence at least $1 - \alpha$, we determine the number of simulations using Hoeffding's inequality: $\Pr(|\hat{p} - p| \geq \varepsilon) \leq 2e^{-2N\varepsilon^2}$. Thus it suffices to choose $N \geq \left\lceil \frac{1}{2\varepsilon^2} \ln \frac{2}{\alpha} \right\rceil$. We focus on probability estimation rather than hypothesis testing (e.g. Wald's sequential probability ratio test), since the goal of the framework is to quantify the probability that a Kappa model satisfies a BLTL property rather than to decide whether it exceeds a given threshold. While sequential estimation techniques could potentially reduce the number of simulations by stopping early, they require careful treatment of optional stopping to maintain statistical guarantees. We here adopt the fixed-sample approach derived from Hoeffding's bound for simplicity and robustness, and we leave the exploration of sequential estimation techniques to future work.

3 Results

Now we begin to discuss the diverse case studies at the center of our SMC framework. Unless otherwise noted, all estimates of satisfaction probabilities are done for confidence level $1-\alpha = 0.99$ and tolerance $\epsilon = 0.05$, which are expressed as error bars enclosing each point estimate our plots. A repository containing our tool is also included in this report[2].

3.1 Case Study I: A Model of Asymmetric Polymerisation

We now revisit in detail the motivating case study of Sect. 1.2.

Biological Context. Protein subunits, referred to as monomers, are structures that may bind to other monomers to form diverse geometric structures. This conformation benefits from many pertinent properties, such as structural stability and biologically-driven function [13] Accordingly, we focus on a small Kappa model of asymmetric polymerisation reported in [6,26].

For convenience, we follow the notation for polymers introduced in [14]. Specifically, we denote by $| \vdash A_i - |$ the quantity of polymers, or chains, of length at least $i+1$. That is, i is the number of agents A in a sequence, where the first agent is bounded (indicated by $\vdash$), and the final agent is free to bind ($-$) to extend the chain.

In each simulation of an experiment, we set the initial pool of monomers of A to 50. We are interested in whether the number of chains $| \vdash A_i - |$ of varying length will exceed 4 during the first 10 time units in an experiment. Formally, we compute $\mathcal{P}_{=?}(\mathbf{F}^{[0,10]}\ (| \vdash A_i - | > 4))$ and $\mathcal{P}_{=?}(\mathbf{G}^{[0,10]}\ (| \vdash A_i - | < 5))$ such that $i \in \{1,2,3,4,5\}$. Following Eq. 4, an example intervention for the finally operator is:

$$\%mod: | \vdash A_i - | > 4\ do\ \$UPDATE\ 'prop\_0'\ 1\quad repeat\ | \vdash A_i - | > 4$$

Here, $\varphi = \varphi' = | \vdash A_i - | > 4$, and $'prop\_0'$ is a Boolean variable (initially set to 0) that we use to monitor when φ is $True$. We also include an intervention to signal to KaSim when to not monitor the state property: $| \vdash A_i - | < 5$ (see Appendix). A similar intervention is used for the state property under the globally operator. When an experiment is complete, we analyze each stochastic simulation trace to assess whether our time bounds $[0, 10]$ have been satisfied over our binary variable.

In Fig. 4a, we report estimates of the satisfaction probability for forming a chain of a varying length during the first 10 time units in 1000 stochastic simulations. As one can observe, for the operator $\mathbf{F}^{[0,10]}$, shorter chains (e.g., $\vdash A_1-$) are more likely in abundance in our experiments when compared to

[2] https://github.com/tatjanapetrov/kappa-smc.

Algorithm 1: BLTL Statistical Model Checking via Kappa Simulation

```
Input: Kappa model M, BLTL formula φ, ε, α
Output: Estimated probability p̂
AP ← ExtractAtomicPropositions(φ);
M′ ← InstrumentModel(M, AP);
N ← ⌈(1/(2ε²)) ln(2/α)⌉;
S ← 0;
for i ← 1 to N do
    τ_i ← SimulateKappa(M′);
    V_i ← τ_i[AP];
    X_i ← 1{Monitor(φ, V_i)};
    S ← S + X_i;
return S/N;
```

Algorithm 2: Offline Monitoring of BLTL

```
Input: Formula φ, AP truth matrix V
Output: true if φ holds at time 0
sat ← Evaluate(φ, V);
return sat[0];
```

Algorithm 3: Generating a Kappa File with Interventions

```
Input: Kappa model κ, atomic propositions AP
Output: Instrumented model κ^I
κ^I ← κ;
for i ← 0 to |AP| − 1 do
    Let AP[i] = (η_i, □_i, η′_i);
    Introduce auxiliary variable a_i;
    Add observable p_i;
    Add intervention: a_i ← 1 if (η_i, □_i, η′_i);
    Add intervention: a_i ← 0 otherwise;
return κ^I;
```

Algorithm 4: Recursive Evaluation of BLTL

```
Input: Formula φ, AP truth matrix V
Output: Boolean vector sat
n ← |V| − 1;
if φ ≡ AP_i then
    return column i of V;
else
    if φ = ¬φ1 then
        return ¬Evaluate(φ1, V);
    else
        if φ = φ1 ∧ φ2 then
            return Evaluate(φ1, V) ∧ Evaluate(φ2, V);
        else
            if φ = G^{≤k} φ1 then
                u ← Evaluate(φ1, V);
                for t ← 0 to n do
                    sat[t] ← ⋀_{j=t}^{min(t+k,n)} u[j];
                return sat;
            else
                if φ = F^{≤k} φ1 then
                    u ← Evaluate(φ1, V);

                    for t ← 0 to n do
                        sat[t] ← ⋁_{j=t}^{min(t+k,n)} u[j];

                    return sat;
                else
                    (φ = φ1 U^{≤k} φ2)
                    u1 ← Evaluate(φ1, V);
                    u2 ← Evaluate(φ2, V);

                    for t ← 0 to n do
                        sat[t] ← ∃j ∈ [t, min(t + k, n)] : u2[j] ∧ ⋀_{i=t}^{j−1} u1[i];
                    return sat;
```

Fig. 3. Algorithms for BLTL statistical model checking of Kappa models. Left column: Monte Carlo estimation, monitoring, and model instrumentation. Right column: recursive evaluation of BLTL formulas.

longer chains (e.g., $\vdash A_5-$). On the contrary, for the operator $\mathbf{G}^{[0,10]}$, it is more likely that longer chains will be in least abundance as opposed to the shorter chains. Note that for each i, the sum $\mathcal{P}_{=?}(\mathbf{F}^{[0,10]}\ (|\vdash A_i - | > 4)) + \mathcal{P}_{=?}(\mathbf{G}^{[0,10]}\ (|\vdash A_i - | < 5)) = 1$. It is worth also noting that such an experiment is manageable in Kappa thanks to its compact representation of agent species, which would become intractable in an analogous CRN model. Also, one would require a different translation for each initial mixture, while our approach remains compact and reusable for any initial mixture.

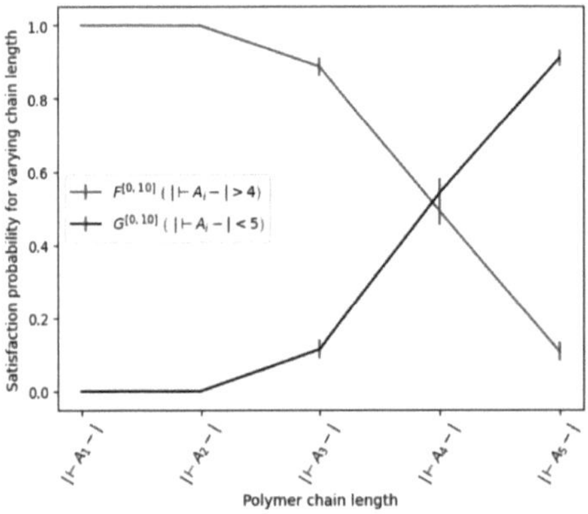

(a) Reachability analyses of the model of polymerizing agents.

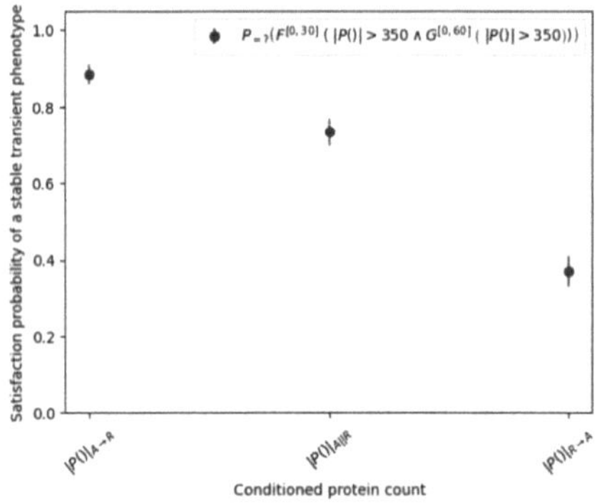

(b) Nested operators analyses of transient behaviour in gene regulatory networks.

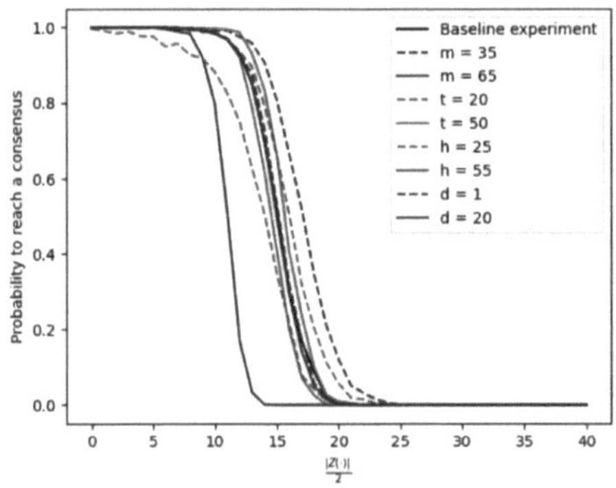

(c) Nested operators analyses for consensus dynamics in swarm robotics.

Fig. 4. Statistical model checking of BLTL properties over three case studies.

3.2 Case Study II: Long-Lived Transients

Our second case study is taken from [27]. The model, shown in link, contains twenty five rules operating over five agent types, which would require 27 species and more than 130 reactions to specify an equivalent mechanism with a CRN.

Biological Context. In a single cell, gene transcription and translation processes are commonly regulated positively or negatively by transcription factors (TFs). TFs themselves are proteins. In [27], the authors showcase a model of biologically implementable gene regulatory circuit which exhibits *long-lived transients.* Long-lived transients are phenotypes which appear stable for an extended period of time, although they are just very slow transients converging to a unique equilibrium state. In the model, two qualitatively different long-lived phenotypes are observed as a consequence to when TFs makes its presence either as an activator or as a repressor. If the activator is present before the repressor, then one seamingly stable behavior is observed, and vice versa. Our goal is to assess the qualitatively different transient phenotypes by means of statistical model checking, thus providing a complementary characterization of this biological behavior. We assess the satisfaction probability of the protein count exceeding and maintaining a particular expression level, which can be expressed using a nested BLTL operator. Accordingly, we set the state property for this threshold as $\varphi = |P()| > 350$. We would like to evaluate the likelihood for this state property to be achieved within 30 min, and held for 60 min. Formally, this is $\mathcal{P}_{=?}(F^{[0,30]}\ (\varphi \wedge G^{[0,60]}\ (\varphi)))$.

In Fig. 4b, we assess the impact of appearance an activating or repressing TF has on obtaining our temporal property φ. Accordingly, we write $A \rightarrow R$ (resp. $R \rightarrow A$) when A (resp. R) appears prior to R (resp. A). When both appear appear concurrently we write $A||R$. In Fig. 4b, we observe indeed that the order at which each TF type appears does impact the satisfaction of our state property, which is consistent with observations reported in [27]. That is, when the activator TF appears before the repressor then our state property is more likely satisfied, when both occur concurrently then is reduces this likelihood, and when reversed the repressor impacts this likelihood even more.

3.3 Case Study III: Nested Temporal Logics in a Model of Consensus

Swarm Robotics Context. We now analyze a swarm robotics case study reported in [21,28]: a subset of robots change and must agree on a decision in a population that includes zealots, robots that don't change their opinion at all. Robots that do change decision must decide between x, y or u (undecided), while zealots can hold only x or y as a decision. This model is referred to as the cross-inhibition model. Accordingly, in [21] the authors model this system as a CRN, and express this model in the PlasmaLab tool [8] to verify BLTL properties of interest. Thus, our objective is to build a Kappa model with interventions of this model to reproduce directly a set of results in the aforementioned paper.

To do so, we first must describe the set of parameters that will allow us to quantify states properties that lead to a stable consensus, that is when a majority of robots agree on a common decision. More specifically, we focus on four parameters: a majority parameter m, corresponding to the minimum percentage of individuals required to reach a consensus; a distance parameter d, which expresses a minimal difference between sub-populations holding a decision x or y; a maximal time to reach a consensus t; and, a minimal amount of time a consensus must be held h. The first two parameters reasons over quantity of patterns, while the latter two parameters are time bounds on BLTL operator.

The first state property that we encode into a Kappa intervention is:

$$\varphi_m^{o\in\{x,y\}} := \frac{|A(a\{o\})|+|Z(z\{o\})|}{|A(\cdot)|+|Z(\cdot)|} > m \tag{5}$$

In Eq. 5, we check whether a fraction of robots (labeled A for robots, and Z for zealots) expressing a decision o (which can be x or y) in the population is greater than the majority parameter m. The second state property we must encode is:

$$\varphi_d^{o\in\{x,y\}} := |A(a\{o\})| + |Z(z\{o\})| - (|A(a\{o'\})| + |Z(z\{o'\})|) > d \tag{6}$$

In Eq. 6, the difference between the number of robots with decision o and the number of robots with decision o', such that $o \neq o'$, must be greater than the distance parameter d. See Appendix for interventions of Eqs. 5 and 6.

Accordingly, in Fig. 4c we use a nested finally and globally operator to estimate the satisfaction probability to reach a consensus in the presence of varying quantities of zealots. First, we keep the number of zealots for each decision equal, $|Z(z\{x\})| = |Z(z\{y\})|$ across each experiment. The baseline experiment is set to $m = 50$, $d = 10$, $t = 35$, and $h = 40$. Formally, the nested operator we estimate is $\mathcal{P}_{=?}(\mathbf{F}^{[0,35]}\mathbf{G}^{[0,40]}(\varphi_m^{o\in\{x,y\}} \wedge \varphi_d^{o\in\{x,y\}}))$. Here, we would like to assess the likelihood of a stable consensus that satisfies the indicated state properties occurs within 35 time units, and holds this consensus for at least 40 time units. We estimate satisfaction probabilities by varying each of the four consensus parameters, one at a time, with varying amounts of zealots. We observe a similar trend to those experiments reported in [21]. In particular, in Fig. 4c we can observe that the distance parameter d is not impacted by varying zealot counts in each experiment when compared to the baseline experiment. However, the majority parameter m experiences the largest shift from the baseline experiment (Table 1).

Table 1. A summary of the various case studies tested using our SMC framework.

Model	# species	# CRNs	# agent(s)	# rule(s)	# traces	Property	Runtime
Polymer	$n = 50$	$O(n^2)$	1	1	1000	Figure 4a	$88.0s$
GRN transient	27	> 130	5	14	1000	Figure 4b	$155.7s$
Consensus	3	8	3	8	1000	Figure 4c	$111.2s$

4 Discussion

In this work, we introduced a formal framework for performing SMC of stochastic rule-based models written in Kappa against BLTL specifications. A key contribution of our approach is that both the modelling and the specification layers operate directly at the level of *patterns*, enabling expressive reasoning over partially specified molecular species while avoiding costly translations to CRNs. By operating natively on patterns, our framework preserves compact representation of agents native to rule-based models, while making these objects amenable to SMC procedures within the BLTL framework. Accordingly, we motivated our approach on a diverse set of case studies in Kappa.

Our current implementation should be regarded as a proof of concept, and several limitations open up promising directions for future work. At present, atomic propositions are monitored within the Kappa engine, while the evaluation of time-bounded temporal operators is performed offline over generated traces. Moreover, the number of simulation runs must be fixed in advance to guarantee statistical precision, which may lead to inefficiencies in practice. Addressing these limitations is an important next step. In particular, integrating online monitoring of temporal operators and adopting adaptive sampling techniques such as sequential hypothesis testing with earlier stopping criteria could improve performance.

Another promising direction is to combine our approach with the abstraction techniques for Kappa rule-based models. Given the extensive work on model reduction in Kappa (for example, [15,20] and [17]), it would be natural to investigate how such abstractions can be leveraged to accelerate statistical verification while preserving correctness guarantees. From a biological perspective, this could enable scalable analysis of large signalling networks, where both structural complexity and stochastic effects play a central role. Similarly, extending the framework towards parameter estimation [3] and synthesis [18] of CTMCs would support systematic studies of robustness, sensitivity, and model calibration in biological systems.

More broadly, our work contributes to bridging formal verification techniques with expressive modelling frameworks based on graph rewriting. We believe that enabling SMC directly over rule-based abstractions opens new opportunities for analysing complex stochastic systems, in particular biological systems where behaviour emerges from local, partially specified interactions. Ongoing work on tool support and integration with existing Kappa-based workflows aims to make these techniques practically accessible to domain scientists.

A Kappa: Syntax and Semantics

In this appendix, we provide detailed formal definitions for Kappa syntax and semantics. For the sake of simplicity, we do not cover the full language. In particular, we have not included agent creation/removal, partially specified binding states, and counters. We refer to [17] for a formal description of Kappa syntax and semantics (not including counters) and to [4] for the treatment of counters.

$$
\begin{array}{lll}
E ::= \epsilon \mid a, E & \text{(expression)} & \\
a ::= A_k(\sigma) & \text{(agent)} & k ::= \mathrm{k} \in \mathbb{N} \ \text{(agent label} \\
\sigma ::= \epsilon \mid s, \sigma & \text{(interface)} & A ::= \mathrm{A} \in \mathcal{A} \ \text{(agent type)} \\
s ::= n\iota\lambda & \text{(site)} & n ::= \mathrm{n} \in \mathcal{S} \ \text{(site name)} \\
\iota ::= \epsilon \mid \{\omega\} & \text{(internal state)} & \omega ::= \mathrm{w} \in \mathbb{I} \ \text{(internal state)} \\
\lambda ::= \epsilon \mid [.] \mid [l] & \text{(binding state)} & l ::= \mathrm{i} \in \mathbb{N} \ \text{(bond label)}
\end{array}
$$

Fig. 5. Syntax for agents.

- $\mathcal{BL}^{\mathbb{E}}(\epsilon) = \emptyset$, $\mathcal{BL}^{\mathbb{E}}(a, E) = \mathcal{BL}^{\mathbb{A}}(a) \cup \mathcal{BL}^{\mathbb{E}}(E)$;
- $\mathcal{BL}^{\mathbb{A}}(A_k(\sigma)) = \mathcal{BL}^{\Sigma}(\sigma)$;
- $\mathcal{BL}^{\Sigma}(\epsilon) = \emptyset$, $\mathcal{BL}^{\Sigma}(s, \sigma) = \mathcal{BL}^{\mathbb{S}}(s) \cup \mathcal{BL}^{\Sigma}(\sigma)$;
- $\mathcal{BL}^{\mathbb{S}}(n\iota\lambda) = \mathcal{BL}^{\Lambda}(\lambda)$;
- $\mathcal{BL}^{\Lambda}(\epsilon) = \emptyset$, $\mathcal{BL}^{\Lambda}([.]) = \emptyset$, $\mathcal{BL}^{\Lambda}([l]) = \{l\}$.

Fig. 6. Binding label occurrences.

- $\mathcal{AL}^{\mathbb{E}}(\epsilon) = \emptyset$, $\mathcal{AL}^{\mathbb{E}}(a, E) = \mathcal{AL}^{\mathbb{A}}(a) \cup \mathcal{AL}^{\mathbb{E}}(E)$;
- $\mathcal{AL}^{\mathbb{A}}(A_k(\sigma)) = \{k\}$.

Fig. 7. Agent label occurrences.

A.1 Refined Syntax

In Fig. 5, we enrich the syntax of Kappa expressions, which were given in Fig. 2 on page 6, to precisely identify each agent in Kappa expressions. To this aim, every agent is labeled with an integer, which we call its agent label. We assume that the agent labels that occur in a given Kappa expression are pair-wisely distinct. We also assume that the agents of a rule are labeled in the same way on the left-hand side and on the right-hand side. This means that two agents at the same position in the left-hand side and the right-hand side of a rule, have the same agent type and the same agent label.

Given a Kappa expression E, we denote as $\mathcal{BL}^{\mathbb{E}}(E)$ the set of binding labels that occur in E (as defined in Fig. 6) and $\mathcal{AL}^{\mathbb{E}}(E)$ the set of agent labels that occur in E (as defined in Fig. 7).

Example 2. We give here some well-formed expressions.

- $A_1(x[.], y[1]), A_2(x[1], y[2]), A_3(x[2], y[.])$;
- $A_1(x[.], y[1]), A_2(x[.], y[1])$;
- $A_1(y[1]), A_2(x[1])$;
- $A_1(y[.]), A_2(x[.])$.

According to Definition 2, all these Kappa expressions are patterns. Their sets of binding labels are respectively $\{1, 2\}$, $\{1\}$, $\{1\}$, and $\emptyset$, while their sets of agent labels are respectively $\{1, 2, 3\}$, $\{1, 2\}$, $\{1, 2\}$, and $\{1, 2\}$.

A.2 Structural Equivalence

Kappa expressions are considered both up to the order of their agents and up to the order of sites within their agents. In addition, binding labels only specify which the binding between site pairs, thus, they can be renamed injectively in a given expression without modifying its meaning.

For this reason, a congruence relation, $\equiv^{\mathbb{E}}$, is introduced, in Fig. 8, to consider expressions up to permutation of agents in expressions and up to permutation of sites in their agents. It is defined by induction over the syntax. Notice that the congruence symbol bears a superscript, which indicates the syntactic class of the elements on which it operates. We will proceed the same way for every operator that we will define in this appendix section. Given an 1-to-1 function π on the set of binding labels $\mathcal{BL}$, the renaming, $\alpha^{\mathbb{E}}_{\pi}(E)$, of the binding labels in an expression E by the function π is defined inductively in Fig. 9 on the syntax of Kappa expressions.

We now have all the materials to define the structural equivalence between Kappa expressions.

Definition 5 (Structural equivalence). *Two Kappa expressions E and E' are structural equivalent if there exists a 1-to-1 function π on the set $\mathcal{BL}$ such that $E \equiv^{\mathbb{E}} \alpha^{\mathbb{E}}_{\pi}(E')$.*

In such a case, we simply write $E \sim^{\mathbb{E}} E'$.

- $\dfrac{}{\epsilon \equiv^{\mathbb{E}} \epsilon}$, $\dfrac{a_1 \equiv^{\mathbb{A}} a_1' \quad a_2 \equiv^{\mathbb{A}} a_2' \quad E \equiv^{\mathbb{E}} E'}{a_1, a_2, E \equiv^{\mathbb{E}} a_2', a_1', E'}$;
- $\dfrac{a \equiv^{\mathbb{A}} a' \quad E \equiv^{\mathbb{E}} E'}{a, E \equiv^{\mathbb{E}} a', E'}$, $\dfrac{E \equiv^{\mathbb{E}} E' \quad E' \equiv^{\mathbb{E}} E''}{E \equiv^{\mathbb{E}} E''}$;
- $\dfrac{\sigma \equiv^{\Sigma} \sigma'}{A_k(\sigma) \equiv^{\mathbb{A}} A_k(\sigma')}$;
- $\dfrac{}{\epsilon \equiv^{\Sigma} \epsilon}$, $\dfrac{}{s, s', \sigma \equiv^{\Sigma} s', s, \sigma}$, $\dfrac{\sigma \equiv^{\Sigma} \sigma'}{s, \sigma \equiv^{\Sigma} s, \sigma'}$, $\dfrac{\sigma \equiv^{\Sigma} \sigma' \quad \sigma' \equiv^{\Sigma} \sigma''}{\sigma \equiv^{\Sigma} \sigma''}$.

Fig. 8. Congruence relation.

- $\alpha^{\mathbb{E}}_{\pi}(\epsilon) = \epsilon$;
- $\alpha^{\mathbb{E}}_{\pi}(a, E) = \alpha^{\mathbb{A}}_{\pi}(a), \alpha^{\mathbb{E}}_{\pi}(E)$;
- $\alpha^{\mathbb{A}}_{\pi}(A_k(\sigma)) = A_k(\alpha^{\Sigma}_{\pi}(\sigma))$;
- $\alpha^{\Sigma}_{\pi}(\epsilon) = \epsilon$;
- $\alpha^{\Sigma}_{\pi}(s, \sigma) = \alpha^{\mathbb{S}}_{\pi}(s), \alpha^{\Sigma}_{\pi}(\sigma)$;
- $\alpha^{\mathbb{S}}_{\pi}(n\iota\lambda) = n\iota\alpha^{\Lambda}_{\pi}(\lambda)$;
- $\alpha^{\Lambda}_{\pi}(\epsilon) = \epsilon$;
- $\alpha^{\Lambda}_{\pi}([.]) = [.]$;
- $\alpha^{\Lambda}_{\pi}[l] = [\pi(l)]$.

Fig. 9. α-conversion of binding label.

Example 3. We have:

$$\begin{aligned}&A_1(x[.], y[1]), A_2(x[1], y[2]), A_3(x[2], y[.])\\ \sim^{\mathbb{E}}\ &A_1(y[1], x[.]), A_2(x[1], y[2]), A_3(x[2], y[.]),\end{aligned}$$

since

$$\begin{aligned}&A_1(x[.], y[1]), A_2(x[1], y[2]), A_3(x[2], y[.])\\ \equiv^{\mathbb{E}}\ &A_1(y[1], x[.]), A_2(x[1], y[2]), A_3(x[2], y[.])\end{aligned}$$

and

$$\begin{aligned}&\alpha^{\mathbb{E}}_{\pi_1}(A_1(y[1], x[.]), A_2(x[1], y[2]), A_3(x[2], y[.]))\\ &= A_1(y[1], x[.]), A_2(x[1], y[2]), A_3(x[2], y[.])\\ &\text{with } \pi_1(1) = 1,\ \pi_1(2) = 2, \text{ and } \pi_1(3) = 3.\end{aligned}$$

Example 4. We have:

$$\begin{aligned}&A_1(x[.], y[1]), A_2(x[1], y[2]), A_3(x[2], y[.])\\ \sim^{\mathbb{E}}\ &A_2(y[1], x[2]), A_3(x[1], y[.]), A_1(x[.], y[2]),\end{aligned}$$

since

$$\begin{aligned}&A_1(x[.], y[1]), A_2(x[1], y[2]), A_3(x[2], y[.])\\ \equiv^{\mathbb{E}}\ &A_2(y[2], x[1]), A_3(x[2], y[.]), A_1(x[.], y[1])\end{aligned}$$

and

$$\begin{aligned}&\alpha^{\mathbb{E}}_{\pi_2}(A_2(y[2], x[1]), A_3(x[2], y[.]), A_1(x[.], y[1]))\\ &= A_2(y[1], x[2]), A_3(x[1], y[.]), A_1(x[.], y[2])\\ &\text{with } \pi_2(2) = 1,\ \pi_2(1) = 2, \text{ and } \pi_2(3) = 3.\end{aligned}$$

Note that equality up to renaming of the binding labels is not compositional (due to potential conflicts between the binding labels). Thus, the relation $\sim^{\mathbb{E}}$ is only an equivalence relation (not a congruence relation).

- $\dfrac{}{E \models^{\mathbb{E}}_{\emptyset} \epsilon}, \dfrac{a \models^{\mathbb{A}}_{\phi} a' \quad E \models^{\mathbb{E}}_{\phi'} E'}{a, E \models^{\mathbb{E}}_{\phi \uplus \phi'} a', E'}$;
- $\dfrac{\sigma \models^{\Sigma} \sigma'}{A_k(\sigma) \models^{\mathbb{A}}_{[k' \mapsto k]} A_{k'}(\sigma')}$;
- $\dfrac{}{\sigma \models^{\Sigma} \epsilon}, \dfrac{s \models^{\mathbb{S}} s' \quad \sigma \models^{\Sigma} \sigma'}{s, \sigma \models^{\Sigma} s', \sigma'}$;
- $\dfrac{\iota \models^{I} \iota' \quad \lambda \models^{\Lambda} \lambda'}{n\iota\lambda \models^{\mathbb{S}} n\iota'\lambda'}$;
- $\dfrac{}{\iota \models^{I} \epsilon}, \dfrac{}{\iota \models^{I} \iota}$;
- $\dfrac{}{\lambda \models^{\Lambda} \epsilon}, \dfrac{}{\lambda \models^{\Lambda} \lambda}$;

Fig. 10. Matching relation.

A.3 Embeddings

As defined in Definition 2 page 6, the patterns are specific Kappa expressions. Several constructions in Kappa are based on identifying a pattern within another. This is achieved thanks to the notion of embedding.

An embedding from a pattern P into a pattern P' is defined by a mapping from the agents in P to some agents in P' such that each agent in P is less specific than its image in P'. This means that the pattern P' may contain more agents, the interface of the common agents may contain more sites, and each site may contain more information in their internal state and in their binding state. After having reordered the agents and the sites and renamed the binding labels in the pattern P' thanks to the equivalence relation $\sim_{\mathbb{E}}$, these requirements are formalized by means of a matching relation $\models_{\phi}^{\mathbb{E}}$ that is defined inductively over the syntax of Kappa expressions in Fig. 10. The subscript ϕ is assembled along the proof of the matching as a function of the agent labels $\mathcal{AL}^{\mathbb{E}}(P)$ of the pattern P into those $\mathcal{AL}^{\mathbb{E}}(P')$ of the pattern P'.

Definition 6 (Embedding). *An embedding from a pattern P into a pattern P' is induced by a function ϕ from the set $\mathcal{AL}^{\mathbb{E}}(P)$ into the set $\mathcal{AL}^{\mathbb{E}}(P')$, whenever there exists a pattern P'' that satisfies both properties:*

1. $P' \sim^{\mathbb{E}} P''$;
2. $P'' \models_{\phi}^{\mathbb{E}} P$.

Example 5. There are two embeddings from the pattern $A_1(y[1]), A_2(x[1])$ to the pattern $A_1(x[.], y[1]), A_2(x[1], y[2]), A_3(x[2], y[.])$.

The first one is induced by the embedding $[1 \mapsto 1, 2 \mapsto 2]$, since

$$A_1(y[1], x[.]), A_2(x[1], y[2]), A_3(x[2], y[.]) \models_{[1\mapsto 1, 2\mapsto 2]}^{\mathbb{E}} A_1(y[1]), A_2(x[1]).$$

The second one is induces by the embedding $[1 \mapsto 2, 2 \mapsto 3]$, since

$$A_2(y[1], x[2]), A_3(x[1], y[.]), A_1(x[.], y[2]) \models_{[1\mapsto 2, 2\mapsto 3]}^{\mathbb{E}} A_1(y[1]), A_2(x[1]).$$

- $\dfrac{}{[E \setminus \epsilon]^{\mathbb{E}} = E}, \quad \dfrac{[a \setminus a']^{\mathbb{A}} = a'' \quad [E \setminus E']^{\mathbb{E}} = E''}{[a, E \setminus a', E']^{\mathbb{E}} = a'', E''};$
- $\dfrac{[\sigma \setminus \sigma']^{\Sigma} = \sigma''}{[A_k(\sigma) \setminus A_{k'}\sigma']^{\mathbb{A}} = A_k(\sigma'')};$
- $\dfrac{}{[\sigma \setminus \epsilon]^{\Sigma} = \sigma}, \quad \dfrac{[s \setminus s']^{\mathbb{S}} = s'' \quad [\sigma \setminus \sigma']^{\Sigma} = \sigma''}{[s, \sigma \setminus s', \sigma']^{\Sigma} = s'', \sigma''};$
- $\dfrac{[\iota \setminus \iota']^{I} = \iota'' \quad [\lambda \setminus \lambda']^{\Lambda} = \lambda''}{[n\iota\lambda \setminus n\iota'\lambda']^{\mathbb{S}} = n\iota''\lambda''};$
- $\dfrac{}{[\iota \setminus \epsilon]^{I} = \iota}, \quad \dfrac{}{[\iota \setminus \iota']^{I} = \iota'};$
- $\dfrac{}{[\lambda \setminus \epsilon]^{\Lambda} = \lambda}, \quad \dfrac{}{[\lambda \setminus [.]]^{\Lambda} = [.]}, \quad \dfrac{}{[\lambda \setminus [l]]^{\Lambda} = [l]};$

Fig. 11. Rewriting.

Two patterns are said to be isomorphic if there exist embeddings from the first one to the second, and conversely. In such a case, the corresponding embeddings are called isomorphisms. An isomorphism between two identical patterns is called an automorphism. The notion of automorphism is important in counting the number of occurrences of a pattern in another.

Definition 7 (Number of occurrences). *Given two patterns P and P', the number of occurrences of the pattern P in the pattern P' is equal to the quotient between the number of embeddings between P and P' and the number of automorphisms of P.*

Example 6. The pattern

$$A_1(x[.], y[1]), A_2(x[1], y[2]), A_3(x[2], y[.])$$

has exactly one automorphism. This automorphism is induced by the mapping

$$[1 \mapsto 1, 2 \mapsto 2, 3 \mapsto 3].$$

The pattern

$$A_1(x[.], y[1]), A_2(x[.], y[1])$$

has exactly two automorphisms. These automorphisms are induced by the following mappings:

$$[1 \mapsto 1, 2 \mapsto 2] \text{ and } [1 \mapsto 2, 2 \mapsto 1].$$

A.4 Rule Applications

A Kappa rule $E_l \xrightarrow{k} E_r$ can be applied to a pattern P along an embedding ϕ from the left-hand side E_l of the rule, into the pattern P. This is obtained by reordering the agents and the sites of P and renaming their binding labels to match the pattern E_l, and then updating the agents in P with any available information in the pattern E_r (except the agent labels which remain unchanged). This last step is formalized by means of a replacement procedure, $[.\setminus.]^{\mathbb{E}}$ which is defined inductively over the syntax in Fig. 11. This construction is well-defined up to the equivalence relation $\sim^{\mathbb{E}}$, which means that the final result does not depend, up to agent and site permutation and up to renaming of binding labels, on the choice of the alignment of agents and sites, nor on the choice of binding labels. In order to ensure that there is no confusion between the biding labels occurring in the rewritten pattern and the ones that are inserted by the rule application, we require that the binding labels that occur in the rewritten pattern and in the right-hand side E_r of the rule, also occur in the left-hand side E_l of the rule.

This is formalized in the following definition.

Definition 8 (Rule application). *Let $E_l \xrightarrow{k} E_r$ be a rule, P be a pattern, and ϕ be an embedding between E_l and P. Let P' be a pattern such that $P \sim^{\mathbb{E}} P'$, $P' \models^{\mathbb{E}} E_l$, and $(\mathcal{BL}^{E_r} \setminus \mathcal{BL}^{E_l}) \cap \mathcal{BL}^{P'} = \emptyset$.*

The application of the rule on the pattern P via the embedding ϕ defines a computation step from the pattern P to the pattern $[P' \setminus E_r]^{\mathbb{E}}$ with the kinetic rate k.

In the previous definition, such a pattern P' actually exists for every embedding ϕ between the pattern E_l and the pattern P. Moreover, up to $\sim^{\mathbb{E}}$, the result does not depend on the choice of this pattern and is effectively a pattern (not just a Kappa expression). In other words, it satisfied the conditions of Definition 2.

There exist several conventions for the kinetic rates. Here we have used the rate constant of the rule. It is also possible to divide this rate constant by the number of automorphisms on the left-hand side E_l of the rule, by the number of automorphisms on the left-hand side E_l of the rule the corresponding function of which also induces an automorphism on the right-hand side E_r of the rule [9].

Example 7. The result of the application of the rule:

$$A_1(y[1]), A_2(x[1]) \xrightarrow{k} A_1(y[.]), A_2(x[.])$$

with the pattern:

$$A_1(x[.], y[1]), A_2(x[1], y[2]), A_3(x[2], y[.])$$

along the embedding that is induced by the mapping:

$$[1 \mapsto 1, 2 \mapsto 2],$$

is equal to the pattern:

$$A_1(y[.], x[.]), A_2(x[.], y[2]), A_3(x[2], y[.]),$$

since

$$A_1(y[1], x[.]), A_2(x[1], y[2]), A_3(x[2], y[.]) \models^{\mathbb{E}}_{[1 \mapsto 1, 2 \mapsto 2]} A_1(y[1]), A_2(x[1])$$

and

$$\begin{aligned}&[A_1(y[1], x[.]), A_2(x[1], y[2]), A_3(x[2], y[.]) \setminus A_1(y[1]), A_2(x[1])]^{\mathbb{E}} \\ &\quad = A_1(y[.], x[.]), A_2(x[.], y[2]), A_3(x[2], y[.]).\end{aligned}$$

Example 8. The result of the application of the rule:

$$A_1(y[1]), A_2(x[1]) \xrightarrow{k} A_1(y[.]), A_2(x[.])$$

with the pattern:

$$A_1(x[.], y[1]), A_2(x[1], y[2]), A_3(x[2], y[.])$$

along the embedding that is induced by the mapping:

$$[1 \mapsto 2, 2 \mapsto 3],$$

is equal to the pattern:

$$A_2(y[.], x[2]), A_3(x[.], y[.]), A_1(x[.], y[2]),$$

since

$$A_2(y[1], x[2]), A_3(x[1], y[.]), A_1(x[.], y[2]) \models^{\mathbb{E}}_{[1\mapsto 2, 2\mapsto 3]} A_1(y[1]), A_2(x[1])$$

and

$$\begin{aligned}[A_2(y[1], x[2]), A_3(x[1], y[.]), A_1(x[.], y[2]) \setminus A_1(y[1]), A_2(x[1])]^{\mathbb{E}} \\ = A_2(y[.], x[2]), A_3(x[.], y[.]), A_1(x[.], y[2]).\end{aligned}$$

Both outcomes are equivalent with respect to the relation $\sim^{\mathbb{E}}$, which is specific to this example. In general, several applications of the same rule on a given pattern leads to different patterns.

Both computation steps have rates k, $\frac{k}{2}$, and $\frac{k}{2}$ depending on the choice for the convention. Indeed the pattern $A_1(y[1]), A_2(x[1])$ has two automorphisms, which are induced by the mappings $[1 \mapsto 1, 2 \mapsto 2]$ and $[1 \mapsto 2, 2 \mapsto 1]$ and since both mappings also induce automorphisms on the pattern $A_1(y[.]), A_2(x[.])$ (Figs. 13 and 14).

A.5 Algebraic Expressions

Binary operation	::=	$+ \mid - \mid * \mid / \mid \hat{} \mid max \mid min \mid n \ mod \ n'$	
Unary operation	::=	log | exp | sin | cos | tan | sqrt	
Constant	::=	π	
Float	::=	$x \in \mathbb{R}$	
Variables	::=	$[E]$	(number of effective events)
	|	$[E-]$	(number of fictitious events)
	|	$[T]$	(simulated physical time)
	|	$[Tsim]$	(cpu time since simulation start)
	|	$\|pattern\|$	(number of occurrence of a pattern)

Fig. 12. Syntax for algebraic expressions in Kappa.

A.6 Boolean Expressions

$$
\begin{aligned}
Boolean - expr &::= algebraic - expr \quad (= \mid < \mid >) \quad algebraic - expr \\
&::= Boolean - expr \quad || \quad Boolean - expr \\
&::= Boolean - expr \quad \&\& \quad Boolean - expr \\
&::= [not] \quad Boolean - expr \\
&::= boolean \\
boolean &::= [True] \\
&::= [False]
\end{aligned}
$$

Fig. 13. Syntax for Boolean expressions in Kappa.

A.7 Intervention Expressions

$$
\begin{aligned}
effect - list &::= effect \mid effect - list \mid \varepsilon \\
effect &::= \$ADD \;\; algebraic - expr \;\; |pattern| \text{ (increment pattern number occurrences)} \\
&::= \$DEL \;\; algebraic - expr \;\; |pattern| \text{ (decrement pattern number occurrences)} \\
&::= \$UPDATE \;\; variable \;\; algebraic - expr \;\; \text{(update variable value)} \\
intervention &::= \text{\%mod: } Boolean - expr \text{ do } effect - list \text{ repeat } boolean - expression
\end{aligned}
$$

Fig. 14. Syntax for interventions in Kappa.

Listing 1.1. A model of asymmetric polymerization

```
%var: k_1 0.01
%agent: A(x, y) // Declaration of species A
'bind_A' A(x[.]), A(y[.]) -> A(x[1]), A(y[1])
    @ k_1 // rule for binding event
%init: 50 A() // Initial quantity of species
   'A'
%obs: 'polymer_A_1' |A(y[_], x[.])| // Track
   the number of chains with at least 2
   agents

%var: 'chain_satisfaction' 0 // Boolean
   variable to track pattern satisfaction
%obs: 'len_poly' 'chain_satisfaction' //
   Track the quantity of the Boolean variable
```

Listing 1.2. A model of long lived transients.

```
//////// Signatures
%agent: D(a1,a2,d,b2,loop{b, ub}) //
   Declaration of agent representing DNA with
    four binding sites: 'a1' and 'a2' for
   binding the activators,
// 'd' and 'b2' for binding the repressor
//(both) or Polymerase (site 'd'), and site '
   loop' which indicates whether the DNA is
   looped
//or not.
%agent: RNAP(d) // Declaration of Polymerase
   with binding site named 'd'
%agent: A(a) // Declaration of activator A
   with binding site named 'a'
%agent: R(d) // Declaration of repressor B
   with binding site named 'd'
%agent: P() // Declaration of protein P

//////// Rules
// numbers (labels) inside '[]' sign denote
   bond identifiers
// for bimolecular reactions, the rate is
   scaled with the average number of
   molecules in
//the cell 'N' in order to convert from units
    'per Mol per sec' to 'per molecule per
   sec'
// POLYMERASE
'rule_1' RNAP(d[.]), D(d[.]) -> RNAP(d[1]), D
   (d[1]) @ on_rnap // RNAP binds,
   bimolecular reaction
'rule_2' RNAP(d[1]), D(d[1]) -> RNAP(d[.]), D
   (d[.]) @ off_rnap // RNAP unbinds PROTEIN
'rule_3' RNAP(d[1]), D(d[1]), . -> RNAP(d[1])
   , D(d[1]), P() @ p_on // P is expressed
   when RNAP is bound
'rule_4' P() -> . @ p_off
```

```
// ACITIVATION
//A binds to the site 'a1' or site 'a2' of
   DNA whenever it is not looped
'rule_5' A(a[.]), D(a1[.], a2, loop{ub}) <->
   A(a[1]), D(a1[1], a2, loop{ub}) @ on_a,
   off_a
'rule_6' A(a[.]), D(a1, a2[.], loop{ub}) <->
   A(a[1]), D(a1, a2[1], loop{ub}) @ on_a,
   off_a
// lopping is immediate when the second
   activator binds
'rule_7' A(a[1]), D(a1[1],a2[.],loop{ub}), A(
   a[.]) <-> A(a[1]), D(a1[1],a2[2],loop{b}),
    A(a[2]) @ loop_a, unloop_a
'rule_8' A(a[1]), D(a1[.],a2[1],loop{ub}), A(
   a[.]) <-> A(a[1]), D(a1[2],a2[1],loop{b}),
    A(a[2]) @ loop_a, unloop_a

// if A is bound to site 'a1', it recruits
   RNAP

'rule_9' A(a[1]), D(a1[1],d[.]), RNAP(d[.])
   -> A(a[1]), D(a1[1],d[2]), RNAP(d[2]) @
   on_rnap_if_a
// INHIBITION
// R binds to site 'd' or site 'b2' of DNA
   whenever it is not looped
// By binding to site 'd', repressor inhibits
    the binding of RNAP to the same site, and
//hence inhibits the expression of the
   protein indirectly
'rule_10' R(d[.]), D(d[.],b2,loop{ub}) <-> R(
   d[1]), D(d[1],b2,loop{ub}) @ on_b, off_b
'rule_11' R(d[.]), D(d,b2[.],loop{ub}) <-> R(
   d[1]), D(d,b2[1],loop{ub}) @ on_b, off_b
// looping is immediate when the second
   repressor binds
```

```
'rule_12' R(d[1]), D(d[1],b2[.],loop{ub}), R(
   d[.]) <-> R(d[1]), D(d[1],b2[2],loop{b}),
   R(d[2]) @ loop_b, unloop_b
'rule_13' R(d[1]), D(d[.],b2[1],loop{ub}), R(
   d[.]) <-> R(d[1]), D(d[2],b2[1],loop{b}),
   R(d[2]) @ loop_b, unloop_b
//////// Variables
//// rates
%var: N 10^9 // the average number of
   molecules in the cell
%var: on_rnap 10^4/N
%var: off_rnap 1.6*0.01
%var: on_rnap_if_a 9*on_rnap
%var: on_b 8.8*10^7/N
%var: off_b 0.19
%var: on_a 8.8*10^7/N
%var: off_a 0.0264
%var: p_on 0.5
%var: p_off 0.001
%var: rnap0 1500 // initial number of RNAP
   molecules
%var: a_add 275
%var: b_add 350
%var: unloop_a off_a/1000
%var: unloop_b off_b/10000

%var: p0 240 // initial number of proteins
%var: b0 0 // initial number of B molecules
%var: a0 0
%var: loop_a on_a
%var: loop_b on_b
//////// Observables

%obs: protein |P()|
%obs: d_active |D(d[1]),RNAP(d[1])|
////////// Perturbation

%mod: alarm 100 do $ADD a_add A(a); // 5400
%mod: alarm 100 do $ADD b_add R(d); // 5460
```

```
%var: p_AR 0 // Proposition for genes.
%obs: 'p_ar' p_AR

%mod: |P()| > 350 do $UPDATE p_AR 1; repeat |
    P()| > 350
%mod: |P()| < 351 do $UPDATE p_AR 0; repeat |
    P()| < 351

///////// Initial conditions
%init: 1 D(d,a1,a2,b2,loop{ub})
%init: rnap0 RNAP(d)
%init: b0 R(d)
%init: a0 A(a)
%init: p0 P()
```

Listing 1.3. A model of consensus in swarm robotics.

```
%var: dec_y 0.01
%var: dec_x 0.01
%var: 'decision_distance' 9
%var: 'minimal_consensus' .50
%var: ZX 24
%var: ZY 24

%agent: A(a{u, y, x})
%agent: Z(z{y, x})

'y_undecided'   A(a{x}), A(a{y}) -> A(a{x}),
    A(a{u}) @ dec_x
'x_undecided'   A(a{x}), A(a{y}) -> A(a{u}),
    A(a{y}) @ dec_y
'decide_x'          A(a{x}), A(a{u}) -> A(a{x
    }), A(a{x}) @ dec_x
'decide_y'      A(a{y}), A(a{u}) -> A(a{y}),
    A(a{y}) @ dec_y

'stubborn_x_1' A(a{y}), Z(z{x}) -> A(a{u}), Z
    (z{x}) @ dec_x
```

```
'stubborn_x_2' A(a{u}), Z(z{x}) -> A(a{x}), Z
   (z{x}) @ dec_x
'stubborn_y_1' A(a{x}), Z(z{y}) -> A(a{u}), Z
   (z{y}) @ dec_y
'stubborn_y_2' A(a{u}), Z(z{y}) -> A(a{y}), Z
   (z{y}) @ dec_y

%obs: X  |A(a{x})| + |Z(z{x})|
%obs: Zx |Z(z{x})|
%obs: Zy |Z(z{y})|
%obs: Y  |A(a{y})| + |Z(z{y})|
%obs: U  |A(a{u})|

%init: 0 A(a{u})
%init: 50-ZX A(a{x})
%init: 50-ZY A(a{y})
%init: ZX Z(z{x})
%init: ZY Z(z{y})

%var: 'size_dec_x' |A(a{x})| + |Z(z{x})|
%var: 'size_dec_y' |A(a{y})| + |Z(z{y})|
%var: 'robot_population' |A()| + |Z()|
%var: 'fraction_x' 'size_dec_x'/'
   robot_population'
%var: 'fraction_y' 'size_dec_y'/'
   robot_population'
%var: 'consensus_x' 0
%var: 'consensus_y' 0
%obs: 'con_x' 'consensus_x'
%obs: 'con_y' 'consensus_y'

%mod: 'fraction_x' > 'minimal_consensus' && '
   size_dec_x' > 'decision_distance' + '
   size_dec_y' do $UPDATE 'consensus_x' 1;
   $UPDATE 'consensus_y' 0; repeat '
   fraction_x' > 'minimal_consensus'
%mod: 'fraction_y' > 'minimal_consensus' && '
   size_dec_y' > 'decision_distance' + '
   size_dec_x' do $UPDATE 'consensus_y' 1;
```

```
    $UPDATE 'consensus_x' 0; repeat '
    fraction_y' > 'minimal_consensus'
%mod: 'consensus_x' = 1 && 'fraction_x' < '
    minimal_consensus' do $UPDATE 'consensus_x
    ' 0; repeat 'fraction_x' < '
    minimal_consensus'
%mod: 'consensus_y' = 1 && 'fraction_y' < '
    minimal_consensus' do $UPDATE 'consensus_y
    ' 0; repeat 'fraction_y' < '
    minimal_consensus'
%mod: 'consensus_x' = 1 && 'size_dec_x' < '
    decision_distance' + 'size_dec_y' + 1 do
    $UPDATE 'consensus_x' 0; repeat '
    decision_distance' + 'size_dec_y' + 1 > '
    size_dec_x'
%mod: 'consensus_y' = 1 && 'size_dec_y' < '
    decision_distance' + 'size_dec_x' + 1 do
    $UPDATE 'consensus_y' 0; repeat '
    decision_distance' + 'size_dec_x' + 1 > '
    size_dec_y'
```

References

1. Andersen, J.L., Flamm, C., Merkle, D., Stadler, P.F.: A software package for chemically inspired graph transformation. CoRR, abs/1603.02481 (2016)
2. Blinov, M., Yang, J., Faeder, J., Hlavacek, W.: Graph theory for rule-based modeling of biochemical networks. In: Lecture Notes in Computer Science - LNCS, vol. 4230, pp. 89–106 (2006)
3. Bouguéon, M.: Modélisation en langage Kappa de la dynamique des cellules étoilées hépatiques durant le développement et la réversion de la fibrose. (Kappa modeling of hepatic stellate cell dynamics during fibrosis development and reversion). PhD thesis, University of Rennes 1, France (2023)
4. Boutillier, P., Cristescu, I., Feret, J.: Counters in Kappa: semantics, simulation, and static analysis. In: Caires, L. (ed.) ESOP 2019. LNCS, vol. 11423, pp. 176–204. Springer, Cham (2019). https://doi.org/10.1007/978-3-030-17184-1_7
5. Boutillier, P., Ehrhard, T., Krivine, J.: Incremental update for graph rewriting. In: Yang, H. (ed.) ESOP 2017. LNCS, vol. 10201, pp. 201–228. Springer, Heidelberg (2017). https://doi.org/10.1007/978-3-662-54434-1_8
6. Boutillier, P., Feret, J., Krivine, J., Fontana, W.: The Kappa Language and Kappa Tools (2019)
7. Boutillier, P., et al.: The Kappa platform for rule-based modeling. Bioinformatics **34**(13), i583–i592 (2018)

8. Boyer, B., Corre, K., Legay, A., Sedwards, S.: Plasma-lab: a flexible, distributable statistical model checking library. In: Joshi, K., Siegle, M., Stoelinga, M., D'Argenio, P.R. (eds.) Quantitative Evaluation of Systems, pp. 160–164. Springer Berlin Heidelberg, Berlin (2013)
9. Camporesi, F., Feret, J., Lý, K.Q.: KaDE: a tool to compile Kappa rules into (Reduced) ODE models. In: Feret, J., Koeppl, H. (eds.) CMSB 2017. LNCS, vol. 10545, pp. 291–299. Springer, Cham (2017). https://doi.org/10.1007/978-3-319-67471-1_18
10. Clarke, E.M., Faeder, J.R., Langmead, C.J., Harris, L.A., Jha, S.K., Legay, A.: Statistical model checking in biolab: applications to the automated analysis of t-cell receptor signaling pathway. In: Heiner, M., Uhrmacher, A.M. (eds.) Computational Methods in Systems Biology, pp. 231–250. Springer Berlin Heidelberg, Berlin (2008)
11. Danos, V., et al.: Graphs, rewriting and pathway reconstruction for rule-based models. In: LIPIcs, FSTTCS 2012, vol. 18, pp. 276–288 (2013)
12. Danos, V., Feret, J., Fontana, W., Krivine, J.: Scalable simulation of cellular signaling networks. In: International Conference on Programming Languages and Systems, pp. 139–157. Springer (2007)
13. Deeds, E.J., Bachman, J.A., Fontana, W.: Optimizing ring assembly reveals the strength of weak interactions. Proc. Natl. Acad. Sci. **109**(7), 2348–2353 (2012)
14. Feret, J.: Model reduction of infinite rule-based models. In: Page, E.H., Uhrmacher, A.M. (eds.) Proceedings of the 39th ACM SIGSIM Conference on Principles of Advanced Discrete Simulation, SIGSIM-PADS 2025, Santa Fe, NM, USA, 23–26 June 2025, pp. 46–55. ACM (2025)
15. Feret, J., Danos, V., Krivine, J., Harmer, R., Fontana, W.: Internal coarse-graining of molecular systems. Proc. Natl. Acad. Sci. **106**(16), 6453–6458 (2009)
16. Feret, J., Henzinger, T., Koeppl, H., Petrov, T.: Lumpability abstractions of rule-based systems. Theoret. Comput. Sci. **431**, 137–164 (2012)
17. Feret, J., Koeppl, H., Petrov, T.: Stochastic fragments: a framework for the exact reduction of the stochastic semantics of rule-based models. Int. J. Softw. Inform., 73 (2013)
18. Hajnal, M., Nouvian, M., Šafránek, D., Petrov, T.: Data-informed parameter synthesis for population Markov chains. In: Češka, M., Paoletti, N. (eds.) Hybrid Systems Biology, pp. 147–164. Springer International Publishing, Cham (2019)
19. Harris, L.A., et al.: BioNetGen 2.2: advances in rule-based modeling. Bioinformatics **32**(21), 3366–3368 (2016)
20. Helms, T., Warnke, T., Maus, C., Uhrmacher, A.M.: Semantics and efficient simulation algorithms of an expressive multilevel modeling language. ACM Trans. Model. Comput. Simul. **27**(2), 1–25 (2017)
21. Klein, J., d'Onofrio, A., Petrov, T.: Exploring consensus robustness in swarms with disruptive individuals. In: Margaria, T., Steffen, B. (eds.) Leveraging Applications of Formal Methods, Verification and Validation. Rigorous Engineering of Collective Adaptive Systems, pp. 33–48. Springer Nature Switzerland, Cham (2025)
22. Kwiatkowska, M., Norman, G., Parker, D.: PRISM 4.0: verification of probabilistic real-time systems. In: Gopalakrishnan, G., Qadeer, S. (eds.) CAV 2011. LNCS, vol. 6806, pp. 585–591. Springer, Heidelberg (2011). https://doi.org/10.1007/978-3-642-22110-1_47
23. Laurent, J., Medina-Abarca, H.F., Boutillier, P., Yang, J., Fontana, W.: A trace query language for rule-based models. In: International Conference on Computational Methods in Systems Biology, pp. 220–237. Springer (2018)

24. Legay, A., Delahaye, B., Bensalem, S.: Statistical model checking: an overview. In: Barringer, H., et al. (eds.) Runtime Verification, pp. 122–135. Springer Berlin Heidelberg, Berlin, Heidelberg (2010)
25. Milios, D., Sanguinetti, G., Schnoerr, D.: Probabilistic model checking for continuous-time Markov chains via sequential Bayesian inference. In: McIver, A., Horvath, A. (eds.) Quantitative Evaluation of Systems, pp. 289–305. Springer International Publishing, Cham (2018)
26. Petrov, T., Feret, J., Koeppl, H.: Reconstructing species-based dynamics from reduced stochastic rule-based models. In: Laroque, C., Himmelspach, J., Pasupathy, R., Rose, O., Uhrmacher, A.M. (eds.) WSC - Winter Simulation Conference - 2012, Berlin, Germany (2012)
27. Petrov, T., Igler, C., Sezgin, A., Henzinger, T.A., Guet, C.C.: Long lived transients in gene regulation. Theoret. Comput. Sci. **893**, 1–16 (2021)
28. Reina, A., Zakir, R., De Masi, G., Ferrante, E.: Cross-inhibition leads to group consensus despite the presence of strongly opinionated minorities and asocial behaviour. Commun. Phys. **6**(1), 236 (2023)
29. Sneddon, M.W., Faeder, J.R., Emonet, T.: Efficient modeling, simulation and coarse-graining of biological complexity with NFsim. Nat. Methods **8**(2), 177–183 (2011)
30. Troják, M., Šafránek, D., Mertová, L., Brim, L.: Parameter synthesis and robustness analysis of rule-based models. In: Lee, R., Jha, S., Mavridou, A., Giannakopoulou, D. (eds.) NASA Formal Methods, pp. 41–59. Springer International Publishing, Cham (2020)
31. Wang, Q.: Formal methods for biological systems: languages, algorithms, and applications (2016)

Efficient Stochastic Trace Generation for Transcription

Arman Ferdowsi[1], Matthias Függer[2(✉)], and Thomas Nowak[2,3]

[1] Faculty of Computer Science, University of Vienna, Vienna, Austria
arman.ferdowsi@univie.ac.at
[2] Université Paris-Saclay, CNRS, ENS Paris-Saclay, LMF, Gif-sur-Yvette, France
mfuegger@lmf.cnrs.fr, thomas@thomasnowak.net
[3] Institut Universitaire de France, Paris, France

Abstract. Bursty transcription in single cells typically produces overdispersed, skewed, and sometimes heavy-tailed expression distributions that are explained by two-state Markov models of the promoters. While the gold standard for simulation is exact stochastic sampling with Gillespie's algorithm, obtaining thousands of timed traces is computationally costly. Surrogate models based on stochastic differential equations (SDEs) are widely used to speed up this simulation process. An example is the Chemical Langevin Equation based on Gaussian noise, which, however, does not capture heavy-tailed noise.

In this work, we present a unified SDE framework that combines deterministic drift, Gaussian fluctuations, and additive sporadic jumps of arbitrary distributions, and provide an open-source Python implementation, `bcrnnoise`. The framework subsumes standard surrogate models and allows for vectorized generation of batches of transcription traces. We assess computational speed and accuracy of common surrogate models along with new models, showing that high accuracy can be obtained while reducing computational cost up to two orders of magnitude.

Keywords: computational biology · transcription · stochastic models · stochastic approximations

1 Introduction

Many biochemical processes show pronounced stochastic behavior at different levels of abstraction. One such process happening in every cell is transcription, the process of producing mRNA from a DNA sequence. Single-cell measurements have repeatedly shown that gene transcription often occurs in episodic bursts, where mRNA is transcribed, followed by pauses of no activity [41]. Direct imaging and sequencing-based assays have quantified burst frequency and size at

---

Supplementary Information The online version contains supplementary material available at https://doi.org/10.1007/978-3-032-30870-2_6.

P. T. Monteiro (Ed.): CMSB 2026, LNBI 16678, pp. 104–121, 2027.
https://doi.org/10.1007/978-3-032-30870-2_6

transcript resolution, revealing behavior that aligns well with a promoter probabilistically toggling between two states [35,36,41]: an active ON state where transcription occurs with a certain rate and an OFF state with no transcription. This so-called two-state telegraph transcription model is widely used [26,27,33,34,41] to capture transcription bursts, an effect that is not explained by the simpler, also commonly used, one-state (constitutive) model [32,39], where transcription occurs at a constant rate.

Such a biochemical system can be readily described within the framework of Chemical Reaction Networks (CRNs) [13,38], where biochemical species interact with each other via reactions. The resulting dynamics $p(x,t)$ of the probability of the species counts being equal to vector x at time t are described by the Chemical Master Equation (CME). The CME is rarely directly used for the generation of traces. The gold standard to numerically solve such models is exact stochastic sampling via Gillespie's algorithm [13]. Computationally, this is expensive even for systems with only a few species like the two-state transcription model. In particular, high event rates, e.g., due to high plasmid copy number and thus many genes being transcribed, lead to slow progress in simulated time, since the state vector is updated at each event. Furthermore, thousands of simulations have to be run to obtain detailed noise profiles of the stochastic process. Indeed, detailed noise characteristics have been used for model discrimination in single-molecule assays, by comparing predicted and observed noise profiles to reject incompatible mechanistic hypotheses and guide experimental design [18].

To address this limitation, computationally faster algorithms are widely used and have been implemented in software packages such as COPASI [20], BasiCO [3], and StochKit [37] the simulation of arbitrary CRNs. Prominent algorithms are discrete-noise approximations such as Tau-leaping [15] where several events are grouped together before updating the system's state and continuous-state surrogates based on Stochastic Differential Equations (SDEs). The Chemical Langevin Equation (CLE) is an example of the latter, replacing reaction-counting fluctuations by Gaussian noise, yielding tractable SDEs for means, variances, spectra, and control-theoretic analyses [12,14,24,38]. While fast, surrogates like the CLE fail to capture the heavy tails and overdispersion characteristic of processes like burst-driven transcription [8,11,29,31,35] and are thus less informative for model discrimination.

Abstract models that account for non-Gaussian behavior have been proposed in the context of transcription. A promising approach is replacing parts of the transcription process with piecewise-deterministic processes [29], which showed improved accuracy on steady-states compared to CLE models. Also, models that study the case of increasing volume $V \to \infty$ with Lévy behavior have been proposed as abstract models [23]. However, fast surrogate models that remain accurate over the complete time trajectory for small cellular volumes and that account for transient effects after activating transcription remain challenging.

Related to this line of work is also analytical progress that has been made for transcription models. For the two-state telegraph model, analytical results are available in generating-function form and yield closed-form moment expressions [21,34], providing an important reference for marginal distributions. However, the work does not explicitly address multi-copy settings as they occur, e.g., in bacteria where a plasmid with a certain copy number carries identical DNA sequences from which transcription occurs.

In particular, activating promoters leads to a transient behavior from all promoters being in the OFF state towards random switching of promoters. Further, these analytic results do not directly enable fast generation of complete traces since they a priori lack fast transition kernels, and correlations between different times, needed for large-scale trace generation and noise-profile comparisons.

Of mention is also research that builds on analytical progress of such models, aiming towards more detailed transcription models beyond the two-state model. Examples are work on models that include other cellular processes for which approximate analytic solutions have been obtained [5], an approximate analytic model for gene expression with stochastic bursts [28] that also includes the translation process from mRNA to protein and a comparison to commonly used diffusion-type models, and an analytic model that includes splicing [17].

Contributions. We propose a unified Lévy–Itô jump-diffusion SDE framework that places common CRN approximate models like Tau-leaping and CLE along compound-Poisson burst surrogates within a single drift–noise specification. Compound-Poisson and, more generally, Lévy jump processes can replace or complement Gaussian diffusion noise terms in SDEs, enabling heavy tails [1,7].

We implemented the SDE framework, making it available as an open-source Python library `bcrnnoise` that provides a common simulation API for physical-unit-aware specification of deterministic, diffusion, and jump processes. The library enables vectorized simulation of large numbers of traces within batches in discrete update steps of some specified time step $\Delta t > 0$, in contrast to sequential simulation of such traces one by one. While we use natively compiled libraries and just-in-time-compilation techniques to speed up the Python code, the focus of this work is on the systematic comparison of noise models for transcription rather than highly optimized CRN simulation.

For comparison with gold standard simulations, the library also implements Gillespie's algorithm.

We compare common and newly proposed surrogate models for the one-state (constitutive) and the two-state (telegraph promoter) transcription models within our framework for computational time and accuracy of their noise profile. For parameterization of the surrogate models we derive analytic formulas from stationary moments (Theorem 1). Our simulations confirm that, for low plasmid copy numbers, CLE approximations of the two-state model show low accuracy. Further, models based on Geometric noise perform relatively well; in particular, if in variants accounting for transient behavior. Finally, a Binomial-Poisson noise model is shown to outperform the widely-used Tau-leaping algorithm for large update-steps $\Delta t > 0$ in terms of accuracy, rendering it a promising candidate for vectorized generation of high numbers of traces within short time at high accuracy: our simulations show up to two orders of magnitude improvement in runtime with high accuracy.

2 Canonical Stochastic Transcription CRNs

We consider the two most-used CRN models of transcription, differing in whether the promoter is constitutively active or switches between discrete activity states, resulting in transcription bursts. We further assume that the gene is present n_p times within a fixed volume V of a cell, e.g., due to the copy number of the gene-bearing plasmid being n_p.

Constitutive One-State Model. Each plasmid constitutively produces mRNA at rate α ($\mathrm{min}^{-1}\,\mathrm{fL}^{-1}$), giving a total transcription rate of αn_p. Transcripts are degraded or diluted at first-order rate δ (min^{-1}). The resulting CRN is given as

$$\emptyset \xrightarrow{\alpha n_\mathrm{p}} \mathrm{mRNA} \qquad \mathrm{mRNA} \xrightarrow{\delta} \emptyset.$$

We assume that initially there is no mRNA in the system.

The exact stationary distribution of the mRNA copy number under this CRN is Poisson with mean $\alpha n_\mathrm{p} V/\delta$ [32,39] (Supplementary Material, Theorem 2).

Telegraph Two-State Model. Each plasmid independently switches between a transcriptionally inactive state (OFF) and an active state (ON) at rates k_on and k_off (min^{-1}), respectively. Only ON plasmids produce mRNA, at rate α (min^{-1}) per active plasmid, and transcripts are degraded as above. Denoting concentrations of ON and OFF plasmids by N_on and N_off, with conservation law $N_\mathrm{on} + N_\mathrm{off} = n_\mathrm{p}/V$, the CRN is

$$\mathrm{Gene_{off}} \xrightarrow{k_\mathrm{on}} \mathrm{Gene_{on}} \qquad \mathrm{Gene_{on}} \xrightarrow{k_\mathrm{off}} \mathrm{Gene_{off}}$$

$$\mathrm{Gene_{on}} \xrightarrow{\alpha} \mathrm{Gene_{on}} + \mathrm{mRNA} \qquad \mathrm{mRNA} \xrightarrow{\delta} \emptyset$$

We assume that initially there is no mRNA in the system and that all genes are in the OFF state. The latter models the scenario where transcription of a gene is activated that is located on multiple copies of a plasmid.

The telegraph model is seen to capture promoter bursting: if $k_\mathrm{off} \gg \alpha$ the ON state is short-lived and mRNA is transcribed in bursts. The exact stationary distribution of mRNA is a Poisson mixture whose mean and variance admit closed-form expressions [34,35] (Supplementary Material, Theorem 3).

Exact Simulation. Both CRNs are simulated exactly via Gillespie's stochastic simulation algorithm (SSA) in `bcrnnoise`, which samples each reaction event in continuous time. The one-state model ($\mathcal{M}_\mathrm{CME}$) tracks a single variable (mRNA count) and fires two reactions (birth and death). The two-state model ($\mathcal{M}_\mathrm{CME,2}$)

tracks three variables (mRNA count and the numbers of ON/OFF promoters) and fires four reactions. In both cases the per-step time (i.e., the inter-event time) is variable and the simulation cost grows with the total reaction rate, which scales with n_p. Benchmarks confirm the expected linear scaling in n_p (Fig. 1a&b). Besides the linear scaling of cost per generated trajectory, simulation of several trajectories is a priori not vectorized and may thus be parallelized only over the number of computing cores.

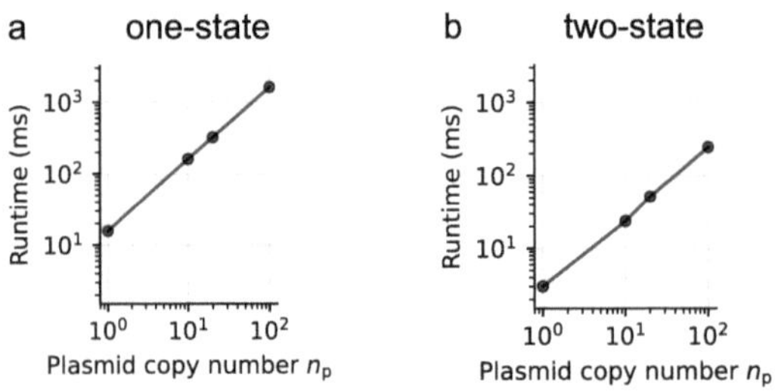

Fig. 1. Gillespie SSA runtime scales linearly with plasmid copy number. Simulation time per trajectory (simulated time 120 min) with Gillespie SSA in `bcrnnoise` for the constitutive one-state model (**a**) and the telegraph two-state model (**b**). Means over 20 runs for n_p from 1 to 100 are shown. Parameters follow experimentally reported parameters [4] (one-state) and [16] (two-state); see Methods for details.

3 Unified Jump-Diffusion Framework

We next introduce a unified SDE framework to express surrogate noise models for transcription. Formalizing them within a unified framework allows us to directly compare models. Further, advantages are ease of switching and prototyping noise models within the corresponding Python implementation `bcrnnoise`.

3.1 SDE Model

Consider a CRN with $n \geq 1$ biochemical species and let X_t be the stochastic n-dimensional vector of the species' concentrations at time $t \geq 0$. Combining deterministic kinetics, Gaussian fluctuations, and sporadic jumps into a Lévy–Itô equation, one obtains

$$dX_t = f(X_{t-})\,dt + B(X_{t-})\,dW_t + \int_{\|z\|<1} z\,\tilde{N}(dt, dz) + \int_{\|z\|\geq 1} z\,N(dt, dz). \quad (1)$$

Here f is the deterministic drift, $B\,dW_t$ the diffusive Gaussian component, and the jump terms encode arrival times and jump sizes through the Lévy measure Π.

One can show that such a combined process is mathematically well-behaved: under mild conditions, it has a unique solution and remains positive in presence of certain boundary conditions for noise (Supplementary Material, Theorem 4). Further, analogous to the CME, analytic equations for the density $p(x,t)$ over species concentration vectors x and time t can be stated (Supplementary Material, Theorem 5). In general, these are intractable to solve analytically, however; much like for the CME.

The Tau-leaping and CLE approximations of the CME are recovered as special cases of Eq. (1). *Tau-leaping* sets $B \equiv 0$ and takes Π to be the reaction-channel jump measure: for each reaction j with propensity $a_j(x)$ and stoichiometric change ν_j, one Poisson random measure N_j contributes jumps of size ν_j/V at rate $a_j(x)V$, yielding a pure-jump process without Gaussian noise and deterministic components (a pure-jump process without Gaussian noise). *CLE* instead sets the jump dynamics to $\Pi \equiv 0$ and replaces each Poisson channel by a Gaussian with the same infinitesimal mean and variance, giving the state-dependent diffusion $B(x)^2 = \sum_j a_j(x)\nu_j^2/V$.

Linear One-Dimensional Transcription Model. While not all surrogate models discussed in this work are one-dimensional, a lower dimensionality of the system's state is of interest towards the goal of a computationally efficient instance of the unified SDE model. We thus consider the ansatz of a linear (Ornstein–Uhlenbeck-type) one-dimensional model for which we will derive moment expressions that will enable parameterization of this simple model via moment-matching to the full model.

The Ornstein–Uhlenbeck-type model is obtained from (1) with a single dimension, where x is the concentration of mRNA, and letting $f(x) = \lambda_0 - \delta x$ with transcription rate $\lambda_0 \geq 0$ and degradation/dilution rate $\delta > 0$. Further, the process W_t is a standard Brownian motion, $N(dt,dz)$ is a Poisson random measure with Lévy measure Π, and $\tilde{N}(dt,dz)$ denotes the compensated measure on $\{0 < z < 1\}$. In the compound-Poisson case, $\Pi(dz) = \kappa\,\nu(dz)$, so bursts arrive at rate κ with jump-size law $Y \sim \nu$. In fact, letting $L_t := \sigma W_t + \int_{0<z<1} z\,\tilde{N}([0,t],dz) + \int_{z\geq 1} z\,N([0,t],dz)$, the stationary solution can be written explicitly as $X_\infty = \frac{\lambda_0}{\delta} + \int_0^\infty e^{-\delta t}\,dL_t$, and moments of X_∞ exist precisely up to the corresponding moments of the Lévy input L_1. A derivation of this representation and the corresponding stationary transform formulas is given in Supplementary Material, Section A.4.

Here, we focus on the compound-Poisson (finite-activity) case, where the burst mechanism is parameterized directly by an arrival rate κ and a jump-size law Y for which we obtain:

Theorem 1 (Stationary transform, moment extraction, and invertibility). *In the compound-Poisson case with $\Pi(dz) = \kappa\,\nu(dz)$ and jump-size law $Y \sim \nu$, writing the jump term in the equivalent uncompensated compound-Poisson form described in Supplementary Material, Theorem 4, the stationary Laplace transform $M_{\mathrm{st}}(s) = \mathbb{E}[e^{-sX_\infty}]$ is*

$$\ln M_{\mathrm{st}}(s) = -\frac{\lambda_0}{\delta}\,s + \frac{\sigma^2}{4\delta}\,s^2 + \frac{\kappa}{\delta}\int_0^s \frac{G_Y(u)-1}{u}\,du, \qquad s \geq 0, \tag{2}$$

where $G_Y(s) = \mathbb{E}[e^{-sY}]$. *If* $\mu_1 = \mathbb{E}[Y]$ *and* $\mu_2 = \mathbb{E}[Y^2] < \infty$, *then*

$$\mathbb{E}[X_\infty] = \frac{\lambda_0 + \kappa\,\mu_1}{\delta}, \qquad \mathrm{Var}(X_\infty) = \frac{\sigma^2 + \kappa\,\mu_2}{2\delta}.$$

Moreover, $-\delta s \frac{d}{ds} \ln M_{\mathrm{st}}(s) - \lambda_0 s + \frac{\sigma^2}{2} s^2 = \kappa\big(1 - G_Y(s)\big)$ *for* $s > 0$, *so, once* $(\lambda_0, \delta, \sigma, \kappa)$ *are fixed, the stationary transform uniquely determines the burst-size transform* G_Y.

The proof of Theorem 1 and the infinite-activity extension are given in Supplementary Material, Section A.4.

Efficient Generation of Traces. Expressing the surrogate models within the unified SDE framework directly allows one to vectorize generation of traces: the SDE is discretized into update steps of a fixed time step $\Delta t > 0$, iteratively applying deterministic, Gaussian, and jump-noise terms to the current state. Instead of updating a single trajectory, states can be updated as vectors of batch sizes, leading to the generation of a large number of trajectories simultaneously. Towards that goal we implemented the `bcrnnoise` framework so that deterministic and noise components support vector formats. For the update of the deterministic component we use basic and efficient first-order Euler integration; higher-order methods or intermediate substeps, while possible, would add significant computational cost and unbalance the treatment of noise and deterministic components with different step sizes. All subsequently discussed models make use of vectorized updates (see Methods for details).

We next discuss surrogate models for the one-state and the two-state model with respect to parameterization, computational cost, and dimensionality of the model's state space; see Supplementary Material, Table 1 for an overview.

3.2 Surrogates for One-State Model

The following surrogate models approximate $\mathcal{M}_{\mathrm{CME}}$ using a single tracked variable (mRNA concentration) and fixed-size time steps. We start with the commonly used surrogates Tau-leaping and CLE.

$\mathcal{M}_{\mathrm{TL}}$: *Tau-leaping.* The model approximates $\mathcal{M}_{\mathrm{CME}}$ by combining reaction counts over a step Δt: mRNA births $N_b \sim \mathrm{Pois}(\alpha n_p V \Delta t)$ and deaths $N_d \sim \mathrm{Pois}(\delta x V \Delta t)$ are chosen independently, and update $\Delta x = (N_b - N_d)/V$ applied. Equivalently, one may draw the total number of events $N \sim \mathrm{Pois}((\alpha n_p + \delta x) V \Delta t)$ and assign births by binomial thinning. The model recovers the SSA as $\Delta t \to 0$. *State:* 1 variable. *Cost per step:* 1 Poisson draw + 1 Poisson/Binomial draw.

$\mathcal{M}_{\mathrm{CLE}}$: *Chemical Langevin Equation.* Replaces the discrete reaction counts with their Gaussian fluctuation limit by applying the state update $\Delta x = (\alpha n_p - \delta x_t)\,\Delta\,\mathrm{t} + \sqrt{(\alpha n_p + \delta x_t)/V}\,\mathrm{d}W_t$. *State:* 1 variable. *Cost per step:* 2 Gaussian draws (one per reaction channel).

$\mathcal{M}_{\text{CLE}^*}$: *Optimised CLE.* This is the first improved model. We collapse the two per-reaction Gaussian channels of $\mathcal{M}_{\text{CLE}}$ into a single draw, exploiting the fact that birth and death noise are independent channels with their sum again being Gaussian with net diffusion coefficient $\sqrt{(\alpha n_p + \delta x)/V}$. It is statistically identical to $\mathcal{M}_{\text{CLE}}$, but improves runtime. *State:* 1 variable. *Cost per step:* 1 Gaussian draw.

$\mathcal{M}_{\text{Geo}}$: *Geometric Bursts.* We also tested a non-Gaussian model with heavier tails. While this model was primarily designed to capture bursts in the two-state model, we added it here for comparison. The model is a compound-Poisson surrogate with geometrically distributed burst sizes $Y \sim \text{Geom}(p)$ arriving at rate κ. To improve computing time, we abstract fast mRNA decay into deterministic linear decay $f(x) = -\delta x$. The parameters κ and p are matched to the first two stationary moments of the reference model. *State:* 1 variable. *Cost per step:* 1 Poisson draw (burst count K) + K geometric draws; The model is expected to be fast if frequently $K = 0$ (i.e., bursts are rare). Since $K \sim \text{Poisson}(\kappa V \,\Delta t)$, so $\mathbb{E}[K] = \kappa V \,\Delta t$, the geometric draws are rare whenever $\kappa V \,\Delta t \ll 1$.

$\mathcal{M}_{\text{BP}}$: *Binomial–Poisson Propagator.* Jahnke and Huisinga [22] gave a closed-form solution of the CME for monomolecular networks. Writing the one-step kernel in copy-number form with $X_t = V x_t$, each of the X_t molecules present at time t survives to $t + \Delta t$ with probability $e^{-\delta \Delta t}$, giving $\text{Bin}(X_t, e^{-\delta \Delta t})$ survivors [25]. New births form a Poisson process of rate $\alpha n_p V$; thinning by survival to $t + \Delta t$ yields $\text{Pois}\big(\frac{\alpha n_p V}{\delta}(1 - e^{-\delta \Delta t})\big)$. Hence, conditional on X_t,

$$X_{t+\Delta t} \sim \text{Bin}\big(X_t,\, e^{-\delta \Delta t}\big) + \text{Pois}\big(n_p \,\tfrac{\alpha V}{\delta}\big(1 - e^{-\delta \Delta t}\big)\big)\,,$$

which is exact for any Δt. Unlike $\mathcal{M}_{\text{TL}}$, which approximates production as $\text{Pois}(\alpha n_p V \,\Delta t)$, ignoring concurrent degradation of newly produced molecules, and therefore has a one-step mean that grows without bound as $\Delta t \to \infty$, $\mathcal{M}_{\text{BP}}$ remains exact at any step size: as $\Delta t \to \infty$, $e^{-\delta \Delta t} \to 0$ so all current molecules degrade, and the Poisson mean converges to $n_p \alpha V/\delta$, giving $X_{t+\Delta t} \sim \text{Pois}(n_p \alpha V/\delta)$, the correct stationary distribution of the birth-death process, regardless of X_t. *State:* 1 variable. *Cost per step:* 1 Binomial draw + 1 Poisson draw.

3.3 Surrogates for Two-State Model

We next discuss surrogates that approximate $\mathcal{M}_{\text{CME},2}$, again starting with the classical Tau-leaping and CLE models. The discussed models differ in how many variables they track and whether the promoter dynamics are simulated stochastically or collapsed analytically.

$\mathcal{M}_{\text{TL},2}$: *Tau-leaping.* The model extends $\mathcal{M}_{\text{TL}}$ to the telegraph model by drawing four independent Poisson counts per step: transcription ($\alpha N_{\text{on}} V \,\Delta t$), degradation ($\delta x V \,\Delta t$), promoter off ($k_{\text{off}} N_{\text{on}} V \,\Delta t$), and promoter on ($k_{\text{on}} N_{\text{off}} V \,\Delta t$). *State:* 3 variables (mRNA, N_{on}, N_{off}). *Cost per step:* 4 Poisson draws.

$\mathcal{M}_{\mathrm{CLE},2}$: *Chemical Langevin Equation.* Extends $\mathcal{M}_{\mathrm{CLE}}$ to the telegraph model by applying the Gaussian fluctuation limit to each of the four reaction channels (transcription, degradation, promoter off, promoter on) independently, with per-reaction diffusion coefficients $\sqrt{f_i/V}$. *State:* 3 variables (mRNA, N_{on}, N_{off}). *Cost per step:* 4 Gaussian draws.

$\mathcal{M}_{\mathrm{CLE}^*,2}$: *Optimized CLE.* As in the one-state model, we collapses reaction noise channels of $\mathcal{M}_{\mathrm{CLE},2}$: one for the mRNA birth–death block and one for the promoter switching block (applied with opposite sign to N_{on} and N_{off}). The model is statistically equivalent to $\mathcal{M}_{\mathrm{CLE},2}$. *State:* 3 variables (mRNA, N_{on}, N_{off}). *Cost per step:* 2 Gaussian draws.

$\mathcal{M}_{\mathrm{Geo}}$: *Geometric Bursts.* As in the one-state benchmark, we consider a compound-Poisson surrogate with geometrically distributed burst sizes $Y \sim \mathrm{Geom}(p)$ and deterministic mRNA degradation $f(x) = -\delta x$. In the two-state setting, the burst parameters are matched to the stationary mean and variance of the telegraph model, but promoter fluctuations are not tracked explicitly. This provides a one-dimensional heavy-tailed surrogate that reproduces the stationary moments of $\mathcal{M}_{\mathrm{CME},2}$ while collapsing all promoter dynamics into an effective burst process. *State:* 1 variable (mRNA). *Cost per step:* 1 Poisson draw + K geometric draws.

$\mathcal{M}_{\mathrm{Geo,A}}$: *Geometric Bursts with Analytical Promoter.* This model also uses geometric burst sizes and deterministic mRNA decay, but improves on $\mathcal{M}_{\mathrm{Geo}}$ by retaining the transient activation of the promoter pool. We reduce the two-state system to a single mRNA variable by replacing the stochastic promoter occupancy $N_{\mathrm{on}}(t)$ with its analytical conditional mean $\frac{\pi_{\mathrm{on}} n_p}{V}\big(1-e^{-(k_{\mathrm{on}}+k_{\mathrm{off}})t}\big)$, which captures the transient warm-up of the promoter pool when starting with all promoters in the OFF state. The geometric burst rate is then modulated proportionally to this deterministic envelope, while the burst-size parameter remains the stationary moment-matched one. *State:* 1 variable (mRNA). *Cost per step:* 1 Poisson draw + K geometric draws.

$\mathcal{M}_{\mathrm{BP},2}$: *Binomial–Poisson Propagator.* We also propose a new extension of $\mathcal{M}_{\mathrm{BP}}$ to the two-state telegraph model. Writing the one-step kernel in copy-number form with $X_t = Vx_t$ and $G_t = VN_{\mathrm{on},t}$, we treat the n_p promoter copies as independent two-state Markov chains [25]. For a single promoter $S_t \in \{0,1\}$,

$$\mathbb{P}(S_{t+\Delta t} = 1 \mid S_t = s) = \pi_{\mathrm{on}} + (s - \pi_{\mathrm{on}})e^{-r\Delta t}, \qquad s \in \{0,1\},$$

with $r = k_{\mathrm{on}} + k_{\mathrm{off}}$ and $\pi_{\mathrm{on}} = k_{\mathrm{on}}/r$. Hence, the exact endpoint ON-probabilities over Δt are $p_{11} = \pi_{\mathrm{on}} + (1-\pi_{\mathrm{on}})e^{-r\Delta t}$ and $p_{01} = \pi_{\mathrm{on}}(1-e^{-r\Delta t})$, and, conditional on G_t,

$$G_{t+\Delta t} \sim \mathrm{Bin}(G_t,\, p_{11}) + \mathrm{Bin}(n_p - G_t,\, p_{01})\,,$$

which is exact for any Δt. Freezing the promoter count at its left-endpoint value G_t, the mRNA update is

$$X_{t+\Delta t} \sim \mathrm{Bin}\big(X_t,\, e^{-\delta\Delta t}\big) + \mathrm{Pois}\big(G_t\, \tfrac{\alpha}{\delta}\big(1 - e^{-\delta\Delta t}\big)\big)\,.$$

Unlike $\mathcal{M}_{\mathrm{BP}}$, whose constant birth rate makes the update exact without further conditioning, this mRNA step assumes the promoter count is constant over $[t, t + \Delta t]$ and becomes exact as $\Delta t \to 0$. Unlike binomial Tau-leaping [6,40], which uses the first-order birth approximation $\mathrm{Pois}(\alpha G_t \Delta t)$, $\mathcal{M}_{\mathrm{BP},2}$ accounts for degradation of molecules produced within the step: the new-survivor mean converges to $G_t\alpha/\delta$ as $\Delta t \to \infty$, the correct conditional stationary copy-number mean given the frozen promoter state. $\mathcal{M}_{\mathrm{BP},2}$ therefore degrades more gracefully than other Tau-leaping variants at large Δt. *State:* 3 variables (mRNA, N_{on}, N_{off}). *Cost per step:* 3 Binomial draws + 1 Poisson draw.

We next derive analytic formulas for parameters for surrogate models where not already given by the initial parameters. The parameterized models were then benchmarked with respect to runtime and accuracy.

3.4 Model Parameterization

Models are parameterized in one of two ways: they use the biological rates directly or they are parameterized by two-moment matching to the stationary mean and variance. We only state formulas for models that do not directly use biological parameters. Moment formulas are stated in concentration units.

For the implemented geometric-burst models, a time step Δt samples $K \sim \mathrm{Poisson}(\kappa V \Delta t)$ burst events, each adding Y/V to the mRNA concentration, where $Y \sim \mathrm{Geom}(p)$ on $\mathbb{N}_0$. Equivalently, in the notation of Theorem 1, the concentration jump law is Y/V and the arrival rate is κV. Hence, with $\lambda_0 = \sigma = 0$, it is $m_\star = \frac{\kappa \mu_1}{\delta}$, $v_\star = \frac{\kappa \mu_2}{2\delta V}$, $\mu_1 = \frac{1-p}{p}$, and $\mu_2 = \frac{(1-p)(2-p)}{p^2}$. Solving for p and κ given a target $(m_\star, v_\star)$ with $2Vv_\star > m_\star$ gives

$$p = \frac{2m_\star}{m_\star + 2Vv_\star}, \qquad \kappa = \frac{m_\star\, \delta\, p}{1-p}. \tag{3}$$

These formulas are instantiated with the one-state target moments below and, independently, with the two-state target moments.

Surrogates for One-State Model. The stationary distribution of $\mathcal{M}_{\mathrm{CME}}$ with n_p constitutive copies is Poisson (Theorem 2), with concentration moments

$$m_{\mathrm{CME}} = \frac{n_p\alpha}{\delta}, \qquad v_{\mathrm{CME}} = \frac{n_p\alpha}{\delta V}. \tag{4}$$

$\mathcal{M}_{\mathrm{CLE}^*}$: diffusion coefficient $B^2(x) = (\alpha n_p + \delta x)/V$.
$\mathcal{M}_{\mathrm{Geo}}$: Substituting Eq. (4) into Eq. (3) yields $p_{\mathrm{CME}} = \frac{2V}{V+2}$ and $\kappa_{\mathrm{CME}} = \frac{2n_p\alpha V}{V+2}$. At $V = 1\,\mathrm{fL}$: $p = 2/3$, $\kappa = 2n_p\alpha/3$. The feasibility condition $v_{\mathrm{CME}} > m_{\mathrm{CME}}/2$ requires $V < 2\,fL$.

Surrogates for Two-State Model. The stationary concentration moments of $\mathcal{M}_{\mathrm{CME},2}$ with n_p promoter copies are (Theorem 3), with $\pi_{\mathrm{on}} := \frac{k_{\mathrm{on}}}{k_{\mathrm{on}}+k_{\mathrm{off}}}$ has $m_{\mathrm{CME},2} = \frac{n_p\, \alpha\, \pi_{\mathrm{on}}}{\delta V} = \frac{n_p\, \alpha\, k_{\mathrm{on}}}{\delta\, (k_{\mathrm{on}}+k_{\mathrm{off}})\, V}$ and $v_{\mathrm{CME},2} = \frac{m_{\mathrm{CME},2}}{V} + \frac{m^2_{\mathrm{CME},2}}{n_p} \frac{k_{\mathrm{off}}}{k_{\mathrm{on}}} \frac{\delta}{\delta+k_{\mathrm{on}}+k_{\mathrm{off}}}$.

$\mathcal{M}_{\text{CLE}^*,2}$: two block-wise diffusion coefficients from CME propensities, $B^2_{\text{mRNA}} = \frac{\alpha N_{\text{on}}+\delta x}{V}$ and $B^2_{\text{sw}} = \frac{k_{\text{off}} N_{\text{on}}+k_{\text{on}} N_{\text{off}}}{V}$, with $N_{\text{off}} = n_p/V - N_{\text{on}}$.

$\mathcal{M}_{\text{Geo}}$: Substituting $(m_\star, v_\star) = (m_{\text{CME},2}, v_{\text{CME},2})$ into Eq. (3) yields $p_{\text{CME},2} = \frac{2\, m_{\text{CME},2}}{m_{\text{CME},2}+2V\, v_{\text{CME},2}}$ and $\kappa_{\text{CME},2} = \frac{m_{\text{CME},2}\, \delta\, p_{\text{CME},2}}{1-p_{\text{CME},2}}$.

$\mathcal{M}_{\text{Geo,A}}$: uses the same burst-size parameter $p_{\text{CME},2}$ and, because all promoters start in the OFF state, the analytical mean active-promoter concentration is $\bar{N}_{\text{on}}(t) = \frac{n_p \pi_{\text{on}}}{V}\left(1 - e^{-(k_{\text{on}}+k_{\text{off}})t}\right)$. Its time-dependent burst propensity is therefore $\kappa_{\text{A}}(t) = \kappa_{\text{CME},2} \frac{\bar{N}_{\text{on}}(t)}{n_p \pi_{\text{on}}/V} = \kappa_{\text{CME},2}\left(1 - e^{-(k_{\text{on}}+k_{\text{off}})t}\right)$. The burst count over one step is sampled as $K \sim \text{Poisson}(\kappa_{\text{A}}(t) V \Delta t)$.

4 Results

The parameterized models were then benchmarked with respect to runtime and accuracy after implementation within the `bcrnnoise` library.

Runtime. We benchmarked runtime by simulating 100 trajectories of length 120 min for each model (30 repeats), varying the plasmid copy number n_p and, for surrogate models, the time step Δt, using literature-derived parameter sets (see Methods). For SDE-based surrogates, the 100 trajectories were generated in a vectorized batch. For the constitutive one-state model (Fig. 2a), all SDE-based surrogates have simulation times one to two orders of magnitude faster than $\mathcal{M}_{\text{CME}}$. Unlike exact $\mathcal{M}_{\text{CME}}$, their maximum runtime does not increase from $n_p = 1$ to 20 and is mainly determined by Δt. For the telegraph two-state model (Fig. 2b), similar observations hold. $\mathcal{M}_{\text{BP}}$ and $\mathcal{M}_{\text{BP},2}$ are seen to perform similarly to $\mathcal{M}_{\text{TL}}$ and $\mathcal{M}_{\text{TL},2}$. Geometric surrogates perform particularly well for the two-state model. Interestingly, $\mathcal{M}_{\text{CLE}^*}$ and $\mathcal{M}_{\text{CLE}^*,2}$ do not significantly improve performance of $\mathcal{M}_{\text{CLE}}$ and $\mathcal{M}_{\text{CLE},2}$, which is attributed to the fact that random draws do not happen in the update loop but are generated in vectors upfront. Representative mRNA concentration trajectories for surrogate models of the constitutive one-state (Fig. 2c) and telegraph two-state (Fig. 2d) models are shown for the plasmid numbers $n_p \in \{1, 20\}$ and the time-steps $\Delta t = 1$ min.

Accuracy. Since surrogates achieved considerable performance boosts, we next tested their accuracy. We chose the same parameter settings as for the runtime benchmarks, generating 10,000 traces for each model to obtain precise noise profiles. Since $\mathcal{M}_{\text{CLE}}$ and $\mathcal{M}_{\text{CLE},2}$ are identically distributed to $\mathcal{M}_{\text{CLE}^*}$ and $\mathcal{M}_{\text{CLE}^*,2}$, we only show the optimized versions. The noise profiles were first tested in their accuracy to match marginal distributions of mRNA over the 120 min duration using Wasserstein-1 distance to the reference models at Δt time increments (Fig. 3a&b, see Methods for details). Early and late time distributions are also shown in the Supplementary Material (Section A.8).

For the one-state model (Fig. 3a), at $n_p = 1$ and fast updates with $\Delta t = 1$ min, surrogates are seen to perform well, with $\mathcal{M}_{\text{TL}}$ and $\mathcal{M}_{\text{BP}}$ being the best.

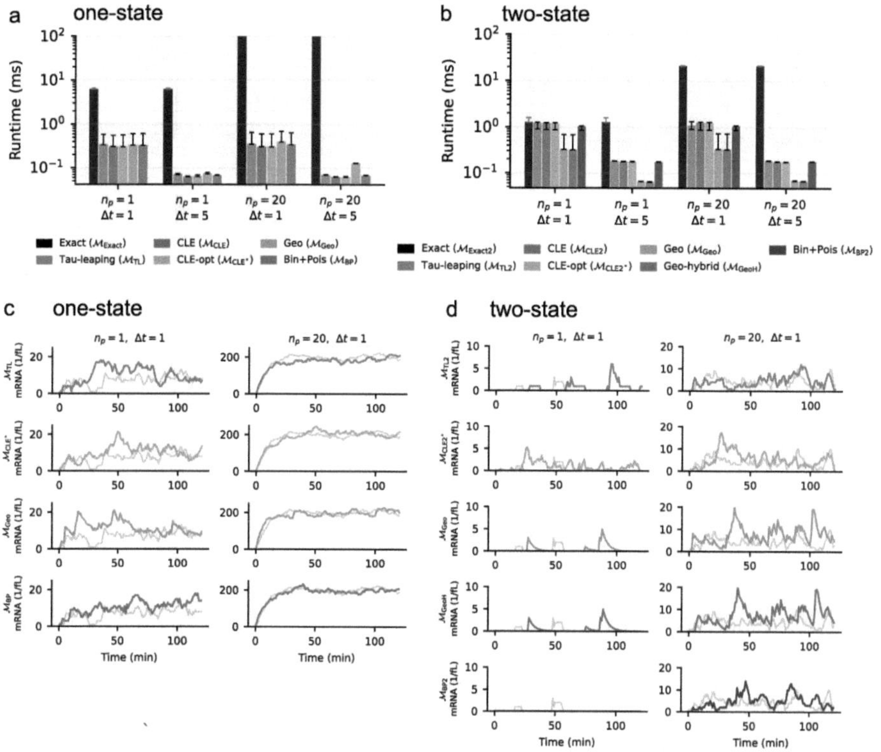

Fig. 2. Runtime and trajectories for surrogate models. (**a**) Constitutive one-state model families benchmarked over 100 generated traces at $n_p \in \{1, 20\}$ and $\Delta t \in \{1\,\text{min}, 5\,\text{min}\}$. Bars show median runtime per trajectory across 30 repeated benchmark batches; error bars indicate the 16th–84th percentiles. (**b**) Telegraph two-state model families under the same conditions. (**c&d**) Example trajectories for surrogate models with reference trajectories from exact models shown (gray).

Increasing the step size to $\Delta t = 5\,\text{min}$, however, considerably degrades accuracy except for $\mathcal{M}_{\text{BP}}$. Similar behavior is observed for higher plasmid number $n_p = 20$, with the degradation for the early (transient) phase being large, except for $\mathcal{M}_{\text{BP}}$.

For the two-state model (Fig. 3b), $\mathcal{M}_{\text{CLE}^*,2}$ is seen to not capture the tailed distribution shapes with Gaussian noise and degrades even more over time. Geometric surrogates perform particularly well along with $\mathcal{M}_{\text{BP},2}$. Interestingly, increasing the step-size to $\Delta t = 5\,\text{min}$ does not lead to a large degradation of accuracy for geometric models; in contrast to $\mathcal{M}_{\text{TL},2}$ where the assumption of small propensity changes during Δt is not accurate anymore. Again, $\mathcal{M}_{\text{BP},2}$ shows excellent performance. For $n_p = 20$ plasmids, the transient phase, after switching on the promoters, is again the most challenging to approximate. The problem is pronounced for $\mathcal{M}_{\text{Geo}}$, whose parameters are fitted to match the steady-state. This was alleviated by our model $\mathcal{M}_{\text{Geo,A}}$ that accounts for the switching-on phase, considerably improving the accuracy.

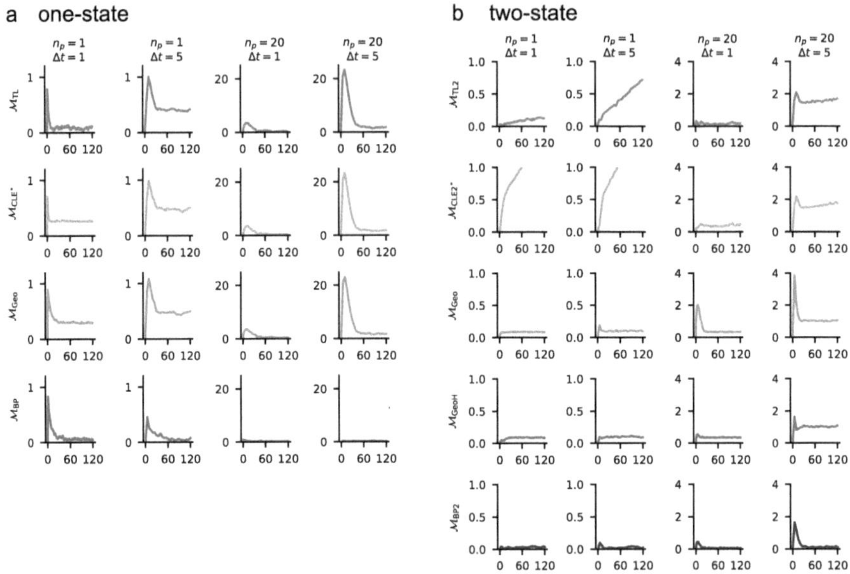

Fig. 3. Wasserstein-1 distance over time for surrogate models. $W_1(t)$ between the marginal mRNA distribution of each surrogate and the exact reference ($\mathcal{M}_{\text{CME}}$ for the constitutive one-state (**a**); $\mathcal{M}_{\text{CME},2}$ for the telegraph two-state (**b**)), estimated from 10,000 trajectories at each recorded time point. Rows: surrogate models; columns: plasmid copy number $n_p \in \{1, 20\}$ and time step $\Delta t \in \{1\,\text{min}, 5\,\text{min}\}$.

We next tested the models' capabilities to capture noise dependencies over time: noise at time t is not expected to be independent of noise at time t' in a model with bursts. We thus computed normalized auto-correlation functions (ACFs) for all surrogate models and compared these to the exact models (see Methods for details). For the constitutive one-state model (Fig. 4a), all surrogates reproduce the reference ACF closely across both copy numbers for the small time-step of 1 min: the exponential decorrelation is captured by all models. For the larger time-step of 5 min, all models achieve acceptable correlation quality for $n_p = 1$, with the winner being the $\mathcal{M}_{\text{BP}}$ model. Increasing plasmid counts to $n_p = 20$ visibly leads to strong underestimation of correlation except for the $\mathcal{M}_{\text{BP}}$ model, which fits exactly the non-trivial correlation.

For the telegraph two-state model (Fig. 4b), the short update-time of 1 min leads to favorable correlation performance for all models, with the geometric models moderately underestimation correlation. When increasing the update step to 5 min, large underestimations of the surrogate models become visible except for our $\mathcal{M}_{\text{BP},2}$ model. Interestingly, both one-dimensional geometric models struggle similarly to capture the slower correlation decline due to bursts within one dimension: $\mathcal{M}_{\text{Geo,A}}$ does not improve over $\mathcal{M}_{\text{Geo}}$ here, despite its superior prediction for marginals.

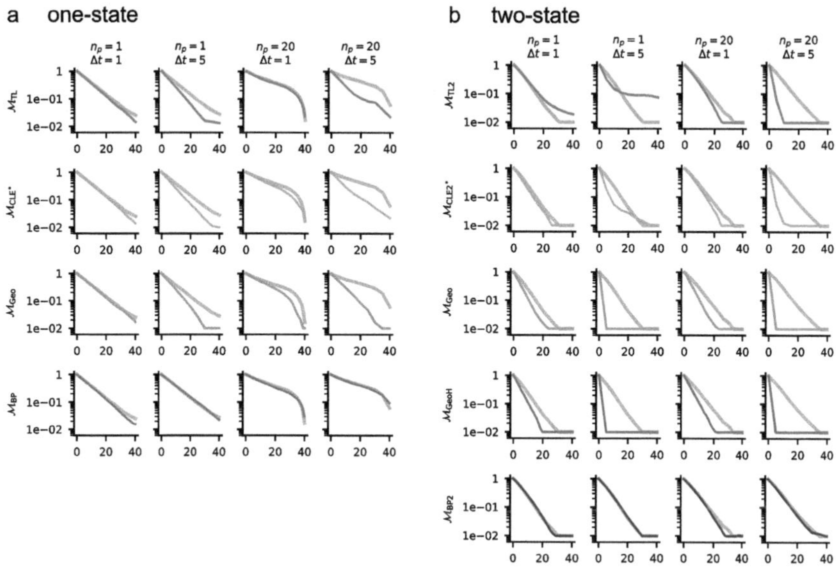

Fig. 4. Autocorrelation functions of surrogate models. Empirical normalized ACF $\rho(\tau)$ of mRNA concentration for the constitutive one-state (**a**) and telegraph two-state (**b**) benchmarks, averaged over 10,000 trajectories. Rows: surrogate models; columns: plasmid copy number $n_p \in \{1, 20\}$ and time step $\Delta t \in \{1\,\mathrm{min}, 5\,\mathrm{min}\}$. The reference ACF ($\mathcal{M}_{\mathrm{CME}}$ or $\mathcal{M}_{\mathrm{CME},2}$) is shown in gray in every panel; the surrogate ACF (log scale) is overlaid in the model color.

5 Methods

Software Implementation. All simulations were performed in our Python library `bcrnnoise` [10] available at https://github.com/BioDisCo/bcrnnoise. The library provides a unified interface for biochemical reaction network simulation under interchangeable noise specifications. A self-contained code listing illustrating this for a constitutive transcription network is given in Section A.6. All physical quantities (rates, concentrations, volumes, and time) are represented as `pint` [19] `Quantity` objects, providing automatic unit consistency checks and conversion throughout the library. We used the `unit-jit` library (https://github.com/BioDisCo/unit-jit) to just-in-time compile `pint` code to floats except at function boundaries. All random-number generation used NumPy. SDE-based models exploit a vectorized Euler–Maruyama kernel: all n trajectories advance simultaneously in a single loop iteration. For the compound-Poisson burst models ($\mathcal{M}_{\mathrm{Geo}}$, $\mathcal{M}_{\mathrm{Geo,A}}$), burst counts are drawn jointly across trajectories and the resulting geometric burst sizes are aggregated without per-trajectory loops using `np.add.reduceat`.

Exact Model Parameters. *One-state* [4]*:* Parameters are drawn from genome-wide median mRNA kinetics in *E. coli* (MG1655) [4]: per-plasmid transcription rate $\alpha = 1.0\,\mathrm{fL}^{-1}\,\mathrm{min}^{-1}$, degradation rate $\delta = 0.1\,\mathrm{min}^{-1}$ (mean mRNA lifetime 10 min). Cell volume was chosen as $V = 1\,\mathrm{fL}$. *Two-state* [16]*:* Parameters are from single-molecule measurements of the λ PRM promoter in *E. coli* [16]: $k_{\mathrm{on}} = 0.027\,\mathrm{min}^{-1}$ (mean OFF duration of 37 min), $k_{\mathrm{off}} = 0.17\,\mathrm{min}^{-1}$ (mean ON duration of 6 min), per-plasmid transcription rate $\alpha = 0.4\,\mathrm{min}^{-1}$, $\delta = 0.2\,\mathrm{min}^{-1}$ (mean mRNA lifetime 5 min), and $V = 1\,\mathrm{fL}$.

Runtime Metrics. Wall-clock times were measured with `time.perf_counter` over 30 batches of 100 trajectories of length $T = 120\,\mathrm{min}$ on a single CPU core (MacBook Pro, Apple M2, 24 GB RAM). Exact reference models ($\mathcal{M}_{\mathrm{CME}}$, $\mathcal{M}_{\mathrm{CME},2}$) used Gillespie simulation with variable step size.

Accuracy Metrics. Distributional accuracy was quantified by the first Wasserstein distance W_1 using `scipy.stats.wasserstein_distance`. The empirical autocorrelation function (ACF) was computed from the same trajectories used for the distributional validation. To avoid transient effects, the first 40 min of each trajectory were discarded. The remaining stationary portion spans $t \in [40\,\mathrm{min}, 120\,\mathrm{min}]$. For each model the unnormalized autocorrelation at integer lag k was estimated as $\hat{C}(k) = \frac{1}{N\,(T_{\mathrm{stat}}-k)} \sum_{i=1}^{N} \sum_{t=1}^{T_{\mathrm{stat}}-k} X_i(t)\, X_i(t+k)$, where $N = 10{,}000$ is the number of trajectories and T_{stat} is the number of retained time points. The ACF was then normalized to $\rho(k) = \frac{\hat{C}(k)-\hat{\mu}^2}{\hat{\sigma}^2}$, with $\hat{\mu}$ and $\hat{\sigma}^2$ the mean and variance over all trajectories and retained time points, so that $\rho(0) = 1$. Lags were evaluated up to 40 min.

6 Conclusion

We introduced a unified jump-diffusion SDE framework for mRNA trace generation in the constitutive and telegraph transcription models. The framework places classical approximations (Tau-leaping, the Chemical Langevin Equation) and compound-Poisson burst surrogates within a single drift–noise specification, and includes new surrogates based on geometric noise and Binomial–Poisson propagators. Implemented in the open-source `bcrnnoise` library, it enables vectorized batch simulation and comparison against exact Gillespie references.

Benchmarking shows that noise-model choice matters greatly for accuracy and efficiency. Gaussian surrogates are fast but lose accuracy in burst-dominated regimes, particularly for the telegraph model and during transient activation. Geometric burst surrogates reproduce marginal distributions substantially better, and an analytical warm-up of promoter activation further improves transient behavior, however perform poorly to capture correlation.

Most notably, Binomial–Poisson propagators combine high accuracy with strong computational performance, remaining accurate where Tau-leaping degrades at coarse time steps. The resulting two-orders-of-magnitude speed-up at near-identical accuracy provides a practical basis for selecting surrogates by observable and biological regime.

Acknowledgments. The research of Arman Ferdowsi was funded in part by CHIST-ERA-22-SPiDDS-07 (TROCI Project), by the Austrian Science Fund (FWF) under grant 10.55776/I6647, and by the Austrian Science Fund (FWF) project DMAC (grant 10.55776/P32431). The research of Matthias Függer and Thomas Nowak was supported by the French National Research Agency (ANR) projects DREAMY (ANR-21-CE48-0003) and COSTXPRESS (ANR-23-CE45-0013), as well as the SAIF project, funded by the "France 2030" government investment plan managed by ANR, under the reference ANR-23-PEIA-0006.

Disclosure of Interests. The authors have no competing interests to declare that are relevant to the content of this article.

References

1. Applebaum, D.: Lévy Processes and Stochastic Calculus, 2nd edn. Cambridge University Press (2009)
2. Aubin, J.P., Da Prato, G.: Stochastic viability and invariance. Annali della Scuola Normale Superiore di Pisa-Classe di Scienze **17**(4), 595–613 (1990)
3. Bergmann, F.T.: Basico: a simplified python interface to copasi. J. Open Source Softw. **8**(90), 5553 (2023)
4. Bernstein, J.A., Khodursky, A.B., Lin, P.H., Lin-Chao, S., Cohen, S.N.: Global analysis of mRNA decay and abundance in Escherichia coli at single-gene resolution using two-color fluorescent DNA microarrays. Proc. Natl. Acad. Sci. **99**(15), 9697–9702 (2002)
5. Cao, Z., Grima, R.: Analytical distributions for detailed models of stochastic gene expression in eukaryotic cells. Proc. Natl. Acad. Sci. **117**(9), 4682–4692 (2020)
6. Chatterjee, A., Vlachos, D.G., Katsoulakis, M.A.: Binomial distribution based τ-leap accelerated stochastic simulation. J. Chem. Phys. **122**(2), 024112 (2005). https://doi.org/10.1063/1.1833357
7. Cont, R., Tankov, P.: Financial Modelling with Jump Processes. Chapman and Hall/CRC (2003)
8. Elowitz, M.B., Levine, A.J., Siggia, E.D., Swain, P.S.: Stochastic gene expression in a single cell. Science **297**(5584), 1183–1186 (2002)
9. Fasen, V., Klüppelberg, C., Lindner, A.: Extremal behavior of stochastic volatility models. In: Stochastic Finance, pp. 107–155. Springer (2006)
10. Ferdowsi, A., Függer, M., Nowak, T.: bcrnnoise: simulate bio-chemical reaction networks with noise (2026). https://github.com/BioDisCo/bcrnnoise
11. Friedman, N., Cai, L., Xie, X.S.: Linking stochastic dynamics to population distribution: an analytical framework of gene expression. Phys. Rev. Lett. **97**(16), 168302 (2006)
12. Gardiner, C.W.: Handbook of Stochastic Methods for Physics, Chemistry and the Natural Sciences. Springer Series in Synergetics (1985)
13. Gillespie, D.T.: Exact stochastic simulation of coupled chemical reactions. J. Phys. Chem. **81**(25), 2340–2361 (1977). https://doi.org/10.1021/j100540a008
14. Gillespie, D.T.: The chemical langevin equation. J. Chem. Phys. **113**(1), 297–306 (2000)
15. Gillespie, D.T.: Approximate accelerated stochastic simulation of chemically reacting systems. J. Chem. Phys. **115**(4), 1716–1733 (2001)

16. Golding, I., Paulsson, J., Zawilski, S.M., Cox, E.C.: Real-time kinetics of gene activity in individual bacteria. Cell **123**(6), 1025–1036 (2005)
17. Gorin, G., Pachter, L.: Modeling bursty transcription and splicing with the chemical master equation. Biophys. J . **121**(6), 1056–1069 (2022)
18. Gorin, G., Vastola, J.J., Fang, M., Pachter, L.: Interpretable and tractable models of transcriptional noise for the rational design of single-molecule quantification experiments. Nat. Commun. **13**(1), 7620 (2022)
19. Grecco, H.: Pint: makes units easy (2012). https://github.com/hgrecco/pint
20. Hoops, S., et al.: Copasi–a complex pathway simulator. Bioinformatics **22**(24), 3067–3074 (2006)
21. Iyer-Biswas, S., Hayot, F., Jayaprakash, C.: Stochasticity of gene products from transcriptional pulsing. Phys. Rev. E (2009)
22. Jahnke, T., Huisinga, W.: Solving the chemical master equation for monomolecular reaction systems analytically. J. Math. Biol. **54**(1), 1–26 (2007). https://doi.org/10.1007/s00285-006-0034-x
23. Jia, C., Zhang, M.Q., Qian, H.: Emergent lévy behavior in single-cell stochastic gene expression. Phys. Rev. E **96**(4), 040402 (2017)
24. van Kampen, N.G.: Stochastic Processes in Physics and Chemistry, 3rd edn. Elsevier (2007)
25. Kendall, D.G.: On the generalized birth-and-death process. Ann. Math. Stat. **19**(1), 1–15 (1948). https://doi.org/10.1214/aoms/1177730285
26. Kepler, T.B., Elston, T.C.: Stochasticity in transcriptional regulation: origins, consequences, and mathematical representations. Biophys. J . **81**(6), 3116–3136 (2001)
27. Ko, M.S.: A stochastic model for gene induction. J. Theor. Biol. **153**(2), 181–194 (1991)
28. Lin, Y.T., Doering, C.R.: Gene expression dynamics with stochastic bursts: construction and exact results for a coarse-grained model. Phys. Rev. E **93**(2), 022409 (2016)
29. Lin, Y.T., Galla, T.: Bursting noise in gene expression dynamics: linking microscopic and mesoscopic models. J. R. Soc. Interface **13**(114), 20150772 (2016)
30. Lindner, A., Maller, R.: Lévy integrals and the stationarity of generalised ornstein-uhlenbeck processes. Stochast. Process. Appl. **115**(10), 1701–1722 (2005)
31. Mahat, D.B., et al.: Single-cell nascent RNA sequencing unveils coordinated global transcription. Nature **631**(8019), 216–223 (2024)
32. Paulsson, J.: Summing up the noise in gene networks. Nature **427**, 415–418 (2004)
33. Paulsson, J.: Models of stochastic gene expression. Phys. Life Rev. **2**(2), 157–175 (2005)
34. Peccoud, J., Ycart, B.: Markovian modeling of gene-product synthesis. Theor. Popul. Biol. **48**(2), 222–234 (1995)
35. Raj, A., Peskin, C.S., Tranchina, D., Vargas, D.Y., Tyagi, S.: Stochastic mRNA synthesis in mammalian cells. PLoS Biol. **4**(10), e309 (2006)
36. Ramsköld, D., et al.: Single-cell new RNA sequencing reveals principles of transcription at the resolution of individual bursts. Nat. Cell Biol. **26**(10), 1725–1733 (2024). https://doi.org/10.1038/s41556-024-01486-9
37. Sanft, K.R., Wu, S., Roh, M., Fu, J., Lim, R.K., Petzold, L.R.: Stochkit2: software for discrete stochastic simulation of biochemical systems with events. Bioinformatics **27**(17), 2457–2458 (2011)
38. Schnoerr, D., Sanguinetti, G., Grima, R.: Approximation and inference methods for stochastic biochemical kinetics–a tutorial review. J. Phys. A: Math. Theor. **50**(9), 093001 (2017)

39. Thattai, M., Van Oudenaarden, A.: Intrinsic noise in gene regulatory networks. Proc. Natl. Acad. Sci. **98**(15), 8614–8619 (2001)
40. Tian, T., Burrage, K.: Binomial leap methods for simulating stochastic chemical kinetics. J. Chem. Phys. **121**(21), 10356–10364 (2004). https://doi.org/10.1063/1.1810475
41. Tunnacliffe, E., Chubb, J.R.: What is a transcriptional burst? Trends Genet. **36**(4), 288–297 (2020)

Mamdani-Driven Fuzzy Reaction Systems

Linda Brodo[2], Moreno Falaschi[1](✉), Fiamma Romagnoli[1], and Elisa B. P. Tiezzi[1]

[1] Department of Information Engineering and Mathematics, University of Siena, Via Roma 56, 53100 Siena, Italy
{moreno.falaschi,fiamma.romagnoli,elisa.tiezzi}@unisi.it
[2] Dipartimento di Scienze Economiche e Aziendali, University of Sassari, Via Muroni 25, 07100 Sassari, Italy
brodo@uniss.it

Abstract. Reaction Systems (RSs) provide a successful qualitative modelling framework inspired by biochemical reactions. In a RS a computation starts from an initial state given by a set of entities and each following computation state is determined by the application of all the enabled reactions to the previous state. RSs can also model the interaction with the environment. Each entity can either be present or absent in a computation state, as a crisp boolean condition, and also reactions are (or not) enabled under crisp conditions. This framework has proved to have many applications for modelling biomedical and computer science systems, but it can become restrictive when laboratory measurements exhibit graded concentrations, partial inhibition, and noise. We thus introduce Mamdani-driven Fuzzy Reaction Systems (M-FRS), as a graded conservative extension of RSs. Each reaction in the style of RSs is now interpreted as a Mamdani rule, and we formalise a single four-stage fuzzy inference cycle (fuzzification, rule evaluation, aggregation, optional defuzzification) which defines a deterministic discrete-time graded update operator. Fuzzy inference yields a discrete dynamical system. As a first case study, we develop a compact M-FRS model of the hypothalamic–pituitary–thyroid axis.

Keywords: Reaction Systems · Fuzzy Systems · Fuzzy Reaction Systems · Systems Biology

1 Introduction

Biochemical regulatory networks are intrinsically reactive systems. Hormonal axes, intracellular signalling pathways, and gene-regulatory circuits continuously receive stimuli, update internal concentrations, and produce downstream responses that influence subsequent evolution. Despite the underlying biochemical complexity, many such systems exhibit a structural regularity that can be described in terms of activation and inhibition relations between entities.

Reaction Systems (RSs), originally introduced in [13], provide an elegant qualitative abstraction of this mechanism. In a RS, given a set of entities S (the

P. T. Monteiro (Ed.): CMSB 2026, LNBI 16678, pp. 122–142, 2027.
https://doi.org/10.1007/978-3-032-30870-2_7

background set) a reaction is specified by a triplet (R, I, P), where R denotes the set of reactants, I the set of inhibitors, and P the set of products, and R, I, P are subsets of S. A reaction is enabled in a state $W \subseteq S$ if and only if all elements of R are present in W and no element of I is present. The global update rule applies all enabled reactions in parallel, producing the next state as union of the products of all enabled reactions. Additionally, when considering interactive computations, a context process (modelling the environment) may also add entities (from the set S) in each computation state, besides those generated by the application of the reactions. This semantics yields a deterministic discrete dynamical system over the finite state space $\mathcal{P}(S)$. The success of RSs lies in its conceptual clarity: it isolates causality from quantitative kinetics, as reactions depend only on facilitation and inhibition, not on rate constants or concentration values. This abstraction makes RSs particularly suitable for qualitative reasoning about biological organisation, causal dependencies, reachability properties, cyclic behaviour, structural feedback patterns, and interaction with the environment. However, crisp 'boolean' set membership in RSs also constitutes a limitation when confronted with empirical biological data. Modern laboratory measurements rarely provide binary information: hormone titres, metabolite concentrations, phosphorylation levels, and gene expression intensities are reported as continuous values and often fluctuate around nominal thresholds. Partial inhibition is common: a molecule may reduce, but not completely suppress, a downstream process. Likewise, activation may be gradual rather than all-or-nothing. Encoding such phenomena in a RS typically requires the introduction of arbitrary thresholds that discretise continuous measurements into "present" or "absent". While technically feasible, this approach reintroduces subjectivity and discards information that may be biologically relevant. The resulting model remains crisp, but the mapping from data to 'boolean' states becomes extrinsic to the formalism. The proposed framework preserves the qualitative reactive structure of Reaction Systems while enriching it with graded quantitative observations interpreted through fuzzy semantics. Although the model allows the use of normalised quantitative data, it does not attempt to reconstruct biochemical kinetics, reaction rates, or continuous-time dynamics. Rather, quantitative observations are translated into graded linguistic descriptions that drive the rule-based evolution of the system.

In this paper we introduce *Mamdani-driven Fuzzy Reaction Systems* (M-FRS), a graded extension of classical RSs that preserves the reaction syntax while replacing the boolean semantics with fuzzy membership degrees in the interval of reals $[0, 1]$. Each reaction is interpreted as a Mamdani rule [21] and a single fuzzy inference step induces a deterministic state-update operator $\Phi : [0, 1]^S \longrightarrow [0, 1]^S$, where S is the background set of entities. This way, fuzzy inference extends the semantics of RSs and yields a discrete fuzzy dynamical system without introducing continuous-time kinetics. We show that M-FRS is conservative with respect to classical RSs under suitable choices of labels and operators: when graded states collapse to boolean values, the induced dynamics coincides with the classical RS update rule.

From Crisp Enabling to Graded Semantics. Fuzzy set theory introduced by Zadeh [28] provides a principled framework for modelling graduality and uncertainty. In the fuzzy setting, each entity is assigned a degree of presence in the unit interval $[0, 1]$, and logical connectives are interpreted via triangular norms (t–norms), t–conorms, and fuzzy negations. Instead of asking whether a reactant is present, one evaluates to what degree it satisfies a linguistic predicate such as *High*. Instead of checking whether an inhibitor is absent, one computes the graded truth value of its negation. Logical conjunction becomes a continuous operator that captures the joint satisfaction of multiple conditions. Fuzzy inference systems [19] have long been used in control engineering [26,27], pattern recognition [20], and biomedical modelling (see e.g. [1,2,17,25]) as they accommodate graduality, noise, and linguistic interpretability. Classical fuzzy inference systems, however, are inherently static: they compute an output for a given input, but they do not define a state-transition semantics by themselves. A standard Mamdani inference cycle [11,21] consists of four stages—fuzzification of numerical inputs, rule evaluation, aggregation of rule outputs, and optional defuzzification to obtain a crisp value—and yields an input–output mapping. This process is typically not iterated. This highlights a fundamental gap between fuzzy inference systems and RSs. The semantics of a RS, in contrast, specifies how system states evolve in discrete computation steps. M-FRS is designed to combine the complementary strengths of fuzzy reasoning and RSs, RSs generate a sequence of states in which Mamdani-style fuzzy reasoning realises a graded extension of each computation step.

Design Principles. The classical reaction structure with triplets (R, I, P) is retained unchanged. At each time step t, the system state is represented by a graded state function $c_t : S \to [0, 1]$, where $c_t(x)$ denotes the normalised degree of presence of entity $x \in S$. Fuzzification is performed by evaluating each value $c_t(x)$ through a family of membership functions associated with linguistic labels (e.g. Low, Medium, High), thus assigning graded truth values to linguistic statements about the entities. The firing strength of a reaction a becomes a value $\rho_a \in [0, 1]$, representing the degree to which the reaction is enabled. It is computed by combining the graded satisfaction of reactants and inhibitors through fuzzy logical operators. A single fuzzy inference cycle defines a state-update operator, which can be iterated to yield a deterministic discrete-time dynamical system over a continuous state space, preserving the reactive semantics of RSs. Thus, quantitative state values are systematically translated into linguistic descriptions before rule evaluation.

Contributions. We introduce the first framework integrating RSs and fuzzy systems. A M-FRS provides a conservative semantic extension of RSs. Under appropriate choices of membership functions and operators, and when graded states collapse to boolean values, the induced dynamics coincides with the classical RS update rule. Conceptually, a M-FRS does not impose thresholds; instead, it captures partial activation and gradual inhibition within a discrete-time framework. To demonstrate the expressiveness of our framework, we construct a compact M-FRS model of the HPT axis, a canonical neuroendocrine feedback system.

Related Work. In the literature there are many examples of applications of fuzzy systems to biomedical problems, e.g. [1,2,17,25]. For instance [2] defines a fuzzy rule-based Mamdani expert system for diagnosing hypothyroidism disorder, using a statistical model of logistic regression. To the best of our knowledge there is no framework integrating Mamdani Fuzzy Systems and RSs. In [22] Manzoni defined a concept of Fuzzy Set for the states of context independent RSs similar to ours, but did not consider Mamdani Fuzzy Systems and did not develop a systematic framework. [22] also did not show case studies. There are several works [5,8,9,23] which extend RSs in order to add quantitative information, 'counting' the entities. All these approaches count in a 'crisp' manner the quantities or use a sort of threshold approximation, but do not describe a fuzzy system.

Structure of the Paper. Section 2 introduces the basic framework of RSs and describes their semantics. Section 3 describes the notion of fuzzy sets and fuzzy logical operators. Section 4 introduces the background on Fuzzy Inference Systems. Section 5 presents our framework of Mamdani Fuzzy Reaction Systems and Sect. 6 describes a model of the hypothalamic–pituitary–thyroid axis. Finally, Sect. 7 presents some conclusion and future work.

2 Reaction Systems

Reaction Systems (RSs) have been introduced as a qualitative computational formalism born in the field of Natural Computing and inspired by the mechanism of reactions in living cells. Here we present the basic notions of RSs. For a complete presentation, we refer the interested reader to the seminal work [13] and for more examples and details to work [6]. RSs are a rather general modelling framework which has been applied in many different fields. Some examples of applications and analyses of RSs are in [3,4,7,10,12,14,15,24]. Hereafter, the term *entities* will denote generic molecular substances (e.g. atoms, molecules) that may be present in the states of a biochemical system.

Let S (the *background set*) be a (finite) set of entities, a *state* is any subset $W \subseteq S$. A *reaction* is a triple $a = (R, I, P)$, where $R, I, P \subseteq S$ are finite, non empty subsets of S and $R \cap I = \emptyset$. The sets R, I, P are the sets of *reactants*, *inhibitors*, and *products*, respectively. The set of all the reactions over S is denoted as $rac(S)$. The result of a reaction $a = (R, I, P)$ on W, denoted by $res_a(W)$, will be P if all reactants are present int W, and all the inhibitors are absent, and it is defined as follows:

$$res_a(W) \triangleq \begin{cases} P & \text{if } R \subseteq W \ \wedge \ I \cap W = \emptyset \\ \emptyset & \text{otherwise} \end{cases} \tag{1}$$

Products P are the outcome of a fired reaction, to be available in the next state. A Reaction System is a pair $\mathcal{A} = (S, A)$ where S is the set of entities, and $A \subseteq rac(S)$ is a finite set of reactions over S. Given $W \subseteq S$, the result of the reactions A on W, denoted $res_A(W)$, is the union of the products of all the reactions in A:

$$res_A(W) \triangleq \cup_{a \in A} res_a(W). \tag{2}$$

Biological systems are open systems that react to environmental stimuli, thus the behaviour of a RS is formalised in terms of an *interactive process*. Let $\mathcal{A} = (S, A)$ be a RS and let $n \geq 0$. An $(n+1)$-steps *interactive process* in $\mathcal{A}$ is a pair $\pi = (\gamma, \delta)$ s.t. $\gamma = \{C_i\}_{i \in [0,n]}$ is the *context sequence* and $\delta = \{D_i\}_{i \in [0,n]}$ is the *result sequence*, where $C_i, D_i \subseteq S$ for any $i \in [0, n]$, $D_0 = \emptyset$, and $D_{i+1} = res_A(D_i \cup C_i)$ for any $i \in [0, n-1]$. The context sequence γ represents the environment, while the result sequence δ is entirely determined by γ and the set of reactions A. We call $\tau = W_0, \ldots, W_n$ the *state sequence*, with $W_i \triangleq C_i \cup D_i$ for any $i \in [0, n]$. Note that each state W_i in τ is the union of the context C_i at step i and the result set $D_i = res_A(W_{i-1})$ from step $i - 1$.

Remark 1. The classical formalization of RSs is based on two assumptions: no permanency, i.e. any entity vanishes unless it is sustained by a reaction; no counting, i.e. the quantity of entities that are present in a cell is not considered. It follows that the result of a computation step does not depend on the order of application of the reactions.

Example 1. Let $\mathcal{A} \triangleq (S, A)$ be a toy RS, where $S \triangleq \{\mathsf{a}, \mathsf{b}, \mathsf{c}, \mathsf{d}\}$ and the reaction set $A \triangleq \{a_1, a_2\}$ contains $a_1 \triangleq (\{\mathsf{a}\}, \{\mathsf{c}\}, \{\mathsf{b}\})$, $a_2 \triangleq (\{\mathsf{b}\}, \{\mathsf{c}\}, \{\mathsf{c}\})$. Then, let $\pi \triangleq (\gamma, \delta)$ a 3−*steps* interactive process where $\gamma \triangleq C_0, C_1, C_2 = \{\mathsf{a}\}, \{\mathsf{a}\}, \emptyset$ and $\delta \triangleq D_0, D_1, D_2 = \emptyset, \{\mathsf{b}\}, \{\mathsf{b}\}, \{\mathsf{c}\}$. The resulting state sequence is $\tau \triangleq W_0, W_1, W_2 = \{\mathsf{a}\}, \{\mathsf{a}, \mathsf{b}\}, \{\mathsf{b}, \mathsf{c}\}$. In fact, $W_0 = C_0$; $D_1 = res_A(W_0) = res_A(\{\mathsf{a}\}) = \{\mathsf{b}\}$ as $en_{a_1}(W_0) \wedge \neg en_{a_2}(W_0)$, then $W_1 = D_1 \cup C_1$; and $D_2 = \{\mathsf{b}, \mathsf{c}\}$ as $en_{a_1}(W_1) \wedge en_{a_2}(W_1)$, then $W_2 = D_2 \cup C_2$. This evolution is depicted in Fig. 1.

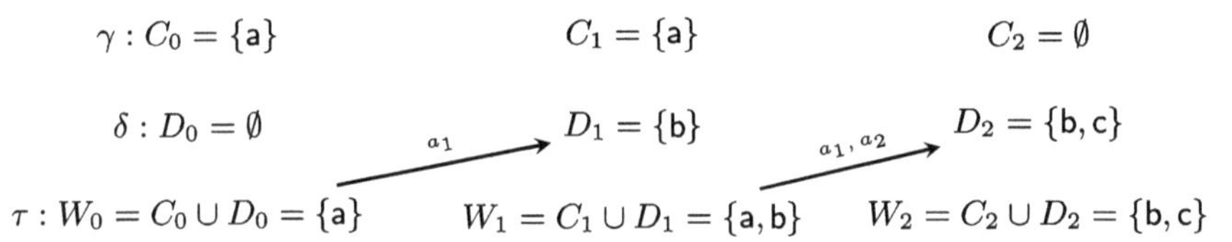

Fig. 1. A graphical representation of the interactive computation of the Example 1.

3 Fuzzy Sets and Basic Operations

Fuzzy set theory provides a natural mathematical framework to formalise graded descriptions [28]. The following definitions will provide the basis for the definition of fuzzy inference systems.

Let X be a universe of discourse. A fuzzy set B on X is characterised by a membership function $\mu_B : X \to [0,1]$, where $[0,1]$ is an interval of Reals, and $\mu_B(x)$ denotes the degree to which x belongs to B. The extreme values $\mu_B(x) = 0$ and $\mu_B(x) = 1$ correspond to complete absence and full membership, respectively. Classical (crisp) sets are recovered as the special case in which $\mu_B(x) \in \{0,1\}$ for all $x \in X$ [19]. In practical applications, the universe of discourse X typically represents the range of possible values of a quantitative variable, often normalised to the unit interval $[0,1]$. In this case, $x \in X$ denotes a numerical value (e.g. a normalised concentration), and membership functions are defined through simple parametric forms. For instance, a triangular membership function with parameters $a < b < c$ is defined as

$$\mu_A(x) = \begin{cases} 0 & x \leq a \vee x \geq c \\ \dfrac{x-a}{b-a} & a < x \leq b \\ \dfrac{c-x}{c-b} & b < x < c \end{cases}$$

where $a, b, c \in [0,1]$ with $a < b < c$. Other shapes can be defined analogously and allow one to encode expert knowledge or empirical ranges in a flexible way. Given two fuzzy sets $A, B \subseteq X$, their intersection, union, and complement are commonly defined as

$$\mu_{A \cap B}(x) = \min\{\mu_A(x), \mu_B(x)\} \qquad \mu_{A \cup B}(x) = \max\{\mu_A(x), \mu_B(x)\} \qquad \mu_{\neg A}(x) = 1 - \mu_A(x)$$

representing the standard fuzzy conjunction, disjunction, and negation [19]. These operators correspond to the standard conservative (minimum) conjunction, liberal (maximum) disjunction, and standard negation, respectively. While the minimum and maximum operators represent two extreme forms of aggregation, many systems exhibit intermediate behaviours, where partially active inputs combine into moderate effects. More generally, graded logical interactions are modelled using t–norms T and their dual t–conorms C. A t–norm is a function $T : [0,1]^2 \to [0,1]$ satisfying commutativity, associativity, monotonicity, and having 1 as neutral element; dually, a t–conorm has 0 as neutral element [19]. From a logical perspective, a fuzzy set A is a graded predicate, and $\mu_A(x)$ represents the truth degree of "x satisfies A". Logical connectives are then defined as

$$\text{AND: } T(\mu_A(x), \mu_B(x)), \qquad \text{OR: } C(\mu_A(x), \mu_B(x)),$$

while negation is represented by the standard complement $1 - \mu_A(x)$. We consider standard continuous t–norms, including Gödel (min), product (ab), and Łukasiewicz ($\max\{0, a+b-1\}$), each inducing a different interpretation of conjunction, with the corresponding t–conorms modelling disjunction.

4 Fuzzy Inference Systems

The fuzzy–set formalism introduced in Sect. 3 provides the basic tools for modelling graded predicates and their interaction within a rule-based framework.

Fuzzy inference systems (FISs) are rule–based computational schemes that evaluate collections of linguistic implications in a systematic manner. A typical rule has the form: IF A_1 AND $\cdots$ AND A_k THEN B, where the antecedents $A_1, \ldots, A_k$ and the consequent B are fuzzy sets. The logical conjunction in the antecedent is interpreted via a chosen t–norm T, while the aggregation of multiple rule outputs is performed through a t–conorm C. The degree to which the antecedent conditions are satisfied determines the firing strength of the rule and, consequently, the activation level of the consequent. Fuzzy inference systems provide a mathematical framework for reasoning with graded information by extending classical Boolean logic to the unit interval $[0, 1]$ [19,26]. Logical connectives are generalised through triangular norms and their dual t–conorms. In the Mamdani scheme [21], both antecedents and consequents are represented as fuzzy sets. The firing strength of each rule modulates its consequent, typically through t–norm–based clipping, and the resulting fuzzy sets are aggregated into a single output set. When required, a defuzzification operator (e.g. centroid, bisector, or mean of maxima) extracts a representative crisp value. Alternative paradigms, such as the Takagi–Sugeno model [27], replace fuzzy consequents with parametric functions of the inputs. However, when structural interpretability and symbolic transparency are central modelling objectives, the Mamdani framework offers a more natural alignment with rule–based causal descriptions. For this reason, we focus on Mamdani inference in this work, leaving extensions to alternative paradigms as future work.

A classical FIS defines a static mapping between inputs and outputs. A dynamical interpretation arises only when the output of one inference step is recursively fed back as input to the next step, thereby inducing a discrete–time state transition operator. This observation is central to our construction: in the next section, we embed a Mamdani inference step into the state-update mechanism of RSs, obtaining a discrete dynamical system driven by fuzzy reasoning.

5 Mamdani-Driven Fuzzy Reaction Systems (M-FRS)

A key design feature of the RS formalism is its qualitative nature: entities are either present or absent, reactions are either enabled or blocked, and system states are represented as sets. However, when modelling real biological systems this Boolean view may sometimes become restrictive [19,20]. Molecular concentrations, regulatory effects, and inhibition mechanisms often vary gradually.

In a fuzzy system, variables may assume intermediate truth values in the unit interval and rules operate over linguistic descriptions such as *Low*, *Medium*, or *High*. Classical FISs compute an output from a given input through a pipeline consisting of fuzzification, rule evaluation, aggregation, and optional defuzzification. However, these systems define static input–output mappings and do not by themselves provide a notion of state evolution over time [21,26].

Here, we combine these two paradigms by introducing the *Mamdani-driven Fuzzy Reaction Systems* (M-FRS). The idea is to replace the classical Boolean evaluation of reactions with a Mamdani-style fuzzy inference step while preserving the behaviour of RSs. Then, reactions retain their triplet structure but reactants and inhibitors are interpreted through presence levels in $[0, 1]$. The resulting framework supports partial enabling of reactions, partial inhibition, noise-tolerant behaviour, and preserves the following key design principles: (1) the classical reaction triplet (R, I, P) is retained unchanged, ensuring backward compatibility with the syntax and behaviour of RSs; (2) each reaction is interpreted as a Mamdani fuzzy rule over linguistic labels (e.g. Low, Medium, High), reusing the standard fuzzy inference pipeline consisting of fuzzification, rule evaluation, aggregation, and optional defuzzification; (3) the rule-based structure of reactions preserves linguistic interpretability, allowing domain experts to inspect statements such as "reactants should be High and inhibitors Low to produce High products"; (4) a single fuzzy inference cycle defines one discrete state update; feeding the resulting state back as input yields a dynamical system that maintains a behaviour in the style of RSs.

5.1 From Boolean Update to a Fuzzy State Map

In a classical RS, at step t, the system is in a state $W_t \subseteq S$, representing the set of entities that are present. The next state is obtained by applying all reactions in parallel, possibly augmented by an external context $C_{t+1} \subseteq S$: $W_{t+1} = \text{res}_A(W_t) \cup C_{t+1}$, as explained in Sect. 2.

Assuming a discrete clock (which follows the computation steps) we can also say that this update rule defines a deterministic discrete-time dynamical system on the finite state space $\mathcal{P}(S)$. First, we first define the framework for the context free case, and then we extend it to the context interactive case. In a M-FRS, at step/time t, the state is represented by a function

$$c_t : S \to [0, 1],$$

where $c_t(x)$ represents a normalised quantitative level associated with entity x, typically obtained from real-valued measurements (e.g. laboratory data) through an appropriate normalisation. These values provide the numerical input to the subsequent fuzzification stage. A function $c : S \to [0, 1]$ is called a *graded state* of the system, representing the degree of presence of each entity. The temporal evolution of the system is described by a deterministic update operator

$$\Phi : [0, 1]^S \to [0, 1]^S, \quad \text{such that} \quad c_{t+1} = \Phi(c_t).$$

Here, $[0, 1]^S$ denotes the set of all graded states of the system. Thus, the operator Φ takes as input the current graded state and returns the next graded state obtained after one fuzzy inference cycle. The operator Φ plays the same role as res_A in the classical setting, mapping the current state to the next one in a single (time) step. The key difference is that reaction enabling and product generation are evaluated through membership degrees and fuzzy logical operators rather than Boolean conditions. The resulting dynamics is deterministic: once the reactions, membership functions, and fuzzy logical operators are fixed, each state

c_t uniquely determines the next state c_{t+1}. Hence, a M-FRS defines a discrete-time dynamical system obtained by iterating a single fuzzy inference step.

Determinism here refers to the operational semantics of the model, rather than to the underlying biological reality. Once the reaction structure, membership functions, and fuzzy logical operators are fixed, the update operator Φ uniquely determines the next graded state. This provides a mathematically well-defined discrete-time dynamics at the chosen level of abstraction, while stochastic effects, parameter uncertainty, and incomplete biological knowledge remain outside our scope.

5.2 One-Step M-FRS Update

The update operator Φ is defined by a Mamdani-style fuzzy inference cycle consisting of four phases: fuzzification, rule evaluation, aggregation, and optional defuzzification. Before describing these phases, we fix the structural components that determine the behaviour of the system:

- $\forall x \in S$, a finite set of linguistic labels L_x, e.g. $\{\text{Low}, \text{Med}, \text{High}\}$;
- $\forall \ell \in L_x$, a membership function $L_{x,\ell} : [0,1] \to [0,1]$ mapping a normalised presence level to a graded truth value;
- a continuous t–norm $T : [0,1]^2 \to [0,1]$ modelling fuzzy conjunction;
- a t–conorm $C : [0,1]^2 \to [0,1]$ modelling fuzzy disjunction;
- a fuzzy negation $N : [0,1] \to [0,1]$, typically chosen as $N(u) = 1 - u$.

Different choices of the triple (T, C, N) (e.g. Gödel, product, or Łukasiewicz operators) induce different graded enabling mechanisms and may lead to different dynamical behaviours of the system. In many fuzzy logical frameworks, t–norms and t–conorms are chosen as dual operators with respect to the selected fuzzy negation, supporting standard De Morgan correspondences between conjunction and disjunction. For this reason, in concrete applications it is often desirable to adopt logically compatible triples (T, C, N). In the examples developed in this paper we use the Gödel pair $(\min, \max)$ together with the standard negation $N(u) = 1 - u$. More generally, the M-FRS framework remains parametric with respect to the choice of (T, C, N), allowing different interpretations of graded conjunction, disjunction, and negation depending on the intended modelling semantics. Once these elements are fixed, the update operator Φ is uniquely determined. Given a current state c_t, one update $t \to t + 1$ proceeds in four phases, as follows:

Phase 1: Fuzzification. In M-FRS, the system state at time t is given by a state function $c_t : S \longrightarrow [0,1]$, where $c_t(x)$ represents a normalised quantitative level associated with entity $x \in S$. For each entity $x \in S$ and each linguistic label $\ell \in L_x$, this numerical value is interpreted through the corresponding membership function

$$\mu_{t,\ell}(x) = L_{x,\ell}\big(c_t(x)\big).$$

The choice of linguistic labels depends on the intended modelling semantics and on the role played by each entity within the considered application domain. In particular, labels associated with reactants, inhibitors, and products encode qualitative conditions such as sufficient activation, inhibitory presence, or normal physiological range. In the case study developed in Sect. 6, these labels are selected according to their biological interpretation. Fuzzification translates numerical degrees of presence into graded linguistic descriptions (e.g. x *is Low*, x *is High*), providing the interface between quantitative states and the rule-based reasoning used in subsequent phases.

Example 2. At time $t = 0$, let the measured leptin level be $LEP = 16.5$, and consider the clinically relevant interval $[a, b] = [0, 30]$. The corresponding normalised state value is

$$c_0(LEP) = \frac{LEP - a}{b - a} = \frac{16.5}{30} \approx 0.55.$$

Note that the values $c_t(x)$ (for $x \in S$) represent a normalised quantitative state and do not yet correspond to a linguistic qualification. Let $L_{\text{Normal}} : [0,1] \to [0,1]$ be a membership function that describes the linguistic label *Normal*, defined as

$$L_{\text{Normal}}(u) = \begin{cases} 0, & u \leq 0.25 \vee u \geq 0.75, \\ \dfrac{2(u - 0.25)}{0.5}, & 0.25 < u < 0.5, \\ \dfrac{2(0.75 - u)}{0.5}, & 0.5 \leq u < 0.75, \end{cases}$$

We obtain

$$\mu_{0,\text{Normal}}(LEP) = L_{\text{Normal}}(0.55) \approx 0.8.$$

Thus, at time $t = 0$, the normalised value of LEP is $c_0(LEP) \approx 0.55$, and LEP is *Normal* with degree approximately 0.8.

Phase 2: Rule Evaluation. We describe how a single reaction is evaluated in a fuzzy setting. Let $a = (R_a, I_a, P_a)$ be a reaction, where $R_a, I_a, P_a \subseteq S$ are the sets of reactants, inhibitors, and products, respectively. The evaluation of a at time t depends on the current graded state $c_t : S \to [0,1]$, which assigns to each entity $x \in S$ a normalised degree of presence. In classical RSs, a is enabled if and only if all its reactants are present and none of its inhibitors is present, that is, $\bigwedge_{x \in R_a}(x \text{ present}) \wedge \bigwedge_{y \in I_a}(y \text{ absent})$.

In M-FRS, the same logical structure is retained, but the predicates "present" and "absent" are interpreted through membership functions and fuzzy logical operators. To quantify reactant availability, fix a linguistic label ℓ_R (e.g. *High*) expressing sufficient presence. For each $x \in R_a$, define

$$\mu_{t,\ell_R}(x) = L_{x,\ell_R}(c_t(x)),$$

and aggregate these values via the t–norm T (here taken as the Gödel minimum):

$$\alpha_a = \min_{x \in R_a} \mu_{t,\ell_R}(x).$$

The value $\alpha_a \in [0,1]$ measures the degree to which all reactants jointly satisfy the required presence condition. For inhibitors, fix a linguistic label ℓ_I (e.g. *High*) representing inhibitory presence. For each $y \in I_a$, define

$$\mu_{t,\ell_I}(y) = L_{y,\ell_I}(c_t(y)).$$

The graded absence of y is obtained through the fuzzy negation $N(u) = 1-u$, yielding $1 - \mu_{t,\ell_I}(y)$. The joint graded absence of all inhibitors is then computed via the t–norm:

$$\delta_a = \min_{y \in I_a} \left(1 - \mu_{t,\ell_I}(y)\right).$$

Thus, $\delta_a \in [0,1]$ represents the degree to which all inhibitors are simultaneously absent. The firing strength of reaction a at time t is defined as $\rho_a = \min\{\alpha_a, \delta_a\}$. The value ρ_a represents the degree of activation of reaction a, i.e. the truth degree of its antecedent in the corresponding fuzzy rule.

Example 3. Consider the reaction a=$(\{LEP\}, \{T3\}, \{TRH\})$ simulating the TRH secretion at the hypothalamic level that is modulated by metabolic signals (LEP) and the endocrine feedback ($T3$). Assume that values at time t=0 are: 2.25 for T3 and the critical relevant interval is $[1, 6]$ pg/ml. The computation of the normalized value of T3 follows the procedure applied for LEP in Example 2. Then we get the normalized state: $c_t(\text{LEP}) = 0.55, \quad c_t(\text{T3}) = 0.25$.

Let the linguistic label ℓ_{T3} = High, and assume the following triangular membership function:

$$L_{\text{High}}(u) = \begin{cases} 0, & u \leq 0.25 \\ \frac{u-0.25}{0.5}, & 0.25 < u < 0.75 \\ 1, & u \geq 0.75 \end{cases}$$

Using the same procedure as in Example 2, we obtain $\mu_{0,\text{Normal}}(\text{LEP}) = 0.8, \quad \mu_{0,\text{High}}(\text{T3}) = 0$.

Now, we compute the absent graded degree of T3: $N(\mu_{0,\text{High}}(T3)) = 1{-}0 = 1$. Since the reaction has a single inhibitor and a single reactant, the joint graded absence of all inhibitors is $\delta_a = \min(1) = 1$, and the joint reactant availability is $\alpha_a = \min(0.8) = 0.8$.

Therefore, the firing strength is $\rho_a = \min\{1, 0.8\} = 0.8$. The reaction is strongly enabled: LEP strongly supports activation, and the absence of T3 does not reduce the firing strength.

The minimum operator admits a natural semantic interpretation. For reactants it implements a limiting–factor principle, where the activation degree of a reaction is determined by the least satisfied reactant condition. For inhibitors it expresses the graded conjunction of inhibitor absence. Consequently, the minimum operator acts as a fuzzy counterpart of logical conjunction, and the least satisfied condition determines the overall firing strength ρ_a.

Unlike classical propositional logic, fuzzy logical operators do not, in general, preserve all Boolean equivalences. Consequently, Boolean formulae that are classically equivalent may yield different graded evaluations under fuzzy interpretations. In the present framework this does not introduce semantic indeterminacy, since M-FRS evaluates explicitly structured reactions rather than arbitrary logical formulae. The syntactic structure of a reaction is therefore considered part of the model specification itself, encoding a specific causal organisation of reactants, inhibitors, and products.

Phase 3: Construction and Aggregation of Consequents. The construction and aggregation phase generalises the union of products in classical Reaction Systems to a graded setting. In the classical model, the product set P_a of a reaction $a = (R_a, I_a, P_a)$ is a crisp subset of S. Thus, $x \in P_a$ means that reaction a contributes entity x to the next state whenever it is enabled. No quantitative amount, rate, or stoichiometry is associated with P_a. Let A be the set of reactions. Fix an entity $x \in S$. Only reactions that produce x may influence its value at the next time step. We therefore define $A_x = \{a \in A \mid x \in P_a\}$. If $A_x = \varnothing$, then no reaction produces x at time $t+1$, and the corresponding aggregated fuzzy set is identically zero. For each reaction $a \in A_x$ firing with strength $\rho_a \in [0,1]$, its contribution to x is interpreted as a fuzzy support for the statement "x is l_P" at time $t+1$, where l_P denotes the designated product label (typically High).

Let $L_{x,l_P} : [0,1] \to [0,1]$ be the corresponding membership function. The individual contribution of reaction a is then given by the clipped membership function

$$u \mapsto T(\rho_a, L_{x,l_P}(u)), \quad u \in [0,1],$$

which reduces to $\min\{\rho_a, L_{x,l_P}(u)\}$ when the Gödel t–norm is adopted. If multiple reactions produce the same entity x, their contributions are combined in parallel via a t–conorm C. The resulting fuzzy set describing the graded support for x at step/time $t+1$ is defined as

$$A_x^{t+1}(u) = \bigvee_{a \in A_x} T\big(\rho_a, L_{x,l_P}(u)\big), \quad u \in [0,1],$$

where the operator $\bigvee$ denotes the aggregation of multiple contributions via the chosen t–conorm C, i.e. it is realised through repeated application of C. The function A_x^{t+1} represents the aggregated fuzzy description of the presence of x at the next (time) step.

Phase 4: Defuzzification. After phase 3, for each entity $x \in S$ we obtain a fuzzy set $A_x^{t+1} : [0,1] \to [0,1]$ describing the graded support for the presence level of x at time $t+1$. To recover a numerical next state $c_{t+1} : S \to [0,1]$, we apply a defuzzification operator to each aggregated fuzzy set. A standard choice is the centroid method:

$$c_{t+1}(x) = \frac{\int_0^1 u\, A_x^{t+1}(u)\, du}{\int_0^1 A_x^{t+1}(u)\, du},$$

whenever $\int_0^1 A_x^{t+1}(u)\,du > 0$, and we set $c_{t+1}(x) = 0$ otherwise. Thus, defuzzification provides the numerical representative of the aggregated fuzzy description needed to define the next graded state.

In Sect. 6 our case study will illustrate all the four phases of the one-step M-FRS update. Now we give the definition of the Mamdani-driven Fuzzy Reaction Systems.

Definition 1 (Mamdani-driven Fuzzy Reaction Systems (M-FRS)). *A Mamdani-driven Fuzzy Reaction System is a structure* $F = (S, A, \{L_x\}_{x \in S}, T, C, N)$, *where*

- S *is a finite set of entities;*
- A *is a finite set of crisp reactions;*
- *for each* $x \in S$, L_x *is a finite set of linguistic labels, each equipped with a membership function* $L_{x,\ell} : [0,1] \to [0,1]$;
- T *is a t–norm,* C *is a t–conorm, and* N *is a fuzzy negation.*

These components induce a deterministic state-transition operator $\Phi : [0,1]^S \to [0,1]^S$, *defined by the fuzzy inference pipeline described in Sect. 5.2. The associated dynamic behaviour is represented by the discrete system* $([0,1]^S, \Phi)$.

Remark 2 (Conservativity). The M-FRS model is conservative with respect to classical RSs under suitable choices of labels and operators. If, for every entity $x \in S$, a single linguistic label Present is chosen with membership function $L_{x,\text{Present}}(u) = u$, and the Gödel operators $(T, C, N) = (\min, \max, 1 - u)$ are adopted, then the graded enabling condition coincides with the Boolean enabling condition on $\{0,1\}$. Moreover, if all graded states satisfy $c_t(x) \in \{0,1\}$ for all $x \in S$, then, under the natural identification between Boolean-valued states and subsets of S, the induced operator Φ coincides with the classical update rule res_A.

Context Extension. Classical RSs admit an explicit context process modelling the influence of the environment on the system evolution. To preserve this aspect, we introduce a context function $\kappa_t : S \to [0,1]$, which assigns to each entity $x \in S$ a degree of external input at step/time t. The function $\kappa_t(x)$ represents the degree to which the entity x is provided by the environment, independently of the internal reaction dynamics. This allows one to model exogenous stimuli, boundary conditions, or external regulatory signals. The context is not subjected to an additional fuzzification step. This choice reflects its role as an exogenous input rather than an internal variable to be interpreted linguistically. While the system state is translated into fuzzy predicates through membership functions, the context directly represents the intensity of external stimuli.

Let $\Phi_{\text{int}} : [0,1]^S \to [0,1]^S$ denote the internal update operator obtained through the fuzzy inference cycle. The full state transition is then defined as follow, where C is the chosen t–conorm:

$$\Phi(c_t, \kappa_{t+1})(x) = C\big(\Phi_{\text{int}}(c_t)(x), \kappa_{t+1}(x)\big), \quad x \in S.$$

This operation combines, for each entity x, two sources of activation: the degree to which x is produced internally and the degree to which it is supplied by the environment. The use of a t–conorm ensures a monotone integration of these contributions, so that increasing either internal production or external input cannot decrease the resulting value. In particular, when $C = \max$, the update rule reduces to the fuzzy counterpart of set-theoretic union in classical RSs.

This yields an open dynamical system in which the evolution is driven by both internal reactions and environmental inputs, extending the interactive semantics of classical RSs to the graded setting.

6 Case Study: A Fuzzy Reaction Model of the HPT Axis

Biological Background: The hypothalamus–pituitary–thyroid (HPT) axis is a canonical endocrine regulatory system governing metabolic homeostasis. The hypothalamus secretes thyrotropin-releasing hormone (TRH), which stimulates the anterior pituitary to release thyroid-stimulating hormone (TSH). In turn, TSH promotes the production of thyroid hormones, primarily triiodothyronine (T3). Circulating T3 exerts negative feedback on both hypothalamic and pituitary levels, inhibiting the production of TRH and TSH. This feedback loop ensures the stabilization of the axis [16]. In addition to hormonal feedback, metabolic signals modulate hypothalamic activity. In particular, leptin (LEP), produced by adipose tissue, reflects energy availability and provides a permissive signal for TRH production [18]. In this case study, we focus on the HPT axis and model how leptin and thyroid hormone feedback regulate the cascade TRH → TSH → T3.

Entities and Qualitative Reaction Structure: Our set of entities is $S = \{LEP, TRH, TSH, T3\}$. The qualitative reaction structure is defined by the following reactions, expressed as triples (R, I, P) of reactants, inhibitors, and products, where only qualitative regulatory relationships are encoded, not kinetic parameters. Each reaction is followed by a brief biological interpretation.

1. $a_1 = (\{LEP\}, \{T3\}, \{TRH\})$: TRH secretion at the hypothalamic level is modulated by metabolic signals and endocrine feedback. Leptin is modelled as a required reactant encoding a permissive signal of energy availability, while thyroid hormone (T3) exerts inhibitory feedback on TRH production. Consequently, TRH production is enabled when leptin levels are adequate and inhibitory feedback from T3 is weak. This reaction captures the integration of long-term energy status (via leptin) with negative endocrine feedback in the regulation of hypothalamic output.
2. $a_2 = (\{TRH\}, \{T3\}, \{TSH\})$: TSH secretion from the anterior pituitary requires stimulation by TRH and is inhibited by thyroid hormone feedback. Thus, TSH production occurs when TRH is present (hypothalamic stimulation), and inhibitory feedback from T3 is sufficiently weak. This reaction represents the pituitary integration step of the endocrine cascade.

3. $a_3 = (\{TSH\}, \varnothing, \{T3\})$: TSH stimulates the thyroid gland to produce thyroid hormones. In this simplified qualitative model, thyroid hormone production depends solely on the presence of TSH and is not subject to additional inhibition. This reaction represents the effector stage of the HPT axis, where pituitary output drives thyroid hormone synthesis.

The reactions have the following qualitative interpretation: adequate leptin levels provide a permissive signal for TRH production, while T3 exerts an inhibitory feedback on this process; TRH stimulates TSH secretion, subject to inhibition by T3; TSH stimulates thyroid hormone production.

Linguistic Labels and Fuzzy Operators: Each entity is associated with a measurable quantitative value (e.g. from blood samples). Since these quantities are expressed in different units and ranges, they are normalized to the unit interval $[0, 1]$, as the universe of discourse for presence levels. For each entity we adopt three linguistic labels: *Low*, *Normal*, and *High*, defined through standard triangular membership functions over a clinically relevant interval $[a, b]$. In the reactions, leptin is evaluated through the label *Normal*, while endocrine variables are evaluated through the label *High*.

$$L_{\text{Low}}(u) = \begin{cases} 1, & u \leq a, \\ \dfrac{b-u}{b-a}, & a < u < b, \\ 0, & u \geq b, \end{cases} \qquad L_{\text{High}}(u) = \begin{cases} 0, & u \leq a, \\ \dfrac{u-a}{b-a}, & a < u < b, \\ 1, & u \geq b. \end{cases}$$

Normal, on the other hand, is defined as a triangular membership function over the interval $[a, b]$, attaining its maximum at the midpoint $(a+b)/2$ and vanishing at the endpoints.

$$L_{\text{Normal}}(u) = \begin{cases} 0, & u \leq a \vee u \geq b \\ \dfrac{2(u-a)}{b-a}, & a < u < \frac{a+b}{2}, \\ \dfrac{2(b-u)}{b-a}, & \frac{a+b}{2} \leq u < b, \end{cases}$$

We adopt Gödel fuzzy operators $T = min$, $C = max$, $N(u) = 1 - u$.

Initial Graded State: we consider an initial graded state representing adequate energy reserves. Leptin is in the normal range, TRH and TSH are at basal levels, and thyroid hormone levels are low. Values are normalized in $[0, 1]$: $c_0(LEP) = 0.55$, $c_0(TRH) = 0.35$, $c_0(TSH) = 0.25$, $c_0(T3) = 0.25$.

One-Step M-FRS Update: we compute a discrete-time update $c_1 = \Phi(c_0)$.

- **Phase 1: Fuzzification.** We adopt the linguistic labels *Low*, *Normal*, and *High* with parameters $a = 0.25$ and $b = 0.75$. The value $\mu_{0,\text{Normal}}(LEP)$ has already been computed in Example 2 and is reported here for completeness.

$$L_{\text{Low}}(u) = \begin{cases} 1, & u \leq 0.25, \\ \dfrac{0.75 - u}{0.5}, & 0.25 < u < 0.75, \\ 0, & u \geq 0.75, \end{cases} \qquad L_{\text{High}}(u) = \begin{cases} 0, & u \leq 0.25, \\ \dfrac{u - 0.25}{0.5}, & 0.25 < u < 0.75, \\ 1, & u \geq 0.75, \end{cases}$$

$$L_{\text{Normal}}(u) = \begin{cases} 0, & u \leq 0.25 \vee u \geq 0.75, \\ \dfrac{2(u - 0.25)}{0.5}, & 0.25 < u < 0.5, \\ \dfrac{2(0.75 - u)}{0.5}, & 0.5 \leq u < 0.75, \end{cases}$$

Evaluating the membership degrees, leptin is interpreted through the linguistic label Normal, representing adequate energy availability:
$\mu_{0,\text{Normal}}(LEP) = \frac{2(0.75-0.55)}{0.5} = 0.8$, $\mu_{0,\text{High}}(TRH) = 0.2$, $\mu_{0,\text{High}}(TSH) = 0$, $\mu_{0,\text{High}}(T3) = 0$.

- **Phase 2: Rule evaluation.** For each reaction we compute the firing strength.

$$\rho_{a_1} = \min\big(\mu_{0,\text{Normal}}(LEP),\, 1 - \mu_{0,\text{High}}(T3)\big) = \min(0.8, 1) = 0.8$$

$$\rho_{a_2} = \min\big(\mu_{0,\text{High}}(TRH),\, 1 - \mu_{0,\text{High}}(T3)\big) = \min(0.2, 1) = 0.2 \qquad \rho_{a_3} = \mu_{0,\text{High}}(TSH) = 0.$$

- **Phase 3: Construction and Aggregation.** For each entity $x \in S$, let $A_x = \{a \in A \mid x \in P_a\}$ be the set of reactions producing x. The aggregated fuzzy output set for x at time $t+1$ is defined as $A_x^{t+1}(u) = C(\{T(\rho_a, L_{x,\ell_P}(u)) \mid a \in A_x\}), u \in [0,1]$, where T is the chosen t-norm (here $T = \min$), ρ_a is the firing strength of reaction a, and L_{x,ℓ_P} is the membership function associated with the product linguistic label. In the present case study we use the linguistic label $\ell_P = \text{High}$. Since each entity is produced by a single reaction, the aggregation reduces to the clipped consequent of that reaction:
TRH: a_1 has firing strength $\rho_{a_1} = 0.8$, therefore $A^1_{TRH}(u) = \min(0.8, L_{\text{High}}(u))$.
TSH: $A^1_{TSH}(u) = \min(0.2, L_{\text{High}}(u))$. $T3 : A^1_{T3}(u) = 0$.
- **Phase 4: Defuzzification.** The crisp concentration at time $t+1$ is obtained by centroid defuzzification: $c_1(TRH) \approx 0.713$, $c_1(TSH) \approx 0.649$, $c_1(T3) = 0$, $c_1(LEP) = 0.55$.
Please note that LEP level is kept constant as we assume that an external context maintains its value; we did not add the context rule to simplify this presentation. Thus, $c_1 = (0.55, 0.713, 0.649, 0)$. The above values are obtained by applying centroid defuzzification to the aggregated fuzzy sets.

Multi-step Evolution. The same four-stage fuzzy inference procedure is iteratively applied to obtain the trajectory of the system. At each step the crisp vector c_t is fuzzified, the reaction rules are evaluated, the fuzzy outputs are aggregated, and the resulting fuzzy sets are defuzzified. This defines a discrete-time dynamical system $c_{t+1} = \Phi(c_t)$. From $c_0 = (0.55, 0.35, 0.25, 0.25)$ we get:

$t = 0 : (0.55, 0.35, 0.25, 0.25)$, $t = 1 : (0.55, 0.713, 0.649, 0)$, $t = 2 : (0.55, 0.713, 0.724, 0.713)$
$t = 3 : (0.55, 0.634, 0.634, 0.725)$ $t = 4 : (0.55, 0.631, 0.631, 0.710)$ $t = 5 : (0.55, 0.635, 0.635, 0.709)$.

The evolution reflects a gradual activation of the HPT endocrine cascade driven by metabolic input. Initially, leptin provides moderate support to TRH production at the hypothalamic level. This stimulation propagates downstream, leading to a progressive increase in TSH secretion at the pituitary level. As TSH rises, thyroid hormone production is initiated, resulting in an increase in T3 levels. The accumulation of T3 introduces negative feedback on both TRH and TSH, reducing their activation strength over time and counterbalancing the upstream stimulation provided by leptin. As a consequence, the system converges toward a stable fixed point in which TRH, TSH, and T3 reach intermediate steady-state levels. This equilibrium reflects a balance between metabolic input, represented by leptin, and endocrine feedback regulation within the HPT axis.

We made a preliminary implementation[1] of the proposed M-FRS update operator in Python, with functions implementing the four phases of the Mamdani inference cycle. This implementation was used to compute the function giving one-step update, and for performing the iterations reported in this section.

Interpretation: This case study highlights some key properties of the M-FRS for the HPT axis:

- Endocrine cascades can be encoded through reactions with graded activation.
- Activation propagates gradually along the regulatory hierarchy (TRH $\rightarrow$ TSH $\rightarrow$ T3), yielding intermediate states rather than abrupt transitions.
- Negative feedback is captured continuously via fuzzy membership functions, with T3 progressively inhibiting upstream reactions.
- External inputs can be added: leptin acts as a permissive signal modulating TRH production.

This example shows that the resulting dynamics is not purely cascade-driven, but emerges from the balance between upstream stimulation and endocrine feedback within the HPT axis.

Dynamical Behaviour. The computed trajectories, see Fig. 2, show a gradual activation of the HPT axis driven by metabolic input and regulated by endocrine feedback. Starting from the initial graded state, leptin (LEP) provides a constant exogenous signal supporting TRH activation at the hypothalamic level. This activation propagates downstream, leading to an increase in TSH secretion and, subsequently, in T3 production. The evolution unfolds over multiple time steps, reflecting the graded nature of the fuzzy inference mechanism: activation

[1] Available in https://www3.diism.unisi.it/~falaschi/FRS/.

propagates along the cascade TRH → TSH → T3 through intermediate states. As T3 accumulates, its inhibitory effect progressively reduces the activation of upstream reactions, decreasing TRH and TSH levels. Thus, the system converges to a stable configuration in which all endocrine variables attain intermediate values, representing a balance between metabolic stimulation and hormonal negative feedback. LEP remains constant along the trajectory, as we assume that the external context keeps it constant.

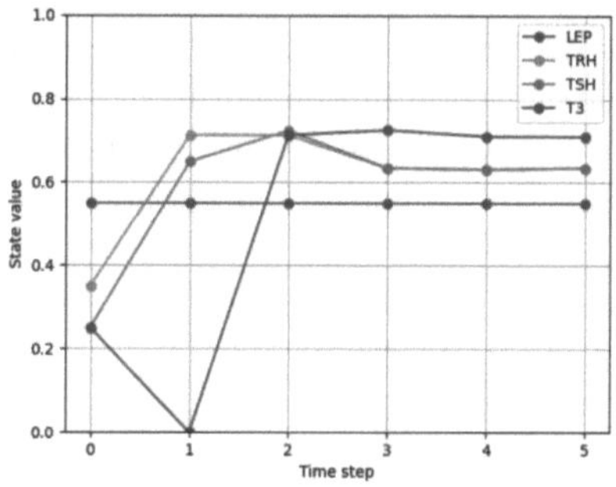

Fig. 2. Trajectories of the HPT axis case study.

7 Conclusions and Future Work

We have introduced M-FRS, a graded extension of RSs that preserves their qualitative reaction structure while enabling the modelling of continuous-valued biological quantities. Our framework integrates fuzzy inference with RSs, yielding a deterministic discrete-time dynamical system over a continuous state space. Our approach maintains the interpretability and compositionality of reaction-based models, while overcoming the limitations of boolean abstractions. In particular, it allows one to capture partial activation, graded inhibition, and smooth propagation of signals. The case study on the HPT axis illustrates how M-FRS can model endocrine cascades and feedback mechanisms in a compact and biologically meaningful way, producing stable dynamics that reflect the balance between metabolic input and hormonal regulation. M-FRS provides a rule-based semantic framework for modelling gradual activation and inhibition within a discrete-time setting. Investigating the expressive power of M-FRS with respect to other qualitative, fuzzy, and reaction-network modelling paradigms constitutes an important direction for future work.

Different choices of fuzzy logical operators may significantly influence the system dynamics. In this work we adopted Gödel operators (min, max, $1-u$), but alternative t–norms and t–conorms, such as product or Łukasiewicz operators, may lead to different graded enabling behaviours and stability properties and need a systematic comparison in the context of M-FRS. Our framework could be extended to alternative fuzzy inference paradigms. While Mamdani inference ensures interpretability and alignment with rule-based reasoning, other models such as Takagi–Sugeno systems could provide a more compact or computationally efficient representation, especially in larger-scale systems. The integration of data-driven approaches is a promising research direction. Learning membership functions or tuning linguistic partitions from experimental or clinical data would enhance the descriptive and predictive capabilities of the model, bridging the gap between qualitative reasoning and quantitative modelling. We also want to improve our preliminary Python implementation to make it more flexible and general. Finally, we want to investigate properties of M-FRS as a dynamical system, such as fixed points, stability, convergence, and sensitivity to perturbations.

Disclosure of Interests. The authors have no competing interests to declare that are relevant to the content of this article.

References

1. Alsharaiah, M.A., Samarasinghe, S., Kulasiri, D.: Proteins as fuzzy controllers: auto tuning a biological fuzzy inference system to predict protein dynamics in complex biological networks. Biosystems **224**, 104826 (2023). https://doi.org/10.1016/j.biosystems.2023.104826
2. Asaad Sajadi, N., Borzouei, S., Mahjub, H., Farhadian, M.: Diagnosis of hypothyroidism using a fuzzy rule-based expert system. Clin. Epidemiol. Glob. Health **7**(4), 519–524 (2019). https://doi.org/10.1016/j.cegh.2018.11.007
3. Azimi, S.: Steady states of constrained reaction systems. Theor. Comput. Sci. **701**(C), 20–26 (2017). https://doi.org/10.1016/j.tcs.2017.03.047
4. Azimi, S., Iancu, B., Petre, I.: Reaction system models for the heat shock response. Fund. Inform. **131**(3–4), 299–312 (2014). https://doi.org/10.3233/FI-2014-1016
5. Bottoni, P., Mitrana, V., Petre, I.: Multiset reaction systems. In: Jiménez López, M.D., Vaszil, G. (eds.) Languages of Cooperation and Communication: Essays Dedicated to Erzsébet Csuhaj-Varjú to Celebrate Her Scientific Career, pp. 179–193. Springer, Cham (2025). https://doi.org/10.1007/978-3-031-97274-4_11
6. Brijder, R., Ehrenfeucht, A., Main, M., Rozenberg, G.: A tour of reaction systems. Int. J. Found. Comput. Sci. **22**, 1499–1517 (2011). https://doi.org/10.1142/S0129054111008842
7. Brodo, L., Bruni, R., Falaschi, M.: Dynamic slicing of reaction systems based on assertions and monitors. In: Hanus, M., Inclezan, D. (eds.) Proceedings of Practical Aspects of Declarative Languages, PADL 2023. Lecture Notes in Computer Science, vol. 13880, pp. 107–124. Springer, Cham (2023). https://doi.org/10.1007/978-3-031-24841-2_8
8. Brodo, L., Bruni, R., Falaschi, M., Gori, R., Levi, F., Milazzo, P.: Exploiting modularity of SOS semantics to define quantitative extensions of reaction systems. In: Aranha, C., Martín-Vide, C., Vega-Rodríguez, M.A. (eds.) TPNC 2021. LNCS, vol. 13082, pp. 15–32. Springer, Cham (2021). https://doi.org/10.1007/978-3-030-90425-8_2

9. Brodo, L., et al.: Quantitative extensions of reaction systems based on SOS semantics. Neural Comput. Appl. **35**(9), 6335–6359 (2023). https://doi.org/10.1007/S00521-022-07935-6
10. Brodo, L., et al.: Causal analysis of positive reaction systems. Int. J. Softw. Tools Technol. Transfer **26**, 509–526 (2024). https://doi.org/10.1007/s10009-024-00757-y
11. Cordón, O.: A historical review of mamdani-type genetic fuzzy systems. In: Trillas, E., Bonissone, P.P., Magdalena, L., Kacprzyk, J. (eds.) Combining Experimentation and Theory: A Hommage to Abe Mamdani, pp. 73–90. Springer, Heidelberg (2012). https://doi.org/10.1007/978-3-642-24666-1_6
12. Corolli, L., Maj, C., Marini, F., Besozzi, D., Mauri, G.: An excursion in reaction systems: from computer science to biology. Theor. Comput. Sci. **454**, 95–108 (2012). https://doi.org/10.1016/j.tcs.2012.04.003
13. Ehrenfeucht, A., Rozenberg, G.: Reaction systems. Fund. Inform. **76**, 1–18 (2006). https://doi.org/10.3233/FUN-2007-751-415
14. Ehrenfeucht, A., Main, M.G., Rozenberg, G.: Combinatorics of life and death for reaction systems. Int. J. Found. Comput. Sci. **21**(3), 345–356 (2010). https://doi.org/10.1142/S0129054110007295
15. Ehrenfeucht, A., Main, M.G., Rozenberg, G.: Functions defined by reaction systems. Int. J. Found. Comput. Sci. **22**(1), 167–178 (2011). https://doi.org/10.1142/S0129054111007927
16. Feldt-Rasmussen, U., Effraimidis, G., Klose, M.: The hypothalamus-pituitary-thyroid (HPT)-axis and its role in physiology and pathophysiology of other hypothalamus-pituitary functions. Mol. Cell. Endocrinol. **525**, 111173 (2021). https://doi.org/10.1016/j.mce.2021.111173
17. Jin, Y., Wang, L.: Fuzzy Systems in Bioinformatics and Computational Biology. Studies in Fuzziness and Soft Computing, vol. 242. Springer (2009). https://doi.org/10.1007/978-3-540-89968-6
18. Kim, M., et al.: The central melanocortin system affects the hypothalamo-pituitary thyroid axis and may mediate the effect of leptin. J. Clin. Investig. **105**(7), 1005–1011 (2000). https://doi.org/10.1172/JCI8857
19. Klir, G.J., Yuan, B.: Fuzzy Sets and Fuzzy Logic: Theory and Applications. Prentice Hall (1995). https://doi.org/10.1021/ci950144a
20. Kosko, B.: Neural Networks and Fuzzy Systems: A Dynamical Systems Approach to Machine Intelligence. Prentice Hall (1992)
21. Mamdani, E.H., Assilian, S.: An experiment in linguistic synthesis with a fuzzy logic controller. Int. J. Man Mach. Stud. **7**(1), 1–13 (1975). https://doi.org/10.1016/S0020-7373(75)80002-2
22. Manzoni, L.: Fuzzy reaction systems. Oral presentation. In: 4th International Workshop on Reaction Systems, Pisa, Italy (2024)
23. Mitrana, V., Paun, M., Petre, I., Prelipcean, A.M.: Quantitative reaction systems. In: 2025 5th International Conference on Innovative Research in Applied Science, Engineering and Technology (IRASET), pp. 1–6. IEEE (2025). https://doi.org/10.1109/IRASET64571.2025.11008263
24. Okubo, F., Yokomori, T.: The computational capability of chemical reaction automata. Nat. Comput. **15**(2), 215–224 (2015). https://doi.org/10.1007/s11047-015-9504-7
25. Ramya, M., Kavitha, A.R.: Mamdani fuzzy inference system based on multi-textural biomarkers for Alzheimer's stage detection. Comput. Methods Biomech. Biomed. Eng. Imaging Vis. **14**(1), 2439278 (2026). https://doi.org/10.1080/21681163.2024.2439278

26. Ross, T.J.: Fuzzy Logic with Engineering Applications. Wiley (2010). https://doi.org/10.1002/9781119994374
27. Takagi, T., Sugeno, M.: Fuzzy identification of systems and its applications to modeling and control. IEEE Trans. Syst. Man Cybern. **15**(1), 116–132 (1985). https://doi.org/10.1109/TSMC.1985.6313399
28. Zadeh, L.A.: Fuzzy Sets, vol. 8. Information and Control (1965). https://doi.org/10.1016/S0019-9958(65)90241-X

Incremental KaSa: Static Analysis of Kappa Models at Edit Time

Rebecca Ghidini and Jérôme Feret(✉)

DI ENS, École Normale Supérieure, PSL, CNRS, INRIA, Paris, France
{rebecca.ghidini,jerome.feret}@info.ens.psl.eu

Abstract. Kappa offers a modeling environment to describe, simulate, and reason about rule-based models. It has been used to model protein-protein interaction networks, especially models of signaling pathways. Kappa comes with a static analyzer, KaSa, to assist the modeler and assess the consistency of the models. Although efficient, KaSa is sometimes too slow to reason while modifying large models or when editing models within the user interface. Here, we propose an incremental version that updates the result of the current analysis at each model modification.

Our approach relies on the use of an abstraction of the relationships between the rules of the model and the properties that they induce. Partial evaluation is used when some rules are removed, to exclude the results that derive from the removed rules. Adding rules is done classically by resuming the iterations of the analysis algorithm. This incremental analysis is available on the command-line or as an electron app, and it is evaluated on examples from the literature.

Keywords: Rule-based modeling · Static analysis · Formal methods

1 Introduction

Kappa is a rule-based modeling language. In Kappa, rules describe the potential interactions (binding/activation) between agent (often protein) instances, which hence gain new capabilities of interactions. Kappa has been used to model signaling pathways (EGFR [10], yeast [18], TGF [19]), self-assembling models (Wnt [15]), epidemic models (COVID [20]), and cell population models (liver cells [4]).

Writing a model may be error-prone. Before simulating, explaining, or reducing a model, one must first determine whether the Kappa model matches what the modeler intended. Static analysis tools, such as KaSa, assist the modeler in this task by detecting modeling flaws. KaSa [5,11,14] infers structural properties about the configurations of protein instances and how they can be connected to each other. It focuses on three kinds of properties: The first one are relations between the states of different sites, either sites that lay on the same protein instance or on two bound instances. E.g., it may infer that when a certain site is bound, then another site is always phosphorylated. It also examines whether a

P. T. Monteiro (Ed.): CMSB 2026, LNBI 16678, pp. 143–151, 2027.
https://doi.org/10.1007/978-3-032-30870-2_8

given protein that has two outgoing bounds is bound twice to the same instance or rather to two different protein instances (e.g., see our case study in Sect. 2). Additionally, it can detect rules that can never be triggered. To derive these properties, KaSa proves that some patterns of interests cannot arise in any execution of the model. It does so by computing a conservative abstraction of all reachable protein complexes. Such an abstraction is necessary because finding all reachable complexes is undecidable in Kappa, as can be shown by reduction to the halting problem in two-counter machines.

In this paper, we present an incremental version of KaSa, in which the analysis result is dynamically updated when rules are inserted, removed, or modified, or when the initial state is changed. As modelers typically work on a small part of the model at a time, we focus on changes in the currently considered submodel. This enables an efficient analysis update, such that the user can get the analysis result on the fly, after each modification of this submodel. Our approach relies on an abstraction of the relationships between the elements of the submodel (rules and initial ingredients) and the properties that they induce. Partial evaluation is used when some rules or initial ingredients are removed. The iterations of the analysis are resumed when rules or initial ingredients are inserted. Modifications are considered as an insertion after a removal.

Our method is mainly based on three elements. 1. The model is separated into small chapters, and the incremental analysis supports only modifications in the current chapter. Changing the current chapter requires more computation time. This is acceptable, since it corresponds to opening a file. 2. KaSa iteratively computes the least solution of a set of Horn clauses. Hence, when new elements are inserted, the iterations are resumed to cope with the added Horn clauses. 3. Based on [13], the analysis computes a symbolic representation based on binary decision diagrams [7,8] of all the results of the analysis for each subset of the elements in the current chapter. This permits the extraction of the analysis result when an element is discarded, without having to revert the effect of the removed Horn clauses.

Our analysis is integrated both in the Kappa graphical interface [6] and in an interactive command-line interface (version 5.0 or later). Executables, guides, and examples are provided in the supplementary information [12].

Related Work. Formal methods have been used to ease the simulation of models, explain their behavior, and reduce their complexity. This paper focuses on static analysis as a method to assist the modeler in the assembling of a model.

Our approach is based on updating the least solution of a dynamic set of Horn clauses, which is equivalent to the reachability problem in dynamic directed hypergraphs. In [1,2,16], this problem is addressed by computing and maintaining the information on the shortest proof for each provable goal [1,2,16]. In contrast, our approach focuses on modifications within a subset, offering a trade-off between which parts of the model can be updated and the cost overhead for computing and maintaining the information for updating the analysis result.

Incremental analysis is also used in model checking: Counter-example guided abstraction refinement splits program executions to ease the proof of their tem-

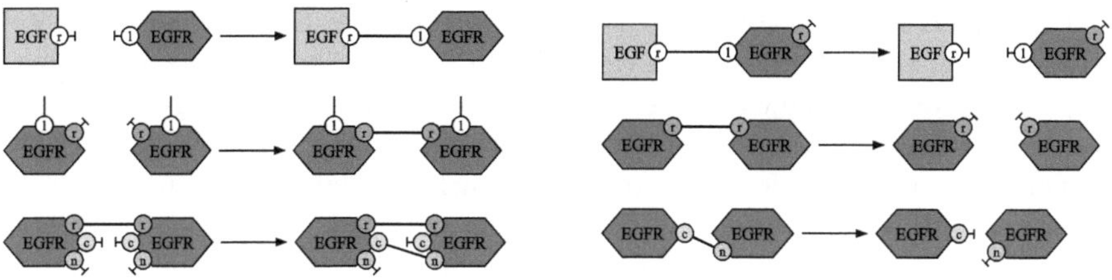

Fig. 1. Some Kappa rules modeling the formation (left column) and the dissociation (right column) of a double bond between two instances of a membrane receptor.

poral specification in each subcase. In [17], the subcase partitioning is updated incrementally when the target program is modified. Differential bisimulations can also be computed by gradually incorporating each differential equation [3]. Note that in this paper, we consider both rule insertion and rule removal, which is out of reach for their approach.

Paper Outline. The paper is organized as follows. A typical use case of incremental analysis for Kappa is given in Sect. 2. Our method for incremental analysis is briefly explained in Sect. 3. The graphic user interface and the command-line tools are described in Sect. 4. Performance is assessed in Sect. 5. More benchmarks are provided in the supplementary information [12].

2 Use Case

We illustrate a typical usage of our incremental analyzer: A modeler is revising a part of a larger model that describes the behavior of membrane receptors for the epidermal growth factor (EGF).

Two types of protein are concerned: Ligand instances (EGF) are represented by colored blue circles and receptor instances (EGFR) are green hexagons. Each receptor instance has four binding sites: one in white (site `l`) to connect with ligand instances, one in blue (site `r`) to bind at the same site of other receptor instances, and the third one in yellow (site `c`) to bind to the fourth one in pink (site `n`) of other receptor instances. The binding rules are depicted in the left column of Fig. 1. From top to bottom, ligand instances bind to the receptor instances to activate them. The activated receptor instances then pairwise bind with a symmetric bond. Lastly, a non-symmetric bond is formed to distinguish the role of the two receptor instances in dimer instances.

A key property in this model part is that it is impossible to chain three receptor instances. To assess this property, the modeler introduces the following fictitious rule:

He expects the analyzer to detect that this rule can never be applied (which is exactly the case).

The modeler then considers rules to break the links between protein instances, e.g. the column on the right in Fig. 1. A ligand instance disconnects from a receptor instance when the blue site of the latter is free. All other sites in receptor instances may be freed without conditions. Yet, with these new rules, the fictitious rule is no longer detected unreachable: either the analysis is not precise enough, or this property is no longer satisfied. The modeler uses the incremental analyzer to check the result of the analysis when one of the four unbinding rules is discarded. In this way, the property of interest is recovered when the second rule is discarded. The modeler replaces it with the following one:

The analysis still alerts that the fictitious rule is unreachable. This proves that the expected property is satisfied in the corrected model.

3 Incremental Analysis

In this section, we briefly describe our incremental analysis.

It is based on a non-incremental analysis [5,11,14]: an abstract interpretation [9] that detects some unreachable patterns. Such patterns cannot occur in any potential execution of the model. Our goal is to incrementally update the result of this analysis when some rules or some initial ingredients are inserted, removed, or modified. Inserting new elements can be performed by resuming the analysis iterations, and so taking into account the patterns that are now reachable or that the analysis cannot prove unreachable due to the approximation.

Removing elements is usually the bottleneck of incremental analyses, because it requires backtracking the analysis to reason about what had been deduced thanks to those elements. This typically relies on data structures that are costly to maintain. Our approach eliminates the need for backtracking, since all necessary computations are performed during initialization. The method is based on an analysis of parametric models [13]. In this analysis, it is possible to condition the presence of a rule or of an initial ingredient to the value of a Boolean parameter. The original static analysis is extended to compute a symbolic representation of the relationships between the Boolean parameter valuations and the analysis output. It is then easy to remove an element that has a corresponding Boolean parameter, just by setting the value of this parameter to false and evaluating the result of the analysis with this additional information.

In order to master the time and memory overhead, we do not assign a Boolean parameter to each rule and each initial ingredient. Following the motivation of the use case (e.g. see in Sect. 2), we instead let the user define the part of the model they are currently focusing on. We call it the *current chapter*. When a rule or an initial ingredient is inserted into the model, it is assigned a Boolean parameter and is then considered to be in the current chapter. Any removal or modification outside the current chapter requires relaunching the whole analysis. Obviously, the size of the current chapter impacts the performance of the analysis, which is evaluated on some examples in Sect. 5.

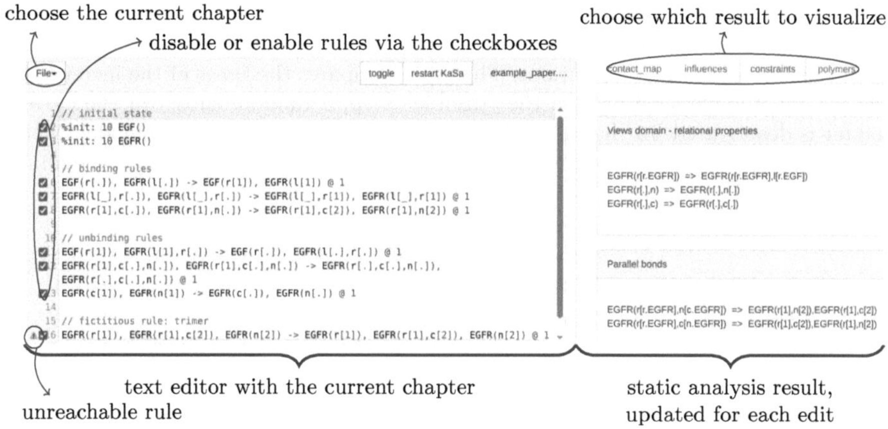

Fig. 2. Screenshot of the incremental KaSa tool with descriptions for each component.

Depending on the choice of the tool distribution, the selection of the current chapter may be implicitly performed by the file system or fine-tuned by means of user annotations. We refer to Sect. 4 for more details about it.

4 Tool Description

The tool is available as a graphical user interface (GUI) in the form of a web application and in command-line. It is written in OCaml. The user interface is compiled via `js_of_ocaml`. The code is available on GitHub (https://github.com/Kappa-Dev/KappaTools) (version 5.0 or later of the Kappa software Suite).

4.1 Web Application

The main features of the web application are described in [6]. We focus here on the use of the incremental analysis. In the GUI, incremental analysis is switched on by default, but it can be switched off in the "Preferences".

Figure 2 shows a screenshot of the web application containing the example model from Sect. 2. The GUI consists of a text editor and the analysis results. A model can be organized into several files. The current chapter is then implicitly defined as the content of the currently opened file. When a model is loaded or a new file is chosen, the reachability analysis is initialized with a Boolean parameter for each rule and each initial ingredient in the current file.

The analysis result is visualized on the right of the text editor, in multiple tabs. The tab "contact map" visualizes all possible bindings between different protein types, while the "influences" tab shows the influences of each rule on other rules, i.e., which rules may form complexes that match with the left-hand side of another rule. The "constraints" tab infers a set of properties about the potential patterns that may occur in the reachable states, such as relationships between sites of a protein or the sites of two bound proteins, and the presence

Table 1. Evaluation results on a Mac Book Pro with an Apple M4 max chip and 48 GB of memory. For each run, 10 rules were randomly chosen as the current chapter. The runtime is the mean of 10 repetitions. The table compares the times of the incremental analysis and the classical one. In the "disable" step, a random subset of the current chapter is deactivated. In the "adding" step, a new rule is added to the model. Model sizes are given in number of rules (each rule being a scheme for a set of reactions).

Model	Nr. of rules	non-incremental	incremental		
		analysis	initial analysis	disable rules	add a rule
`tgf_v19`	96	0.0772	0.116	0.0128	0.0381
`tgf_20180419`	291	0.2	0.227	0.00479	0.0868
`wnt_20151228`	355	0.895	1.02	0.0655	0.364
`wnt_20170322`	1469	3.54	3.86	0.0125	1.59
`korkut_20170113`	3915	3.22	3.24	0.0737	0.119
`korkut_20170206`	5749	13.4	13.5	0.2	1.18

of double bonds. The last tab ("polymers") informs the user if the model can form polymers of arbitrary length. KaSa also detects dead rules, i.e., rules that can never be applied because their left-hand side can never be formed in this particular model. When dead rules are found, warnings appear in the text editor.

Initially, the value of each Boolean parameter is set to 'true', i.e., all rules are enabled. This value can be modified by means of checkboxes, and the result of the analysis is updated accordingly. The user can therefore temporarily disable a rule to test its influences on the output, and then re-enable it efficiently. Elements can also be freshly added to the text editor, or fully deleted. KaSa then detects the change and updates the analysis result incrementally.

4.2 Command-Line Tool

The command-line tool offers more control on the part of the model that can be modified without having to restart the whole analysis. Its input is made up of some Kappa files. The current chapter can be specified by wrapping the chosen elements in the directive `%working_set:[...]`, or by adding a command-line option (`---current-chapter`) listing the files that represent the current chapter.

When the tool is launched, it performs the initial analysis and then prints the analysis result as text. Next, it is possible to enable or disable some elements of the current chapter or to update a file and to print the analysis result for the updated version of the model. The update is rejected when an element outside the current chapter is removed or modified.

5 Evaluation

Now, we assess the overhead induced by computing the information required for incremental updates, and the speedup obtained during model alterations.

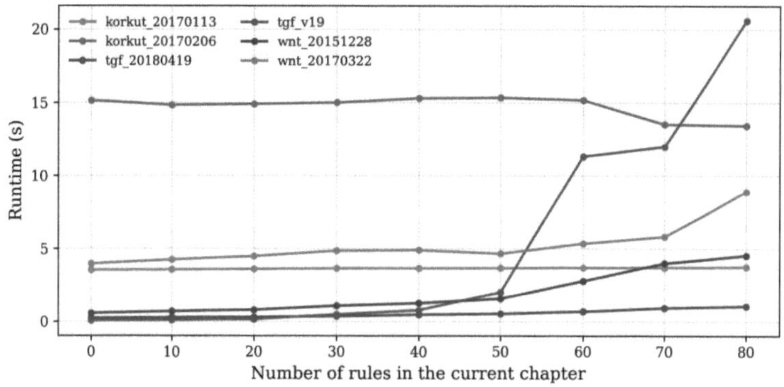

Fig. 3. Runtimes on a Mac Book Pro with an M4 max chip and 48 GB of memory of the initial static analysis for the six models, with different chapter sizes. Each plot denotes the mean of the runtimes of 10 repetitions.

We tested the analysis on under-construction versions of models, since the goal is to assist the modeling process. We consider two intermediary versions of a model of the TGF pathway [19], two intermediary versions of a first model of the Wnt signaling pathway and two intermediary versions of a second model of the Wnt signaling pathway, that we call "korkut" [15]. The considered TGF model was fully handwritten by human inspection of the literature. The first Wnt model was generated manually with the help of scripts. The korkut model was developed in two steps: large versions of the model were automatically assembled from the literature, before being carefully curated by hand with the help of analysis tools. We have chosen early versions in this curation process, which explains the large number of rules compared to the final model version described in [15]. Models are provided in the supplementary information [12].

For each version of each model, we chose 10 random rules as the current chapter. Then, we measured the runtime of computing the initial analysis, of deactivating a random subset of the current chapter, and of adding a new rule. We compared the runtimes with the ones of the non-incremental analysis. The results are shown in Table 1. We observe that the initial run of the incremental static analysis is slightly costlier than the non-incremental one (for 10 rules in the current chapter). Deactivating and reactivating the rules is always computed in much less than a second in each considered model. This is therefore considerably faster than recomputing the analysis from the beginning. The cost of adding a rule is smaller than half of the cost of the non-incremental analysis for the smaller models, but the benefit is more important for the larger ones.

Now we investigate the impact of the current chapter size on the runtime of the analysis initialization. The results are shown in Fig. 3. For the biggest model (korkut, 5749 rules), the analysis time is up to 15 s almost independently of the size of the current chapter. For the 19th version of the TGF model, the computation time strongly depends on the size of the current chapter. It takes 0.07 s with an empty current chapter and 20.6 s in average with initial chapters of 80 rules. It is worth noting that both models exhibit a very different causal profile: In the second version of the korkut model, the causality is mostly flat, whereas the 19th version of the TGF pathway exhibits long causal chains. Additionally, the computation time is sometimes deeply impacted by the random selection of the current chapter, which explains the decreasing at the end of the plot in the second version of the korkut model.

6 Conclusion

We have presented an incremental version of the Kappa static analyzer, KaSa. The modeler can now select the part of the model that they want to work with, and the analyzer then dynamically updates the result when this part is modified. To achieve this, the analyzer maintains an implicit description of the analysis result for each subpart of this modifiable part of the model. Element removals are processed directly by requesting the corresponding result. Element insertions are done by resuming the iterations of the analysis. The tool is available as a web application or in the command-line [12].

Our approach offers a trade-off between the size of the editable subpart and the overhead cost for computing and maintaining the additional information.

References

1. Ausiello, G., Franciosa, P.G., Frigioni, D.: Directed hypergraphs: problems, algorithmic results, and a novel decremental approach. In: Theoretical Computer Science. ICTCS 2001. LNCS, vol. 2202, pp. 312–328. Springer, Berlin, Heidelberg (2001). https://doi.org/10.1007/3-540-45446-2_20
2. Ausiello, G., Franciosa, P.G., Frigioni, D., Giaccio, R.: Decremental maintenance of reachability in hypergraphs and minimum models of horn formulae. In: Leong, H.W., Imai, H., Jain, S. (eds.) ISAAC 1997. LNCS, vol. 1350, pp. 122–131. Springer, Heidelberg (1997). https://doi.org/10.1007/3-540-63890-3_14
3. Bacci, G., Bacci, G., Larsen, K.G., Tribastone, M., Tschaikowski, M., Vandin, A.: Efficient local computation of differential bisimulations via coupling and up-to methods. In: 36th Annual ACM/IEEE Symposium on Logic in Computer Science, LICS 2021, Rome, Italy, June 29 - July 2, 2021, pp. 1–14. IEEE (2021). https://doi.org/10.1109/LICS52264.2021.9470555
4. Bouguéon, M., et al.: A rule-based multiscale model of hepatic stellate cell plasticity: critical role of the inactivation loop in fibrosis progression. PLoS Comput. Biol. **20**(7), 1011858 (2024). https://doi.org/10.1371/JOURNAL.PCBI.1011858
5. Boutillier, P., et al.: KaSa: a static analyzer for kappa. In: Češka, M., Šafránek, D. (eds.) CMSB 2018. LNCS, vol. 11095, pp. 285–291. Springer, Cham (2018). https://doi.org/10.1007/978-3-319-99429-1_17
6. Boutillier, P., et al.: The kappa platform for rule-based modeling. Bioinform. **34**(13), i583–i592 (2018). https://doi.org/10.1093/BIOINFORMATICS/BTY272
7. Bryant, R.E.: Graph-based algorithms for boolean function manipulation. IEEE Trans. Comput. **35**, 677–691 (1986)
8. Clarke, E.M., McMillan, K.L., Zhao, X., Fujita, M., Yang, J.C.: Spectral transforms for large boolean functions with applications to technology mapping. Form. Methods Syst. Des. **10**(2/3), 137–148 (1997). https://doi.org/10.1023/A:1008695706493

9. Cousot, P., Cousot, R.: Systematic design of program analysis frameworks. In: Aho, A.V., Zilles, S.N., Rosen, B.K. (eds.) Conference Record of the Sixth Annual ACM Symposium on Principles of Programming Languages, San Antonio, Texas, USA, January 1979, pp. 269–282. ACM Press (1979). https://doi.org/10.1145/567752.567778
10. Danos, V., Feret, J., Fontana, W., Harmer, R., Krivine, J.: Rule-based modelling of cellular signalling. In: Caires, L., Vasconcelos, V.T. (eds.) CONCUR 2007 - Concurrency Theory, 18th International Conference, CONCUR 2007, Lisbon, Portugal, September 3-8, 2007, Proceedings. LNCS, vol. 4703, pp. 17–41. Springer, Cham (2007). https://doi.org/10.1007/978-3-540-74407-8_3
11. Danos, V., Feret, J., Fontana, W., Krivine, J.: Abstract interpretation of cellular signalling networks. In: Logozzo, F., Peled, D.A., Zuck, L.D. (eds.) Verification, Model Checking, and Abstract Interpretation. VMCAI 2008. LNCS, vol. 4905, pp. 83–97. Springer, Berlin, Heidelberg (2008). https://doi.org/10.1007/978-3-540-78163-9_11
12. Feret, J., Ghidini, R.: Supplementary information. http://www.di.ens.fr/~feret/Incremental-KaSa-tool-paper/
13. Feret, J., Ghidini, R.: Reachability analysis for parametric rule-based models. In: Fages, F., Pérès, S. (eds.) Computational Methods in Systems Biology. CMSB 2025. LNCS, vol. 15959, pp. 153–173. Springer, Cham (2025). https://doi.org/10.1007/978-3-032-01436-8_9
14. Feret, J., Lý, K.Q.: Reachability analysis via orthogonal sets of patterns. In: Sanguinetti, G., Safránek, D. (eds.) Proceedings of SASB 2018, the 7th International Workshop on Static Analysis and Systems Biology, University of Edinburgh, September 7, 2016. Electronic Notes in Theoretical Computer Science, vol. 335, pp. 27–48. Elsevier (2018). https://doi.org/10.1016/J.ENTCS.2018.03.007
15. Gyori, B., Bachman, J., Subramanian, K., Muhlich, J., Galescu, L., Sorger, P.: From word models to executable models of signaling networks using automated assembly. Mol. Syst. Biol. **13** (2017)
16. Ramalingam, G., Reps, T.: An incremental algorithm for a generalization of the shortest-path problem. J. Algorithms **21**(2), 267–305 (1996). https://doi.org/10.1006/jagm.1996.0046
17. Rothenberg, B., Dietsch, D., Heizmann, M.: Incremental verification using trace abstraction. In: Podelski, A. (ed.) Static Analysis. SAS 2018. LNCS, vol. 11002, pp. 364–382 Springer, Cham (2018). https://doi.org/10.1007/978-3-319-99725-4_22
18. Suderman, R., Deeds, E.J.: Machines vs. ensembles: effective MAPK signaling through heterogeneous sets of protein complexes. PLoS Comput. Biol. **9**(10) (2013). https://doi.org/10.1371/JOURNAL.PCBI.1003278
19. Théret, N., Feret, J., Hodgkinson, A., Boutillier, P., Vignet, P., Radulescu, O.: Integrative models for tgf-β signaling and extracellular matrix. In: Ricard-Blum, S. (ed.) Extracellular Matrix Omics. Biology of Extracellular Matrix, vol. 7, pp. 209–225. Springer, Cham (2020). https://doi.org/10.1007/978-3-030-58330-9_10
20. Waites, W., et al.: Compositional modelling of immune response and virus transmission dynamics. Philos. Trans. R. Soc. A: Math. Phys. Eng. Sci. **380**(2233), 20210307 (2022). https://doi.org/10.1098/rsta.2021.0307

Constraint-Based Modeling and Molecular Computation

Inferring Minimal Culture Media Using Biologically Constrained Combinatorial Optimization

Moana Aulagner(✉), Samuel Blanquart, and Anne Siegel

Univ Rennes, Inria, CNRS, IRISA UMR 6074, Rennes, France
moana.aulagner@inria.fr

Abstract. Inferring culture media that enable specific metabolic functions is a challenging problem due to the vast combinatorial search space induced by all the possible subsets of compounds and reactions within a metabolic network. Existing scalable approaches based on flux optimization or combinatorial enumeration do not integrate prior biological knowledge to tailor the media to the cell physiological context. We introduce a method that solves culture media inference constrained by biological observation and knowledge as a combinatorial optimization problem, implemented using Answer Set Programming (ASP). This method combines four heuristics that progressively restrict the search space toward biologically supported solutions: (i) identify the target synthesis subnetwork achieving target compounds production, (ii) compute the parsimonious network merging the minimal reaction sets contextualized with the provided constraints, (iii) enumerate minimal media from this reduced search space, and (iv) detect and filter out the self activating internal compounds from the solution space, required for algorithmic reasons but not informative as environmental inputs. We evaluate this approach on different genome-scale metabolic networks and test varying biological constraints and heuristic combinations to assess the method's scalability. This method provides a knowledge-driven and scalable enumeration of minimal culture media, combining logical reasoning, minimality optimizations, as well as knowledge and topology-based constraints to address the combinatorial complexity of the reverse ecology problem.

Keywords: Answer set programming · Culture medium inference · Metabolic networks · Context-specific metabolism · Network expansion

1 Introduction

Reverse ecology aims to infer the minimal or most plausible environmental inputs that enable specific metabolic functions [9,11,15]. When modeled on genome-scale metabolic networks (GSMNs), this problem amounts to identifying subsets of compounds that allow the production of target metabolites. GSMNs typically involve 1,000 to 2,000 metabolites [8] and the search space grows exponentially with the number of candidate metabolites, in the unrestricted case, making exhaustive enumeration of minimal media challenging [12].

P. T. Monteiro (Ed.): CMSB 2026, LNBI 16678, pp. 155–177, 2027.
https://doi.org/10.1007/978-3-032-30870-2_9

Flux Balance Analysis (FBA) approaches formulate culture media inference as a linear or mixed-integer optimization problem [14] to identify minimal nutrient sets satisfying growth or production objectives (*e.g.*, using [4]). In this framework, RIPTiDe [10] contextualizes flux distributions by integrating transcriptomic data to better align GSMN predictions with biological observations. It weights reaction fluxes by transcript abundances, highlighting active GSMN pathways under specific physiological conditions. Likely culture media can be post processed from exchange fluxes inferred by RIPTiDe [18]. While effective, these methods are parameter-sensitive, rely on well-curated models, and typically return a limited number of solutions without exhaustively exploring the space. Graph-based algorithms can enumerate minimal media for small networks [1], but do not scale to large GSMNs with thousands of reactions. Combinatorial approaches based on network expansion (NE) [3] enable enumeration of candidate media as *seed* sets ensuring target reachability. Seeds represent the initial compounds available to the system, *i.e.*, the culture medium, from which metabolic response is discretely simulated [2], defining the *scope* of reachable metabolites. A valid seed set therefore ensures that targeted compounds belong to the resulting scope. The Seed2LP approach [7] combines qualitative discrete reasoning with quantitative FBA to infer candidate culture media from GSMNs. Unlike traditional FBA methods, Seed2LP frames medium inference as a combinatorial optimization problem based on the NE framework, enabling exploration of multiple valid qualitative solutions. However, this leads to a combinatorial explosion of the solution space. To address this, Seed2LP heuristically samples candidate media, generating a limited subset of solutions for subsequent FBA evaluation within a reasonable timeframe.

We introduce MEDORA, a knowledge-constrained combinatorial framework for culture media inference based on Answer Set Programming (ASP). Inspired by the contextualization of metabolic networks using a single type of biological data introduced in [10], MEDORA integrates multiple biological constraints on both compounds and reactions, derived from prior knowledge and experimental observations directly into the enumeration process. In contrast to Seed2LP, which samples the solution space without biological contextualization, MEDORA exhaustively enumerates minimal media using four optimization strategies reducing the combinatorial complexity while improving the biological consistency of the predicted culture media. In this work, we present these heuristics, the types of biological data used for contextualization, and the performance of the method on four metabolic networks of varying sizes.

2 Background

This section introduces MEDORA's formal framework for inferring minimal context-specific culture media (MCSCM) from GSMNs, covering ASP for optimization, Boolean simulation via the NE algorithm, and the concepts of *restricted scope* and *target synthesis networks* to contextualize metabolic subnetworks and media according to biological information.

The Answer-Set Programming Formalism. MEDORA is implemented using Answer-Set Programming (ASP) as its core solving method [19]. ASP is a declarative programming paradigm for solving combinatorial optimization problems. The ASP solver Clingo [6] implements Boolean constraints and check constraint satisfiability. This approach enables subset-minimal or cardinal minimal optimization. An ASP program consists of atoms (the knowledge base) and rules that define choices and constraints. Optimization statements allow selecting minimal or maximal solutions. ASP is particularly suitable for metabolic reasoning because it allows combining logical constraints, reachability conditions, and multi-objective optimization [5,16,17,20].

Modeling Metabolic Networks with Hypergraph Structures. A *metabolic network (MN)* $\mathbf{N} = (\mathbf{M}, \mathbf{R})$ is a directed hypergraph, where the set of nodes $\mathbf{M}$ corresponds to compounds and the set of hyperedges $\mathbf{R}$ corresponds to reactions. Each reaction $r \in \mathbf{R}$ connects a set of input compounds $\text{reactant}(r) \subseteq \mathbf{M}$ to a set of output compounds $\text{product}(r) \subseteq \mathbf{M}$. The compounds in $\text{reactant}(r)$ are called *reactants* of r, and those in $\text{product}(r)$ are called *products* of r. Let $r^+, r^- \in \mathbf{R}$ be two reactions such that $\text{product}(r^+) = \text{reactant}(r^-)$ and $\text{product}(r^-) = \text{reactant}(r^+)$. The reactions r^+ and r^- then define the forward and backward directions of a *reversible* reaction. MEDORA generates ASP facts encoding the directed hypergraph of a metabolic network from user-provided SBML files.

Estimating Producible Compounds According to a Subnetwork of the Metabolic Network. The NE algorithm approximates metabolism activity as a recursive traversal of a MN starting from a set of available compounds [3]. In this work we use a refined version of the NE algorithm in order to apply it specifically on relevant parts of the whole MN. For any predetermined subnetwork $\overline{\mathbf{R}} \subset \mathbf{R}$, and any set of compounds $\mathbf{S} \subseteq \mathbf{M}$, the *scope of* $\mathbf{S}$ *restricted to* $\overline{\mathbf{R}}$ represents the set of all compounds (respectively, reactions) that can be produced (respectively, activated) from $\mathbf{S}$ through a recursive sequence of reactions within the considered subnetwork $\overline{\mathbf{R}}$. Two complementary projections of the scope can be considered, $\text{Scope}_{\mathbf{M}}(\mathbf{S}, \overline{\mathbf{R}})$ which denotes the set of metabolites producible from $\mathbf{S}$, and $\text{Scope}_{\mathbf{R}}(\mathbf{S}, \overline{\mathbf{R}})$ which denotes the set of reactions activated during the expansion process. They are formally defined in Eq. (1).

$$
\begin{aligned}
&\text{Scope}_{\mathbf{M}}(\mathbf{S}, \overline{\mathbf{R}}) = \bigcup_{i=0}^{k} \mathbf{M}_i \qquad \text{Scope}_{\mathbf{R}}(\mathbf{S}, \overline{\mathbf{R}}) = \bigcup_{i=1}^{k} \mathbf{R}_i \\
&\qquad\qquad \mathbf{M}_0 = \mathbf{S} \\
&\text{with} \qquad \mathbf{R}_{i+1} = \{r \in \overline{\mathbf{R}} \mid \text{reactant(r)} \subseteq \mathbf{M}_i\} \quad \forall i \geq 0 \\
&\qquad\qquad \mathbf{M}_i = \text{product}(\mathbf{R}_i)\, \forall i \geq 1 \quad \text{and } \mathbf{M}_{k+1} = \mathbf{M}_k.
\end{aligned}
\tag{1}
$$

Backtracking Reactions and Compounds Involved in Targets Synthesis. Let $\overline{\mathbf{R}} \subseteq \mathbf{R}$ be a subnetwork and $\mathbf{T} \subseteq \mathbf{M}$ a set of targeted compounds. The *target synthesis network of* $\mathbf{T}$ *constrained to* $\overline{\mathbf{R}}$, denoted by $\text{SynthNet}(\mathbf{T}, \overline{\mathbf{R}})$, is the pair $(\mathbf{M}_{syn}, \mathbf{R}_{syn})$ consisting of the set of compounds $\mathbf{M}_{syn} \subseteq \mathbf{M}$ and the set of reactions $\mathbf{R}_{syn} \subseteq \overline{\mathbf{R}}$ that can contribute, directly or indirectly, to the production of at least one compound in $\mathbf{T}$. It is formally defined in Eq. (2). Figure 1 (step I) shows a small MN and an example of target synthesis network for compound T, including all compounds and reactions enabling T's synthesis. The recursive calculation of both the scope (Eq. (1)) and target synthesis network (Eq. (2)) are encoded using two constraints in ASP, sufficient to model recursivity and initiation constraints (see Listing 1.1).

$$\begin{aligned}
&\text{SynthNet}(\mathbf{T},\overline{\mathbf{R}}) = \left(\text{SynthNet}_{\mathbf{M}}(\mathbf{T},\overline{\mathbf{R}}), \text{SynthNet}_{\mathbf{R}}(\mathbf{T},\overline{\mathbf{R}})\right)\\
&\text{with} \quad \text{SynthNet}_{\mathbf{R}}(\mathbf{T},\overline{\mathbf{R}}) = \bigcup_{i=1}^{k} \mathbf{P}_i \qquad \text{SynthNet}_{\mathbf{M}}(\mathbf{T},\overline{\mathbf{R}}) = \bigcup_{i=1}^{k} \mathbf{M}_i \\
&\qquad\quad \mathbf{P}_1 = \{r \in \overline{\mathbf{R}} \mid \text{product}(r) \cap \mathbf{T} \neq \emptyset\}\\
&\text{and} \quad \mathbf{M}_i = \textstyle\bigcup_{r \in \mathbf{P}_i} \left(\text{reactant}(r) \cup \text{product}(r)\right) \quad \forall i \geq 0\\
&\qquad\quad \mathbf{P}_{i+1} = \{r \in \overline{\mathbf{R}} \mid \text{product}(r) \cap \mathbf{M}_i \neq \emptyset\}\, \forall i \geq 1 \quad \text{and } \mathbf{P}_{k+1} = \mathbf{P}_k.
\end{aligned} \tag{2}$$

Listing 1.1. Simplified ASP encoding for constrained scope and target synthesis network: predicate `seed/1` defines initial seed compounds, while predicate `subnetwork/1` specifies subnetwork constraints. This encoding structure is reused across encodings for different seed sets and subnetworks.

```
%Constrained scope computation : initiation with seed and recursive network expansion constrained by the subnetwork
   scope_M(S) :- seed(S).
   scope_M(S) :- product(S,Rw), subnetwork(Rw), scope_M(S2) : reactant(S2,Rw).
   scope_R(Rw) :- subnetwork(Rw), scope_R(S) : reactant(S,Rw).
%Constrained Target Synthesis Network computation: initiation and recursive backward network expansion with conjunctive rules
   synth_net(S1,Rw,R,S2) :- reactant(S1,Rw), product(S2,Rw), reaction(Rw,R), reaction_producing_target(Rw), subnetwork(Rw).
   synth_net(S1,Rw,R,S2) :- reactant(S1,Rw), product(S2,Rw), synth_net(S2,Rw2,R2,S3), reaction(Rw,R), subnetwork(Rw).
```

3 Contextualizing Media Inference with Biological Data

The goal of MEDORA is to infer the composition of *minimal context-specific culture media* (MCSCM) that enable the production of targeted compounds while integrating experimental data and prior biological knowledge. Those additional biological constraints lead to the definition of *context-specific metabolic networks*, defined as subnetworks (i) able to produce the targeted compounds according to the MN topology (ii) restricted to minimal sets of reactions consistent with the biological observations, and (iii) activated by a minimal set of medium compounds also consistent with these observations. This section presents how MEDORA encodes the inference of MCSCM as a sequence of ASP optimization tasks. We define the input biological data, compute the *parsimonious network* (minimal reaction sets satisfying constraints), and derive minimal media - each defining a context-specific MN activated via NE. Figure 1 (steps II–III) illustrates these concepts.

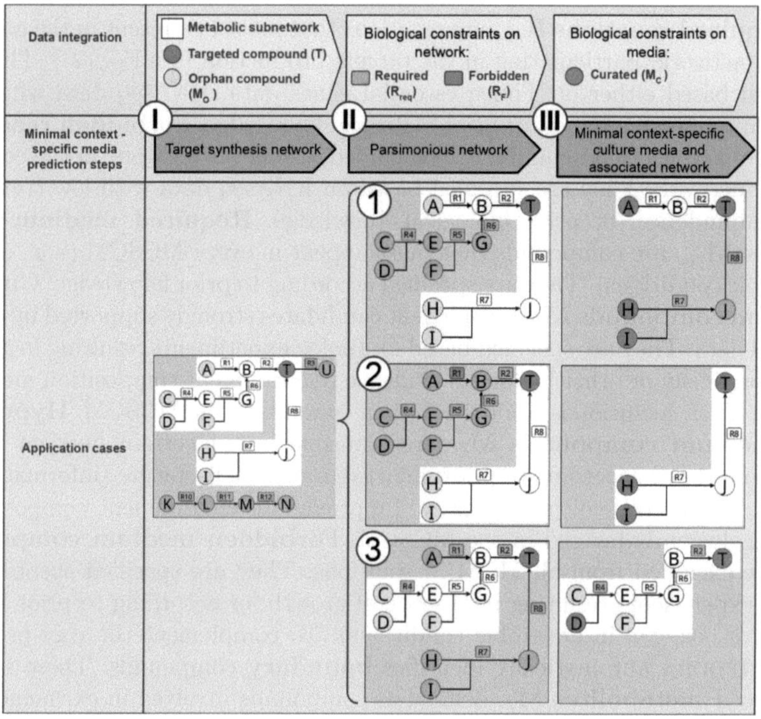

Fig. 1. Three successive optimization steps under varying biological constraints, with each computed subnetwork highlighted in white. **I. Target synthesis network** determination from the MN and target compounds. **II. Parsimonious network** computation, integrating reaction constraints for three cases: *no constraint*, *forbidden reaction* (`R1`), and *required reactions* (`R2`, `R4`). **III. Minimal context-specific culture media** (MCSCM) computation, involving curated compounds (`A`, `D`, `H`, `I`). The putative media are (`A`), (`H`, `I`), and (`C`, `D`, `F`) for cases 1, 2, and 3, respectively.

3.1 Biological Constraints in Media Inference

To achieve the computation of MCSCM, the method first takes as input a MN $\mathbf{N} = (\mathbf{M}, \mathbf{R})$ and second a set of *targeted compounds*, $\mathbf{T} \subseteq \mathbf{M}$. Targeted compounds are expected to belong to the scope of the inferred culture media. They are specified according to biomass composition for instance but can also include any targeted compound of biological interest (*e.g.*, secondary metabolites). Third, MEDORA can integrate as input several types of biological constraints, modeled by a parameter **BiolParam**, converted in ASP facts by MEDORA to serve as constraints for the MCSCM problem. The MN in SBML format and the target compounds **T** are the only required inputs; all other data are optional.

$$\mathbf{BiolParam} = (\mathbf{R}_{req}, \mathbf{R}_F, \mathbf{M}_{req}, \mathbf{M}_C, \mathbf{M}_H, \mathbf{M}_F) \tag{3}$$

Required reactions $\mathbf{R}_{req}$ are reactions that must be present in the context-specific network, participating in the targets production (see Eq. (2)). They are specified based either on TnSeq essential genes data, RNAseq data with high transcriptomic abundance, or prior biological knowledge. **Forbidden reactions $\mathbf{R}_F$** are reactions that should not be included, whenever possible, in the context-specific network. They are specified based on RNAseq data with low transcriptomic abundance, or prior biological knowledge. **Required medium compounds $\mathbf{M}_{req}$** are compounds that must appear in every MCSCM (*e.g.*, oxygen in aerobic conditions). They are specified according to prior knowledge. **Curated medium compounds $\mathbf{M}_C$** are nutrient candidates strongly supported by experimental data. They are specified based on Biolog experiments resulting in growth of the organism or other biological evidence (environment composition measurements). Their inclusion is prioritized when computing the MCSCM. **Hypothetical medium compounds $\mathbf{M}_H$** are plausible but uncertain nutrient candidates considered according to prior knowledge such as literature (information on similar strains) or ecological context (approximate environment composition). Their inclusion is favored in the MCSCM. **Forbidden medium compounds $\mathbf{M}_F$** are excluded from all MCSCM solutions. They are specified according to Biolog experiments resulting in absence of growth, or according to prior knowledge (*e.g.*, oxygen in anaerobic conditions). To complement the user-provided data, MEDORA automatically identifies **boundary** compounds. These include **imported metabolites $\mathbf{M}_I$**, defined as compounds involved in exchange reactions - reversible reactions with no product - and **orphan compounds $\mathbf{M}_O$**, defined as compounds that are consumed but never produced by any reaction in the MN. Their computation is detailed in Listing 1.4 of Appendix 2. Both can be included as candidate medium compounds.

The candidate medium compounds are prioritized in the following order: $\mathbf{M}_{req} > \mathbf{M}_C > \mathbf{M}_H > \mathbf{M}_I > \mathbf{M}_O$. The imported compounds refer to those automatically inferred by MEDORA and can be reclassified by the user as any other higher category to increase their impact on the resulting media composition.

3.2 Parsimonious Network

Admissible Synthesis Networks. These networks encompass all reaction sets consistent with biological evidence and MN topology. Given a MN $\mathbf{N} = (\mathbf{M}, \mathbf{R})$ and a set of target compounds $\mathbf{T}$, a set of reactions $\mathbf{R}_{adm}$ is called an admissible network for targets synthesis if it satisfies the six following conditions, formalized in Eq. (4) and encoded in ASP in Listing 1.2.

i All reactions of $\mathbf{R}_{adm}$ belong to the synthesis network SynthNet$(\mathbf{T}, \mathbf{R})$ of $\mathbf{T}$.
ii The admissible synthesis network $\mathbf{R}_{adm}$ contains all reactions which import or consume a candidate compound in $\mathbf{Med}_{cand}$, that is, required, curated, hypothetical nutrients, and boundary metabolites: $\mathbf{Med}_{cand} = \mathbf{M}_{req} \cup \mathbf{M}_C \cup \mathbf{M}_H \cup \mathbf{M}_I \cup \mathbf{M}_O$.
iii Both instances of a reversible reaction cannot simultaneously belong to $\mathbf{R}_{adm}$.

iv When restricting the network to $\mathbf{R}_{adm}$, the targets $\mathbf{T}$ are producible from the set of candidate media $\mathbf{Med}_{cand}$.
v All required reactions $\mathbf{R}_{req}$ belonging to the synthesis network SynthNet $(\mathbf{T}, \mathbf{R})$ also belong to the admissible synthesis network of $\mathbf{T}$, restricted to $\mathbf{R}_{adm}$.
vi For any reaction in the synthesis network SynthNet$(\mathbf{T}, \mathbf{R})$, if this reaction has at least one $\mathbf{M}_{req}$ as reactant, then it must belong to the synthesis network of T restricted to $\mathbf{R}_{adm}$.

$$\text{IsAdmissibleSynthesisNetwork}(\mathbf{M}, \mathbf{R}, \mathbf{T}, \mathbf{R}_{adm}) = 1 \text{ iff} \tag{4}$$
$$\begin{cases} \text{(i)} & \mathbf{R}_{adm} \subseteq \text{SynthNet}(\mathbf{T}, \mathbf{R}) \\ \text{(ii)} & \{r \in \text{SynthNet}_{\mathbf{R}}(\mathbf{T}, \mathbf{R}) \mid \text{reactant}(r) \cap \mathbf{Med}_{cand} \neq \emptyset\} \subseteq \mathbf{R}_{adm} \\ & \qquad \text{with } \mathbf{Med}_{cand} = \mathbf{M}_{req} \cup \mathbf{M}_C \cup \mathbf{M}_H \cup \mathbf{M}_I \cup \mathbf{M}_O \\ \text{(iii)} & r \in \mathbf{R}_{adm}, r^- \notin \mathbf{R}_{adm} \text{where } r^- \text{ is the symmetric reaction of } r \\ \text{(iv)} & \mathbf{T} \subseteq \text{Scope}_{\mathbf{M}}(\mathbf{Med}_{cand}, \mathbf{R}_{adm}) \\ \text{(v)} & \mathbf{R}_{req} \cap \text{SynthNet}_{\mathbf{R}}(\mathbf{T}, \mathbf{R}) \subseteq \text{SynthNet}(\mathbf{T}, \mathbf{R}_{adm}) \\ \text{(vi)} & \{r \in \text{SynthNet}_{\mathbf{R}}(\mathbf{T}, \mathbf{R}) \mid \text{reactant}(r) \cap \mathbf{M}_{req} \neq \emptyset\} \\ & \qquad \subseteq \text{SynthNet}_{\mathbf{R}}(\mathbf{T}, \mathbf{R}_{adm}) \end{cases}$$

Parsimonious Network. The parsimonious network contextualized by user-provided candidate media compounds, required reactions, and forbidden reaction is the union of all minimal admissible synthesis networks, determined by two minimization criteria: minimizing forbidden reactions and minimizing reactions unrelated to target production. It thus summarizes all minimal reaction combinations consistent with the user's input data (Eq. (5) and Eq. (6)).

$$\text{ParsimoniousNetworkFamily}(\mathbf{R}, \mathbf{T}, \mathbf{R}_{req}, \mathbf{R}_F, \mathbf{Med}_{cand}) =$$
$$\underset{\substack{\mathbf{R}_{adm} \subseteq \mathbf{R} \mid \\ \text{IsAdmissibleSynthesis} \\ \text{Network}(\mathbf{M}, \mathbf{R}, \mathbf{T}, \mathbf{R}_{adm}) = 1}}{\arg\min} \begin{pmatrix} \text{size}(\mathbf{R}_F \cap \mathbf{R}_{adm}), \\ \text{size}(\mathbf{R}_{adm} \setminus \{r \in \mathbf{R}_{adm} \mid \text{product}(r) \cap \mathbf{T} \neq \emptyset\}) \end{pmatrix} \tag{5}$$

$$\text{ParsNetwork}(\mathbf{R}, \mathbf{T}, \mathbf{R}_{req}, \mathbf{R}_F, \mathbf{Med}_{cand}) = \bigcup_{\substack{\mathbf{R}_{min} \in \text{ParsimoniousNetworkFamily} \\ (\mathbf{R}, \mathbf{T}, \mathbf{R}_{req}, \mathbf{R}_F, \mathbf{Med}_{cand})}} \mathbf{R}_{min} \tag{6}$$

Figure 1 (step II) illustrates the computation of parsimonious networks - defined as the union of admissible synthesis networks - for three constraint cases: *no constraint* (Case 1), selecting two admissible networks ((`A`,`B`,`T`); (`R1`,`R2`)) and ((`H`,`I`,`J`,`T`); (`R7`,`R8`)); *one forbidden reaction* (`R1`, Case 2), selecting only ((`H`,`I`,`J`,`T`); (`R7`,`R8`)); and *two required reactions* (`R2`, `R4`, Case 3), yielding the parsimonious network ((B,C,D,E,F,G,T); (R2,R4,R5,R6)). Figure 2 in Appendix 1 details the successive steps involved in the computation of the parsimonious network.

ASP Encoding. Listing 1.2 (lines L1–7) defines the solution space of admissible synthesis networks and two associated integrity constraints. Line L1 defines the target synthesis network, identifying metabolites S and reactions R involved in producing the targeted compounds (Eq. (2)). Reversible reactions are represented bidirectionally, differentiated by R_w. The search space is restricted to reactions and compounds within the target synthesis network (L3), satisfying Eq. (4)(i). Integrity constraints ensure that reactions consuming candidate media compounds are included in the admissible set (L5), and that both directions (R_{w1} and R_{w2}) of the same reaction R cannot be selected simultaneously (L7), enforcing conditions (ii) and (iii) of Eq. (4).

The second part encodes the recursive constraints of Eq. (4)(iv)/(v)/(vi) on the admissible network topology. Medium compounds in the admissible network are identified (L9–10) to compute its restricted scope (L11), which must reach all targeted compounds (L13), enforcing Eq. (4)(iv). The restricted target synthesis network (L14) must include all required reactions (L16) or those involving at least one required reactant (L17), enforcing Eq. (4)(v) and Eq. (4)(vi).

The third part (L18–25) defines the search for parsimonious networks among admissible candidates. Forbidden reactions are identified (L19), along with admissible reactions not directly contributing to target production (L21). Two optimization criteria exclude non-minimal networks: the first (24) minimizes forbidden reactions with highest priority, while the second (L25) minimizes non-target-producing reactions as in Eq. (5). Finally, Eq. (6) is enforced directly using the Clingo command option `-enum-mode=brave`, which computes the union of all solutions.

Listing 1.2. ASP encoding of admissible and parsimonious synthesis networks

```
1  %[Define synth_net_target(S1,Rw,R,S2)] Replicate Listing 1.1 (Lines 6-7) and
   substitute reaction(Rw,R) to subnetwork(Rw).
2  %Selection of an admissible subset of the target synthesis network
3     { adm(S1,Rw,R,S2) : synth_net_target(S1,Rw,R,S2) }.
4  %Reaction consuming nutrients must be in admissible synthesis network
5     :- reaction_consum_nutrient(Rw), not adm(_,Rw,_,_).
6  %Two reverse reactions cannot belong to the admissible network
7     :- adm(_,Rw1,R,_), adm(_,Rw2,R,_), Rw1!=Rw2.
8  %Identify the medium compounds in the admissible network to compute scope_adm
9     med_adm(S) :- med_cand(S), adm(S,_,_,_), not target(S), not_forb_med(S).
10    med_adm(S) :- med_cand(S), adm(_,_,_,S), not target(S), not_forb_med(S).
11 %[Define scope_adm_M(S)]. Replicate Listing 1.1(Lines 2-3) and substitute
   med_adm(S) to seed(S) and  adm(_,Rw,_,_) to subnetwork(Rw) .
12 %scope_adm_M contains all producible targeted compounds.
13    :- prod_target(S), not scope_adm_M(S).
14 %[Define synth_net_target_adm(S1,Rw,R,S2)] Replicate Listing 1.1 (Lines 6-7)
   and substitute adm(_,Rw,_,_) to subnetwork(Rw).
15 %The admissible SynthNet must contain all required reactions and reactions
   with a required reactant.
16       :- req_reaction_synth_net(R), not synth_net_target_adm(_,_,R,_).
17       :- req_reactant_synth_net(Rw), not synth_net_target_adm(_,Rw,_,_).
18 % Excludes admissible networks not minimal in forbidden reaction
19    forb_adm(R) :- forb(R), adm(_,_,R,_).
```

```
% Excludes admissible networks not minimal in reactions not producing targets
  non_producing_target(Rw) :- adm(_,Rw,R,_), not produce_target(R).

% optimization
  #minimize {1@2,R:forb_adm(R)}.
  #minimize {1@1,R:non_producing_target(R)}.
```

3.3 Minimal Context-Specific Culture Media (MCSCM)

The specification of MCSCM holds in two steps. First, we identify an admissible culture media. Then among all admissible ones, we identify the minimal through a four steps minimization taking into account user data. This algorithm returns MCSCM that are both topologically valid and consistent with user data. It also returns the MCSCM's associated networks.

Admissible Culture Medium. Let $\mathbf{Med}_{adm} \subset \mathbf{M}$ be a subset of metabolic compounds. We define $\mathbf{R}_{med}$ to be the set of reactions activated from $\mathbf{Med}_{adm}$ within the parsimonious network $\text{ParsNetwork}(\mathbf{R}, \mathbf{T}, \mathbf{R}_{req}, \mathbf{R}_F, \mathbf{Med}_{cand})$

$$\mathbf{R}_{med} = \text{Scope}_{\mathbf{R}}(\mathbf{Med}_{adm}, \text{ParsNetwork}(\mathbf{R}, \mathbf{T}, \mathbf{R}_{req}, \mathbf{R}_F, \mathbf{Med}_{cand})).$$

The set of metabolites $\mathbf{Med}_{adm}$ is said to be an *admissible culture medium* when the three following constraints hold. They are formally defined in Eq. (7) and encoded in the ASP listing 1.3.

i The set $\mathbf{Med}_{adm}$ is a subset of the candidate medium compounds set, contains all required medium compounds $\mathbf{M}_{req}$ and excludes forbidden medium compounds $\mathbf{M}_F$.
ii All targeted compounds $\mathbf{T}$ are producible by at least one reaction in $\mathbf{R}_{med}$, *i.e.*, they belong to the products of $\mathbf{R}_{med}$.
iii All required in $\mathbf{M}_{req}$ and $\mathbf{R}_{req}$ belonging to the target synthesis network $\text{SynthNet}(\mathbf{T}, \mathbf{R})$ also belong to the admissible synthesis network of $\mathbf{T}$, restricted to $\mathbf{R}_{med}$.

$$\text{IsAdmissibleMedium}(\mathbf{M}, \mathbf{R}, \mathbf{T}, \mathbf{BiolParam}, \mathbf{Med}_{adm}) = 1 \tag{7}$$
$$\Leftrightarrow \begin{cases} \text{(i)} & \mathbf{M}_{req} \subseteq \mathbf{Med}_{adm} \subseteq \mathbf{Med}_{cand} \setminus \mathbf{M}_F \\ \text{(ii)} & \mathbf{T} \subseteq \bigcup_{r \in \mathbf{R}_{med}} \text{product}(r) \\ \text{(iii)} & (\mathbf{M}_{req}, \mathbf{R}_{req}) \cap \text{SynthNet}(\mathbf{T}, \mathbf{R}) \subseteq \text{SynthNet}(\mathbf{T}, \mathbf{R}_{med}) \end{cases}$$
$$\text{with } \mathbf{R}_{med} = \text{Scope}_{\mathbf{R}}(\mathbf{Med}_{adm}, \text{ParsNetwork}(\mathbf{R}, \mathbf{T}, \mathbf{R}_{req}, \mathbf{R}_F, \mathbf{Med}_{cand}))$$
$$\text{and } \mathbf{BiolParam} = (\mathbf{R}_{req}, \mathbf{R}_F, \mathbf{M}_{req}, \mathbf{M}_F, \mathbf{M}_C, \mathbf{M}_H)$$

Context-Specific Optimal Media. Optimal media $\mathbf{Med}_{opt}$ are admissible media $\mathbf{Med}_{adm}$ that are minimal with respect to four successive minimization criteria, which prioritize the exclusion of non-required and non-curated compounds:

i minimization of the number of medium compounds outside the sets of required compounds $\mathbf{M}_{req}$, and user-defined compounds $\mathbf{M}_C$ and $\mathbf{M}_H$;
ii minimization of the number of non-required compounds, when required compounds $\mathbf{M}_{req}$ are specified;
iii minimization of the number of compounds outside the curated set $\mathbf{M}_C$;
iv minimization of the total number of compounds in the considered medium.

$$\mathbf{Med}_{opt}(\mathbf{M}, \mathbf{R}, \mathbf{T}, \mathbf{BiolParam}) = \underset{\substack{\mathbf{Med}_{adm} \subseteq \mathbf{M} | \\ \text{IsAdmissibleMedium}(\mathbf{M}, \\ \mathbf{R}, \mathbf{T}, \mathbf{BiolParam}, \mathbf{Med}_{adm}) = 1}}{\arg\min} \begin{pmatrix} \text{size}\left(\mathbf{Med}_{adm} \setminus (\mathbf{M}_{req} \cup \mathbf{M}_C \cup \mathbf{M}_H)\right), \\ \text{size}\left(\mathbf{Med}_{adm} \setminus \mathbf{M}_{req}\right) \text{ if } \mathbf{M}_{req} \neq \emptyset, \\ \text{size}\left(\mathbf{Med}_{adm} \setminus \mathbf{M}_C\right), \\ \text{size}\left(\mathbf{Med}_{adm}\right) \end{pmatrix} \quad (8)$$

$\mathbf{Med}_{opt}(\mathbf{M}, \mathbf{R}, \mathbf{T}, \mathbf{BiolParam})$ is the family of minimal context-specific culture media (MCSCM). Figure 1 (step III) illustrates the MCSCMs derived from three parsimonious network examples: Case 1 selects (A) - smaller than (H, I) - activating the subnetwork ((A,B,T);(R1,R2)). Case 2 identifies (H,I) as the sole minimal medium, activating subnetwork ((H,I,J,T);(R7,R8)). Case 3 reaches required reactions R2, R4 and target T via a minimal medium (C,D,F) - two curated compounds and one orphan - activating subnetwork ((B,C,D,E,F,G,T);(R2,R4,R5,R6)).

Listing 1.3. ASP Encoding of Admissible and Minimal Context-Specific Media

```
% [Include Listing 1.2]
% Selection of a candidate medium within the parsimonious network
   { med_adm_pars(S) : med_cand_pars(S), not forb_med(S)}.
% Required medium compounds must be included
   :- req_med_synth_net(S), not med_adm_pars(S).
% [Generate pars_network] execute Listing 1.2 with the Clingo command option
  -enum-mode=brave and encode the output as pars_network
% [Define scope_adm_M_pars(S) & scope_adm_R_pars(Rw)]. Duplicate Listing 1.1(
  L2-4) replacing seed(S) with med_adm_pars(S) & subnetwork(Rw) with
  pars_network(Rw)
% scope_adm_M_pars contains all producible targeted compounds.
   :- target(S), not scope_adm_M_pars(S).
% [Define synth_net_target_adm_pars(S1,Rw,R,S2)] Duplicate Listing 1.1(L6-7)
  replacing subnetwork(Rw) with scope_adm_R_pars(Rw).
% Include all required reactions and compounds
   :- req_reaction_synth_net(R), not synth_net_target_adm_pars(_,_,R,_).
   :- med_req_synth_net(S), not synth_net_target_adm_pars(S,_,_,_).
% Compounds outside required / curated / hypothetical sets
   outside_bio_data(S) :- med_adm_pars(S), not med_req_syn_net(S), not
  curated(S), not hypothetical(S).
% Compounds outside required set
   outside_required(S) :- med_adm_pars(S), not med_req_syn_net(S).
% Compounds outside curated set
   outside_curated_only(S) :- med_adm_pars(S), not curated(S).

%Optimization priorities
    #minimize {1@4,S:outside_bio_data(S)}.
```

```
23    #minimize {1@3,S:outside_required(S), has_required }.
24    #minimize {1@2,S:outside_curated_only(S)}.
25    #minimize {1@1,S:med_adm_pars(S)}.
```

ASP Encoding. Listing 1.3 defines the solution space of admissible culture media and their integrity constraints (L1-6) as in Eq. (7)(i). The search space (L3) selects medium compounds compatible with the parsimonious network and not user-forbidden, while L6 ensures all required medium compounds are included (integrity constraint). The second part (L7-13) encodes recursive constraints: the scope is computed from the selected medium and restricted to the parsimonious network (L7), must reach all targeted compounds (L9) as in Eq. (7)(ii). The restricted target synthesis network (L10) must retain all required compounds and reactions (L12–13) as in Eq. (7)(iii). The third part (L14-25) defines the search for MCSCM (Eq. (8)). Medium compounds are classified based on user data (L15-19). Optimization criteria prioritize minimizing non-user-supported (L22), non-required (L23), non-curated (L24) and total medium compounds (L25).

3.4 Heuristics for Computing and Enumerating of Optimal Media

Unlike Flux Balance Analysis (FBA), the NE algorithm requires a predefined set of initial compounds to propagate producibility recursively. For compounds in cyclic reaction chains, activation is paradoxical: they must be consumed to be produced, and produced to be consumed. If omitted from the initial set, essential internal pathways may remain inactive, leading to incomplete or infeasible models. To address this, MEDORA introduces a preprocessing step to identify Self-Activated Internal Compounds (SAICs)–compounds necessary for their own reachability. While algorithmically essential, SAICs do not always correspond to real environmental inputs. MEDORA simplifies this by assuming SAICs are always present in candidate media, reducing complexity without biological justification (see Appendix 2, Fig. 4 for details).

Enriching the Set of Medium Candidates with Self-Activated Internal Compounds (SAIC). We define the set of *primers* $\mathbf{P} \subset \mathbf{M}$ as the union of all minimal scope-initiating sets that maximize the reachability of the NE algorithm Eq. (9). Similarly, we compute the set of *reverse primers* $\mathbf{P}_{rev} \subset \mathbf{M}$ by applying the backward NE, or *reverse scope* (see Appendix), as shown in Eq. (10). Unlike the forward scope, the reverse scope propagates network expansion backward, maximizing the reachability of upstream compounds. Because it relies on conjunctive formulae, it is more restrictive than Target Synthesis Network (Eq. (2)), which uses disjunctive formulae.

$$\mathcal{P} = \arg\max_{\mathbf{A} \subset \mathbf{M}}(\,\text{size}(\text{Scope}_{\mathbf{M}}(\mathbf{A}, \mathbf{R}) \setminus \mathbf{A})\,) \qquad \mathbf{P} = \bigcup_{\mathbf{A} \in \mathcal{P}} \mathbf{A} \tag{9}$$

$$\mathcal{P}_{rev} = \arg\max_{\mathbf{B} \subset \mathbf{M}}(\,\text{size}(\text{RevScope}_{\mathbf{M}}(\mathbf{B}, \mathbf{R}) \setminus \mathbf{B}))\} \qquad \mathbf{P}_{rev} = \bigcup_{\mathbf{B} \in \mathcal{P}_{rev}} \mathbf{B}\,) \tag{10}$$

Self-Activated Internal Compounds (SAICs) are defined as the intersection of forward and reverse primers (Eq. (11)). This computation is implemented as an ASP optimization problem (Listing 1.4, See Appendix).

$$\mathbf{M}_{SAIC} = \mathbf{P} \cap \mathbf{P}_{rev} \tag{11}$$

As illustrated in Fig. 3 (Appendix 2), activation sets $A \in \mathcal{P}$ comprise both boundary compounds (orphans and imported compounds) and SAICs: boundary compounds initiate metabolic pathways, enabling maximal downstream production, whereas SAICs prevent premature termination of scope expansion. Thus, maximizing NE reachability inherently accounts for both components. This intuition is supported by the three properties presented (proofs provided in Appendix 2).

$$\forall\, \mathbf{A} \in \mathcal{P}, \quad \forall m \in \mathbf{A} \text{ then } m \notin \text{Scope}(\mathbf{A} \setminus \{m\}) \tag{12}$$

$$\forall\, \mathbf{B} \in \mathcal{P}_{rev}, \quad \forall m \in \mathbf{B} \text{ then } m \notin \text{RevScope}(\mathbf{B} \setminus \{m\}) \tag{13}$$

$$\forall\, m \in \mathbf{M}_{SAIC}, \exists r_1, r_2 \in \mathbf{R} \;\; \text{s.t} \;\; m \in \mathit{reactant}(r_1) \cap \mathit{product}(r_2) \tag{14}$$

According to Eq. (12), primers include all compounds that are essential for maximal NE expansion: removing any primer from the set reduces the scope (and similarly for reverse primers according to Eq. (13)). Property (14) states that SAICs are internal compounds, distinct from boundary entry points ($\mathbf{P} \backslash \mathbf{M}_{SAIC}$) which include the orphans $\mathbf{M}_O$ and imported compounds $\mathbf{M}_I$. SAICs also differ from upstream compounds ($\mathbf{P}_{rev} \setminus \mathbf{M}_{SAIC}$), some of which are dead-ends.

Reducing Combinatorial Complexity via SAICs Masking. While SAICs are computationally essential, they inflate solution counts due to combinatorial redundancy arising from alternative SAIC combinations (Fig. 4). To address this, we assume all SAICs are present in every candidate medium and exclude them from the reported solutions. This masking eliminates algorithmically driven combinations, thereby highlighting biologically relevant compounds.

In the ASP encoding, masking is implemented by modifying the optimization constraints (Eq. (7)(i)): the admissible medium $\mathbf{Med}_{adm}$ excludes $\mathbf{M}_{SAIC}$, while the Scope is initialized by both $\mathbf{Med}_{adm}$ and $\mathbf{M}_{SAIC}$.

Three Heuristics for Computing Minimal Media According to Biological Knowledge.

- **Media computation based on user-defined biological data**. This is computed by applying the ASP encoding from Listings 1.1, 1.2 and 1.3. Therefore, the candidate medium set is the one defined in Eq. (4)

$$\mathbf{Med}_{cand} = \mathbf{M}_{req} \cup \mathbf{M}_C \cup \mathbf{M}_H \cup \mathbf{M}_I \cup \mathbf{M}_O.$$

- **Media computation based on user-defined biological data and SAIC without masking**. This computation extends the ASP encodings in Listings 1.1, 1.2, 1.3, 1.4 by modifying Listing 1.3 to include SAICs in the candidate medium set in the constraints associated with Eq. (4).

$$\mathbf{Med}_{cand} = \mathbf{M}_{SAIC} \cup \mathbf{M}_{req} \cup \mathbf{M}_C \cup \mathbf{M}_H \cup \mathbf{M}_I \cup \mathbf{M}_O \quad \text{in Eq.(4)(ii)}$$

- **Media computation based on user-defined biological data and SAIC with masking.** This computation uses modified versions of the ASP encodings in Listings 1.1, 1.2, 1.3, 1.4, by introducing masking constraints to modify Eqs. (4) and (7) (see modifications in Appendix 2).

$$\begin{aligned} \mathbf{Med}_{cand} &= \mathbf{M}_{SAIC} \cup \mathbf{M}_{req} \cup \mathbf{M}_C \cup \mathbf{M}_H \cup \mathbf{M}_I \cup \mathbf{M}_O && \text{in Eq.(4)(ii)} \\ \mathbf{M}_{req} &\subseteq \mathbf{Med}_{adm} \subseteq \mathbf{Med}_{cand} \setminus (\mathbf{M}_F \cup \mathbf{M}_{SAIC}) && \text{in Eq.(7)(i)} \\ \mathbf{R}_{med} &= \text{Scope}_{\mathbf{R}}((\mathbf{Med}_{adm} \cup \mathbf{M}_{SAIC}), \\ &\qquad \text{ParsNetwork}(\mathbf{R}, \mathbf{T}, \mathbf{R}_{req}, \mathbf{R}_F, \mathbf{Med}_{cand})) && \text{in Eq.(7)(ii)} \end{aligned}$$

4 Experiments

Experimental Design. Experiments were conducted on four genome-scale metabolic networks: three *E. coli* models from the BiGG database (`e_coli_core`: 72 metabolites, 95 reactions; `IJO1366`: 1,805 metabolites, 2,583 reactions; `IML1515`: 1,877 metabolites, 2,712 reactions) and one *R. leguminosarum* model from [18] (`iCS1224`: 984 metabolites, 1,257 reactions). For `IML1515`, experiments used both core and complete biomass formulations. MEDORA was executed under multiple configurations to evaluate the impact of biological constraints and SAIC parameters on computation time, solution count, and sizes of computed media and networks, with a 45-min time limit per run. Input conditions varied by biological data availability. Without data, only the network and biomass targets were provided. With data, curated compounds (exchange metabolites for *E. coli*) and aerobic/anaerobic constraints were added. The aerobic/anaerobic reactions were identified based on the `e_coli_core` model description [13] (9 aerobic/8 anaerobic; equivalent reactions manually mapped for larger models). For *R. leguminosarum*, curated metabolites (Biolog data), hypothetical compounds (rhizospheric metabolome), and required reactions (TnSeq essential genes) were extracted from [18] and included to the model. SAIC handling was also tested: experiments were performed with/without SAIC as candidate compounds, and with SAIC unmasked or masked. For completeness, all models were also processed using Seed2LP without biological constraints (see Appendix 3). Experimentations have been performed on a machine with an Intel Cori7-1365U CPU with 30 GB of RAM. (sourcecode: https://github.com/Moana63/MEDORA).

Execution Time Decreases with the Introduction of Biological Data and Masking of SAICs. As expected, excluding SAICs from candidate media in MEDORA yielded no solutions (data not shown). Without biological data, both Seed2LP and unmasked MEDORA completed within the 45 min limit only for the smallest models, `e_coli_core` and `iCS1224` (Appendix 3, Table 2). As in Table 1 (column *Time(s)*), unmasked MEDORA runs without data lasted 3 s for `e_coli_core` and 36 min for `iCS1224`, whereas integrating biological data reduced execution times to under 2 min for `iCS1224`. For the large-scale models `IJO1366` and `iML1515`, introducing biological data reduced execution times below the 45 min limit in most conditions, with unmasked runs completing in

16.6–40 min, except for iML1515 under aerobic conditions. Applying both biological constraints and SAIC masking further reduced execution times below the 45min limit for all models. For IJO1366 and iML1515, masked runs with data completed in 1.8–11.7 min. In iCS1224, masking reduced runtime from 36 min to 6.8 min without data (compared to 54 min for Seed2LP). Overall, biological constraints and SAIC masking substantially improved scalability, enabling MEDORA to enumerate minimal media in large GSMNs.

The Number of Solutions Decreases with SAIC Masking. As in Table 1 (column *#Sol*), MEDORA SAIC masking consistently reduced the number of enumerated solutions across all models. For e_coli_core with biological data, solu-

Table 1. Performance summary of experiments. The column *MN* refers to the metabolic network used in each experiment. *BioDat* specifies the biological condition used. *Masked* indicates whether SAICs were masked of not. *Time(m)* reports the total computation time in minutes. *#Sol* corresponds to the number of feasible solutions obtained. *MedSize* represents the minimal medium size. *MedBio* and *MedSAIC* represent the proportion of biological input and SAIC compounds present in the union of all computed media, respectively. Finally, ActiMN refers to the proportion of the network reactions that are activated across all solutions.

MN	BioDat	Masked	Time(m)	#Sol	MedSize	MedBio	MedSAIC	ActiMN
e_coli_core	no	no	<1	2	7	25%	63%	48%
e_coli_core	no	yes	<1	1	3	67%	0%	49%
e_coli_core	aero	no	<1	28	9	40%	47%	61%
e_coli_core	anaero	no	<1	24	8	36%	50%	56%
e_coli_core	aero	yes	<1	8	4	75%	0%	61%
e_coli_core	anaero	yes	<1	7	3	71%	0%	56%
IJO1366	no	no	>45	/	/	/	/	/
IJO1366	no	yes	>45	/	/	/	/	/
IJO1366	aero	no	16.6	768	45	62%	28%	18%
IJO1366	anaero	no	40	2048	43	66%	28%	19%
IJO1366	aero	yes	3.3	12	40	86%	0%	19%
IJO1366	anaero	yes	1.8	32	38	91%	0%	19%
IML1515_core	no	no	>45	/	/	/	/	/
IML1515_core	no	yes	>45	/	/	/	/	/
IML1515_core	aero	no	>45	/	/	/	/	/
IML1515_core	anaero	no	31.3	1536	40	64%	23%	20%
IML1515_core	aero	yes	11.7	216	35	82%	0%	20%
IML1515_core	anaero	yes	2.1	48	36	84%	0%	20%
IML1515_complete	no	no	>45	/	/	/	/	/
IML1515_complete	no	yes	>45	/	/	/	/	/
IML1515_complete	aero	no	>45	/	/	/	/	/
IML1515_complete	anaero	no	33	1536	44	76%	16%	26%
IML1515_complete	aero	yes	4.6	108	41	96%	0%	26%
IML1515_complete	anaero	yes	2.5	48	39	96%	0%	26%
iCS1224	no	no	36	144	45	63%	28%	33%
iCS1224	no	yes	6.8	3	36	87%	0%	34%
iCS1224	yes	no	1.7	32	54	59%	29%	49%
iCS1224	yes	yes	1.7	2	41	83%	0%	50%

tion counts decreased from 24–28 in unmasked conditions to 7–8 when masked. In `iCS1224`, masking reduced the number of solutions from 144 to 3 without biological data, and from 32 to 2 with biological data. In `iCS1224`, Seed2LP returned 192–11,719 solutions depending on parameters, and the union of enumerated solutions contained a high proportion of compounds identified as SAICs by MEDORA (61% and 37%, respectively; Appendix 3, Table 2, column *Med-SAIC*). For the large-scale models `IJO1366` and `iML1515`, unmasked MEDORA conditions produced 768–2,048 solutions, whereas masked conditions reduced the solution space to 12–216 solutions. Overall, SAIC masking substantially reduced the combinatorial explosion induced by internal compounds, improving interpretability while preserving minimal media computation within the NE formalism.

Biological Data and SAIC Masking Increase the Biological Consistency of Inferred Media. As shown in Table 1 (column *MedBio*), the proportion of biological compounds in inferred media increased when biological data is included and SAICs are masked. For `e_coli_core`, it goes from 67% to 75% in aerobic conditions and to 71% in anaerobic conditions. In `iCS1224`, this proportion slightly decreased from 87% to 83% because the union of solutions expanded following the activation of 277 required reactions. For all other models, biologically supported compounds represented more than 60% of inferred media in unmasked conditions and more than 80% in masked conditions. As in Table 1 (columns *MedSize* and *ActiMN*), minimal medium size remained stable across conditions, with fewer than 10 compounds for small networks and 40–50 compounds for large-scale models. SAIC masking reduced medium size by excluding these compounds from inferred media, while slightly increasing the proportion of activated reactions by assuming all SAICs as activated. Activated reaction proportions ranged from 19–26% in `IJO1366` and `iML1515`, 30–50% in `iCS1224`, and 50–60% in `e_coli_core`, with further increases when biological data were integrated. The high proportion in `e_coli_core` reflects its interconnected structure and numerous cofactor targets, whereas the increase in activated reactions when including biological data in `iCS1224` is explained by the inclusion of 277 required reactions from TnSeq data. Compared to MEDORA, Seed2LP inferred smaller minimal media with a lower proportion of biologically supported compounds (Appendix 3, Table 2). Overall, MEDORA improves the biological contextualization of inferred media and metabolic subnetworks by both relaxing strict minimality to integrate biological data and identifying SAICs for masking.

5 Conclusion

Our results show that MEDORA uniquely integrates observations at both reaction and compound levels, making it suitable for interpreting diverse experimental data - including RNAseq, TnSeq, Biolog, and metabolomic experiments. Following [10], in which active subnetworks and exchanges fluxes are computed according to reaction-level gene expression, MEDORA provides a comprehensive framework for cross-analyzing multiple sources of evidence, offering deeper insights into metabolic processes. From a computational perspective, discrete simulation of metabolic networks using the Network Expansion formalism necessitates the activation of both external media compounds and internal compounds essential for interdependent pathways. Manual curation of these internal compounds is impractical for genome-scale networks due to their complexity. To address this, we introduce the concept of Self-Activated Internal Compounds (SAICs), which are automatically identified by MEDORA and masked during minimal media computation to prevent combinatorial explosion. Leveraging Answer Set Programming, MEDORA efficiently computes all possible solutions while extracting biologically relevant information. The heuristics implemented for SAIC computation, masking, and contextualization of media inferences with biological observations significantly reduce the solution space, enabling the exhaustive enumeration of minimal culture media, a critical advancement for metabolic network analysis. Future work will include a comparison with the ranges of reaction fluxes predicted by RIPTiDe [10], requiring post-processing steps, since it neither enumerates solutions nor directly infers culture media composition.

Acknowledgments. This study was funded by Inria-Inrae PhD supports, ANR/ France 2030 20-PCPA-0004 DEEP IMPACT project.

Disclosure of Interests. The authors have no competing interests to declare that are relevant to the content of this article.

Appendix 1: Detailed Computation of the Parsimonious Network (Complement to Sect. 3.2)

Computation of the Parsimonious Network. Figure 2 details on several examples the successive steps for computing the parsimonious network. **I. Candidate network** selection within the Target Synthesis Network of `T`. **II. Admissible network** identification under two main conditions: (i) the *scope* initiated by candidate medium compounds (`A`, `C`, `F`, `G`) within the candidate network activates the required reaction `R4` and produces the target `T`; (ii) the *Target Synthesis Network of T restricted to the candidate network* (in purple) activates `R4`. Cases 1 and 2 satisfy both conditions and are admissible. Cases 3 and 4 satisfy condition (i) but not condition (ii), as `R4` is not activated in the restricted Target Synthesis Network. **III. Parsimonious network** computation as the union of all minimal admissible networks. Cases 1 and 2 are minimal and their union define the parsimonious network.

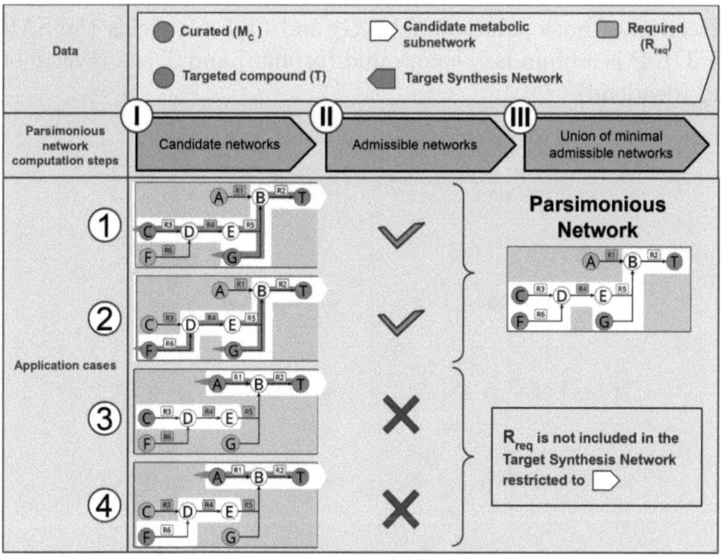

Fig. 2. Three successive steps for computing the parsimonious network, with candidate subnetworks highlighted in white. (Color figure online)

Appendix 2: SAIC Computation (Complement to Sect. 3.4)

Definition and Illustration of Reverse Scope. The reverse scope is defined as follows.

$$\text{RevScope}_{\mathbf{M}}(\mathbf{T}, \overline{\mathbf{R}}) = \bigcup_{i=0}^{k} \mathbf{M}_i \qquad \text{RevScope}_{\mathbf{R}}(\mathbf{T}, \overline{\mathbf{R}}) = \bigcup_{i=1}^{k} \mathbf{R}_i$$

$$\text{with} \quad \begin{aligned} \mathbf{M}_0 &= \mathbf{T} \\ \mathbf{R}_{i+1} &= \{r \in \overline{\mathbf{R}} \mid \text{product(r)} \subseteq \mathbf{M}_i\} \quad \forall i \geq 0 \\ \mathbf{M}_i &= \text{reactant}(\mathbf{R}_i) \quad \forall i \geq 1 \end{aligned} \tag{15}$$

and k is such that $\mathbf{M}_{k+1} = \mathbf{M}_k$.

Figure 3 illustrates the computation of primers and reverse primers based on scope and RevScope. The right panel shows primer identification via scope expansion. Valid solutions must maximize the number of reachable compounds. The first two examples are invalid, as some compounds remain neither selected as primers nor reached (white nodes). The last two examples are valid: compound P, combined with F or G, enable maximal reachability. The left panel shows reverse primer identification using RevScope. Valid solutions must again maximize reachable compounds. The two first example are invalid as some compounds remain neither selected as primers nor reached (white nodes). The last two are valid: compound T, combined with F or G, achieve maximal reachability.

The intersection of both solutions (P,F,G) and (T,F,G) yields the SAICs compounds (F,G). P is a boundary compound (orphan) and T is a reverse boundary compound (deadend).

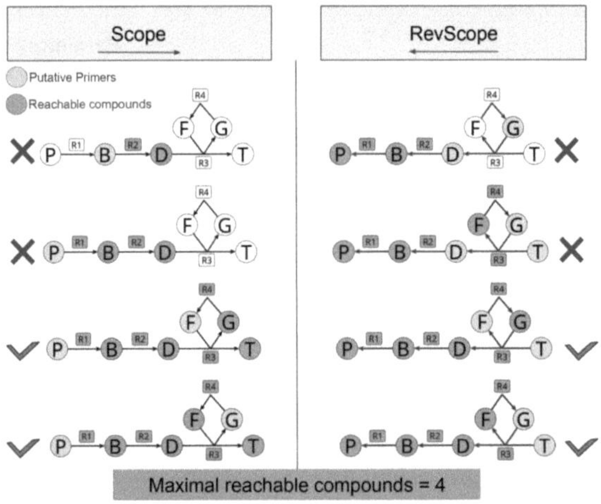

Fig. 3. Computation of primers and reverse primers by maximizing reachability of the scope and reverse scope, which are then used to compute SAICs.

ASP Encoding for SAIC Computation. MEDORA identifies SAICs by first selecting a candidate subset (L2), then recursively extending the forward scope while accounting for reversibility (L4–L7) as in Eq. (9). Reachable compounds are defined as non-selected primers (L9), and the optimization (L12) selects primer sets that maximize their number. The same process is repeated by substituting the forward scope by the reverse scope in L13–L23 to encode Eq. (10). SAICs are identified as the intersection of primers and reverse primers (L26) as in Eq. (11). Orphans and importable compounds are identified at L28 and L30 respectively.

Listing 1.4. Simplified ASP encoding of the primers and SAICs computation

```
1  %Select a subset of primer candidate
2    {primer(S) : candidate(S)}.
3  %Compute forward scope
4    scope(S) :- primer(S).
5    scope(S) :- product(S,R,_), reaction(R,_), scope(S2) : reactant(S2,R,_).
6  %Include reversibility
7    scope(S) :- reactant(S,R,_), reaction(R,_), reversible(R,_), scope(S2) :
       product(S2,R,_).
8  %Reachable compounds
9    reachable(S) :- scope(S), not primer(S).
10 %Maximization of reachability
11   #maximize { 1@1, S : reachable(S) }.
12 %Select a subset of reverse primer candidate
13   {primer_rev(S) : candidate_rev(S)}.
```

```
%Compute backward scope
  scope_rev(S) :- primer_rev(S).
  scope_rev(S) :- reactant(S,R,_),reaction(R,_), scope_rev(S2) : product(S2,R,_).
%Include reversibility
  scope_rev(S) :- product(S,R,_), reaction(R,_), reversible(R,_), scope_rev(S2) : reactant(S2,R,_).
%Reachable compounds
  reachable_rev(S) :- scope_rev(S), not primer_rev(S).
%Maximization of reachability
  #maximize { 1@1, S : reachable_rev(S) }.

%Identification of SAIC
saics(S) :- primer(S), primer_rev(S).
%Identification of orphans
   orphans(S) :- not product(S,_,_), reactant(S,_,_).
%Identification of importable compounds
   import(S) :- reaction(R,_), reactant(S,R,_), not product(_,R,_).
```

Proofs of Eq. (12), (13), (14). Let $m \in A \in \mathcal{P}$. Assume that $m \in \text{Scope}(A \setminus \{m\})$. Let $\bar{A} = A \setminus m$.

Since $m \in \text{Scope}(A \setminus \{m\})$ we have that $\text{Scope}(\bar{A}) = \text{Scope}(A)$. From $m \in \text{Scope}(A \setminus \{m\})$ and $m \in A$ we also deduce that

$$\begin{aligned}
\text{Scope}(\bar{A}) \setminus \bar{A} &= \text{Scope}(A) \cap \text{comp}(A \setminus \{m\}) \\
&= \text{Scope}(A) \cap (\text{comp}(A) \cup \{m\}) \\
&= (\text{Scope}(A) \setminus A) \cup \text{Scope}(A) \cup \{m\} \\
&= (\text{Scope}(A) \setminus A) \cup \{m\}.
\end{aligned}$$

This yields that $\text{size}(\text{Scope}(\bar{A}) \setminus \bar{A}) = \text{size}(\text{Scope}(A) \setminus A) + 1$ which is impossible. Equation (12) can be proved with a similar reasoning.

To prove Eq. (14), let $m \in \mathbf{M}_{SAIC}$. There exists $A \in \mathcal{P}$ with $m \in A$ such that $\text{Scope}(A) \setminus A$ is maximal. Assuming that m is the reactant of no reaction in $\mathbf{R}$ yields that $\text{Scope}(\{m\}) = \emptyset$, therefore $\text{Scope}(A) = \text{Scope}(A \setminus \{m\})$ and $\text{Scope}(A \setminus \{m\}) \setminus (A \setminus \{m\}) = \{m\} \cup \text{Scope}(A) \setminus A$ has a greater size than $\text{Scope}(A) \setminus A$. A similar reasoning with RevScope yield that m is the product of at least one reaction.

Masking SAIC. The left panel of Fig. 4 shows a toy metabolic network with boundary compounds (`A,B,C`) and SAICs (`Y,Z`) that produce each other through reactions (`R2,R5,R4,R6`). The Network Expansion requires all reactants of a reaction to be present for activation; thus, `R1` cannot be activated without (`A,B`) and `R3` without (`A,C`), and `R2` cannot be activated without (`D,Y`) and `R4` without (`E,Z`). To produce both target compounds `T1` and `T2`, two alternative *unmasked* media are available, both including all boundary compounds (`A,B,C`) to initiate the recursion and either SAIC `Y` or `Z` to sustain it internally. As illustrated in the right panel, *masking* SAICs removes them from the enumeration process and reduces the number of solutions from two to one in this simplified example.

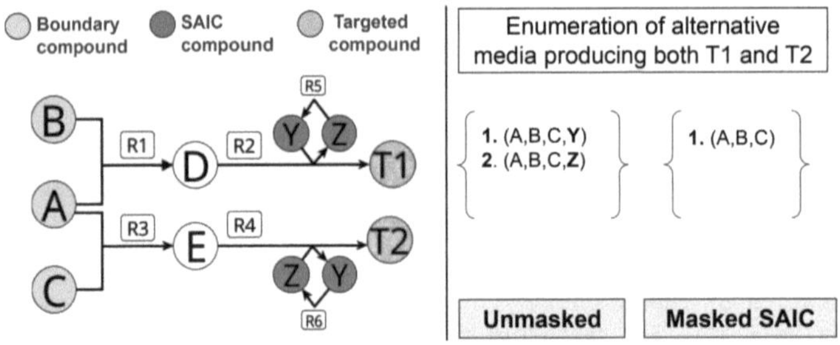

Fig. 4. Impact of masking SAICs.

ASP Encoding for Masking SAIC. Two modifications have to be made to Listing 1.3 to mask SAICs

- The search space (L3 of Listing 1.3) is replaced by a selection of medium compounds compatible with the parsimonious network, not user-forbidden *and not SAICs.*
  {`med_adm_pars(S): med_cand_pars(S), not forb_med(S), not cpd_SAIC(S)`}.
- the admissible scope, initiated by the selected medium *and the SAICs*, and restricted to the parsimonious network. Therefore L6 in Listing 1.3) is replaced by

```
% [Define scope_adm_M_pars(S) & scope_adm_R_pars(Rw)]. Duplicate
Listing 1.1(L2-4) replacing seed(S) with med_adm_pars(S) and
cpd_SAIC(S) & subnetwork(Rw) with pars_network(Rw)
```

Appendix 3: Seed2LP Experiments (Complement to Sect. 4)

Seed2LP was applied to the same four models as MEDORA using two heuristics reported to achieve the highest completion rates within 45 min [7]: (i) *reasoning* mode, which searches for solutions under NE formalism, and (ii) *guess_check_div* mode (GC_{div}), which searches for solutions consistent with FBA. A 45-minute time limit was set. Exchange reactions were optionally included, and enumeration was limited to 100 solutions to reduce computation time. For `iCS1224`, an additional run was performed without time or solution limits.

Table 2. Performance summary of Seed2LP experiments. The column *MN* refers to the metabolic network used in each experiment. *Heuristic* specifies the solving strategy applied (e.g., reasoning, guess_check_div). *Exch.Incl.* indicates whether exchange/import reactions from the SBML model are included in the medium computation. *SolLim* denotes the maximum number of solutions to enumerate before cutoff. *Time(m)* reports the total computation time in minutes. *#Sol* corresponds to the number of feasible solutions obtained. *MedSize* represents the minimal medium size. *MedBio* and *MedSAIC* represent the proportion of biological input compounds and SAIC compounds present in the union of all computed media, respectively.

MN	Heuristic	Exch.Incl.	SolLim	Time(m)	#Sol	MedSize	MedBio	MedSAIC
e_coli_core	GC_{div}	yes	100	<1	0	/	/	/
e_coli_core	GC_{div}	no	100	<1	2	6	14%	71%
e_coli_core	reasoning	yes	100	<1	2	4	0%	100%
e_coli_core	reasoning	no	100	<1	12	6	30%	50%
iCS1224	GC_{div}	yes	100	>45	/	/	/	/
iCS1224	GC_{div}	no	100	30.4	100	21	33%	20%
iCS1224	reasoning	yes	no	0.3	192	4	0%	61%
iCS1224	reasoning	no	100	9.9	100	21	32%	17%
iCS1224	reasoning	no	no	54	11719	21	19%	37%
IJO1366	GC_{div}	yes	100	>45	/	/	/	/
IJO1366	GC_{div}	no	100	>45	/	/	/	/
IJO1366	reasoning	yes	100	>45	/	/	/	/
IJO1366	reasoning	no	100	>45	/	/	/	/
IML1515	GC_{div}	yes	100	>45	/	/	/	/
IML1515	GC_{div}	no	100	>45	/	/	/	/
IML1515	reasoning	yes	100	>45	/	/	/	/
IML1515	reasoning	no	100	>45	/	/	/	/

Two models (`e_coli_core` and `iCS1224`) completed within the time limit in most configurations. No FBA-feasible solution were found for `e_coli_core` under GC_{div} with exchanged reactions (Table 2, column *#Sol*), while the same configuration for `iCS1224` exceeded the time limit (Table 2, column *Time(s)*).

Seed2LP produced small media overall (Table 2, column *MedSize*), ranging from 4–6 compounds for `e_coli_core` and 4–21 for `iCS1224`. This reflects its ability to include internal metabolites as candidate compounds, enabling pathway initiation at intermediate steps and reducing the need to activate upstream reactions. In contrast, MEDORA restricts candidates to user data, boundary compounds and SAICs.

The proportion of biologically supported compounds (Table 2, column *MedBio*) was consistently lower than MEDORA's, ranging from 0–30% for `e_coli_core` and 0–33% for `iCS1224`, depending on the heuristic and options.

Seed2LP also included SAICs in its solutions (Table 2, column *MedSAIC*), with proportions varying from 17% to 100%.

For `iCS1224`, two configurations yielded a substantially larger number of solutions (Table 2, column *MedSize*), from 192 (reasoning with exchange reactions) to 11,719 (reasoning without exchange reactions and without limits). This increase likely reflects combinatorial variation involving SAICs (61% and 37% content respectively) and the wider number of possible media compounds included by Seed2LP.

References

1. Andrade, R., et al.: Enumeration of minimal stoichiometric precursor sets in metabolic networks. Algorithms Mol. Biol. **11**(1), 25 (2016). https://doi.org/10.1186/s13015-016-0087-3
2. Borenstein, E., Kupiec, M., Feldman, M.W., Ruppin, E.: Large-scale reconstruction and phylogenetic analysis of metabolic environments. Proc. Natl. Acad. Sci. USA **105**(38), 14482–14487 (2008). https://doi.org/10.1073/pnas.0806162105
3. Ebenhöh, O., Handorf, T., Heinrich, R.: Structural analysis of expanding metabolic networks. Genom. Inform. **15**(1), 35–45 (2004). International Conference on Genome Informatics
4. Ebrahim, A., Lerman, J.A., Palsson, B.O., Hyduke, D.R.: COBRApy: COnstraints-based reconstruction and analysis for python. BMC Syst. Biol. **7**(1), 74 (2013). https://doi.org/10.1186/1752-0509-7-74
5. Frioux, C., Fremy, E., Trottier, C., Siegel, A.: Scalable and exhaustive screening of metabolic functions carried out by microbial consortia. Bioinformatics **34**(17), i934–i943 (2018). https://doi.org/10.1093/bioinformatics/bty588
6. Gebser, M., Kaminski, R., Kaufmann, B., Schaub, T.: Multi-shot ASP solving with clingo. Theory Pract. Logic Program. **19**(1), 27–82 (2019). https://doi.org/10.1017/S1471068418000054
7. Ghassemi Nedjad, C., Bolteau, M., Bourneuf, L., Paulevé, L., Frioux, C.: Seed2LP: seed inference in metabolic networks for reverse ecology applications. Bioinformatics **41**(4), btaf140 (2025). https://doi.org/10.1093/bioinformatics/btaf140
8. Gu, C., Kim, G.B., Kim, W.J., Kim, H.U., Lee, S.Y.: Current status and applications of genome-scale metabolic models. Genom. Biol. **20**(1), 121 (2019). https://doi.org/10.1186/s13059-019-1730-3
9. Handorf, T., Christian, N., Ebenhöh, O., Kahn, D.: An environmental perspective on metabolism. J. Theor. Biol. **252**(3), 530–537 (2008). https://doi.org/10.1016/j.jtbi.2007.10.036
10. Jenior, M.L., Moutinho, T.J.J., Dougherty, B.V., Papin, J.A.: Transcriptome-guided parsimonious flux analysis improves predictions with metabolic networks in complex environments. PLoS Comput. Biol. **16**(4), e1007099 (2020). https://doi.org/10.1371/journal.pcbi.1007099
11. Levy, R., Borenstein, E.: Reverse ecology: from systems to environments and back. In: Advances in Experimental Medicine and Biology, vol. 751, pp. 329–345 (2012). https://doi.org/10.1007/978-1-4614-3567-9_15
12. Nikoloski, Z., Grimbs, S., Selbig, J., Ebenhöh, O.: Hardness and approximability of the inverse scope problem. In: Crandall, K.A., Lagergren, J. (eds.) WABI 2008. LNCS, vol. 5251, pp. 99–112. Springer, Heidelberg (2008). https://doi.org/10.1007/978-3-540-87361-7_9

13. Orth, J.D., Fleming, R.M.T., Palsson, B.Ø.: Reconstruction and use of microbial metabolic networks: the core *Escherichia coli* metabolic model as an educational guide. EcoSal Plus **4**(1) (2010). https://doi.org/10.1128/ecosalplus.10.2.1. https://journals.asm.org/doi/10.1128/ecosalplus.10.2.1
14. Orth, J.D., Thiele, I., Palsson, B.: What is flux balance analysis? Nat. Biotechnol. **28**(3), 245–248 (2010). https://doi.org/10.1038/nbt.1614. https://www.nature.com/articles/nbt.1614
15. Parter, M., Kashtan, N., Alon, U.: Environmental variability and modularity of bacterial metabolic networks. BMC Evol. Biol. **7**(1), 169 (2007). https://doi.org/10.1186/1471-2148-7-169
16. Prigent, S., et al.: Meneco, a topology-based gap-filling tool applicable to degraded genome-wide metabolic networks. PLOS Comput. Biol. **13**(1), e1005276 (2017). https://doi.org/10.1371/journal.pcbi.1005276. https://journals.plos.org/ploscompbiol/article?id=10.1371/journal.pcbi.1005276
17. Schaub, T., Thiele, S.: Metabolic network expansion with answer set programming. In: Hill, P.M., Warren, D.S. (eds.) ICLP 2009. LNCS, vol. 5649, pp. 312–326. Springer, Heidelberg (2009). https://doi.org/10.1007/978-3-642-02846-5_27
18. Schulte, C.C.M., Ramachandran, V.K., Papachristodoulou, A., Poole, P.S.: Genome-scale metabolic modelling of lifestyle changes in rhizobium leguminosarum. mSystems **7**(1), e0097521 (2022). https://doi.org/10.1128/msystems.00975-21
19. Shah, N.: Knowledge representation, reasoning and declarative problem solving by C. Baral, Cambridge University Press, 2003. J. Funct. Program. **14**(5), 588–589 (2004). https://doi.org/10.1017/S0956796804215325. https://www.cambridge.org/core/product/identifier/S0956796804215325/type/journal_article
20. Thuillier, K., Baroukh, C., Bockmayr, A., Cottret, L., Paulevé, L., Siegel, A.: Learning boolean controls in regulated metabolic networks: a case-study. In: Cinquemani, E., Paulevé, L. (eds.) CMSB 2021. LNCS, vol. 12881, pp. 159–180. Springer, Cham (2021). https://doi.org/10.1007/978-3-030-85633-5_10

On the Design of an Analog-Dyadic Converter CRN

Mathieu Hemery(✉)

Inria Saclay Ile de France, EPI Lifeware, Palaiseau, France
mathieu.hemery@inria.fr

Abstract. The Chemical Reaction Networks (CRN) interpreted through the differential semantics, even when restricted to elementary reactions with mass action law kinetics, form a Turing-complete language. This means that any computable real function can thus be programmed, and in fact compiled, in an abstract CRN that will compute it with an arbitrarily high precision. In this computational framework, the information carriers are the molecular concentrations, the required precision is given as input, and the output concentration is guaranteed to satisfy the required precision. On the other hand, one can be interested in estimating the derivative of an unknown input signal or in reading the concentration value of an input molecular species. By nature, such problems can only be approximated with a finite precision. Hence, the computation framework proposed previously cannot be applied and we need to design and analyze custom CRNs to perform these tasks. In this paper, we present an analog-dyadic converter CRN which takes as input one molecular concentration (in $[0, 1]$ but not necessarily computable), and produces as output a sequence of "on" and "off" spikes corresponding to some extent to the sequence of bits in the dyadic representation of the input concentration. We provide a detailed analysis of the source of errors and their behavior when varying the reactions rate constants. We conclude by sketching a possible design for a reader module that takes as input an arbitrary concentration and a desired precision and outputs a dyadic encoding approximating the value of the concentration with the desired precision. We leave as an open question to prove the correctness of our construction.

1 Introduction

Turing machine is a concrete, albeit unpractical, model for the theoretical study of computers' possibilities. A computer being any machine able to perform calculations [14]. Its interest resides in its simplicity as it is composed of one or several infinite tapes, a head, a finite set of symbols to be written on these tapes and a finite set of rules. Despite this sobriety, the Church-Turing thesis states that Turing machine is one form of the universal computer in the sense that any function that can be computed by a computer of any sort can also be computed by it.

P. T. Monteiro (Ed.): CMSB 2026, LNBI 16678, pp. 178–200, 2027.
https://doi.org/10.1007/978-3-032-30870-2_10

A less known ancestor of mechanical computing is the integrating machine of James Thomson (the brother of Lord Kelvin) [13] which later became the differential analyzer and the *General Purpose Analog Computer* (GPAC) with the work of Shannon [12] and others. The central idea in *analog computing* is to represent the mathematical values of the computation through physical quantities, be it electrical or mechanical ones, and perform operations on them through the physical manipulation of these quantities. The idea, at this time, was mainly to reproduce the behavior of the model of interest by building a more convenient analog system obeying the same laws and then perform measurements directly on this "maquette". While very efficient, particularly in terms of energy expenditure, this framework is also limited in its representative power. Indeed, the solutions that can be *generated* by such a machine are necessarily constrained by their physical embodiment. In particular, they are always analytic [3], which seems to exclude GPAC as a model equivalent to Turing machine.

However, in [7] and [1], Graça, Bournez *et al.* realize the *tour de force* to show that GPAC and thus Polynomial Ordinary Differential Equation (PODE) can have the same expressing power as a Turing machine and are thus a Turing complete framework. The central idea was to consider that the function represented by the machine with variables $\mathbf{x}$ is not the relation: $t \mapsto \mathbf{x}$ – where the function is generated by the machine – but $\mathbf{x}(t = 0) \mapsto \lim_{t\to\infty} \mathbf{x}(t)$ – where the function is computed at the limit. This is significant because PODE is a purely mathematical notion. If the Church-Turing thesis is correct, it implies that the computational power of any physical machine may be defined through a purely mathematical setting.

Building upon these works, our team has shown that through the differential semantics, chemical reaction networks (CRN) can implement arbitrary PODE and are thus also a Turing complete framework able to perform any computation [6]. These results drive us to study the theoretical and practical aspects of CRN seen as a programming language. This leads us to propose a complete pipeline that compile mathematical functions to elementary CRN [5] and to study the theoretical aspect of the intermediate operation of quadratization [9].

A natural question that is both theoretically interesting and practically relevant is the method used to read the result of the computation once the machine has reached the desired precision. It is to shed some light on this aspect that we propose the present paper.

We present here an analog-dyadic converter that relies entirely on elementary reactions of chemical species. We take great care to propose an implementation that uses as few species and reactions as possible while still performing its function with accuracy and robustness. The main idea is to receive the concentration of a species as input and display a sequence of binary spikes that represents the encoding of the initial concentration as a dyadic number. Hence, allowing a "physical observation" of the initial concentration value with increasing precision as the number of spikes increases.

From a more theoretical point of view, this constitutes a central and non-trivial part of the realization of an analog computer, be it with CRN or PODE.

Indeed, the possibility to compute a quantity is of no use if we cannot read the result. But given the undecidability of the comparison, it is not evident that this task is actually possible. A careful analysis shows that our device can only reach a certain precision that depend upon the rate constants and the initial input. This validity domain exhibits a fractal pattern. Fortunately, by tuning the rate constants, we can expand the validity domain and it seems possible to reach an arbitrary precision, hence allowing us to build a reader module that complete the computation module of [6].

Finally, this work is also an attempted step toward the study of the Hartmanis-Stearns conjecture formulated in 1965 and still pending [8]. This conjecture posits that only the rational or transcendental numbers can be computed in real time, in the sense that for a real x, there exists a multi-tape Turing machine taking p as input and returning as output a rational r approximating x with a precision 2^{-p} in a time $O(p)$.

Interestingly, the simple CRN:

$$\emptyset \xrightarrow{5} X, \quad X^2 \xrightarrow{1} \emptyset, \tag{1}$$

is such that X converges exponentially fast toward the irrational but algebraic number $\sqrt{5}$. It is "simply" a matter of retrieving this information. We will see at the end of this article that this is possible with a PODE either with bounded concentrations and a time scaling like $o(p^2)$ or with concentration and time scaling like $o(p)$. Hence, the Hartmanis-Stearns conjecture reduces to: "How can we relate the time of a bounded PODE to the one of a multi-tape Turing machine?"

The plan of this article is the following. First, we will remind the main mathematical tools and aspects needed to understand the notion of CRN and the dyadic representation of numbers, thus setting the notations. We will then present the functioning of the converter and explain the different elements that allow it to perform its function in a robust way. After that, we will perform an-in depth analysis of the main causes of precision loss in order to determine what is the expected precision and how it scales with the different parameters of the model. We finally use this analysis to show how we might alter this device to produce a reader module, completing the computation framework of Fages et al.

2 Notation and Computation Framework

2.1 Chemical Reaction Network

Chemical Reaction Network is a well-established framework used by chemists and biologists to represent the interactions of chemical components and study the various behaviors and properties that emerge from these interactions.

Formally, a CRN is given as a set of species and a set of reactions. These reactions are tuples composed of two multisets of species, the reactants $\mathcal{R}$ and the products $\mathcal{P}$, and a function f indicating the rate at which the reaction takes place.

Once a CRN is provided, it is possible to interpret it using several semantics: boolean, stochastic, differential, etc. It is this flexibility that gives CRN its modeling power, as the same description may be used through a great variety of tools coming from various domains of science.

In this paper, we will only use the *differential semantics* that consists in deriving a set of ordinary differential equations (ODE) from the CRN. For each species, we attribute a variable representing its concentration and build its derivative by collecting the rates of each reaction in which it participates and multiply it by its signed stoichiometric coefficient (its index in the multiset of products minus its index in the one of reactants).

We moreover restrict ourselves to *Mass Action Law* where rate functions are parameterized by a single positive number k (the rate constant) and are given by the product of the concentrations of all its reactants multiplied by the constant k. In this case, we obtain Polynomial ODE (PODE). We will use the standard notation with an arrow going from reactants to products and an upper index indicating the rate constant if it is different from one:

$$\mathcal{R} \xrightarrow{k} \mathcal{P}.$$

The differential semantics provides a canonical mapping from CRN to ODE that uniquely associates a set of differential equations to each CRN. For example, the CRN: $A + B \xrightarrow{k} A + 2C$ is associated to the PODE

$$\dot{A} = 0, \quad \dot{B} = -kAB, \quad \dot{C} = +2kAB. \tag{2}$$

A natural question is then: does there exist an inverse mapping? And the answer is: yes, but!

Yes, for any ODE $\mathcal{E}$ that uses only elementary mathematical functions, we can construct a CRN such that a subset of the variables of its associated ODE through the canonical mapping exaclty admits the same solution as $\mathcal{E}$ [11]. For mathematical variables A that may be negative, it is possible to split them between their positive (A_p) and negative (A_n) parts and build a CRN for which the observable $A_p - A_n$ will exactly follow the initial ODE $\mathcal{E}$ [6,10]. But, this mapping is not canonical and there is quite a lot of play for the "implementation" of a particular ODE. This is both a curse, because it gives us a lot of arbitrary choices to make in order to provide a particular CRN, and a boon, because it allows us to add additional constraints that may bring us desirable properties upon the constructed CRN.

We study Mass Action Law for two reasons. First, it emerges quite naturally from collision theory, making them "more elementary" than other rate functions. These are indeed often coarse-grained approximations of the behavior of more complex Mass Action Law CRN (see [15] for a historical review on Mass Action kinetics). More surprisingly, it has been shown that Mass Action Law CRNs interpreted through the differential semantic are Turing complete in the following sense [6]:

Theorem 1. *For any computable function $f : \mathbb{R}^k \to \mathbb{R}$, there exist a finite CRN with mass action law kinetics, over a set of species S_i and a polynomial function p such that, if $S_i(t = 0) = p(x)$, then the unique solution of the differential semantics interpretation of the CRN is such that*

$$\forall t > 1, |S_1(t) - f(x)| < S_2(t), \lim_{t\to\infty} S_2(t) = 0.$$

Said otherwise, for any computable function, we can construct a CRN over a finite number of species that encodes the input upon the initial concentration of its constituent species, and output the result of the computation as the concentration of the first species at the end of time while also providing a bound on the error on the second species.

It is here natural to ask how, at the end of the computation, we can read the result encoded in the concentration of a chemical species? This is precisely the question that motivates this paper and for that we will need to introduce the notion of dyadic number.

2.2 Dyadic Notation

The set of dyadic numbers denoted $\mathbb{D}$ is the one of numbers that can be expressed as a fraction whose denominator is a power of two, that is:

$$\mathbb{D} = \left\{ x | \exists n, p \in \mathbb{Z} \times \mathbb{N}, x = \frac{n}{2^p} \right\}.$$

It is a subset of the rational numbers.

By construction, a dyadic number have a natural finite representation which is the binary equivalent of decimal, for u and d the largest and smallest needed powers: $x = \sum_{p=d}^{u} b_p 2^p$, where $b_p \in \{0, 1\}$ and of course, u and d can both be positive or negative.

For example:

$$\begin{aligned} 1.8984375 &= 1 + \frac{1}{2} + \frac{1}{4} + \frac{1}{8} + \frac{0}{16} + \frac{0}{32} + \frac{1}{64} + \frac{1}{128} \\ &= 1.1110011_2 \end{aligned} \tag{3}$$

It is easy to see that $\mathbb{D}$ is dense in $\mathbb{R}$ in the same way that the rationals or the decimals are. As for the decimals, a real number always has at least one (possibly infinite) dyadic representation. They are thus a convenient set to represent real numbers in a framework where the number of symbols in the numeration system is scarce, the same way that binary allows representing integers with only two symbols.

We now have all the elements to present the basic structure of our converter.

3 The Analog-Dyadic Converter

The purpose of the dyadic converter is, starting from a species, the concentration of which is between 0 and 1, to "write" the dyadic representation of this initial

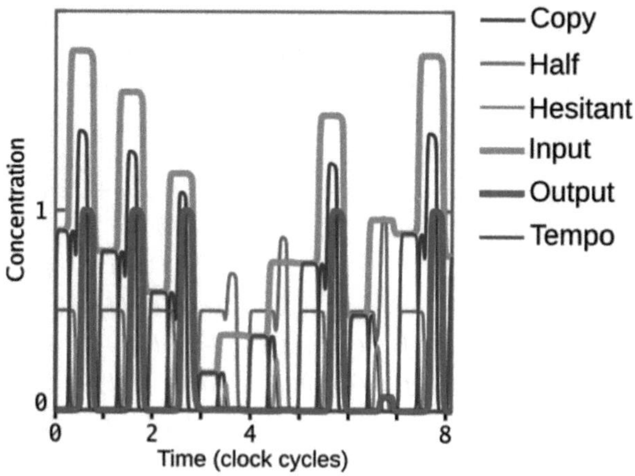

Fig. 1. Time course of the dyadic converter through 8 complete cycles of the clock. During the kth cycle, the *Output* species (in bold red) spikes or not according to the comparison of the *Input* species (in bold orange) to a threshold species. Here we can see that the output is 11100101. Note that this is different from the expected result as, $\text{Input}(t = 0) = 0.9 = 0.11100110\ldots_2$. The 6 first bits are correct, but we suffer from an error on the 7th one. The cause of these errors, and how to mitigate them, will be discussed in this paper. (Color figure online)

concentration as a sequence of binary spikes in the concentration of one species (here named "Output"). An example of this behavior is shown in Fig. 1.

The main idea is simply to follow the same steps as those of the typical algorithm used to convert a number to its dyadic representation. In a nutshell, we first compare the current value of the input to one half and write a one or a zero accordingly. Then, in order to pass to the next bit, we need to zoom in. This can be done by doubling the input and subtracting one if necessary to keep it between 0 and 1. Then we loop.

The reactions of the dyadic converter are a bit more involved as they include ancillary species to perform the function with the constraints of chemical implementation. The pseudocode along with its CRN implementation is given in Table 1.

3.1 Overview

Our conversion module is composed of five interacting parts: a clock, a copy, a comparison, a subtraction and a cleaning mechanism.

The purpose of the clock is to play the role of a musical director. It coordinates all the other reactions as they should be activated in order to correctly perform the desired behavior. This is achieved by having a set of species that alternate active and passive phases in a predefined order and use them to catalyze all the reactions of the other parts.

Table 1. Description of the operations performed by the dyadic converter module given with a pseudocode representation along with the CRN implementation. For clarity, the clock and its regulation are not represented here. The exact model is given in (9).

	Pseudocode	CRN
Copy	$Copy := Input$	$Input \rightarrow Input + Tempo$
&	$Input := 2 * Input$	$Tempo \rightarrow \emptyset$
Doubling		$Tempo \rightarrow Copy + Input$
	$Half := \frac{1}{2}$	$\emptyset \rightarrow Half, Half \xrightarrow{2} \emptyset$
Comparison	$Half := 0$ if $Half < Copy$	$Copy + Half \rightarrow 2Hesitant$
	$Copy := 0$ if $Half > Copy$	$Hesitant + Half \rightarrow 2Half$
		$Hesitant + Copy \rightarrow 2Copy$
Spiking	$Output := 1$ if $Copy$	$Copy + Inactive \leftrightarrow Copy + Output$
Subtraction	$Input := Input - Output$	$Output + Input \rightarrow Inactive$

The copy reactions allow us two different effects. First, it creates a copy of the input that can be destroyed during the comparison step without losing the value of the input that should be passed (up to some modifications) from one cycle to the next. It also allows us to double the value of the input.

The comparison scheme is based upon the classical mechanism of *approximate majority* [4]. It compares with good precision the value of the Copy to a predefined threshold, here: one half. While a more simple comparison could have been implemented with a simple bidegradation, the approximate majority scheme is here preferred for its robustness and the strength of its signal. Indeed, at the end of the computation the reminding species is always higher than one half, hence ensuring an easy reading. Of course, this mechanism is not perfect, and it takes time to discriminate, especially between close concentrations, a phenomenon that is the core of Sect. 4.2.

The subtraction reaction is a simple bidegradation. It relies on an output species that is activated if and only if the input is higher than one half based on the result of the previous comparison mechanism. This has two benefits: first, it creates a robust output signal that is simply 0 or 1. Second, as it goes to 1 independently of its previous value, it provides us with the unitary value that should be subtracted from the input to start the next cycle of the dyadic conversion as explained in the pseudocode.

The cleaning reactions finally simply remove the intermediate species in order to start the next cycle with null concentration. This step is facultative as these species are set by the different reactions to their desired values independently of their initial concentrations. However, cleaning them ease the analysis of the model.

We will now take a bit more time to present in detail the two more involved elements of the CRN, namely the clock and the comparison module.

3.2 Clock

It is now known for some time that you can easily generate a sine and cosine with 4 species and 6 reactions [6]. In this CRN, the 4 species are the positive and negative parts of the trigonometric functions while the reactions are, for four of them, the catalytic production of the next species, the two others being bidegradations of the positive and negative parts.

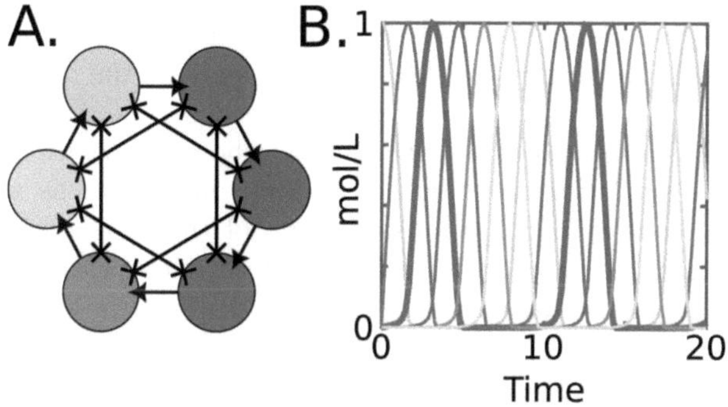

Fig. 2. A. Schematic representation of a six-step clock. Each species activates the next one and participates in a bidegradation (here depicted as a two crossed connector) with its second neighbor. **B.** The time course of the CRN presented in panel A. with corresponding colors. Activations have rates $k_{\text{clock}} = 1$ while degradations have rates $k_f = 1000$. At $t = 0$ one of the species (here light blue) has an initial concentration of 1. The violet species has been highlighted only to ease the readability of the behavior of a single species. (Color figure online)

Surprisingly and as presented in Fig. 2, this is not limited to 4 species. For any $n \geq 4$, the CRN:

$$T_i \xrightarrow{k_{\text{clock}}} T_i + T_{i+1}, \quad T_i + T_{i+2} \xrightarrow{k_f} \emptyset, \tag{4}$$

where the indices $i \in [1, n]$ and should be understood modulo n and the rate k_f is high enough to ensure that bidegrations strongly dominate other reactions, also exhibits an oscillatory behavior. Even more beautiful, it gives us an n-clock where all the species alternates between an "active" sinusoidal behavior corresponding to one "bump" and a "dormant" null behavior where it simply waits to be activated again.

By using each of these species as a catalyst for other reactions, we can associate a part of the CRN of Table 1 to a particular time of the n-clock, the same way the circadian clock regulates the activity of pathways in cells.

For a computer scientist, our clock is thus of a surprising kind as one complete cycle of the clock does not correspond to one elementary operation of the system – as it would in a traditional computer with a clock used for synchronizing the different parts – but to a full cycle of operations leading to the computation of one bit of the dyadic encoding.

For a perfect computation, the steps of the conversion should be performed sequentially and independently. The main problem is that our clock is such that two consecutive species, T_i and T_{i+1} display a strong overlap, as can be seen in Fig. 2. Even the overlap between T_i and T_{i+2} may be too important when strong guarantees are needed: typically when the two steps are likely to create a positive feedback loop that may lead to an exponential divergence as is the case for the two reactions of the copy mechanism: $Input \rightarrow Input + Tempo$ and $Tempo \rightarrow Copy + Input$. To avoid that, we can always let more steps of the clock pass between such reactions. We may also increase the rate constant k_f as it helps to soothe this unwanted overlap.

As this work is also a proof of principle for a short device, we try to minimize the use of such insulation mechanisms to keep our device as streamlined as possible. In the context of a formal derivation of the theoretical possibility of CRN computation, we should find a better clock with proven bounds on the concentration during the passive phase.

3.3 Thresholding with Approximate Majority

The comparison relies first on the production of a threshold species (H for Half):

$$\emptyset \xrightarrow{k_n} H, \quad H \xrightarrow{k_d} \emptyset, \tag{5}$$

that will converge to the ratio: $\frac{k_n}{k_d}$. In our case, we use $k_d = 2k_n$ to obtain a one half ratio. This step is perform as an initialization and realized during the first step of the clock.

Then during step 5, an approximate majority scheme is performed where the species of interest A[1] is compared to the H species through the formation of an undecided U species:

$$A + H \xrightarrow{k_1} 2U, \quad U + A \xrightarrow{k_2} 2\,A, \quad U + H \xrightarrow{k_2} 2\,H. \tag{6}$$

In model (9), we set $k_1 = k_2 = k_{\mathrm{AM}} = 10$. We keep them different here for the analysis.

The differential semantics of this reaction system gives us the following ODE:

$$\begin{aligned}\dot{A} &= -k_1 AH + k_2 UA,\\ \dot{H} &= -k_1 AH + k_2 UH,\\ \dot{U} &= 2k_1 AH - k_2 U(A + H).\end{aligned} \tag{7}$$

The approximate majority is well known to converge to a steady state where the species that was initially the more abundant between A and H will

[1] To avoid cluttering the notation of this section, we use A and a for the study of the approximate majority in its own. In the full CRN, the species to be compared will be *Copy*. Similarly, the undecided U species is named Hesitant in the full CRN.

be the only one remaining with a concentration equal to the sum of the two initial ones. That is, we have when $t \to \infty$:

$$\begin{cases} A = A_0 + H_0, \quad H = 0 & \text{if } A_0 > H_0, \\ A = A_0, \quad H = H_0 & \text{if } A_0 = H_0, \\ A = 0, \quad H = A_0 + H_0 & \text{if } A_0 < H_0. \end{cases} \tag{8}$$

Using this scheme, we can thus test if the initial concentration of A was below or above the threshold H just by testing its presence at the end of the process. This supposes, that the approximate majority dynamic had enough time to converge. Or at least that, if it should be 0, the eventual traces of the A species are low enough to remain undetected. This question will be treated in length in Sect. 4.2.

Now that we have presented all the elements, let us see how they perform together.

3.4 Dyadic Converter

The full CRN of our converter is given by:

$$\begin{aligned}
\forall i \in [1,8] T_i &\xrightarrow{k_{\text{clock}}} T_i + T_{i+1}, & \forall i \in [1,8] T_i + T_{i+2} &\xrightarrow{k_f} \emptyset, \\
Input + T_1 &\xrightarrow{k_{\exp}} Input + T_1 + Tempo, & Tempo + T_1 &\xrightarrow{k_{\exp}} T_1, \\
T_1 &\xrightarrow{k_{\exp}} T_1 + Half, & T_1 + Half &\xrightarrow{2k_{\exp}} T_1, \\
T_4 + Tempo &\xrightarrow{k_{\exp}} T_4 + Input + Copy, & T_5 + Copy + Half &\xrightarrow{k_{\text{AM}}} T_5 + 2 \cdot Hesitant, \\
T_5 + Hesitant + Half &\xrightarrow{k_{\text{AM}}} T_5 + 2 \cdot Half, & T_5 + Hesitant + Copy &\xrightarrow{k_{\text{AM}}} T_5 + 2 \cdot Copy, \\
T_6 + Copy + Inactive &\xrightarrow{k_{\exp}} T_6 + Copy + Output, & T_7 + Tempo &\xrightarrow{k_{\exp}} T_7, \\
T_7 + Copy &\xrightarrow{k_{\exp}} T_7, & T_7 + Half &\xrightarrow{k_{\exp}} T_7, \\
T_8 + Input + Output &\xrightarrow{k_{\exp}} T_8 + Inactive. & &
\end{aligned} \tag{9}$$

With the initial condition: $T_1 = 1, Inactive = 1$ and of course $Input = I_0$. For this paper, we set: $k_{\text{clock}} = 1, k_{\text{AM}} = k_{\exp} = 10, k_f = 1000$.

In Fig. 3, we illustrate the behavior of the model through one full cycle of the clock depending on whether I_0, the initial value of the input, is below or above the threshold of $\frac{1}{2}$ and thus whether the output species should spike or not. We can see that at the end of step 4, the *Copy* species now has the value I_0 and *Input* itself has doubled its value. Then the *Copy* is compared to $Half$ and thus set back to 0 in the first case, while it goes to $\frac{1}{2} + I_0$ in the second one. The presence or absence of *Copy* at this time activates (or not) the production of *Output* to its target value of 1. It is this unitary (or null) value which is then subtracted to the current value of *Input* to set it to its value for the next iteration of the clock, that is either $2I_0$ or $2I_0 - 1$.

We just show that our simple CRN is able to display the desired behavior by implementing the pseudocode of Table 1 to output at least the first bit of the dyadic encoding of its input. We have also seen that this network is susceptible

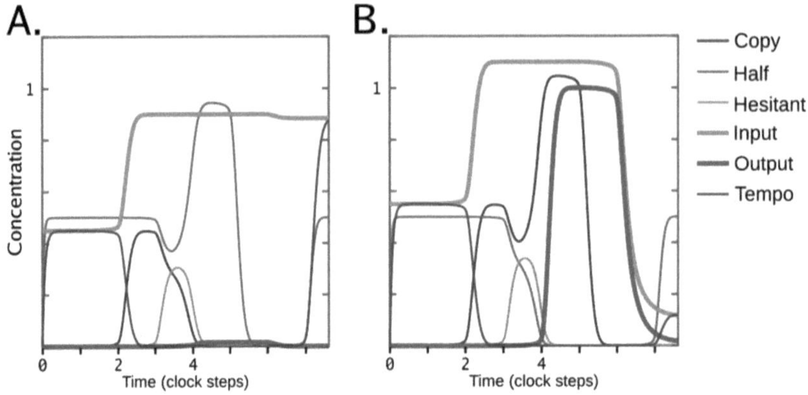

Fig. 3. Numerical integration of one full cycle of the clock for two different initial conditions. One where the *Input* species is slightly below (**A.**) the $\frac{1}{2}$ threshold and one where it is slightly above (**B.**).

of making mistakes. After a certain time, the initial precision is lost and the bits no longer correspond to the exact representation. We call *precision* the number of correct bits that the CRN is able to output. This quantity depends on the parameters of the CRN and the value of the initial input.

We will now take time to determine what are the main sources of such discrepancies and how we can control them. We will thus determine the influence of the parameters of the CRN on these errors and give some theoretical bounds upon the precision of our conversion device.

In particular, we will estimate the validity domain of our device. Indeed, we have seen that the precision we can achieve depends on both the input and the rate constants. For a given set of parameters $(k_{\text{clock}}, k_{\text{exp}}, k_{\text{AM}}, k_f)$, it is this attainable precision as a function of the input that we want to determine.

4 Detailed Analysis

Our analysis of the errors relies on three properties:

- Converging exponential have had enough time to reach a precision ϵ with respect to their target value during one step of the clock (see Sect. 4.1 but also Appendix A.3).
- The different steps of the clock are well separated. This avoids any leakage between successive steps. As this is only approximately the case for our clock example, we may have to modify the clock to ensure a better insulation.
- The Approximate Majority mechanism had enough time to discriminate between its two constituents up to a precision $\delta^\star$ (see Sect. 4.2 and Appendix A.2).

Conceptually, the two first properties may be thought as the use of a perfect clock where the pieces of cosine have been replaced by rectangular signals of amplitude 1 and duration τ. Hence, the different parts of the module are activated at full intensity for a constant duration before being switched off. For this reason, we rely on the parameter τ as a convenient parameter to describe the clock. As shown in Appendix A.3, we have the relation $\tau = \frac{2}{k_{\text{clock}}}$.

For the last property, we will see that it creates a constraint on the different rate constants of the reactions.

4.1 Premature Halting

The main culprit in terms of error is the premature halting of the reactions before they reach their asymptotic steady states. Note that this error is unavoidable as the exact computation is only performed in infinite time due to the framework of "computation at the limit".

Most differential equations involved in the dyadic converter harbor converging exponential with a rate k_{exp} as solutions. Knowing this allows us to compute the bounds on the value of the different species during the time evolution of one cycle of our converter module as a function of the input value I_0. This allows us to bound I_f the value of *Input* at the end of the clock cycle (the full detail of this derivation is given in Appendix A.1):

$$\begin{cases} I_f \in [2I_0 - 3\epsilon, 2I_0] & \text{if } I_0 < \frac{1}{2}, \\ I_f \in [2I_0 - 1 - 2\epsilon, 2I_0 - 1 + \epsilon] & \text{if } I_0 > \frac{1}{2}. \end{cases} \tag{10}$$

where $\epsilon = e^{-k_{\text{exp}}\tau}$.

An error of order 3ϵ after each cycle means that the value of the Input after n cycles has accumulated an error like:

$$e_n = 3\left(2^n - 1\right)\epsilon.$$

Thus if we still want a good precision at step p, this means that we want $3 \cdot 2^p \epsilon \ll 1$ and for this, we have to impose: $k_{\text{exp}}\tau \gg p$.

Reaching the pth cycle asks for a time $T(p) \propto \tau p$, and as we have $\tau \propto p$ by our previous computation, we conclude that reaching a given precision asks for a time that scales quadratically:

$$T(p) \propto \frac{p^2}{k_{\text{exp}}}. \tag{11}$$

However, the premature halting of the converging exponential is not the only cause of errors that can be perpetrated by our converter. The other main cause of errors being the incapacity to distinguish between two similar concentrations when the input and threshold species are too close, that is, when the input is near one half and this is what we discuss in the next section.

4.2 Comparison

Analyzing the ODEs of the approximate majority 6, (see Appendix A.2 for the full derivation), we deduce that the system does not have the time to reach a proper convergence when the initial value is too close from one half. Introducing $\delta \geq 0$ as $I_0 = \frac{1}{2} \pm \delta$ we can derive that when $k_1 \gg k_2$, there exists a threshold $\delta^\star$ given by:

$$\log(\delta^\star) = -\frac{\log(4r^2)}{1+\sqrt{2}} - \frac{k_2\tau}{1+\sqrt{2}} \tag{12}$$

such that starting with a lower value for δ indicates that the approximate majority mechanism will at time τ be in a state where the species that should be close to 0 is actually higher than r. For ensuring the bounds of the previous section, we need $r < \frac{\epsilon}{\tau k_{\text{exp}}}$. Note that this relation introduce a dependency between the error sources, lowering ϵ also lower r which leads to higher $\delta^\star$.

When $\delta < \delta^\star$ the comparison mechanism will not have the time to converge properly, this removes $[\frac{1}{2} - \delta^\star, \frac{1}{2} + \delta^\star]$ from the validity domain for precision 1. During the next cycle, the same phenomenon appears, creating two new forbidden intervals: $[\frac{1}{4} - \frac{\delta^\star}{2}, \frac{1}{4} + \frac{\delta^\star}{2}]$ and $[\frac{3}{4} - \frac{\delta^\star}{2}, \frac{3}{4} + \frac{\delta^\star}{2}]$ for the precision 2. And the same process repeats at each clock cycle, creating the fractal pattern of the validity domain represented in black in Fig. 4A. For this picture, we choose: $\delta^\star = e^{-\frac{10 \cdot 1}{3}} \simeq 0.036$.

To conclude on the behavior of the approximate majority scheme, it has to be said that with a finite number of molecules, the stochastic aspect of this CRN would also impose some limit. We would have to set a limit on fault tolerance: "I want my discrimination to be correct in at least 99% of the cases" and this would translate into a new limit δ_{stoch} with a behavior similar to $\delta^\star$, effectively setting a limit to how far we could lower $\delta^\star$.

Now let us check if these theoretical considerations are valid once we start making numerical simulations of our device.

4.3 In Practice

To evaluate the actual quality of the response, we perform extensive numerical simulations, always using model (9) for 1000 different values of the initial input in the range $[0, 1]$. We then automatically extract the presence or absence of the 10 first spikes[2] recovering to the effective encoding (which may be different from the mathematical exact one).

We propose two different measures to determine the precision of our model:

- The *precision* defined as the first bit where the model makes an error (depicted in red in Fig. 4A),

[2] For this analysis, we consider a spike to be present if the Output species spikes above a threshold of $\frac{1}{3}$ thus making a pessimist assumption about the ability of the reader to discriminate intermediate value. It could be interesting to add an *unclear* state for these intermediate values and see how this allows to catch the precision loss of the module.

- The *error* defined as the signed difference between the actual number and the number encoded by the dyadic representation output by the model (see Fig. 4B).

For example, in the simulation presented in Fig. 1, the input is $0.9 = 0.1110011001100\ldots_2$ and the output of the model is $0.11100101\ldots_2 = 0.8945$. In this case, the precision is 7 and the error is -0.0055.

Precision and *error* are two different measures and a low precision is only a piece of evidence for a high error. Think of 0.500002 and 0.49995 which differ very slightly despite a difference as early as the first digit. It is thus important for us to look at both.

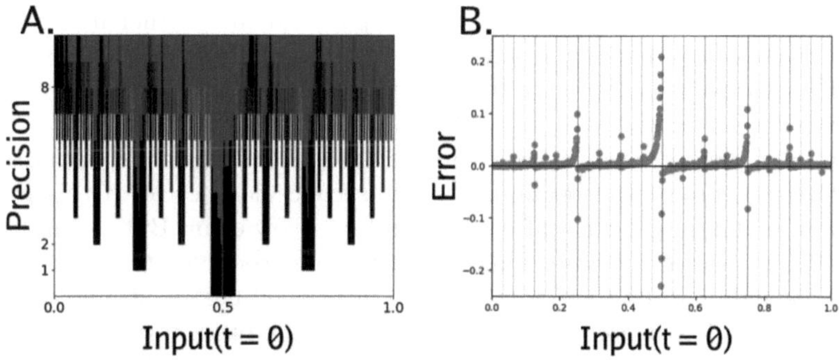

Fig. 4. Analysis of the actual behavior of the converter module for $k_{\text{clock}} = 1$ and $k_{\text{exp}} = k_{\text{AM}} = 10$ and 1000 different values of the input between 0 and 1. The system is then numerically integrated, and the spikes are automatically detected to determine the system response over 10 full cycles of the clock. **A.** Comparison between the theoretical precision of the approximate majority analysis (in black) and the actual precision of the full CRN as measured after numerical integration (in red). **B.** *Error* of the dyadic converter as a function of the initial input. (Color figure online)

We can see on the panel **A.** that the actual precision is more subtle than the theoretical picture presented in black. This is because of the presence of errors due to premature halting but also due to our choice to present a streamlined CRN with as few reactions as possible and to take low values for the rate constants. This allows us to show explicitly the behavior of our converter in its different error regimes.

First, it needs to be emphasized that both panels in Fig. 4 exhibit the fractal pattern discussed above. Moreover and as expected, the precision is essentially bounded by the results of our AM analysis. We also see that the effect of premature halting is more important for high values of the input, explaining the lower precision near 1. (This is also true for error, but is difficult to see due to the scale of the figure.)

Let us now discuss briefly the behaviors of the CRN that were not covered by our previous analysis. To derive our computation, we tried to estimate a lower bound on precision and rely on two hypotheses: first, a pessimistic approach to the error, since as soon as the parameter δ was below the critical threshold, we consider the system to be faulty, and second, an exact value for the quantity to be compared. Sadly, both assumptions are false.

Manifestly, errors are not ineluctable inside this black region, but being too close to $\frac{1}{2}$ indeed incurs a loss of precision as the system is halted before it reaches consensus. First, we can see that the error is the worst slightly below one half. This comes from the fact that the Half species we compare to suffer from the premature convergence effect discussed in Sect. 4.1. For this set of parameters, the actual threshold seems to be around 0.496.

The way the approximate majority errors affect the result is also interesting. Indeed, due to the continuous nature of our computation, around one half, it is possible to see "aborted" spikes of the Output that are neither 0 nor 1. This kind of behavior can be seen around time 80 in Fig. 1. Through the subtraction part, this error propagates to the Input species meaning that the next cycle start with an incorrect input.

Typically, just after the one half threshold, we would expect the input species to be close to zero at the beginning of the second clock cycle. If this was the case, we would only get zeros after that, and so, a low error. But as can be seen on panel **B.**, it is not the case. This creates the hyperbolic pattern that appears around one half and, by the fractal pattern mentioned before, around all dyadic numbers with a low denominator as indicated by the black vertical lines.

Let us now talk about the scaling of these errors with the different rates of our model. Amusingly, the responses of the system to a tuning of the different rates are not independent. While we would have thought that a large increase in k_{exp} without modifying k_{AM} would reduce the source of error to only the problematic cases around one half – and its fractal successors – it is not what actually happens. Indeed, a high k_{exp} makes the spiking reaction so sensitive, that even a residual fraction of the Copy species is detected and trigger the spike as revealed in Eq. 12.

Conversely, increasing only k_{AM} effectively narrows the problematic fractal region by decreasing $\delta^\star$ until the precision is essentially limited by the problem of premature halting. Hence, effectively increasing the precision necessitates to increase k_{exp} while keeping $k_{\text{AM}} \gg k_{\text{exp}}$.

All this can be used to build a *reader* module, completing the computation module of Fages et al.

4.4 Building a Reader Module

Theorem 1 ensures that for any computable function f, we can build a CRN on species $\mathbf{S}$ such that for any x, the first species converges to $S_1 \to f(x)$ and the second species, which is positive, decreases and converges to 0, controls the error: $|S_1 - f(x)| < S_2$. For a desired precision ϵ we can wait until $S_2(t^\star) = \frac{\epsilon}{2}$ and return any value past this point in time. We choose to stop the computing device at a particular time $t \geq t^\star$ and denote $\tilde{f}(x) = S_1(t)$. Then you need to start the reading device. A prototype of linker CRN is presented in Appendix A.4 that allows to let the computing CRN converge before halting it and starting the reader module.

The difficulty is that $\tilde{f}(x)$ is *a priori*, an ordinary real. There is no reason why it should be computable. We only know that it approaches the result with the aforementioned precision. Starting from the converter CRN, we can build a reader module that takes this value as input along with the precision ϵ and produces an observable behavior allowing the user to construct a dyadic number d such that $|d - \tilde{f}(x)| \leq \frac{\epsilon}{2}$. Hence, we have with d a dyadic approaching $f(x)$ with the desired precision ϵ as outlined in Fig. 5.

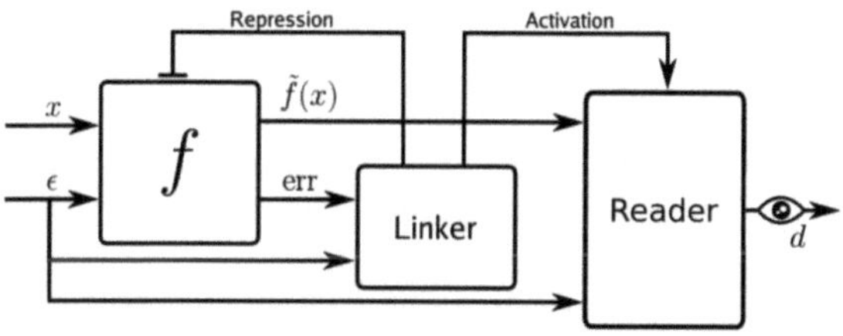

Fig. 5. Schematic figure of a complete analog machine to compute the function f. The first module takes as input x and the desired precision ϵ and outputs a (possibly not computable) value $\tilde{f}(x)$ while also providing its current estimation of the error on err. A linker module halts the computation once the precision is reached and activates a reader module that takes both the output of the previous module and the desired precision and returns a physically observable signal which allows us to construct a dyadic d encoding the result with desired precision.

To reach this precision, we need to have both $\epsilon \geq e^{-k_{\exp}\tau}$ and $\epsilon \geq e^{\frac{-k_{\mathrm{AM}}\tau}{1+\sqrt{2}}}$. We suppose that we are given the precision as a species with a concentration p such that $\epsilon = e^{-p}$. We thus need $k_{\mathrm{AM}} > \frac{3p}{\tau}$ and $k_{\exp} > \frac{p}{\tau}$. To allow the CRN to adapt automatically to the desired precision, the idea is to introduce a catalyst species to tune the rates at which the reactions take place, in order to obtain a satisfying precision. In practice, we may simply use p as the tuning species.

The approximate majority part, for example, would thus become:

$$\begin{aligned}
T_5 + P + Copy + Half &\xrightarrow{3k_{\mathrm{AM}}} T_5 + P + 2 \cdot Hesitant,\\
T_5 + P + Hesitant + Half &\xrightarrow{3k_{\mathrm{AM}}} T_5 + P + 2 \cdot Half, \qquad (13)\\
T_5 + P + Hesitant + Copy &\xrightarrow{3k_{\mathrm{AM}}} T_5 + P + 2 \cdot Copy.
\end{aligned}$$

And similarly for all the reactions involving $k_{\exp}$ and k_{AM}.

To conclude this section on the reader module. The attentive reader may see a contradiction between the quadratic time discussed in Sect. 4.1, and the fact that we can adapt to arbitrary precision without modifying the clock in this section (hence achieving a $o(p)$ time). The crucial difference lies in the bounds of the ODE. When adjusting the time of the clock, all the solutions of the

ODE are bounded by a constant (2 in practice). While in the reader module, the concentration of the precision species increases with the precision (quite obviously). However, we should also stress that it is unclear how exactly the complexity of the PODE/CRN computation framework can be related to that of conventional computation on a Turing machine, apart from the characterization of the polynomial time complexity class [2].

5 Conclusion

In this paper, we have presented a CRN converter that allows us to read an analog input such as the concentration of a chemical species by displaying its dyadic representation as a series of binary spikes on the concentration of an output species. We also conduct an in-depth analysis of the precision that is theoretically possible to reach with such a device according to the tuning of the three main types of rates that appear in the reaction: the clock k_{clock}, the approximate-majority k_{AM} and the basic operations k_{exp}. In particular, we show that for fixed k_{exp} and k_{AM} adjusting the clock leads to a reading time that increases quadratically with the desired precision while keeping all the concentration within constant bounds.

We thus have contributed to both theoretical questions exposed in the introduction.

Concerning the computation with PODE, we have shown that it is indeed possible to construct a PODE that takes in input a bounded concentration and a desired precision and returns the dyadic encoding of a number approaching the input with the desired precision. Provided that we prove bounds on the behavior of the clock and the halter module on a formal level, this would validate the computational framework proposed in [6] on a more practical level.

Regarding the Hartmanis-Stearns conjecture, this clarifies the picture. If it is possible to compute the value of an algebraic irrational number in real time, it is actually more difficult to read the output value once the computation has reached a sufficient precision. Indeed, the reader module is either bounded by a constant and quadratic in the precision needed or linear in time but bounded by a variable that scales like the precision. The difficult question to determine how these behaviors may be related to the number of transitions of a multi-tape Turing machine is still pending.

This work could be extended in several directions. The most interesting one would be to replace the clock with a handshaking mechanism. The idea would be to wait until sufficient precision is reached before launching the next step of the computation. This would allow for a kind of dynamical adjustment of the time spent on the different cycles, going fast when the input is close to 0 or 1 and taking more time when the comparison is difficult.

It is also unclear if this CRN is optimal in terms of time and space complexity for the desired behavior. As this kind of analog framework is relatively new, very few works exist to determine such bounds and even, what are the relevant quantities to look at. In [2], Pouly proposes the length of the solution curve and shows that it allows us to characterize the P-time class. But how it is possible to build other classes of complexity inside the analog computation framework and how to relate them to the ones of the logical complexity is still a field largely unexplored.

Finally, we also start working at the other end of the chain: looking at how we can build a concentration satisfying a desired precision from a dyadic encoding as input. As we try to ensure some form of robustness with respect to the timing and intensity of the spikes, this work is surprisingly more difficult than the one discussed here. But it is in a good way and may be the subject of a short communication in future work.

A Appendix

A.1 Precision Computation

Most differential equations involved in the dyadic converter harbor converging exponential as solutions, that is, functions of the form:

$$f(t) = f_\infty + (f_0 - f_\infty)\, e^{-k_{\exp} t},$$

where f_0 is the value of the concentration at $t = 0$, f_∞ is the desired steady state, and $k_{\exp}$ is the rate constant of the reaction. For model (9), this covers all the reactions for which the rate is set to "rate".

Thus, if we suppose that the reactions are active for a time larger than τ, the function is stopped at a value closer to f_∞ than: $f_\infty + (f_0 - f_\infty)e^{-k_{\exp}\tau}$, introducing the adimensional quantity $\epsilon = e^{-k_{\exp}\tau}$ we can bound the final value f_τ by (in the case where $f_0 < f_\infty$):

$$f_\tau \in [f_0 + (f_0 - f_\infty)\epsilon, f_\infty] \tag{14}$$

Knowing this allows us to compute the bounds on the value of the different species during the time evolution of one cycle of our converter module as presented in Table 2; and at the end, the concentration I_f of the Input species at the end of one clock cycle as a function of its concentration I_0 at the start of the cycle, specifically:

$$\begin{cases} I_f \in [2I_0 - 3\epsilon, 2I_0] & \text{if } I_0 < \frac{1}{2}, \\ I_f \in [2I_0 - 1 - 2\epsilon, 2I_0 - 1 + \epsilon] & \text{if } I_0 > \frac{1}{2}. \end{cases} \tag{15}$$

Table 2. Bounds on the concentration of the main species of the dyadic converter after the end of the different steps. When needed, we point to the cases where the output species have spiked (I) or not (O). Minus signs indicate that the value does not have changed.

	Input	Tempo	Copy	Half	Output
Step 0	I_0	0	0	0	0
Step 1	I_0	$[I_0(1-\epsilon), I_0]$	-	$[\frac{1}{2}(1-\epsilon), \frac{1}{2}]$	-
Step 4	$[I_0 + I_0(1-\epsilon)^2, 2I_0]$	$[0, I_0(1-\epsilon)]$	$[I_0(1-\epsilon)^2, I_0]$	-	-
Step 5 (O)	-	-	$[0, \frac{\epsilon}{\tau k_{\text{exp}}}]$	$\simeq I_0 + \frac{1}{2}$	-
Step 5 (I)	-	-	$\simeq I_0 + \frac{1}{2}$	$[0, \frac{\epsilon}{\tau k_{\text{exp}}}]$	-
Step 6 (O)	-	-	-	-	$[0, \epsilon]$
Step 6 (I)	-	-	-	-	$[1-\epsilon, 1]$
Step 7	-	$[0, \epsilon]$	$[0, \epsilon]$	$[0, \epsilon]$	-
Step 8 (O)	$[I_0 + I_0(1-\epsilon)^2 - \epsilon, 2I_0]$	-	-	-	$[0, \epsilon]$
Step 8 (I)	$[I_0 + I_0(1-\epsilon)^2 - 1, 2I_0 - 1 + \epsilon]$	-	-	-	$[0, \epsilon]$

Considering the worst case with an error of order 3ϵ this means that at each step, the value of the Input accumulated an error like: $e_{n+1} = 2e_n + 3\epsilon$, so that after n steps, the error scales like:

$$e_n = 3\left(2^n - 1\right)\epsilon,$$

thus if we still want good precision at step p, this means that we have to impose:

$$\begin{aligned} 3 \cdot 2^p \epsilon &\ll 1, \\ e^{-k_{\text{exp}}\tau} &\ll 2^{-p}, \\ k_{\text{exp}}\tau &\gg p. \end{aligned} \tag{16}$$

Now, reaching step p asks for a time $T(p) = 8\tau p$ as the clock cycle comports eight steps. As we have $\tau \propto p$ by our previous computation, we can conclude that reaching a given precision asks for a time that scales quadratically:

$$T(p) \propto \frac{p^2}{k_{\text{exp}}}. \tag{17}$$

A.2 Convergence of Approximate Majority

Let us remind the ODEs associated to the model (6):

$$\begin{aligned} \dot{A} &= -k_1 AH + k_2 UA \\ \dot{H} &= -k_1 AH + k_2 UH \\ \dot{U} &= 2k_1 AH - k_2 U(A+H) \end{aligned} \tag{18}$$

The obvious conserved quantity ($A + H + U = C_t$) allows us to introduce the reduced variables: $a = \frac{A}{C_t}$, $u = \frac{U}{C_t}$ and $(1 - a - u)$ as the equivalent for H. We obtain the equations[3]:

$$\begin{aligned} \dot{a} &= -k_1(a(1-a-u)) + k_2ua & a(t=0) &= \alpha \\ \dot{u} &= 2k_1(a(1-a-u)) - k_2u(1-u) & u(t=0) &= 0 \end{aligned} \tag{19}$$

Once again a change of variable is necessary to simplify these equations, we use the variable $\tilde{a} = a + \frac{u}{2}$, giving:

$$\begin{aligned} \dot{\tilde{a}} &= k_2u(\tilde{a} - \frac{1}{2}) \\ \dot{u} &= 2k_1(\tilde{a} - \frac{u}{2})(1 - \tilde{a} - \frac{u}{2}) - k_2u(1-u) \end{aligned} \tag{20}$$

Supposing that $k_1 \gg k_2$ allows us to approximate u as a fast variable with the equilibrium given by:

$$u = \left(\sqrt{4\tilde{a}(1-\tilde{a})+1} - 1\right), \tag{21}$$

that we can plug in the equation of $\tilde{a}$. As this equation is separable, we obtain the relation:

$$\begin{aligned} k_2t + c_1 = &-\log(\sqrt{s}-1) - log(\sqrt{s} - 2\tilde{a} - 1) + (1+\sqrt{2})\log(\sqrt{s} - 2\sqrt{2}\tilde{a} + 2\tilde{a} - 1) \\ &-(\sqrt{2}-1)\log(\sqrt{s} + 2(1+\sqrt{s})\tilde{a} - 1) = f_i(\tilde{a}) \end{aligned} \tag{22}$$

where for readability, we denote: $\sqrt{4\tilde{a}(1-\tilde{a})+1} = \sqrt{s}$ and c_1 is an integration constant that should be computed from the initial condition. The function f_i is symetrical under the relation $\tilde{a} \to 1 - \tilde{a}$ and describes the evolution of the system over time. That is, if we want a final value r while starting at $\tilde{a}_0$, we have to wait for a time: $t = \frac{f_i(r) - f_i(\tilde{a}_0)}{k_2}$. In our case, we have a fixed time τ a precision requirement r and want to determine how close we can be to one half to still reach it. That is, we want to know δ such that:

$$k_2\tau = f_i(r) - f_i(\frac{1}{2} - \delta).$$

An expansion around both $r \ll 1$ and $\delta \ll 1$ gives us:

$$\begin{aligned} k_2\tau &= -\log 4r^2 - (1+\sqrt{2})\log\delta \\ \log\delta &= -\frac{\log 4r^2}{1+\sqrt{2}} - \frac{k_2\tau}{1+\sqrt{2}} \end{aligned} \tag{23}$$

From this, we can estimate the scaling of the critical threshold, below which the approximate majority is not able to discern the majority species as a function of k_2 and τ:

$$\delta^\star \propto \exp -\frac{k_2\tau}{1+\sqrt{2}}. \tag{24}$$

[3] To be exact, we should also replace k_1 and k_2 by their rescaled version $\tilde{k} = kC_t$, we omit this detail for the sake of readability.

All this derivation has been done under the assumption that $k_1 \gg k_2$ which is the most natural one. To be complete, suppose that $k_1 \ll k_2$. We can easily prove that, once again, u equilibrates quickly near 0 giving us: $u = \frac{2k_1}{k_2}\tilde{a}(1-\tilde{a})$ and inserting it in the equation over $\tilde{a}$ we have:

$$\dot{\tilde{a}} = 2k_1\tilde{a}(1-\tilde{a})(\tilde{a}-\frac{1}{2}). \tag{25}$$

In this simpler case, we have the analytical solution:

$$\tilde{a}(t) = \frac{4e^{c_0} + e^{k_1 t} \pm \sqrt{4e^{c_0+k_1 t} + e^{2k_1 t}}}{2(4e^{c_0} + e^{k_1 t})}, \tag{26}$$

where c_0 is the integration constant that can be derived from the initial condition. The two important elements to remark are that the $\pm$ sign depends on whether α is initially higher or lower than one half and that the system follows the same kind of sigmoidal pattern as previously, starting by a slow phase to escape the intermediate region followed by an exponential convergence toward one of the two attractors that are 0 and 1.

From this, we can derive the same kind of relation as previously:

$$\delta^\star \propto e^{-\frac{k_1\tau}{2}}.$$

A.3 Integrating over a Cosine

We approximate the sine wave of our clock by square signal to ease the analysis. Actually, we can pretty easily compute the equivalent of our $\epsilon = \exp -\tau k_{\text{exp}}$ quantity for a sinusoidal wave of frequency ω.

Let us use the activator species T to activate two reactions, thus creating a simple steady state for the molecule R (for reporter): $T \xleftrightarrow{k_{\text{exp}}} T + R$ and use a sinusoidal profile:

$$T(t) = \begin{cases} \sin t\omega\pi & \text{if } t \in [0, \omega^{-1}] \\ 0 & \text{otherwise} \end{cases} \tag{27}$$

The associated ODE is: $\dot{A} = k_{\text{exp}}T(1-A)$ that is separable, and thus we easily obtain:

$$A_\infty = 1 - e^{-\frac{2k_{\text{exp}}}{\omega\pi}} = 1 - \epsilon. \tag{28}$$

Hence, in our case where $\omega = \pi^{-1}$, we simply have $\epsilon = e^{-2k_{\text{exp}}}$ where k_{exp} is the rate constant of the main reaction of the current step. Or said otherwise, the sine wave is equivalent to a square signal of duration $\tau = 2$.

A.4 Linker CRN

The following CRN presents a prototype of linker CRN that allows to use our reader CRN on the output of a computing CRN as presented by Fages et al. Here, y is the species mimicking the precision of the main CRN, a is an activator that spikes when the desired precision p is reached. Finally, s_{compute} and s_{read} represent the two species of the switch that turns the whole CRN from computing to reading mode by catalyzing every reactions in their respective parts.

$$\begin{aligned} y + s_{\text{compute}} &\xrightarrow{1} s_{\text{compute}}, & a &\leftrightarrow \emptyset, \\ y + a + p &\xrightarrow{2k_f} y + 2 \cdot a + p, & 2 \cdot y + a &\xrightarrow{k_f} 2 \cdot y, \\ 2 \cdot p + a &\xrightarrow{k_f} 2 \cdot p, & & \\ s_{\text{compute}} + a &\xrightarrow{1} s_{\text{read}} + a, & s_{\text{compute}} + s_{\text{read}} &\xrightarrow{1} 2 \cdot s_{\text{read}}. \end{aligned} \tag{29}$$

With at $t = 0$, $s_{\text{compute}} = 1$ and $a = 1$.

References

1. Bournez, O., Campagnolo, M.L., Graça, D.S., Hainry, E.: Polynomial differential equations compute all real computable functions on computable compact intervals. J. Complex. **23**(3), 317–335 (2007)
2. Bournez, O., Graça, D.S., Pouly, A.: Polynomial time corresponds to solutions of polynomial ordinary differential equations of polynomial length. In: 43rd International Colloquium on Automata, Languages, and Programming, ICALP 2016, 11–15 July 2016, Rome, Italy. LIPIcs, vol. 55, pp. 109:1–109:15. Schloss Dagstuhl - Leibniz-Zentrum fuer Informatik (2016)
3. Bournez, O., Graça, D.S., Pouly, A.: On the functions generated by the general purpose analog computer. Inf. Comput. (2017)
4. Cardelli, L., Csikász-Nagy, A.: The cell cycle switch computes approximate majority. Sci. Rep. **2**, 09 (2012)
5. Fages, F., Hemery, M., Soliman, S.: On biocham symbolic computation pipeline for compiling mathematical functions into biochemistry. ACM Commun. Comput. Algebra **58**(2), 15–22 (2025)
6. Fages, F., Le Guludec, G., Bournez, O., Pouly, A.: Strong turing completeness of continuous chemical reaction networks and compilation of mixed analog-digital programs. In: CMSB 2017: Proceedings of the Fifteenth International Conference on Computational Methods in Systems Biology. LNCS, vol. 10545, pp. 108–127. Springer (2017)
7. Graça, D.S., Costa, J.F.: Analog computers and recursive functions over the reals. J. Complex. **19**(5), 644–664 (2003)
8. Hartmanis, J., Stearns, R.E.: On the computational complexity of algorithms. Trans. Am. Math. Soc. **117**, 285–306 (1965)
9. Hemery, M., Fages, F., Soliman, S.: On the complexity of quadratization for polynomial differential equations. In: Abate, A., Petrov, T., Wolf, V. (eds.) CMSB 2020. LNCS, vol. 12314, pp. 120–140. Springer, Cham (2020). https://doi.org/10.1007/978-3-030-60327-4_7
10. Hemery, M., Fages, F., Soliman, S.: Compiling elementary mathematical functions into finite chemical reaction networks via a polynomialization algorithm for ODEs. In: Cinquemani, E., Paulevé, L. (eds.) CMSB 2021. LNCS, vol. 12881, pp. 74–90. Springer, Cham (2021). https://doi.org/10.1007/978-3-030-85633-5_5
11. Hemery, M., Fages, F., Soliman, S.: A polynomialization algorithm for elementary functions and odes, and their compilation into chemical reaction networks. In: CASC 2021: Computer Algebra in Scientific Computing, Proceedings of Short Papers (2021)

12. Shannon, C.E.: Mathematical theory of the differential analyser. J. Math. Phys. **20**, 337–354 (1941)
13. Thomson, J.: On an integrating machine having a new kinematic principle. Van Nostrand's Eclectic Eng. Mag. (1869-1879) **15**(94), 301 (1876)
14. Turing, A.M., et al.: On computable numbers, with an application to the entscheidungsproblem. J. Math **58**(345–363), 5 (1936)
15. Voit, E.O., Martens, H.A., Omholt, S.W.: 150 years of the mass action law. PLoS Comput. Biol. **11**(1), e1004012 (2015)

Analog Computation with Transcriptional Networks

David Doty[1], Mina Latifi[1(✉)], and David Soloveichik[2]

[1] University of California Davis, Davis, CA, USA
{doty,milatifi}@ucdavis.edu
[2] The University of Texas at Austin, Austin, TX, USA
david.soloveichik@utexas.edu

Abstract. Transcriptional networks represent one of the most extensively studied types of systems in synthetic biology. Although the completeness of transcriptional networks for digital logic is well-established, *analog* computation plays a crucial role in biological systems and offers significant potential for synthetic biology applications. While transcriptional circuits typically rely on cooperativity and highly nonlinear behavior of transcription factors to regulate protein *production*, they are often modeled with simple linear *degradation* terms. In contrast, general analog dynamics require both positive and negative nonlinear terms, seemingly necessitating control over not just transcriptional (i.e., production) regulation but also the degradation rates of transcription factors.

Surprisingly, we prove that controlling transcription factor production (i.e., transcription rate) without explicitly controlling degradation is mathematically complete for analog computation, achieving equivalent capabilities to systems where both production and degradation are programmable. We demonstrate our approach on several examples including oscillatory and chaotic dynamics, analog sorting, memory, PID controller, and analog extremum seeking. Our result provides a systematic methodology for engineering novel analog dynamics using synthetic transcriptional networks without the added complexity of degradation control and informs our understanding of the capabilities of natural transcriptional circuits.

We provide a compiler, in the form of a Python package that can take any system of polynomial ODEs and convert it to an equivalent transcriptional network implementing the system *exactly*, under appropriate conditions.

Keywords: Analog computing · Transcriptional network · Gene regulatory network · Polynomial differential equation

1 Introduction

A *transcription factor* X is a protein that regulates the transcription (DNA $\rightarrow$ RNA) of a gene coding for a protein Y, either increasing the rate of production

P. T. Monteiro (Ed.): CMSB 2026, LNBI 16678, pp. 201–233, 2027.
https://doi.org/10.1007/978-3-032-30870-2_11

of Y (activation) or decreasing it (repression). Y could itself be another transcription factor. A *transcriptional network* is a set of transcription factors that regulate each other in this way.

Complex transcriptional networks have been extensively studied in synthetic biology to implement specific mathematical functions and behaviors, such as oscillation [17], bistability [20], Boolean logic [28], and analog function computation [15,36]. Many of these studies use transcription factors characterized by first-order (linear) degradation dynamics. Linear degradation provides an accurate model for studying promoter dynamics in bacteria, particularly in the context of transcriptional rate variability due to growth conditions and extrinsic factors [34].

Various techniques can potentially be employed to construct transcriptional networks with arbitrary complexity and wiring. One such approach is CRISPR interference (CRISPRi), a gene repression method that silences specific genes without altering DNA sequences [33]. CRISPRi has been used to design synthetic gene circuits, including logic circuits, bistable networks (toggle switches), stripe pattern formation using incoherent feed-forward loops (IFFL), and oscillators [19,35]. In addition to CRISPRi, CRISPR activation (CRISPRa) methods have been developed to activate genes by attaching transcriptional activator domains to dCas9 [13,24]. CRISPRa has been used in the design of synthetic systems, such as signal amplification [39]. Recent studies have shown that dual-mode CRISPRa/i architectures can simultaneously enable gene activation and repression within the same system [26]. Gene regulatory networks can also be implemented in controlled *in vitro* transcriptional systems, such as the synthetic oscillators demonstrated in [23], where interacting DNA templates and transcriptional reactions produce dynamic regulatory behavior.

These studies suggest that transcriptional networks are an expressive and reliable target for implementing analog computation and other sophisticated dynamical behaviors in cells, i.e., a useful *in vivo* programming language. However, the theoretical limits to their power are poorly understood: *How* expressive are these networks? What class of analog computations are they able to achieve? To answer these questions, we must formalize a precise model of transcriptional networks. There are various related approaches to this [16], typically using Hill functions [1] to control the production rate (positive terms of $\frac{dx}{dt}$) of a transcription factor X (with concentration x) and having a single negative term $-\gamma x$, for some constant $\gamma > 0$, i.e., linear degradation.

The latter constraint follows from the idea that, although mechanisms exist to regulate the *production* of X with other transcription factors, *decay* typically occurs through two mechanisms: degradation by proteases, and cell division that increases volume, effectively decreasing concentrations. When proteases act non-specifically[1] and/or the latter mechanism is dominant—the regime studied in this paper—the degradation constant γ is the same for all transcription factors.

In contrast to this uniform linear decay, most of the interesting nonlinear behavior in typical transcriptional networks happens in the production

[1] Section 6 discusses this assumption in more detail.

rates. We model these as any *nonnegative Laurent polynomial*, a generalization of multivariate polynomials to allow negative integer exponents, for instance $x^2y^{-3}+4zw^{-1}+5$, where negative-exponent factors are repressors and positive-exponent factors are activators. (While this formal class unrealistically allows arbitrarily many activators and repressors per promoter, Theorem 4 shows that the construction can be reduced to monomials of the form $\alpha\frac{a_1a_2}{r}$, corresponding to at most two activators and one repressor, without loss of computational power.) These positive Laurent-polynomial production rates relate to broader power-law kinetic formalisms that allow negative exponents (often without restricting them to integers), including S-system models in Biochemical Systems Theory [41] and generalized-mass-action/power-law systems in CRNT [3,6,27]. We justify in Appendix A.1 our choice of production rates as approximable by the more standard Hill functions.

Polynomial ordinary differential equations (ODEs) are a noteworthy class of analog computational models, which have received far more theoretical attention than transcriptional networks. As shown by Claude Shannon [38], polynomial ODEs are equivalent to the GPAC (general purpose analog computer) model that Shannon defined to model the capabilities of the differential analyzer machine invented by Vannevar Bush [10] to automate numerical solution of differential equations. It is known [38, Theorem XI] (see also corrected proof in [32, Footnote 12]) that ODEs defined by non-hypertranscendental functions[2] can be converted into an equivalent set of polynomial ODEs (possibly over a larger set of variables), such that the variables in the polynomial ODEs corresponding to the original variables have the same trajectories.[3] Furthermore, polynomial ODEs have recently been discovered to have essentially maximal *digital* computational power, being able to simulate arbitrary Turing machines [7]. Being so expressive, polynomial ODEs are an attractive target for implementation by other analog models of computation.

Compared to polynomial ODEs, the primary limitation of transcriptional networks is that the ODE for a transcription factor X has exactly one negative term and it is of the linear form $-\gamma x$, where γ is the same for all transcription factors. In contrast, polynomial ODEs can have arbitrarily complex negative terms. It thus appears difficult to simulate arbitrary polynomial ODEs with a system that has such a strong limitation on its negative terms.

---

[2] Non-hypertranscendental functions are those that are solutions of algebraic differential equations. This includes all algebraic functions such as polynomials, Laurent polynomials, and $\sqrt{x}$, as well as some transcendental functions such as exponential, logarithm, trigonometric, and hyperbolic functions, but excluding, for example, the gamma function Γ generalizing factorial (for positive integer n, $\Gamma(n) = (n-1)!$) to complex inputs.

[3] For example, the non-polynomial ODE $x' = \sqrt{x}$ is equivalent to the polynomial ODEs $x' = y$ and $y' = 1/2$, letting $y = \sqrt{x}$. Evidently $x' = y$, and by the chain rule, $y' = \frac{d\sqrt{x}}{dt} = \frac{d\sqrt{x}}{dx} \cdot \frac{dx}{dt} = \frac{1}{2\sqrt{x}} \cdot \mathrm{y} = \frac{1}{2\sqrt{x}} \cdot \sqrt{x} = 1/2$ as chosen.

Surprisingly, our main result, Theorem 2 (Sect. 3), shows that "almost"[4] any system of polynomial ODEs whose variables stay nonnegative can be "ratio-implemented" by a transcriptional network. This means that for each variable x in the original ODEs, there is a pair of transcription factors $X^\top, X^\perp$ ("X-top" and "X-bottom"), such that for all times t, $\frac{x^\top(t)}{x^\perp(t)} = x(t)$, where $x^\top(t), x^\perp(t)$ represent the concentrations of $X^\top, X^\perp$ at time t respectively. Intuitively, the reason that this ratio representation of values helps is that, if all transcription factors decay at rate γ for the same amount of time, this preserves all ratios between them.

The nonnegativity requirement is not a fundamental limitation. One can use a *dual-rail* representation (c.f., [12,30]), in which each variable x is encoded as the difference of two nonnegative quantities $x^+ - x^-$, allowing arbitrary real values to be represented while maintaining nonnegativity of all variables. This also avoids issues with variables approaching zero in non-Hungarian form, since both x^+ and x^- remain positive even when their difference converges to zero. In some of our examples such as the sine-cosine oscillator, we use a simpler ad-hoc trick of "shifting values up" to maintain nonnegativity; see Sect. 5. (This is not a general-purpose technique since it requires a lower bound on the negative values to know how much to shift; for example since sine and cosine are at least -1, we shift up by 2, and could shift by any $\alpha > 1$, to maintain positivity.)

A naïve implementation of the ratio-representation idea has the property that even if the variables of the original ODEs stay bounded (both above by some finite upper bound u, and also bounded away from 0 by some lower bound $\ell > 0$), the transcription factors could either diverge to ∞ or converge to 0, despite the ratios $\frac{x^\top}{x^\perp}$ staying in the interval (ℓ, u). (This simpler construction is shown in the proof of Theorem 2 as an intuitive warmup to the full construction.) Our construction (see Algorithm 1) overcomes this obstacle, maintaining the useful property that if the original variables were bounded in some interval (ℓ, u), then the new transcription factor variables are bounded in some (possibly larger) interval (ℓ', u'). The precise condition is somewhat complex and captured in Definitions 4 to 6.

Next (Theorem 4, Sect. 4), we show how to trade off "complexity" in this construction. It is reasonable to worry that using arbitrarily many activators and repressors on a single promoter site pushes the regulation model too far. We show how to modify the construction of Algorithm 1 so that each Laurent monomial term is at most of the form $\alpha\frac{a_1 a_2}{r}$, i.e., each promoter site is regulated by at most two activators (a_1, a_2) and one repressor (r). The tradeoff is that additional transcription factors must be introduced in addition to the pair $x_i^\top, x_i^\perp$ for each original polynomial ODE variable x. This is done by first converting the polynomial ODEs to have extra variables $z_{i,j}$ corresponding to the j'th monomial on the right-hand side of $\dot{x}_i$. Each such new variable then would get its own pair

[4] The condition we require the polynomial ODEs to satisfy, other than staying nonnegative, is that any variable that starts at 0 or converges to 0 must have a "Hungarian form" ODE, which roughly means "is the ODE of some chemical reaction network"; see Definition 2.

of transcription factors $z_{i,j}^{\top}, z_{i,j}^{\perp}$. One additional constraint for this construction to work is that all variables must start strictly positive, though we are unsure if this is truly necessary or simply helps our proof, whereas Theorem 2 allows "Hungarian" variables (Definition 2) to start at 0 before becoming positive.

Finally, we provide a compiler that implements the main construction of Theorem 2, the Python package `ode2tn` [29]. All examples in Sect. 5 were simulated using `ode2tn`.

We note prior unpublished work studying the computational power of transcriptional networks for analog computation with a different approximation of Hill-function kinetics than in the current paper [40].

2 Preliminaries

Throughout this paper, for a real variable x, a function of time t, we sometimes write x' to denote $\frac{dx}{dt}$, the derivative of x with respect to t.

We recall the definition of a Laurent polynomial, which generalizes the idea of a (multivariate) polynomial to allow negative integer exponents.

Definition 1 (Laurent polynomial). *A* Laurent polynomial *is of the form:* $p(x_1, \ldots, x_n) = \sum_{k=1}^{\ell} c_k \prod_{i=1}^{n} x_i^{e_{k,i}}$, *where each* $c_k \in \mathbb{R}$ *and* $e_{k,i} \in \mathbb{Z}$ *(not necessarily positive). If each* $c_k \geq 0$, *we say* p *is* nonnegative. *If* $\ell = 1$, *we say* p *is a* Laurent monomial.

For example $\frac{x^2}{y^3} + 4z^5 + \frac{5}{x} - \frac{6}{w^2}$ is a Laurent polynomial consisting of four Laurent monomials. It is not nonnegative because the coefficient of the last monomial is -6. Note that a (standard) polynomial is a Laurent polynomial with all $e_{k,i} \geq 0$. We similarly say a polynomial is *nonnegative* if all of its coefficients $c_k \geq 0$.

We now define a class of ODEs that are of interest because they correspond precisely to the class of ODEs that represent the dynamical systems known as chemical reaction networks (CRNs) [12]. We follow the convention throughout this paper that for a chemical species X (including transcription factors discussed below) written in uppercase, its concentration is represented by the same lowercase letter x. CRNs consist of reactions among abstract species such as $A + 2B \xrightarrow{k} 3C$. Each reaction's rate is the product of its reactant concentrations and the *rate constant* written above the arrow, and each species X has a positive (respectively, negative) derivative term for each reaction net producing (resp., consuming) X. For example, the reaction above would correspond under the standard mass-action model of kinetics to the ODEs $a' = -kab^2, b' = -2kab^2, c' = 3kab^2$.

A negative term for x' means in the reaction that contributes to that term, X is net consumed, thus is a reactant, implying x must appear as a factor in the negative term, motivating the following definition, originating from [22], with terminology taken from [12].

Definition 2. *A system of polynomial ODEs over variables $x_1, \ldots, x_n$ is in* Hungarian form *for a particular variable x_i if there are nonnegative polynomials p_i^+ and q_i^- such that*

$$x_i' = p_i^+(x_1, \ldots, x_n) - x_i \cdot q_i^-(x_1, \ldots, x_n).$$

In other words q_i^- consists of the negative terms of x_i', divided by x_i. We say that a system of polynomial ODEs is in *Hungarian form* (without reference to a variable) if it is in Hungarian form for all its variables. In fact, a system of ODEs is in Hungarian form if and only if it is the set of ODEs describing the kinetics of some CRN [22]. It is also known that a set of polynomial ODEs is in Hungarian form if and only if, for all nonnegative initial conditions, the variables stay nonnegative.

2.1 Transcriptional Networks

Intuitively, a transcriptional network is a system of chemical species, called *transcription factors*, where each factor X is produced at a rate depending on other factors, and decays at rate γx, where $\gamma > 0$ is the same for all transcription factors. The factors regulating X's production rate p are either *activators*, increasing p, or *repressors*, decreasing p (Fig. 1). We allow the production rate to be an arbitrary Laurent polynomial whose variables are transcription factor concentrations; this choice is justified in Appendix A.1.

Definition 3. *A* transcriptional network *is a system of ordinary differential equations (ODEs) over variables $x_1, \ldots, x_n$ representing* transcription factor *concentrations*

$$\begin{aligned} x_1' &= p_1(x_1, x_2, \ldots x_n) - \gamma x_1 \\ x_2' &= p_2(x_1, x_2, \ldots x_n) - \gamma x_2 \\ &\vdots \\ x_n' &= p_n(x_1, x_2, \ldots x_n) - \gamma x_n, \end{aligned}$$

where each p_i is a nonnegative Laurent polynomial, and $\gamma > 0$ is called the decay constant.

Positive exponent factors such as a or a^2 in Laurent polynomials for x' imply that A is an activator for X; negative exponent factors such as $\frac{1}{r}$ imply that R is a repressor for X.

3 Transcriptional Networks Can Implement Nonnegative Polynomial ODEs

This section demonstrates how transcriptional networks can implement any system of polynomial ordinary differential equations (ODEs) with the caveats given

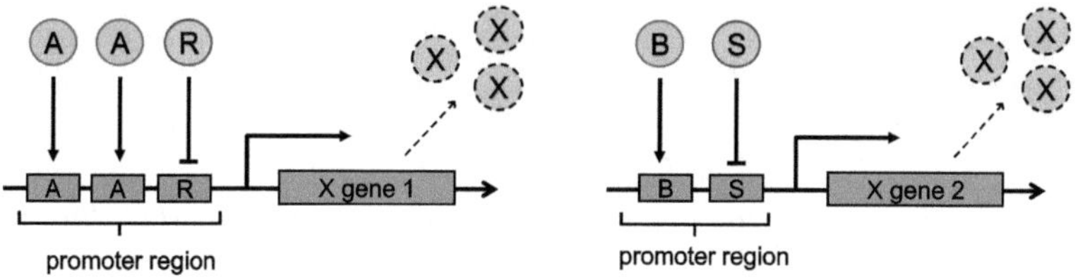

Fig. 1. The transcription factors, activator A and repressor R, regulate X gene 1 (shown on the left) controlling the production rate of protein X (assumed to be produced instantly on translation, though in reality only an mRNA strand would be produced by transcription, and subsequent ribosomal translation of the mRNA into a protein would be necessary to produce X). Similarly, activator B and repressor S, regulate X gene 2 (shown on the right). Each transcription factor has a specific binding site on the promoter, allowing it to bind independently of the other transcription factors. In cells, X may or may not be a transcription factor itself; in this paper we assume that all genes encode transcription factors. Based on Definition 3, the ODE for transcription factor X is $x' = a^2/r + b/s - \gamma x$. (Uppercase letters denote transcription factors, and lowercase letters denote their concentrations.)

in Theorem 2. The key concept is that variables x_i in the original system are represented as a ratio of two transcription factor concentrations $x_i = x_i^\top / x_i^\perp$. This ratio representation seems natural in the context of identical linear decay since it remains unchanged when both the numerator and denominator decrease at the same first-order rate (i.e., $-\gamma x_i^\top$ and $-\gamma x_i^\perp$).

However, we must develop technical machinery to address the following questions: (1) How to control the production rate of $X_i^\top$ and $X_i^\perp$ to ensure that the ratio $x_i = x_i^\top / x_i^\perp$ traces the original trajectory? (2) Note that the ratio representation may correctly represent the value x_i, but both the numerator and denominator go to infinity or to zero. Clearly transcription factors must remain bounded, and, further, we cannot expect the system to be reliable if the ratio is represented with very small values in both the numerator $x_i^\top$ and denominator $x_i^\perp$ to represent a much larger x_i, since small values are subject to more environmental noise.[5] How can we avoid such instability?

A *trajectory of a dynamical system* (e.g., a set of polynomial ODEs) over a set of variables $x_1, \ldots, x_n$ is a function $\rho : \mathbb{R}_{\geq 0} \to \mathbb{R}^n$, where $\rho(t)_i$ is the value of x_i at time t, also written as $x_i(t)$. The trajectory may not be defined over all time; then we allow $\rho : [0, t_{\max}) \to \mathbb{R}^n$ for $t_{\max} \in \mathbb{R}_{\geq 0} \cup \infty$.[6]

[5] That said, it is realistic to expect that the original ODEs might converge x_i to 0; in which case the transcriptional network should of course converge $x_i^\top$ to 0 as well.

[6] For most systems $t_{\max} = \infty$. However, even natural systems such as CRNs can have pathological behavior: for example the reaction $2X \to 3X$, starting with $X(0) = 1$, has solution $X(t) = 1/(1-t)$, so that $\lim_{t \to 1} X(t) = \infty$. However, this trajectory is defined and finite on the bounded domain $[0, 1)$ (i.e., $t_{\max} = 1$), and indeed, the construction of Theorem 2 applied to that CRN gives a transcriptional network where $\lim_{t \to 1} x^\top(t)/x^\perp(t) = \infty$, yet $x^\top(t)$ and $x^\perp(t)$ are finite for all $t < 1$.

Definition 4. *Let $t_{\max} \in \mathbb{R}_{\geq 0} \cup \infty$ and let $\rho : [0, t_{\max}) \to \mathbb{R}^n_{\geq 0}$ be a trajectory of a dynamical system defined for all $t \in [0, t_{\max})$. We say a transcriptional network $\mathcal{F}$* ratio-implements *ρ if each variable x_i of ρ is mapped to a pair of transcription factors $X_i^\top, X_i^\perp$ of $\mathcal{F}$ such that $\mathcal{F}$ is defined on $[0, t_{\max})$ and the following holds.*[7] *For each variable x_i of ρ, for any $x_i^\top(0) \in \mathbb{R}_{\geq 0}$, $x_i^\perp(0) \in \mathbb{R}_{>0}$ such that $x_i(0) = x_i^\top(0)/x_i^\perp(0)$, for all future times $0 < t < t_{\max}$, $x_i(t) = x_i^\top(t)/x_i^\perp(t)$.*

Of course, the underlying polynomial ODEs may diverge to ∞ or converge to 0 for some variables; if so then certainly the transcriptional network must do the same (e.g., sending x to 0 either by sending $x^\top$ to 0 or $x^\perp$ to ∞). However, if the original variables stay bounded in an open interval (ℓ, h) for $0 < \ell < h < \infty$, then we would like the transcription factors to stay bounded in this way as well.

Definition 5. *A trajectory ρ is* bounded-above *on a set of variables X if for all $x \in X$, there is $b_{\max}$ such that for all $t \in [0, t_{\max})$, $x(t) < b_{\max}$ (i.e., $x(t)$ does not diverge, i.e., $\sup_{0 \leq t < t_{\max}} x(t) < \infty$). Similarly, ρ is* bounded-positive *on a set of variables X if for all $x \in X$, there is $b_{\min} > 0$ such that for all $t \in [0, t_{\max})$, $x(t) > b_{\min}$. We say ρ is* bookended *on a set of variables X if it is both bounded-above and bounded-positive on X.*

When we omit the set of variables X, then bounded-above, bounded-positive, and bookended means with respect to all the variables $X = \{x_1, \ldots, x_n\}$.

Definition 6. *Suppose a transcriptional network $\mathcal{F}$ ratio-implements a trajectory ρ. We say that $\mathcal{F}$ ratio-implements ρ* stably *if the trajectory of $\mathcal{F}$ is bounded-positive on the set of all $x_i^\perp$, and if ρ being bounded above on all variables implies that $\mathcal{F}$ is bounded above on all variables (thus bookended on all $x_i^\perp$).*

Note that the final part of Definition 6 does not follow from the first and the correctness of the ratio-representation: it is possible that in ρ some variable x_i goes to 0, yet possibly $\mathcal{F}$ ratio-implements this by letting $x_i^\perp$ go to ∞. We want to avoid this, since it is unrealistic to have concentrations approach ∞.

Note that if ρ diverges on even a single variable, then possibly any transcription factor concentration $x_i^\top$ or $x_i^\perp$ can diverge while maintaining the correct ratio $x_i = x_i^\top/x_i^\perp$. On the other hand if ρ does not diverge, then every transcription factor in a stable ratio-implementation remains bounded-above. Ensuring that $x_i^\perp$ is bounded-positive avoids the other issue identified at the beginning of this section: the possibility that both $x_i^\top$ and $x_i^\perp$ go to zero while maintaining the correct ratio.

We note that to show an implementation of a bounded-above ρ is stable, it suffices to show that the $x_i^\perp$ are bookended.

[7] Certainly if $x_i(t)$ is defined for all $t \in [0, t_{\max})$, so must be $x_i^\top$ and $x_i^\perp$ for their ratio to obey $x_i(t) = x_i^\top(t)/x_i^\perp(t)$ on that interval, but the definition allows (as in Theorem 4, for instance) to introduce auxiliary variables, and these must be defined on that interval as well.

Observation 1. *Due to the correctness of ratio-implementation, i.e., maintaining that* $x_i(t) = \frac{x_i^\top(t)}{x_i^\perp(t)}$ *for all* $t \in [0, t_{\max})$, *if* $x_i^\perp$ *is bookended, then* x_i *is bounded-above if and only if* $x_i^\top$ *is bounded-above.*

In other words, if we interpret diverging as a "realism" constraint, then a stable implementation is precisely as realistic as the ODEs being implemented.

One could generalize the definition of ratio-implementation to other representations, including the direct representation where each variable x in the original dynamical system is represented directly by a transcription factor x, or perhaps a mix of the ratio representation for some variables and the direct representation for others. For simplicity, we state the definition in terms of the ratio representation studied in this paper. However, in the "extremum-seeking" example in Appendix D.5, we use a mixed representation.

Our main theorem says that a transcriptional network can implement arbitrary polynomial ODEs from any initial condition that stays nonnegative, so long as any variable whose ODE is not in Hungarian form stays bounded away from 0. (Note that staying bounded away from 0 means starting strictly positive, and also not converging to 0.) We note that γ is a parameter of Algorithm 1, not an output, since in general $b_{\max}$ is uncomputable from the ODEs and initial conditions, due to the ability of polynomial ODEs to simulate Turing machines [7]. A full proof of Theorem 2 is given in Appendix B.

Algorithm 1: Construction of a transcriptional network $\mathcal{F}(\gamma)$ from polynomial ODEs $P = (p_1, \ldots, p_n)$, with $\mathbf{x}(t) = (x_1(t), \ldots, x_n(t))$ representing the variables at time t. Note that the input is just the system of polynomial ODEs, but the constant γ below is chosen also based on bounds from a trajectory from specific initial conditions.

Rewrite each polynomial p_i as $x_i' = p_i^+(x_1, x_2, \ldots, x_n) - p_i^-(x_1, x_2, \ldots, x_n)$ where p_i^+ and p_i^- are non-negative polynomials.

For each x_i include two transcription factors $X_i^\top$ and $X_i^\perp$ with initial concentrations $x_i^\top(0) \geq 0$ and $x_i^\perp(0) > 0$ such that: $x_i(0) = \frac{x_i^\top(0)}{x_i^\perp(0)}$.

Construct the transcriptional network as:

$$\frac{dx_i^\top}{dt} = \beta x_i^\top / x_i^\perp + p_i^+ x_i^\perp - \gamma x_i^\top \tag{1}$$

$$\frac{dx_i^\perp}{dt} = \beta + p_i^- {x_i^\perp}^2 / x_i^\top - \gamma x_i^\perp \tag{2}$$

where $\beta > 0$ is any positive constant. γ is a parameter of the construction and must obey $\gamma > \max_i \sup_{t \geq 0} p_i^-(\mathbf{x}(t))/x_i(t)$. Equations (1) and (2) are assumed to be fully simplified; see Remark 2 and Remark 3.

Theorem 2. *Let* P *be a system of polynomial ODEs over the set of variables* $\mathcal{X}$ *that is in Hungarian form for the subset of variables* $\mathcal{X}_h \subseteq \mathcal{X}$ *(possibly empty* *set). Then there is a transcriptional network $\mathcal{F}(\gamma)$, constructed by Algorithm 1, such that for every upper-bound $b_{\max} > 0$, and every lower-bound $b_{\min} > 0$, there is $\gamma > 0$, such that for every nonnegative trajectory ρ of P that is bounded-above by $b_{\max}$ on $\mathcal{X}_h$ and bookended by $b_{\max}$ and $b_{\min}$ on $\mathcal{X} \setminus \mathcal{X}_h$, $\mathcal{F}(\gamma)$ stably ratio-implements ρ.*

Since we allowed the definition of transcriptional networks to have arbitrary Laurent polynomials (a strict superset of polynomials) as production rates, we could also have simulated arbitrary systems of ODEs with Laurent polynomials for each derivative. In other words, p_i^+ and p_i^- could be nonnegative Laurent polynomials.[8] This fact will be used later in Theorem 4.

We now argue that by slightly strengthening the conditions on the variables (requiring all variables, even Hungarian, not to start at 0 or approach 0) we can assume the original ODE system has Laurent polynomials.

Theorem 3. *Let P be a system of Laurent polynomial ODEs over the set of variables $\mathcal{X}$. Then there is a transcriptional network $\mathcal{F}(\gamma)$, constructed by Algorithm 1 with p_i^+ and p_i^- being nonnegative Laurent polynomials, such that for every upper-bound $b_{\max} > 0$ and every lower-bound $b_{\min} > 0$, there is $\gamma > 0$ such that for every trajectory ρ of P that is bookended by $b_{\max}$ and $b_{\min}$ on $\mathcal{X}$, $\mathcal{F}(\gamma)$ stably ratio-implements ρ.*

Remark 1. Our main construction in Algorithm 1 replaces each variable x in the polynomial ODEs with a pair of transcription factors (variables in a new set of Laurent polynomial ODEs) $X^\top, X^\perp$, such that for all t, $x(t) = \frac{x^\top(t)}{x^\perp(t)}$, the so-called "ratio representation" of x. It is also possible to inter-convert between these formats *without* replacing variables.

We have $x^\top$ and $x^\perp$ in a transcriptional network, but there is no transcription factor that directly represents the value x. Suppose we want a third transcription factor to *directly* represent the original value x, in addition to representing x indirectly via the ratio $\frac{x^\top}{x^\perp}$. Then we can introduce a new transcription factor $\hat{X}$ with ODE $\hat{x}' = \gamma(\frac{x^\top}{x^\perp} - \hat{x})$. The larger is γ, the more closely $\hat{x}$ tracks $x = \frac{x^\top}{x^\perp}$. (Recall from the proof of Theorem 2 that γ must be bounded away from 0, but it does not need to be bounded above, so we are free to set γ arbitrarily large to make $\hat{x}$ track x arbitrarily closely.) Note that this remains a transcriptional network, since the positive term is a Laurent monomial and the negative term is $-\gamma\hat{x}$ as required. We employ a similar trick in Appendix D.5, introducing a transcription factor x to track the value $\frac{z^\top}{z^\perp} + a\frac{p^\top}{p^\perp}$.

Conversely, if we have a single variable x in a transcriptional network, we can let $x^\top(0) = x(0)$, $x^\perp(0) = 1$, with $x^{\top\prime} = x'$ and $x^{\perp\prime} = \gamma - \gamma x^\perp$, which maintains

[8] Note that we could handle even more functions on the right-hand side of the ODEs (any non-hypertranscendental functions) by first converting to a system of polynomial ODEs [32]. However, the construction of Algorithm 1 works *directly* as shown (without any initial pre-transformation of the ODEs) on Laurent polynomials, hence could result in a simpler final transcriptional network than one obtained by first converting to polynomial ODEs.

the stronger condition that $x(t) = \frac{x^\top(t)}{x^\perp(t)}$ for all t (i.e., $\frac{x^\top}{x^\perp}$ "tracks" x with zero lag).

Remark 2. When applying the construction in Algorithm 1, algebraic simplification should be performed on the right-hand side of (1) and (2), reducing all rational expressions to lowest terms. This prevents having redundant fractions such as $\frac{x_i^\perp}{x_i^\perp}$, which would imply that $x_i^\perp$ acts simultaneously as both an activator and a repressor. Moreover, when a variable x_i is permitted to approach 0 (i.e., when x_i is Hungarian; see Theorem 2), this simplification is essential as shown in the next remark.

Remark 3. Note that a Hungarian form polynomial ODE can be written $x_i' = p_i^+ - x_i q_i^-$, where p_i^+ and q_i^- are arbitrary nonnegative polynomials in $x_1, \ldots, x_n$ (q_i^- being p_i^- with the common x_i factored out.) In this case Eq. (2) simplifies to $x_i^{\perp\prime} = \beta + q_i^- x_i^\perp - \gamma x_i^\perp$. Note that $x_i^\top$ no longer appears in the denominator; consequently, even when x_i (and hence $x_i^\top$) approaches 0, $x_i^\top$ is not a vanishing repressor in the actual transcriptional network, preserving the Hill-function regime of Appendix A.1 (see Remark 4).

4 Simplification of Transcriptional Network Limiting Activators and Repressors Per Promoter

The model of Laurent monomials to describe the effect of these on production rate may break down with a large number of activators and repressors on a single promoter site (see Appendix A.1). Thus a disadvantage of the construction of Algorithm 1 is that each transcription factor promoter can end up regulated by many activators and many repressors, corresponding to having many terms in the numerator and/or denominator of a single Laurent monomial, possibly pushing the model too far. To mitigate this concern, in this section we describe a way to simplify the construction such that each promoter is controlled by at most one repressor and at most two activators, i.e., each Laurent monomial will be of the form $\alpha\frac{a_1 a_2}{r}$ for two activators a_1, a_2 and a repressor r (possibly some of a_1, a_2, r may be missing).

We use a technique motivated by the methods of polynomial quadratization [11]—converting polynomial ODEs to have degree at most two. Importantly, however, we cannot simply compose the existing quadratization constructions with ours. Indeed, simply running the quadratized polynomial ODEs through our construction, would result in Laurent monomials of numerator degree 4 and denominator degree 3 (e.g., if the p_i^- term is the degree 2 monomial $x_j x_k$, then the middle monomial of (2) would be $\frac{x_j^\top}{x_j^\perp}\frac{x_k^\top}{x_k^\perp}\frac{{x_i^\perp}^2}{x_i^\top}$). Instead, we must carefully set up the initial polynomial ODE transformation to ensure cancellation of terms within the construction of Algorithm 1 will limit the degree of the numerator to at most 2 and denominator to at most 1.

We note that the conditions required on the ODEs of Theorem 4 are more stringent than those of Theorem 2, requiring all variables to start positive and stay bounded away from 0 (bounded-positive, Definition 5). This avoids some divide-by-zero problems in the construction, as shown in the full proof given in Appendix C.

Theorem 4. *Let P be a system of polynomial ODEs over the set of variables $\mathcal{X}$. Then there is a transcriptional network $\mathcal{F}(\gamma)$, whose every positive term is a Laurent monomial of the form $\alpha\frac{a_1 a_2}{r}$, where each a_1, a_2, r is a transcription factor or the constant 1. such that for every upper-bound $b_{\max} > 0$ and every lower-bound $b_{\min} > 0$, there is $\gamma > 0$, such that for every trajectory ρ of P that is bookended by $b_{\max}$ and $b_{\min}$ on $\mathcal{X}$, $\mathcal{F}(\gamma)$ stably ratio-implements ρ.*

5 Examples

We illustrate our main construction (Eqs. (1) and (2)) from Algorithm 1 on several example systems of polynomial ODEs. Code producing the plots is available at https://github.com/UC-Davis-molecular-computing/ode2tn/blob/main/notebook.ipynb. Additional examples are shown in Appendix D.

Unless explained otherwise, the plots of variables such as x are showing the value $\frac{x^\top}{x^\perp}$ over time for the underlying transcription factors $x^\top$ and $x^\perp$.

5.1 Sine-Cosine Oscillator

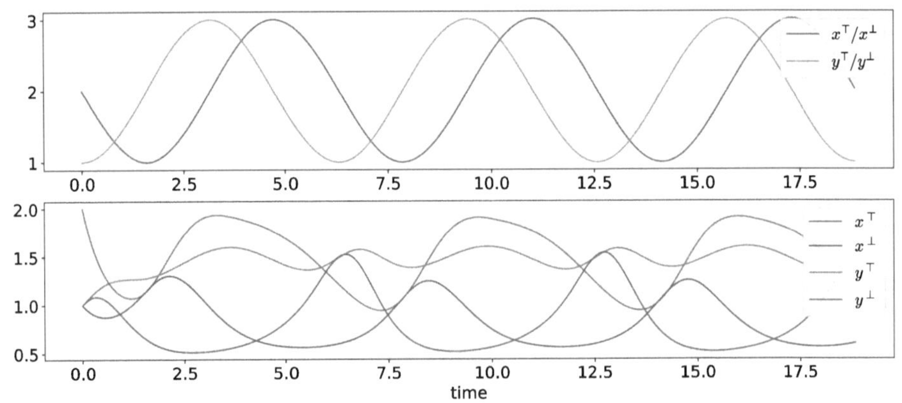

Fig. 2. Plot of "shifted positive" sine-cosine oscillator implemented with a transcriptional network. There are two subplots: the first shows the "original" variables x, y (i.e., the computed ratios $x^\top/x^\perp$ and $y^\top/y^\perp$). The second subplot shows underlying transcription factor variables $x^\top, x^\perp, y^\top, y^\perp$.

The sine-cosine oscillator is the system

$$x' = y$$
$$y' = -x$$

since we can write $x' = \sin(t)' = \cos(t) = y$ and $y' = \cos(t)' = -\sin(t) = -x$. However, this takes negative values, whereas transcription factor concentrations must be nonnegative. This could be solved with the so-called *dual-rail* representation [14] where negative values x can be represented as the difference of two positive values $x = x^+ - x^-$. However, it is simpler in this case simply to "shift" the oscillator upwards to stay positive. The following system, starting with $x = 2, y = 1$ (i.e., initial conditions where each variable starts 2 higher than originally), will oscillate between a maximum amplitude of 3 and a minimum amplitude of 1; see Fig. 2. It works by replacing variable v by $v-2$ wherever it appears in the ODEs.

$$
\begin{aligned}
x' &= y - 2 \\
y' &= -x + 2
\end{aligned}
$$

Recall we must choose a constant γ to apply the construction of Algorithm 1, which must be greater than the maximum value taken by any p_i^-/x_i. Here we think of $x_1 = x$ and $x_2 = y$. In this case, $p_1^- = 2$ (negative term for x') and $p_2^- = x$ (negative term for y'). We have $2/x \le 2$ (the case $i = 1$) and it turns out that $x/y < 2.5$ for all values in the trajectory of this oscillator. Thus choosing $\gamma = 2.5$ suffices to ensure all transcription factors stay bounded. In subsequent examples we omit a detailed analysis and simply pick a γ that appears empirically to keep the transcription factors bounded; note that the argument of the proof of Theorem 2 gives a sufficient but not necessary condition for choosing γ; for example, although x/y does sometimes exceed 2, it appears in practice that setting $\gamma = 2$ also keeps the transcription factors bounded.

After applying the construction of Algorithm 1, i.e., using Eqs. (1) and (2) to generate the ODEs for ${x^\top}', {x^\perp}', {y^\top}'$, and ${y^\perp}'$ based on the ODEs for x' and y' above (where we can take x above to be x_1, and take y above to be x_2, in the proof of Theorem 2), this generates the transcriptional network:

$$
\begin{aligned}
{x^\top}' &= \frac{x^\top}{x^\perp} + \frac{x^\perp y^\top}{y^\perp} - 2.5x^\top & \qquad {x^\perp}' &= 1 + 2\frac{{x^\perp}^2}{x^\top} - 2.5x^\perp \\
{y^\top}' &= \frac{y^\top}{y^\perp} + 2y^\perp - 2.5y^\top & \qquad {y^\perp}' &= 1 + \frac{x^\top {y^\perp}^2}{x^\perp y^\top} - 2.5y^\perp
\end{aligned}
$$

and initial values $x^\top(0) = 2, \quad x^\perp(0) = 1, \quad y^\top(0) = 1, \quad y^\perp(0) = 1.$

6 Conclusion

A central message of this paper concerns the role of degradation. Nonlinear protein degradation can be a source of effective cooperativity, enabling behaviors such as bistability and oscillation [9]; however, we have shown that no such degradation nonlinearity is *required* for analog completeness—common first-order decay suffices when transcriptional production is programmable as a positive Laurent polynomial.

We chose polynomial ODEs as an implementation target for the reasons explained in the introduction: they are ubiquitous, well-understood, and equivalent to other natural analog computing models such as GPAC [38] as well as being computationally powerful [7]. However, since we allowed the definition of transcriptional networks to have arbitrary Laurent polynomials (a strict superset of polynomials) as production rates, we could also have simulated arbitrary systems of ODEs with Laurent polynomials for each derivative. Note that we could handle even more functions on the right-hand side of the ODEs (any non-hypertranscendental functions) by first converting to a system of polynomial ODEs [32]. However, the construction of Algorithm 1 works *directly* as shown (without any initial pre-transformation of the ODEs) on Laurent polynomials, hence could result in a simpler final transcriptional network than one obtained by first converting to polynomial ODEs.

Going the other direction, we can ask how restricted production rates can be while maintaining their computational power. As discussed in Appendix A.1, Laurent polynomials can approximate Hill functions, but inexactly. In particular, the approximation carries a speed-accuracy tradeoff in the sense that the approximation works in the limit of some Hill dissociation constants being large or small, which translates into needing to speed up the maximal production rate to "make room" for such extreme constants. It would be interesting to explore the details of this tradeoff, or other ways of approximating more commonly-used production rates with Laurent polynomials. It would also be interesting to explore the computational power of Hill functions more directly.

6.1 Discussion on Implementation

Although our results establish theoretical guarantees, real-world implementation of these transcriptional networks would face several practical challenges. Many of the simplifying assumptions made in our framework may differ from constraints of experimental settings. In this section, we discuss these differences in more detail and highlight several open questions that arise when considering potential implementations.

One assumption made in Appendix A.1 is that all activators of a gene must be simultaneously present and bound to the promoter to initiate transcription. In reality, activators may bind independently, contributing additively to transcriptional activation, or they may bind cooperatively, producing nonlinear or synergistic effects that cannot be inferred from individual binding probabilities alone [13,43].

Another assumption we made is that the binding strengths of activators and repressors are significantly different. In reality, this is not always the case. For example, when using CRISPRa/i systems, such fine-tuned control over binding strength is not easily achievable. While certain techniques, such as introducing mismatches in the guide RNA, can partially adjust binding affinity, this tuning is not possible when a transcription factor acts as both an activator and a repressor for different genes.

Our construction assumes all transcription factors degrade at the same rate. While appropriate for degradation due to dilution, proteases are known to degrade different proteins at different rates [4], due for instance to the "N-terminal residue", the first amino acid in the peptide chain. However, since CRISPR is one promising implementation route and all such transcription factors are actually made of the same protein (Cas9 or a variant), differing only in the guide RNA strand, such systems might in fact have roughly equal degradation rates even due to proteases. Also, it would be interesting to consider systems in which different transcription factors X_i have different degradation rates $-\gamma_i x_i$, both under the model that we assume the engineer can choose degradation rates, and under the model that degradation rates are chosen adversarially. More generally, biological degradation can be enzyme-mediated and nonlinear rather than simple first-order decay [9]; while our main result shows such richness is not *required* for analog completeness, characterizing what additional advantages (e.g., smaller circuits, faster convergence, or robustness to noise) it might confer is an interesting open question.

These observations point to several open directions. We note that our assumption that the presence of any repressor among multiple possible repressors is sufficient to prevent transcription is reasonable [1,5]. Based on this, we can consider different models for studying transcriptional networks:

1. **Repressor-only networks:** transcriptional regulation is achieved exclusively through repressors, and gene expression occurs only in the absence of any bound repressor.
2. **Limited-activation networks:** each gene promoter may be regulated by multiple repressors but by at most one activator, introducing a simple layer of transcriptional activation while retaining the dominance of repression.
3. **Additive-regulation networks:** multiple activators and repressors can act on the same promoter, and activators' combined influence on transcription is assumed to be additive, without cooperative or synergistic effects.
4. **Single activation and repression networks:** Each gene promoter can be regulated by at most one activator and at most one repressor.
5. **Single transcription factor networks:** Each gene promoter can be regulated by at most one transcription factor, either a repressor or an activator.

Acknowledgments. We thank Ophelia S Venturelli for our earlier collaboration on related approaches to analog computation with transcriptional networks, which provided important context for the present work. DD and ML were supported by NSF awards 2211793, 1900931 and DoE award DE-SC0024467. DS was supported by NSF awards 2200290, SemiSynBio III: GOALI, DoE award DE-SC0024467, and a Schmidt Sciences Polymath Award.

Disclosure of Interests. The authors have no competing interests to declare that are relevant to the content of this article.

A Proofs for Sect. 2 (Preliminaries)

A.1 Justification of Laurent Polynomials as Class of Production Rates

When the binding of the activator A is weak yet the binding of the repressor R is strong, it is common to approximate the transcription rate as proportional to the ratio a/r; see, for example, ref. [21] and [1, Section 10.4]. We now present a self-contained argument, generalizing this approximation to multiple activators and repressors, and several copies of the same transcription factor gene, resulting in the Laurent polynomial form of transcription rate.

Transcription factors are proteins that bind to a specific DNA sequence, known as a *promoter region*, to regulate the transcription of a nearby gene [1], ultimately influencing the amount of protein the gene encodes. These transcription factors can function as activators, increasing the rate of transcription (production), or as repressors, decreasing it. Each transcription factor undergoes decay due to a combination of dilution (due to cell division) and active degradation. For the purposes of this work, we assume that the rate of degradation is the same for every transcription factor (i.e., dilution or degradation by non-specific enzymes), implying a *uniform linear decay* rate γ across all transcription factors.

A transcriptional network describes the interactions between transcription factors and their target genes, where the transcription factors regulate genes that themselves encode *other transcription factors*. Thus all transcription factors are produced at a rate determined entirely by the current concentrations of transcription factors in the network. An activator A of a transcription factor X increases X's production rate, and a repressor R decreases X's production rate (Fig. 1).

The mechanism of regulation of X is by influencing the rate at which RNA polymerase can bind to the promoter region upstream of the gene for X. If the RNA polymerase successfully binds and transcribes, i.e. creates an mRNA strand representing X, then more X will be produced (after the mRNA is translated into the protein X by a ribosome, assumed in this model to happen negligibly soon after transcription.) Transcription factors affect production rate by influencing the probability that an RNA polymerase successfully binds and transcribes. There is some chance that a polymerase will detach on its own before successfully beginning transcription; activators help the polymerase stick around for longer and increase the chances of successful transcription. Repressors simply block the polymerase by getting in the way.

These influences of a transcription factor on its target gene can be described using a Hill function, which is derived from the probability of the transcription factor binding to the gene's promoter region. The Hill functions for an activator A and a repressor R, with respective concentrations a and r, are defined as follows. Here, $K_A, K_R \in \mathbb{R}^+$ respectively represent activation and repression coefficients, $\alpha_a, \alpha_r \in \mathbb{R}^+$ denote maximal promoter activity:

$$H(a) = \alpha_a \frac{a}{K_A + a} \tag{3}$$

$$H(r) = \alpha_r \frac{K_R}{K_R + r} \tag{4}$$

The term $\frac{a}{K_A+a}$ denotes the probability that the activator A is bound to the promoter. Similarly, the term $\frac{K_R}{K_R+r}$ denotes the probability that the repressor R is not bound. This expression arises from the equivalence $1 - \frac{r}{K_R+r} = \frac{K_R}{K_R+r}$.

The fully general Hill function also has a "cooperativity" constant c, appearing as an exponent in the terms above like K_A^c and a^c. In this paper we assume the non-cooperative case of $c = 1$. In other words, each transcription factor binds independently to its own specific binding site on the promoter, without being influenced by the presence of other transcription factors binding to the same gene.

We also assume that a transcription factor X can potentially be produced by multiple copies of its gene, each of which, due to different promoter regions upstream of each copy, is regulated by different transcription factors.[9] Suppose that a transcription factor X is encoded in m different copies $\{g_1, g_2, ..., g_m\}$ of the gene, each regulated by multiple transcription factors, with the i'th copy having activators $\mathcal{A}_i \subseteq \mathcal{F}$ and repressors $\mathcal{R}_i \subseteq \mathcal{F}$. Then the production rate of X can be expressed as:

$$\sum_{i=1}^{m} \alpha_i \prod_{A \in \mathcal{A}_i} \frac{a}{K_A + a} \prod_{R \in \mathcal{R}_i} \frac{K_R}{K_R + r}$$

We can simplify this summation if we factor out K_R's from the numerator and include them in the constant $(\alpha_i' = \alpha_i \prod_{R \in \mathcal{R}_i} K_R)$ to get

$$\sum_{i=1}^{m} \alpha_i' \prod_{A \in \mathcal{A}_i} \frac{a}{K_A + a} \prod_{R \in \mathcal{R}_i} \frac{1}{K_R + r}$$

We note that if K_R is assumed to be very small and factored out for each repressor, then the coefficient varies more significantly as the number of repressors increases. To show that a wide range of coefficients in a Laurent monomial can be achieved, we introduce a modified construction in Sect. 4 that restricts each promoter to have only a fixed number of repressors and activators.

Remark 4. Suppose $\mathcal{A} = \{A_1, A_2, \ldots, A_m\}$ and $\mathcal{R} = \{R_1, R_2, \ldots, R_l\}$ respectively represent the sets of activators and repressors associated with a specific promoter. If the activation coefficients (K_{A_i}) are large enough compared to the activator's concentration, and the repression coefficients (K_{R_j}) are small enough compared to the repressor's concentration, then the transcriptional rate of this

[9] This is ultimately our justification to go from single-term Laurent monomials to multi-term Laurent polynomials; each gene copy contributes additively to the production rate. Most of this section justifies the use of Laurent monomials, in place of products of Hill functions, for describing the regulation of a single copy.

promoter is proportional to the ratio of the product of the activator concentrations to the product of the repressor concentrations, which is a Laurent monomial.

$$\alpha_i' \prod_{A_i \in \mathcal{A}} \frac{a_i}{K_{A_i} + a_i} \prod_{R_j \in \mathcal{R}} \frac{1}{K_{R_j} + r_j} \approx \alpha_i'' \frac{\prod_{A_i \in \mathcal{A}} a_i}{\prod_{R_j \in \mathcal{R}} r_j}.$$

Note that if a repressor approaches zero, then no finite value of K_{R_j} will satisfy the approximation. Thus we need to make sure that repressors stay bounded away from zero (see Remark 3).

In other words, in the limit of large K_{A_i} and small K_{R_j}, the probability of activator binding decreases while the probability of repressor binding increases, and thus the rate of transcription decreases. Mathematically, we can assume that the maximal promoter activity α increases to balance the effect, but physically there is a resulting speed-accuracy tradeoff that is worth further exploration.

Remark 4 justifies our use of nonnegative Laurent polynomials as the class of production rates available in programming transcriptional networks. By nonnegative we mean that all the Laurent monomials have nonnegative coefficients, corresponding to the control of the rate of production.

B Proofs for Sect. 3 (Transcriptional Networks Can implement Nonnegative Polynomial ODEs)

Theorem 2. *Let P be a system of polynomial ODEs over the set of variables $\mathcal{X}$ that is in Hungarian form for the subset of variables $\mathcal{X}_h \subseteq \mathcal{X}$ (possibly empty set). Then there is a transcriptional network $\mathcal{F}(\gamma)$, constructed by Algorithm* 1, *such that for every upper-bound $b_{\max} > 0$, and every lower-bound $b_{\min} > 0$, there is $\gamma > 0$, such that for every nonnegative trajectory ρ of P that is bounded-above by $b_{\max}$ on $\mathcal{X}_h$ and bookended by $b_{\max}$ and $b_{\min}$ on $\mathcal{X} \setminus \mathcal{X}_h$, $\mathcal{F}(\gamma)$ stably ratio-implements ρ.*

Proof. We begin with a simpler "warmup" construction that ratio-implements ρ, but not stably, before describing how to modify it to be stable. By grouping positive and negative terms together, any polynomial $p(\mathbf{x})$ can be written as $p^+(\mathbf{x}) - p^-(\mathbf{x})$, where p^+ and p^- are polynomials with all nonnegative coefficients. Thus any polynomial ODE can be expressed as

$$x_i' = p_i^+(x_1, x_2, \ldots, x_n) - p_i^-(x_1, x_2, \ldots, x_n).$$

x_i can be represented as the ratio of two transcription factors $x_i^\top$ and $x_i^\perp$: $x_i = \frac{x_i^\top}{x_i^\perp}$, where the initial concentrations of $X_i^\top$ and $X_i^\perp$ are any nonnegative values such that the ratio $x_i^\top / x_i^\perp$ is the desired initial value of $x_i = \rho(0)_i$. For brevity in the equations below, we write p_i^+ to denote $p_i^+(x_1, \ldots, x_n)$, and similarly for p_i^-.

We claim that the following transcriptional network ratio-implements ρ, where $\gamma > 0$ is a constant to be determined later.

$$x_i^{\top\prime} = p_i^+ x_i^\perp - \gamma x_i^\top \tag{5}$$
$$x_i^{\perp\prime} = p_i^- x_i^\perp / x_i - \gamma x_i^\perp \tag{6}$$

Note that (6) can be equivalently written $x_i^{\perp\prime} = p_i^- {x_i^\perp}^2 / x_i^\top - \gamma x_i^\perp$; here, $x_i^\top$ and $x_i^\perp$ are transcription factor concentrations, whereas x_i is the abstract value $\frac{x_i^\top}{x_i^\perp}$ but is not itself the concentration of any transcription factor in the system. (See Remark 4 for how to introduce such a transcription factor whose concentration is $\frac{x_i^\top}{x_i^\perp}$, if that is desired.) To justify that this transcriptional network ratio-implements ρ, we must show that $\frac{d(x_i^\top / x_i^\perp)}{dt} = p_i^+ - p_i^-$.

$$\begin{aligned}
\frac{d(x_i^\top / x_i^\perp)}{dt} &= \frac{x_i^{\top\prime} x_i^\perp - x_i^\top x_i^{\perp\prime}}{{x_i^\perp}^2} && \text{quotient rule} \\
&= \frac{x_i^{\top\prime}}{x_i^\perp} - \frac{x_i^\top x_i^{\perp\prime}}{{x_i^\perp}^2} \\
&= \frac{p_i^+ x_i^\perp - \gamma x_i^\top}{x_i^\perp} - \frac{x_i^\top (p_i^- x_i^\perp / x_i - \gamma x_i^\perp)}{{x_i^\perp}^2} && \text{substituting by (5) and (6)} \\
&= p_i^+ - \frac{\gamma x_i^\top}{x_i^\perp} - p_i^- + \frac{\gamma x_i^\top}{x_i^\perp} = p_i^+ - p_i^- .
\end{aligned}$$

The transcriptional network given here, though it satisfies Definition 4, has an important problem: It is not a stable ratio-implementation by Definition 6. To see this, consider Eq. (6). We can rewrite it as

$$\frac{dx_i^\perp}{dt} = x_i^\perp (p_i^- / x_i - \gamma).$$

Note that if $p_i^- / x_i - \gamma$ remains sufficiently positive (respectively, negative) for sufficient time, then the value $x_i^\perp$ over that timescale will exponentially increase (resp., decrease). Thus, while the ratio $x_i^\top / x_i^\perp$ can remain in a positive bounded interval (i.e., bound by (ℓ, h) for $0 < \ell < h < \infty$), both the numerator and denominator can either increase without bound (if $p_i^- / x_i - \gamma$ stays positive) or converge to 0 (if $p_i^- / x_i - \gamma$ stays negative). While in some cases it might be possible to tune the dynamics such that the system oscillates between these two regimes, in general this is difficult and the transcription factor concentrations $x_i^\top$ and $x_i^\perp$ will tend to both exponentially increase or go to zero. Thus we choose $\gamma > \max_i \sup_{t \geq 0} p_i^- (\mathbf{x}(t)) / x_i(t)$. For this it suffices to choose $\gamma > C b_{\max}^k / b_{\min}$, where C is the maximum number of monomials in any Laurent polynomial ODE, and k is the maximum degree; thus $C b_{\max}^k$ upper bounds the value $p_i^- (\mathbf{x}(t))$ for any t.

We now show a modified construction (see Algorithm 1) that also satisfies the definition of stable ratio-implementation (Definition 6). Recall that ρ is bounded-above on all x_i variables. Recall that Definition 6 requires that we show all $x_i^\top, x_i^\perp$ transcription factor concentrations are bounded above, and furthermore, all $x_i^\perp$ are also bounded-positive.

To fix this problem, we include a positive constant β in the production rate of $x_i^\perp$ and change the transcriptional network to:

$$\begin{aligned}\frac{dx_i^\top}{dt} &= \beta x_i + p_i^+ x_i^\perp - \gamma x_i^\top \\ \frac{dx_i^\perp}{dt} &= \beta + p_i^- x_i^\perp / x_i - \gamma x_i^\perp\end{aligned}$$

Similarly to (6), (8) is equivalent to writing ${x_i^\perp}' = \beta + p_i^- {x_i^\perp}^2 / x_i^\top - \gamma x_i^\perp$. We now justify why we add the term βx_i into the production rate of (1): Since we are adding a term to (6) we must introduce an additive term, call it α, to (5) to cancel out the effect and make sure $\frac{d(x_i^\top / x_i^\perp)}{dt} = p_i^+ - p_i^-$. Below we show $\alpha = \beta x_i$.

$$\frac{dx_i^\top}{dt} = \alpha + p_i^+ x_i^\perp - \gamma x_i^\top \tag{7}$$

$$\frac{dx_i^\perp}{dt} = \beta + p_i^- x_i^\perp / x_i - \gamma x_i^\perp \tag{8}$$

$$\begin{aligned}\frac{d(x_i^\top / x_i^\perp)}{dt} &= \frac{{x_i^\top}' x_i^\perp - x_i^\top {x_i^\perp}'}{{x_i^\perp}^2} && \text{quotient rule} \\ &= \frac{{x_i^\top}'}{x_i^\perp} - \frac{x_i^\top {x_i^\perp}'}{{x_i^\perp}^2} \\ &= \frac{\alpha + p_i^+ x_i^\perp - \gamma x_i^\top}{x_i^\perp} - \frac{x_i^\top (\beta + p_i^- x_i^\perp / x_i - \gamma x_i^\perp)}{{x_i^\perp}^2} && \text{substituting (7), (8)} \\ &= \frac{\alpha}{x_i^\perp} + p_i^+ - \frac{\gamma x_i^\top}{x_i^\perp} - p_i^- + \frac{\gamma x_i^\top}{x_i^\perp} - \frac{x_i^\top \beta}{{x_i^\perp}^2} \\ &= \frac{\alpha x_i^\perp - x_i^\top \beta}{{x_i^\perp}^2} + p_i^+ - p_i^-\end{aligned}$$

For the above expression to equal $p_i^+ - p_i^-$ as required, we must have $\alpha x_i^\perp - \beta x_i^\top = 0$, i.e., $\alpha = \beta \frac{x_i^\top}{x_i^\perp} = \beta x_i$, completing the justification for adding the term βx_i in (1).

Now we explain why the addition of the β term to $x_i^\perp$ prevents the problem identified above. First, we claim that each $x_i^\perp$ term is bounded-positive. Looking at (2), we have two cases. In the first case, if $x_i^\perp$ starts above β/γ, then $x_i^\perp$ cannot go under β/γ, since its production rate is at least β and its degradation rate is $\gamma x_i^\perp$. In the second case assume $x_i^\perp < \beta/\gamma$; then $x_i^{\perp\prime} > 0$, i.e., it will increase towards β/γ. Thus $x_i^\perp$ is unconditionally bounded-positive.

We now want to establish that $x_i^\perp$ is also bounded above, i.e., $x_i^\perp$ is bookended, provided that γ is sufficiently large. Write Eq. (2) as

$$\frac{dx_i^\perp}{dt} = \beta + x_i^\perp(p_i^-/x_i - \gamma) = \beta - b(t)x_i^\perp$$

where we define $b(t) = \gamma - p_i^-/x_i$. If we ensure that $b(t) > b_{\min}$ for some $b_{\min} > 0$, then if ever $x_i^\perp > \beta/b_{\min} > \beta/b(t)$, then $x_i^{\perp\prime} < 0$, so it will decrease. This establishes that $x_i^\perp$ is bounded above.

It remains to establish that $b(t) > b_{\min}$ for some $b_{\min} > 0$. We now do a case analysis. For the first case, assume that all the variables in ρ are bounded-above. As long as p_i^-/x_i is also bounded above, i.e., for some constant c, $p_i^-/x_i < c$, then we can set $\gamma > c$ to ensure $b(t) = \gamma - p_i^-/x_i > \gamma - c = b_{\min} > 0$.

How can we ensure that p_i^-/x_i is bounded above? First, let us consider the case that the original system of polynomial ODEs (P) is in Hungarian form for x_i. Then $p_i^-/x_i = q_i^-$ for some nonnegative polynomial q_i^-. Since we have assumed that all the variables in ρ are bounded-above, q_i^- is bounded-above as well, and we can set γ larger than the maximum value ever taken on by any q_i^- for $1 \le i \le n$. This choice of γ is sufficient to ensure that $b(t) > b_{\min}$.

On the other hand, consider the case that P is not Hungarian form for x_i. The problem is that if x_i approaches zero, p_i^-/x_i may approach infinity since, unlike the Hungarian case, x_i is not a factor in p_i^- canceling $1/x_i$. Thus we explicitly disallow non-Hungarian variables to approach 0, as stated in the condition of the theorem. Similarly to the above, all variables being bounded above implies p_i^- is also bounded above. Since x_i cannot approach 0, this means that p_i^-/x_i is bounded above, and we similarly choose γ to be greater than its maximum value.

Note that because each $x_i^\perp$ is bookended, by our assumption that all x_i are bounded-above, Observation 1 establishes that each $x_i^\top$ is also bounded above, obeying the constraints to make this a stable ratio-implementation by Definition 6. □

Theorem 3. *Let P be a system of Laurent polynomial ODEs over the set of variables $\mathcal{X}$. Then there is a transcriptional network $\mathcal{F}(\gamma)$, constructed by Algorithm 1 with p_i^+ and p_i^- being nonnegative Laurent polynomials, such that for every upper-bound $b_{\max} > 0$ and every lower-bound $b_{\min} > 0$, there is $\gamma > 0$ such that for every trajectory ρ of P that is bookended by $b_{\max}$ and $b_{\min}$ on $\mathcal{X}$, $\mathcal{F}(\gamma)$ stably ratio-implements ρ.*

Proof. The proof is very similar to Theorem 2, and the construction, Algorithm 1, is identical, since Algorithm 1 expresses the rates as ratios of the polynomials p^+, p^-, and the transcription factor concentrations, which remain Laurent polynomials even if p^+, p^- are Laurent polynomials to begin with. The extra hypothesis on variables not starting at or approaching 0 handles the fact that, for a Laurent monomial with a nontrivial denominator $\frac{1}{d}$, if d is 0, then the monomial would be undefined. □

C Proofs for Sect. 4 (Simplification of Transcriptional Network Limiting Activators and Repressors Per Promoter)

Theorem 4. *Let P be a system of polynomial ODEs over the set of variables $\mathcal{X}$. Then there is a transcriptional network $\mathcal{F}(\gamma)$, whose every positive term is a Laurent monomial of the form $\alpha\frac{a_1 a_2}{r}$, where each a_1, a_2, r is a transcription factor or the constant 1. such that for every upper-bound $b_{\max} > 0$ and every lower-bound $b_{\min} > 0$, there is $\gamma > 0$, such that for every trajectory ρ of P that is bookended by $b_{\max}$ and $b_{\min}$ on $\mathcal{X}$, $\mathcal{F}(\gamma)$ stably ratio-implements ρ.*

Proof. Here we take advantage of the fact that Algorithm 1 actually can process arbitrary Laurent polynomials (not merely polynomials) (see Theorem 3), since we first modify P to a system of ODEs with Laurent polynomial right-hand sides.

Consider a polynomial ODE system

$$\frac{dx_i}{dt} = p_i(x_1, \dots, x_n) = \sum_{j=1}^{k_i} \alpha_{i,j} M_{i,j} \tag{9}$$

where each $M_{i,j}$ is a monomial in the variables $x_1, \dots, x_n$. For all monomials $M_{i,j}$, we introduce new variables $z_{i,j}$ and set their ODE to ensure that at all times $t \geq 0$,

$$z_{i,j}(t) = \frac{x_i(t)}{M_{i,j}(t)}. \tag{10}$$

Since each $x_i(0) > 0$, we have $M_{i,j}(0) > 0$ and $z_{i,j}(0) > 0$. Then (9) can be rewritten as

$$\frac{dx_i}{dt} = \sum_{j=1}^{k_i} \alpha_{i,j} \frac{x_i}{z_{i,j}} = x_i \sum_{j=1}^{k_i} \frac{\alpha_{i,j}}{z_{i,j}}. \tag{11}$$

We now derive the ODE equations for $z_{i,j}$ via the logarithmic derivative: for any positive differentiable function f, the quantity $\dot{f}/f = \frac{d}{dt}\ln f$ converts products and quotients into sums and differences. Write $M_{i,j} = x_1^{e_1} \cdots x_n^{e_n}$. Then applying the identity $\dot{f}/f = \frac{d}{dt}\ln f$ a few times,

$$\begin{aligned}\frac{\dot{z}_{i,j}}{z_{i,j}} &= \frac{d}{dt}\ln z_{i,j} = \frac{d}{dt}\ln\frac{x_i}{M_{i,j}} = \frac{d}{dt}\ln x_i - \frac{d}{dt}\ln M_{i,j} = \frac{\dot{x}_i}{x_i} - \frac{d}{dt}\ln M_{i,j} \\ &= \frac{\dot{x}_i}{x_i} - \frac{d}{dt}\ln(x_1^{e_1}\cdots x_n^{e_n}) = \frac{\dot{x}_i}{x_i} - \frac{d}{dt}\sum_{\ell=1}^{n} e_\ell \ln x_\ell = \frac{\dot{x}_i}{x_i} - \sum_{\ell=1}^{n} e_\ell \frac{d}{dt}\ln x_\ell \\ &= \frac{\dot{x}_i}{x_i} - \sum_{\ell=1}^{n} e_\ell \frac{\dot{x}_\ell}{x_\ell}.\end{aligned} \tag{12}$$

Dividing (11) by x_i (and changing j to m) shows that $\frac{\dot{x}_i}{x_i} = \sum_{m=1}^{k_i} \frac{\alpha_{i,m}}{z_{i,m}}$, and likewise for each x_ℓ. Substituting this into the right side of (12) and multiplying through by $z_{i,j}$ yields

$$\frac{dz_{i,j}}{dt} = z_{i,j} \left[\sum_{m=1}^{k_i} \frac{\alpha_{i,m}}{z_{i,m}} - \sum_{\ell=1}^{n} e_\ell \sum_{m=1}^{k_\ell} \frac{\alpha_{\ell,m}}{z_{\ell,m}} \right], \tag{13}$$

Since all variables are bookended in the trajectory by assumption, Eq. (10) implies that $z_{i,j}$ is bookended as well. Importantly, each term of $\dot{z}_{i,j}$ in (13) is simply $\lambda \frac{z_{i,j}}{z_{\ell,m}}$ for some constant coefficient λ; this will be key in transforming this ODE system to a transcriptional network with a limited number of activators and repressors.

If the initial conditions satisfy $z_{i,j}(0) = x_i(0)/M_{i,j}(0)$ for all i, j, then these equalities are preserved for all time: the derivation above shows that $x_i/M_{i,j}$ satisfies the same ODE as $z_{i,j}$, so uniqueness of solutions implies $z_{i,j}(t) = x_i(t)/M_{i,j}(t)$ for all t. Hence along every such trajectory $M_{i,j} = x_i/z_{i,j}$, and (11) reproduces the original polynomial system exactly.

Now collect all variables x_i and $z_{i,j}$ into a single list

$$y_1, \ldots, y_N.$$

Then the system described by (11) and (13) can be written in the form

$$\frac{dy_a}{dt} = \sum_{b=1}^{N} \lambda_{a,b} \frac{y_a}{y_b}, \qquad a = 1, \ldots, N, \tag{14}$$

for suitable real constants $\lambda_{a,b}$.

For each a, b, define

$$\lambda_{a,b}^{+} = \max\{\lambda_{a,b}, 0\}, \qquad \lambda_{a,b}^{-} = \max\{-\lambda_{a,b}, 0\}.$$

Then $\lambda_{a,b} = \lambda_{a,b}^{+} - \lambda_{a,b}^{-}$, where $\lambda_{a,b}^{+}, \lambda_{a,b}^{-} \geq 0$, and we have

$$\frac{dy_a}{dt} = \sum_{b=1}^{N} \lambda_{a,b}^{+} \frac{y_a}{y_b} - \sum_{b=1}^{N} \lambda_{a,b}^{-} \frac{y_a}{y_b}. \tag{15}$$

For each variable y_a, include two transcription factors $Y_a^\top$ and $Y_a^\perp$ with positive initial concentration such that $y_a = \frac{Y_a^\top}{Y_a^\perp}$. Construct the transcriptional network from (15) by applying Algorithm 1:

$$\frac{dY_a^\top}{dt} = \beta \frac{Y_a^\top}{Y_a^\perp} + \sum_{b=1}^{N} \lambda_{a,b}^{+} \frac{Y_a^\top Y_b^\perp}{Y_b^\top} - \gamma Y_a^\top \tag{16}$$

$$\frac{dY_a^\perp}{dt} = \beta + \sum_{b=1}^{N} \lambda_{a,b}^{-} \frac{Y_a^\perp Y_b^\perp}{Y_b^\top} - \gamma Y_a^\perp. \tag{17}$$

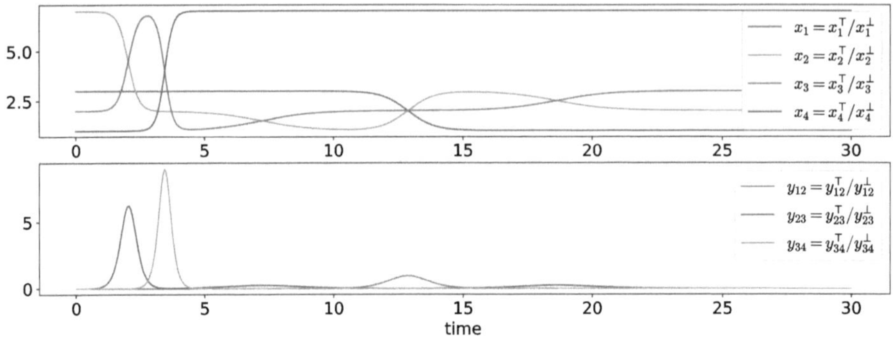

Fig. 3. Bubble sort system with four variables $x_1 = 3$, $x_2 = 7$, $x_3 = 2$, $x_4 = 1$ and we start $y_{1,2} = y_{2,3} = y_{3,4} = 0.01$. The $y_{i,i+1}$ value spikes when it is swapping x_i and x_{i+1}. (Though there are conditions under which the plot does not look like discrete swaps separated in time.) As in Fig. 2, each variable is the computed ratio of two transcription factors.

Here β is any positive constant, and γ is a positive constant chosen once for the whole network and trajectory as in Algorithm 1. Every positive term appearing in (16)–(17) is of one of the forms

$$\sigma, \qquad \sigma u, \qquad \frac{\sigma u}{v}, \qquad \frac{\sigma u v}{w},$$

for constant σ and transcription factor concentrations u, v, w, completing the construction. □

D Proofs for Sect. 5 (Examples)

For subsequent examples, we will not show the values of the underlying $v^\top, v^\perp$ variables, but for the sine-cosine system, they can also be seen in Fig. 2.

D.1 Bubble Sort

This is a system introduced by Paul and Hüper [31], which implements a sorting algorithm reminiscent of the discrete bubble sort. The goal is to sort the values $x_1, \ldots, x_n$. Variables $y_{i,i+1}$ are intended to swap the values of x_i and x_{i+1} if they are out of order.[10]

[10] That said, this is not exactly an implementation of bubble sort, since swaps do not occur in discrete sequential steps. For instance, if started with values in reverse order such as $x_1 = 10, x_2 = 9, \ldots, x_{10} = 1$, the ODEs will change all values in what appears to be one "step".

The ODEs for this system are

$$\begin{aligned}
x_1' &= -y_{1,2} \\
x_2' &= y_{1,2} - y_{2,3} \\
x_3' &= y_{2,3} - y_{3,4} \\
&\vdots \\
x_{n-1}' &= y_{n-2,n-1} - y_{n-1,n} \\
x_n' &= y_{n-1,n} \\
y_{1,2}' &= y_{1,2}(x_1 - x_2) \\
y_{2,3}' &= y_{2,3}(x_2 - x_3) \\
&\vdots \\
y_{n-1,n}' &= y_{n-1,n}(x_{n-1} - x_n)
\end{aligned}$$

The initial values of the x_i's represent the values that need to be sorted, and the initial values of all $y_{i,i+1}$'s are $\varepsilon > 0$. Since these ODE's are not in Hungarian form, we assume that x_i's have positive initial values. Figure 3 shows an example after we apply the construction given in Algorithm 1.

D.2 Schlögl System

The Schlögl chemical reaction network [37] is given by the reactions

$$\begin{aligned}
X &\xrightarrow{1} X + Y \\
3Y &\underset{k_2}{\overset{k_1}{\rightleftharpoons}} 2Y \\
Y &\xrightarrow{k_3} \emptyset
\end{aligned}$$

Note: this network is presented differently in [37]. There, our species Y is called X, and our species X is called C. Also, unit rate constants are assumed, so the rate constants k_1, k_2, k_3 above are imitated by extra reactants that are assumed to be held at a fixed concentration despite being consumed in each reaction.

This corresponds to the ODE $y' = x - (k_1 y^3 - k_2 y^2 + k_3 y)$. In our plots, $k_1 = 11, k_2 = 16.5, k_3 = 6.5$. Note that the system does not change x. One thinks of this system as implementing a "1-bit memory" (a.k.a. hysteresis) in the sense that if we imagine an external controller altering x, say by raising it and then lowering it back to its original value, then the value of y converges to a different value than it was at before altering x. This can be seen by inspecting the phase-space diagram in Fig. 4. Figure 5 shows an example where we change the value of x in a sequence where the new value of y depends on whether y was previously large (close to 1) or previously small (close to 0).

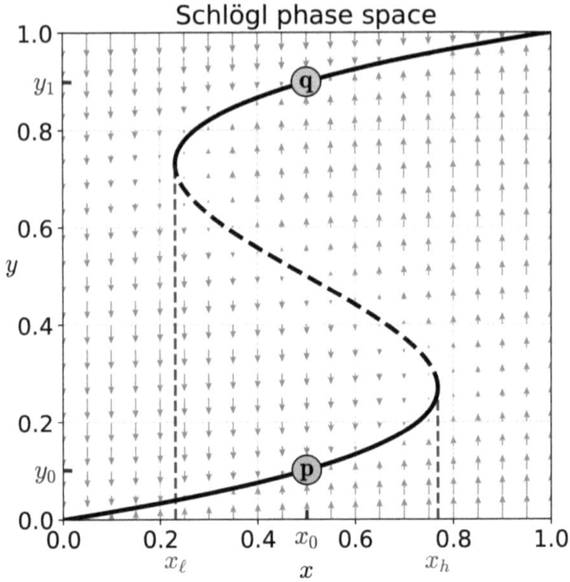

Fig. 4. Phase-space diagram of the Schlögl CRN of Appendix D.2. The black curve is the plot of the function $x = f(y) = 11y^3 - 16.5y^2 + 6.5y$, mirrored around the line $y = x$. No reaction changes X; we think of X as "externally controlled" as a way to influence Y through the reactions. For any point (x, y) in the plane, the vector arrows show the direction of y', pushing Y up if to the right of the curve (blue arrows) and down otherwise (orange arrows). Imagine for example we start at point $\mathbf{p} = (x_0, y_0)$. If we then move X above the value x_h, Y converges to the upper solid part of the black curve. If we subsequently lower the value of X to its original coordinate x_0, Y will converge at a different point $\mathbf{q} = (x_0, y_1)$ above $\mathbf{p}$, remembering that we changed X, despite returning X to its original value. Symmetrically, if we lower the value of X below the threshold x_ℓ, and raise it back again to its original value, we restore the system back to point $\mathbf{p}$. This dynamic process is shown in Fig. 5. The dashed portion of the curve shows unstable fixed points of the CRN; the solid portions are stable fixed points. (Color figure online)

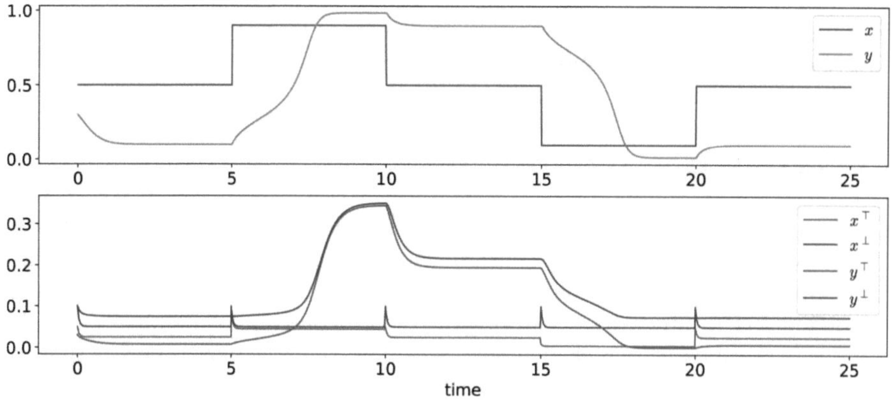

Fig. 5. Plot of Schlögl system with parameters $k_1 = 11, k_2 = 16.5, k_3 = 6.5$, with "resets" of the x variable. x starts at 0.5 (x_0 in Fig. 4). y starts "small", which makes y converge to ≈ 0.1 (y_0 in Fig. 4). At time 5 we set x "large" ($= 0.9$, by setting $x^\top = 0.09$ and $x^\perp = 0.1$), and y follows (reaching $y \approx 0.984$ such that $f(y) = 0.9$). We then set x back to 0.5 at time 10, which causes y to converge to $y_1 \approx 0.9$. We then set x below x_ℓ at time 15, then raise it back to 0.5 for a second time at time 20, and the system remembers that we previously made x low, returning y to low (≈ 0.1). In the top plot, x and y are the computed ratios of the transcription factors.

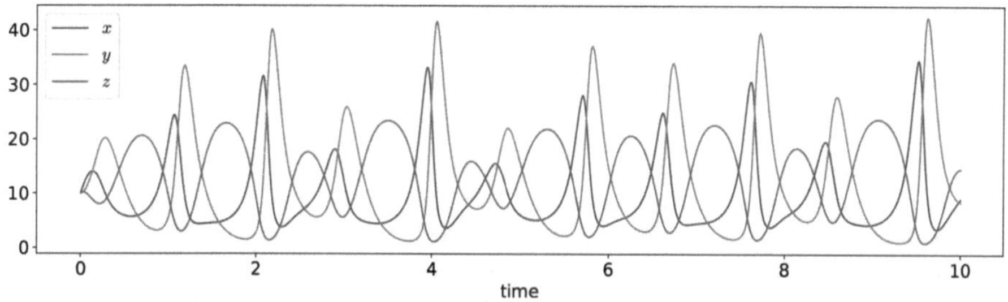

Fig. 6. Willamowski-Rössler chemical reaction network with rate constants given in Appendix D.3 and initial concentrations $x(0) = 10$, $y(0) = 10$ and $z(0) = 10$. x, y, and z are the computed ratios of their respective transcription factors.

D.3 Willamowski-Rössler System (Chaotic)

The Willamowski-Rössler system [42] is a nonlinear dynamical system derived from the reactions

$$X \underset{0.5}{\overset{30}{\rightleftharpoons}} 2X$$

$$X + Y \xrightarrow{1} 2Y$$

$$Y \xrightarrow{10} \emptyset$$

$$X + Z \xrightarrow{1} \emptyset$$

$$Z \underset{0.5}{\overset{16.5}{\rightleftharpoons}} 2Z$$

This system exhibits chaotic behavior, meaning its trajectories are highly sensitive to initial conditions and can show unpredictable yet structured patterns over time. See Fig. 6.

D.4 PID Controller

A proportional–integral–derivative (PID) controller is a feedback-based mechanism widely used to maintain continuous control and automatic adjustments in machines and processes. The PID controller consists of three components: proportional (P), integral (I), and derivative (D) control. As a simple example, consider a thermostat, which demonstrates how the PID controller uses these three elements to maintain the temperature at the desired set point. Biomolecular integral and PID controllers are an active area in synthetic biology and molecular control [2,8,18].

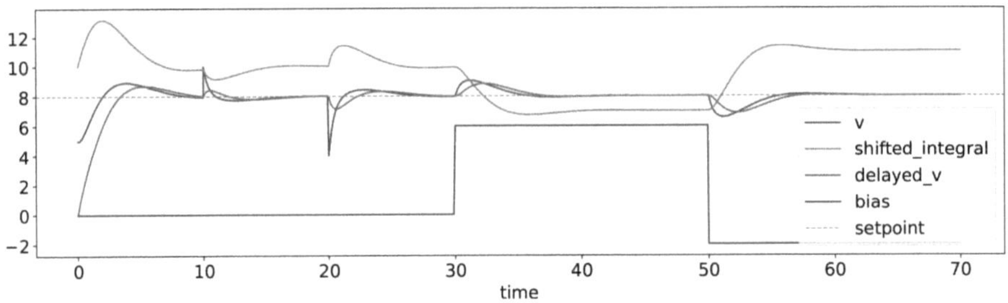

Fig. 7. PID controller, attempting to keep v at a setpoint of 8 (called σ in the main text), in response to external disturbances, with PID coefficients $P = 1.5, I = 1, D = 1$. At time 10, we perturb v, increasing it to 10 (by setting $v^\top = 10$ and $v^\perp = 1$), and at time 20, we perturb v again, similarly decreasing it to 4, each representing an ephemeral disturbance to the system. At time 30, we perturb v in a more permanent way, by adding a constant "bias" term of 6 to its ODE, which remains in v's ODE for all times $30 \leq t \leq 50$, at which point we shift the bias to -2.

The controller first considers the difference (error) between the setpoint and the measured temperature. The output signal of this part is proportional to the size of the error. The integral term sums the error over time, addressing steady-state errors that proportional control alone cannot resolve. For example, when the temperature consistently remains below the setpoint, the integral term increases the output to fix this problem. The derivative term considers the rate of change of the error. This helps predict temperature trends and adjust the output signal to avoid overshoot. See Fig. 7.

There are coefficients P, I, D corresponding to the proportional, integral, and derivative terms. Let the setpoint be σ (a constant), and let v be the value we want to maintain at the setpoint. The variable i represents the integral of the error shifted up by the constant μ so that it stays non-negative; when we need the integral itself, we use the value $i-\mu$. The derivative term is represented as follows. First, d represents a "delayed v", lagging behind v by some amount controlled by the constant λ. Therefore, the expression $v - d$ is an approximation of the derivative of v, and $d-v$ represents the derivative of the error $\frac{d}{dt}(\sigma - v) = -\frac{dv}{dt}$. The ODEs to achieve these are

$$\begin{aligned} v' &= P(\sigma - v) + I(i - \mu) + D(d - v) \\ i' &= \sigma - v \\ d' &= \lambda(v - d) \end{aligned}$$

We can start with $d(0) = 0$, $v(0)$ being any positive value, and $i(0) = \mu$.

D.5 Extremum Seeking Feedback Scheme

This system originates with [25]. This is an "extremum-seeking" system. There is some "objective function" f assumed to be unknown to us. The goal is to adjust the value of a variable in the ODEs until it finds a local maximum of f. Figure 8 shows a function $f(x)$ with two local maxima. The goal of the system is, starting with a variable x, for x to hill-climb to the nearest local maximum of f.

In our setting, we think of f as an unknown process that, based on the current concentration of some transcription factor X, produces a transcription factor F characterized by some unknown function f. In other words, if X has concentration x, F has concentration $f(x)$. We imagine F is some natural reagent whose production we wish to maximize. Our goal is to maximize the concentration of F by adjusting X, without knowing how F depends on X. (i.e., the standard black-box optimization problem, but the computation of the optimization must be done by ODEs rather than by a standard algorithm).

The following ODEs achieve this by using a sine-cosine oscillator (on variables p and q) to move $z + ap$ up or down from the current value of z, with constants $\omega = 3$ (period of oscillation), $\lambda = 0.3$, $a = 0.1$ (amplitude of oscillation), $k = 0.15$ (rate of convergence). x' is set so that x tracks $z + ap$. Intuitively, this works in the following way: p goes up and down from $+1$ to -1. When p is positive, the ap term in x' drags x up slightly (say to x_h), and when p is negative, the ap term drags x down slightly (say to $x_\text{l} < x_\text{h}$). If $f'(x) > 0$ (i.e., f has positive slope, so we should increase x to find the local maximum to the right), then this means that $f(x_\text{h})p$ when $p = 1$ (the positive term in w') will have larger magnitude than $|f(x_\text{l})p|$ when p is -1. Thus, since the push to increase w when p is positive is stronger than the push to decrease w when p is negative, the net effect pushes w higher. Symmetry logic shows that when $f'(x) < 0$ (the slope is negative, so we should *decrease* x to reach the local maximum to the left), the net effect will be to push w lower.

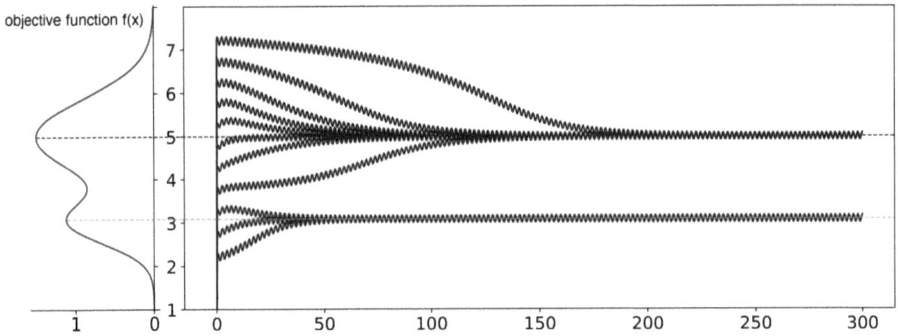

Fig. 8. Extremum seeking feedback scheme. The objective function is $f(x) = e^{-2(x-3)^2} + e^{-2(x-5)^2/3}$, with local maxima at $x \approx 3.08$ and $x \approx 5$. (f's graph shown rotated 90°C counterclockwise) This plot shows transcription factor x's trajectory with various initial values between 2.5 and 7.5. (Outside of that interval, the slope of f is sufficiently close to 0 to severely delay the time required for x to find the maxima.)

$$\begin{aligned} p' &= \omega q \\ q' &= -\omega p \\ w' &= -\lambda w + f(x)p \\ z' &= kw \\ x' &= \gamma(z + ap - x) \end{aligned}$$

with initial values $p = 0, q = 1, w = 0, x = 0$, and the initial value of z represents where to start the search for a local maximum.

However, as with our simpler example with just the sine-cosine oscillator in Sect. 5.1, Theorem 2 only allows us to implement nonnegative trajectories. We follow the same approach as Sect. 5.1, shifting the oscillator implemented by p and q (as well as w, which also goes negative in the above system) up by 2 to keep it nonnegative, oscillating between a peak of 3 and a trough of 1, by shifting the initial values of p, q, w up by 2. Then, when we want to reference the original (possibly negative) value of p, q, or w, we reference the value minus 2. We also similarly shift z down by $2a$ (explained below):

$$\begin{aligned} p' &= \omega(q - 2) \\ q' &= -\omega(p - 2) \\ w' &= -\lambda(w - 2) + f(x)(p - 2) \\ z' &= k(w - 2) \\ x' &= \gamma(z + 2a + a(p - 2) - x) = \gamma(z + ap - x) \end{aligned}$$

with initial values $p = 2, q = 3, w = 1, x = 0$, and $z =$ the desired starting value for the search minus ap.

We shift z down by $2a$ for the following reason. We will apply the construction of Theorem 2 to the variables p, q, w, z, but *not* to x, because as discussed above, we use x as a model of an *existing* transcription factor X that influences some other transcription factor F in a way we don't control, such that F's concentration at any time is $f(x)$. But for x to obey the constraints in our model of transcriptional networks, its ODE must have a single negative term $-\gamma x$. By shifting z down by $2a$, we change the reference to it in x's ODE to $z + 2a$, which cancels the term $-2a$ due to the upward shift of p, restoring that x has a single negative term $-\gamma x$ as required.

Note also that we have written $f(x)$, even though $f(x)$ may not be a Laurent polynomial as required by the definition of transcriptional networks. What we are modeling is that the environment rapidly adjusts the concentration $f(x)$ of transcription factor F based on the concentration x of X. Although we have no control over the production of F itself, we can use it to regulate other transcription factors. This is done using our compiler by placing a placeholder symbol `f_placeholder`, applying the construction to the resulting ODEs while instructing the compiler to ignore `f_placeholder` (i.e., do not make top and bottom versions of it, and do not put any ODE for it in the transcriptional network ODEs), and then substitute the actual (non-polynomial) expression for f afterwards before simulating the ODEs. See the example notebook in the code repository for details [29].

Figure 8 shows the transcriptional network starting with various initial values of z, showing how x changes over time. In each case x immediately shoots up to z, before converging (with some oscillation) to one of the two local maxima.

References

1. Alon, U.: An Introduction to Systems Biology: Design Principles of Biological Circuits. Chapman and Hall/CRC (2019)
2. Aoki, S.K., Lillacci, G., Gupta, A., Baumschlager, A., Schweingruber, D., Khammash, M.: A universal biomolecular integral feedback controller for robust perfect adaptation. Nature **570**(7762), 533–537 (2019)
3. Arceo, C.P.P., Jose, E.C., Marin-Sanguino, A., Mendoza, E.R.: Chemical reaction network approaches to biochemical systems theory. Math. Biosci. **269**, 135–152 (2015)
4. Bachmair, A., Finley, D., Varshavsky, A.: In vivo half-life of a protein is a function of its amino-terminal residue. Science **234**(4773), 179–186 (1986)
5. Bintu, L., et al.: Transcriptional regulation by the numbers: models. Curr. Opinion Genet. Dev. **15**(2), 116–124 (2005)
6. Boros, B., Hofbauer, J., Müller, S., Regensburger, G.: The center problem for the Lotka reactions with generalized mass-action kinetics. Qual. Theory Dyn. Syst. **17**(2), 403–410 (2018)
7. Bournez, O., Graça, D.S., Pouly, A.: Polynomial time corresponds to solutions of polynomial ordinary differential equations of polynomial length. J. ACM **64**(6) (2017)
8. Briat, C., Gupta, A., Khammash, M.: Antithetic integral feedback ensures robust perfect adaptation in noisy biomolecular networks. Cell Syst. **2**(1), 15–26 (2016)
9. Buchler, N.E., Gerland, U., Hwa, T.: Nonlinear protein degradation and the function of genetic circuits. Proc. Natl. Acad. Sci. **102**(27), 9559–9564 (2005)

10. Bush, V.: The differential analyzer. A new machine for solving differential equations. J. Franklin Inst. **212**(4), 447–488 (1931)
11. Bychkov, A., Pogudin, G.: Optimal monomial quadratization for ODE systems. ACM Commun. Comput. Algebra **54**(3), 119–123 (2020)
12. Cardelli, L., Tribastone, M., Tschaikowski, M.: From electric circuits to chemical networks. Nat. Comput. **19**, 237–248 (2020)
13. Chavez, A., et al.: Highly efficient Cas9-mediated transcriptional programming. Nat. Methods **12**(4), 326–328 (2015)
14. Chen, H.-L., Doty, D., Reeves, W., Soloveichik, D.: Rate-independent computation in continuous chemical reaction networks. J. ACM **70**(3) (2023)
15. Daniel, R., Rubens, J.R., Sarpeshkar, R., Lu, T.K.: Synthetic analog computation in living cells. Nature **497**(7451), 619–623 (2013)
16. de Jong, H.: Modeling and simulation of genetic regulatory systems: a literature review. J. Comput. Biol. **9**(1), 67–103 (2002)
17. Elowitz, M.B., Leibler, S.: A synthetic oscillatory network of transcriptional regulators. Nature **403**(6767), 335–338 (2000)
18. Filo, M., Kumar, S., Khammash, M.: A hierarchy of biomolecular proportional-integral-derivative feedback controllers for robust perfect adaptation and dynamic performance. Nat. Commun. **13**(1), 2119 (2022)
19. Gander, M.W., Vrana, J.D., Voje, W.E., Carothers, J.M., Klavins, E.: Digital logic circuits in yeast with CRISPR-dCas9 NOR gates. Nat. Commun. **8**(1), 15459 (2017)
20. Gardner, T.S., Cantor, C.R., Collins, J.J.: Construction of a genetic toggle switch in Escherichia coli. Nature **403**(6767), 339–342 (2000)
21. Goentoro, L., Shoval, O., Kirschner, M.W., Alon, U.: The incoherent feedforward loop can provide fold-change detection in gene regulation. Mol. Cell **36**(5), 894–899 (2009)
22. Hárs, V., Tóth, J.: On the inverse problem of reaction kinetics. In: Farkas, M., Hatvani, L. (eds.) Qualitative Theory of Differential Equations. Colloquia Mathematica Societatis János Bolyai, vol. 30, pp. 363–379. North-Holland, Amsterdam (1981)
23. Kim, J., Winfree, E.: Synthetic in vitro transcriptional oscillators. Mol. Syst. Biol. **7**(1), 465 (2011)
24. Konermann, S., et al.: Genome-scale transcriptional activation by an engineered CRISPR-Cas9 complex. Nature **517**(7536), 583–588 (2015)
25. Krstić, M., Wang, H.-H.: Stability of extremum seeking feedback for general nonlinear dynamic systems. Automatica **36**(4), 595–601 (2000)
26. Moon, S.Y., Kim, M.R., An, N.-Y., Noh, M.H., Lee, J.Y.: Dual-mode CRISPRa/i for genome-scale metabolic rewiring in escherichia coli. Nucleic Acids Res. **53**(15), gkaf818 (2025)
27. Müller, S., Feliu, E., Regensburger, G., Conradi, C., Shiu, A., Dickenstein, A.: Sign conditions for injectivity of generalized polynomial maps with applications to chemical reaction networks and real algebraic geometry. Found. Comput. Math. **16**(1), 69–97 (2016)
28. Nielsen, A.A., et al.: Genetic circuit design automation. Science **352**(6281), aac7341 (2016)
29. ode2tn python package. https://github.com/UC-Davis-molecular-computing/ode2tn
30. Oishi, K., Klavins, E.: Biomolecular implementation of linear I/O systems. IET Syst. Biol. **5**(4), 252–260 (2011)

31. Paul, S., Hüper, K.: Analog rank filtering. IEEE Trans. Circ. Syst. I Fund. Theory Appl. **40**(7), 469–476 (1993)
32. Pour-El, M.B.: Abstract computability and its relation to the general purpose analog computer (some connections between logic, differential equations and analog computers). Trans. Am. Math. Soc. **199**, 1–28 (1974)
33. Qi, L.S., et al.: Repurposing CRISPR as an RNA-guided platform for sequence-specific control of gene expression. Cell **152**(5), 1173–1183 (2013)
34. Rudge, T.J., et al.: Characterization of intrinsic properties of promoters. ACS Synth. Biol. **5**(1), 89–98 (2016)
35. Santos-Moreno, J., Tasiudi, E., Stelling, J., Schaerli, Y.: Multistable and dynamic CRISPRi-based synthetic circuits. Nat. Commun. **11**(1), 2746 (2020)
36. Sarpeshkar, R.: Analog synthetic biology. Philos. Trans. Roy. Soc. A Math. Phys. Eng. Sci. **372**(2012), 20130110 (2014)
37. Schlögl, F.: Chemical reaction models for non-equilibrium phase transitions. Z. Phys. **253**(2), 147–161 (1972)
38. Shannon, C.E.: Mathematical theory of the differential analyzer. J. Math. Phys. **20**(1–4), 337–354 (1941)
39. Tanenbaum, M.E., Gilbert, L.A., Qi, L.S., Weissman, J.S., Vale, R.D.: A protein-tagging system for signal amplification in gene expression and fluorescence imaging. Cell **159**(3), 635–646 (2014)
40. Venturelli, O.S., Soloveichik, D.: Completeness of transcriptional repressor networks operating in the unsaturated regime. https://www.solo-group.link/papers/complete_transcription.pdf
41. Vilela, M., Chou, I.-C., Vinga, S., Vasconcelos, A.T.R., Voit, E.O., Almeida, J.S.: Parameter optimization in S-system models. BMC Syst. Biol. **2**, 35 (2008)
42. Willamowski, K.-D., Rössler, O.: Irregular oscillations in a realistic abstract quadratic mass action system. Zeitschrift für Naturforschung A **35**(3), 317–318 (1980)
43. Zhang, Y., et al.: CRISPR/gRNA-directed synergistic activation mediator (SAM) induces specific, persistent and robust reactivation of the HIV-1 latent reservoirs. Sci. Rep. **5**(1), 16277 (2015)

Metabolic Transformation Algorithm: A Systems Biology Approach to Aging and Alzheimer's Disease

Bruno Sá[1], Catarina Gomes[1], and Miguel Rocha[1,2(✉)]

[1] Centre of Biological Engineering, University of Minho, Braga, Portugal
[2] Labbels | Associate Laboratory, University of Minho, Braga, Guimarães, Portugal
mrocha@di.uminho.pt

Abstract. Aging and Alzheimer's disease are complex multifactorial processes driven by interacting genetic and metabolic mechanisms, for which single-gene approaches often fail to capture system-level behaviour. Systems biology addresses this challenge by integrating omics data with genome-scale metabolic models (GSMMs) to identify candidate interventions. The Metabolic Transformation Algorithm (MTA) and its robust variant rMTA use constraint-based modelling to predict perturbations that shift a system from a disease-associated toward a healthier metabolic state. To move beyond single-gene prioritization, we applied EA-rMTA, an evolutionary extension of rMTA that searches the combinatorial knockout space by optimizing the robust Transformation Score.

We evaluated the framework in two case studies: lifespan-extending *unc-62* knockdown in *Caenorhabditis elegans* and early-onset Alzheimer's disease (EOAD) in human cortex. In both settings, rMTA found biologically coherent targets and pathway-level signatures consistent with known hallmarks of aging and neurodegeneration. EA-rMTA further identified compact and interpretable multi-gene intervention strategies that outperformed single-gene deletions in shifting the metabolic state toward the desired phenotype.

Together, these results show that evolutionary search extends metabolic transformation analysis beyond single-gene perturbations and enables the discovery of experimentally tractable combinatorial intervention hypotheses. More broadly, the framework provides a computational strategy for generating systems-level therapeutic hypotheses in aging, neurodegeneration, and other multifactorial disorders.

Keywords: Metabolic Transformation Algorithm · Constraint-based metabolic models · Aging · Alzheimer's disease · Caenorhabditis elegans

1 Introduction

Aging is characterized by a progressive loss of physiological integrity and increased vulnerability to disease, including neurodegeneration, cardiovascular

B. Sá and C. Gomes—These authors contributed equally to this work.

P. T. Monteiro (Ed.): CMSB 2026, LNBI 16678, pp. 234–262, 2027.
https://doi.org/10.1007/978-3-032-30870-2_12

disorders, and cancer [7,8,14,30,49]. Because aging emerges from interactions across genes, proteins, metabolites, and tissues, it is better understood as a systems-level process than as a purely chronological phenomenon. In this context, systems biology provides a useful framework for studying how coordinated changes in biological networks give rise to age-associated phenotypes [40,76].

The Metabolic Transformation Algorithm (MTA) [81] and its robust version, Robust Metabolic Transformation Algorithm (rMTA) [72], are promising computational tools for identifying metabolic perturbations that shift a model from a source state toward a desired target state. By integrating Genome-scale Metabolic Model (GSMM) with Differential Gene Expression (DGE) data from healthy and diseased conditions, these methods prioritize perturbations whose predicted flux changes are capable of shifting cellular metabolism toward a desired phenotypic. Unlike approaches centered on cell destruction, such as many cancer therapies and antibiotics [9,24], MTA-based methods aim to restore metabolic function. Many phenotypes relevant to aging and neurodegeneration are polygenic and involve overlapping metabolic pathways, making single-gene interventions insufficient due to redundancy and compensatory responses. This motivates the use of Evolutionary Algorithm rMTA (EA-rMTA) [70], which extends rMTA from single-gene ranking to the exploration of combinatorial perturbation spaces by optimizing the rMTA metric, Robust Transformation Score (rTS).

Neurodegenerative disorders such as Alzheimer's Disease (AD) are major conditions associated with aging and are marked by progressive neuronal dysfunction and loss [26,48]. Although often framed as proteinopathies, they also involve metabolic dysfunction, immune dysregulation, and synaptic decline [42,65]. Model organisms remain essential for dissecting these mechanisms, and *C. elegans* is particularly valuable because of its short lifespan, genetic tractability, conserved pathways, and well-characterized nervous system [27,34,38,79]. Among longevity-associated genes in *C. elegans*, the transcriptional cofactor *unc-62* is especially relevant. Knockdown of *unc-62* by RNA interference extends lifespan by approximately 30–40%, even when initiated during adulthood, making it a useful perturbation for uncovering metabolic changes associated with aging [15,73].

In this study, we apply rMTA and EA-rMTA to two complementary biological contexts: lifespan-associated *unc-62* knockdown in *C. elegans* and Early Onset Alzheimer's Disease (EOAD) in human cortex transcriptomic data. By integrating transcriptomic data with GSMMs, we use rMTA to identify single-gene perturbations associated with desired metabolic transformations and EA-rMTA to search for multi-gene combinations that improve the rTS. Across these two systems, we show that evolutionary metabolic transformation analysis recovers biologically coherent pathways and prioritizes compact combinatorial perturbation sets, providing a systems-level strategy for studying metabolic mechanisms in aging and neurodegeneration.

2 Materials and Methods

2.1 Datasets and Metabolic Models

Two GSMMs were used in this study: iCEL1314 for *C. elegans* [80] and Recon3D for human metabolism [6]. Blocked reactions were identified and removed using COBRApy [19] to improve model consistency before omics integration. For the *C. elegans* case study, transcriptomic data for *unc-62* knockdown were obtained from Gene Expression Omnibus (GEO) series GSE39574 and comprised three RNA-seq replicates. For AD, transcriptomic data were obtained from GEO series GSE203206, comprising 47 human cortex RNA-seq samples (8 controls, 19 EOAD, and 20 Late Onset Alzheimer's Disease (LOAD)). Only control and EOAD samples were considered in this study.

2.2 Differential Expression and Model Reconstruction

Differential expression analysis was performed with `limma`. For *C. elegans*, control and *unc-62* knockdown samples were compared using an adjusted p-value threshold of 0.1, following rMTA recommendations to obtain approximately 100–200 altered reactions. For EOAD, controls were compared with EOAD samples using an adjusted p-value threshold of 0.05. Biological replicates were averaged at the transcript level and mapped to model genes. Context-specific metabolic models were then reconstructed with Troppo using the Integrative Metabolic Analysis tool (iMAT) algorithm [59,85]. For each reconstructed model, 2,000 flux samples were generated using the COBRApy implementation of Artificial Centering Hit-and-Run (ACHR). The average of these samples was used to estimate the reference flux distribution, v^{ref}, for downstream rMTA analyses.

2.3 MTA and rMTA Workflow

MTA identifies perturbations that can transform a metabolic model from a source state toward a desired phenotypic state [72,81]. In our *C. elegans* case, the transformation direction was instead defined to reproduce the metabolic signature associated with the long-lived *unc-62* knockdown state.

First, a flux description of the source state is obtained. Expression data from the source condition are integrated with the generic GSMM using iMAT, producing a context-specific model. Because multiple feasible flux distributions can satisfy the same constraints, 2,000 flux samples are generated and averaged to define the reference flux vector, v^{ref}.

Second, the desired transformation is translated from gene expression to reaction-level constraints. Differentially expressed genes between source and target states are mapped to model reactions using GPR rules. Together with the sign of each reference flux in v^{ref}, reactions are classified into three sets: R_F, reactions expected to change in the forward direction; R_B, reactions expected to change in the backward direction; and R_S, reactions expected to remain approximately unchanged.

Third, each candidate knockout is simulated in the model. A mixed-integer quadratic programming problem then searches for a feasible post-perturbation flux distribution, v^{res}, that induces significant flux changes in R_F and R_B while minimizing deviations in R_S. The significance threshold for each reaction is denoted ϵ_i, and the trade-off between changing target reactions and preserving unchanged reactions is controlled by α.

Fourth, the resulting perturbation is scored. The Transformation Score (TS) rewards flux changes that occur in the desired direction and penalizes changes in the opposite direction, normalized by deviations in reactions that should remain unchanged. A more positive TS therefore indicates a stronger model transformation toward the target state.

rMTA makes this score more conservative by evaluating each knockout under three complementary scenarios [72]. The best-case score (Best-case Transformation Score (bTS)) corresponds to the original MTA transformation toward the target state. The worst-case score (Worst-case Transformation Score (wTS)) swaps the target-direction reaction sets and measures whether the same perturbation could also reinforce the source state. The MOMA score (MOMA Transformation Score (mTS)) estimates a more realistic post-perturbation response by minimizing the deviation from v^{ref}. These values are combined into the robust Transformation Score,

$$\text{rTS} = \text{mTS} \cdot [k\,(\text{bTS} - \text{wTS})]^a \tag{1}$$

where $k = 100$ and $a = 1$ only when bTS > 0, mTS > 0, and wTS < 0; otherwise $a = 0$ and rTS falls back to mTS. Thus, high rTS values prioritize perturbations that move the model toward the target state while showing limited capacity to move it back toward the source state. In this study, rMTA used $\alpha = 0.66$, as in previous MTA/rMTA applications.

2.4 EA-rMTA and Post-processing

To extend rMTA beyond single-gene perturbations, we applied EA-rMTA, which uses an evolutionary algorithm to optimize multi-gene knockout combinations according to the rTS [70]. Instead of evaluating one deleted gene at a time, each candidate solution represents a set of simultaneous gene deletions. Solutions are encoded as binary vectors over the model genes, where 1 denotes a knockout and 0 denotes an intact gene. The fitness of each vector is the rTS obtained after applying all encoded knockouts to the model.

The evolutionary search proceeds through the standard population-based cycle. An initial population of fixed-size knockout sets is generated, each individual is evaluated with the rTS fitness function, and higher-scoring individuals are preferentially selected as parents. Uniform crossover recombines knockout patterns between parent solutions, while bit-flip mutation introduces local changes. After these operators, a repair function enforces the maximum number of allowed knockouts by removing excess deleted genes. A refresh step introduces new random individuals in each generation to maintain diversity and reduce premature convergence. The best solutions are retained through fitness-based replacement.

After optimization, EA-rMTA solutions were simplified to improve interpretability and distinguish core contributors from genes with only marginal score gains. Starting from a high-scoring solution, each gene was removed temporarily and the rTS was recomputed. The gene whose removal caused the smallest reduction in rTS was then removed permanently, and this procedure was repeated until further pruning produced a marked score decrease. The resulting compact sets are reported as core perturbation sets that preserve most of the multi-gene score.

The final EA-rMTA analyses used the following configurations. For *C. elegans*, the population size was 512, with 250 generations, refresh fraction 0.5, a maximum of 20 knockouts, and repair enabled. For EOAD, the population size was 400, with 100 generations, refresh fraction 0.75, a maximum of 10 knockouts, and repair enabled.

2.5 Enrichment Analysis

Functional interpretation was performed with GSEApy [21]. Enrichment analysis tests whether a selected gene set is overrepresented in curated pathways, ontologies, disease annotations, or drug signatures. Two rMTA-derived gene sets were considered: all genes with positive rTS values and the top 10% highest-ranked genes. Enrichr was used for the human analysis and WormEnrichr for the *C. elegans* analysis. Enriched terms were filtered using adjusted $p < 0.05$ and ranked by combined score.

3 Results and Discussion

3.1 C. Elegans

Differentially Expressed Genes. Differential gene expression analysis identified 129 significantly altered genes between control and *unc-62* knockdown worms, with 74 upregulated and 55 downregulated genes (Fig. 1). The volcano plot highlights the genes with the strongest expression changes. These results show that *unc-62* knockdown induces a substantial transcriptional response, providing the basis for subsequent integration with the metabolic model and rMTA.

rMTA. The rMTA analysis generated a ranked list of candidate genes associated with the metabolic response to *unc-62* knockdown. The top-ranked candidates are summarized in Table 1. Several of these genes converge on biological functions previously linked to aging and longevity, suggesting that rMTA captures biologically meaningful aspects of the pro-longevity metabolic state.

Notably, *bre-4* and *ger-1* encode enzymes involved in glycosylation processes that mediate toxin binding at the cell surface [2,68]. Their inhibition confers resistance to environmental toxins, paralleling the effect of *unc-62* knockdown, which reduces internal protein aggregation by limiting yolk protein accumulation [15,74]. This convergence suggests a broader role for toxin resistance, both internal and external, in lifespan regulation.

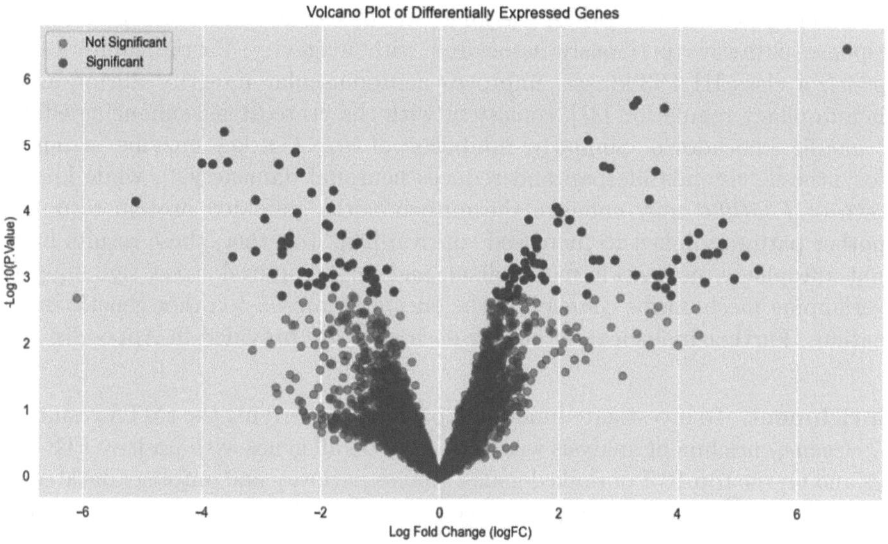

Fig. 1. Volcano plot of differential gene expression analysis showing significantly upregulated and downregulated genes in *unc-62* knockdown worms compared to controls.

Table 1. Top-ranked genes from the rMTA analysis in *C. elegans* under *unc-62* knockdown.

Rank	WormBase ID	Gene	Description
1	WBGene00000283	cah-5	Putative carbonic anhydrase 5
2	WBGene00006932	vps-34	Phosphatidylinositol 3-kinase catalytic subunit type 3
3	WBGene00016629	C44B7.7	Gamma-glutamylcyclotransferase
4	WBGene00000269	bre-4	Beta-1,4-N-acetylgalactosaminyltransferase bre-4
5	WBGene00001823	hap-1	Inosine triphosphate pyrophosphatase
6	WBGene00022393	abhd-12	2-arachidonoylglycerol hydrolase ABHD12
7	WBGene00003476	mtm-3	Myotubularin-related protein 3
8	WBGene00013301	Y57G11C.3	Putative 6-phosphogluconolactonase
9	WBGene00009138	F25H9.6	Flavoprotein domain-containing protein
10	WBGene00014203	ZK1058.3	Putative galactose-1-phosphate uridylyltransferase
11	WBGene00004092	ppt-1	Palmitoyl-protein thioesterase 1
12	WBGene00019813	ger-1	GDP-L-fucose synthase
13	WBGene00016957	atic-1	5-aminoimidazole-4-carboxamide ribonucleotide formyltransferase

Other genes in the rMTA ranking are linked to metabolic and stress-response pathways previously associated with longevity. Partial inhibition of *vps-34*, a class III PI3-kinase, improves neuromuscular integrity during aging via autophagy regulation [31], consistent with the proteostasis-enhancing effects of *unc-62* knockdown. Similarly, inhibition of *atic-1*, a key enzyme in purine biosynthesis, extends lifespan and reduces neuronal damage [64], while knockdown of *F25H9.6* may enhance the mitochondrial unfolded protein response, another pathway linked to increased survival [29]. Together, these results highlight autophagy, nucleotide metabolism, and mitochondrial stress signalling as overlapping mechanisms connecting the effects of *unc-62* to other genetic interventions. Further biological details for each gene are provided in Appendix 1.1.

Enrichment. To investigate functional patterns underlying the rMTA results in *C. elegans*, enrichment analysis was performed on all genes with positive rTS values and on the top 10% of ranked genes. Across pathway and ontology databases, both gene sets showed strong convergence on mitochondrial processes, including oxidative phosphorylation, NADH–ubiquinone electron transport, fatty acid metabolism, and mitochondrial protein quality control. These pathways are key regulators of lifespan in *C. elegans*, influencing ATP production, redox balance, ROS signalling, and activation of mitochondrial stress responses such as the UPR_{mt} [86]. Enrichment in fatty acid-related pathways further reflects the role of lipid remodelling in maintaining membrane integrity and signalling during aging [60]. Carbohydrate and amino acid metabolism also emerged prominently. Enrichment in the pentose phosphate pathway, glycine/serine/threonine metabolism, and amino sugar and nucleotide sugar metabolism highlighted processes supporting redox buffering, proteostasis, and methylation capacity. These pathways are established regulators of stress resistance, detoxification, and epigenetic control of longevity [3,37,44,47].

Analysis of the top 10% high-confidence subset further emphasized pathways linked to coenzyme and acetyl-CoA metabolism, including pantothenate and CoA biosynthesis, fatty acid oxidation, and histone acetylation. These findings suggest a central role for metabolic–epigenetic coupling in longevity, whereby metabolic processes regulate chromatin state and transcriptional flexibility [5,32,69]. Finally, several enriched categories aligned directly with the transcriptional response to *unc-62* knockdown, as well as with top-ranked rMTA genes such as *F25H9.6*, *bre-4*, and *ger-1*. This consistency supports the interpretation that the metabolic changes identified by rMTA reflect biologically coherent modules involved in energy balance, proteostasis, and glycan remodelling. Full enrichment plots and database-specific analyses are provided in Appendix 1.2.

EA-rMTA. In *C. elegans*, baseline rMTA identified a best single-gene knockout with an rTS of 0.7170, setting the single-perturbation reference for this case study. EA-rMTA improved this score, with the optimized configuration consistently producing multi-gene knockout solutions that reached rTS values of approximately 1.4409 (Table 2).

Table 2. Comparison of rMTA and EA-rMTA outcomes in *C. elegans.* EA-rMTA results correspond to the optimized configuration (max knockouts = 20, repair enforced, refresh rate = 0.5).

Approach	Best rTS
Single-gene knockout (baseline rMTA)	0.7170
EA-rMTA (optimized multi-gene knockout)	1.4409

Iterative pruning of high-scoring EA-rMTA solutions revealed that many deletions were redundant. Near-optimal scores were maintained until candidate sets were reduced to approximately 7–12 genes, after which rTS values declined sharply (Fig. 2). Notably, all independent high-scoring solutions converged to a common point of 12 genes during pruning, indicating that relatively small gene sets were sufficient to capture the metabolic improvements achieved by larger knockout combinations.

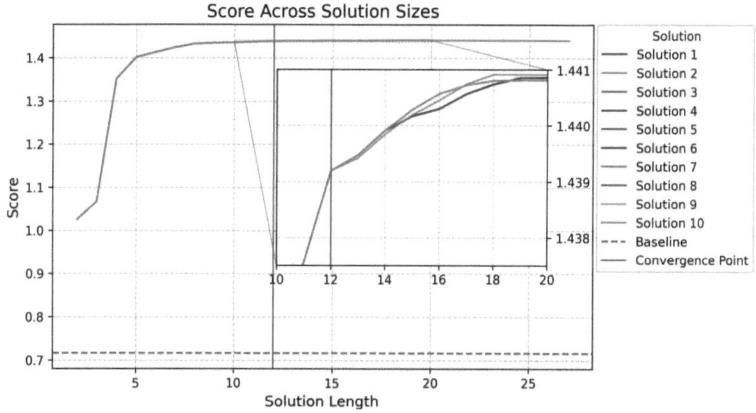

Fig. 2. Iterative pruning of EA-rMTA solutions in *C. elegans.* Fitness values remained close to the maximum until solutions were reduced to 7–12 knockouts, after which performance dropped markedly. All solutions converged at a length of 12.

From this analysis, a recurring core of seven genes emerged as major contributors to near-optimal performance (Table 3). Although most of these genes produced only modest or negligible effects individually, their combined simulated deletion generated strong synergistic improvements in the system-wide rTS. This pattern highlights the cooperative nature of metabolic regulation, where small-effect genes collectively modulate flux distributions in ways that single-gene perturbations cannot capture.

Table 3. Core gene set identified by EA-rMTA pruning in *C. elegans*. Single-gene rTS values are shown for reference.

Gene (Symbol)	Single-gene rTS
WBGene00015778 (*got-2*)	0.6152
WBGene00012326	0.0137
WBGene00001077 (*dpy-18*)	0.0131
WBGene00002879 (*let-754*)	0.0026
WBGene00015553 (*trxr-1*)	–0.0002
WBGene00009824 (*gpdh-1*)	–0.0020
WBGene00009119 (*ndk-1*)	–0.0059

The functions of these core genes span energy homeostasis, redox regulation, amino acid metabolism, and structural integrity, all of which correspond to established hallmarks of aging. For example, thioredoxin reductase (*trxr-1*) contributes to redox balance, while *got-2* and *ndk-1* participate in mitochondrial and nucleotide metabolism. These connections suggest that EA-rMTA not only identifies high-performing model perturbation combinations, but also reveals functional modules that may collectively drive the longevity phenotype observed in *unc-62* knockdown worms. Further biological details for each gene are provided in Appendix 1.3.

3.2 Alzheimer's Disease

Differentially Expressed Genes. Differential gene expression analysis of the EOAD dataset examined a total of 24,055 genes. Among these, 134 genes were significantly upregulated and 260 were significantly downregulated in EOAD samples compared to controls, indicating a marked transcriptional shift associated with the disease state.

As shown in Fig. 3, the volcano plot highlights the genes with the strongest differential expression between EOAD and healthy controls. These findings show that EOAD is characterized by substantial transcriptional alterations, establishing the basis for subsequent integration with the Recon3D metabolic model and rMTA.

rMTA. Application of the rMTA pipeline to the EOAD context-specific model generated a ranked list of candidate genes based on their rTS. The top three genes are summarized in Table 4.

Table 4. Top-ranked genes from the rMTA analysis in EOAD.

Symbol	Full Name	rTS
RFK	Riboflavin kinase	5.4578
PHGDH	Phosphoglycerate dehydrogenase	3.7170
SLC22A8	Solute carrier family 22 member 8	3.2815

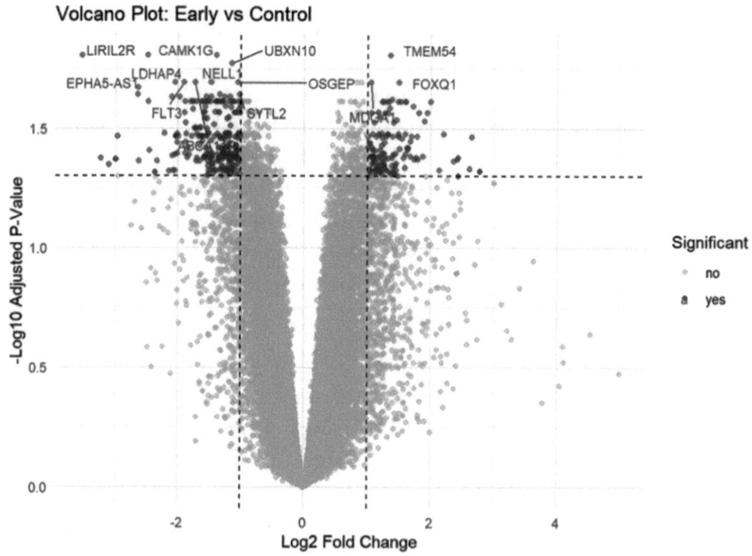

Fig. 3. Volcano plot of differential gene expression analysis comparing EOAD and control samples. Significantly upregulated and downregulated genes are highlighted.

The top candidates, *RFK*, *PHGDH*, and *SLC22A8*, map respectively to riboflavin metabolism, serine biosynthesis, and metabolite transport at the blood–brain barrier, processes tightly linked to mitochondrial dysfunction, oxidative stress, and altered glucose and neurotransmitter metabolism in Alzheimer's disease [1,11,12,46]. Taken together, these findings highlight riboflavin metabolism, serine biosynthesis, and metabolite transport as convergent mechanisms disrupted in EOAD, consistent with major disturbances in energy homeostasis and oxidative stress. Detailed functional annotations for these genes are provided in Appendix 2.1.

Enrichment. To investigate functional patterns associated with the EOAD rMTA signature, we performed pathway and ontology enrichment on (i) all genes with positive rTS values and (ii) the top 10% of genes ranked by rTS. Across KEGG, WikiPathways, Reactome, HumanCyc, and Elsevier pathway databases, both gene sets showed highly concordant enrichment for mitochondrial oxidative phosphorylation, with a strong focus on respiratory chain Complex I and electron transport chain activity.

In addition to oxidative phosphorylation, we observed consistent enrichment of pathways related to branched-chain amino acid degradation, fatty acid β-oxidation, and cofactors such as ubiquinone and coenzyme A, suggesting shifts in mitochondrial substrate use and electron carrier availability in EOAD. Ontology-based analyses localized these signals to NADH dehydrogenase activity and mitochondrial respiratory chain Complex I, while disease annotations linked the rMTA gene sets to primary mitochondrial disorders such as NADH:Q(1) oxidoreductase deficiency and Complex I deficiency. Drug signature enrichment repeatedly highlighted metformin hydrochloride, in line with its known effects on Complex I and redox balance [45].

Taken together, these enrichment analyses identify mitochondrial Complex I as the dominant functional axis underlying the EOAD rMTA signature. Convergent evidence from pathways, ontologies, drug signatures, and disease links highlights impaired respiratory chain activity, deficits in electron carriers, and compensatory reliance on amino acid and fatty acid catabolism. Compared with the broader metabolic flexibility observed in the *C. elegans* analysis, EOAD displays a more focused disruption of mitochondrial function. Full enrichment results are provided in Appendix 2.2.

EA-rMTA. In the Alzheimer's case study, integration of the evolutionary algorithm into rMTA increased the best rTS from 5.4578 to 6.4798 (Table 5). This gain reflects the ability of the EA-driven search to uncover multi-gene perturbation sets that surpass the effects of individual model perturbations, reinforcing the value of combinatorial search in complex disease contexts.

Table 5. Comparison of rMTA and EA-rMTA outcomes in EOAD. EA-rMTA results correspond to the optimized configuration (max knockouts = 10, repair enforced, refresh rate = 0.75).

Approach	Best rTS
Single-gene knockout (baseline rMTA)	5.4578
EA-rMTA (optimized multi-gene knockout)	6.4798

Iterative simplification analyses demonstrated that most of the model score could be preserved with approximately five knockouts, beyond which additional deletions contributed little benefit (Fig. 4). This reduction highlights the feasibility of identifying compact, experimentally tractable intervention strategies.

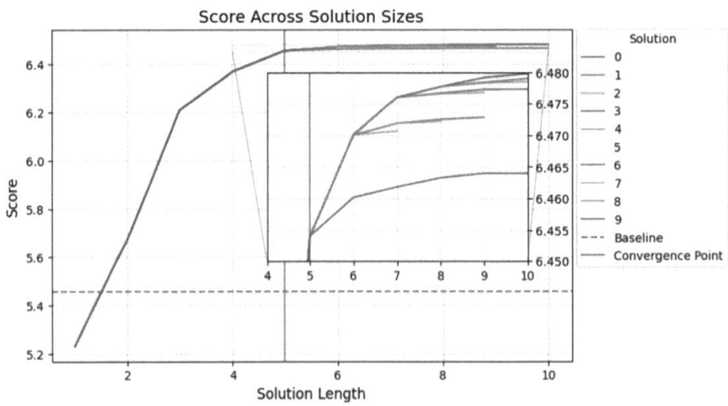

Fig. 4. Iterative pruning of EA-rMTA solutions in EOAD. Fitness values remained near maximum until solutions were reduced to approximately five genes, after which performance declined sharply.

Importantly, while high-scoring genes such as *PSPHP1* and *PGM2L1* retained strong individual model scores, the optimization process also revealed contributions from low-scoring genes such as *GLYCTK* and *PGK1*, whose effects became apparent only in synergistic multi-gene contexts (Table 6).

Table 6. Representative single-gene rTS values for genes identified during EA-rMTA solution simplification in EOAD. Detailed functional annotations of the top individual genes are provided in Appendix 2.3.

Gene	Full Name	Single-gene rTS
ABCA3	ATP binding cassette subfamily A member 3	0.308
GLYCTK	Glycerate kinase	0.278
PGK1	Phosphoglycerate kinase 1	0.308
PSPHP1	Phosphoserine phosphatase pseudogene 1	5.232
PGM2L1	Phosphoglucomutase 2 like 1	4.287

Biological interpretation of these results highlights the diversity of processes contributing to EA-rMTA performance. For example, *PSPHP1*, is annotated as a pseudogene, shares the same GPR rule in the model as *PSPH* and thereby participates in L-serine biosynthesis, a pathway essential for neurotransmitter and membrane lipid production [39,57]. Its strong rTS value is therefore consistent with increasing evidence linking serine metabolism to synaptic function in AD. Similarly, *PGM2L1*, involved in glucose 1,6-bisphosphate synthesis, is highly expressed in the brain and shows downregulation in AD neurons [10,56,82], supporting its interpretation as a model-prioritized metabolic vulnerability.

By contrast, context-dependent contributors such as *GLYCTK* and *PGK1* scored poorly as individual knockouts yet added disproportionately in multi-gene solutions. *PGK1*, a glycolytic enzyme with emerging neuroprotective roles, has been shown to reduce Amyloid-Beta (Aβ) aggregation and remodel hippocampal proteomes in early AD [10,78,82]. Its inclusion in high-performing EA-rMTA sets suggests that strengthening glycolytic resilience may synergize with other metabolic interventions. *GLYCTK*, linked to serine and fructose metabolism, is not directly associated with AD, but pathogenic variants are implicated in neurological disorders such as D-glyceric aciduria [66], suggesting that subtle modulation of this pathway may enhance combinatorial benefits.

Finally, *ABCA3*, a transporter with poorly defined brain functions, appears only in combinatorial contexts with negligible individual effect. Its recurrent emergence is noteworthy given altered expression of ATP-binding cassette transporters in neurodegenerative diseases, including frontotemporal dementia and AD-related settings [17,36]. This points to underexplored transport mechanisms that could indirectly shape neuronal metabolism.

Taken together, these findings show that EA-rMTA enhances rMTA by uncovering cooperative genetic interactions relevant to Alzheimer's pathology.

The identification of compact, synergistic multi-gene subsets that outperform single-gene perturbations underscores the value of evolutionary search for disentangling polygenic and pathway-level mechanisms underlying neurodegenerative disease.

4 Conclusions

In this study, we applied rMTA and its evolutionary extension Evolutionary Algorithm (EA)-rMTA to two distinct biological contexts: lifespan-extending *unc-62* knockdown in *C. elegans* and EOAD. Across both case studies, the results show that metabolic transformation analysis captures biologically meaningful signatures of aging and disease, while evolutionary search reveals synergistic multi-gene interactions that are not accessible through single-gene approaches alone.

In *C. elegans*, rMTA highlighted candidate model perturbations and pathways linked to autophagy, metabolic regulation, stress responses, and mitochondrial function, all of which are closely associated with longevity. Enrichment analysis further converged on oxidative phosphorylation, redox balance, and related metabolic processes, reinforcing the biological coherence of the inferred pro-longevity state. EA-rMTA showed that compact multi-gene subsets captured most of the model score obtained by larger knockout sets, emphasizing the importance of synergistic interactions in shaping metabolic resilience.

For EOAD, rMTA found candidate perturbations linked to riboflavin metabolism, serine biosynthesis, and metabolite transport. Enrichment analysis also pointed to mitochondrial dysfunction, especially respiratory-chain Complex I impairment, oxidative phosphorylation, and coenzyme metabolism. EA-rMTA further showed that compact multi-gene perturbation sets outperformed single-gene perturbations by combining strong individual targets with context-dependent contributors. These results support the relevance of cooperative metabolic interactions in AD.

Together, these findings highlight the value of EA-rMTA as a systems biology framework for prioritizing interpretable combinatorial perturbation hypotheses in complex metabolic phenotypes. By combining constraint-based metabolic modelling, transcriptomic integration, and evolutionary optimization, the method provides a practical strategy for studying polygenic and pathway-level mechanisms in complex metabolic phenotypes. Beyond the specific insights gained in aging and AD, our results establish EA-rMTA as a generalizable framework with potential applications in aging, neurodegeneration, and other multifactorial diseases.

Acknowledgements. This work was supported by the BioNext project Integrated Platform for Sustainable Biotechnologies and Digital Transition – reference NORTE2030-FEDER-02698600, funded through NORTE 2030, Portugal 2030, and the European Structural and Investment Funds. This work was also supported by the Portuguese Foundation for Science and Technology (FCT) under the scope of the strategic funding of the UIDB/04469/2025 research unit, DOI: 10.54499/UID/04469/2025.

Data Availability Statement. All source code and examples used on this study are publicly available on GitHub, at https://github.com/BrunoAGSa/MTA.

Appendix 1. *C. elegans* – Additional Results

Appendix 1.1: rMTA Extended Gene Annotations

The following notes provide detailed biological background for the top-ranked genes identified by rMTA in *C. elegans*, complementing the integrative discussion presented in the main text.

cah-5 encodes a member of the carbonic anhydrase family, enzymes that catalyze the reversible hydration of carbon dioxide and play critical roles in pH regulation, anion transport, and water balance. Fluorescence microscopy studies show that *cah-5* is expressed in neurons and the intestine, suggesting functional roles in the nervous system and digestive tract [67], similar to *unc-62*, which is prominently expressed in the intestine.

vps-34 encodes a class III phosphatidylinositol 3-kinase, essential for endocytic sorting, engulfment, and autophagy. Partial inhibition of this gene in adult worms improves neurotransmission and muscle integrity, ameliorating motor aging [31]. This effect resembles that of *unc-62* knockdown in adulthood, which also extends lifespan.

bre-4 encodes a beta-1,4-N-acetylgalactosaminyltransferase. Its expression increases during aging in wild-type worms, suggesting a role in the aging process [41]. *bre-4* also plays an essential role in forming glycolipid receptors on intestinal plasma membranes, which are required for binding and uptake of Cry proteins such as Cry5Ba. Inhibition of this gene confers resistance to this toxin [2]. While increased *bre-4* expression correlates with aging, it is unclear if its inhibition extends lifespan. Similar to *unc-62*, whose knockdown reduces detrimental protein accumulation, *bre-4* knockdown confers resistance to toxins.

The ortholog of human ***hap-1*** in *C. elegans* is *trak-1*, associated with neuronal function. Knockout mice lacking *hap-1* do not survive postnatally, and therefore the impact in adult mice is unknown [58]. In contrast, *trak-1* knockout worms develop normally without significant behavioral deficits [52]. There is no evidence that reducing *hap-1*/*trak-1* expression extends lifespan.

abhd-12 encodes a serine hydrolase primarily involved in lipid metabolism. In humans, mutations in *ABHD12* cause PHARC, a neurodegenerative disorder characterized by polyneuropathy, hearing loss, ataxia, retinosis pigmentosa, and cataracts [22]. Similar effects are observed in mice [4]. There is currently no information on *abhd-12* in *C. elegans*, but its role in lipid metabolism could influence aging, as seen in mammalian models.

mtm-3 encodes a myotubularin-related phosphatase involved in autophagy. Similar to other autophagy-defective mutants, loss of *mtm-3* reduces survival, indicating its role in stress response [77]. Like *unc-62* knockdown, which is lethal in larvae, *mtm-3* knockdown also leads to reduced survival.

F25H9.6 is the ortholog of phosphopantothenoylcysteine decarboxylase, involved in Coenzyme A biosynthesis [16]. Knockdown of *F25H9.6* may enhance the mitochondrial unfolded protein response (UPR^{mt}), which is associated with increased lifespan [29]. Similar to *unc-62* knockdown, *F25H9.6* knockdown could also extend lifespan.

ppt-1 encodes palmitoyl-protein thioesterase 1, an enzyme involved in depalmitoylation of proteins. In humans, mutations in *PPT1* cause infantile neuronal ceroid lipofuscinosis (INCL), a neurodegenerative disease [75]. In *C. elegans*, *ppt-1* mutations result in mild developmental and reproductive phenotypes, as well as abnormal mitochondrial morphology [62]. RNAi knockdown of *ppt-1* decreases median lifespan [20].

ger-1 encodes GDP-L-fucose synthase, essential for fucosylation processes. Mutations in this gene affect pathogen resistance, preventing binding of the *Coprinopsis cinerea* lectin 2 (CCL2) toxin [68]. Similar to *bre-4*, *ger-1* knockdown confers resistance to toxins.

atic-1 encodes a bifunctional enzyme involved in purine biosynthesis. Overexpression of *atic-1* decreases lifespan, while inhibition increases lifespan and reduces neuronal damage [64]. Like *unc-62* knockdown, *atic-1* knockdown extends lifespan.

Appendix 1.2: Detailed Enrichment Analyses

To investigate functional patterns associated with the rMTA results, enrichment analysis was performed on two gene sets: (i) all genes with positive rTS values and (ii) the top 10% of genes ranked by rTS.

For the complete set of positive rTS genes, enrichment analysis revealed strong associations with mitochondrial processes, including oxidative phosphorylation, NADH–ubiquinone electron transport, mitochondrial protein processing, and fatty acid elongation (Fig. 5). These categories encompass mitochondrial ATP synthesis and respiratory chain activity, which are central to lifespan regulation in *C. elegans* through their effects on energy production, ROS balance, and activation of mitochondrial stress responses such as the UPR_{mt} [86]. Enrichment in fatty acid elongation further highlights the role of lipid remodelling in maintaining membrane integrity and signalling during aging [60].

KEGG pathway analysis supported these findings, showing significant enrichment in the *pentose phosphate pathway*, *amino sugar and nucleotide sugar metabolism*, and *glycine, serine, and threonine metabolism* (Fig. 6). The PPP supports redox balance and stress resistance through NADPH generation and UPR_{mt} signalling, while amino sugar and nucleotide sugar metabolism connects nutrient status to proteostasis via UDP-GlcNAc–dependent protein modification and O-GlcNAc cycling [3,44]. Similarly, glycine, serine, and threonine metabolism feeds into methionine cycle activity, regulating methylation capacity and extending lifespan [37,47].

When restricting the analysis to the top 10% of rTS-ranked genes, enriched biological processes included fatty acid oxidation, coenzyme metabolism, histone acetylation, and neuronal migration (Fig. 7). Fatty acid oxidation and coenzyme metabolism reflect the importance of metabolic flexibility and energy balance,

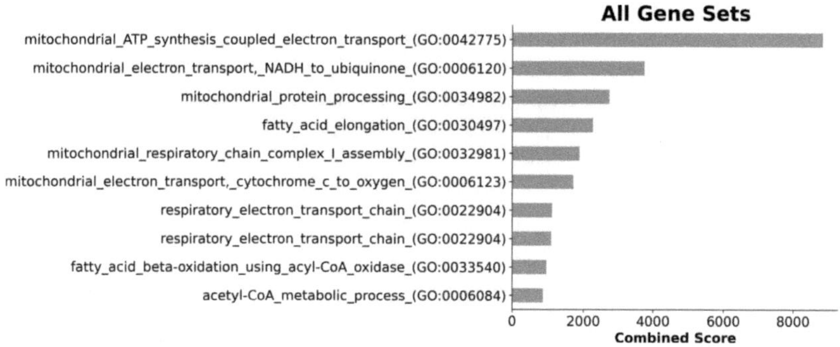

Fig. 5. Enrichment analysis of all positive rTS genes in *C. elegans*. Top enriched processes include mitochondrial energy metabolism and fatty acid elongation. Results are ranked by combined enrichment score.

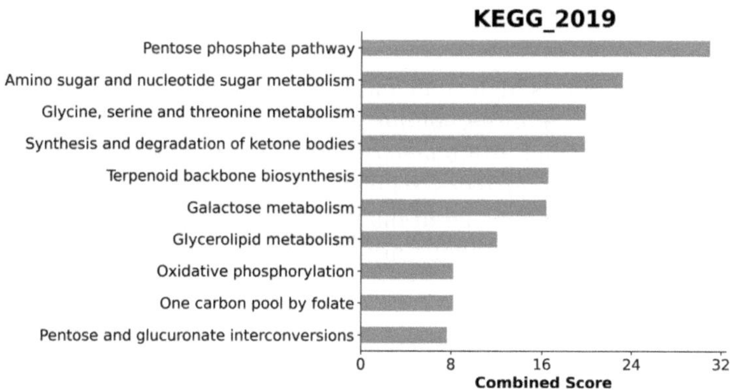

Fig. 6. KEGG pathway enrichment of all positive rTS genes in *C. elegans*. Strong enrichment was observed in the pentose phosphate pathway, amino sugar and nucleotide sugar metabolism, and glycine/serine/threonine metabolism.

both of which influence lifespan and stress resilience in *C. elegans* [32,69]. Enrichment in histone acetylation points to the role of epigenetic regulation in aging, as chromatin remodelling depends on acetyl-CoA availability for histone acetyltransferases, thereby linking metabolism to transcriptional control of longevity and proteostasis [5].

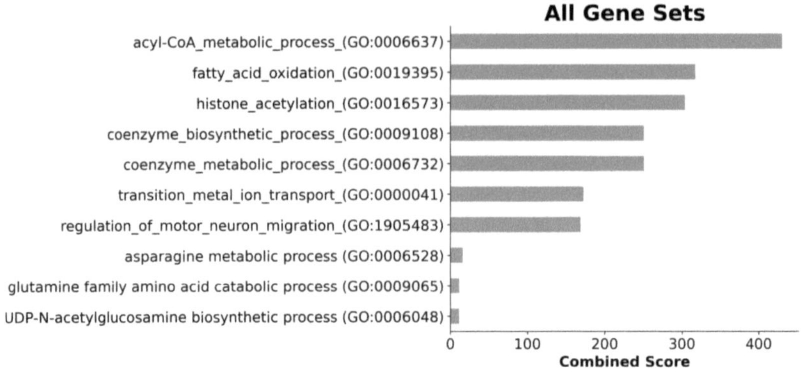

Fig. 7. Enrichment analysis of the top 10% rTS-ranked genes in *C. elegans*. Significant processes include fatty acid oxidation, coenzyme metabolism, histone acetylation, and neuronal migration.

KEGG analysis of this high-confidence subset further revealed enrichment in the *pentose phosphate pathway*, *amino sugar and nucleotide sugar metabolism*, *galactose metabolism*, and *pantothenate and CoA biosynthesis* (Fig. 8). These findings reinforce themes of redox regulation and protein quality control identified in the full gene set, but additionally highlight coenzyme and acetyl-CoA metabolism as central hubs coupling mitochondrial activity to epigenetic remodelling.

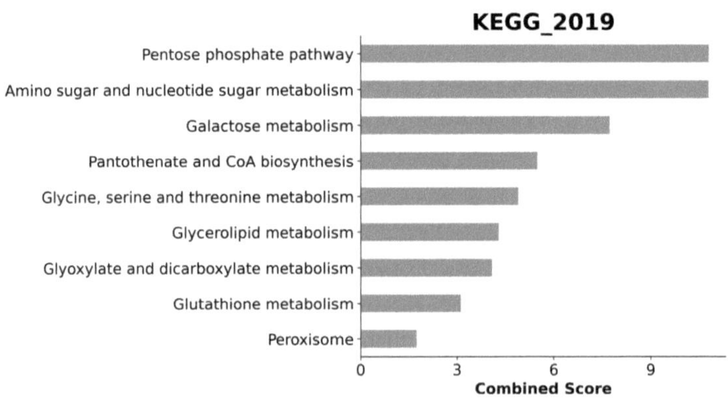

Fig. 8. KEGG pathway enrichment of the top 10% rTS-ranked genes in *C. elegans*. Strong associations were observed with the pentose phosphate pathway, amino sugar and nucleotide sugar metabolism, galactose metabolism, and pantothenate and CoA biosynthesis.

Together, these analyses show that genes prioritized by rMTA converge on mitochondrial function, redox regulation, and metabolic and epigenetic coupling. These pathways are tightly linked to lifespan regulation in *C. elegans*, suggesting that rMTA effectively captures biological processes central to aging and proteostasis.

Importantly, these enrichment patterns complement the results of differential expression and rMTA ranking. The transcriptional response to *unc-62* knockdown included genes associated with autophagy, nucleotide metabolism, and mitochondrial stress signalling, all of which were reflected in the enriched categories detected here. For example, mitochondrial energy metabolism and fatty acid oxidation processes resonate with the identification of *F25H9.6* and other mitochondrial regulators in the rMTA ranking. Likewise, enrichment of glycosylation and sugar metabolism-related pathways connects directly to the ranked genes *bre-4* and *ger-1*, which mediate toxin resistance via glycan remodelling. Finally, the prominence of coenzyme and acetyl-CoA metabolism provides a mechanistic link to the epigenetic regulation inferred from histone acetylation enrichment, integrating metabolic flexibility with chromatin-level control of longevity.

Appendix 1.3: EA-rMTA Extended Analysis and Gene Annotations

The following notes provide biological context for the core subset of seven genes consistently identified by EA-rMTA as major contributors to near-optimal performance in multi-gene knockout solutions. While their individual knockouts produced only modest effects, their synergistic interactions yielded substantial improvements in the robust Transformation Score (rTS), underscoring the polygenic nature of aging regulation in *C. elegans.*

gpdh-1 encodes a glycerol-3-phosphate dehydrogenase involved in osmotic and metabolic stress responses. Neuronal knockdown extends lifespan under high-glucose conditions, implicating *gpdh-1* in the regulation of longevity [54].

trxr-1 encodes thioredoxin reductase (TRX-1), a key enzyme in redox homeostasis. Alterations in thioredoxin pathways influence both mean and maximum lifespan, highlighting its importance in oxidative stress regulation [53].

got-2 likely encodes an L-aspartate:2-oxoglutarate aminotransferase, influencing aspartate metabolism and mitochondrial function. Human orthologs are critical for neurological development [35], suggesting conserved roles in energy and neuronal metabolism.

WBGene00012326 encodes a putative NADH-dependent glutamate synthase. Glutamate metabolism is central to neuronal signalling and energy balance, linking this gene to pathways relevant for aging and stress adaptation [51].

let-754 likely encodes an adenylate kinase, which regulates ATP/ADP ratios. This balance is essential for metabolic health and stress tolerance, implicating the gene in cellular energy regulation [83].

ndk-1 encodes a nucleoside diphosphate kinase that influences MAPK signalling and vulval development. Large-scale RNAi studies indicate that downregulation of *ndk-1* can extend lifespan [50].

dpy-18 encodes the catalytic alpha-subunit of collagen prolyl 4-hydroxylase, an enzyme required for cuticle collagen maturation. Although best known for its "dumpy" phenotype, partial knockdown may alter longevity-related signalling pathways [13,71].

Appendix 2. Alzheimer's – Additional Results

Appendix 2.1: rMTA Extended Gene Annotations

The following notes provide detailed biological background for the top-ranked genes identified by rMTA in EOAD, complementing the integrative discussion presented in the main text.

RFK, encoding riboflavin kinase, achieved the highest transformation score. This enzyme plays a central role in flavin metabolism and mitochondrial electron transport, and its upregulation has been reported in AD-affected brain regions [1, 46]. This finding supports the notion that *RFK* upregulation reflects an adaptive response to oxidative stress, aligning with the well-documented contribution of redox imbalance to neurodegeneration.

PHGDH, which catalyzes the first step of the serine biosynthesis pathway, was also prioritized. Elevated *PHGDH* expression has been linked to cognitive decline and synaptic dysfunction in late-stage AD [11]. Because serine metabolism bridges glycolysis and neurotransmitter production, targeting this pathway may help restore both energy metabolism and synaptic function.

Finally, ***SLC22A8***, a solute carrier implicated in metabolite transport and blood–brain barrier regulation, emerged as a top hit. Its downregulation in AD models has been associated with neuroinflammation and impaired metabolite exchange [12], indicating that restoring *SLC22A8* activity could enhance neurovascular and metabolic balance.

Appendix 2.2: EOAD Enrichment: Detailed Pathway, Ontology, and Disease Analyses

For the complete set of positive rTS genes, enrichment converged strongly on mitochondrial processes, particularly oxidative phosphorylation, electron transport chain activity, and Complex I assembly across KEGG and WikiPathways (Fig. 9A,C). These pathways are long-recognized hallmarks of Alzheimer's pathogenesis, where impaired respiratory chain function contributes to reduced ATP production, redox imbalance, and excessive ROS generation, ultimately driving oxidative stress, synaptic failure, and neuronal degeneration [23,63]. HumanCyc analysis highlighted enrichment in valine, leucine, and isoleucine degradation, while Reactome also identified fatty acid β-oxidation (Fig. 9B,D), both of which suggest dysregulated mitochondrial substrate use as a compensatory response to glucose hypometabolism. Elsevier pathways emphasized ubiquinone biosynthesis (Fig. 9E), consistent with the critical role of CoQ as an electron carrier; CoQ deficiency is known to exacerbate Complex I dysfunction and compromise mitochondrial flux [33,55,61].

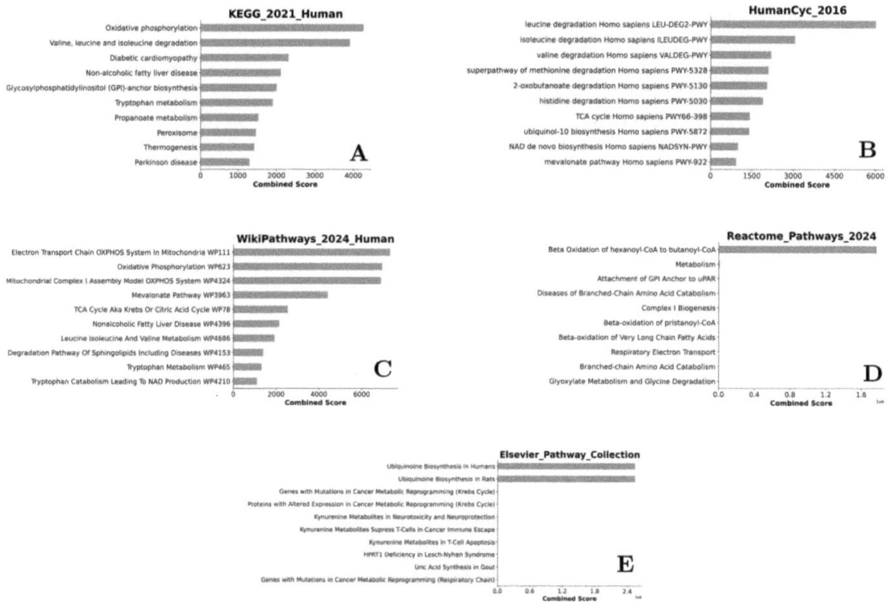

Fig. 9. Enrichment analysis of all positive rTS genes in Alzheimer's disease across multiple pathway databases. (A) KEGG, (B) HumanCyc, (C) WikiPathways, (D) Reactome, (E) Elsevier. Processes converge on oxidative phosphorylation, branched-chain amino acid degradation, fatty acid oxidation, and ubiquinone biosynthesis.

Ontology-based analyses reinforced these results. GO molecular functions were dominated by NADH dehydrogenase activity. Cellular component terms localized enrichment to mitochondrial respiratory chain Complex I (Fig. 10A, B). Together, these findings identify Complex I as the core functional axis affected in EOAD. Disease enrichment via DisGeNET linked the gene set to mitochondrial disorders, including NADH:Q(1) oxidoreductase deficiency and mitochondrial Complex I deficiency (Fig. 10D), emphasizing mechanistic overlap between EOAD and primary mitochondrial pathologies [25,84]. Drug signature analysis identified *metformin hydrochloride* (Fig. 10C), consistent with emerging evidence that metformin modulates Complex I activity, improves redox balance, and influences glucose and mitochondrial metabolism [45].

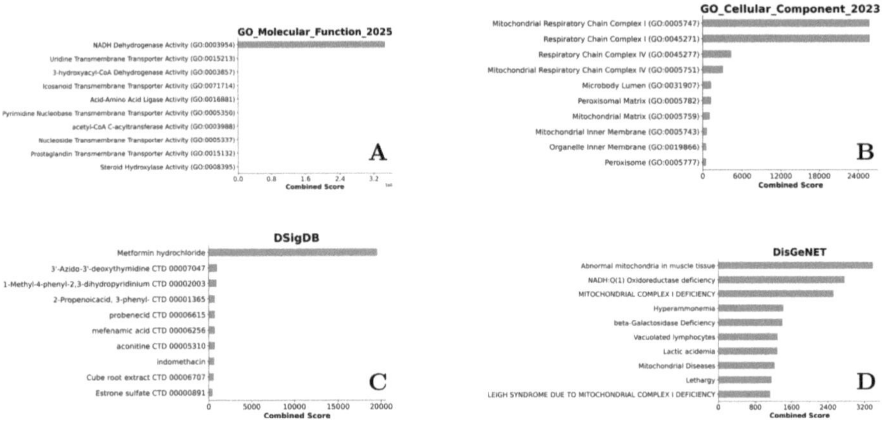

Fig. 10. Ontology and disease enrichment analysis of all positive rTS genes in Alzheimer's disease. (A) GO Molecular Function (NADH dehydrogenase activity), (B) GO Cellular Component (mitochondrial respiratory chain Complex I), (C) DSigDB (metformin hydrochloride), (D) DisGeNET (mitochondrial disorders, including NADH:Q(1) oxidoreductase deficiency and mitochondrial Complex I deficiency).

Analysis of the top 10% rTS-ranked genes sharpened these observations. KEGG, WikiPathways, and Reactome analyses again pointed to oxidative phosphorylation, Complex I biogenesis, and mitochondrial respiratory chain activity (Fig. 11A,C,D). HumanCyc highlighted coenzyme A biosynthesis, implicating cofactor supply as an additional constraint on metabolic flux, while Elsevier enrichment pointed to disease contexts such as MELAS syndrome and cancer-associated respiratory chain impairment (Fig. 11B,E). These signals underscore the parallels between EOAD and primary mitochondrial disorders, where OXPHOS assembly defects are central to pathology [28,43]. Notably, enrichment of retrograde endocannabinoid signalling links metabolic reprogramming to synaptic regulation, consistent with evidence implicating this pathway in neurotransmission, neuroinflammation, and cognitive decline in AD [18].

Ontology and disease annotations for this high-confidence subset again centered on mitochondrial processes. GO molecular functions reinforced NADH dehydrogenase activity, while cellular component terms pinpointed Complex I (Fig. 12A,B). DSigDB again prioritized metformin hydrochloride (Fig. 12C), strengthening the case for translational relevance. DisGeNET enrichment highlighted disorders such as mitochondrial Complex I deficiency and abnormal mitochondrial morphology, further supporting the centrality of respiratory chain impairment in EOAD (Fig. 12D).

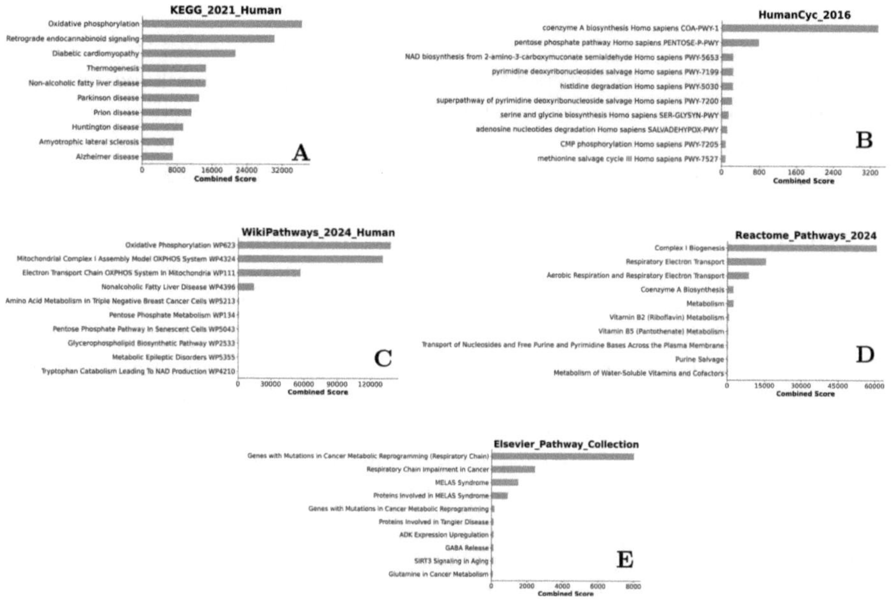

Fig. 11. Enrichment analysis of the top 10% rTS-ranked genes in Alzheimer's disease. (A) KEGG, (B) HumanCyc, (C) WikiPathways, (D) Reactome, (E) Elsevier. Processes converge on oxidative phosphorylation, Complex I biogenesis, and coenzyme metabolism.

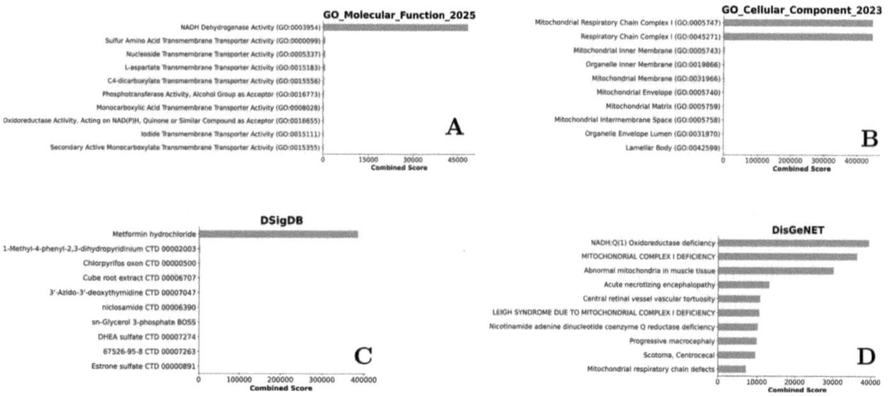

Fig. 12. Ontology and disease enrichment analysis of the top 10% rTS-ranked genes in Alzheimer's disease. (A) GO Molecular Function (NADH dehydrogenase activity), (B) GO Cellular Component (mitochondrial respiratory chain Complex I), (C) DSigDB (metformin hydrochloride), (D) DisGeNET (mitochondrial disorders including mitochondrial Complex I deficiency and abnormal mitochondria in muscle tissue).

Appendix 2.3: EA-rMTA Extended Gene Annotations

The following notes provide biological context for the genes identified by EA-rMTA in EOAD as contributors to high-performing multi-gene knockout solutions. While many of these genes showed only modest or no effects as single knockouts, their synergistic interactions generated substantial improvements in the robust Transformation Score (rTS), underscoring the polygenic nature of AD.

ABCA3 encodes an ATP-binding cassette transporter primarily involved in pulmonary surfactant metabolism, but it is also expressed in the brain. Its neurological functions remain poorly defined, though altered expression has been reported in frontotemporal lobar degeneration [36]. While not directly linked to AD, its presence in neurodegenerative contexts suggests possible relevance [17].

GLYCTK encodes glycerate kinase, which catalyzes the conversion of D-glycerate to 2-phosphoglycerate within serine and fructose metabolism. Pathogenic variants are associated with D-glyceric aciduria, a metabolic disorder with neurological symptoms [66]. Although no direct association with AD has been established, its metabolic role suggests potential indirect involvement.

PGK1 encodes phosphoglycerate kinase 1, a glycolytic enzyme with emerging neuroprotective roles. Recent studies indicate that PGK1 activation reduces Aβ aggregation and pathological protein condensates [10,82]. Proteomic analyses also implicate PGK1 in hippocampal remodelling during early AD, and in vitro assays suggest direct Aβ binding [78].

PSPHP1 is a non-coding pseudogene with no known protein-coding function. However, in the metabolic model it shares the same gene–protein–reaction (GPR) association as *PSPH*, catalyzing the final step of L-serine biosynthesis [39]. L-serine is a precursor for neurotransmitters and brain-specific phospholipids essential for synaptic function. Dysregulation of this pathway has been linked to cognitive impairment in AD models [57]. Although the role of *PSPHP1* remains unclear, its association with serine metabolism warrants further attention.

PGM2L1 encodes phosphoglucomutase 2-like 1, an enzyme involved in the synthesis of glucose 1,6-bisphosphate, and is highly expressed in the brain. Loss-of-function mutations are associated with neurodevelopmental syndromes [56]. While no direct link to AD has been established, transcriptomic analyses report *PGM2L1* downregulation in neurons from AD patients and models [10,82], suggesting possible involvement in disease-associated metabolic shifts.

References

1. Andjelkovic, A.V., Situ, M., Citalan-Madrid, A.F., Stamatovic, S.M., Xiang, J., Keep, R.F.: Blood-brain barrier dysfunction in normal aging and neurodegeneration: mechanisms, impact, and treatments. Stroke **54**(3), 661–672 (2023). https://doi.org/10.1161/STROKEAHA.122.040578, https://www.ahajournals.org/doi/10.1161/STROKEAHA.122.040578, publisher: American Heart Association

2. Barrows, B.D., Haslam, S.M., Bischof, L.J., Morris, H.R., Dell, A., Aroian, R.V.: Resistance to bacillus thuringiensis toxin in caenorhabditis elegans from loss of fucose. J. Biol. Chem. **282**(5), 3302–3311 (2007)
3. Bennett, C.F., et al.: Transaldolase inhibition impairs mitochondrial respiration and induces a starvation-like longevity response in Caenorhabditis elegans. PLOS Genetics **13**(3), e1006695 (2017). https://doi.org/10.1371/journal.pgen.1006695, https://dx.plos.org/10.1371/journal.pgen.1006695
4. Blankman, J.L., Long, J.Z., Trauger, S.A., Siuzdak, G., Cravatt, B.F.: Abhd12 controls brain lysophosphatidylserine pathways that are deregulated in a murine model of the neurodegenerative disease pharc. Proc. Natl. Acad. Sci. **110**(4), 1500–1505 (2013)
5. Bradshaw, P.C.: Acetyl-CoA metabolism and histone acetylation in the regulation of aging and lifespan. Antioxidants **10**(4), 572 (2021). https://doi.org/10.3390/antiox10040572, https://www.mdpi.com/2076-3921/10/4/572
6. Brunk, E., et al.: Recon3D enables a three-dimensional view of gene variation in human metabolism. Nat. Biotechnol. **36**(3), 272–281 (2018). https://doi.org/10.1038/nbt.4072, https://www.nature.com/articles/nbt.4072
7. Calcinotto, A., Kohli, J., Zagato, E., Pellegrini, L., Demaria, M., Alimonti, A.: Cellular senescence: aging, cancer, and injury. Physiol. Rev. **99**(2), 1047–1078 (2019). https://doi.org/10.1152/physrev.00020.2018, https://www.physiology.org/doi/10.1152/physrev.00020.2018
8. Campisi, J.: Aging, cellular senescence, and cancer. Annu. Rev. Physiol. **75**(1), 685–705 (2013). https://doi.org/10.1146/annurev-physiol-030212-183653, https://www.annualreviews.org/doi/10.1146/annurev-physiol-030212-183653
9. Chavali, A.K., D'Auria, K.M., Hewlett, E.L., Pearson, R.D., Papin, J.A.: A metabolic network approach for the identification and prioritization of antimicrobial drug targets. Trends Microbiology **20**(3), 113–123 (2012). https://doi.org/10.1016/j.tim.2011.12.004, https://linkinghub.elsevier.com/retrieve/pii/S0966842X11002241
10. Chen, H., Li, Y., Gao, J., Cheng, Q., Liu, L., Cai, R.: Activation of Pgk1 results in reduced protein aggregation in diverse neurodegenerative conditions. Mol. Neurobiol. **60**(9), 5090–5101 (2023). https://doi.org/10.1007/s12035-023-03389-6
11. Chen, X., et al.: PHGDH expression increases with progression of Alzheimer's disease pathology and symptoms. Cell Metab. **34**(5), 651–653 (2022). https://doi.org/10.1016/j.cmet.2022.02.008
12. Chestnykh, D., et al.: Acid sphingomyelinase activity suggests a new antipsychotic pharmaco-treatment strategy for schizophrenia. Mol. Psychiatry (2025). https://doi.org/10.1038/s41380-025-02893-6
13. Cho, J.Y., Choi, T.W., Kim, S.H., Ahnn, J., Lee, S.K.: Morphological characterization of small, dumpy, and long phenotypes in caenorhabditis elegans. Mol. Cells **44**(3), 160–167 (2021)
14. Cohen, A.A., et al.: A complex systems approach to aging biology. Nature Aging **2**(7), 580–591 (2022). https://doi.org/10.1038/s43587-022-00252-6, https://www.nature.com/articles/s43587-022-00252-6
15. Curran, S.P., Ruvkun, G.: Lifespan regulation by evolutionarily conserved genes essential for viability. PLoS Genet. **3**(4), e56 (2007)
16. Daugherty, M., et al.: Complete reconstitution of the human coenzyme a biosynthetic pathway via comparative genomics. J. Biol. Chem. **277**(24), 21431–21439 (2002)

17. De Roeck, A., Van Broeckhoven, C., Sleegers, K.: The role of *ABCA7* in Alzheimer's disease: evidence from genomics, transcriptomics and methylomics. Acta Neuropathol. **138**(2), 201–220 (2019). https://doi.org/10.1007/s00401-019-01994-1
18. Di Marzo, V., Stella, N., Zimmer, A.: Endocannabinoid signalling and the deteriorating brain. Nat. Rev. Neurosci. **16**(1), 30–42 (2015)
19. Ebrahim, A., Lerman, J.A., Palsson, B.O., Hyduke, D.R.: Cobrapy: constraints-based reconstruction and analysis for python. BMC Syst. Biol. **7**, 1–6 (2013)
20. Edmonds, M.J., Morgan, A.: A systematic analysis of protein palmitoylation in caenorhabditis elegans. BMC Genomics **15**, 1–16 (2014)
21. Fang, Z., Liu, X., Peltz, G.: Gseapy: a comprehensive package for performing gene set enrichment analysis in python. Bioinformatics **39**(1), btac757 (2023)
22. Fiskerstrand, T., et al.: Mutations in abhd12 cause the neurodegenerative disease pharc: an inborn error of endocannabinoid metabolism. Am. J. Hum. Genetics **87**(3), 410–417 (2010)
23. Fišar, Z., et al.: Activities of mitochondrial respiratory chain complexes in platelets of patients with alzheimer's disease and depressive disorder. Mitochondrion **48**, 67–77 (2019). https://doi.org/10.1016/j.mito.2019.07.013, https://www.sciencedirect.com/science/article/pii/S1567724918301107, mitochondria in Health and Disease – Part 2
24. Folger, O., Jerby, L., Frezza, C., Gottlieb, E., Ruppin, E., Shlomi, T.: Predicting selective drug targets in cancer through metabolic networks. Mol. Syst. Biol. **7**(1), 501 (2011). https://doi.org/10.1038/msb.2011.35, https://www.embopress.org/doi/10.1038/msb.2011.35
25. Gao, H., et al.: Mitochondrial complex i deficiency induces alzheimer's disease-like signatures that are reversible by targeted therapy. Alzheimer's Dementia **21**(8), e70519 (2025)
26. Glass, C.K., Saijo, K., Winner, B., Marchetto, M.C., Gage, F.H.: Mechanisms underlying inflammation in neurodegeneration. Cell **140**(6), 918–934 (2010). https://doi.org/10.1016/j.cell.2010.02.016, https://linkinghub.elsevier.com/retrieve/pii/S0092867410001686
27. Green, R.A., et al.: Expression and imaging of fluorescent proteins in the C. Elegans gonad and early embryo. Methods Cell Biol. **85**, 179–218. Elsevier (2008). https://doi.org/10.1016/S0091-679X(08)85009-1, https://linkinghub.elsevier.com/retrieve/pii/S0091679X08850091
28. Gropman, A., Uittenbogaard, M., Chiaramello, A.: The mitochondrial neurodegenerative diseases melas and lhon-plus: how translational research converts challenges into therapeutic opportunities and clinical trial design (p2-5.004). Neurology **98**(18_supplement), 968 (2022)
29. Haeussler, S., Yeroslaviz, A., Rolland, S.G., Luehr, S., Lambie, E.J., Conradt, B.: Genome-wide rnai screen for regulators of uprmt in caenorhabditis elegans mutants with defects in mitochondrial fusion. G3 **11**(7), jkab095 (2021)
30. Hoeijmakers, J.H.: DNA damage, aging, and cancer. N. Engl. J. Med. **361**(15), 1475–1485 (2009). https://doi.org/10.1056/NEJMra0804615, http://www.nejm.org/doi/abs/10.1056/NEJMra0804615
31. Hu, Z., et al.: Partial inhibition of class iii pi3k vps-34 ameliorates motor aging and prolongs health span. PLoS Biol. **21**(7), e3002165 (2023)
32. Ishii, N., et al.: Coenzyme Q10 can prolong C. Elegans lifespan by lowering oxidative stress. Mech. Ageing Dev. **125**(1), 41–46 (2004). https://doi.org/10.1016/j.mad.2003.10.002, https://linkinghub.elsevier.com/retrieve/pii/S0047637403001982

33. Ju, Y., Li, S., Kong, X., Zhao, Q.: Exploring fatty acid metabolism in alzheimer's disease: the key role of cpt1a. Sci. Rep. **14**(1), 31483 (2024)
34. Kaletta, T., Hengartner, M.O.: Finding function in novel targets: C. Elegans as a model organism. Nat. Rev. Drug Discov. **5**(5), 387–399 (2006). https://doi.org/10.1038/nrd2031, https://www.nature.com/articles/nrd2031
35. van Karnebeek, C.D., et al.: Bi-allelic got2 mutations cause a treatable malate-aspartate shuttle-related encephalopathy. Am. J. Hum. Genetics **105**(3), 534–548 (2019)
36. Katzeff, J.S., Lok, H.C., Bhatia, S., Fu, Y., Halliday, G.M., Kim, W.S.: ATP-binding cassette transporter expression is widely dysregulated in frontotemporal dementia with TDP-43 inclusions. Front. Mol. Neurosci. **15**, 1043127 (2022). https://doi.org/10.3389/fnmol.2022.1043127, https://www.ncbi.nlm.nih.gov/pmc/articles/PMC9663841/
37. Kim, J., Jo, Y., Cho, D., Ryu, D.: L-threonine promotes healthspan by expediting ferritin-dependent ferroptosis inhibition in C. elegans. Nat. Commun. **13**(1), 6554 (2022). https://doi.org/10.1038/s41467-022-34265-x, https://www.nature.com/articles/s41467-022-34265-x
38. Kim, W., Underwood, R.S., Greenwald, I., Shaye, D.D.: OrthoList 2: a new comparative genomic analysis of human and *Caenorhabditis elegans* Genes. Genetics **210**(2), 445–461 (2018). https://doi.org/10.1534/genetics.118.301307, https://academic.oup.com/genetics/article/210/2/445/5931030
39. King, Z.A., et al.: BiGG models: a platform for integrating, standardizing and sharing genome-scale models. Nucleic Acids Res. **44**(D1), D515–D522 (2016). https://doi.org/10.1093/nar/gkv1049, https://academic.oup.com/nar/article-lookup/doi/10.1093/nar/gkv1049
40. Kirkwood, T.B.L.: Systems biology of ageing and longevity. Philos. Trans. R. Soc. B: Biol. Sci. **366**(1561), 64–70 (2011). https://doi.org/10.1098/rstb.2010.0275, https://royalsocietypublishing.org/doi/10.1098/rstb.2010.0275
41. Kremer, J., Brendel, C., Mack, E.K.M., Mack, H.I.D.: Expression of β-1, 4-galactosyltransferases during aging in caenorhabditis elegans. Gerontology **66**(6), 571–581 (2020)
42. Lamptey, R.N.L., Chaulagain, B., Trivedi, R., Gothwal, A., Layek, B., Singh, J.: A review of the common neurodegenerative disorders: current therapeutic approaches and the potential role of nanotherapeutics. Int. J. Mol. Sci. **23**(3), 1851 (2022). https://doi.org/10.3390/ijms23031851, https://www.mdpi.com/1422-0067/23/3/1851
43. Lashley, T., et al.: Extensive anti-coa immunostaining in alzheimer's disease and covalent modification of tau by a key cellular metabolite coenzyme a. Front. Cell. Neurosci. **15**, 739425 (2021)
44. Lee, B.E., Suh, P.G., Kim, J.I.: O-GlcNAcylation in health and neurodegenerative diseases. Exp. Mol. Med. **53**(11), 1674–1682 (2021). https://doi.org/10.1038/s12276-021-00709-5, https://www.nature.com/articles/s12276-021-00709-5
45. Liao, W., Xu, J., Li, B., Ruan, Y., Li, T., Liu, J.: Deciphering the roles of metformin in alzheimer's disease: a snapshot. Front. Pharmacol. **Volume 12 - 2021** (2022). https://doi.org/10.3389/fphar.2021.728315, https://www.frontiersin.org/journals/pharmacology/articles/10.3389/fphar.2021.728315
46. Liu, S., Chen, H., He, X.D., Yang, X.O.: Glucometabolic-related genes as diagnostic biomarkers and therapeutic targets for alzheimer's disease and type 2 diabetes mellitus: a bioinformatics analysis. Neurol. Res. Int. **2024**, 5200222 (2024). https://doi.org/10.1155/2024/5200222

47. Liu, Y.J., et al.: Glycine promotes longevity in Caenorhabditis elegans in a methionine cycle-dependent fashion. PLOS Genetics **15**(3), e1007633 (2019). https://doi.org/10.1371/journal.pgen.1007633, https://dx.plos.org/10.1371/journal.pgen.1007633
48. Livingston, G., et al.: Dementia prevention, intervention, and care: 2020 report of the lancet commission. The Lancet **396**(10248), 413–446 (2020). https://doi.org/10.1016/S0140-6736(20)30367-6, https://linkinghub.elsevier.com/retrieve/pii/S0140673620303676
49. López-Otín, C., Blasco, M.A., Partridge, L., Serrano, M., Kroemer, G.: The hallmarks of aging. Cell **153**(6), 1194–1217 (2013). https://doi.org/10.1016/j.cell.2013.05.039, https://linkinghub.elsevier.com/retrieve/pii/S0092867413006454
50. Mansfeld, J., et al.: Branched-chain amino acid catabolism is a conserved regulator of physiological ageing. Nat. Commun. **6**(1), 10043 (2015)
51. Maragakis, N.J., Rothstein, J.D.: Glutamate transporters: animal models to neurologic disease. Neurobiol. Dis. **15**(3), 461–473 (2004)
52. Mercer, K.B., et al.: A c. elegans homolog of huntingtin-associated protein 1 is expressed in chemosensory neurons and in a number of other somatic cell types. J. Mol. Neurosci. **37**, 37–49 (2009)
53. Miranda-Vizuete, A., González, J.C.F., Gahmon, G., Burghoorn, J., Navas, P., Swoboda, P.: Lifespan decrease in a caenorhabditis elegans mutant lacking trx-1, a thioredoxin expressed in asj sensory neurons. FEBS Lett. **580**(2), 484–490 (2006)
54. Mo, J., et al.: Intestinal gpdh-1 regulates high glucose diet induced lifespan extension in aged worms. PeerJ **11**, e15845 (2023)
55. Montine, T.J., Morrow, J.D.: Fatty acid oxidation in the pathogenesis of alzheimer's disease. Am. J. Pathol. **166**(5), 1283–1289 (2005)
56. Morava, E., et al.: Impaired glucose-1, 6-biphosphate production due to bi-allelic pgm2l1 mutations is associated with a neurodevelopmental disorder. Am. J. Hum. Genetics **108**(6), 1151–1160 (2021)
57. Murtas, G., Marcone, G.L., Sacchi, S., Pollegioni, L.: L-serine synthesis via the phosphorylated pathway in humans. Cell. Mol. Life Sci. **77**(24), 5131–5148 (2020). https://doi.org/10.1007/s00018-020-03574-z
58. Norflus, F., Bu, J., Guyton, E., Gutekunst, C.A.: Behavioral analysis of the huntingtin-associated protein 1 ortholog trak-1 in caenorhabditis elegans. J. Neurosci. Res. **94**(9), 850–856 (2016)
59. Oliveira, A., Ferreira, J., Vieira, V., Sá, B., Rocha, M.: Troppo: tissue-specific reconstruction and phenotype prediction using omics data. Bioinformatics Advances **5**(1), vbaf113 (2025). https://doi.org/10.1093/bioadv/vbaf113
60. Papsdorf, K., Brunet, A.: Linking lipid metabolism to chromatin regulation in aging. Trends Cell Biol. **29**(2), 97–116 (2019). https://doi.org/10.1016/j.tcb.2018.09.004, https://www.sciencedirect.com/science/article/pii/S0962892418301594
61. Polis, B., Samson, A.O.: Role of the metabolism of branched-chain amino acids in the development of alzheimer's disease and other metabolic disorders. Neural Regen. Res. **15**(8), 1460–1470 (2020)
62. Porter, M.Y., Turmaine, M., Mole, S.E.: Identification and characterization of caenorhabditis elegans palmitoyl protein thioesterase1. J. Neurosci. Res. **79**(6), 836–848 (2005)
63. Reiss, A.B., et al.: Mitochondria in alzheimer's disease pathogenesis. Life **14**(2) (2024). https://doi.org/10.3390/life14020196, https://www.mdpi.com/2075-1729/14/2/196

64. Riedinger, C., et al.: High-glucose toxicity is mediated by aicar-transformylase/imp cyclohydrolase and mitigated by amp-activated protein kinase in caenorhabditis elegans. J. Biol. Chem. **293**(13), 4845–4859 (2018)
65. Ross, C.A., Poirier, M.A.: Protein aggregation and neurodegenerative disease. Nat. Med. **10**(S7), S10–S17 (2004). https://doi.org/10.1038/nm1066, https://www.nature.com/articles/nm1066
66. Sass, J.O., et al.: D-glyceric aciduria is caused by genetic deficiency of D-glycerate kinase (GLYCTK). Human Mutation **31**(12), 1280–1285 (2010). https://doi.org/10.1002/humu.21375
67. Sherman, T.A., Rongali, S.C., Matthews, T.A., Pfeiffer, J., Nehrke, K.: Identification of a nuclear carbonic anhydrase in caenorhabditis elegans. Biochimica et Biophysica Acta (BBA)-Molecular Cell Research **1823**(4), 808–817 (2012)
68. Stutz, K., Kaech, A., Aebi, M., Künzler, M., Hengartner, M.O.: Disruption of the c. elegans intestinal brush border by the fungal lectin ccl2 phenocopies dietary lectin toxicity in mammals. PLoS One **10**(6), e0129381 (2015)
69. Sun, Y., et al.: Cordycepin extends the longevity of Caenorhabditis elegans via antioxidation and regulation of fatty acid metabolism. Eur. J. Pharmacol. **994**, 177388 (2025). https://doi.org/10.1016/j.ejphar.2025.177388, https://linkinghub.elsevier.com/retrieve/pii/S0014299925001426
70. Sá, B., Oliveira, A., Rocha, M.: Evolutionary algorithms for metabolic transformation through multi-gene knockout optimization. In: Proceedings of the Genetic and Evolutionary Computation Conference, pp. 1489–1496. ACM, NH Malaga Hotel Malaga Spain (2025). https://doi.org/10.1145/3712256.3726477, https://dl.acm.org/doi/10.1145/3712256.3726477
71. Topf, U., Chiquet-Ehrismann, R.: Genetic interaction between caenorhabditis elegans teneurin ten-1 and prolyl 4-hydroxylase phy-1 and their function in collagen iv-mediated basement membrane integrity during late elongation of the embryo. Mol. Biol. Cell **22**(18), 3331–3343 (2011)
72. Valcárcel, L.V., Torrano, V., Tobalina, L., Carracedo, A., Planes, F.J.: rMTA: robust metabolic transformation analysis. Bioinformatics **35**(21), 4350–4355 (2019). https://doi.org/10.1093/bioinformatics/btz231, https://academic.oup.com/bioinformatics/article/35/21/4350/5421511
73. Van Auken, K., et al.: Roles of the homothorax/meis/prep homolog unc-62 and the exd/pbx homologs ceh-20 and ceh-40 in c. Elegans embryogenesis. Development **129**(22), 5255–5268 (2002). https://doi.org/10.1242/dev.129.22.5255, https://doi.org/10.1242/dev.129.22.5255
74. Van Nostrand, E.L., Sánchez-Blanco, A., Wu, B., Nguyen, A., Kim, S.K.: Roles of the developmental regulator unc-62/homothorax in limiting longevity in caenorhabditis elegans. PLoS Genet. **9**(2), e1003325 (2013)
75. Vesa, J., et al.: Mutations in the palmitoyl protein thioesterase gene causing infantile neuronal ceroid lipofuscinosis. Nature **376**(6541), 584–587 (1995)
76. Wood, L.B., Winslow, A.R., Strasser, S.D.: Systems biology of neurodegenerative diseases. Integr. Biol. **7**(7), 758–775 (2015). https://doi.org/10.1039/C5IB00031A, https://academic.oup.com/ib/article/7/7/758-775/5199019
77. Wu, Y., et al.: Pi 3 p phosphatase activity is required for autophagosome maturation and autolysosome formation. EMBO Rep. **15**(9), 973–981 (2014)
78. Yadikar, H., Ansari, M.A., Abu-Farha, M., Joseph, S., Thomas, B.T., Al-Mulla, F.: Deciphering early and progressive molecular signatures in alzheimer's disease through integrated longitudinal proteomic and pathway analysis in a rodent model. Int. J. Mol. Sci. **25**(12), 6469 (2024). https://doi.org/10.3390/ijms25126469, https://www.ncbi.nlm.nih.gov/pmc/articles/PMC11203991/

79. Yan, G., et al.: Network control principles predict neuron function in the Caenorhabditis elegans connectome. Nature **550**(7677), 519–523 (2017). https://doi.org/10.1038/nature24056, https://www.nature.com/articles/nature24056
80. Yilmaz, L.S., Li, X., Nanda, S., Fox, B., Schroeder, F., Walhout, A.J.: Modeling tissue-relevant *Caenorhabditis elegans* metabolism at network, pathway, reaction, and metabolite levels. Mol. Syst. Biol. **16**(10), e9649 (2020). https://doi.org/10.15252/msb.20209649, https://www.embopress.org/doi/10.15252/msb.20209649
81. Yizhak, K., Gabay, O., Cohen, H., Ruppin, E.: Model-based identification of drug targets that revert disrupted metabolism and its application to ageing. Nat. Commun. **4**(1), 2632 (2013). https://doi.org/10.1038/ncomms3632, https://www.nature.com/articles/ncomms3632
82. Zhang, Q., et al.: Glycolysis-enhancing α1-adrenergic antagonists are neuroprotective in Alzheimer's disease. biorxiv: the Preprint Server for Biology, p. 2025.04.03.647018 (2025). https://doi.org/10.1101/2025.04.03.647018
83. Zhang, S., et al.: Adenylate kinase ak2 isoform integral in embryo and adult heart homeostasis. Biochem. Biophys. Res. Commun. **546**, 59–64 (2021)
84. Zhu, X., Perry, G., Smith, M.A., Wang, X.: Abnormal mitochondrial dynamics in the pathogenesis of alzheimer's disease. J. Alzheimers Dis. **33**(s1), S253–S262 (2012)
85. Zur, H., Ruppin, E., Shlomi, T.: iMAT: an integrative metabolic analysis tool. Bioinformatics **26**(24), 3140–3142 (2010). https://doi.org/10.1093/bioinformatics/btq602
86. Ősz, F., Nazir, A., Takács-Vellai, K., Farkas, Z.: Mutations of the electron transport chain affect lifespan and ros levels in c. Elegans. Antioxidants **14**(1) (2025). https://doi.org/10.3390/antiox14010076, https://www.mdpi.com/2076-3921/14/1/76

Causal Inference and Multi-Omics Integration

Metabolic Flux Inference in a Cheese Microbial Community via ComFI: A Biology-Informed Approach for Time-Resolved Multi-omics Integration

Sthyve Tatho[1,2](✉), Valentina Baldazzi[3,4], and Simon Labarthe[1,2]

[1] Univ. Bordeaux, INRAE, BIOGECO, 33610 Cestas, France
[2] Inria, University of Bordeaux, INRAE, Talence, France
sthyve.tatho@inria.fr, simon.labarthe@inrae.fr
[3] Université Côte d'Azur, INRAE, ISA, Sophia-Antipolis, France
valentina.baldazzi@inrae.fr
[4] Inria, Université Côte d'Azur, INRAE, CNRS, MACBES, Sophia-Antipolis, France

Abstract. Microbial communities play a central role in many bioprocesses with key applications in food fermentation, waste treatment, human and animal well-being, plant protection or metabolite transformation in industrial bioprocesses. However, the metabolic microbial interactions driving the community dynamics remain difficult to characterize because of their complexity and their temporal variability. Recent advances in sequencing and analytical technologies now provide time-resolved multi-omics data at the community scale providing key insights into the mechanisms shaping the community dynamics. However, integrating these heterogeneous data in an interpretable way to decipher species-specific metabolic activity and microbial interactions remains a major challenge in the study of microbial communities.

We introduce the *community metabolic flux inference* (comFI) method, a mathematical framework for inferring the metabolic fluxes of individual microorganisms from community-level longitudinal data. The method formulates flux estimation as a biology-informed constrained inference problem that combines observed microbial abundances and extracellular metabolite exchange data, with metabolic constraints encoded in a metabolic model and transcriptomic-based lasso regularization terms.

We evaluated comFI on synthetic datasets generated from dynamic models of microbial communities involving three *Escherichia coli* mutant strains. The comFI method showed a very good reconstruction accuracy for exchange fluxes, intracellular metabolic fluxes distribution, metabolic pathway activation patterns and strain contribution. We also applied the method to experimental cheese fermentation data involving three bacteria (*Lactococcus lactis*, *Lactobacillus plantarum*, and *Propionibacterium freudenreichii*), combining abundance measurements, targeted metabolomics and metatranscriptomics data. The comFI framework enabled to recover previously identified interaction patterns, and to reconstruct latent intracellular flux states for individual microorganisms alongside with their respective metabolic contributions within the community, consistently with the omics data and known physiology.

P. T. Monteiro (Ed.): CMSB 2026, LNBI 16678, pp. 265–287, 2027.
https://doi.org/10.1007/978-3-032-30870-2_13

All together, we demonstrate that comFI provides a practical framework for recovering the metabolic activity of individual microorganisms from community-scale multi-omics time-resolved data.

1 Introduction

Microbial communities, whether associated with animal or human hosts, food fermentation processes, soils, aquatic environments, or plants, play a central role in many biological, environmental, and industrial processes [19,25]. However, understanding their functioning remains challenging because community behaviour emerges from complex and dynamic interspecies interactions, metabolite exchanges, and environmental feedbacks. In particular, disentangling the specific contribution of each species within the community and characterizing its intracellular activity remain major open questions [14,19].

Recent advances in molecular biology and analytical technologies now make it possible to generate large amounts of time-resolved omics data, including genomics, transcriptomics, metabolomics, and microbial abundance measurements [2,8,15,18]. These data provide opportunities to study microbial ecosystems, but they also challenge the use of traditional microbial community modelling approaches. Ecological models, such as generalized Lotka–Volterra, consumer-resource, and Monod-type models [4,6], can integrate population abundance and, in some cases, metabolite data to describe microbial dynamics at a coarse-grained level. However, they generally regard microorganisms as black boxes, focusing on net effects on growth, substrate consumption, and product formation, without explicitly representing intracellular metabolism. As a consequence, they are not naturally suited for integrating functional omics data such as metatranscriptomics.

In contrast, constraint-based approaches, including flux balance analysis (FBA), flux variability analysis (FVA), parsimonious FBA (pFBA), and metabolic flux analysis (MFA), provide a mechanistic description of intracellular metabolic networks. However, standard FBA-derived methods often rely on strong optimality assumptions, such as biomass or energy maximization [4,15], and are not designed to directly infer community-scale metabolic activity from time-resolved experimental data. MFA is closer to data-driven inference but it typically relies on fluxomic data with labeled metabolites, which are costly and difficult to obtain, especially when fluxes vary dynamically over multiple time-scales [1,11].

These limitations become even more critical when considering microbial communities, where the number of interacting species, metabolic pathways, and exchange processes increase significantly. In such systems, the integration of metatranscriptomic data is particularly important, as it provides functional information on reaction activity that can help constrain otherwise underdetermined flux inference problems. However, incorporating metatranscriptomic profiles together with abundance and metabolomic data into a single mathematical framework remains both conceptually and computationally challenging.

In this context, we introduce **comFI**, for *community metabolic flux inference*, a biology-informed framework for metabolic flux inference in microbial communities that integrates time-resolved multi-omics data, including microbial abundances, extracellular metabolite measurements, and metatranscriptomic profiles. By combining community-level observations with intracellular stoichiometric constraints and transcriptomics informed regularization, comFI is designed to infer species-specific metabolic fluxes and metabolic exchanges within microbial communities.

We present the mathematical formulation of the method and evaluate its predictive ability through a systematic benchmark study, based on simulated datasets covering different ecological configurations. Importantly, we also apply comFI to a real cheese fermentation consortium composed of *Lactococcus lactis*, *Lactobacillus plantarum*, and *Propionibacterium freudenreichii*, using longitudinal measurements of microbial abundances, targeted extracellular metabolomics, and transcriptomic data. This application illustrates the practical relevance of the framework on experimental community data and shows its ability to recover previously identified interaction patterns, reconstruct latent intracellular flux states for each microorganism, quantify their respective metabolic contributions within the consortium, and identify the metabolic pathways involved during cheese fermentation.

2 Materials and Methods

2.1 Description of the ComFI Approach

The comFI approach aims to infer species-specific intracellular flux distributions from measurements collected at the community scale. These correspond to aggregated exchange rates summing up consumption (R_s) and production rates (R_p) of exometabolites resulting from the net metabolic activity of multiple microorganisms as well as species-specific growth rates (R_b). Together, these quantities constitute the observed inputs of the model , as illustrated in Fig. 1 **A**.

At each time point t, the model distinguishes between the observed community-level exchange rate of a metabolite m, denoted $R_{m,t}$, and the microorganism-specific *per-capita* exchange flux, denoted $\nu_{m,t}^{(b)}$, for microorganism b in $\mathcal{B}_m$ where $\mathcal{B}_m$ is a community of N_b microbial species. The objective of comFI is to reconstruct the full set of intracellular and exchange fluxes $\nu_t := (\nu_t^{(b)})_{b\in\mathcal{B}_m}$ for all microorganisms in the community consistently with both the observed data and the metabolic constraints of each organism. The inference problem is formulated as the following constrained optimization problem:

$$\hat{\nu}(t) := \arg\min_{\nu_t} \sum_{m\in\mathcal{M}} \left\| R_{m,t} - \sum_{b\in\mathcal{B}_m} \mathcal{X}_t^{(b)} \nu_{m,t}^{(b)} \right\|_2^2 + \lambda \mathcal{R}(\nu_t | w_t)$$
$$\text{subject to} \begin{cases} S^{(b)} \nu_t^{(b)} = 0, \\ C_{\min,t}^{(b)} \leq \nu_t^{(b)} \leq C_{\max,t}^{(b)}, \end{cases} \qquad b = 1, \ldots, N_b. \tag{1}$$

where the first term of the objective function measures the discrepancy between the observed growth and community-level exchange rates and the model prediction, defined as the sum of the predicted organism-specific contributions weighted by observed biomass $\mathcal{X}_t^{(b)}$. Overall, the above formulation defines a high-dimensional inference problem, since the number of unknown fluxes is typically much larger than the number of available measurements. Therefore, prior biological knowledge is required to obtain identifiable and biologically plausible solutions. In comFI, this information is introduced through constraints and regularization. First, structural constraints imposed by the stoichiometry of the metabolic network are expressed by the relation $S^{(b)}\nu_t^{(b)} = 0$, which enforces the steady-state assumption and ensures mass conservation at the intracellular level. Note that, like in classical dFBA, exchange reactions are not included in the mass-conservation constraints. Instead, community-scale net exchange reactions are fitted on the spline time derivatives, allowing overall flux dynamics for the whole network. Second, a transcriptomic-based regularization term $\mathcal{R}(\nu_t|w_t)$ is introduced to guide the solution toward biologically relevant states. Although both ridge ($\mathcal{R}(\nu_t) = \|\nu_t\|_2^2$) and lasso ($\mathcal{R}(\nu_t) = \|\nu_t\|_1$) penalties could be considered, we retained a weighted lasso-type regularization ($\mathcal{R}(\nu_t|w_t) = \|w_t\nu_t\|_1$) based on the principle of metabolic parsimony (see below the definition of the transcriptomic-derived weights w_t). The hyperparameter λ is chosen using a min-max criteria balancing the two terms of the loss function (see Appendix SI 2). This choice promotes transcriptomic-guided sparse flux distributions and favors biologically interpretable solutions. Lastly, the bounds $C_{\min,t}^{(b)}$ and $C_{\max,t}^{(b)}$ restrict fluxes to feasible ranges based on metabolic knowledge.

For shared substrate metabolites consumed by multiple organisms, the lower bound on each organism's import flux is dynamically adjusted to reflect competition for resources, with the following assumptions. When the substrate is in excess, the limiting parameter is physiological uptake parameter intrinsic to the consumer physiology. When the substrate is depleted and starts to be limiting, we compute the maximal amount of available metabolite per capita of consumer and per time unit. This hypothesis corresponds to a fair resource sharing assumption that allows unbiased constraint definition among community members. We note that once common constraints are defined, the solver may allocate different uptake flux to render contrasted physiology among micro-organisms. The constraints read:

$$C_{\min,t}^{(b,m)} = \max\left(\nu_{\text{intr}}^{(b,m)}, -\frac{\mathcal{X}_t^{(m)}}{\Delta_t \sum_{b' \in \mathcal{B}_m} \mathcal{X}_t^{(b')}}\right). \tag{2}$$

Here, $C_{\min,t}^{(b,m)}$ is the lower bound defining the feasible import flux range of metabolite m for microorganism b at time t, $\mathcal{X}_t^{(m)}$ is the observed concentration of metabolite m, $\mathcal{B}_m$ is the set of microorganisms able to consume m, and Δ_t is the characteristic uptake time scale. The second term in Eq. (2) represents the maximal per capita uptake rate that would deplete the available extracellular amount of m over the time interval Δ_t, assuming that this resource is shared among all competing biomass. The intrinsic bound $\nu_{\text{intr}}^{(b,m)}$ represents the maximal uptake capacity of microorganism b when metabolite m is not limiting. Since import fluxes are negative, the maximum operator selects the most restrictive lower bound between the intrinsic uptake capacity and the resource-limited uptake capacity. Numerical exploration showed that comFI outcome was weakly sensitive to this constraint. The main quantities involved in Eq. (1) and Eq. (2) are summarized in Table 1

2.2 Transcriptomic Data Integration

Metatranscriptomic data provide insightful information on intracellular activities and can help guide the inference of internal fluxes. To incorporate this additional layer of information, metatranscriptomic measurements obtained at the gene scale are projected onto each reaction through *gene–protein–reaction* (GPR) rules: for each reaction r, a GPR rule is defined with a logical formula linking the genes involved in the expression of the reaction. The logical AND operator links genes that are jointly required for a reaction to be activated, while the OR operator links alternative genes. The reaction-level transcript count is obtained with the GPR, by replacing the AND (resp. OR) operator by the min (resp. max) operator between gene transcript counts. This transformation yields a set of reaction-scale transcripts T_t that can be integrated into the inference problem through the weighted regularization function [13]:

$$\mathcal{R}(\nu_t \mid w_t) := \|w_t \nu_t\|_1 \quad \text{where} \quad w_t = \frac{k}{1 + \exp\left(r \cdot (|T_t| - s)\right)}. \tag{3}$$

Here, w_t is defined with a logistic function parametrized with s, the transcription threshold used to distinguish reactions that are likely to be active from those that are likely to be inactive, k the maximal value and r which tunes the slope of the function. This weighted formulation allows to penalize weakly expressed reactions, favoring null flux inference for these function. Since it is a penalty (and not a strong constraint), reactions without transcript that are needed for the overall outcome of the network can still be associated with non-zero flux. See Table 2 in appendix for logistic function parameter values.

2.3 Dimensionless Problem

To facilitate inference accuracy, we introduce a dimensionless version of problem (1). We set the scaling factors

$$\sigma_{1_t}^{-1} = \frac{1}{R_t}, \qquad \sigma_{2_t}^{(b)} = \frac{R_t^{(b)}}{\mathcal{X}_t^{(b)}}.$$

The scaling factor $\sigma_{1_t}^{-1}$ normalizes the rates of the state variables, bringing them to a common scale and improving numerical conditioning. The factor $\sigma_{2_t}^{b}$ correspondingly rescales the flux variables within the biomass equations, ensuring consistency between flux magnitudes and biomass-specific rates.

The renormalized optimization problem is

$$\begin{aligned} \hat{\nu}_t = \arg\min_{\tilde{\nu}_t} \; & \left\| \tilde{R}_t - \tilde{B}_t \tilde{\nu}_t \right\|_2^2 + \lambda \mathcal{R}(w_t \tilde{\nu}_t) \\ \text{subject to} & \begin{cases} \tilde{S}\tilde{\nu}_t = 0, \\ \tilde{\nu}_{\min,t} \le \tilde{\nu}_t \le \tilde{\nu}_{\max,t}, \end{cases} \end{aligned} \tag{4}$$

with

$$\tilde{R}_t = \sigma_{1_t}^{-1} R_t, \quad B_t \nu_t = \sum_{b \in \mathcal{B}_m} \mathcal{X}_t^{(b)} \nu_t^{(b)}, \quad \tilde{B}_t = \sigma_{1_t}^{-1} B_t \sigma_{2_t}, \quad \tilde{\nu}_t = (\sigma_{2_t})^{-1} \nu_t$$

and

$$\tilde{S} = S\sigma_{2_t}, \quad \tilde{\nu}_{\min,t} = (\sigma_{2_t})^{-1} C_{\min,t}, \quad \tilde{\nu}_{\max,t} = (\sigma_{2_t})^{-1} C_{\max,t}.$$

The resulting sparse quadratic program is solved with OSQP [23] (`v0.6.7`).

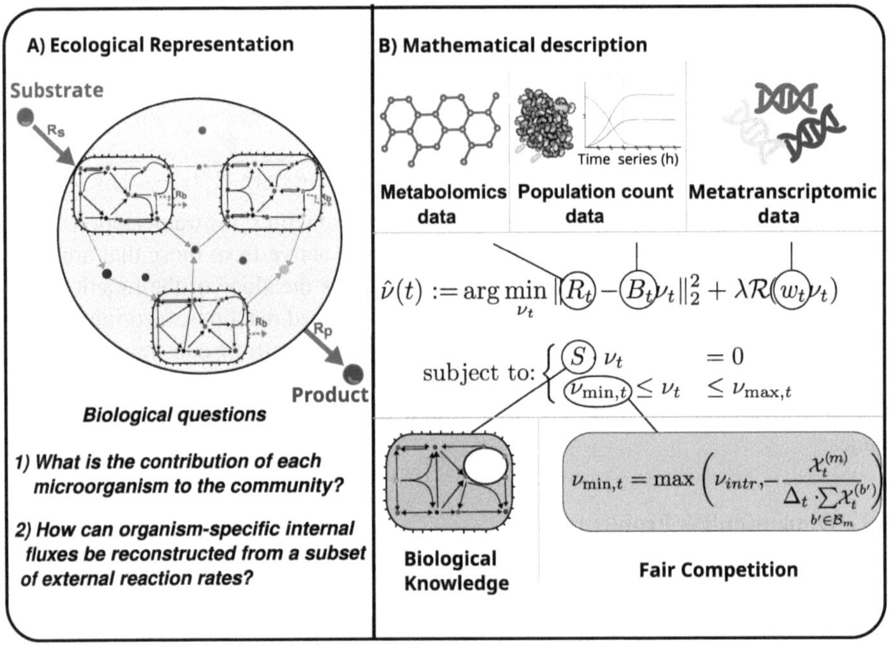

Fig. 1. comFI for the reconstruction of metabolic fluxes in microbial communities. comFI enables the inference of exchange fluxes and intracellular flux distributions from measured uptake and production rates. A) From community-scale consumption (R_s) and production (R_p) rates, together with individual growth rates, member-specific uptake and production rates are reconstructed, along with the associated intracellular metabolic fluxes. **B)** Mathematical formulation of the framework, including data integration into the optimization model, incorporation of biological knowledge through the stoichiometric matrix, and enforcement of a fair competition assumption via lower bounds on substrate uptake.

2.4 Data Preprocessing

Targeted quantitative exo-metabolomics and microbial counts respectively measure metabolite and biomass densities. However, problem (1) is formulated using observed rates. To recover smooth temporal derivative estimates, we perform spline smoothing

[21,24] using the spline $\mathbf{S_{p,m}}(t) = \sum_{i=0}^{n-1} B_{i,k,\tau}(t)\, c_{i,m}$, where $B_{i,k,\tau}$ denotes the B-spline basis functions of degree k, and c_i the associated coefficients, defined for metabolite m.

The coefficients are obtained by minimizing the weighted penalized least squares criterion

$$J(c) = \frac{1}{2}\sum_{j=1}^{N_t}\sum_{i=1}^{N_{r,j}} w_j(\varphi(t_j))\left(\mathbf{S_{p,m}}(\varphi(t_j)) - X^{obs}_{i,m,\varphi(t_j)}\right)^2 + \frac{\lambda_s}{2}\int_a^b \left(\frac{d^2\mathbf{S_{p,m}}(\varphi(t_j))}{dt^2}\right)^2 dt,$$

where N_t is the number of distinct time points, $N_{r,j}$ the number of replicates at time t_j, X^{obs}_{i,m,t_j} the i-th observed replicate of metabolite m concentration at time t_j, and w_j a weight assigned to time point t_j [12,16]. The parameter λ_s controls the smoothness trade-off. Spline smoothing was implemented using pyGAM package [22].

The default PyGAM method for smoothing parameter selection was used, except when a log transformation of time has been applied. In the latter case, spline smoothing parameter has been selected by PyGAM using a grid search in the interval $[0, 1]$, separately for each extracellular metabolite (see Fig. 11 for spline fitting results).

After spline computation, metabolite evolution rate are computed with time derivation of the splines

$$R_{m,t} = \varphi'(t)\partial_t \mathbf{S_{p,m}}(\varphi(t))$$

2.5 Benchmark Construction

Benchmarking Increasingly Complex Biological Interactions. We constructed a synthetic dataset representing microbial communities with three levels of ecological complexity (see Fig. 2 top). Each community comprises three microorganisms and illustrates a distinct interaction pattern: (1) **co-cons**: all microorganisms share a limiting resource but produce different metabolites; (2) **Co-pro**: microorganisms consume individual resources, and jointly produce the same metabolite; (3) **cross-feeding**: one organism benefits from the metabolic by-product of another.

Synthetic Bacterial and Metabolite Densities. To model bacterial metabolism, we used the iJO1366 genome-scale metabolic model of *Escherichia coli* str. K-12 substr. MG1655, available from the BiGG database (http://bigg.ucsd.edu/models/iJO1366). We manually modified this model by knocking out genes and reactions identified in [20] as enhancing the production of specific metabolites (valine, alanine, acetate) from glucose, malate and alanine. These modifications allowed us to generate the three ecological scenarios depicted in Fig. 2. Community dynamics were simulated using dynamic flux balance analysis (dFBA) [17], which predicts temporal variations in metabolic fluxes. Simulations were performed with the `dfba_sampling` package [10] version `0.2.1` (https://gitlab.inria.fr/slimmest/python-dfba-sampling), built on the COBRApy Python library [9] version `0.29.1`. Initial conditions were chosen to reflect biologically relevant metabolite concentrations (expressed in $mmol.L^{-1}$), and simulations were run from $t_{\text{initial}} = 0$ to $t_{\text{final}} = 9$ time units.

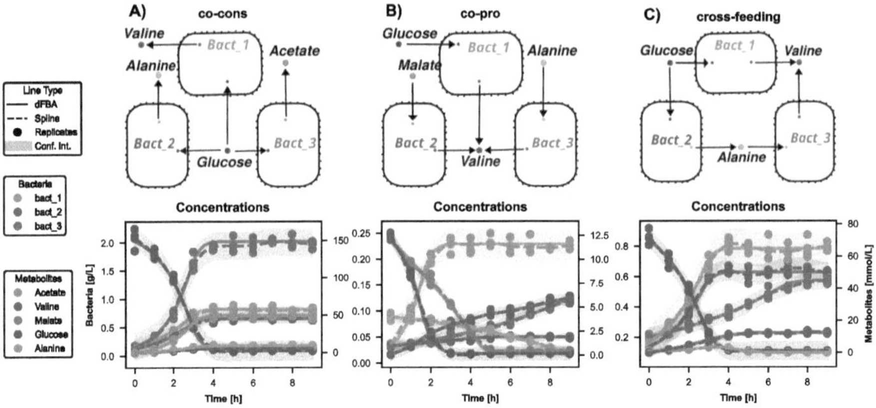

Fig. 2. Synthetic data for comFI benchmark. Schematic representation of increasingly complex ecological interactions from A) to C). For each scenario, we display: the schematic representation of the community **at the top** and the simulation **at the bottom**. The dFBA ground truth solution (solid lines), the noisy measurements used as comFI input (dots, 3 replicates at 10 evenly spaced time points), and the spline reconstruction (dotted lines) with its confidence cone (shaded area).

The resulting ground truth fluxes are shown in Fig. 2 (solid lines). From these, we generated noisy measurements by adding replicates: for each of the 10 evenly spaced time points, we created three noisy observations (dots) to serve as input to comFI. The spline reconstruction (dotted lines) and its confidence cone, obtained during the comFI preprocessing step, are also displayed.

Synthetic Metatranscriptomics Data. We derived synthetic metatranscriptomic data directly from the internal fluxes computed during the dFBA simulations. The absolute value of the flux is used as the reaction metatranscriptomic count in Eq. (3) to compute the comFI regularization using parameters value indicated in Table 2. This approach provides complete knowledge of reaction activity, as we have access to the exact flux values.

2.6 Application on a Fermentative Cheese Community

The second case study focuses on a controlled microbial consortium composed of *L. lactis* biovar *diacetylactis* CIRM-BIA1206, *L. plantarum* CIRM-BIA465, and *P. freudenreichii* CIRM-BIA122 [3]. These strains were selected for their metabolic complementarity and their contribution to flavor formation during cheese ripening.

Experimental monitoring covered the entire cheese-making and ripening process, taking approximately 1200 h (7 weeks). Population dynamics were quantified as colony-forming units per gram (CFU/g), and converted to gram of biomass per liter of milk (g/L) using the approximation that a bacteria is a μm^3 volume of water. Substrate consumption (lactose and citrate) and organic acid production (lactate, acetate, propionate, and succinate) were quantitatively measured by high-performance liquid chromatography (HPLC) using dedicated standards.

To penalize intracellular flux inference, we integrated metatranscriptomic (RNA-seq) data collected at five key time points: Cm, molding ($t = 19.5$ h); Cdm, demolding ($t = 40$ h); C0w, start of ripening ($t = 60$ h); C4w, fourth week of ripening ($t = 732$ h); and C7w, seventh week of ripening ($t = 1236$ h).

We note that bacterial inoculation during cheese processing was performed sequentially: lactic acid bacteria (i.e. starter) were introduced at $t = 0$, followed by *P. freudenreichii* (ripening bacteria) at $t = 18$ h. Bacterial population measurements were obtained from at least four biological replicates, whereas biochemical assays and transcriptomic profiling were performed on two biological replicates. Full data description is available here [3].

3 Results

We evaluated the performance of the comFI framework on both synthetic and experimental datasets. We first assessed its ability to reconstruct exchange and intracellular fluxes in controlled simulated communities, where reference flux distributions are available. We then examined its capacity to recover species-specific metabolic activity from experimental multi-omics data.

3.1 ComFI Accurately Predicts Flux Distribution from Synthetic Data

We analyzed the performance of comFI on simulated microbial communities under different ecological scenarios.

Reconstruction of Exchange Fluxes. We first evaluated the reconstruction of individual exchange fluxes i.e. consumption and production rates of extracellular metabolites on the co-cons scenario where microorganisms jointly consume glucose and produce distinct metabolites. In this scenario, the species-level consumption of glucose is poorly determined, since community-scale net consumption rates are observed, while individual consumption are unobserved latent states. Though, the reconstructed exchange fluxes closely matched the reference dFBA simulations as shown in Fig. 3 left upper panel, where the reconstruction achieved an R^2 score of 0.96. In the co-pro scenario, where microorganisms consume distinct substrates and jointly contribute to valine production, the reconstruction also showed strong agreement with the reference data, with an R^2 score of 0.92 (Fig. 3 left central panel). The cross-feeding scenario is more complex, since it involves a cross-feeding between two species mediated by alanine with additional co-consumption of glucose and co-production of valine (see Fig. 2). However, the reconstruction achieved a comparable R^2 score of 0.95 (Fig. 3 left lower panel). Taken together, these results show that comFI accurately reconstructs exchange fluxes across contrasted ecological configurations, including competition, co-production, and cross-feeding.

Reconstruction of Internal Fluxes. We next evaluated the reconstruction of intracellular fluxes. Figure 3 central panel compares simulated fluxes with inferred values across all reactions and time points, corresponding to more than 7,500 reactions in total. The reconstruction accuracy was high across all scenarios, with R^2 scores of 0.99, 0.96, and 0.95 for the three communities, respectively. To further assess whether reactions were correctly classified as active or inactive, we evaluated classification performance (Fig. 3 right panel) using a flux threshold of $s = 10^{-5}$. In the co-cons case, 23,792 inactive reactions were correctly classified (true negative rate: 99%), and 1,583 active reactions were correctly identified (true positive rate: 83%). In the co-pro case, 22,265 inactive reactions were correctly classified (true negative rate: 95%), and 2,461 active reactions were correctly identified (true positive rate: 97%). In the cross-feeding case, 23,921 inactive reactions were correctly classified (true negative rate: 99%), and 1,442 active reactions were correctly identified (true positive rate: 97%). These results indicate that comFI recovers not only exchange dynamics but also intracellular flux states with high accuracy in the simulated benchmark. Additionnaly, reaction activity patterns are accurately recovered, indicating that the transcriptomic-based regularization correctly pruned inactive reactions during inference, achieving remarkable true negative rates.

Contribution by Organism. The contribution of each microorganism was quantified by integrating inferred fluxes over time. In the co-cons scenario, Bact_1 accounts for 27.9% of total glucose consumption, Bact_2 for 22.1%, and Bact_3 for 50.0% with respectively 2.1%, 0.9%, 1.6% of relative error (see Fig. 8). In the co-pro scenario, the contributions are more evenly distributed: Bact_1 contributes 29.2%, Bact_2 contributes 33.4%, and Bact_3 contributes 37.4% with respectively 1.0%, 38.6%, 20.4% of relative error. In the cross-feeding scenario, alanine production is attributed to Bact_2 (48.6%), while alanine consumption is attributed to Bact_3 (51.4%) with respectively 1.4%, 1.3% of relative error. Valine production is shared between Bact_2 (44.6%) and Bact_1 (55.4%) with respective relative error of 25 and 20%. Glucose consumption is attributed to Bact_1 (61.0%) and Bact_2 (39.0%) with relative error of 11 and 13% (see Fig. 8). Alanine consumption exceeds alanine production over the course of the simulation, as shown in Fig. 4. Overall, the synthetic benchmark shows that comFI can recover both flux magnitudes and species-level contributions from aggregated community measurements, including in settings involving shared resources and complex metabolite exchanges.

3.2 ComFI Disentangles Microbial Activity During Cheese Production

We next applied comFI to the cheese fermentation community described in [15], composed of *Lactococcus lactis*, *Lactobacillus plantarum*, and *Propionibacterium freudenreichii*. This consortium was previously analyzed using a dFBA-based framework [15], and provides a relevant experimental case study to investigate how comFI attributes metabolic roles within a microbial community. The monitored extracellular metabolites included lactose, lactate, acetate, citrate, propionate, and succinate.

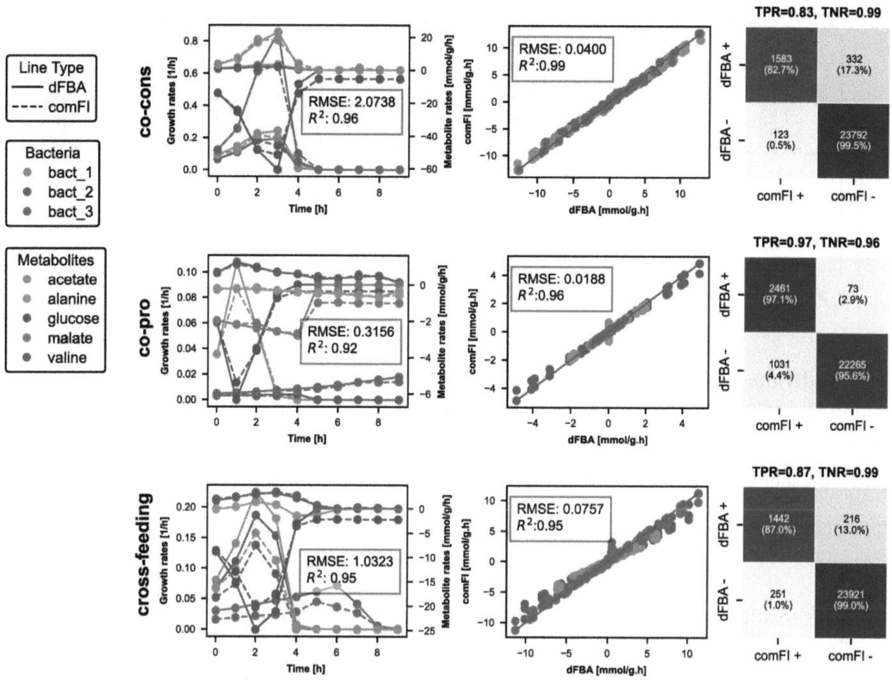

Fig. 3. Comparison between dFBA ground-truth fluxes and comFI estimates across the three ecological scenarios of the synthetic benchmark. The three rows correspond to the different benchmark scenarios. ***Left panel:*** *exchange flux reconstruction.* Exchange fluxes are shown at each time point for the different microorganisms, metabolites, and biomass variables. ***Central panel:*** *intracellular flux reconstruction.* Reference dFBA fluxes of all model reactions (x-axis) are plotted against the corresponding comFI estimates (y-axis). The bisector $y = x$ is shown in red, together with the corresponding R^2 and RMSE values. ***Right panel:*** *reaction activity classification.* Confusion matrices summarize the proportion of correctly and incorrectly predicted active and inactive reactions. Performance is reported using the true positive rate (TPR) and true negative rate (TNR), defined as $\mathrm{TPR} = \frac{\mathrm{TP}}{\mathrm{TP+FN}}, \quad \mathrm{TNR} = \frac{\mathrm{TN}}{\mathrm{TN+FP}}$.

ComFI Reconstructs Exchange Fluxes and Organism Contributions During Cheese Processing. Species-specific exchange reactions were reconstructed at each time step (Fig. 5 top), together with overall bacterial contribution to the fate of targeted metabolites (Fig. 5 bottom), achieving a coefficient of determination of $R^2 = 0.80$ for exchange-flux reconstruction between spline-smoothed rates and comFI estimates (Fig. 6, A). The inferred organism-level contributions indicate that lactose consumption is dominated by *L. lactis* (93.5%), with smaller contributions from *P. freudenreichii* (3.7%) and *L. plantarum* (2.8%) (Fig. 5 bottom). Citrate consumption is attributed to *L. lactis* (85.9%) and *P. freudenreichii* (14.1%). Lactate production is largely associated with *L. lactis* (92.6%), followed by *P. freudenreichii* (4.5%) and *L. plantarum* (2.9%). Acetate production is more evenly distributed across the community, with contributions of 44.2% for *L. lactis*, 19.2% for *P. freudenreichii*, and 35.5% for *L. plantarum*. Over-

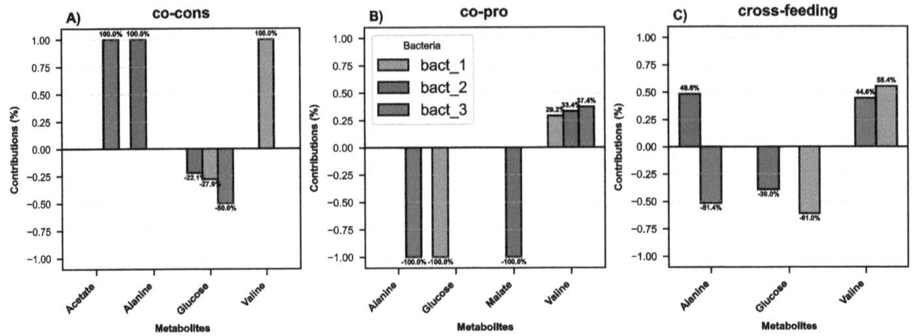

Fig. 4. Individual contributions to shared metabolite fluxes. The relative contribution of each microorganism to the consumption or production of a shared metabolite is computed by integrating biomass-weighted exchange fluxes over time. For a shared metabolite m and a microorganism b, we represent $\frac{\int_0^T \nu_{m,t}^{(b)} \mathcal{X}_t^{(b)}\, dt}{\sum_{b_i} \left| \int_0^T \nu_{m,t}^{(b_i)} \mathcal{X}_t^{(b_i)}\, dt \right|}$. Negative fluxes represent consumption, while positive ones represent production.

all, these results indicate that *L. lactis* is the main contributor to the dominant carbon transformations captured in this dataset, while acetate production appears to involve a broader participation of the three community members. These results are consistent with previous results obtained with dFBA [15].

ComFI Predicts Internal Flux Distribution, Consistently with Transcriptomic Data During High Microbial Activity. In the experimental setting, reference intracellular fluxes are not available. We therefore assessed the consistency between inferred reaction activity and transcriptomic measurements. A reaction was considered as a true positive when the corresponding transcript was expressed and comFI inferred the reaction to be active; false positives, true negatives, and false negatives were defined accordingly. To account for the temporal structure of the fermentation, we distinguished two phases: an early dynamic phase (`Cm`, `Cdm`, and `C0w`), corresponding to rapid lactose consumption, and a later stationary phase (`C4w` and `C7w`), corresponding to ripening. During the early phase, comFI achieved a true negative rate of 69.3% of reactions, indicating that comFI correctly carved the metabolic network according to the metatranscriptomic profiles. Meanwhile, 4,451 reactions were classified as both expressed and active, corresponding to a true positive rate of 59.1% (Fig. 6, B). During the stationary phase, the true positive rate was degraded (40.8%) but the true negative rate was maintained at a correct value of 60.7% (Fig. 6, C).

ComFI Recovers Known Microbial Physiology. Intracellular flux predictions allow to map predicted flux on metabolic pathways (Fig. 7). During early phase, *L.lactis*, the most active bacteria, mainly consumes lactose through tagatose pathway, rather than leloir pathway, hence producing high levels of lactate, and low levels of butanediol and diacetyl, responsible for a buttery flavour, as expected [15]. The other lactic acid bacteria, *L.plantarum* rather uses Leloir pathway for lactose degradation, branching to glycolysis and lactate production, correctly recovering expected physiology [15]. Finally, *P.freudenreichii* mainly uptakes lactate to produce propionate through the Wood-Werkman pathway, a characteristic of this species. Finally, good correspondances are observed when comparing comFI prediction to transcription profiles for key reactions related to lactose and lactate metabolism (see Fig. 9).

A notable result is that several reactions (`2131pyrpp` in *P. freudenreichii*, `ACLS` and `LACZ` in *L. lactis*, and `ACLS` in *L. plantarum*) that previously required manual flux-bound adjustments to achieve the expected growth and production behaviour [15] can now be automatically inferred by comFi without further adjustements. Taken together, these results suggest that comFI recovers intracellular activity patterns that remain coherent with transcriptomic information and known physiology, while reducing the need for manual adjustment of selected reaction bounds in classical dFBA approaches.

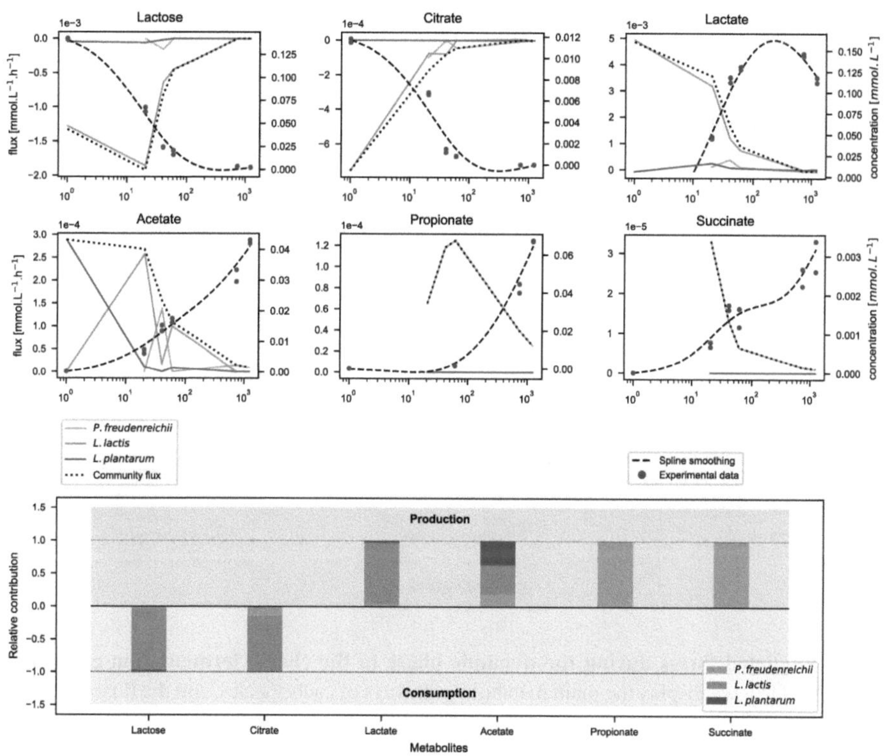

Fig. 5. Exchange-flux reconstruction and organism-level contributions in the cheese fermentation community. Top Comparison between spline-smoothed exchange rates and comFI estimates for the monitored extracellular metabolites. **Bottom** Relative contribution of each microorganism to substrate consumption and metabolite production, computed by time integration of the inferred biomass-weighted exchange fluxes.

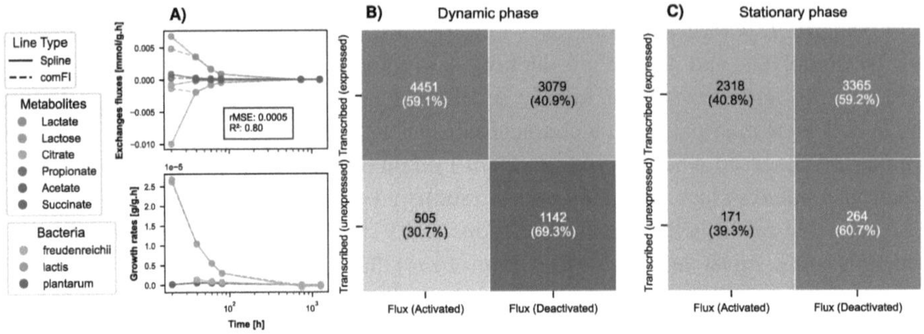

Fig. 6. Exchange rate reconstruction and consistency between inferred intracellular activity and transcriptomic data in the cheese fermentation community. A) Predicted (dotted lines) and observed (plain lines) growth (lower panel) and metabolic exchange rates (upper panel) are displayed, together with overall R^2. B) Confusion matrices summarize the agreement between transcript expression and predicted reaction activity during the early dynamic phase (`Cm`, `Cdm`, `C0w`). C) Confusion matrices showing the same agreement during the later stationary phase (`C4w`, `C7w`).

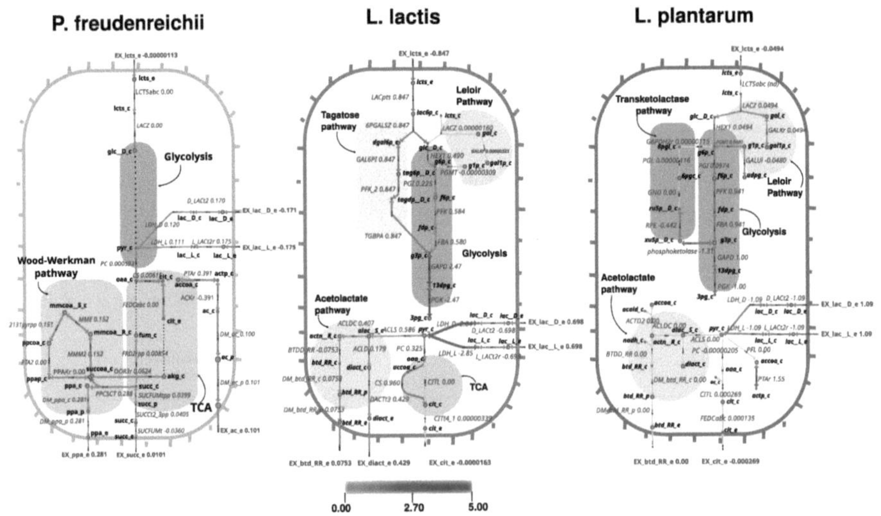

Fig. 7. Predicted fluxes during the dynamic phase in the cheese fermentation community Following [15], we display the main metabolic pathways of each species, and the fluxes predicted by comFI.

4 Discussion

Analysis of microbial communities is challenging due the high number of interacting species, metabolic exchanges and environmental feedbacks shaping the community behaviour. To address this challenge, we developed the community metabolic flux inference (comFI) method, a new mathematical framework for inferring the metabolic fluxes of individual microorganisms from community-level data. Application to synthetic data showed that comFI can accurately reconstruct exchange fluxes, intracellular fluxes, and species-level metabolic contributions across several ecological interaction regimes, including competition, co-production, and cross-feeding. We then applied comFI to a cheese fermentation consortium of three bacteria, to further illustrate the practical relevance of the approach in an experimental context. Although no ground-truth intracellular fluxes are available in this case, the inferred exchange patterns and the intracellular flux distributions fits known physiology. Furthermore, the consistency between transcriptomic signals and predicted reaction activity supports the biological plausibility of the reconstructed metabolic states. The recovery of flux through reactions that previously required manual tuning in classical dFBA [15] is particularly encouraging, as it suggests that comFI may reduce the need for ad hoc intervention when analyzing community metabolism.

In this context, the incorporation of metatranscriptomic information through regularization provides an additional layer of biological guidance, helping to select flux distributions that are consistent with observed gene expression patterns. More generally, this regularized formulation also gives comFI an implicit denoising effect. Experimental measurements of metabolite concentrations and derived exchange rates are typically affected by noise. Transcript abundance itself may be affected by limited sequencing depth, transcript instability, low read counts, incomplete annotation, or imperfect mapping between genes and reactions. By enforcing metabolic consistency through stoichiometric and bound constraints, comFI produces flux estimates that reconcile potentially conflicting measurements, leading to smoother and more coherent solutions. As a result, the optimization problem may identify a reaction flux even when the corresponding transcript is weakly expressed or not detected. In this sense, the method can be viewed not only as an inference framework but also as a biologically informed filtering approach.

Despite these promising results, several issues may affect the quality of comFI predictions. First, extracellular metabolite rates are not directly observed but rather estimated through the spline-based preprocessing step, hence inducing estimation uncertainties. In particular, the smoothing regularization parameter directly affects the inferred rates. A small value allows the spline to closely fit the measured concentrations, enhancing the risk of overfitiing, noisy oscillations and degraded derivative estimates. Conversely, a large value produces smoother derivatives but may attenuate short transient phases of consumption or production. This choice is important because errors introduced at this step propagate to the inferred net exchange rates.

Second, because the method is based on net exchange rates, its application may become difficult when the dynamics of extracellular metabolites is close to stationary. This is indeed what happens in the cheese fermentation data. During the early dynamic phase (`Cm`, `Cdm`, and `C0w`), when lactose is available and metabolic activity is high, the agreement between transcriptomic data and predicted reaction activity is satisfactory. In contrast, during the later stationary phase (`C4w` and `C7w`), the method fails to identify expressed reactions as active, while still capturing inactive reactions associated with weakly expressed transcripts. This behaviour could partially come from an incorrect choice for transcriptomic threshold separating activated and inactivated reactions, including uncertainties in the ground truth activation labeling. More probably, this behavior could be interpreted in light of the fact that comFI operates on exchange rates, that is, on temporal derivatives of measured concentrations. When extracellular concentration profiles reach a plateau, the inferred consumption or production rates become close to zero, and the optimization problem is driven by weak dynamic signals. Under these conditions, many reactions may remain transcriptionally expressed while carrying little or no flux in the inferred solution. Biologically, a near-constant concentration profile does not necessarily imply the absence of activity in the system; rather, it may reflect a balance between production and consumption, or other compensatory processes that are not directly visible from net rate measurements alone. We finally note that, while the transcriptomic-based regularization effectively prunes metabolic predictions for unexpressed reactions, it fails to favor non-zero flux for highly expressed reactions. This limitation arises because the lasso penalty is specifically designed to enforce sparsity, rather than to promote non-zero solutions.

Third, the choice of the regularization term and transcriptomic weighting functions can influence the inferred flux distributions and may require dataset-specific calibration. In this work, we selected the regularisation parameter using the min–max criterion, which identifies a compromise between fidelity to the data and regularization-induced sparsity. This choice provides a balanced solution, but the parameter could also be adjusted depending on the modeling objective. For instance, a smaller regularization parameter may be preferred when the priority is to remain as close as possible to the measured metabolomic data, whereas a larger value may be useful when the goal is to identify a reduced set of dominant reactions and emphasize sparse metabolic states. An illustrative example of this trade-off is provided by the experimental data set. If the min–max criterion selects a regularization parameter λ achieving a trade-off between metabolic exchange-rate reconstruction $R^2 = 0.80$ and transcriptomics, a vanishing λ induces better reconstruction with R^2 values up to 0.93. Conversely, increasing λ gave more influence to the transcriptomic penalty and improved the identification of reactions associated with weak transcriptomic support, with a true negative rate up to $TNR = 0.87$, at the cost of a strong degradation of metabolomic data reconstruction (R^2 down to -0.59, see Fig. 10 for parameter selection paths).

Another limitation of comFI concerns experimental validation and practical identifiability of the system. Community-level exchange rates provide aggregate constraints on the sum of species-level metabolic contributions, whereas the unknown fluxes are defined at the level of individual organisms and include both exchange and intracellular reactions. As a result, the inverse problem is intrinsically underdetermined when relying solely on metabolomic data. In comFI, this underdetermination is mitigated by integrating stoichiometric constraints, time-dependent flux bounds, and transcriptomics-informed regularization. These constraints transform the problem into a mathematically well-posed one: the non-degenerate weighted lasso regularization provides a theoretical guarantee of the identifiability of the quadratic program. However, due to low weight values for certain parameters, practical identifiability may not always be achieved. Validation should ideally be performed using ground-truth values of internal fluxes, typically obtained via fluxomics. Yet, acquiring fluxomics data for dynamic microbial communities remains a frontier in the field. Nevertheless, the comFI solution can be interpreted as a biologically plausible flux distribution, selected by the regularized optimization problem to reconcile metabolomic and transcriptomic data in a consensus framework, with metabolomic and transcriptomic data reconstruction as an indirect indicator of the validity of the consensus.

Finally, the method relies on the availability and quality of metabolic reconstructions for each microorganism, which may not always be accessible or accurate. Despite a continuous improvement of databases and network reconstruction methods, there is still issues for accurate reconstruction of metabolic models for rare bacteria or microorganisms of other kingdoms (like yeasts or fungi) [5].

5 Conclusion

We introduced comFI, a community metabolic flux inference framework designed to reconstruct species-specific metabolic activity from community-level longitudinal data. Across simulated communities, the method accurately recovered exchange fluxes, intracellular fluxes, reaction activity states, and organism-level contributions. In a real cheese fermentation consortium, comFI also yielded biologically coherent exchange patterns and recovered relevant intracellular activity signatures.

These results support the use of comFI as a practical tool for studying microbial community metabolism from multi-omics data. More generally, the framework opens perspectives for investigating microbial interactions and functions in complex microbial ecosystems where direct flux measurements remain inaccessible.

6 Code

The source code, configuration files, example workflows, and SBML models are available in the `comFI` repository: (https://gitlab.inria.fr/mistic/comfi/).

Acknowledgments. This study was funded by the French National Research Agency (ANR) under the project MISTIC (ANR-22-PEAE-0011), as part of the PEAE 2022 program.

Disclosure of Interests. The authors have no competing interests to declare that are relevant to the content of this article.

SI 1 Notations and Parameter Values

A table recapitulating the different notations used in this paper is presented in Table 1. Logistic function parameters (see Eq. (3)) for transcriptomics-based penalty are given in Table 2 for the synthetic and the cheese community data.

Table 1. Parameters used in the comFI formulation.

Symbol	Type	Meaning
$\mathcal{M}$	Set	Set of metabolites measured at the community level.
$R_{m,t}$	Data	Observed community-level exchange rate of metabolite m at time t.
$\mathcal{B}_m$	Set	Set of microorganisms that can exchange metabolite m.
$\mathcal{X}_t^{(b)}$	Data	Biomass density or abundance of microorganism b at time t.
$\nu_t^{(b)}$	Unknown	Flux vector of microorganism b at time t, including intracellular and exchange fluxes.
$\nu_{m,t}^{(b)}$	Unknown	Exchange flux of metabolite m for microorganism b at time t.
$S^{(b)}$	Model parameter	Stoichiometric matrix associated with microorganism b.
$C_{\min,t}^{(b)}, C_{\max,t}^{(b)}$	Constraints	Lower and upper bounds defining feasible flux ranges for microorganism b.
$\mathcal{R}(\nu_t)$	Regularization	Penalty term used to guide the solution toward biologically plausible flux states.
λ	Hyperparameter	Weight controlling the trade-off between data fitting and regularization.
$\mathbf{S_{p,m}}(t)$	Function	Spline-smoothed temporal profile used to estimate concentrations and derivatives of metabolite m.
N_b	Integer	Number of microorganisms in the community.
$\nu_{\text{intr}}^{(b,m)}$	Constraint	Intrinsic lower bound on the import flux of metabolite m by microorganism b when the metabolite is not limiting.
$\dfrac{\mathcal{X}_t^{(m)}}{\Delta_t \sum_{b' \in \mathcal{B}_m} \mathcal{X}_t^{(b')}}$	Constraint	Resource-limited biomass-specific uptake capacity for metabolite m at time t.
Δ_t	Parameter	Characteristic time scale over which extracellular uptake is evaluated.

SI 2 Hyperparameter Selection

The comFI problem involves a regularization parameter λ that controls the trade-off between reconstruction of the growth and metabolomic data (first term of the loss function in Eq. (1)) and the metatranscriptomic-based lasso term (second term of Eq. (1)). This hyperparameter thus tunes the consistency between targeted exo-metabolomics, growth and metatranscriptomics data. Its selection is made with an automatic procedure based on a unified min–max criterion [7].

Table 2. Parameters fixed a priori and hyperparameters selected for the simulated datasets and the cheese fermentation dataset.

	param.	Description	Simulated	Cheese community
spline smooth.	ω	time point weights	$\omega(t) = 1$	$\omega(t) = \begin{cases} 4 & \text{if } t = 0 \text{ or } t = T, \\ 1 & \text{elsewhere} \end{cases}$
	φ	time warping	$\varphi(t) = t$	$\varphi(t) = \log(t + \epsilon),\ \epsilon = 6$
	λ_s	smoothing hyperparameter	0.6	$\lambda_s \in [0.1, 1]$
	N_k	knot number	20	9
comFI	r	logistic function slope for lasso weight w_t	25	2
	s	logistic function threshold for lasso weight w_t	10^{-5}	8
	k	weight capacity w_t	2	1
	λ	hyperparameter balancing metabolomics, growth, and metatranscriptomics data	**co-cons**: 9.236 **co-pro**: 25.929 **cross-feeding**: 573.615	0.148

A discrete set of candidate parameter values $\Lambda = \{\lambda_1, \ldots, \lambda_n\}$ is defined, consisting of 30 logarithmically spaced values in the interval $[10^{-8}, 10^5]$. For each λ_i, we compute d_i:

$$d_i = \max\Big(\|\tilde{R} - \tilde{B}\tilde{\nu}\|_2^2,\ \|w\,\sigma_2\,\tilde{\nu}\|_1 \Big),$$

where the first term quantifies the deviation from the data, while the second term quantifies the transcriptomic-weighted sparsity of the intracellular metabolic flux distribution.

The selected regularization parameter is then defined as

$$\lambda^* = \arg\min_{\lambda_i \in \Lambda} d_i.$$

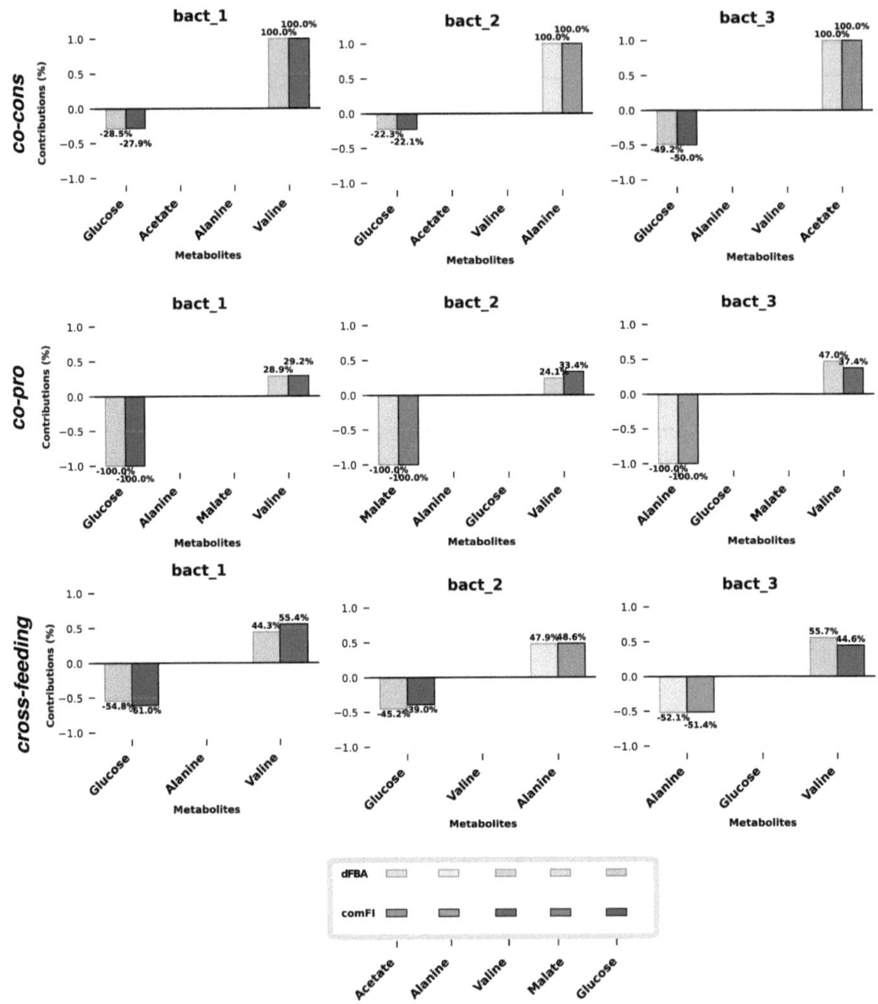

Fig. 8. Individual metabolite contributions for each organism. Each panel corresponds to one organism and compares the metabolite-specific contributions from ground-truth dFBA with the corresponding comFI predictions.

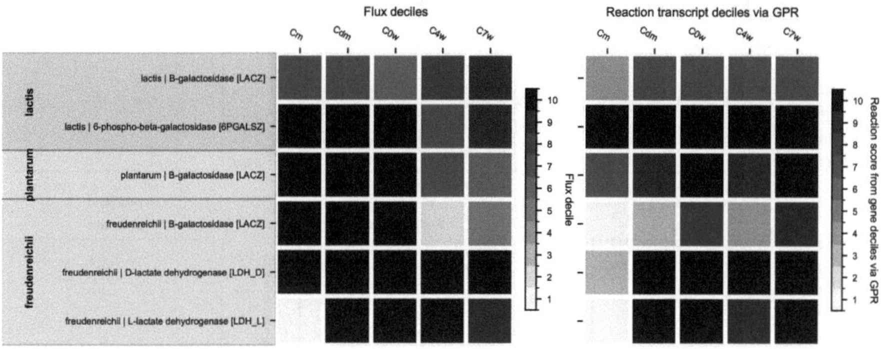

Fig. 9. Correspondance for comFI prediction and reaction expression for selected reactions. We present for selected reactions related to lactose and lactate metabolism the comFI-predicted fluxes (left) and the corresponding transcript levels (right). For each heatmap, the values are stratified (deciles) and colorcoded accordingly. The values are expressed at each time step (columns).

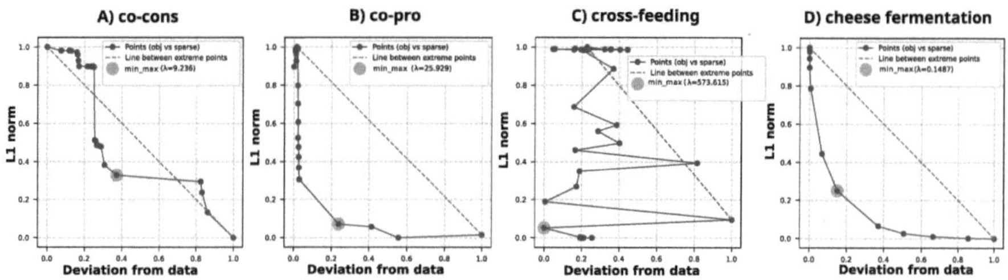

Fig. 10. Choice of the comFI regularization parameter λ in simulated and cheese fermentation data. Selection of the regularization parameter using the min–max criterion for the different datasets: **A)** co-cons, **B)** co-pro, **C)** cross-feeding, and **D)** cheese fermentation. The criterion was used to identify a compromise between the reconstruction of community-level exchange rates and the transcriptomic regularization term.

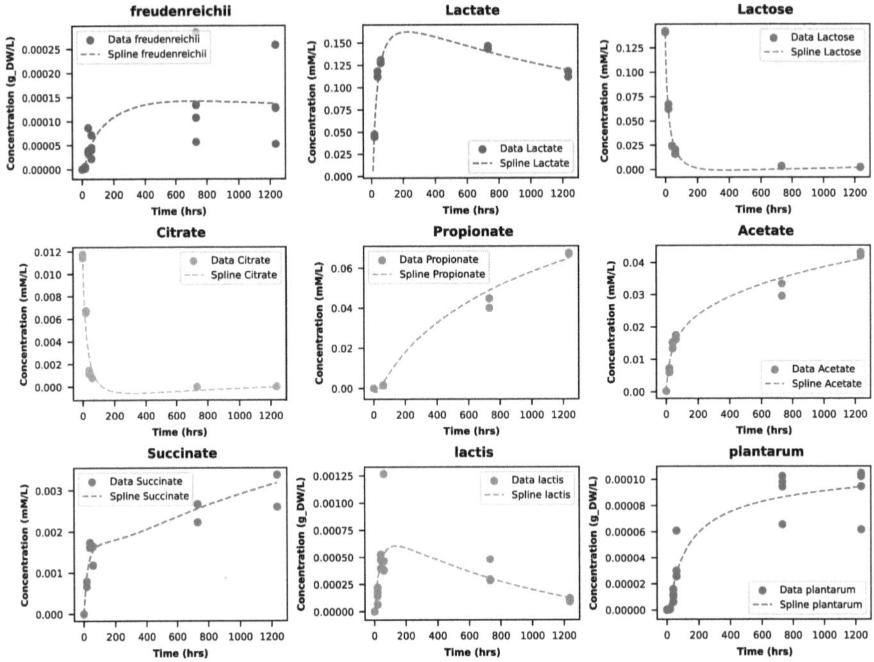

Fig. 11. Spline smoothing of metabolite concentrations and microbial growth trajectories in the cheese fermentation dataset. The figure illustrates the penalized spline fits used to preprocess the experimental time-series data prior to exchange-rate estimation. Fitted splines were used to compute extracellular exchange rates as temporal derivatives of the smoothed concentration profiles.

References

1. Antoniewicz, M.R.: A guide to metabolic flux analysis in metabolic engineering: methods, tools and applications. Metab. Eng. **63**, 2–12 (2021)
2. Brunner, J.D., Gallegos-Graves, L.A., Kroeger, M.E.: Inferring microbial interactions with their environment from genomic and metagenomic data. PLoS Comput. Biol. **19**(11), e1011661 (2023)
3. Cao, W., et al.: Fine-tuning of process parameters modulates specific metabolic bacterial activities and aroma compound production in semi-hard cheese. J. Agric. Food Chem. **69**(30), 8511–8529 (2021)
4. Carr, A.V., et al.: Emergence and disruption of cooperativity in a denitrifying microbial community. ISME J. **19**(1), wraf093 (2025)
5. Cerk, K., et al.: Community-scale models of microbiomes: articulating metabolic modelling and metagenome sequencing. Microbial Biotechnol. **17**(1), e14396 (2024). https://doi.org/10.1111/1751-7915.14396. https://sfamjournals.onlinelibrary.wiley.com/doi/10.1111/1751-7915.14396
6. Chesson, P.: Macarthur's consumer-resource model. Theor. Popul. Biol. **37**(1), 26–38 (1990)
7. Coello, C.A.C., Lamont, G.B., Veldhuizen, D.A.V.: Evolutionary Algorithms for Solving Multi-objective Problems. Springer (2007)

8. Ebrahim, A., et al.: Multi-omic data integration enables discovery of hidden biological regularities. Nat. Commun. **7**(1), 13091 (2016). https://doi.org/10.1038/ncomms13091
9. Ebrahim, A., Lerman, J.A., Palsson, B.O., Hyduke, D.R.: COBRApy: COnstraints-Based reconstruction and analysis for python. BMC Syst. Biol. **7**(1), 74 (2013). https://doi.org/10.1186/1752-0509-7-74
10. Frioux, C., et al.: Accelerating metabolic models evaluation with statistical metamodels: application to salmonella infection models. ESAIM Proc. Surv. **73**, 187–217 (2023). https://doi.org/10.1051/proc/202373187
11. Gerken-Starepravo, L., et al.: An MIQP framework for metabolic pathways optimisation and dynamic flux analysis. Digit. Chem. Eng. **2**, 100011 (2022). https://doi.org/10.1016/j.dche.2022.100011. https://www.sciencedirect.com/science/article/pii/S2772508122000023
12. Gu, C., Wahba, G.: Smoothing spline anova with component-wise Bayesian. J. Comput. Graph. Stat. **2**(1), 97–117 (1993). https://doi.org/10.1080/10618600.1993.10474601
13. Jenior, M.L., Moutinho, T.J., Jr., Dougherty, B.V., Papin, J.A.: Transcriptome-guided parsimonious flux analysis improves predictions with metabolic networks in complex environments. PLoS Comput. Biol. **16**(4), e1007099 (2020)
14. Kreimer, A., Doron-Faigenboim, A., Borenstein, E., Freilich, S.: Netcmpt: a network-based tool for calculating the metabolic competition between bacterial species. Bioinformatics **28**(16), 2195–2197 (2012). https://doi.org/10.1093/bioinformatics/bts323
15. Lecomte, M., et al.: Revealing the dynamics and mechanisms of bacterial interactions in cheese production with metabolic modelling. Metab. Eng. **83**, 24–38 (2024). https://doi.org/10.1016/j.ymben.2024.02.014. https://www.sciencedirect.com/science/article/pii/S1096717624000302
16. Lestari, B., Budiantara, I.N., Sunaryo, S., Mashuri, M.: Spline smoothing for multi-response nonparametric regression model in case of heteroscedasticity of variance. J. Math. Stat. **8**, 377–384 (2012). https://doi.org/10.3844/jmssp.2012.377.384. https://thescipub.com/abstract/jmssp.2012.377.384
17. Mahadevan, R., Edwards, J.S., Doyle, F.J.: Dynamic flux balance analysis of diauxic growth in escherichia coli. Biophys. J. **83**(3), 1331–1340 (2002)
18. Ofek-Lalzar, M., Sela, N., Goldman-Voronov, M., Green, S.J., Hadar, Y., Minz, D.: Niche and host-associated functional signatures of the root surface microbiome. Nat. Commun. **5**(1), 4950 (2014)
19. Pacheco, A.R., Vorholt, J.A.: Resolving metabolic interaction mechanisms in plant microbiomes. Curr. Opin. Microbiol. **74**, 102317 (2023). https://doi.org/10.1016/j.mib.2023.102317. https://www.sciencedirect.com/science/article/pii/S1369527423000541
20. Pande, S., et al.: Fitness and stability of obligate cross-feeding interactions that emerge upon gene loss in bacteria. ISME J. **8**(5), 953–962 (2013). https://doi.org/10.1038/ismej.2013.211
21. Pansu, P.: Courbes b-splines (2004). https://www.math.u-psud.fr/~pansu/web_maitrise/bsplines.pdf
22. Servén, D., Brummitt, C., Abedi, H.: hlink: dswah/pygam: v0.8.0 (2018). https://doi.org/10.5281/zenodo.1476122
23. Stellato, B., Banjac, G., Goulart, P., Bemporad, A., Boyd, S.: OSQP: an operator splitting solver for quadratic programs. Math. Program. Comput. **12**(4), 637–672 (2020). https://doi.org/10.1007/s12532-020-00179-2
24. Wang, Y.: Smoothing Splines: Methods and Applications. CRC Press (2011)
25. Widder, S., et al.: Challenges in microbial ecology: building predictive understanding of community function and dynamics. ISME J. **10**(11), 2557–2568 (2016)

GRNgen: A Generator of Gene Regulatory Networks Fitting Graph and Motif Properties

Alexandre Tan-Lhernould[1,2], Thierry Dorval[1], and François Fages[2](✉)

[1] Institut Servier d'Innovation Thérapeutique, Gif-sur-Yvette, France
tlalex@hotmail.fr
[2] Inria, EPI Lifeware, Palaiseau, France
francois.fages@inria.fr

Abstract. Gene Regulatory Networks (GRNs) constitute a useful abstraction of complex molecular mechanisms responsible for cell behaviors, cell differentiation, and various diseases. Advances in high-throughput transcriptomics, such as single cell RNA sequencing data, have enabled unprecedented access to large-scale gene expression data. However, the manual reconstruction of GRNs from such data and literature is a hard task, and the automatic reconstruction by GRN inference algorithms remains a major challenge to analyze and validate. Previous work revealed that the performances of GRN inference algorithms vary significantly according to network topology, degree distribution and motif preponderance. The analysis of sensitivity to those properties requires the generation of synthetic GRNs of various forms, and expression data obtained by simulation. Since the seminal works of Barabási and Albert on the scale-free power-law distribution of connectivity degrees in GRNs, and of Alon and Milo on the particular distributions and significance of small network motifs, various random graph models have been developed to try to capture those particular features. In this paper, we show that a relaxed version of the directed configuration model (RDCM) does allow us to generate random GRNs fitting the graph properties and motif distributions of several large GRNs of the literature: Human-TRRUST, h-ESC, m-ESC, m-DC, and to a lesser extent Yeast and *E. coli*, thanks to the variance of the results, and despite the discrepancies previously observed in terms of the mean in that random graph model. This is shown with GRNgen, a Python package which takes as input the number of nodes with for each node its in-degree and out-degree, the average path length, diameter, number of arcs and 7 important motif counts, and generates as output a set of random GRNs ranked by their fit to the input properties. We present our results for the generation of 1,000 samples for each of our reference GRNs, and provide elements of comparison with other generators.

Keywords: Gene regulatory networks · Random graphs · Network motifs · Directed configuration model

P. T. Monteiro (Ed.): CMSB 2026, LNBI 16678, pp. 288–307, 2027.
https://doi.org/10.1007/978-3-032-30870-2_14

1 Introduction

Gene Regulatory Networks (GRNs) have been introduced by Kaufmann [13] and Thomas [32,33] as a useful abstraction of complex gene activation and repression mechanisms to explain cell differentiation in terms of the multiple stable states that can exist in the Boolean dynamics of a gene network. Today GRNs and Chemical Reaction Networks (CRNs) [9] are the main formalisms used in computational systems biology to understand the biomolecular mechanisms behind cellular behavior, differentiation, and many diseases [28].

Rapid advances in high-throughput transcriptomics have granted unprecedented access to large-scale gene expression data, leading to a growing interest in gene regulatory network (GRN) inference methods to help or go beyond manual building. Several approaches have been developed [19] such as methods based on information theory (PIDC [7]), regression (GRNboost2 [24]), or dynamical models (SCODE [20]). However, the reconstruction of GRN models from such data is a hard task and the automatic reconstruction by GRN inference algorithms remains a major challenge to analyze and validate.

In many studies, evaluations rely on indirect comparisons to literature-derived networks, using enrichment in databases like RegulonDB [29] or KEGG [17]. But such datasets lack the status of true gold standards and often introduce uncertainty in performance interpretation.

One first difficulty in benchmarking and evaluating GRN inference algorithms is the scarcity of experimental datasets for which we know the ground truth network. While a few exceptions exist, such as the IRMA dataset [6] which captures both biological and technical noise from cells with engineered circuits, they are very limited in scale and not representative of more realistic, genome-wide conditions in human or other complex organisms. The DREAM5 challenge [31] provided a pivotal benchmarking effort, evaluating inference methods on large synthetic data under various experimental settings. However, the synthetic datasets used were derived from small organisms (e.g., *E. coli*, *S. cerevisiae*) using GeneNetWeaver [30], and do not scale to the complexity of mammalian transcriptomes (e.g. ~20,000 genes in humans). Interestingly, DREAM5 revealed that algorithm performance varies significantly depending on network topology [31].

In this context, the creation of synthetic datasets offers a unique opportunity to benchmark the performance of GRN inference algorithms and perform sensitivity analyses under controlled conditions. Since the seminal work of Barabási and Albert on the scale-free, power-law distribution of node degrees in biological networks [3,4], and the subsequent discovery by Milo and Alon regarding the functional significance of small network motifs [1,2,23], various random graph models have been developed to capture these structural features. General models, such as the Directed Configuration Model (DCM) [25], allow for the generation of graphs with a prescribed degree sequence, yet they are limited in certain cases for simple graphs (no self-loops nor multi-edges) without adaptation. Similarly, edge switching algorithms [18,22] offer a robust way to randomize networks while preserving degrees, but their efficiency depends heavily on the optimization of acceptance-rejection probabilities to maintain specific topological constraints.

Based on different random graph models, specialized GRN generators have been proposed. SysGenSim [27] focuses primarily on generating scale-free or Erdős-Rényi topologies, which may not account for real-world GRNs that deviate from strict power-law distributions. SynTReN [34] and GeneNetWeaver [30], rely on the extraction of sub-graphs from existing reference networks like *E. coli* or *S. cerevisiae*. While biologically grounded, those approaches limit the synthetic network to the size of the source organism which is different from mammalian architectures. FFLatt [36] was introduced to specifically address motif enrichment, notably the Feed-Forward Loop but focus primarly on this feature. More recently, GeneSpider2 [12] improves upon this by "stitching" together small Barabási-Albert networks to maintain sparsity and clustering. Although they all reproduce some important GRN properties, they remain limited to the choice of particular properties of specific interest.

To overcome this kind of difficulties, deep generative models such as Generative Adversarial Networks (GANs) have gained popularity as alternative machine learning approaches to network synthesis [11]. These frameworks are designed to learn latent structural patterns from a training set of existing graphs to generate new instances. However, their application to GRNs remains challenging, as deep generative models are heavily dependent on the availability of large-scale high-quality training datasets which remain relatively scarce in biology.

In this paper, we show that a relaxed version of the directed configuration models (RDCM) which allows us to deviate from the node degrees given as input, does allow us to generate random GRNs fitting the graph properties and motif distributions of several large GRNs of the literature: Human-TRRUST [14], h-ESC [21], m-ESC [21], m-DC [21], and to a lesser extent Yeast [21] and *E. coli* [30,35]. This is due to the sufficiently high variance that is obtained in the results, despite the important discrepancies observed on the average properties in the directed configuration model, especially for the motif count means [2,23].

In the next Section, we formally define a GRN as an unsigned directed simple graph, and we list the ten graph properties of interest that will be used to measure the similarity with a reference GRN in an optimization function. In Sect. 3, we present our Relaxed version of the Directed Configuration Model (RDCM) with the random GRN generation algorithm implemented in GRNgen, a Python package freely available at https://github.com/TLAlex/GRNgen, together with the examples presented in this paper. GRNgen takes as input the number of nodes and for each node its in-degree and out-degree, plus optionally 3 other graphical properties and 7 motif distribution criteria, and generates as output a given number of random GRNs ranked by their fit to the input properties. In Sect. 4, we present our results for the generation of 1,000 samples for each of our 7 reference GRNs, and discuss the performance of GRNgen when increasing the number of samples. Finally, we conclude on our results to generate random GRNs similar to human and mouse GRNs of the literature, the lesser performance obtained on Yeast and *E. coli* GRNs, and the potential use of GRNgen in generative AI and evaluation of GRN inference algorithms.

2 GRNs as Unsigned Directed Graphs and Properties of Interest

Since not all the GRNs of the literature distinguish between positive and negative influences between genes, and it is already interesting to consider the distribution of unsigned motifs, we shall restrict ourselves here to GRNs with unsigned directed arcs:

Definition 1. *A GRN is a directed graph $G = (V, A)$ where V is a set of (gene) vertices, $A \subseteq V \times V$ is a set of (influence) arcs with no self-loop (and no multi-arc, i.e. a simple graph) and such that there exists an undirected path between all pairs of vertices, i.e. G is weakly connected.*

In a digraph G, the distance $d(u, v)$ from vertex u to vertex v is the length of the shortest path from u to v, or $+\infty$ if there is no such directed path. Let us denote by $P(G) = \{(u, v) \in V \times V \mid 0 < d(u, v) < +\infty\}$ the set of pairs of distinct vertices that are connected.

In order to generate random GRNs similar to a reference GRN $G = (V, A)$ where $v = |V|$, we shall consider as input

- the sequences of in-degrees, $d^i : [1, v] \rightarrow [0, v-1]$, and out degrees, $d^o : [1, v] \rightarrow [0, v-1]$, given for each vertex,

plus a list of ten objective values, $P_1, \ldots, P_{10} \in \mathbb{R}^+$ representing the GRN properties of interest, first:

P_1 the *average path length* $\bar{l} = \frac{1}{|P(G)|} \cdot \sum_{(u,v) \in P(G)} d(u, v)$

P_2 the *diameter* $d = max_{(u,v) \in P(G)} d(u, v)$

Clearly, many other standard graph properties can be derived from the sequence of in-out degrees of each vertex:

- the *inward degree distribution* $[0, v-1] \rightarrow [0, v]$,
- the *outward degree distribution* $[0, v-1] \rightarrow [0, v]$,

P_3 the number of arcs $a = |A| = \sum_{v \in V} d^i(v) = \sum_{v \in V} d^o(v)$.

It is worth noting that the number of arcs P_3 will be considered as an objective value to fit, because our generation algorithm, described in the next section, may not exactly follow the sequence of in-out degrees given as input.

We also consider the numbers of the following 7 unsigned directed regulation motifs between 3 different vertices $A, B, C \in V$, first introduced in [23]:

P_4 the number of Cascades, of the form A → B → C;
P_5 Feed Forward Loops, A → B → C ← A;
P_6 Fan-Ins, A → B ← C;
P_7 Fan-Outs A ← B → C;
P_8 Mutual-Ins A ↔ B ← C;
P_9 Mutual-Outs A ↔ B → C;
P_{10} Regulating-Mutuals of the form A ↔ B → C ← A.

Of course, more motifs could be considered such as bi-fan motifs or 4-node feed-forward loops, as well as signed motifs distinguishing activation from repression links. Counting the number of motifs in a graph is however computationally intensive, with the complexity scaling with both the size of the graph and the motif size (see Proposition 1 and [26]). This is the reason why, in this paper, we restrict ourselves to the above list of 7 unsigned 3-node directed motifs.

The ten properties we consider are all positive numbers but have different scales. To measure the similarity between a random GRN and a reference GRN, we consider the *relative difference* of each property:

$$\delta_i = \frac{P_i - O_i}{P_i + O_i} \tag{1}$$

where P_i is the value of the ith property in the random GRN, and O_i is the objective value of the ith property in the reference GRN. We have $\Delta_i \in [-1, 1]$ with value 0 when $P_i = O_i$. A loss function can then be defined simply by the weighted sum of the relative differences of the different properties:

$$\Delta = \sum_{i=1}^{10} w_i.\delta_i \tag{2}$$

where w_i is the weight given to property P_i a higher value to make it more important, or 0 to ignore property P_i. For the sake of the evaluation of GRNgen reported in Sect. 4, all weights will be equal to 1, $w_i = 1$.

3 Relaxed Directed Configuration Model and GRNgen Generator Algorithm

To address the high failure rates commonly encountered when generating simple directed graphs with strict degree sequences [10], we propose a Relaxed Directed Configuration Model (RDCM) which prevents generation process failure by allowing a controlled deviation from the initial in-degree sequence given as input. The RDCM generation process described in Algorithm 1 follows two main steps:

1. **Stub Matching with Relaxation:** For each source vertex u, the algorithm attempts to satisfy its out-degree $d^o(u)$ by selecting vertices from a set of potential target vertices. A target is eligible if it does not create a self-loop

or a duplicate arc. If the number of eligible targets with available in-stubs is insufficient, the algorithm performs a **Relaxation Step**: it randomly selects a vertex and increments its in-stub count. This "relaxed" approach guarantees that the out-degree of every vertex is eventually satisfied, resulting in a valid simple graph.

2. **Weak Connectivity Enforcement:** Once all arcs are placed, any remaining isolated components are merged through random arc additions until the graph forms a single weakly connected component.

Algorithm 1. Core RDCM generator

Input: sequence of In and Out Degrees $d^i, d^o : V \to 0, \ldots, |V| - 1$

$A \leftarrow \emptyset$
for all vertex $u \in V$ **do**
    $k \leftarrow d^o(u)$
    $T \leftarrow \{v \in V \mid v \neq u, d^i(v) > 0 \text{ and } (u, v) \notin A\}$
    while $|\{v \in T\}| < k$ **do**
        $w \leftarrow \text{random\_element}(V \setminus \{u\})$
        $d^i(w) \leftarrow d^i(w) + 1$ ▷ Constraint relaxation
        $T \leftarrow T \cup w$
    end while
    $\{v_1, \ldots, v_k\} \leftarrow \text{random\_elements}(k, T)$
    $A \leftarrow A \cup \{(u, v_1), \ldots, (u, v_k)\}$
    for all $j \in \{1, \ldots, k\}$ **do**
        $d^i(v_j) \leftarrow d^i(v_j) - 1$
    end for
end for
while $\exists\ u, v \in V$ not weakly connected **do**
    $A \leftarrow A \cup \{(u, v)\}$ ▷ Constraint relaxation
end while
return $G = (V, A)$.

Algorithm 2. GRNgen

Input: sequence of In and Out Degrees $d^i, d^o : V \to 0, \ldots, |V| - 1$

i) the sequence of In-Out Degrees: $d^i, d^o : V \to 0, \ldots, |V| - 1$,
ii) the objectives for the 10 properties described in the previous section and their weight $(w_1, P_1, \ldots, w_{10}, P_{10})$,
iii) the number n of random graphs to generate;

call n times Algorithm 1 with the first input to generate n GRNs
return the list of n GRNs ranked by the error function Eq. 2.

Proposition 1. *GRNgen runs in time $O(n.v^3)$ where n is the number of samples and v the number of vertices considered as input.*

Proof. Clearly, GRNgen iterates n times the generation process of Algorithm 1 which builds a graph by iterating the connections of vertices in time $O(v^2)$. Then the ranking of the results involves the counting of the motifs over three vertices which is the most costly operation in time $O(v^3)$ n times.

4 Evaluation

4.1 Reference GRNs

To evaluate the capability of GRNgen to generate realistic GRNs, we consider seven GRNs of the literature: Human-TRRUST [14], h-ESC (human Embryonic Stem Cell) [21], m-ESC (mouse Embryonic Stem Cell) [21], m-DC (mouse Dendritic Cell) [21], Yeast [21], *E. coli* [30] and a second *E. coli* GRN from [35]. The selection of these reference GRNs reflects a variety of organisms, cell types and also construction methods by either text mining (Human-TRRUST) or CHIP-seq data (h-ESC, m-ESC, m-DC, Yeast) or mixture of data (*E. coli*) allowing us to evaluate the performance and limits of GRNgen in different contexts. Furthermore, the Human-TRRUST, Yeast, and *E. coli* GRNs are global in the sense that they aggregate networks representing the union of known interactions within the cells of one species. In contrast, the h-ESC, m-ESC, and m-DC GRNs are cell type specific in the sense that they capture the regulatory subnetworks involved in one specific cell type where not all genes are expressed. This selection thus provides a reasonable benchmark of diverse GRNs across a significant scale, ranging from 1,477 nodes and 3,578 edges (*E. coli* [30]) to 9,371 nodes and 76,929 edges (m-DC).

Furthermore, these GRNs exhibit a heterogeneous range of degree distributions which, except the cases of Human-TRRUST and Yeast, can significantly deviate from a power-law with heavy tail distribution, see Figs. 2, 3, 4, 6 and 7, where the power-law part is far from a straight line on a log-log scale. We also observe significant asymmetries between in-degree and out-degree distributions in most networks, with the notable exception of Human-TRRUST. Specifically in m-DC, the number of potential regulators is an order of magnitude smaller than the number of regulated targets resulting in flat out-degree distribution as shown in Fig. 4.

4.2 Comparison with GRNgen Random Networks

For each reference GRN, we generate 1,000 graphs using GRNgen with the in- and out-degrees for each vertex, d^i, d^o, and the 10 objective graph and motif counts to rank the results. Table 1 shows, for each reference GRN, the number of nodes, the ratio of GRNs presenting a loss below 1.0, and the mean computation times in seconds, given with standard deviation, on a virtual machine equipped with an Intel Cascade Lake processor (4 vCPUs) and 16 GB of RAM, for both

Table 1. For each reference GRN and 1000 GRNgen samples, number of nodes, ratio of GRNs with a loss below 1, and mean computation times in seconds with standard deviation for generating one graph and for computing the loss.

Dataset	Nodes	Ratio loss ≤ 1	Generation time	Loss function time
m-DC [21]	9371	0.70	20.25 (5.81)	1059.74 (19.73)
h-ESC [21]	6532	0.63	1.09 (0.37)	68.79 (1.42)
m-ESC [21]	6124	0.53	0.97 (0.32)	60.77 (0.89)
h-TRRUST [14]	2012	0.26	0.22 (0.02)	4.76 (0.06)
Yeast [21]	1703	0.02	0.04 (0.01)	2.90 (0.08)
E. coli [35]	1532	0.00	0.07 (0.02)	2.65 (0.03)
E. coli [30]	1477	0.00	0.06 (0.01)	2.52 (0.04)

generating one graph (Algorithm 1) and computing the loss value. This shows that GRNgen succeeds in reproducing with a low loss value the mammalian GRNs (Human-TRRUST, h-ESC, m-ESC, m-DC), moreover in large proportion ranging from 70% for mDC to 26% for Human-TRRUST, while 1000 samples are not enough to reproduce Yeast and *E. coli* GRNs.

Figure 1 shows the Human-TRRUST GRN of [14] and the best ranked GRN generated by GRNgen over the 1,000 samples. Both visualizations utilize the Yifan Hu force-directed layout [15], which spatializes nodes by equilibrating local attractive and global repulsive forces. The values of the properties are normalized using the relative difference which is bounded between $[-1, 1]$, where 0 corresponds to an exact fit with the reference. The straight dark lines indicate the mean value of each property. While the mean values may deviate significantly from the reference properties, especially for the Mutual-In and Mutual-Out motifs, the dispersion of the ensemble already shows a covering of the reference values with 1,000 samples only. Interestingly, the profiles of the relative difference for the top 5 ranked graphs, indicated by one line, are aligned near the zero-axis. This demonstrates that GRNgen is capable of generating specific networks that simultaneously satisfy the multiple criteria. The two last tables compare the in-degree and out-degree distributions on a double logarithmic scale. The colored dots represent the inward (left) and outward (right) degree distributions of the reference Human-TRRUST GRN. The grey dashed lines correspond to a random subset of 100 samples GRNgen networks from the 1,000 generated samples. The y-axis represents the distribution $P(d)$ of vertices with degree d (x-axis). Although GRNgen does not strictly enforce the input vertex degree sequence, the resulting ensemble consistently preserves the shape of the power-law with heavy-tail distribution of the reference network, with some more variations for the low numbers of the heavy tail.

The ensemble of synthetic graphs generated by GRNgen successfully reproduces the diverse range of global topologies observed across the reference datasets. Notably, several networks exhibit a highly ordered, concentric spatialization (Figs. 2, 3, and 4), where peripheral nodes arrange into distinct annular

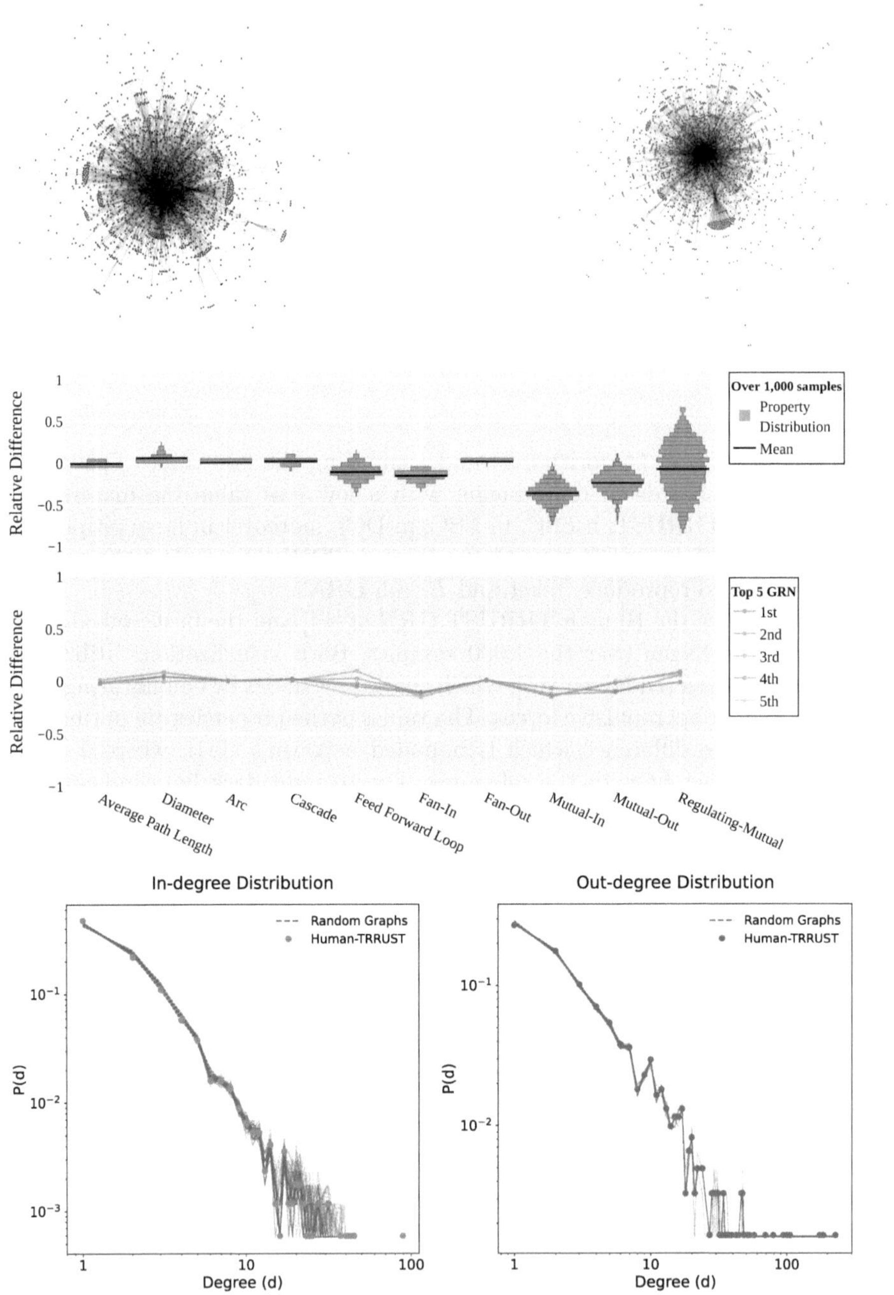

Fig. 1. Comparison of the Human-TRRUST GRN [14] (left) with the best GRN over 1,000 samples (right), the distribution of relative differences, the relative differences for the 5 best GRNs, and the degree distributions for 100 randomly selected samples.

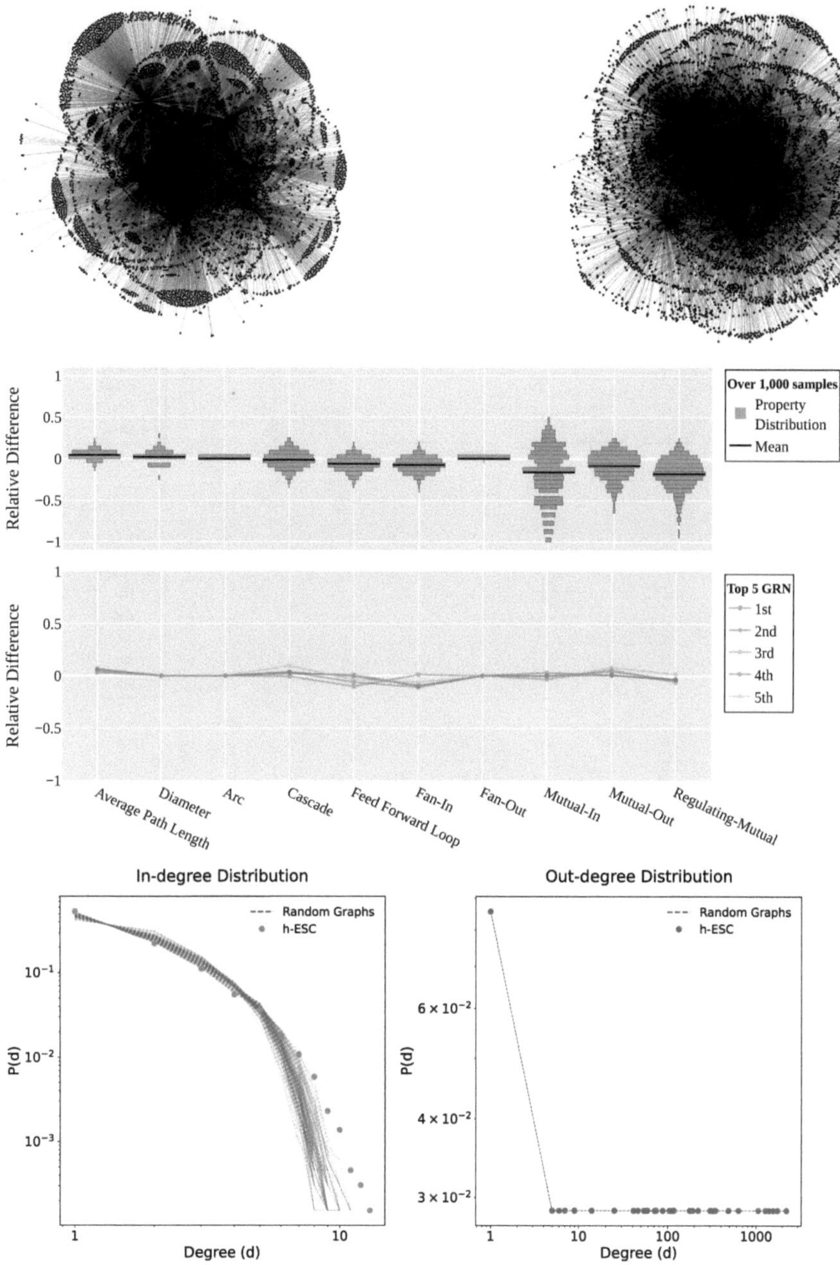

Fig. 2. Comparison of h-ESC [21] (left) with the best GRN over 1,000 samples (right), the distribution of relative differences, the relative differences for the 5 best GRNs, and the degree distributions for 100 randomly selected samples.

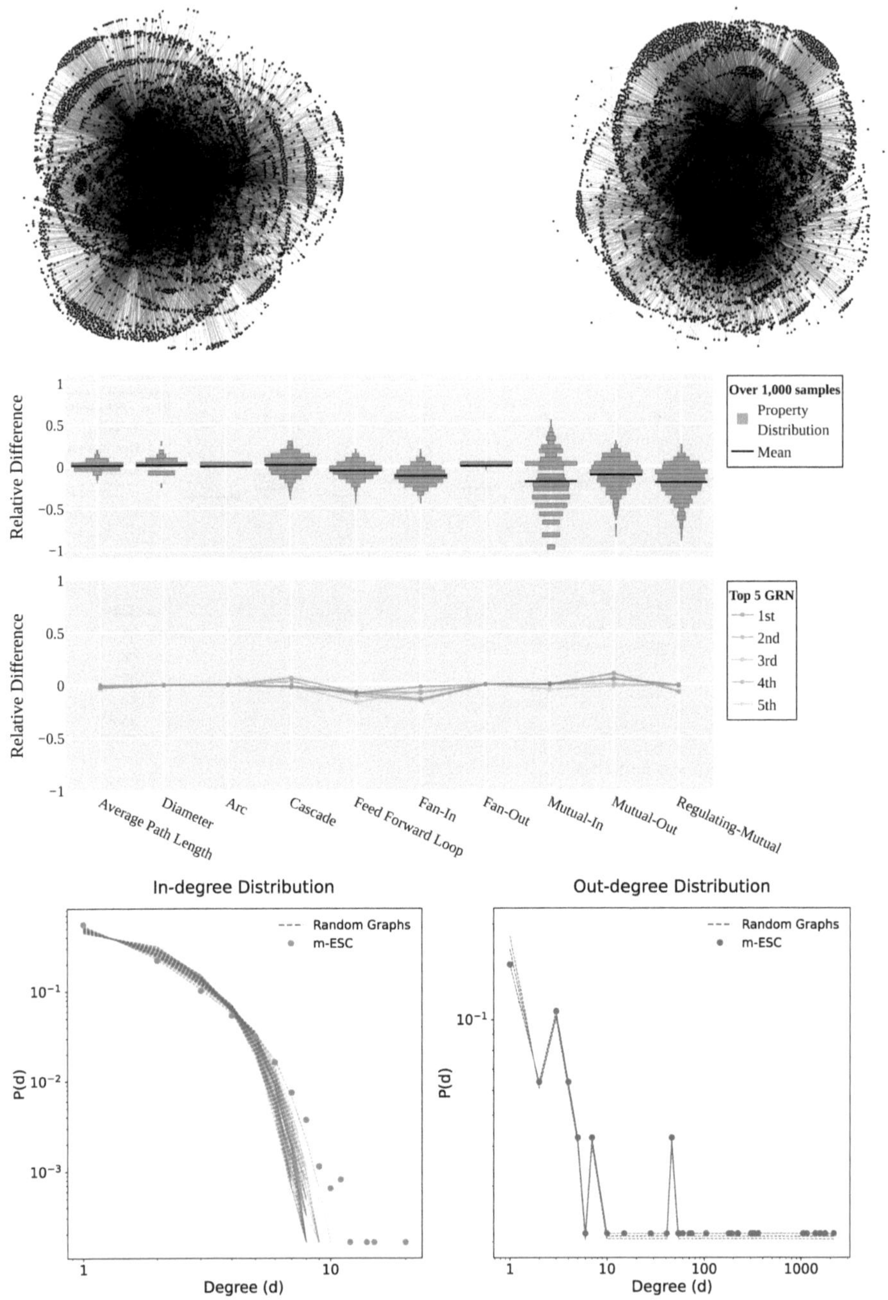

Fig. 3. Comparison of m-ESC [21] (left) with the best GRN over 1,000 samples (right), the distribution of relative differences, the relative differences for the 5 best GRNs, and the degree distributions for 100 randomly selected samples.

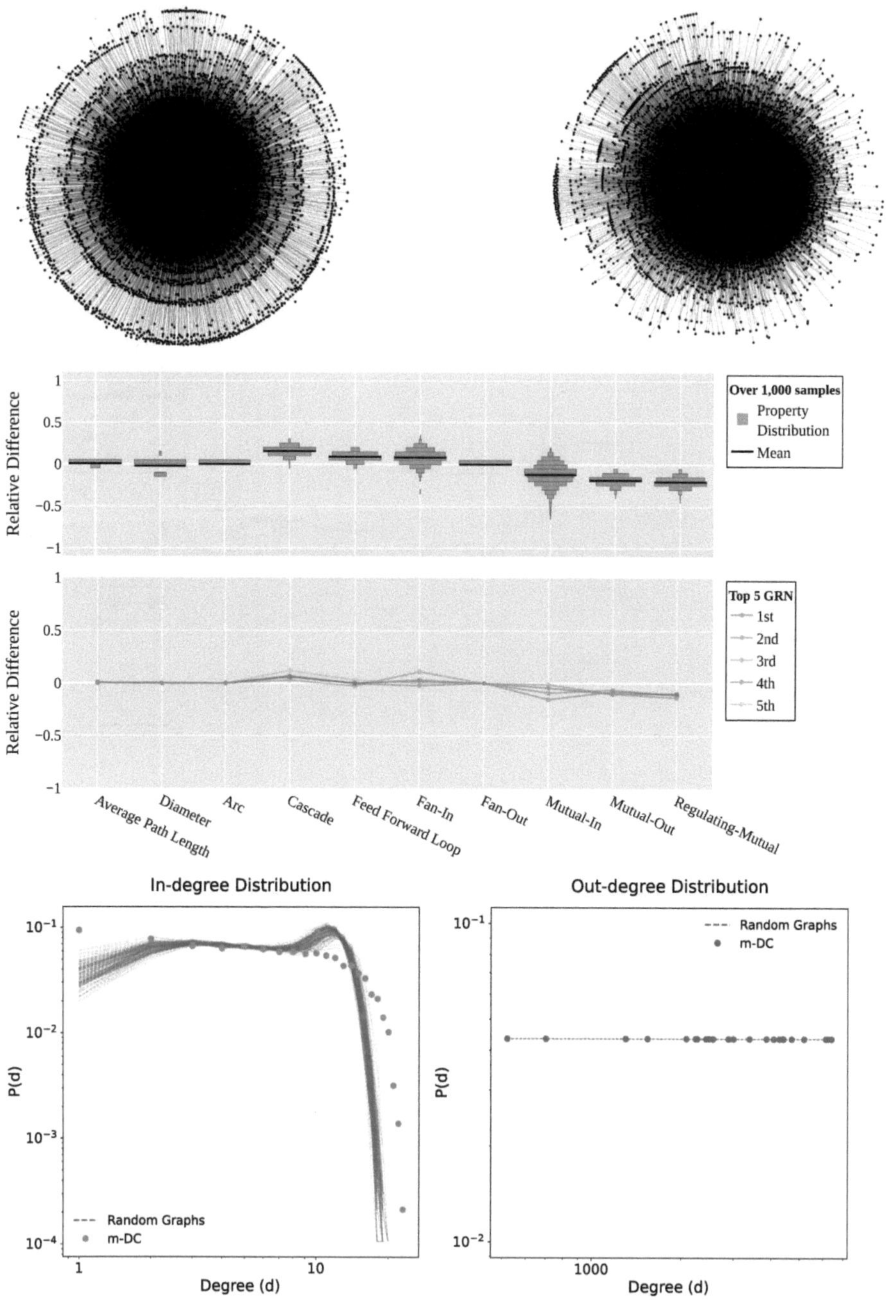

Fig. 4. Comparison of m-DC [21] (left) with the best GRN over 1,000 samples (right), the distribution of relative differences, the relative differences for the 5 best GRNs, and the degree distributions for 100 randomly selected samples.

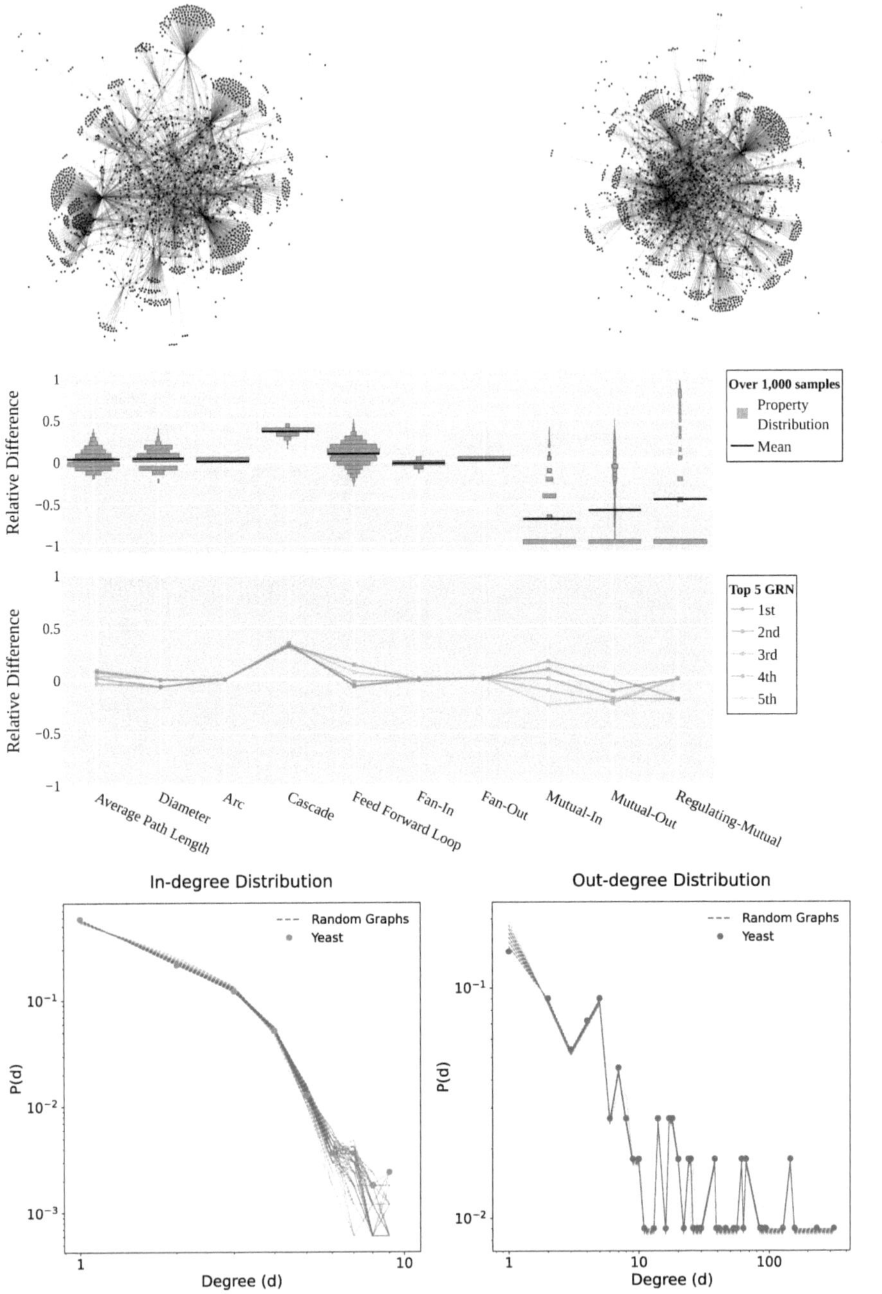

Fig. 5. Comparison of Yeast [21] (left) with the best GRN over 1,000 samples (right), the distribution of relative differences, the relative differences for the 5 best GRNs, and the degree distributions for 100 randomly selected samples.

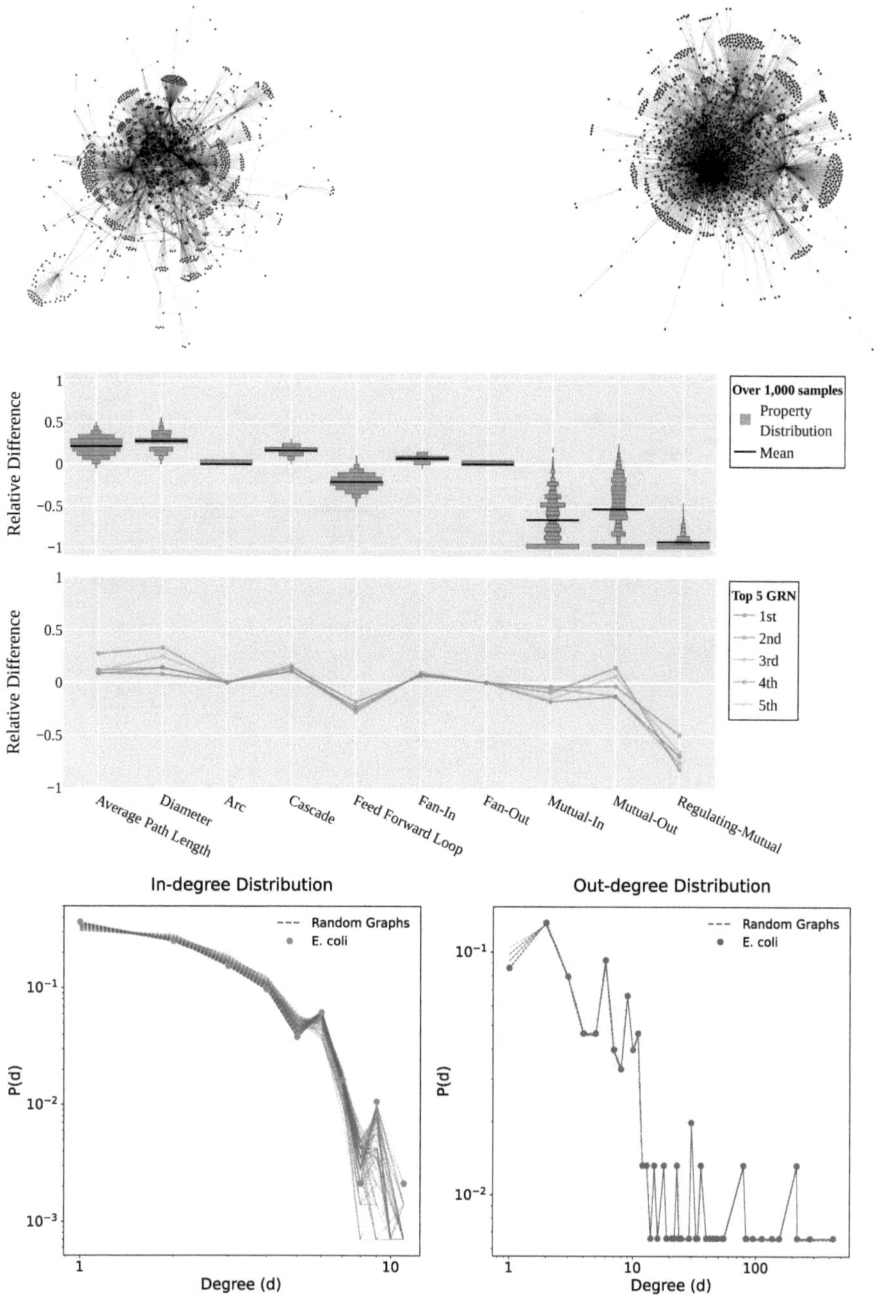

Fig. 6. Comparison of *E. coli* from [30] (left) with the best GRN over 1,000 samples (right), the distribution of relative differences, the relative differences for the 5 best GRNs, and the degree distributions for 100 randomly selected samples.

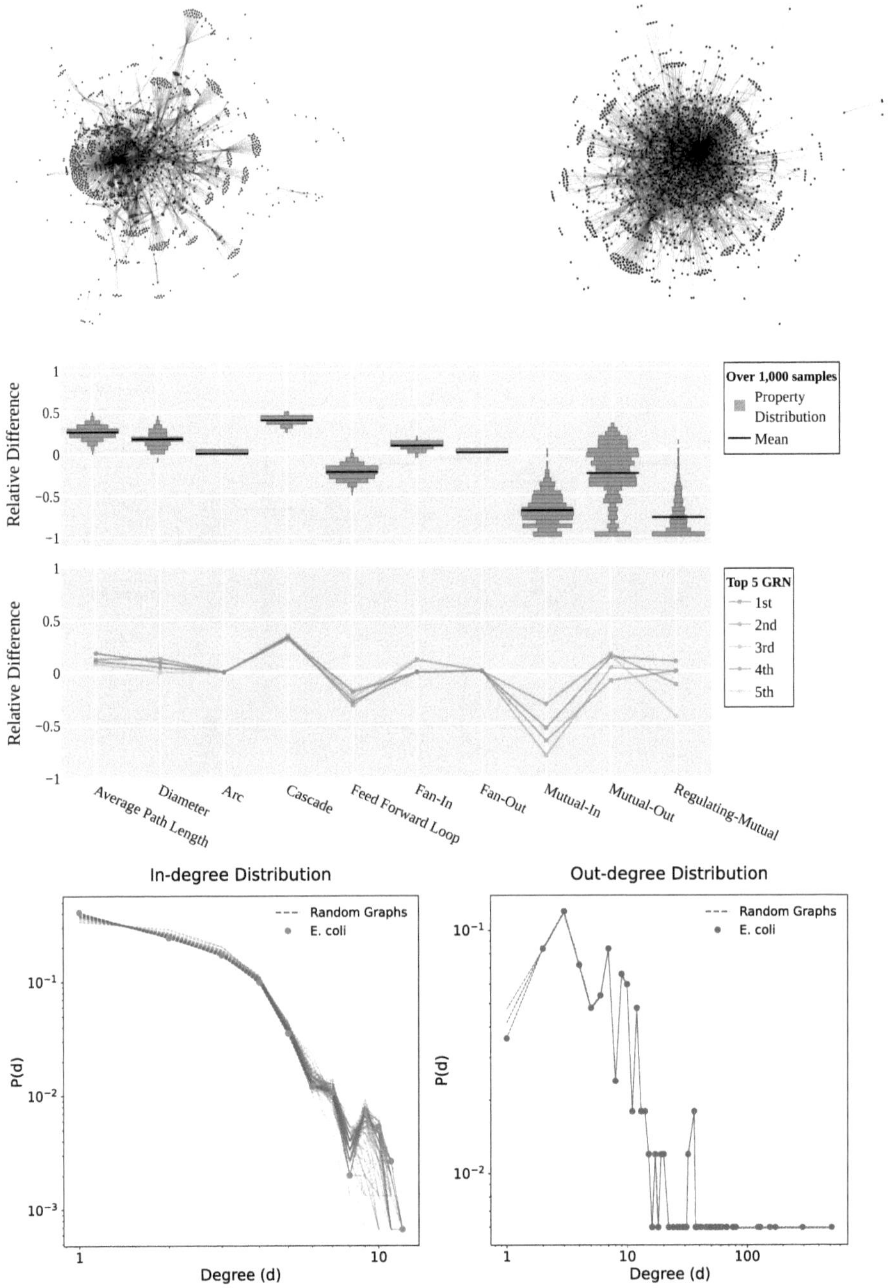

Fig. 7. Comparison of *E. coli* from [35] (left) with the best GRN over 1,000 samples (right), the distribution of relative differences, the relative differences for the 5 best GRNs, and the degree distributions for 100 randomly selected samples.

layers surrounding a high-density core. This pattern is characteristic of networks dominated by a few massive hubs that govern a large population of low-degree leaf nodes located at the periphery. In contrast, the networks in Fig. 1 appear more diffuse; while hubs remain visible, connectivity is more evenly distributed than in the aforementioned datasets. Finally, the spatialization of the reference datasets in Figs. 5, 6 and 7 reveals high network modularity. Rather than a singular core, these graphs present distinct topological clusters that branch outward, representing functional sub-networks within the global GRN architecture. This modularity is well-reproduced by GRNgen, with the exception of the *E. coli* dataset from [30], suggesting that the in-/out-degree distributions alone does not capture the specific local clustering and modular densities of this network.

Path-related properties, specifically average path length and diameter, are accurately maintained across the mammalian datasets. Furthermore, the stability of the arc count confirms that the necessary step of connecting isolated nodes does not significantly compromise the structural fidelity of GRNgen. Similarly, the in-degree relaxation process does not appear to distort the architecture, as evidenced by the consistent in-/out-degree distributions between the reference and generated ensembles. Conversely, motif distributions exhibit different behavior. While the ensemble mean does not always align systematically with the reference, the dispersion of the generated networks almost always encompasses the reference value.

On the other hand, the results given on Yeast and *E. coli* datasets in Figs. 5, 6 and 7), show difficulties with our approach to reproduce all properties with 1,000 samples only with only 2% of the graphs falling below the threshold of 1.00 total loss for the Yeast dataset and none for the *E. coli* datasets (Table 1). For Yeast, the distributions of the cascade, mutual-in, mutual-out and regulating mutual motifs significantly deviate from the reference value. However, the best random GRN does correctly reproduce the reference properties with the exception of the cascade motif which remains over-represented with 2681 instead of 1366 cascade motifs. By increasing the ensemble size to 10,000 graphs, the dispersion across all topological metrics increases, nevertheless the cascade motif distribution remains offset and still fails to overlap with the reference value. For the *E. coli* dataset from [30], the cascade count is quite well reproduced, but it is the regulating-mutual motif which is under-represented, with a value of 79 instead of 433. For the *E. coli* dataset from Fig. 6, it is the cascade and mutual-in motifs which are respectively over (5547 vs 2817) and under (16 vs 53) represented in the best generated GRN. It is hazardous to try to explain why our random graph model is better suited to reproduce mammalian GRNs than those GRNs from unicellular organisms, Yeast and *E. coli*. Nevertheless, one can hypothesize that this is a direct consequence of the fundamental difference that exist in the complexity of the underlying gene regulation mechanisms in those two different categories of cells, especially concerning the presence or not of intermediary layers, including mRNA alternative splicing, post-transcriptional maturation, and nuclear-cytoplasmic transport. For instance, it is shown in [8] that while unicellular eukaryotes and prokaryotes display minimal RNA splicing, mammals and birds exhibit the highest levels of alternative splicing. This provides a possible explanation for the difference of performance of RDCM for reproducing those two categories of GRNs.

4.3 Comparison with Other GRN Generators

In network science, preferential attachment models, such as the Barabási-Albert model [3], are effective for generating scale-free topologies. They are however limited to power-law degree distributions with heavy tails which is not really the case of our reference GRNs apart from Human-TRRUST and Yeast. On Human-TRRUST, the adaptation of Barabási-Albert growth model for directed graphs, using Bollobás algorithm [5], on 10 samples shows a mean loss of 4.83 in the range [4.22, 5.30] against a mean loss of 1.17 in the range [0.89, 1.40] for GRNgen on also 10 random samples (the mean loss is 0.54 in the range [0.46, 0.59] for the best 10 samples over 1000 samples). This difference in performance illustrates the benefit of using the sequence of in- and out-degrees given per node in GRNgen input, whereas Bollobás algorithm generates directed scale-free properties using specific, yet less informative, growth parameters for in- and out-degrees.

We also compared the performance of GRNgen and FFLatt [36] on the Human-TRRUST dataset. GRNgen significantly outperforms FFLatt which exhibits a mean loss of 4.17 in the range [3.98, 4.39], still far higher than the range of [0.89, 1.40] for the 10 samples of GRNgen. It is worth noting, however, that the design obective of FFLatt is to generate networks specifically enriched in vertices participating in feed forward loop, and not to fit a particular number of properties as with GRNgen.

Another popular approach is the edge-rewiring (or switching) method [22]. This method can take as input any degree distribution, but the fitting of motif distributions requires careful calibration of several hyperparameters, in particular the burn-in period which depends on the mixing time that is not well defined, and the acceptance-rejection ratios for swaps. Our experiments with rewiring strategies did not yield superior structural fidelity, despite higher computational complexity.

Finally, as mentioned in the introduction, deep generative models like GANs are fundamentally constrained by the requirement for extensive training datasets which are not available today for GRNs. There exist promising methods in that field to circumvent the training dataset limitation by learning graph properties from only one graph [11]. Such approach would however be limited when willing to capture properties concerning rare local structures.

5 Conclusion and Perspectives

In this study, we demonstrated that the Relaxed Directed Configuration Model (RDCM) implemented in GRNgen provides a quite general framework for generating synthetic GRNs, especially in the context of mammalian cells. By permitting controlled deviations from the node degrees given as input, our approach is able to generate random GRN reproducing important topological features of GRNs of the literature created by different methods, such as Human-TRRUST, h-ESC, m-ESC, and m-DC.

Our results show that, while the ensemble mean for certain properties, in particular motif distributions as previously observed, may significantly deviate from the GRN reference, the variance in the GRNs generated by GRNgen with the RDCM model ensures that the reference properties of mammalian GRNs are almost always contained within the ensemble's dispersion. This finding validates our initial hypothesis: the flexibility of the relaxation process allows GRNgen to explore a sufficiently broad topological space to encompass the specific local architectures of realistic GRNs.

These good results are more difficult to achieve with our approach for the *E. coli* and Yeast GRNs, where the generation of 1,000 samples is not sufficient to fully cover the properties of those networks. Better results can be obtained by increasing the number of samples, but the lack of constraints to better guide the generation of similar networks makes RDCM not very efficient in those cases of unicellular organisms which may justify the use of other algorithms based on specific motif enrichment.

The ability to select individual networks from the GRNgen ensemble that exhibit near-zero relative differences across multiple topological metrics, but also a variety of networks with properties around the reference, makes GRNgen ensemble networks great candidate networks for topological sensitivity analysis of GRN inference algorithms, in order to better understand the hard instances and provide insights for their improvement. For instance, our on-going work focusses on the GRN inference algorithm GENIE3 [16], using asynchronous Boolean state transition traces obtained by simulation of synthetic GRNs generated by GRNgen, to explore the sensitivity of the accuracy of the inference to the presence of particular graph and motif properties. Furthermore, the ability of GRNgen to generate artificial GRNs limited to realistic structures, paves the way to the creation of GRN inference models based on generative AI methods using a very large variety of training simulation data.

Acknowledgements. We are grateful to the ANRT CIFRE for partly funding the PhD thesis of the first author, to Hervé Isambert and Simon de Givry for their comments in the Thesis Committee, to Mathieu Hemery, Sylvain Soliman and Benjamin Zoller for insightful discussions, and to the anonymous reviewers of CMSB for their useful feedback.

References

1. Alon, U.: Network motifs: theory and experimental approaches. Nat. Rev. Genet. **8**(6), 450–461 (2007)
2. Alon, U.: An Introduction to Systems Biology: Design Principles of Biological Circuits. Chapman and Hall/CRC (2019)
3. Barabási, A.-L.: Network Science. Cambridge University Press (2016)

4. Barabási, A.-L., Albert, R.: Emergence of scaling in random networks. Science **286**(5439), 509–512 (1999)
5. Bollobás, B., Borgs, C., Chayes, J.T., Riordan, O.: Directed scale-free graphs. In: SODA, vol. 3, Baltimore, MD, United States, pp. 132–139 (2003)
6. Cantone, I., et al.: A yeast synthetic network for in vivo assessment of reverse-engineering and modeling approaches. Cell **137**(1), 172–181 (2009)
7. Chan, T.E., Stumpf, M.P.H., Babtie, A.C.: Gene regulatory network inference from single-cell data using multivariate information measures. Cell Syst. **5**(3), 251–267 (2017)
8. De la Fuente, R., DıÌĄaz-Villanueva, W., Arnau, V., Moya, A.: Alternative splicing across the tree of life. Elife **13**, RP94802 (2025)
9. Fages, F., Martinez, T., Rosenblueth, D., Soliman, S.: Influence networks compared with reaction networks: semantics, expressivity and attractors. IEEE/ACM Trans. Comput. Biol. Bioinform. (2018)
10. Fosdick, B.K., Larremore, D.B., Nishimura, J., Ugander, J.: Configuring random graph models with fixed degree sequences. SIAM Rev. **60**(2), 315–355 (2018)
11. Gamage, A., Chien, E., Peng, J., Milenkovic, O.: Multi-motifgan (mmgan): motif-targeted graph generation and prediction. In: ICASSP 2020-2020 IEEE International Conference on Acoustics, Speech and Signal Processing (ICASSP), pp. 4182–4186. IEEE (2020)
12. M Garbulowski, et al. Genespider2: large scale GRN simulation and benchmarking with perturbed single-cell data. NAR Genomics Bioinform. **6**(3), lqae121 (2024)
13. Glass, L., Kauffman, S.A.: The logical analysis of continuous, non-linear biochemical control networks. J. Theor. Biol. **39**(1), 103–129 (1973)
14. Han, H., et al.: Trrust v2: an expanded reference database of human and mouse transcriptional regulatory interactions. Nucleic Acids Res. **46**(D1), D380–D386 (2018)
15. Yifan, H.: Efficient, high-quality force-directed graph drawing. Math. J. **10**, 37 (2005)
16. Huynh-Thu, V.A., Irrthum, A., Wehenkel, L., Geurts, P.: Inferring regulatory networks from expression data using tree-based methods. PLoS ONE **5**(9), e12776 (2010)
17. Kanehisa, M., Furumichi, M., Sato, Y., Matsuura, Y., Ishiguro-Watanabe, M.: KEGG: biological systems database as a model of the real world. Nucleic Acids Res. **53**(D1), D672–D677 (2025)
18. Kannan, R., Tetali, P., Vempala, S.: Simple Markov-chain algorithms for generating bipartite graphs and tournaments. Random Struct. Algorithms **14**(4), 293–308 (1999)
19. Marku, M., Pancaldi, V.: From time-series transcriptomics to gene regulatory networks: a review on inference methods. PLoS Comput. Biol. **19**(8), e1011254 (2023)
20. Matsumoto, H., et al.: SCODE: an efficient regulatory network inference algorithm from single-cell RNA-seq during differentiation. Bioinformatics **33**(15), 2314–2321 (2017)
21. McCalla, S.G., et al.: Identifying strengths and weaknesses of methods for computational network inference from single-cell RNA-seq data. G3 Genes Genomes Genet. **13**(3), jkad004 (2023)
22. Milo, R., Kashtan, N., Itzkovitz, S., Newman, M.E., Alon, U.: On the uniform generation of random graphs with prescribed degree sequences. arXiv preprint cond-mat/0312028 (2003)

23. Milo, R., Shen-Orr, S., Itzkovitz, S., Kashtan, N., Chklovskii, D., Alon, U.: Network motifs: simple building blocks of complex networks. Science **298**(5594), 824–827 (2002)
24. Moerman, T., et al.: Grnboost2 and arboreto: efficient and scalable inference of gene regulatory networks. Bioinformatics **35**(12), 2159–2161 (2019)
25. Molloy, M., Reed, B.: A critical point for random graphs with a given degree sequence. Random Struct. Algorithms **6**(2–3), 161–180 (1995)
26. Patra, S., Mohapatra, A.: Review of tools and algorithms for network motif discovery in biological networks. IET Syst. Biol. **14**(4), 171–189 (2020)
27. Pinna, A., Soranzo, N., Hoeschele, I., de la Fuente, A.: Simulating systems genetics data with SysGenSIM. Bioinformatics **27**(17), 2459–2462 (2011)
28. Saint-Antoine, M.M., Singh, A.: Network inference in systems biology: recent developments, challenges, and applications. Curr. Opin. Biotechnol. **63**, 89–98 (2020)
29. Salgado, H., et al.: Regulondb v12. 0: a comprehensive resource of transcriptional regulation in *E. coli* k-12. Nucleic Acids Res. **52**(D1), D255–D264 (2024)
30. Schaffter, T., Marbach, D., Floreano, D.: GeneNetWeaver: in silico benchmark generation and performance profiling of network inference methods. Bioinformatics **27**(16), 2263–2270 (2011)
31. Marbach, D., et al.: Wisdom of crowds for robust gene network inference. Nat. Methods **9**(8), 796–804 (2012)
32. Thomas, R.: Boolean formalisation of genetic control circuits. J. Theor. Biol. **42**, 565–583 (1973)
33. Thomas, R., Kaufman, M.: Multistationarity, the basis of cell differentiation and memory. Chaos **11**(1), 170–195 (2001)
34. Van den Bulcke, T., et al.: Syntren: a generator of synthetic gene expression data for design and analysis of structure learning algorithms. BMC Bioinform. **7**(1), 43 (2006)
35. Wolf, I.R., Simões, R.P.,, Valente, G.T.: Three topological features of regulatory networks control life-essential and specialized subsystems. Sci. Rep. **11**(1), 24209 (2021)
36. Zhivkoplias, E.K., Vavulov, O., Hillerton, T., Sonnhammer, E.L.L.: Generation of realistic gene regulatory networks by enriching for feed-forward loops. Front. Genet. **13**, 815692 (2022)

Consensus Enhances Individual Causal Models: A Use Case on Lung Cancer Driven by Cellular Pathways

Arnaud Lang[1(✉)], Rodrigo Henrique Ramos[2], Safaa Al-Ali[3], Mohammad Reza Mousavi[4], Anna Calissano[5], and Irene Balelli[1]

[1] Inria Center at Université Côte d'Azur, Epione Team, Sophia Antipolis, France
{arnaud.lang,irene.balelli}@inria.fr

[2] Federal Institute of São Paulo, São Carlos, São Paulo, Brazil
ramos@ifsp.edu.br

[3] Univ. Bordeaux, CNRS, Inria (Carmen Team), Bordeaux INP, IMB, UMR 5251, IHU Liryc, 33400 Talence, France
safaa.al-ali@inria.fr

[4] King's College London, Strand, London WC2R 2LS, UK
mohammad.mousavi@kcl.ac.uk

[5] University College London, London, UK
a.calissano@ucl.ac.uk

Abstract. Discovering reliable cause-and-effect relationships in real-world medical data is an open challenge. Classical Causal Discovery (CD) algorithms used to solve this task rely on strict assumptions that are rarely met in complex real-world scenarios with limited expert knowledge - the functional form of the causal relationships, the data distribution, the causal sufficiency. Thus, the reliability of CD algorithms can significantly drop, compromising the interpretability of the results and the trustworthiness of downstream decision-making. To overcome these limitations, we introduce the concept of *consensus causal model* to combine various CD algorithms and enhance their accuracy. Our consensus model can be efficiently constructed from a set of heterogeneous causal graph objects through a homogenisation step, ensuring semantic compatibility with the original edge definitions and enabling meaningful information exchange. To showcase the proposed method, we analyze a lung cancer dataset combining patient-level information such as smoking habits and age, and we study their effect on the onset and development of the disease, the tumor stage, and cellular pathway mutations. By applying multiple classical CD algorithms, we observe significant structural inconsistencies and heterogeneity across individual graphs. We demonstrate that the consensus causal model, unlike the individual models, effectively aggregates the strengths of each algorithm while mitigating their uncertainties. The resulting model reveals biologically validated causal relationships between risk factors, mutations, and pathways that isolated algorithms fail to capture, thereby underscoring the value of consensus causal modelling as a robust alternative to single-model selection for causal discovery.

P. T. Monteiro (Ed.): CMSB 2026, LNBI 16678, pp. 308–333, 2027.
https://doi.org/10.1007/978-3-032-30870-2_15

Keywords: Causal Discovery · Consensus Causal Models · Benchmark · Knowledge-based systems · Cancer Genomics · Cancer Patient Data · Cellular Pathways

1 Introduction

The growing complexity and the mostly opaque nature of artificial intelligence models have been raising concerns about their interpretability, explainability, and trustworthiness. Consequently, there is increasing interest in causality, a field that aims to move beyond correlations and uncover the mechanisms underlying data generation, thus providing enhanced predictive power and enabling reasoning about interventions and counterfactuals. This makes causality particularly relevant in critical domains such as e-healthcare [20,33], where potentially high-risk questions should be reliably answered, while caring for trust-building between the system (computational models for clinical decision-making support) and multiple users (clinicians, nurses, physicians, and importantly, patients). While controlled experiments such as randomized clinical trials remain the gold standard for establishing causality, they are often costly, time-consuming, or even infeasible due to ethical issues. This has motivated the development of computational approaches to infer causal relationships across the retained features of interest directly from observational data, by combining domain knowledge and data-extracted insights: *Causal Discovery* (CD) [17].

Reliably performing CD in real-world settings turns out to be an extremely challenging task [10]. Indeed, the theoretical identifiability of CD algorithms (*i.e.*, the guarantee of recovering the *true* underlying causal graph given sizeable, good-quality data) is tightly related to a strict compliance of the data with some difficult-to-achieve assumptions. Those assumptions can span the type and shape of the causal relationships between variables, the nature and additivity of the independent variable-specific error term, or the observation of an exhaustive set of causal variables (*cf.* causal sufficiency, see Sect. 2.1). Moreover, real-world (e.g., healthcare) datasets are often incomplete, noisy, or biased, further affecting practical identifiability.

In the absence of a robust strategy for assessing whether a dataset satisfies the specific assumptions required as a minimum to guarantee the theoretical identifiability of a given CD algorithm, it can be dangerous to rely on its results to draw conclusions, particularly in critical areas such as health. The simultaneous application of multiple CD strategies could reveal more consistent patterns and help researchers formulate more informed and cautious interpretations. In this work, we propose to move from an individual to a multiple models approach by aggregating the causal information yielded from several CD algorithms, rather than arbitrarily selecting a single model as the best representative one. The driving motivation is that we do not dispose of enough expert knowledge to decide on one unique model. Therefore, we introduce the concept of a *consensus causal model*, which will be obtained by first mapping CD outputs to a universal causal graph representation, facilitating the sharing of information, and then merging these homogenized causal graphs, each of them providing its partial yet valuable view of the same reality. The consensus causal model is expected to convey a richer and more informative structure, while naturally enabling a heuristic measure of the associated confidence, and overall improving trustworthiness.

We evaluate our approach on a high-impact use case: lung cancer. Cancer is a complex disease that emerges from the intricate interplay of mutations accumulated over time that corrupt cell pathways. Factors such as smoking and age can influence the emergence of the disease and contribute to its heterogeneous progression. The increasing availability of (public) cancer data enables the development of many statistical studies exploring, for instance, the relationships between mutations, cellular pathways, and risk factors. CD can enhance these findings by moving from correlational to causal associations, thus bringing crucial insights for designing tailored treatments. In a recent paper, [34] proposed to analyse data from lung cancer, including patient data, tumor stage, driver genes, and cellular pathways, and apply the classical Peter-Clark (PC) algorithm [41] to discover causal associations from the patient to the genomic level. This allowed to reinforce confidence in some already known causal associations between patient and tumor data, while suggesting new potential causal relationships. Nevertheless, the choice of PC as the backbone of their pipeline for CD on lung cancer has not been discussed, and this is not an isolated example (*e.g.*, [22,24]). In this work, we consider the dataset analyzed in [34]. We demonstrate that applying several classical CD methods generates a strong heterogeneity across the resulting causal graphs, emphasizing the risks of relying on a single method when expert knowledge is not available. Certain causal relationships are more consistently discovered than others, and a clear cause-and-effect directionality can sometimes be extremely hard to establish. This motivates a frequency-based aggregation approach, in which edges are weighted by their observation frequency, yielding a more robust and informative estimate of the underlying causal structure.

The paper is organised as follows. In Sect. 2, we provide a brief introduction to causality, describe the CD algorithms included in our method, and present our method to build the consensus causal model. We also include a description of the dataset on lung cancer that we will consider in this study. Section 3 first presents the analysis of the observed heterogeneity within the set of discovered causal graphs obtained by running our CD benchmark. Then, we build our consensus model and provide a biological validation of the consensus graph, highlighting the relevance of our method as a valid and low-cost strategy for obtaining more comprehensive and accurate insights in our use case. Section 4 concludes the paper with some suggestions for future work.

2 Materials and Methods

2.1 Background on Probabilistic Causality

Given two random variables (rvs) X_i, X_j, a common-sense definition of causality can be stated as follows: if X_i causes X_j, then an intervention on X_i will affect X_j, whereas the inverse does not hold. Considering a set of rvs $\mathbf{X}$, a convenient way of representing causal relationships consists of a directed graph $\mathcal{G} = (\mathbf{X}, E)$, where E contains all directed edges relating nodes in $\mathbf{X}$: if X_i causes X_j, then $\mathcal{G}$ will contain a directed edge $X_i \rightarrow X_j$, *i.e.*, $(X_i, X_j) \in E$ (the order matters), we say that X_i is a parent of X_j and denote Pa_j the set of direct causes of X_j. We assume that a causal graph is *acyclic*, meaning that there exists no set of consecutive edges in E starting and ending in the same node: in this case, we talk of a Directed Acyclic Graph (DAG) (see [32] for an overview on the topic). The indirected graph associated with $\mathcal{G}$ is called the *skeleton*. Causal discovery aims to uncover, from data, the DAG underlying the causal data generation mechanism. Let $\mathbf{X}$ be a set of causal variables (sometimes called *endogenous*) and $\mathbb{P}$ a probability distribution over $\mathbf{X}$. Learning the causal DAG over $\mathbf{X}$ means learning how the data sampled from the distribution $\mathbb{P}$ has been generated. We can connect probability and causality by looking at the (in)dependencies and conditional (in)dependencies in $\mathbb{P}$. The *Causal Markov Condition* allows to make a link between the causal graph and the probability distribution through conditional independence.

Definition 1. *Let $\mathcal{G} = (\mathbf{X}, E)$ be a causal graph, and $\mathbb{P}$ a probability distribution over $\mathbf{X}$ generated by $\mathcal{G}$. $\mathcal{G}$ and $\mathbb{P}$ satisfy the* ***Causal Markov Condition (CMC)*** *iff for every X_i in $\mathbf{X}$, $X_i \perp\!\!\!\perp \mathbf{X} \setminus (Des_i \cup \mathrm{Pa}_i) | \mathrm{Pa}_i$ (read: X_i is independent of $\mathbf{X} \setminus (\mathrm{Des}_i \cup \mathrm{Pa}_i)$ given Pa_i).*

The Markov Condition entails the following factorization of the joint probability distribution:

$$\mathbb{P}(\mathbf{X}) = \prod_{X_i \in \mathbf{X}} \mathbb{P}(X_i | \mathrm{Pa}_i). \tag{1}$$

We also recall the definition of *Faithfulness*, required by most CD algorithms for identifiability:

Definition 2. *Let $\mathcal{G} = (\mathbf{X}, E)$ be a causal graph, and $\mathbb{P}$ a probability distribution over $\mathbf{X}$ generated by $\mathcal{G}$. $\mathcal{G}$ and $\mathbb{P}$ satisfy the* ***Faithfulness Condition*** *iff the only conditional independencies in $\mathbb{P}$ are the ones entailed by the CMC applied to $\mathcal{G}$. In this case, we say that $\mathbb{P}$ is* ***faithful*** *to $\mathcal{G}$.*

Given a graph $\mathcal{G}$, the CMC yields a list of conditional independencies for $\mathbb{P}$ to satisfy. Nevertheless, additional independencies can emerge due to specific parameter choices or constraints, leading to *unfaithful* distributions. A further discussion about these conditions connecting causality to probability can be found in [41]. We conclude by defining *causal sufficiency*, which is a theoretical assumption that is rarely satisfied in real-world settings, despite being often required to ensure CD identifiability.

Definition 3. *A set $\mathbf{X}$ of rvs is* ***Causally Sufficient (CS)*** *iff every common cause of any two or more variables in $\mathbf{X}$ is in $\mathbf{X}$.*

2.2 Causal Discovery Benchmark

In this work, we consider 8 classical CD algorithms, which can be classified into 4 categories: constraint-based, score-based, functional-based, and permutation-based. All these methods are implemented in the Python library `causal-learn`, which we will use for the results section. The code and datasets are all publicly available on GitHub. Below, we provide a brief description of each considered CD algorithm, of which a summary is given in Table 1.

Constraint-Based. Constraint-based methods rely on statistical tests for conditional independence to discover the causal graph. Among constraint-based methods, we consider the following candidates:

PC. Peter-Clark (PC) [41] is one of the most popular CD algorithms. It starts with a complete undirected graph and recursively prunes off edges based on conditional independence. PC assumes **Faithfulness** and **Causal Sufficiency**. Its output is a Partially Directed Graph, consisting of both directed and undirected edges, undirected edges being those for which PC wasn't able to establish any orientation.

FCI. Fast Causal Inference (FCI) [42] is a relaxation of the PC algorithm that does not assume **Causal Sufficiency**. FCI outputs a Partial Ancestral Graph, which can contain different types of edges, including partially oriented edges or bidirected edges, which indicate the possible existence of unobserved common causes (confounders).

Several conditional independence tests can be used, and should be carefully considered depending on the data. Specifically, the χ^2-test and G^2-test [44] are better suited for discrete data. For continuous data, we should use e.g., the Fisher-z test [15], which is particularly well suited for data with linear causal relationships and a Gaussian distribution, or a kernel-based test [48], which is more flexible in terms of the expected functional form of the causal relationship.

Score-Based. Score-based algorithms rely on the definition of a score for measuring the goodness of fit of the graph with respect to the observed distribution. We consider the following score-based methods:

GES. Greedy Equivalent Search (GES) [8] starts from an empty graph, and iteratively adds edges entailing an improved score result (forward phase). It then performs a backward search, where edges are removed whenever this operation implies a better scoring. GES assumes **Faithfulness** and **Causal Sufficiency**.

ExactSearch. ExactSearch [39] relies on decomposable scores and uses dynamic programming to compute *every* local score (i.e., a score for each pair of variables and its candidate set of parents). `causal-learn` also implements a refined version of ExactSearch (A^*) [47], which further improves the search method efficiency.

As for constraint-based algorithms, several scores can be proposed and adapted to the data types. The BIC score [37] is classically proposed, and is particularly well-suited for continuous data with linear causal relationships and Gaussian distributions. For discrete data, the Dirichlet score (BDeu) [5] can be used. Finally, a *general score* [19] based on kernels can be proposed for continuous data, without requiring assumptions on the form of the causal relationships.

Functional-Based. Functional-based methods rely on a functional definition of causality, which means specifying a function f which describes the form of the causal dependency: given f, X causes Y is denoted by $Y = f(X) + \epsilon$, where ϵ is a noise variable, independent of X and typically centered. We consider the following methods, based on linear assumptions:

DirectLiNGAM. DirectLiNGAM [38] assumes a *linear non-Gaussian acyclic model* (LiNGAM), meaning a linear function f to describe causality, and a non-Gaussian random noise. DirectLiNGAM performs least squares regressions of each variable on the others, computes the residuals, and tests independence between residuals and variables to finally establish the causal order. It assumes **Causal Sufficiency**.

RCD-LiNGAM. Repetitive Causal Discovery LiNGAM (RCD-LiNGAM) [27] relaxes the causal sufficiency assumptions of DirectLiNGAM, and admits the existence of unobserved variables. As its name suggests, this method is also based on a linear non-Gaussian assumption.

Permutation-Based. Within this category, we consider methods based on Sparsest Permutation (SP) [35]. SP proposes to use conditional independence to associate a unique DAG to a causal order of the set of variables, investigated through permutation. The aim is to identify the permutation yielding the sparsest DAG (i.e., the one with the smallest number of edges). SP's identifiability requires **Causal sufficiency** and a strictly weaker **Faithfulness** constraint.

GRaSP. Greedy Relaxations of SP (GRaSP) [23] replaces the exhaustive permutations search of SP with a more efficient permutation space travelling method, making the algorithm more scalable for highly connected graphs.

BOSS. Best Order Score Search (BOSS) [2] introduces and leverages a novel technique known as Grow-Shrink Trees (GST) [2] to construct the unique DAG associated to a permutation, ensuring scalability for high-dimensional data.

Permutation-based methods also require the specification of a score to assess the quality of the considered graphs. The same scores already discussed for score-based methods apply here.

Table 1. CD algorithms benchmark. (**CS** = Causal Sufficiency)

Algorithm	Type	Faithfulness	CS	Reference
PC	Constraint-based	✓	✓	[41]
FCI		✓	✗	[42]
GES	Score-based	✓	✓	[8]
ExactSearch		✓	✓	[39] [47]
DirectLiNGAM	Functional-based	✗	✓	[38]
RCD-LiNGAM		✗	✗	[27]
GRaSP	Permutation-based	✗	✓	[23]
BOSS		✗	✓	[2]

2.3 Consensus Causal Model

To build our consensus causal model, we first perform a homogenisation step, and map all output causal graphs to a universal causal graph representation characterized through a binary adjacency matrix, enabling coherent information exchange between CD algorithms and aggregation of their heterogeneous outputs. Indeed, as detailed in Sect. 2.2,

CD algorithm outputs may present different types of predicted edges (directed, bidirected, undirected, partially directed). For the sake of interoperability, bidirected and undirected edges are mapped into two symmetric 1 entries in the corresponding binary adjacency matrix, under the convention that symmetric entries in the consensus matrix will be interpreted as an identified association between the two involved nodes, which can be either causal (directed or mediated) or anti-causal (e.g., through latent confounding); symmetric entries on the consensus will be graphically represented as undirected. On the other hand, partially directed edges are homogenized to directed, to strengthen the information contained therein of a forbidden direction. A similar approach was adopted e.g. in [36], for scoring purposes and comparison against ground truth.

Given a set of homogenized binary adjacency matrices sharing the same edge-type conventions, the consensus causal model is computed by their arithmetic average. This leads to a weighted consensus graph, where weights denote edge observation frequencies, and bring information on the consistency of the discovered causal associations. It is worth noticing that our choice of a binary mapping is particularly effective here since it naturally encourages orientation over simple skeleton discovery. Finally, for the sake of a cleaner graphical representation, we consider a majority voting strategy to solve orientation conflicts, whenever possible: we retain the edge direction corresponding to the larger weight between the two possible directions, and keep an edge undirected whenever the two directions have equal weight. Of note, our consensus graph is not constrained to be acyclic, and may allow for cyclic relationships if not actively prohibited (only self-loops are forbidden by construction). Nevertheless, consensus weights provide valuable information for edge pruning. Figure 1 schematically illustrates how the consensus is built.

Aggregating multiple causal graphs has already been proposed (e.g., [10]), but this procedure is typically performed by adding/removing edges based on a threshold (typically set to 50%). The resulting graph is then interpreted as a binary structure. On the contrary, our consensus model learns from all considered CD methods and combines all discovered edges within a weighted structure that conveys a heuristic measure of confidence: higher (respectively, lower) weights indicate more (respectively, fewer) occurrences across the set of causal graphs. The resulting consensus structure is both denser and more informative, providing potentially new insights together with an associated level of uncertainty. While the main focus of the current study concerns the analysis of the lung cancer data described in the following section, Appendix A.3 contains some exemplifying results in a controlled simulation study, comparing the performance of the consensus graph with individual algorithms. Overall, experiments conducted on synthetic data show that our consensus graph and its weighted structure effectively allows to drive attention towards the most relevant causal structures, reaching performances comparable to the best-scoring models.

2.4 Lung Cancer Data

Dataset Creation. The data extraction and dataset construction follow the same pipeline used in [34]. We combined patient- and tumor-level data obtained from a lung cancer study [6] available on cBioPortal [16] with genomic information derived from somatic

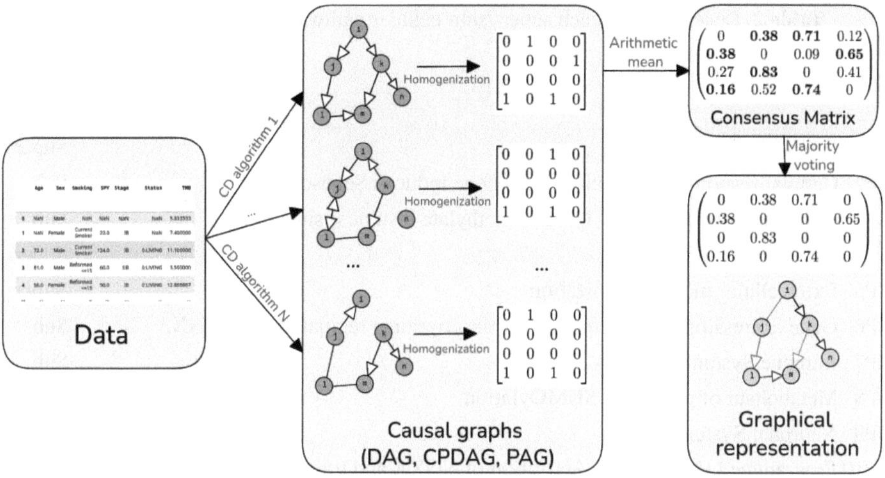

Fig. 1. Diagram explaining the construction of the consensus causal model

mutations and with the hierarchical organization of cellular pathways provided by Reactome [30]. Using the concept of Super Pathways [13], which groups cellular functions into hierarchical structures, we intersected their gene sets with each patient's mutated driver genes. Only mutations in known driver genes [11,29] were considered, reducing the dimensionality of the genomic feature space and increasing the biological relevance of the associations. For each patient and for each Super Pathway or Sub-pathway, we evaluated whether the intersection between mutated genes and pathway genes was statistically significant, retaining only statistically significant associations. Table 2 shows the cellular pathways that have been finally retained, and the reference number we will use for graphical representations in Sect. 3. This procedure yielded a reduced and structured dataset that integrates clinical and tumor information (6 features), and genomic data (12 cellular pathways), illustrated in Table 3. We dispose of 1044 subjects in total.

Further details on the variable reduction, subgroup decomposition, and aggregation steps can be found in [34], which fully documents the original pipeline.

Missing Data Handling. Most existing CD algorithms need to be fed with complete datasets (*i.e.*, with no missing entries), to learn the underlying causal DAG. While the cellular pathways data is complete (a missing record implies no mutation has been observed for this sample, so we can safely replace it with 0), the 6 features reporting patient- and tumor-level data are of heterogeneous nature (continuous and categorical) and contain up to 20% of missing values (see Supplementary Fig. 6). A simple, straightforward solution consists of removing every sample containing at least one missing entry. Nevertheless, this entails a significant loss of information, since more than 30% of the samples are partially corrupted. An alternative approach implies performing missing data imputation prior to the CD task. Several methods of missing data imputation exist, and can be broadly classified into two categories: univariate and multivariate imputation. The first one independently considers one feature at a time and uses

Table 2. Description of each super-/sub- cellular pathway retained for this study.

Ref.	Description	Super/ Sub
SP1	Cell-Cell communication	Super
SP2	Cellular responses to stimuli – Oncogene Induced Senescence	Sub
SP3	Chromatin organization – PKMTs methylate histone lysines	Sub
SP4	Developmental Biology	Super
SP5	Extracellular matrix organization	Super
SP6	Gene expression (Transcription) – Transcriptional regulation by RUNX3	Sub
SP7	Immune System – Dectin-2 family	Sub
SP8	Metabolism of proteins – SUMOylation	Sub
SP9	Neuronal System	Super
SP10	Programmed Cell Death – Activation of NOXA and translocation to mitochondria	Sub
SP11	Signal Transduction	Super
SP12	Vesicle-mediated transport – Scavenging by Class H Receptors	Sub

Table 3. Dataset encompassing patient- and tumor-level data, adapted from [34]. **SPY**: Smoking Pack Years. **SP**: Super-/Sub-pathway. *Sex*, *Smoking*, *Status*, and *Stage* are by nature binary or categorical variables, while the remaining variables are continuous (Ref = Reformed).

Patient	Patient- and tumor-level data						Genomic level data			
	Sex	Age	Smoking	SPY	Stage	Status	SP1	SP2	···	SP12
p1	Male	41	Ref>15	20	IA	Living	2	0	0	0
p2	Male	51	Ref≤15	10	IIIA	Deceased	0	5	0	1
p3	Female	65	Ref	12	IIIB	Living	2	0	7	0
...	Female	83	Current	32	V	Deceased	1	0	0	1
p1044	Male	67	Ref>15	40	IIA	Living	3	2	1	0

the observed values in each feature containing missing entries to replace them, such as the *mean imputation*. Multivariate imputation instead uses all the observed features in the dataset to impute missing values, such as the k-Nearest Neighbors (k-NN) algorithm [3], which we decided to use in this work. To account for heterogeneous data types, we chose the Heterogeneous Euclidean-Overlap Metric (HEOM) [45] to define the nearest neighbors.

Definition 4. *Let* $\mathbf{x} = (x_d)_{d=0,\ldots,D}$ *and* $\mathbf{y} = (y_d)_{d=0,\ldots,D}$ *be two D-dimensional samples, composed of continuous and categorical features. Their HEOM distance,* $d_{\text{HEOM}}(\mathbf{x}, \mathbf{y})$, *is defined as follows:*

$$d_{\mathrm{HEOM}}(\mathbf{x},\mathbf{y}) = \sqrt{\sum_{d=1}^{D} d(x_d, y_d)^2}, \text{where } d(x_d, y_d) = \begin{cases} \begin{cases} 0 \textit{ if } x_d = y_d \\ 1 \textit{ otherwise} \end{cases} & \textit{if } d \textit{ is categorical} \\ \\ \dfrac{|x_d - y_d|}{\max_d - \min_d} & \textit{if } d \textit{ is continuous} \end{cases}$$

$\max_d$ *(resp.* $\min_d$*) are the maximum (resp. the minimum) of the d-th feature across all samples.*

We equipped the k-NN algorithm with the HEOM distance to find the k nearest neighbors ($k = 5$ in this work) of each sample $\mathbf{x} = (x_d)_{d=0,\ldots,D}$ with a missing entry for at least one feature, x_{d^*} in our dataset. If x_{d^*} is continuous, we impute its value using the mean of the $d^{*\text{th}}$ feature over the set of nearest neighbors; otherwise, we impute by the most frequent value. This process has the advantage of preserving the original distribution of the data (see Supplementary Fig. 5).

In Sect. 3 we will refer to the dataset from which partially observed samples have been removed as *Filtered*, and the dataset in which missing entries have been imputed as *Imputed.*

Prior Knowledge. Some CD algorithms allow for the injection of prior knowledge about existing (resp. forbidden) causal relationships: this can greatly facilitate the causal discovery task in terms of both accuracy and computational load. Concerning our specific application, we dispose of limited, yet informative, prior information concerning some variables about patient and tumor data. Specifically, we can assert that *Age* and *Sex* should have no parents variable (*i.e.*, their in-degree is 0), while *Status* should have no children (*i.e.*, its out-degree is 0) as the patients' outcome should not cause any of the variables considered. In Sect. 3 we will associate the mention *prior* whenever this prior knowledge has been provided as additional input to the CD algorithm.

3 Results

3.1 Individual Causal Models Display Substantial Heterogeneity

We generated a total of 44 causal graphs relating the 6 features of patient and tumor data and the 12 cellular pathways. Each graph resulted from the application of a CD algorithm with specific hyperparameter choices (i.e., the conditional independent test or the score, as described in Sect. 2.2). To prevent over-weighting a given CD method, we deduplicate identical causal graphs whenever they result from the same method run with different hyperparameter choices, leading to a final population of 38 candidate individual causal models. We propose several strategies to merge the obtained causal graphs, detailed in Table 4. We build a consensus causal model for each strategy.

Figure 2 shows several interesting metrics evaluated within each set of causal graphs from Table 4, which offer a quantitative measure of the observed heterogeneity across individual causal models. We firstly consider the Structural Hamming Distance (SHD, top left panel), a reference distance to compare the structure of two (partially) directed

Table 4. Strategies for causal graph merging. n denotes the number of graphs included in each set.

Strategy	Which graphs to be merged together?	n
St.1	All causal graphs	38
St.2	Causal graphs obtained using prior knowledge	9
St.3	Causal graphs obtained on the *Filtered* dataset	18
St.4	Causal graphs obtained on the *Imputed* dataset	18

graphs, which counts the number of edge deletions, insertions, or flips needed to turn one graph into the other. We evaluate the SHD between each pair of causal graphs within every merging strategy. One can see that the minimum obtained SHD between any 2 discovered causal graphs is 25 for *St.2*, with an average SHD above 30 for the other merging strategies. This highlights the high variability of the discovered causal structures and, consequently, emphasizes the challenge of relying on a specific causal graph candidate. Supplementary Fig. 7 further supports the heterogeneity statement.

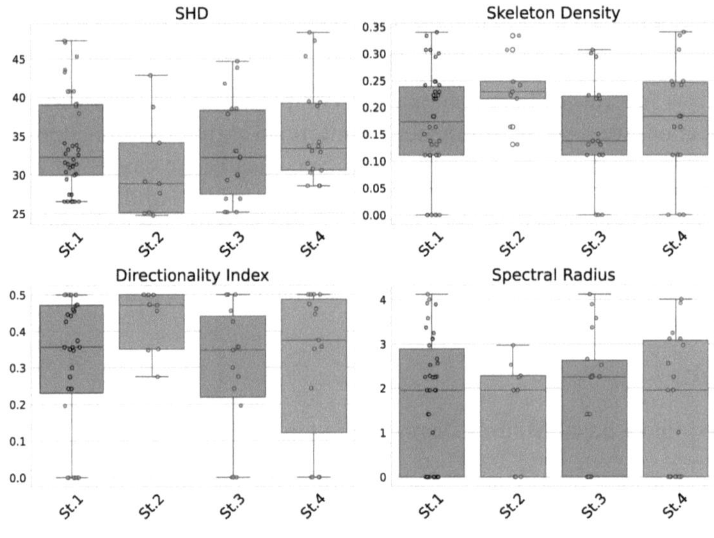

Fig. 2. Boxplot reporting some graph metrics per merging strategy. (Top left) Structural Hamming distance (SHD). (Top right) Skeleton density. (Bottom left) Directionality index. (Bottom right) Spectral radius.

Figure 2 also conveys another relevant piece of information: the importance of prior knowledge. Indeed, causal graphs in *St.2*, obtained by specifying the role of some strategic nodes (Sect. 2.4), display a significantly higher directionality index (the ratio between purely directed *vs* undirected edges) and skeleton density (the overall number of discovered edges) with respect to the other strategies. This suggests that the injected prior knowledge has strongly contributed to orienting edges, while supporting CD in robustly identifying meaningful relationships across the observed variables. To further stress the relevance of prior knowledge, we have also assessed the spectral radius of all discovered causal graphs. *St.2* shows a milder spectral radius: of note, a small spectral radius corresponds to a graph closer to being acyclic, and a small total vertex degree.

Finally, one can observe that the imputation process performed in *St.4* does not seem to lead to more stable discovered causal structures compared to *St.3*, where incomplete entries have been removed, with a consequent significant reduction of the dataset size. One possible explication can come from the nature of the missing mechanism, whose analysis is out of the scope of the current work.

3.2 The Consensus Causal Model Offers Rich Biological Insights

We build the consensus causal model following the procedure described in Sect. 2.3. We use St. 2 to build the consensus, because, as commented in Sect. 3.1, it shows a significantly higher directionality index. In Fig. 4, we compare the consensus model, where edge weights are denoted by color intensity, with the causal graph obtained by [34] applying PC. For the sake of completeness, Supp. Figure 7 further shows the full weighted consensus matrices as heatmaps, before applying the voting strategy for orientation. The consensus causal model appears substantially denser than the reference one, in some cases explaining some previously found direct associations (e.g., *SP12—SP4*) through more complex paths. This opens up a deeper discussion on the complex network relating cellular pathways and patient-level information in lung cancer.

Fig. 3. (a) Most frequent edges (%) connecting patient and tumor level data with cellular pathways variables in *St.1*. (b) Average out-degree of the 'Smoking' variable by strategy stratified by patient and tumor variables vs cellular pathways variables.

Several edges observed in the consensus model are supported by previous external studies. For instance, in clinical oncology, cancer stage is one of the strongest predictors of survival, with advanced stages generally associated with poorer outcomes. In the consensus causal model, we observe a collider structure *Stage* $\rightarrow$ *Status* $\leftarrow$ *Smoking*, meaning the edge *Smoking* $\rightarrow$ *Status* persists even after conditioning on stage and

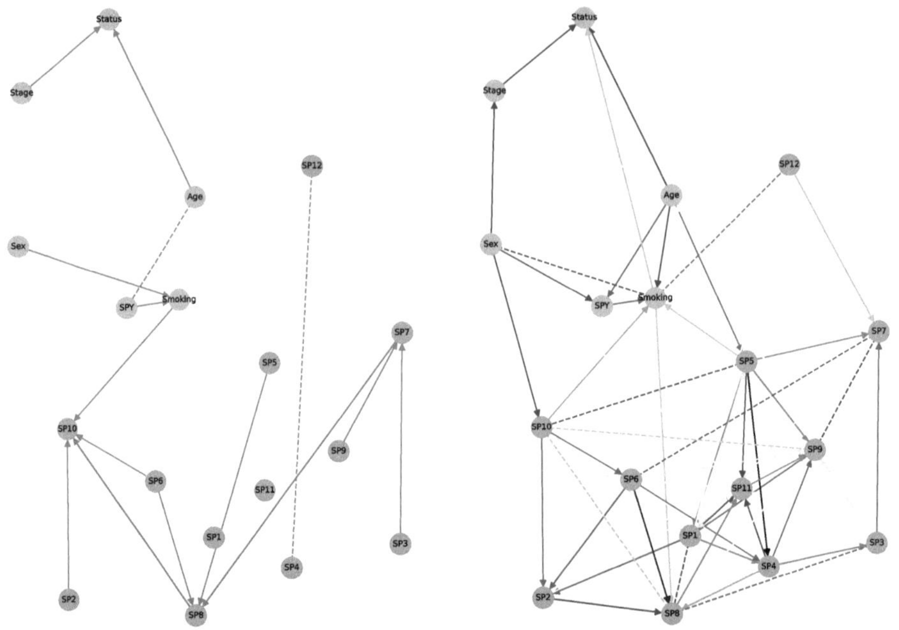

Fig. 4. (Left) Causal graph from [34] and (Right) our consensus causal graph from *St.2*. Dashed edges are undirected edges; edge color intensity in the consensus causal model corresponds to the frequency of the edge occurrence.

all other available features. This pattern suggests that smoking contributes independently to survival outcomes rather than acting solely through the stage progression. Evidence from independent studies supports this interpretation, since continued smoking after cancer diagnosis has been associated with significantly higher mortality [7,9]. This causal association was not identified in the individual causal model from [34].

The causal relationships from the patient and tumor level data towards cellular pathways are mostly mediated by *Age*, *Sex*, and *Smoking*, as underlined in Fig. 3(a). Specifically, more than 40% of the considered individual causal models have identified the causal association *Age→SP5: Extracellular Matrix Organization*, which were not observed in [34]. Extracellular Matrix (ECM) is a large network of proteins and other molecules that surround, support, and give structure to cells and tissues in the body. Previous studies show that aging is strongly linked to changes in the ECM, including reduced remodeling capacity, altered collagen structure, and increased stiffness of the surrounding tissue environment [21,43]. With increasing age, the ECM undergoes irregular and progressive modifications across different tissues, and these alterations are increasingly recognized as contributors to disease states, including cancer [28]. Importantly, the remodeled matrix in aged tissue can create physical and biochemical conditions that support tumor growth and metastatic spread. In addition, these ECM changes may act as a barrier to therapeutic response, limiting the effectiveness of both conventional treatments and immune-based interventions [4]. Similarly, the causal association

Sex→SP10: Programmed Cell Death – Activation of NOXA and translocation to mitochondria, absent in the reference graph from [34], has been recovered by over 30% of individual causal discovery algorithms queried for consensus. The existence of this causal relationship is supported by several external works (e.g., [25]), highlighting sex differences in cell death pathways, including in cancer, with implications on sex-related differences in anti-programmed cell death protein 1 therapy [12].

Also, smoking habits are identified as strongly altering several cellular pathways, underlying the key role it plays in lung cancer: this central role is further stressed by Fig. 3(b), where we report the average out-degree of *Smoking* per merging strategy. Among consistently discovered causal relationships, *Smoking→SP10* was already observed in [34]. It is well documented that cigarette smoke causes mitochondrial damage and can trigger intrinsic cell-death programs [14,40]. Meanwhile, NOXA is a stress-responsive pro-apoptotic protein that acts at the mitochondria. When activated, it helps initiate mitochondrial cell death by blocking survival proteins, which ultimately triggers apoptosis [1,31]. Our consensus model also suggests that *Smoking* causally influences the cellular pathway *SP8: Metabolism of proteins – SUMOylation*. SUMOylation is a general protein-modification process that helps regulate fundamental cellular functions such as cell growth, migration, responses to stress, and processes related to pulmonary diseases, including cancer [46,49]. Studies have shown that exposure to cigarette smoke alters SUMOylation patterns in different cell types, including lung cells and immune cells, indicating that smoking can directly interfere with this protein-regulation system [18,50]. This relationship was missing in the individual model from [34]. Of note, in the consensus model plot in Fig. 4, the reverse direction (*SP10→Smoking*) is reported due to the voting strategy used for edge orientation. Nevertheless, as depicted in Fig. 3(a), the more reasonable causal flow *Smoking→SP10* is correctly recovered by more than 30% of the considered CD algorithms: in this case, prior knowledge should have been preferred over voting to discriminate the best orientation. The voting strategy could also have been responsible for some observed edge reversals between our consensus graph and that of [34]. This is, for instance, the case for SP2 and SP10, for which our consensus associates a stronger weight to the *SP10→SP2* direction (0.7) with respect to the other one (0.4).

A remark should be spent on the role within the consensus model (as well as the reference graph by [34]) of the tumor-level nodes *Stage* and *Status*. Surprisingly, there is no discovered direct or indirect relationship between such nodes and any of the cellular pathways, indicating that corruption of the cellular functions is not identified as causally affecting cancer development or the outcome of the patient. This behavior has also been observed when summarizing the information on genetic disregulation into a single node, Tumor Mutational Burden (TMB - see Supplementary Sect. A.2): TMB is identified in the consensus model as a direct effect of *Smoking*, *Age*, and *Sex*, with no children. This may be partially explained by the fact that our dataset only comprises diseased samples: the inclusion of healthy samples in the study would have possibly allowed highlighting the counterfactuals and hence, other mechanistic relationships between cellular pathways deregulation and lung cancer.

Finally, as noted earlier, the consensus causal graph appears substantially denser than the graph reported in [34], especially in the cellular pathways subgraph. All causal relationships identified between pathways can be explained thanks to the intersection of cancer driver genes: cellular pathways sharing deregulated molecular components are more likely to appear as connected in the causal graph. One example of these patterns is the causal edge observed from *SP10: Programmed Cell Death – Activation of NOXA and translocation to mitochondria* to *SP2: Cellular responses to stimuli – Oncogene Induced Senescence*. In the Reactome hierarchy, these belong to broader functional categories (*Programmed Cell Death* and *Cellular Responses to Stimuli*), while the ones analyzed here represent more specific sub-pathways nested within them. These two sub-pathways share the cancer drivers *TP53* and *TFDP1* [11], which have been associated with regulatory roles in both apoptotic and senescence-related mechanisms. The presence of shared driver genes suggests potential biological cross-talk, and the fact that this relationship appears as a directed edge in our model indicates that the CD algorithms successfully captured this underlying functional dependency. Moreover, all causal pathways across cellular pathways include at least one among *SP5*, *SP8*, *SP10*, *SP12*, all related to *Smoking*.

More generally, despite density might be perceived as a drawback in CD in relation to a higher false positive rate, the trade-off between sensitivity and specificity in causal discovery for biomedical data remains an open question, and largely depends on the intended downstream task. The weighted causal structure of our consensus causal model conveys richer information than a classical binary adjacency matrices, enabling tuning the level of sparsity. For instance, if the graph is intended to be used to guide experimental validation, sparser structures are preferable in order to focus resources on a small number of targets. In this case, only edges with high weights would be retained. Conversely, when aiming for a more comprehensive, system-level understanding, overly aggressive pruning may discard important regulatory relationships: edges with lower weights may still be relevant and should be kept. A related discussion on the trade-off between false positives and false negatives in a medical context is provided in [26], where it motivates the development of a variant of the PC algorithm that allows the user to control the false discovery rate rather than the independence test power. Notably, in our experiments on simulated data (see supplementary Fig. 14), a threshold of 50% provides a reasonable balance between these two objectives.

4 Conclusions

Our work tackles the challenging problem of causal discovery in complex biomedical contexts, where the ground truth is missing, and the compliance of data with the strong assumptions required for causal identifiability are hard to prove. To overcome the difficulties encountered by causal discovery in such contexts, we propose a consensus causal model obtained by aggregating the outputs of multiple causal discovery algorithms based on the consistency of their causal associations. The construction of the consensus departs from the usual binary representation in causal discovery in favor of a continuous perspective, which enables a heuristic quantification of uncertainty in the inferred relationships. The case study of lung cancer allows us to demonstrate the effectiveness of our ensemble strategy as the consensus model recovers most causal relationships previously established by [34] while also providing additional rich and biologically valid insights into the causal relationships linking *Age* and *Smoking* to cellular functions. Overall, the proposed consensus representation aggregates multiple levels of causal evidence into a single object, thereby offering greater flexibility and interpretability for downstream applications. Despite the consensus model already yields an informal measure of confidence, in future work we aim to fully embrace the paradigm of ensemble causal learning and investigate more refined strategies for merging causal graphs, together with a rigorous approach to uncertainty quantification for causal discovery and mechanisms to enforce acyclicity in the aggregated structure.

Acknowledgements. This work was supported by the French government through the National Research Agency (ANR) RHU Talent project (ANR-23-RHUS-0015) and by the Inria-UCL associate team GRAPH-CURE.

A Appendix

A.1 Supplementary Figures

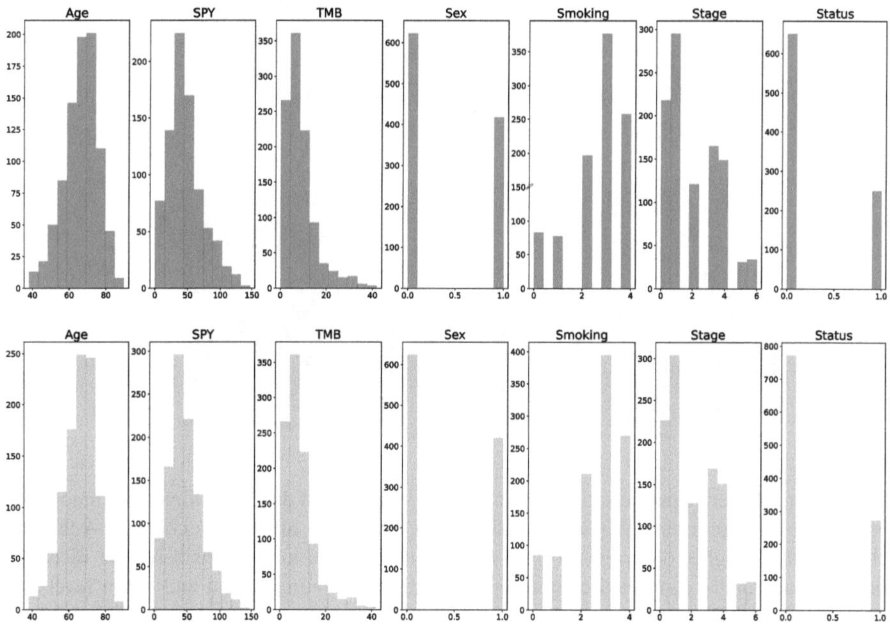

Fig. 5. Data distribution. Top line: original dataset. Bottom line: distribution after imputation.

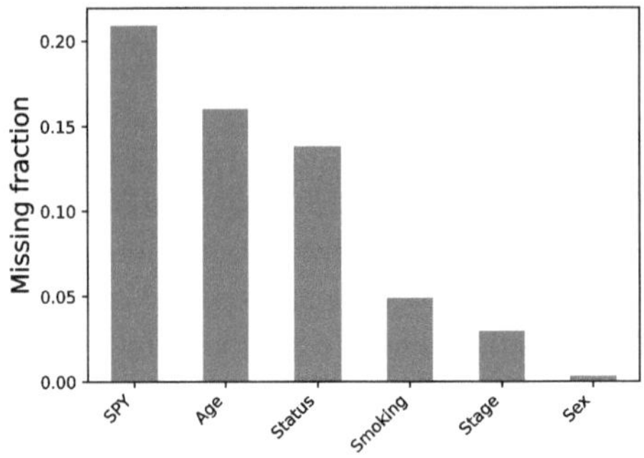

Fig. 6. Prevalence of missing data across all features within the patient and tumor dataset.

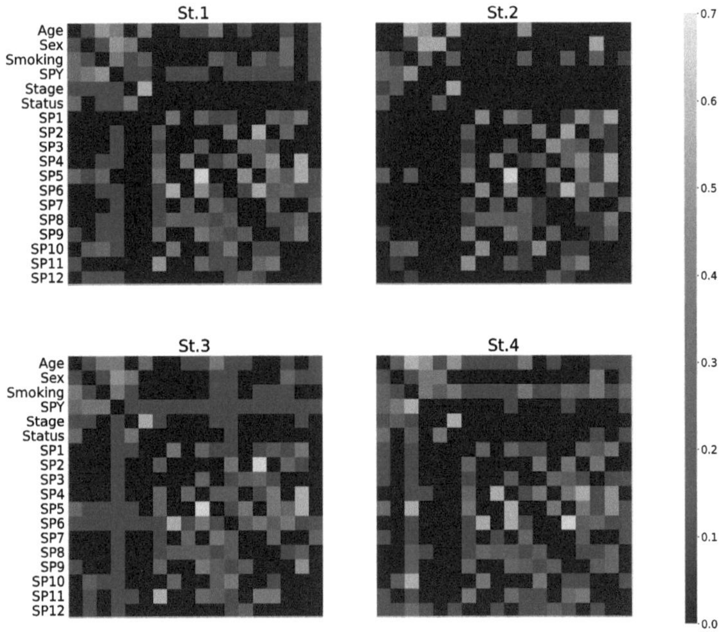

Fig. 7. Mean adjacency matrices per merging strategy on the full dataset (patient and tumor data, and genetic level information). Causality direction corresponds to: row → column. A brighter color denotes a higher occurrence of the corresponding edge in the considered set of causal graphs. Two strongly connected components emerge, one relating patient and tumor level data and one relating cellular pathways.

A.2 A Focus on Patient- and Tumor-Level Variables

Here, we restrict ourselves to the 6 features of patient and tumor level data, and additionally consider Tumor Mutational Burden (TMB) as a proxy of the total degree of genetic mutations affecting cellular pathways, available for all samples in our dataset.

As for the main study, consensus causal models are built following the merging strategies introduced in Sect. 3.

Figure 8 shows the mean adjacency matrices within each group of causal graphs, highlighting again the variability of the discovered causal structures. This can be further appreciated by looking at Fig. 9, upper left panel, which shows pairwise Structural Hamming Distance (SHD). As for the main study, a straightforward conclusion one can draw from the results shown in Fig. 9 is the importance of injecting some (limited) prior knowledge into the CD approach. Indeed, causal graphs analysed in *St.2* (with priors) display a significantly high skeleton density and directionality index, coupled with a smaller spectral radius, suggesting the discovery of a more stable acyclic and still dense graph. Figure 10 also shows the fraction of strongly connected graphs (i.e., where each node is accessible from any other node in the graph): none of the graphs discovered using prior knowledge are strongly connected, while approximately 5.5% of the graphs from the other merging strategies are.

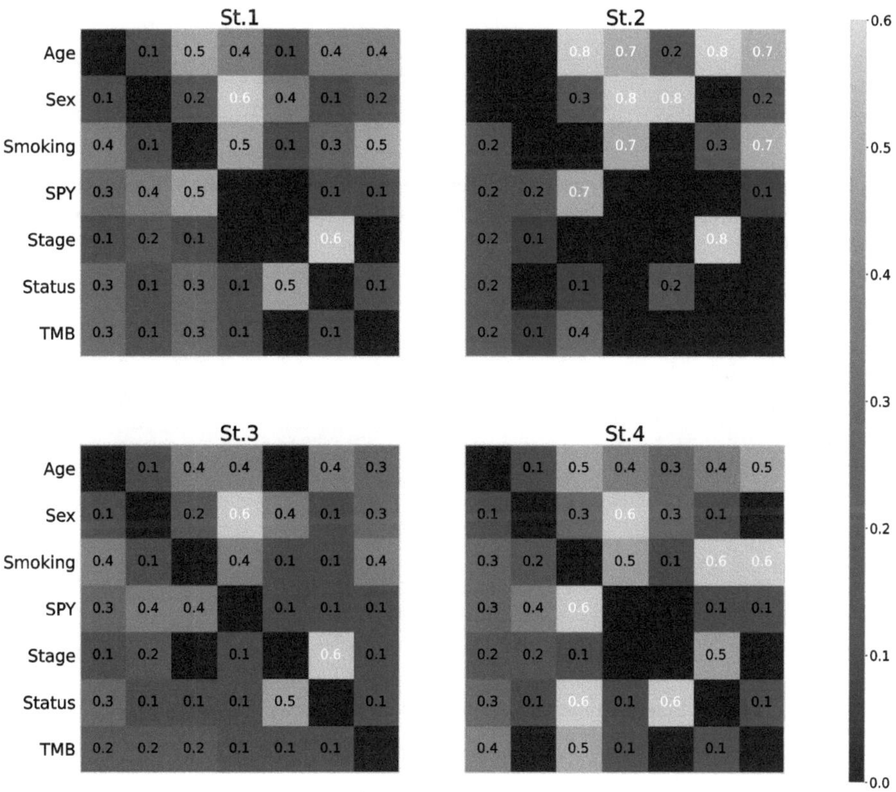

Fig. 8. Mean adjacency matrices per merging strategy on the full dataset (patient and tumor data, and genetic level information). Causality direction corresponds to: row → column. A brighter color denotes a higher occurrence of the corresponding edge in the considered set of causal graphs.

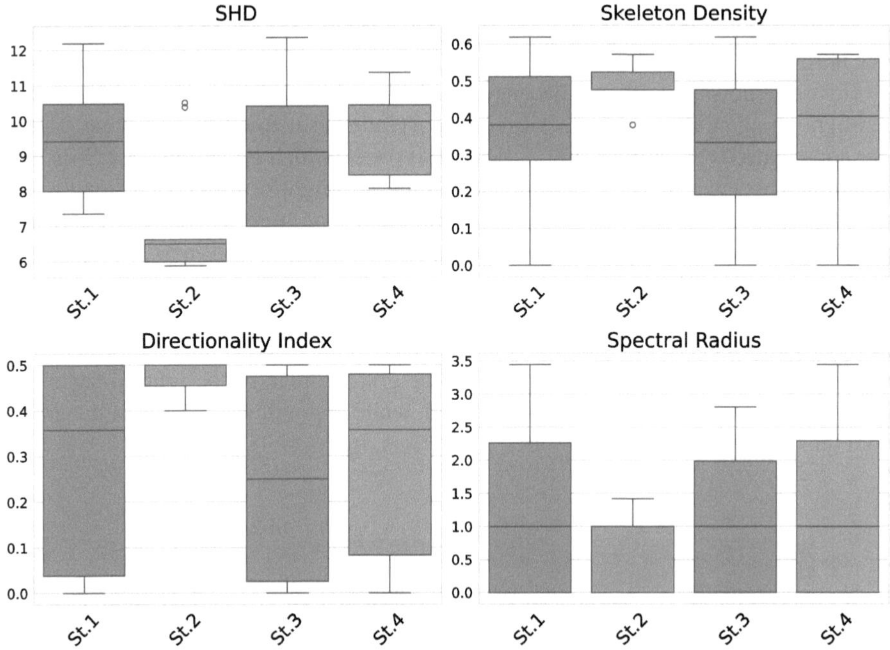

Fig. 9. Boxplot reporting some graph metrics per merging strategy. (Top left) Structural Hamming distance (SHD). (Top right) Skeleton density. (Bottom left) Directionality index. (Bottom right) Spectral radius.

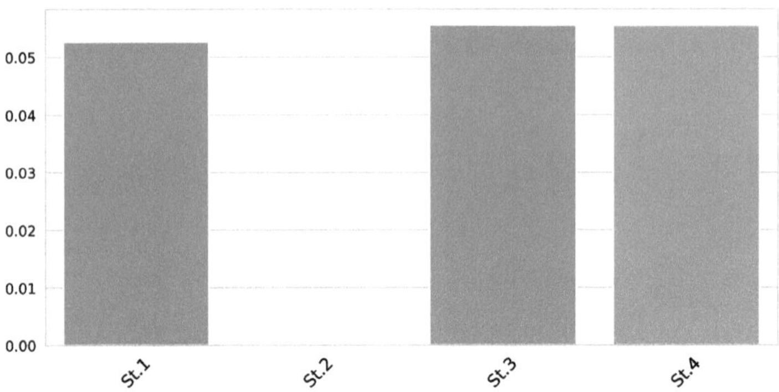

Fig. 10. Fraction of strongly connected graphs per merging strategy.

Finally, Fig. 11 compares the causal graph obtained in the original work by [34] using PC with our consensus causal model obtained using *St.2*. Again, the reference graph appears as a subgraph of our consensus model, and misses some very relevant causal associations, such as the collider structure *Stage* → *Status* ← *Smoking*, already commented in Sect. 3.2. Moreover, one can clearly see that *Smoking*, *Age*, and *Sex* are all parent nodes of *TMB*, thus supporting their role in the causal deregulation of cellular pathways.

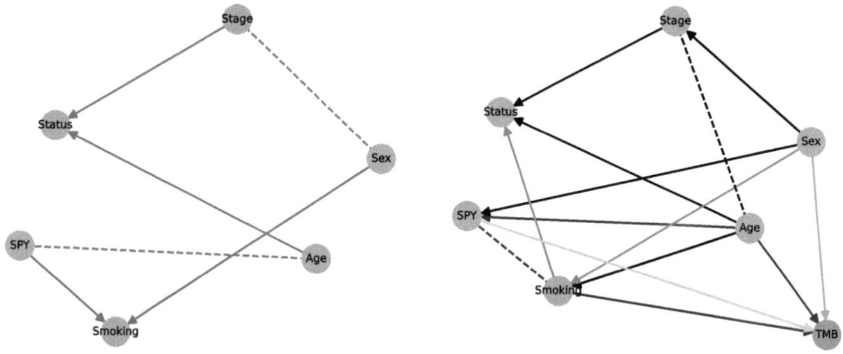

Fig. 11. (Left) Causal graph from [34] and (Right) our consensus causal graph from *St.2*. Dashed edges denote undirected edges; edge color intensity in the consensus causal model corresponds to the frequency of the edge occurrence. [34] did not consider TMB in their study, so it only appears on the consensus model.

A.3 Controlled Simulation Experiments

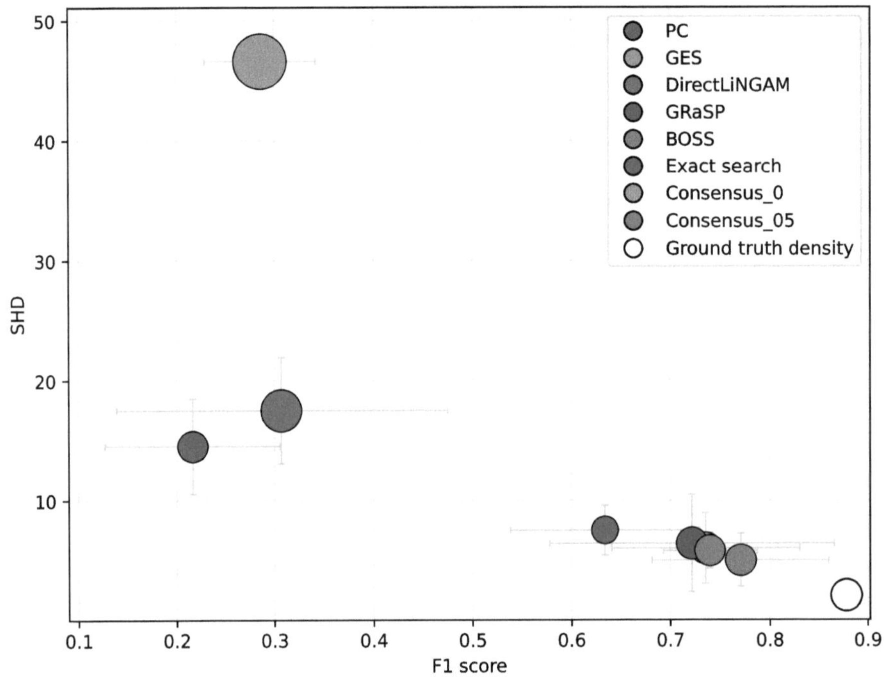

Fig. 12. SHD and F1 score comparing the benchmark CD algorithms and the consensus one. 10 independent datasets of 1000 samples each were randomly generated from 8-node causal graphs, using linear causal relationship ($f(x) = x$), and independent centered Gaussian noise with standard deviation $\sigma = 0.1$. Filled dots represent the mean score over the 10 runs for each method, and error bars represent the corresponding standard deviations. The size of each filled dot is proportional to the average density of the algorithm's output. The empty dot in the top-right corner provides a measure of the average density of the ground truth, as a reference.

To assess the performance of our consensus approach, we perform controlled experiments using synthetic data, with a known ground-truth causal graph, since in real-world settings, this is usually not available. To do so, we proceed as follows:

1. We generate a DAG by randomly generating its adjacency matrix using Erdős–Rényi model for DAGs, and ensuring acyclicity. To do so, we specify the mean density of the desired causal graph through a parameter $p \in]0, 1[$, that corresponds to the parameter of a Bernoulli law for each entry in the adjacency matrix.
2. Given the DAG, samples for each variable X_i are obtained from its parents' set PA_i through a functional transformation f_i and a random independent additive noise variable ϵ_i:

$$X_i = \sum_{X_j \in PA_i} f_i(X_j) + \epsilon_i \tag{2}$$

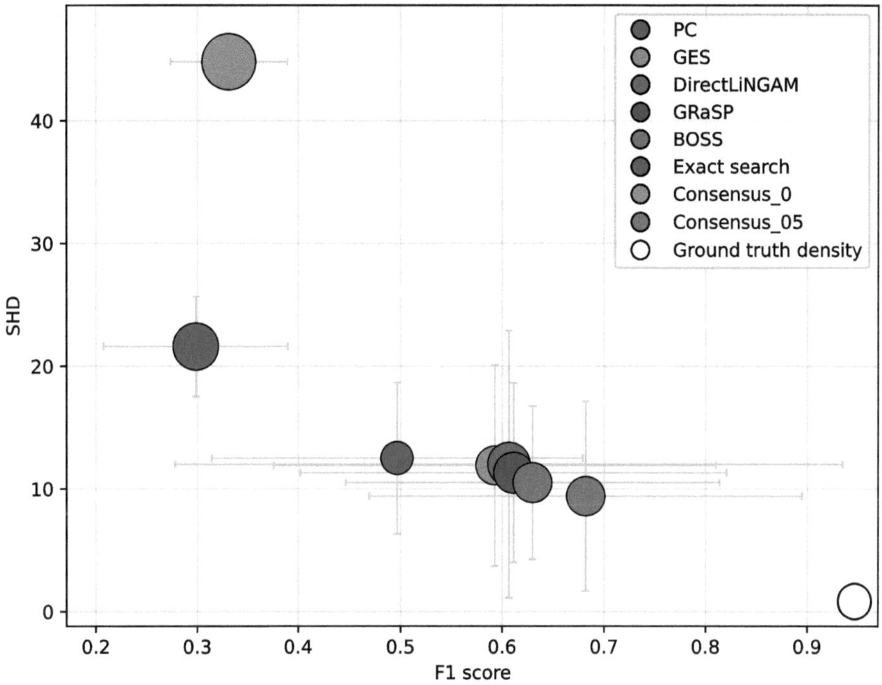

Fig. 13. SHD and F1 score comparing the benchmark CD algorithms and the consensus one. 10 independent datasets of 1000 samples each were randomly generated from 8-node causal graphs, using non-linear causal relationship (f is randomly chosen among non-linear functions), and independent Uniform noise scaled by $\sigma = 0.1$. Filled dots represent the mean score over the 10 runs for each method, and error bars represent the corresponding standard deviations. The size of each filled dot is proportional to the average density of the algorithm's output. The empty dot in the bottom-right corner provides a measure of the average density of the ground truth, as a reference.

In our experiments, we use $f_i = f$, for different specifications of f.

In Figs. 12, 13 we show results from two simulation studies. In both cases, we fixed the number of variables in each random graph to 8, and the parameter of the Bernoulli distribution to $p = 0.4$, which means that the average number of edges in the ground truth is $\frac{8(8-1)}{2}0.4 = 11.2$. Figure 12 refers to the simple case of linear Gaussian data, while Fig. 13 refers to the non-linear non-Gaussian one, in the case of the non-linear non-Gaussian, the function f in (2) is randomly chosen among the following functions: ReLU, sigmoid, logarithmic, exponential, sinus, hyperbolic tangent and quadratic. For each setting, we randomly generated 10 datasets following the steps described above, and compare each individual causal discovery algorithm and our consensus model against the ground truth by reporting the Structural Hamming Distance (SHD), the F1 score, and a relative measure of the density of the output graph. Since all features were continuous in all synthetic dataset discussed here, PC were run with the

Fisher-Z independence test, while the BIC score was used for GES, GRaSP, and BOSS. Finally, we used the search method 'astar' for Exact search.

As a reference, in both Figures, we plot the score of the consensus model where each edge was kept irrespective of its weights (Consensus_0, in pink), which, as expected, obtains a high SHD and low F1 score due to its high density. Nevertheless, one can clearly see that if we fixed a 0.5 threshold for edge pruning, the consensus model (Consensus_05, in gray) significantly improves both scores, indicating that the weights provide relevant information about the pertinence of each edge (and their directions, accounted by SHD). This is particularly striking in the non-linear case (Fig. 13), where Consensus_05 consistently improves both scores, outperforming the individual approaches. This also demonstrates the flexibility of the consensus since dataset in the non-linear setting are generated through different functional form of the causal relationship (i.e. the function f). Concerning the density of the learned graphs (given by the dots' sizes in both figures), the thresholded consensus graph shows a density consistent with that of the ground truth DAG (the empty dot).

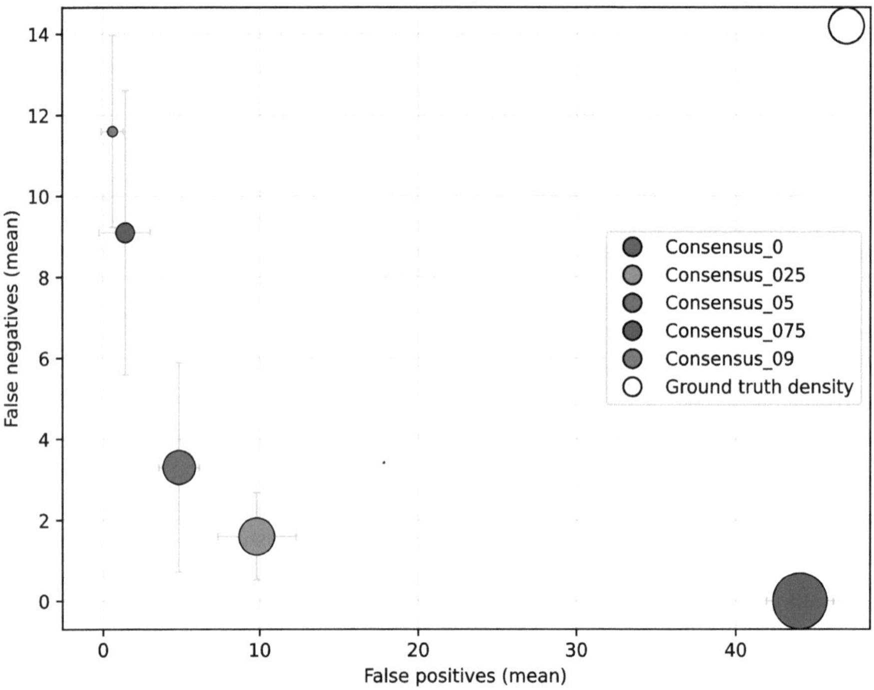

Fig. 14. False positives and False negatives for different threshold consensus. 10 independent datasets of 1000 samples each were randomly generated from 8-node causal graphs, using linear causal relationship ($f(x) = x$), and independent centered Gaussian noise with standard deviation $\sigma = 0.1$. Filled dots represent the mean score over the 10 runs for each method, and error bars represent the corresponding standard deviations. The size of each filled dot is proportional to the average density of the consensus. The empty dot in the top-right corner provides a measure of the average density of the ground truth, as a reference.

Additional extensive controlled simulation experiments were performed (results not shown) by varying several key parameters: number of nodes, sample size, noise coefficient, noise distribution, functional form of the causal relationship, data discretization. In all settings, we were able to reach similar conclusions as the ones shown here. Overall, these results support the relevance of our proposed consensus approach and provide motivation for ensemble causal discovery.

References

1. Albert, M.C., Brinkmann, K., Kashkar, H.: Noxa and cancer therapy: tuning up the mitochondrial death machinery in response to chemotherapy. Mol. Cell. Oncol. **1**(1), e29906 (2014)
2. Andrews, B., Ramsey, J., Sánchez-Romero, R., Camchong, J., Kummerfeld, E.: Fast scalable and accurate discovery of DAGs using the best order score search and grow-shrink trees. In: Advances in Neural Information Processing Systems (2023)
3. Batista, G.E.D.A.P.A., Monard, M.C.: A study of k-nearest neighbour as an imputation method. In: Soft Computing System: Design, Management and Applications (2002)
4. Boaru, D.L., et al.: Extracellular matrix dysregulation in aging, calcification, and cancer diseases: insights into cellular senescence, inflammation, and novel therapeutic strategies. Int. J. Biol. Sci. **21**(15), 6808 (2025)
5. Buntine, W.: Theory refinement on Bayesian networks. In: Proceedings of the Seventh Conference on Uncertainty in Artificial Intelligence (UAI 1991), pp. 52–60. Morgan Kaufmann (1991)
6. Campbell, J.D., et al.: Distinct patterns of somatic genome alterations in lung adenocarcinomas and squamous cell carcinomas. Nat. Genet. **48**(6), 607–616 (2016)
7. Chellappan, S.: Smoking cessation after cancer diagnosis and enhanced therapy response: mechanisms and significance. Curr. Oncol. **29**(12), 9956–9969 (2022)
8. Chickering, D.M.: Optimal structure identification with greedy search. J. Mach. Learn. (2002)
9. Cinciripini, P.M., et al.: Survival outcomes of an early intervention smoking cessation treatment after a cancer diagnosis. JAMA Oncol. **10**(12), 1689–1696 (2024)
10. Constantinou, A., et al.: Open problems in causal structure learning: a case study of covid-19 in the UK. Expert Syst. Appl. **234**, 121069 (2023)
11. Dressler, L., et al.: Comparative assessment of genes driving cancer and somatic evolution in non-cancer tissues: an update of the network of cancer genes (NCG) resource. Genome Biol. **23**(1), 35 (2022)
12. Duma, N., et al.: Sex differences in tolerability to anti-programmed cell death protein 1 therapy in patients with metastatic melanoma and non-small cell lung cancer: are we all equal? Oncologist **24**(11), e1148–e1155 (2019)
13. Fabregat, A., et al.: The reactome pathway knowledgebase. Nucleic Acids Res. **46**(D1), D649–D655 (2018)
14. Fetterman, J.L., Sammy, M.J., Ballinger, S.W.: Mitochondrial toxicity of tobacco smoke and air pollution. Toxicology **391**, 18–33 (2017)
15. Fisher, R.A.: On the "probable error" of a coefficient of correlation deduced from a small sample. Metron **1**, 3–32 (1921)
16. Gao, J., et al.: Integrative analysis of complex cancer genomics and clinical profiles using the cbioportal. Sci. Signal. **6**(269), PL1 (2013)
17. Glymour, C., Zhang, K., Peter, S.: Review of causal discovery methods based on graphical models. Front. Genet. (2019)

18. Gross, T.J.: A microrna processing defect in smokers' macrophages is linked to sumoylation of the endonuclease dicer. J. Biol. Chem. **289**(18), 12823–12834 (2014)
19. Huang, B., Zhang, K., Lin, Y., Schölkopf, B., Glymour, C.: Generalized score functions for causal discovery. In: Proceedings of the 24th ACM SIGKDD International Conference on Knowledge Discovery & Data Mining, pp. 1551–1560 (2018)
20. Joshi, S., et al.: AI as an intervention: improving clinical outcomes relies on a causal approach to ai development and validation. J. Am. Med. Inform. Assoc. **32**(3), 589–594 (2025)
21. Kehlet, S.N., et al.: Age-related collagen turnover of the interstitial matrix and basement membrane: implications of age-and sex-dependent remodeling of the extracellular matrix. PLoS ONE **13**(3), e0194458 (2018)
22. Kotoku, J., et al.: Causal relations of health indices inferred statistically using the directlingam algorithm from big data of osaka prefecture health checkups. PLoS ONE **15**(12), e0243229 (2020)
23. Lam, W.Y., Andrews, B., Ramsey, J.: Greedy relaxations of the sparsest permutation algorithm. In The 38th Conference on Uncertainty in Artificial Intelligence (2022)
24. Le, T.D., et al.: Inferring microRNA-mRNA causal regulatory relationships from expression data. Bioinformatics **29**(6), 765–771 (2013)
25. Li, H., Pin, S., Zeng, Z., Wang, M.M., Andreasson, K.A., McCullough, L.D.: Sex differences in cell death. Ann. Neurol. **58**(2), 317–321 (2005)
26. Li, J., Wang, Z.J.: Controlling the false discovery rate of the association/causality structure learned with the PC algorithm. J. Mach. Learn. Res. **10**, 475–514 (2009)
27. Maeda, T.N., Shimizu, S.: RCD: repetitive causal discovery of linear non-gaussian acyclic models with latent confounders. In: International Conference on Artificial Intelligence and Statistics (2020)
28. Marino, G.E., Weeraratna, A.T.: A glitch in the matrix: age-dependent changes in the extracellular matrix facilitate common sites of metastasis. Aging Cancer **1**(1–4), 19–29 (2020)
29. Martínez-Jiménez, F., et al.: A compendium of mutational cancer driver genes. Nat. Rev. Cancer **20**(10), 555–572 (2020)
30. Milacic, M., et al.: The reactome pathway knowledgebase 2024. Nucleic Acids Res. **52**(D1), D672–D678 (2024)
31. Morsi, R.Z., Hage-Sleiman, R., Kobeissy, H., Dbaibo, G.: Noxa: role in cancer pathogenesis and treatment. Curr. Cancer Drug Targets **18**(10), 914–928 (2018)
32. Pearl, J.: Causality. Cambridge University Press (2009)
33. Prosperi, M., et al.: Causal inference and counterfactual prediction in machine learning for actionable healthcare. Nat. Mach. Intell. **2**(7), 369–375 (2020)
34. Ramos, R.H., Simao, A., Mousavi, M.R.: Causal model discovery in cancer guided by cellular pathways. In: International Conference on Computational Methods in Systems Biology, pp. 174–195. Springer (2024)
35. Raskutti, G., Uhler, C.: Learning directed acyclic graphs based on sparsest permutations. Stat (2018)
36. Rehak, J., Falkenstein, A., Doehner, F., Beyerer, J.: Metrics for the evaluation of learned causal graphs based on ground truth. In: ML4CPS–Machine Learning for Cyber-Physical Systems. UB HSU (2024)
37. Schwarz, G.: Estimating the dimension of a model. Ann. Stat. **6**(2), 461–464 (1978)
38. Shimizu, S., et al.: Directlingam: a direct method for learning a linear non-gaussian structural equation model. J. Mach. Learn. (2011)
39. Silander, T., Myllymaki, P.: A simple approach for finding the globally optimal Bayesian network structure. In: Proceedings of the Twenty-Second Conference on Uncertainty in Artificial Intelligence (2006)
40. Song, Q., Chen, P., Liu, X.M.: The role of cigarette smoke-induced pulmonary vascular endothelial cell apoptosis in COPD. Respir. Res. **22**(1), 39 (2021)

41. Spirtes, P., Glymour, C.N., Scheines, R., Heckerman, D.: Causation, Prediction, and Search. MIT Press (2000)
42. Spirtes, P., Meek, C., Richardson, T.: Causal inference in the presence of latent variables and selection bias. In: Proceedings of the Eleventh Conference on Uncertainty in Artificial Intelligence, Montreal, Quebec, Canada, 18–20 August 1995, pp. 499–506. Morgan Kaufmann (1995)
43. Statzer, C., Park, J.Y.C., Ewald, C.Y.: Extracellular matrix dynamics as an emerging yet understudied hallmark of aging and longevity. Aging Dis. **14**(3), 670 (2023)
44. Tsamardinos, I., Brown, L.E., Aliferis, C.F.: The max-min hill-climbing Bayesian network structure learning algorithm. Mach. Learn. **65**(1), 31–78 (2006)
45. Wilson, D.R., Martinez, T.R.: Improved heterogeneous distance functions. J. Artif. Intell. Res. **6**, 1–34 (1997)
46. Yang, Y., et al.: Protein sumoylation modification and its associations with disease. Open Biol. **7**(10) (2017)
47. Yuan, C., Malone, B.: Learning optimal Bayesian networks: a shortest path perspective. J. Artif. Intell. Res. (2013)
48. Zhang, K., Peters, J., Janzing, D., Schölkopf, B.: Kernel-based conditional independence test and application in causal discovery. In: Proceedings of the 27th Conference on Uncertainty in Artificial Intelligence (UAI 2011), pp. 804–813. AUAI Press (2011)
49. Zheng, X., Wang, L., Zhang, Z., Tang, H.: The emerging roles of sumoylation in pulmonary diseases. Mol. Med. **29**(1), 119 (2023)
50. Zhou, H., et al.: Cigarette smoke extract stimulates bronchial epithelial cells to undergo a sumoylation turnover. BMC Pulm. Med. **20**(1), 276 (2020)

Graph Learning Models for Temporal Gene Expression Prediction and the Role of Interactions Topology

Alessandro Dipalma(✉), Alessio Micheli, Paolo Milazzo, Francesco Simonetti, and Domenico Tortorella

Department of Computer Science, University of Pisa, Largo B. Pontecorvo 3, 56127 Pisa, Italy
alessandro.dipalma@phd.unipi.it

Abstract. Predicting gene expression dynamics is challenging due to the complex regulatory interactions within high-dimensional datasets. We evaluate predictive models that integrate temporal patterns with gene–gene networks, comparing a state-of-the-art approach based on Protein-Protein Interaction (PPI) networks from STRING with models utilizing data-driven network inference. Our results show that inferred networks can enhance accuracy over static biological priors. However, simpler models treating genes independently often achieve comparable performance. This suggests that for the considered datasets, the added complexity of explicit gene–gene interactions does not always translate into superior predictive power, opening to further investigations on the most effective ways to represent and leverage biological connectivity in forecasting tasks.

Keywords: Temporal gene expression · Graph Neural Networks · PPI networks

1 Introduction

Understanding how gene activity [9] evolves over time is essential for studying cellular processes, disease mechanisms and responses to external stimuli. High-throughput transcriptomic technologies allow measuring the expression levels of thousands of genes across multiple time points, producing high-dimensional temporal data that reflect the dynamic state of biological systems.

Since genes interact through complex regulatory mechanisms their activity cannot be accurately modeled independently. Biological interaction networks provide a natural relational structure where nodes represent genes and edges describe functional dependencies [21].

The problem of inferring functional dependencies from longitudinal data is widely studied in the context of computational systems biology. Often, it has been addressed through approaches aiming at inferring gene regulatory networks

P. T. Monteiro (Ed.): CMSB 2026, LNBI 16678, pp. 334–350, 2027.
https://doi.org/10.1007/978-3-032-30870-2_16

[1,5,7,11,16], typically expressed as Boolean Networks. The inferred networks can then be analyzed in order to identify relevant attractors [10], controllers [23] and to investigate properties such as robustness [14,20], causality [4] and gene importance [18]. Moreover, Boolean network simulation techniques [17] allow predicting long-term behaviors and investigating the effects of perturbations due to mutations or gene knock-out.

The interplay between the description of gene interaction in terms of networks and the availability of Temporal Gene Expression Datasets (TGED) can be captured by a representation of the system in terms of temporal signals evolving on graphs. Recent advances in spatio-temporal deep learning have enabled predictive modeling on such structured data. Architectures combining Graph Neural Networks (GNNs) [2] and Recurrent Neural Networks (RNNs) [15] have shown promising results by jointly learning relational representations and temporal dynamics. These approaches typically rely on prior biological knowledge bases [3], such as STRING [22], to define gene interaction networks. However, curated biological networks are designed to capture general-purpose interactions and are not tailored to specific experimental conditions. As a result, they may include weak or noisy connections that limit predictive performance. This limitation is particularly relevant when modeling gene expression dynamics under condition-specific or anomalous biological states.

Figure 1 provides an overview of the considered task. Given a sequence of gene expression measurements, interaction information is integrated to model dependencies among genes. The model then learns temporal patterns from observations up to time t in order to predict gene expression values at time $t+1$.

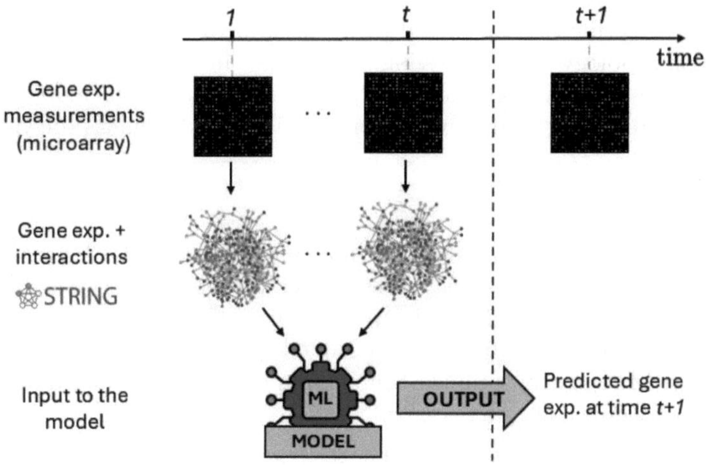

Fig. 1. Gene expression measurements (e.g., from microarray data) are combined with gene interaction information, which can be derived from prior knowledge sources such as STRING. The resulting representations are used as input to the model, which learns temporal dependencies from observations up to time t and predicts gene expression values at time $t+1$.

In this work, we investigate whether constructing graph topologies directly from gene expression signals can provide more informative relational structures for forecasting tasks. We hypothesize that data-driven graph construction better captures statistical dependencies among genes, leading to improved representation learning and prediction accuracy.

Experimental results on multiple gene expression datasets reveal two main findings. First, models leveraging data-driven graph construction strategies consistently outperform those relying on curated biological networks, confirming that dataset-specific topologies provide more informative relational structures for prediction. Second, we observe an additional performance improvement when replacing graph-based relational learning with independent gene representations generated through simple feedforward networks.

This second result indicates that, for the considered datasets, learning high-quality feature representations can be more beneficial than explicitly modeling gene interactions. Overall, these findings suggest that the advantages of graph-based inductive biases strongly depend on the quality and task-relevance of the underlying graph structure.

2 Methods

This section describes the methodological framework adopted to evaluate predictive models for temporal gene expression forecasting. We first introduce the datasets used in the study and formally define the prediction task. We then present the graph construction strategies, distinguishing between knowledge-based and data-driven approaches.

Next, we describe the considered model architectures, designed to assess the role of graph topology and embedding mechanisms in capturing spatio-temporal dependencies. Finally, we outline the experimental protocol, including data representation, forecasting setup, evaluation metrics, and training procedures.

2.1 Datasets

Two publicly available temporal gene expression datasets (TGED) were selected from established repositories, including ArrayExpress and the Gene Expression Omnibus. Both provide time-resolved transcriptomic measurements capturing the dynamics of gene activity across multiple biological conditions, with a sufficient number of regularly sampled time points that allow proper data splitting for the model validation (see Sect. 2.5).

DS1-BC *(E-TABM-631)* [8]. This dataset contains genome-wide gene expression profiles of the hormone-responsive ZR-75-1 human breast cancer cell line under estrogen stimulation. After hormone deprivation, cells were exposed to 17β-estradiol and expression levels were measured at 13 time points over 32 h, enabling the observation of both early signaling events and sustained transcriptional responses. Gene expression was quantified using Illumina WG-6 microarrays. The dataset was released in preprocessed form, including normalization across arrays, log-transformation, and removal of low-confidence probes. The final dataset comprises 9,593 genes and exhibits a relatively broad dynamic range due to log-ratio normalization.

DS2-LK *(GSE270332)* [19]. This dataset measures gene expression dynamics of K562 human leukemia cells during cell-cycle progression. Cells were synchronized and RNA samples were collected at 24 time points spanning approximately one complete cell cycle. Expression levels were obtained using high-throughput RNA sequencing (RNA-seq) on the Illumina HiSeq platform. The released dataset includes STRIPE-corrected measurements, which remove technical artifacts and provide stable expression estimates within a consistent dynamic range. Approximately 13,000 genes are included in the processed dataset, offering a comprehensive view of transcriptional regulation during cell division.

2.2 Problem Formulation

We consider the task of predicting future gene expression levels across all genes given past observations. Formally, a TGED of length T over the genes set V is made up of individual genes' expression time series $x^{(i)}$, with $i \in \{1, ..., |V|\}$. Each gene expression time series $x^{(i)}$ is made up of the individual gene expression time points $x_t^{(i)} \in \mathbb{R}$, with $t \in \{1, \ldots, T\}$.

Given a TGED, we define the temporal graph $\{G_t\}_{t=1}^{T}$, where each time point is the graph $G_t = (V, E, X_t)$. Here, V is the set of genes, E represents gene–gene interactions, and $X_t \in \mathbb{R}^{|V|}$ denotes node features (gene expression values) observed at time t. Note that the graph topology is fixed, hence for every two snapshots $G_{t_1} = (V_1, E_1, X_{t_1})$ and $G_{t_2} = (V_2, E_2, X_{t_2})$ in the same sequence, it holds $V_1 = V_2$ and $E_1 = E_2$.

Given past observations up to time t, the objective is to predict gene expression values at the next time step:

$$(G_1, \ldots, G_t) \rightarrow G_{t+1}.$$

2.3 Graph Construction

For both datasets, we construct two types of graphs: (1) knowledge-based graphs, constructed retrieving gene-gene interactions from STRING [22], and (2) data-driven graphs where gene interactions edges are obtained computing various statistical metrics directly on the temporal gene expression dataset.

STRING Graphs Construction. After mapping gene identifiers from the filtered gene sets (Sect. 3.1) to STRING identifiers, all direct interactions among the genes in the datasets were retrieved using the `experiments` and `database` evidence channels. To analyze the effect of network density, two confidence thresholds from the STRING database were considered: 0.4 and 0.7. In STRING, the confidence score reflects the strength and reliability of the evidence supporting a protein–protein interaction, integrating sources such as experimental data, curated databases, co-expression, and computational predictions. A threshold of 0.4 (medium confidence) includes a broader set of interactions, capturing more potential biological relationships, but also incorporating less strongly supported links. In contrast, a threshold of 0.7 (high confidence) retains only the most reliable interactions, resulting in a more stringent and biologically robust network. Importantly, the set of nodes (genes) remains the same across thresholds, while the number of edges varies depending on the selected confidence level, directly affecting network density.

Figure 2 illustrates the overall pipeline for STRING-based graph construction. Table 1 reports the resulting graph sizes. Lower thresholds produce denser networks, while stricter confidence levels substantially reduce the number of retained interactions.

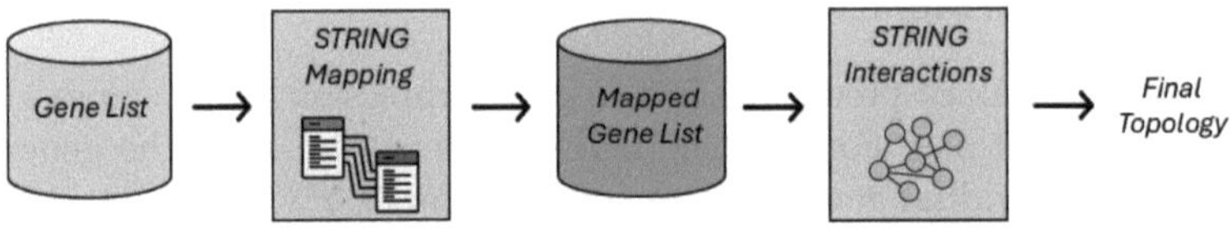

Fig. 2. Pipeline for STRING-based graph construction. The gene symbols on the GSE data are resolved via the STRING mapping APIs. For successfully mapped genes, all the direct interactions are retrieved. The set of interactions constitutes the edges of the training graph.

Table 1. Graph sizes obtained from STRING interactions at different confidence thresholds

Dataset	Threshold	Nodes	Edges
DS1-BC	0.4	848	4819
DS1-BC	0.7	848	1485
DS2-LK	0.4	1464	8148
DS2-LK	0.7	1464	2818

Data-Driven Graphs Construction. For each pair of time series $(x^{(i)}, x^{(j)})$, a similarity score $s_{ij} = M(x^{(i)}, x^{(j)})$ is computed using a chosen metric M that quantifies temporal association. Pairs are then ranked by the M and we retain the top-k scoring pairs for each gene. The retained pairs constitute the set of edges $E_{M,k}$ of the data-driven graph $G_{M,k} = (V, E_{M,k})$.

We consider several similarity metrics to construct data-driven graphs:

- **[CORR] Pearson correlation:** measures linear dependence between two gene expression profiles, assigning higher similarity to genes with similar temporal trends.
- **[CORR W.] Correlation as edge weights:** the Pearson correlation is additionally used as the weight of the retained connections, resulting in a sparse weighted adjacency matrix where edge weights reflect the strength of temporal co-expression.
- **[CORR CR.] Cross-correlation:** captures time-lagged dependencies by considering the maximum correlation between two signals over a range of temporal shifts.
- **[PBS] Phase-Based Synchronization:** measures similarity based on the consistency of phase differences between gene expression signals, capturing synchronized oscillatory behavior over time [25].
- **[DTF] Directed Transfer Function:** estimates directed interactions between genes using a multivariate autoregressive model, where similarity reflects the strength of influence from one gene to another across frequencies [24].
- **[HYBRID] Hybrid Similarity:** combines the best-performing data-driven similarity metric (selected among those above) with network topology from the STRING graph, weighting expression-based similarity according to the topological proximity between genes.

Edge counts are tuned to control graph sparsity and systematically assess its effect on embedding quality and prediction performance. All graph construction is performed only on training data to avoid information leakage from validation or test sets.

2.4 Model Architectures

To evaluate the impact of graph topology and embedding strategies on forecasting performance, we build upon a state-of-art spatio-temporal architecture, NeTOIF [12], that we use as reference model. Starting from this baseline, we design simplified variants with progressively reduced structural inductive bias in order to isolate the contribution of graph-based relational learning.

NeTOIF (GNN + BiLSTM). NeTOIF (Network-based approach for Temporal Omics data Imputation and Forecasting) is a spatio-temporal framework that jointly models structural dependencies among genes and their temporal evolution. At each time step, gene expression values are mapped onto a gene interaction graph where nodes represent genes and edges encode biological relationships. Formally, let $G_t = (V, E, X_t)$ be the graph at time step t, where X_t denotes the node features. A Graph Convolutional Network (GCN) [13] is applied independently at each time step to extract node embeddings by aggregating information from neighboring genes. For each node $i \in V$, this can be written as

$$h_t^{(i)} = \text{GNN}\left(x_t^{(i)}, \{x_t^{(j)} : j \in \mathcal{N}(i)\}\right),$$

where $\mathcal{N}(i)$ denotes the neighbors of node i in the interaction graph.

Through this message-passing mechanism, each embedding captures both individual gene activity and contextual information from interacting genes. The learned embeddings are combined with the original input features through a skip connection controlled by a weighting parameter α:

$$\tilde{h}_t^{(i)} = \alpha h_t^{(i)} + (1 - \alpha)x_t^{(i)}.$$

The resulting representations are sequentially processed by a Bidirectional Long Short-Term Memory (BiLSTM) network, which models temporal dependencies in both forward and backward directions:

$$H = \text{BiLSTM}\left(\tilde{H}_1, \tilde{H}_2, \ldots, \tilde{H}_T\right),$$

where $\tilde{H}_t$ denotes the matrix collecting the representations of all nodes at time step t. The temporal output is then used to forecast gene expression values at the next time step.

MLP-NeTOIF. To assess the importance of graph-based relational learning, we replace the GCN encoder with a node-wise MultiLayer Perceptron (MLP), while keeping the temporal module unchanged. For each node i at time t, embeddings are computed independently as

$$h_t^{(i)} = \text{MLP}(x_t^{(i)}),$$

without message passing or topological aggregation.

As in NeTOIF, a skip connection controlled by α combines learned embeddings with projected input features. The resulting temporal representations are then processed by the same BiLSTM module used in the reference architecture.

BLSTM (Temporal Baseline). Finally, we consider a purely temporal baseline that completely removes the embedding stage. Linearly transformed gene expression values are directly provided to a BiLSTM, which is solely responsible for modeling temporal dynamics and producing predictions. This configuration allows us to isolate the contribution of embedding mechanisms and structural inductive biases. Figure 3 highlights the key architectural differences: NeTOIF employs graph-based message passing to generate node embeddings, MLP-NeTOIF relies on independent node-wise embeddings without relational aggregation, and BLSTM operates directly on raw temporal signals without any embedding stage.

2.5 Experimental Setup

This section describes the experimental framework adopted to evaluate the proposed models for gene expression forecasting. We first define the data splitting strategy and the sliding-window forecasting protocol designed to preserve temporal dependencies. Then, we present the model configurations and the evaluation procedure used to ensure a fair and reproducible comparison across methods

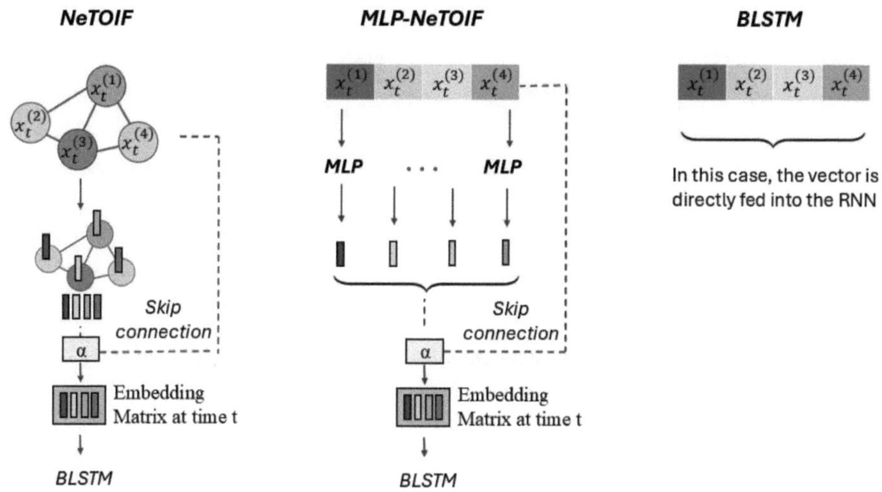

Fig. 3. High-level architectural comparison. Each model receives gene expression values at time step t as input.

Data Splitting and Forecasting Protocol. Due to the temporal nature of gene expression data, random splits would violate causality. Therefore, datasets are divided into contiguous temporal segments, with earlier observations used for training and the most recent windows reserved for validation and testing.

Samples are generated using a sliding-window forecasting protocol. Let $\{G_t\}_{t=1}^{T}$ denote the temporal graph sequence. Given a window length n, the model receives n consecutive graphs as input to predict the next one:

$$(G_t, G_{t+1}, \ldots, G_{t+n-1}) \rightarrow G_{t+n}.$$

The window is then shifted forward by one time step to produce overlapping samples, maximizing the number of training instances while preserving temporal order. For example, with $n = 3$, the first sample is

$$(G_1, G_2) \rightarrow G_3$$

and the next is

$$(G_2, G_3) \rightarrow G_4,$$

and so on. Figure 4 illustrates the sliding-window mechanism for the case $n = 3$.

Evaluation Protocol. All model variants in Sect. 2.4 are evaluated under the same protocol. NeTOIF is tested on STRING topology, with varying confidence threshold and all data-driven graph variants, with multiple graph densities (top-k edges). BLSTM and MLP-NeTOIF are evaluated using only gene expression time series, as they are topology agnostic models. Predictive performance is

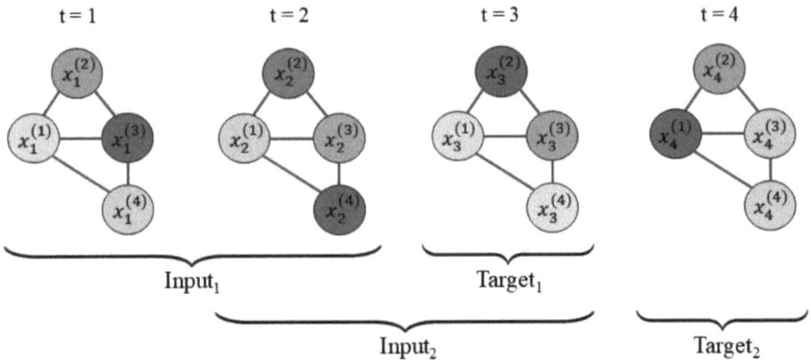

Fig. 4. Sliding-window forecasting protocol with window length $n = 3$. Consecutive temporal graphs are used to predict the next time step.

evaluated using the Mean Squared Error (MSE), computed across all genes and predicted time steps.

All models are trained using the same optimization strategy to ensure a fair comparison. Hyperparameters are selected via grid search on the validation set over model-specific configurations, including hidden layers' dimensions (16 to 256 units), number of layers, dropout (0.1–0.3), learning rate ($5{\cdot}10^{-4}$–$5{\cdot}10^{-3}$), epochs (500–1000), batch size (0–10), and weight decay (10^{-5}–10^{-3}). For architectures including the α parameter, multiple configurations are evaluated. The complete list of hyperparameters for all the models is provided in Appendix A1. Each experiment is repeated seven times with different random seeds, and the mean and standard deviation of the MSE are reported.

3 Results

This section presents the experimental evaluation of the proposed models across two gene expression datasets (DS1-BC and DS2-LK). We compare the three architectures presented in Sect. 3: (i) NeTOIF, combining GNN-based embeddings with temporal modeling; (ii) MLP-NeTOIF, a node-wise embedding variant without message passing; and (iii) a purely temporal BiLSTM baseline.

3.1 Global Performance

This section reports the predictive performance of the considered architectures following the experimental protocol described in Sect. 2.5. We evaluate NeTOIF under different graph construction strategies and sparsity levels and compare it against MLP-NeTOIF and the purely temporal BLSTM baseline. Rather than detailing each dataset separately, results are presented jointly to highlight consistent trends and dataset-specific differences across experimental settings. Note that due to different value ranges and distributions, likely arising from distinct preprocessing and normalization procedures, the MSE scores obtained on the two datasets have different magnitudes.

Tables 2 and 4 report NeTOIF performance graph topology construction strategies and sparsity levels for the two datasets. Columns indicate the number of retained edges (top-k), which controls graph sparsity. Tables 3 and 5 compare STRING-based NeTOIF with non-graph baselines.

Table 2. NeTOIF performance on DS1-BC with different data-driven graph construction strategies and sparsity levels. Columns report the number of retained edges (top-k). Values indicate MSE (mean ± std over test timesteps).

Corr Metric	#Edges			
	1250	2500	5000	7500
CORR	.0479 ± .0018	.0471 ± .0019	.0470 ± .0001	.0472 ± .0005
CORR W.	.0474 ± .0012	.0481 ± .0012	.0466 ± .0004	.0472 ± .0005
CORR CR.	.0469 ± .0005	**.0462 ± .0009**	.0470 ± .0012	.0468 ± .0012
PBS	.0482 ± .0011	.0470 ± .0007	.0474 ± .0009	.0477 ± .0004
DTF	.0472 ± .0005	.0468 ± .0007	.0464 ± .0008	.0466 ± .0005
HYBRID	.0475 ± .0005	.0481 ± .0015	.0473 ± .0004	.0470 ± .0008

Table 3. Comparison between STRING-based NeTOIF and non-graph baselines on DS1-BC. Statistical significance ($^{*}p < 0.05$, $^{**}p < 0.01$, $^{***}p < 0.001$) is computed via t-test against best performing model.

Model	Edges	MSE (mean ± std)
NeTOIF (STRING $\geq$ 0.4)	4819	.0501 ± .0007***
NeTOIF (STRING $\geq$ 0.7)	1485	.0534 ± .0002***
NeTOIF (Best Topology)	2500	.0462 ± .0009**
MLP-NeTOIF	–	**.0449 ± .0010**
BLSTM	–	.0576 ± .0004***

Results across DS1-BC and DS2-LK provide a coherent picture of the respective roles of data-driven graphs, embedding transformations, and message passing. Data-driven graphs consistently improve performance compared to the original STRING topology. Differences among graph construction strategies are minimal and no single method dominates across sparsity levels, indicating that improvements mainly derive from removing weak or noisy interactions rather than from specific connectivity patterns.

Comparisons with the purely temporal BLSTM baseline show that incorporating a learned embedding stage is generally beneficial. In DS1-BC, all NeTOIF variants outperform BLSTM. In DS2-LK, improvements depend on graph quality, as only higher-confidence STRING interactions outperform the temporal

Table 4. NeTOIF performance on DS2-LK with different data-driven graph construction strategies and sparsity levels. Columns report the number of retained edges (top-k). Values indicate MSE (mean ± std over test timesteps).

Corr Metric	#Edges			
	2000	4000	8000	10000
CORR	.3969 ± .0267	.3971 ± .0277	.4026 ± .0214	.3961 ± .0180
CORR W.	.4012 ± .0252	.3985 ± .0265	.4032 ± .0212	.4012 ± .0199
CORR CR.	.4066 ± .0204	.3939 ± .0204	.3950 ± .0252	.3945 ± .0265
PBS	.4102 ± .0017	.4141 ± .0088	.4072 ± .0010	.4127 ± .0227
DTF	.3954 ± .0262	**.3924 ± .0259**	.3962 ± .0275	.3946 ± .0281
HYBRID	.4133 ± .0073	.4256 ± .0084	.4101 ± .0083	.4232 ± .0442

Table 5. Comparison between STRING-based NeTOIF and non-graph baselines on DS2-LK. Statistical significance ($^{*}p < 0.05$, $^{**}p < 0.01$, $^{***}p < 0.001$) is computed via t-test against best performing model.

Model	Edges	MSE (mean ± std)
NeTOIF (STRING ≥ 0.4)	8148	$.425 \pm .001^{**}$
NeTOIF (STRING ≥ 0.7)	2818	$.412 \pm .036^{*}$
NeTOIF (Best Topology)	4000	$.392 \pm .026^{*}$
MLP-NeTOIF	–	**.377 ± .018**
BLSTM	–	$.420 \pm .028^{*}$

baseline. Despite varying graph topologies, NeTOIF produces similar performance across configurations, suggesting that message passing is not the primary driver of predictive accuracy. This is confirmed by the strong results of MLP-NeTOIF, which removes graph connectivity and instead relies on node-wise MLP embeddings. MLP-NeTOIF achieves the best performance on both datasets, indicating that predictive power mainly arises from embedding transformations rather than structural propagation.

Graph structure has been shown to often act as a denoising mechanism, with its contribution depending on the quality of node representations. Recent studies, such as [6], indicate that when high-quality embeddings are available, graph convolutions provide limited additional gain, and that graph structure learning is particularly beneficial in low-label or low-signal regimes.

3.2 Supplementary Analyses

To provide additional evidence supporting the global results, we perform a set of complementary analyses aimed at better understanding model behavior and the role of graph structure.

Performance Stratification over Common Temporal Expression Patterns. For each gene, we compute three temporal descriptors: monotonicity, variability, and oscillation. These labels are not used as input features but serve to construct groups of nodes sharing similar temporal dynamics, allowing performance comparisons across different gene behaviors.

Let $x^{(i)} = (x_1^{(i)}, \ldots, x_T^{(i)})$ denote the temporal expression profile of gene i. The descriptors are defined as:

$$\text{Monotonicity:} \quad \mathcal{M}_i = \rho_s(x^{(i)}), (1, \ldots, T)) \tag{1}$$

$$\text{Variability:} \quad \mathcal{V}_i = \frac{\text{Var}(x^{(i)})}{\max(x^{(i)}) - \min(x^{(i)})} \tag{2}$$

$$\text{Oscillation:} \quad \mathcal{O}_i = \#\text{sign changes} \cdot \text{Var}(\Delta x^{(i)}) \tag{3}$$

where ρ_s is the Spearman rank correlation coefficient. The term $\Delta x_t^{(i)} = x_{t+1}^{(i)} - x_t^{(i)}$ represents the first-order temporal differences, while #sign changes counts the number of sign reversals between consecutive differences. Var(·) denotes the variance. The descriptor continuous values are discretized into three balanced categories (low, medium, high) for downstream analysis.

This stratification is introduced to verify whether specific architectures perform better on particular temporal patterns. For instance, one might expect simpler models such as MLP-NeTOIF to perform better on nearly flat or weakly varying expression profiles, while graph-based models could benefit more dynamic patterns. However, results presented in Fig. 5 show that this is not the case. Across all temporal categories performance differences among architectures preserve the same relative ranking observed in the global evaluation. No architecture exhibits specialized advantages or weaknesses for specific temporal behaviors. This indicates that performance differences are driven by general modeling capacity rather than sensitivity to particular gene dynamics.

Graph Homophily and Structural Effects. The same temporal labels are further used to assess graph structural properties through homophily analysis, measuring the tendency of connected nodes to exhibit similar temporal behaviors. This analysis serves two purposes: (i) validating the effect of data-driven graph structures, and (ii) verifying whether architectural performance aligns with known properties of Graph Neural Networks.

Results presented in Table 6 confirm that data-driven graphs exhibit consistently higher homophily than the original STRING networks. Moreover, GNN-based architectures show improved performance on graphs with stronger homophilic structure, supporting the interpretation that constructing edges from temporal expression improves relational coherence while removing noisy interactions. These results indicate that data-driven graphs improve predictive performance, which is accompanied by an increase in graph homophily. As known from the literature, GNNs generally perform better on graphs with higher homophily, where structural coherence facilitates effective information aggregation.

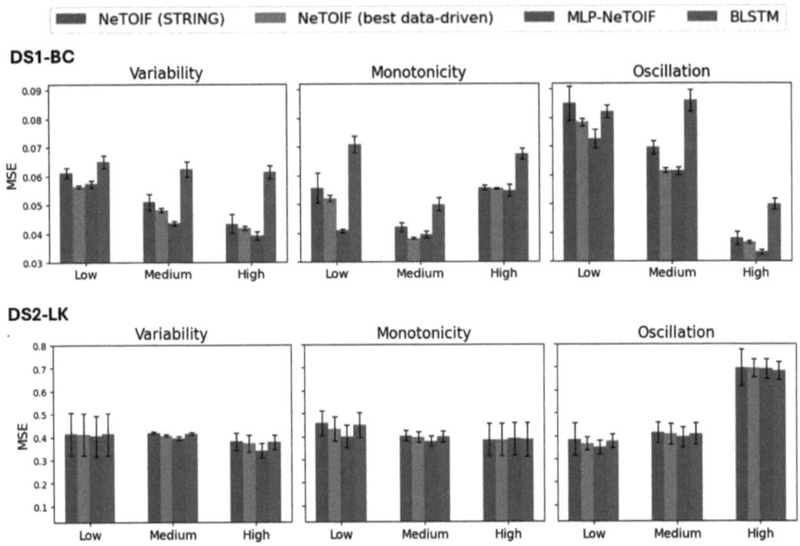

Fig. 5. The first row shows results on the DS1-BC dataset, while the second row shows DS2-LK. In both cases, the plots report the Mean Squared Error (MSE) across node feature classes for the features Variability, Monotonicity, and Oscillation.

Table 6. Homophily values w.r.t. common temporal gene expression patterns, measured on STRING and the best data driven graphs for each dataset.

Dataset	Graph Type	Variability	Monotonicity	Oscillation
DS1-BC	STRING	0.3932	0.3826	0.5032
	Best data-driven	0.4532	0.4611	0.6295
DS2-LK	STRING	0.4594	0.3388	0.5112
	Best data-driven	0.5149	0.6112	0.8112

3.3 Learnable Edge Weights Analysis

To assess the contribution of message passing, we run experimental training where each edge in the network has a learnable weight. Intuitively, the learning process should associate useless and noisy edges with low weights, while edges with predictive power should retain a higher magnitude. We train NeTOIF over the best data-driven topology initializing the fully learnable edge weights to 0.5 and optimized end-to-end. For both datasets (DS1-BC and DS2-LK), we analyze the evolution of the L2 norm of the edge weight matrix during training and the final distribution of the learned edge weights.

Figures 6a and 6b show the results for the two datasets. In both cases, the L2 norm consistently decreases during training, indicating a progressive reduction in the strength of message passing. At convergence, the learned edge weights are strongly concentrated around zero. These findings suggest that, when allowed full

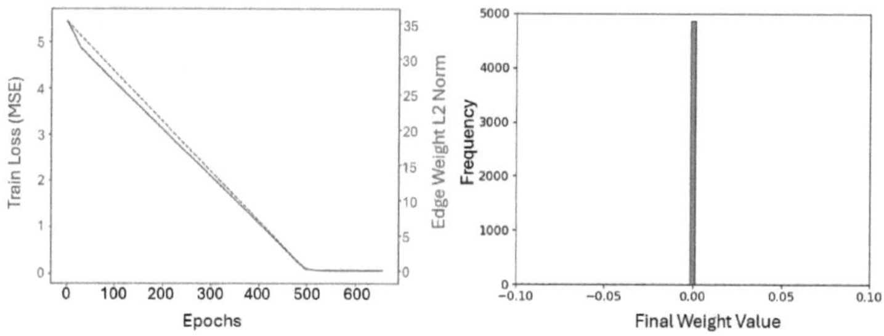

(a) DS2-LK: (left) evolution of the L_2 norm of the learnable edge weight matrix during training; (right) final distribution of the learned edge weights, which appear as a single stripe due to the very narrow value range (−0.0006 to 0.0006).

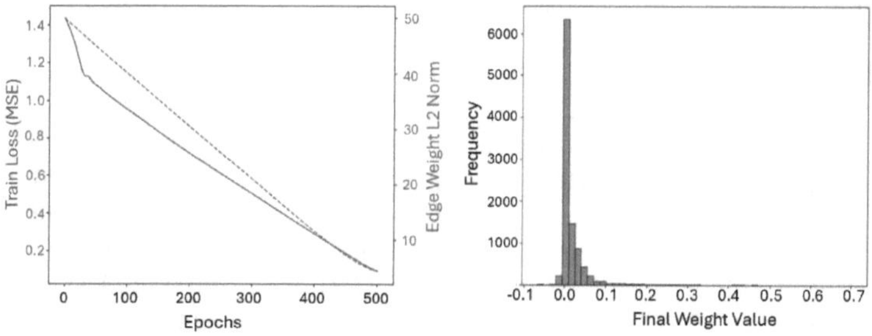

(b) DS2-LK: (left) evolution of the L_2 norm of the learnable edge weight matrix during training; (right) final distribution of the learned edge weights.

Fig. 6. NeTOIF (best data-driven) on DS2-LK. Comparison of the evolution of the L_2 norm of the learnable edge weight matrix during training and the final distribution of the learned edge weights across two runs. The first subfigure highlights the extremely narrow value range of the learned weights.

flexibility, the model suppresses graph propagation and relies primarily on node-level feature transformations (i.e., an MLP-like mechanism). This is a further indication that the graph structure plays a limited role in the final predictive performance, while node features are the main source of information.

4 Conclusions and Future Work

This study investigated the prediction of temporal gene expression dynamics through spatio-temporal learning models that exploit gene interaction networks. Results show that constructing dataset-specific graph topologies leads to consistent improvements over standard knowledge-based networks. Graphs derived from gene expression data better capture task-relevant relationships, allowing models to achieve higher forecasting accuracy. An additional key finding is that complex graph-based embedding mechanisms are not always necessary. Models generating independent node-wise embeddings often achieve comparable or superior performance to architectures that explicitly propagate information across gene interaction networks. This suggests that, for the considered datasets, predictive information is largely encoded in gene-specific temporal patterns rather than in extensive relational dependencies.

Importantly, these findings do not imply that biological interaction networks are ineffective in general. Knowledge-based resources such as STRING provide valuable prior information, but their broad and general-purpose nature may introduce noisy or weakly relevant connections for specific experimental settings. Our results suggest that tailoring interaction topologies to the dataset or biological context could further enhance the effectiveness of graph-based models.

Overall, the study highlights that the design of graph topology and embedding strategies plays a more critical role than model complexity alone. These findings encourage careful evaluation of when structured relational modeling is most beneficial for temporal gene expression prediction (Table 7).

Acknowledgments. Research partly supported by: Project DEEP-GRAPH, funded by the Italian Ministry of University and Research (MUR) PRIN 2022 (project code: 2022YLRBTT, CUP: I53C24002440006); Project PAN-HUB, funded by the Italian Ministry of Health (POS 2014–2020, project ID: T4-AN-07, CUP: I53C22001300001). Moreover, by following two projects funded by the EU under the NextGeneration-EU programme PNRR-M4C2-Investimento 1.3, Partenariato Esteso [PE00000013], "FAIR-Future Artificial Intelligence Research"-Spoke 1 "Human-centered AI"; and PNRR-M4C2-Investimento 1.5, Ecosistema dell'Innovazione [ECS00000017], "THE-Tuscany Health Ecosystem"-CUP [I53C22000780001]-Spoke 6 "Precision medicine & personalized healthcare".

Appendix

A1. Hyperparameters Search Spaces

Table 7. Grid searches hyperparameters.

Hyperparameter	applies to	values
GNN hidden dim	NeTOIF	16, 32, 64, 128, 256
GNN layers	NeTOIF	1, 2, 3
Node hidden dim	MLP-NeTOIF	16, 32, 64, 128, 256
RNN hidden dim	All	16, 32, 64, 128, 256
RNN layers	All	1, 2
Dropout	All	0.1, 0.2, 0.3
Learning rate	All	5e-4, 1e-3, 5e-3
Epochs	All	500, 750, 1000
Batch size	All	0, 5, 10
Alpha	NeTOIF, MLP-NeTOIF	0.1, 0.2, 0.3, 0.5
Weight decay	All	1e-5, 1e-4, 1e-3

References

1. Akutsu, T., Miyano, S., Kuhara, S.: Identification of genetic networks from a small number of gene expression patterns under the boolean network model. In: Biocomputing'99, pp. 17–28. World Scientific (1999)
2. Bacciu, D., Errica, F., Micheli, A., Podda, M.: A gentle introduction to deep learning for graphs. Neural Netw. **129**, 203–221 (2020). https://doi.org/10.1016/j.neunet.2020.06.006
3. Bajpai, A.K., et al.: Systematic comparison of the protein-protein interaction databases from a user's perspective. J. Biomed. Inform. **103**, 103380 (2020). https://doi.org/10.1016/j.jbi.2020.103380
4. Barbuti, R., Gori, R., Milazzo, P.: Encoding boolean networks into reaction systems for investigating causal dependencies in gene regulation. Theoret. Comput. Sci. **881**, 3–24 (2021)
5. Beneš, N., Brim, L., Huvar, O., Pastva, S., Šafránek, D.: Boolean network sketches: a unifying framework for logical model inference. Bioinformatics **39**(4), btad158 (2023)
6. Chen, X., Wang, S., et al.: Disentangling and re-evaluating the effectiveness of graph structure learning for GNNs. In: Proceedings of the AAAI Conference on Artificial Intelligence (2023). https://doi.org/10.1609/aaai.v37i1.25277
7. Chevalier, S., et al.: Data-driven inference of boolean networks from transcriptomes to predict cellular differentiation and reprogramming. NPJ Syst. Biol. Appl. **11**(1), 105 (2025)
8. Dimitrakopoulou, K., Dimitrakopoulos, G.N., Sgarbas, K.N., Bezerianos, A.: Tamoxifen integromics and personalized medicine: dynamic modular transformations underpinning response to tamoxifen in breast cancer treatment. Omics J. Integrat. Biol. **18**(1), 15–33 (2014)
9. Gibney, E.R., Nolan, C.M.: Epigenetics and gene expression. Proc. Nutr. Soc. **69**(1), 1–6 (2010). https://doi.org/10.1017/S002966510999153X
10. Hopfensitz, M., Müssel, C., Maucher, M., Kestler, H.A.: Attractors in boolean networks: a tutorial. Comput. Stat. **28**(1), 19–36 (2013)
11. Huynh-Thu, V.A., Geurts, P.: dyngenie3: dynamical genie3 for the inference of gene networks from time series expression data. Sci. Rep. **8**(1), 3384 (2018)
12. Jing, X., Zhou, Y., Shi, M.: Dynamic graph neural network learning for temporal omics data prediction. IEEE Access **10**, 116241–116252 (2022). https://doi.org/10.1109/ACCESS.2022.3218027. https://ieeexplore.ieee.org/abstract/document/9932591
13. Kipf, T.N., Welling, M.: Semi-supervised classification with graph convolutional networks. In: International Conference on Learning Representations (ICLR) (2017). https://doi.org/10.48550/arxiv.1609.02907
14. Li, F., Long, T., Lu, Y., Ouyang, Q., Tang, C.: The yeast cell-cycle network is robustly designed. Proc. Natl. Acad. Sci. **101**(14), 4781–4786 (2004)
15. Lipton, Z.C., Berkowitz, J., Elkan, C.: A critical review of recurrent neural networks for sequence learning. arXiv (2015). https://doi.org/10.48550/arxiv.1506.00019
16. Marku, M., Pancaldi, V.: From time-series transcriptomics to gene regulatory networks: a review on inference methods. PLoS Comput. Biol. **19**(8), e1011254 (2023)
17. Naldi, A., Hernandez, C., Abou-Jaoudé, W., Monteiro, P.T., Chaouiya, C., Thieffry, D.: Logical modeling and analysis of cellular regulatory networks with ginsim 3.0. Front. Physiol. **9**, 646 (2018)

18. Pham, G., Milazzo, P.: Gene importance assessment based on shapley values for boolean networks: validation and scalability analysis. In: International Symposium: From Data to Models and Back, pp. 19–33. Springer (2024)
19. Pourmorady, A.D., et al.: RNA-mediated symmetry breaking enables singular olfactory receptor choice. Nature **625**(7993), 181–188 (2024)
20. Rizk, A., Batt, G., Fages, F., Soliman, S.: A general computational method for robustness analysis with applications to synthetic gene networks. Bioinformatics **25**(12), i169–i178 (2009)
21. Rout, T., Mohapatra, A., Kar, M.: A systematic review of graph-based explorations of PPI networks: methods, resources, and best practices. Netw. Model. Anal. Health Inform. Bioinform. **13**(1), 29 (2024). https://doi.org/10.1007/s13721-024-00467-0
22. Szklarczyk, D., et al.: The string database in 2023: protein-protein association networks and functional enrichment analyses for any sequenced genome of interest. Nucleic Acids Res. **51**, D638–D646 (2022). https://doi.org/10.1093/nar/gkac1000
23. Thuillier, K., Baroukh, C., Bockmayr, A., Cottret, L., Paulevé, L., Siegel, A.: Learning boolean controls in regulated metabolic networks: a case-study. In: International Conference on Computational Methods in Systems Biology, pp. 159–180. Springer (2021)
24. ufvceiec: Eegraph: An open-source tool for EEG-based graph analysis (2024). https://github.com/ufvceiec/EEGRAPH. Accessed 01 Apr 2026
25. Zhang, Y.X., Jiang, M., Li, P., He, C.: Global analysis of phase locking in gene expression during cell cycle: the potential in network modelling. BMC Syst. Biol. **4**, 167 (2008). https://doi.org/10.1186/1752-0509-4-167

Multi-view Clustering of Transcriptomics and Methylomics Data Elucidates Glioma Molecular Stratification

Carolina Pé-Curto[1], Roberta Coletti[2], and Marta B. Lopes[1,2,3,4(✉)]

[1] NOVA School of Science and Technology (NOVA FCT), Universidade NOVA de Lisboa, 2829-516 Caparica, Portugal
marta.lopes@fct.unl.pt

[2] Center for Mathematics and Applications (NOVA Math), NOVA FCT, Universidade NOVA de Lisboa, 2829-516 Caparica, Portugal

[3] UNIDEMI, Department of Mechanical and Industrial Engineering, NOVA FCT, Universidade NOVA de Lisboa, 2829-516 Caparica, Portugal

[4] Laboratório Associado de Sistemas Inteligentes (LASI), 4800-058 Guimarães, Portugal

Abstract. Gliomas are the most common type of brain tumor in adults and are associated with poor prognosis and high mortality. Despite technological advances, their classification remains challenging in both clinical practice and research, highlighting the need for improved molecular subtyping to enhance diagnosis and treatment. In this study, we systematically evaluate the robustness of current glioma classification using a reproducible pipeline for unsupervised patient stratification. We apply multiple multi-view clustering methods, namely, CIMLR, intNMF, and moCluster, to cluster glioma patients based on transcriptomics and methylomics data. All methods consistently distinguished glioblastoma (GBM) from lower-grade gliomas, with survival analysis confirming poorer outcomes for GBM clusters, in line with clinical expectations. The best partition was obtained with CIMLR, closely aligning with the 2021 WHO classification of central nervous system tumors. In contrast, intNMF identified three clusters with distinct survival distributions, suggesting additional biological heterogeneity that warrants further investigation. To enhance robustness and better capture tumor complexity, we implemented consensus clustering to integrate results across methods. This integrative approach yielded well-defined groups with improved concordance to established glioma subtypes compared to individual methods. Notably, the consensus solution identified more clusters than the traditional classification, revealing deeper molecular characterization and providing a framework to refine glioma classification. Furthermore, we identified key molecular features supported by the literature, including both established and emerging biomarkers. Overall, our findings underscore the value of multi-omics integration and consensus clustering in refining glioma classification, supporting the discovery of novel biomarkers to improve diagnostics, prognostics, and patient outcomes.

Keywords: Glioma · Multi-omics · Multi-view clustering · Data integration · Consensus clustering

P. T. Monteiro (Ed.): CMSB 2026, LNBI 16678, pp. 351–372, 2027.
https://doi.org/10.1007/978-3-032-30870-2_17

1 Introduction

Glioma is the most common form of Central Nervous System (CNS) tumors [35, 39]. In recent years, its classification has seen major changes, ending in 2021 with the publication of an updated version of the World Health Organization (WHO) Classification of CNS Tumors. Currently, three adult-type diffuse gliomas are diagnosed: oligodendroglioma (IDH-mutant; 1p/19q codeletion), astrocytoma (IDH-mutant), and GBM (IDH-wild-type; presence of additional histological features and/or genetic parameters) [19, 22].

Despite advances in the molecular classification of gliomas, patient outcomes remain discouraging. High-grade gliomas, such as GBM, continue to exhibit median survival times of approximately 15 months. A significant challenge in the treatment of these tumors is their intratumoral heterogeneity, which contributes to therapeutic resistance and high relapse rates. This highlights the need for a more precise stratification of glioma patients, to identify molecularly distinct subgroups that may benefit from tailored therapeutic interventions.

The growing availability of omics information from cancer patients offers the means for a deeper understanding of the molecular mechanisms behind glioma heterogeneity. The joint integration of multi-omics data is essential to fully understand complex biological phenomena that cannot be explained by single-omics [3, 5, 38]. However, multi-omics data inherently exhibit heterogeneity and high dimensionality, characterized by a huge number of variables for a limited number of observations, which leads to statistical and computational challenges [4].

Multi-view integration methods, also referred to as multi-table or multi-modal methods, are promising for performing clustering based on multi-omics data, as they enable discerning shared patterns across different molecular layers and improve clustering performance. Given the high dimensionality of omics data, many algorithms focus on dimensionality reduction or similarity matrices for clustering [25]. Some known dimensionality reduction algorithms are based on matrix factorization, such as iCluster [29], iCluster+ [24] and moCluster [23], and Nonnegative Matrix Factorization (NMF) such as integrative Nonnegative Matrix Factorization (intNMF) [5]. On the other hand, Similarity Network Fusiom (SNF) [33], and Cancer Integration via Multikernal Learning (CIMLR) [28] are cases of clustering algorithms based on similarity matrices.

Since individual methods have distinct strengths and weaknesses, integrating their results is expected to produce a compensatory effect, enhancing overall performance [7, 36]. Consensus clustering, also known as ensemble clustering, aims to combine multiple partitions into a single, robust clustering solution [9, 10, 31]. To evaluate the consensus, two main strategies are commonly employed. The first is a median partition-based approach, which aims to identify a solution that maximizes similarity among the base clusterings using an appropriate distance measure. The second is a patient co-occurrence-based approach, which evaluates how consistently the same patient is assigned to the same cluster across different methods [1, 20].

Clustering algorithms are widely used in cancer research to identify disease subtypes. The moCluster method has been applied to datasets from colorectal cancer [23], breast cancer [6], murine liver, liver cancer and obesity [25]. TCGA glioma data has also been analyzed using intNMF [5,8] and CIMLR [28] methods to identify patient groups. However, these studies relied on earlier versions of the WHO CNS classification, which may limit the clinical relevance and accuracy of their findings under current diagnostic standards.

The objectives of this study were to develop a reproducible pipeline for unsupervised patient stratification based on multi-omics data, systematically evaluate multiple multi-view clustering methods and integrate their results through consensus clustering, and identify the key molecular features characterizing the resulting patient subgroups. To achieve this, transcriptomics and methylomics from The Cancer Genome Atlas (TCGA) were analyzed. The selected multi-view methods represent classes of methods which are dimension reduction-based (intNMF and moCluster), similarity/graph-based (CIMLR), and statistical-based (moCluster) methods. Each method simultaneously performs cluster identification and variable selection, which is critical to achieving the study objectives. Following cluster identification through the selected methods, a final consensus clustering assessment was performed to aggregate and find a general agreement between the algorithms, allowing for a more robust solution. In addition, a survival analysis was performed to elucidate the clinical relevance of the glioma clusters identified and their implications for patient prognosis.

This integrative approach aims to provide a better understanding of glioma heterogeneity and offer insights to develop personalized therapeutic strategies for patients sharing the same molecular characteristics. Although developed for glioma, the proposed analysis pipeline may be applicable to other multi-omics datasets or disease contexts.

2 Materials and Methods

2.1 Data

The multi-omics datasets used in this study comprise transcriptomics (RNA-sequencing) and methylomics (DNA methylation) glioma data available from the TCGA, with patient labels updated following the latest WHO classification guidelines [19,22]. A total of 527 patients (249 astrocytomas, 166 oligodendrogliomas, and 112 GBM) were considered, corresponding to those shared by the methylomics and transcriptomics datasets. The final data accounted for 20201 genes and 301541 CpG sites in the transcriptomics and methylomics datasets, respectively, after the removal of constant variables, probes related to sexual chromosomes, and cross-reactive and polymorphic CpGs. In addition, survival data were retrieved from the TCGA.

The omics datasets were normalized to ensure that the results were not skewed towards the data with a wider range [8]. Specifically, for the CIMLR and intNMF methods, the transcriptomic data was normalized so that it ranged from 0 to 1, by dividing by the maximum value; the methylation data, which already lay within this range, required no further transformation. For the moCluster method, both datasets were standardized (with z-score) and then divided by the first singular value, as recommended.

2.2 Analysis Pipeline

The pipeline developed includes an initial step for data collection and preprocessing, followed by the application of three multi-view clustering algorithms. Each individual clustering method was initially implemented considering 3 clusters, to allow validation by comparing the identified clusters with the adult-type gliomas based on the 2021 WHO classification of CNS tumors. Subsequently, the optimal number of clusters for each method was identified by varying the number of clusters and computing the separation cost and the gap statistic for CIMLR and moCluster, respectively. For intNMF, various numbers of clusters were tested, and the optimal k chosen based on the evaluated metrics (see Sect. 2.3). The analysis of the separation cost function identified an optimal number of clusters as 4 for both CIMLR (cluster ranged from 3 to 14), and intNMF (evaluated for 3–6 clusters). For moCluster, a number from 3 to 6 cluster was evaluated by varying the level of sparsity, identifying 5 as the optimal number of patient grouping.

Next, consensus clustering was performed by considering the best result from each multi-view clustering method and applying average-linkage agglomerative clustering with the traditional co-association matrix as the consensus function. This approach was selected because it outperform methods that maximize cluster similarity [1], and it aligns with our goal of identifying patients consistently clustered together for subsequent molecular characterization of a potentially novel glioma stratification.

Finally, a comprehensive evaluation phase was carried out, including cluster validation metrics, comparison with known clinical glioma types, a literature review of the identified clusters and selected features, and survival analysis of the resulting clusters.

2.3 Evaluation of Clustering Results

To evaluate the clustering performance from multi-view and consensus clustering, four main steps were considered: i) comparison of predicted clusters with diagnostic labels based on the 2021 WHO CNS classification; ii) use of cluster validation measures, namely, the Adjusted Rand Index (ARI), Normalized Mutual Information (NMI), Calinski-Harabasz Index (CHI), Dunn Index (DI), and Average Silhoutte Width (ASW); iii) literature review on relevant features associated with glioma; and iv) survival analysis to assess the prognostic value of the clusters. Kaplan-Meier curves were computed, with the statistical significance of the difference in survival between the curves assessed via the log-rank test.

3 Results and Discussion

3.1 Multi-view Clustering

Table 1 shows the cluster validation measures for each multi-view method. Considering the supervised measures (ARI and NMI), the best clustering performance was obtained for CIMLR, followed by moCluster and intNMF. For the unsupervised measures (CHI, DI and ASW), CIMLR again performed better, but intNMF was superior to moCluster. The increase of the number of clusters determined a decrease in the clustering performance in all methods. However, large ASW values were obtained also for CIMLR and intNMF with 4 clusters, indicating that a strong structure is still present with more groups, and suggesting the potential existence of additional patient stratification [14].

Table 1. Cluster validation measures for each multi-view method (ARI, Adjusted Rand Index; NMI, Normalized Mutual Information; CHI, Calinski-Harabasz Index; DI, Dunn Index; ASW, Average Silhouette Width).

Metric	CIMLR3	CIMLR4	intNMF3	intNMF4	moCluster3	moCluster5
ARI	0.610		0.235		0.365	
NMI	0.604		0.314		0.399	
CHI	64 540	38 544	8 179	1 301	684.603	154.070
DI	8.370	5.075	0.231	0.098	0.019	0.034
ASW	0.954	0.940	0.921	0.734	0.600	0.228

Since CIMLR produced better results, we focus on the corresponding outcome to discuss differences and similarities between the known versus the estimated patient grouping. The results of intNMF and moCluster are available in the appendix Sect. B.

The confusion matrix showing a comparison between the predicted and true glioma patient labels can be found in Table 2. When considering three clusters, the CIMLR method identifies patient groups that are well aligned with the 2021 WHO classification of adult-type glioma. Some overlap is observed between astrocytoma and GBM, as well as between astrocytoma and oligodendroglioma, an expected result given the known molecular and histological similarities between these pairs. Considering the estimated optimal number of 4 clusters, the method identifies three main groups predominantly composed of patients with the same glioma type. This reinforces the alignment of the modern classification with molecular characteristics, supporting the validity of the current diagnostic guidelines. The remaining cluster 3 comprises a subgroup of astrocytomas and oligodendrogliomas.

Table 2. Confusion matrices for CIMLR showing the correspondence between the clusters identified (rows) and the true glioma types (columns). Each block of rows, separated by horizontal lines, corresponds to the method applied by searching for a different number of clusters. The number of rows in each block varies according to the number of clusters identified in the corresponding results.

	Cluster	Astrocytoma	GBM	Oligodendroglioma	Total
CIMLR (3 clusters)	1	30	1	157	188
	2	35	111	9	155
	3	184	0	0	184
CIMLR (4 clusters)	1	36	0	137	173
	2	182	0	0	182
	3	28	1	27	56
	4	3	111	2	116

Figure 1 provides a graphical overview of patients grouping. The top panels (Figs. 1a and 1b) show the similarity matrices between the patients, where red means strong similarity, and yellow means low similarity. Above the matrices, two colored lines indicate the known glioma types and the identified clusters, respectively. When three clusters are considered (Fig. 1a), three blocks are clearly visible in the similarity matrix, each associated to one cluster. Cluster 1 (top red bar) and cluster 2 (top green bar) are predominantly oligodendrogliomas (top blue bar) and GBMs (top dark blue bar), while cluster 3 (top purple bar) is entirely composed of astrocytomas (top light blue bar). However, clusters 1 and 2 also contain subgroups of patients exhibiting high similarity and classified with other glioma types. For example, both clusters include astrocytomas forming distinct blocks in the similarity matrix, while differing from the astrocytomas in cluster 3. Also, cluster 2 contains two distinct blocks with particularly high similarity, both composed of GBM patients. Although these patterns confirm the molecular affinities of patients with the same diagnosis, they also highlight the need for further refinement of glioma classification through the definition of molecular subtypes.

When considering four clusters (Fig. 1b), the similarity matrix reveals a clear four-block structure, with clusters 1 and 2 showing the same pattern of clusters 1 and 3 of the three-cluster scenario. The main difference is the definition of clusters 3 and 4, respectively composed of LGGs and GBMs. In particular, cluster 3 groups astrocytomas and oligodendrogliomas that show strong similarity despite their different diagnoses. This result suggests the potential presence of a distinct molecular profile within this subgroup of LGGs, warranting further investigation.

The bottom part of the figure (Figs. 1c and 1d) depicts the similarity graphs, with clusters indicated by different colors. This representation supports the observations from the similarity matrices, as patients from the same cluster form cohesive groups, with the presence of tightly clustered regions of nodes in those cases where potential subgroups can be identified.

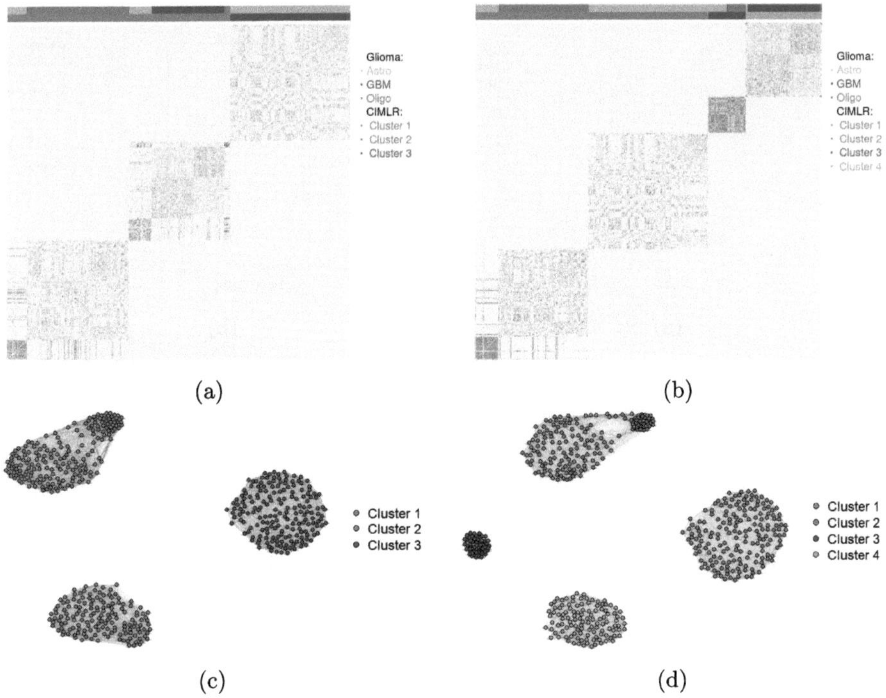

Fig. 1. CIMLR result: **(a)** Similarity matrix with true glioma types and the 3 CIMLR clusters identified. **(b)** Similarity matrix with true glioma types and the 4 CIMLR clusters identified. **(c)** Similarity graph for the 3 CIMLR clusters. **(d)** Similarity graph for the 4 CIMLR clusters.

3.2 Survival Analysis

Kaplan-Meier survival curves were obtained to assess the clinical significance of the estimated clusters. The statistical significance of differences between the survival distributions of the clusters was evaluated by pairwise log-rank tests performed with Benjamini–Hochberg (BH) correction for multiple testing. The significance threshold was set at 0.05.

Figure 2 shows the Kaplan-Meier curves of each cluster identified by CIMLR with three (Fig. 2a) and four clusters (Fig. 2b). In both scenarios, one cluster consistently shows significantly poorer overall survival, with survival differences that are statistically significant compared to the other clusters. This cluster is primarily composed of GBM samples, reflecting the known aggressiveness of this glioma type compared to LGGs. On the other hand, the differences of the

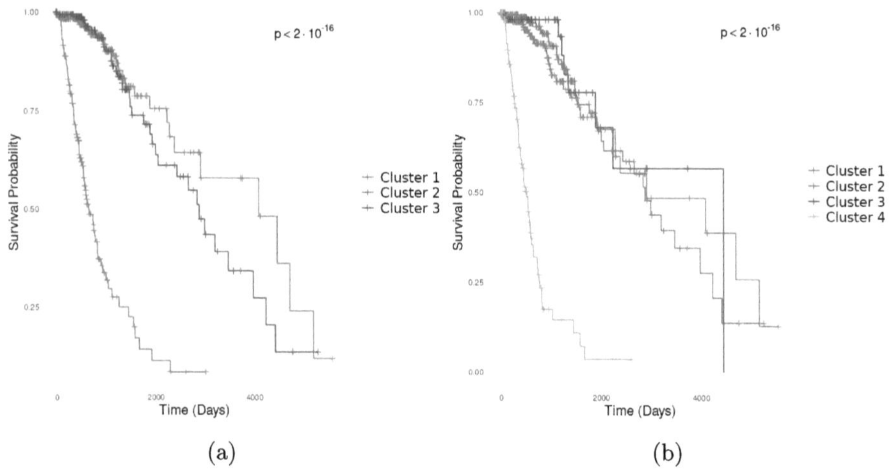

Fig. 2. Kaplan-Meier survival curves for **(a)** CIMLR method with 3 clusters, **(b)** CIMLR with 4 clusters. The events are represented with a vertical line in each curve and the p-values were calculated using the log-rank test. The complete results of pairwise log-rank tests are available at Appendix Sect. C.

survival curves of the other clusters are not statistically significant. While this result could indicate that the clustering obtained has limited prognostic value in the distinction of LGG classes, it is consistent with the clinical outcomes showing that astrocytomas and oligodendrogliomas have similar prognoses. Notably, although clustering is not designed to stratify survival outcomes, it effectively identifies molecular signatures that capture intrinsic glioma heterogeneity. These signatures, even if not directly related to survival, provide critical insight for personalized treatment strategies by characterizing tumor biology at a molecular level.

For the survival analysis of the clusters identified by intNMF and moCluster we refer to the Appendix Sect. C.

3.3 Consensus Clustering

To guarantee a consistent comparison of patient groupings, consensus clustering was applied to the results obtained from CIMLR, intNMF, and moCluster using three clusters. Due to the lower clustering performance of moCluster, and to ensure that only robust and well-supported clustering structures contributed to the final consensus, an additional analysis was performed considering only the results from CIMLR and intNMF.

The initial step in consensus clustering involved constructing a co-association matrix using the outputs from the multi-view clustering methods (Fig. 3). In the 3-methods consensus clustering case, the heatmap reveals several prominent dark blocks along the diagonal (Fig. 3a), indicating groups of patients that were consistently clustered together across the three different methods. This result is confirmed by the 2-methods consensus clustering case (Fig. 3b), which however reveals a more consistent patient clustering across methods, thereby facilitating the identification of a clear dendrogram cut and the interpretation of the resulting groups.

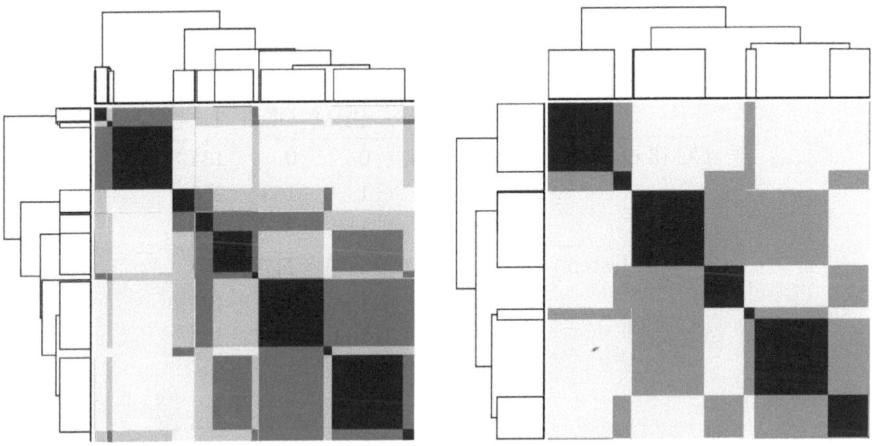

Fig. 3. Heatmap of the co-association matrix from the **(a)** 3 and **(b)** 2 multi-view methods with corresponding dendrograms.

After constructing the co-association matrix and converting it into a dissimilarity matrix, average-link hierarchical clustering was employed to the resulting distance matrix. The dendrograms from the average-link hierarchical clustering are depicted in Fig. 3, above the corresponding heatmaps. To investigate the heterogeneity of glioma beyond the known glioma types, we determined the most suitable number of clusters according to the consensus between three and two methods. Using a threshold applied to the dendrograms, we identified, for the three-method and two-method cases, respectively, 5 and 3 patient clusters that are characterized by high intra-group similarity and low inter-group dissimilarity.

Focusing on consensus clustering with three clusters, it is possible to compare the obtained groups with the known diagnostic labels through supervised measures. Both ARI and NMI resulted higher than those obtained by the single methods (Table 1), respectively, 0.63 and 0.64, suggesting an improved ability of consensus clustering to identify biologically meaningful molecular differences and produce more reliable patient groupings. Considering the unsupervised measures, we obtained CHI = 840.44, DI = 0.50, and ASW = 0.67. Although these values are lower than those obtained by the single multi-view methods, they still indicate a well-defined clustering structure, with good cohesion and separation [14]. Interestingly, consistent results are obtained for consensus clustering with five clusters, with CHI = 798.52, DI = 0.33, and ASW = 0.59, suggesting that the method maintains a stable clustering structure while capturing increased intratumor heterogeneity.

The confusion matrix in Table 3 shows the distribution of the glioma types across the identified clusters.

Table 3. Confusion matrix for the known glioma types versus the consensus clustering (CC) result with 3 clusters (based on two methods), and 5 clusters (based on three methods).

	Cluster	Astro	GBM	Oligo	Total
CC (3 clusters)	1	184	0	0	184
	2	41	1	163	205
	3	24	111	3	138
CC (5 clusters)	1	137	0	117	254
	2	73	1	30	104
	3	18	109	2	129
	4	21	2	15	38
	5	0	0	2	2

For consensus clustering with three clusters, the confusion matrix reveals 3 clusters mainly characterized by one glioma type, with some overlap between LGG (cluster 2) and astrocytoma and GBM types (cluster 3). When considering five clusters we observe the presence of three clusters, namely clusters 2, 3, and 5, that are predominantly composed of a single glioma type (Table 3). Notably, cluster 5 contains only two patients, both oligodendrogliomas. While this potentially suggests a subgroup with a distinct molecular profile, the very small cluster size precludes any robust biological or clinical interpretation. The remaining clusters consist of a mixture of astrocytomas and oligodendrogliomas, indicating a higher degree of heterogeneity that deserves further studies.

Regarding individual multi-view methods, Kaplan-Meier curves were estimated for consensus clustering outputs (Fig. 4). In case of consensus clustering with three clusters (Fig. 4a), the results are aligned with the one obtained for the single methods, with significant differences in survival between cluster 3 (yellow) and the remaining two ($p_{13}, p_{23} < 2 \times 10^{-16}$), while clusters 1 and 2 are not statistically different ($p_{12} = 0.47$).

In contrast, we can observe some differences in the survival curves obtained for the five estimated clusters (Fig. 4b). In agreement with the other results, the cluster mainly composed of GBMs, i.e., cluster 3 (yellow), shows a distinct and accentuated drop in survival probability. Pairwise comparisons with the BH correction were performed, resulting in statistical differences for cluster pairs 1–3, 2–3, and 3–4 ($p_{13}, p_{23} < 2 \times 10^{-16}$, $p_{34} = 9.9 \times 10^{-8}$, respectively), while the difference among the other curves was found not significant. Interestingly, cluster 5 (orange), which is composed of only two oligodendroglioma patients, also shows poor survival, in contrast to the usual prognosis for this glioma type. This unexpected result may suggest the presence of underlying molecular differences affecting survival captured by clustering. However, given the limited sample size, this finding should be interpreted strictly as exploratory. Further validation in larger cohorts would be required to assess whether this pattern is reproducible.

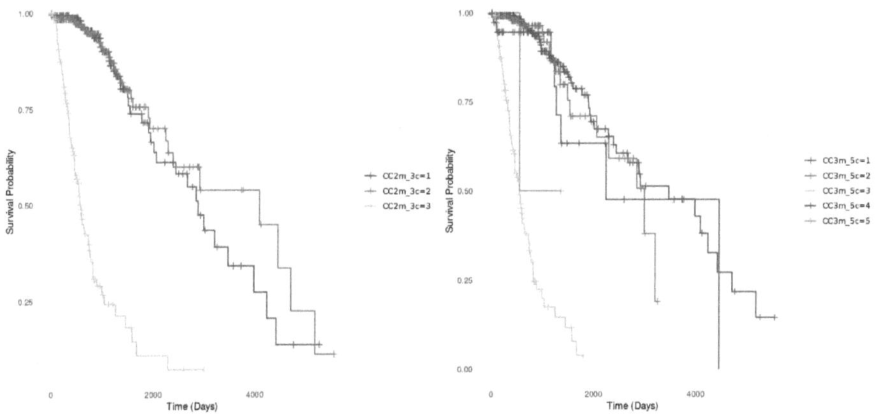

(a) (b)

Fig. 4. Kaplan-Meier curves for the **(a)** 5 and **(b)** 3 predicted consensus clusters. The events were represented with a vertical line in each curve and the *p*-values were calculated using the log-rank test. For both plots, at a significance of 5% the survival distributions of the predicted clusters are not equal.

3.4 Relevant Features

The applied clustering methods allow for the selection of variables relevant for the definition of the identified clusters. Due to the low performances of moCluster (Table 1), this analysis is focused on the variables identified by CIMLR and intNMF. The CIMLR method selected, with a significance of 5 %, 188 583 (58.61 %) and 183 887 (57.15 %) variables for the 3-cluster and 4-cluster cases, respectively, with 179 215 features shared between the two sets. Notably, most of the top-ranked variables are methylomics features, with the first transcriptomics feature in the 75th (*SNAP91*) and 991st (*KIAA0495*) positions for 3 and 4 clusters, respectively. While this result may be biased by the considerably higher number of methylomics variables compared to transcriptomics, it may also indicate a stronger contribution of methylomic features to glioma group separation. This observation is further supported by the 2D visualization of the two omics in a variable subspace generated using t-distributed Stochastic Neighbor Embedding (t-SNE) (Fig. 6), where the methylomics-based representation provides a clearer separation of the clusters.

For the intNMF method, each (sparse) omics-specific coefficient matrix was studied to determine cluster-specific variables (i.e., variables with zero coefficients in all clusters but one). To interpret the relevance of each variable and allow comparison, the coefficients were normalized in each omics matrix by dividing by the maximum value in the corresponding matrix. Figure 5 shows the barplot that resumes the relevance of transcriptomics (RNA) and methylomics (DNA) features in each cluster. The coefficients, ranging from 0 to 1, represent the relative importance of each feature. When considering three clusters (Fig. 5a), we observe that cluster 1, primarily composed of astrocytomas, is almost exclusively characterized by transcriptomic features. In contrast, cluster 2, which includes a mix of LGGs, is mainly defined by methylomic variables. Cluster 3, comprising mostly GBM patients, shows a more balanced contribution from both data types, though with a slight predominance of transcriptomics. Notably, most cluster-specific variables exhibit relatively low coefficients, except for the methylomic features in cluster 2, which display values above 0.8—indicating the presence of highly relevant variables.

When considering 4 clusters (Fig. 5b), intNMF produces clusters more closely aligned with the known glioma types, particularly by splitting the previous cluster 2 into two distinct clusters: cluster 2, predominantly composed of astrocytomas, and cluster 3, mainly consisting of oligodendrogliomas. This outcome, combined with the variable selection performed, may offer insights for improving glioma type characterization and identifying potential targets for glioma-type-specific therapies. For instance, our results suggest that cluster 3 is primarily defined by methylomic features, highlighting methylation as a potentially informative omics layer for explaining oligodendroglioma. Conversely, cluster 2 shows a more balanced contribution from both transcriptomic and methylomic features, although the methylomic layer demonstrates slightly higher relevance, with coefficients above 0.5. The remaining two clusters show patterns consistent with those observed in the three-cluster scenario.

On a consensus clustering perspective, and focusing on the 3 clusters for the 2 methods, some of the top 10 most common relevant variables for each method, based on their contribution to clustering performance, were thoroughly investigated and highlighted in Table 4. Furthermore, the cluster-specific variables from the intNMF method with 3 clusters are all from cluster 2, which is characterized solely by astrocytoma and oligodendroglioma types, meaning that the identified common variables could be only separating LGG from GBM. To complement our feature analysis, some non-consensus variables whose role seems to be pertinent were also highlighted in Table 4.

Table 4. CpG sites selected by the multi-view methods, along with their corresponding genes and known roles in gliomas and other cancers or diseases, when applicable.

CpGsite	Gene	Method	Role in gliomas	Role in cancer or other disease [a]
cg00681103	*CFLAR*	intNMF3, CIMLR3, CIMLR4	Gene significantly correlated with overall survival [18]; decreased expression in LGG compared to non-tumor [27]	
cg17130504	*LZTS2*	intNMF3, CIMLR3, CIMLR4	Up-regulated in LGG and down-regulated in GBM [37].	
cg20452714	*ARTN*	intNMF3, CIMLR3, CIMLR4		Linked to increased tumor size, quick relapse, and shorter survival in hepatocellular carcinoma (primary liver cancer), as well as promoting drug resistance [12].
cg17759443	*ADAM33*	intNMF3, CIMLR3, CIMLR4		Known biomarker for different types of cancer, such as breast cancer [21] and gastric cancer [15].
cg15472784	*KIAA0495*	intNMF3, CIMLR3, CIMLR4	Highlighted by [32] Role in distinguishing GBM, and was found down-regulated in astrocytoma.	
cg07201456	*CHST6*	intNMF3, CIMLR3, CIMLR4	Known molecular factor having a significant negative correlation with the prognosis and survival of glioma patients [40].	
cg21819468	*PDPN*	intNMF3, CIMLR3, CIMLR4	A high expression was thought to be negatively correlated with prognosis, however, recent findings suggest that the gene itself did not have a direct factor in response to treatment, and it is hypothesized that the previous correlation was due to other underlying pathways [34].	
cg20944305	*P2RY1*	intNMF3, CIMLR3, CIMLR4	Up-regulated in high-grade gliomas [16].	
cg05784314	*SLC27A3*	intNMF3, CIMLR3, CIMLR4	High expression has been connected to worse outcomes in GBM [17]	
cg08971281	*PTRF*	intNMF3, CIMLR3, CIMLR4	High *PTRF* mRNA expression is linked with increased malignancy, particularly in high-grade gliomas and IDH wildtype tumors, indicating a link to poor prognosis [30].	
cg02578560	*TTBK1*	CIMLR4, CIMLR3	[2] identified the *TTBK1* gene as downregulated in primary GBM compared to normal brain tissues, suggesting a potential role for *TTBK1* in GBM, yet it is highlighted that further studies are necessary to determine if the low expression of the gene is related to primary GBM tumor growth.	No strong association with cancer [13], but playing an important part in neurodegenerative diseases, such as Alzheimer's and Parkinson's disease [26].
cg18222083	*TMEM106A*	CIMLR4, CIMLR3	Recently highlighted in a glioma classification problem by influencing the distinction of GBM and identified as a potential novel biomarker [32].	Proven to decrease cell proliferation and migration in kidney and lung cancer [11]

[a] For genes without a well-established role in gliomas.

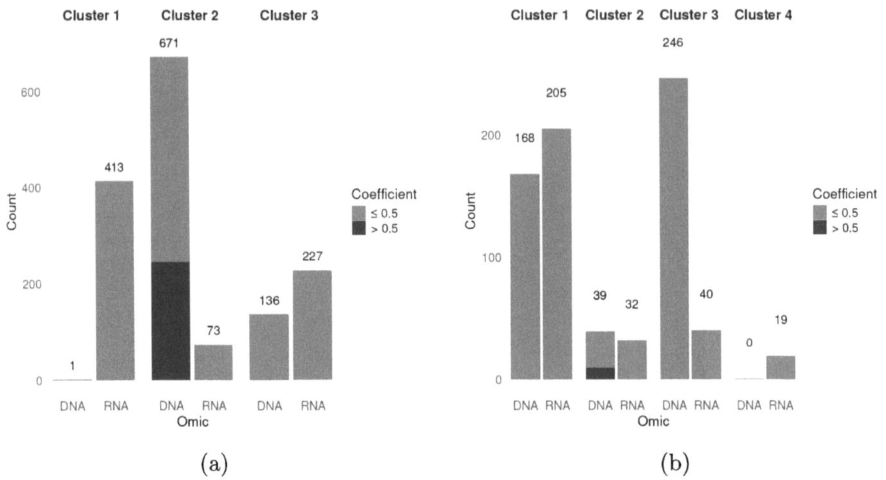

Fig. 5. Bar plots showing the number of cluster-specific variables for each omic in **(a)** the 3 clusters' solution and **(b)** the 4 clusters' solution of intNMF. Bars are divided based on whether the normalized coefficient is above or below 0.5.

4 Conclusion

The present study developed a pipeline for unsupervised patient stratification from multi-omics data, using state-of-the-art multi-view clustering methods applied to glioma transcriptomics and methylomics profiles. A consensus clustering approach based on the co-association matrix and average-linkage hierarchical clustering was used to integrate the results across methods and identify robust patient subgroups. Although developed in the context of glioma, the proposed framework is not disease-specific and can be extended to other cancer types or complex diseases with available multi-omics data.

Among the evaluated methods, CIMLR achieved the best performance, producing well-defined and cohesive clusters. All methods consistently distinguished GBM from LGG cases, placing them in separate clusters. This separation was confirmed by survival analysis, which associated the GBM cluster to poorer outcomes, consistent with clinical expectations. Although, in most of the cases of study, no significant survival differences were observed among the LGG clusters, this aligns with current clinical knowledge suggesting similar prognoses between astrocytomas and oligodendrogliomas. Importantly, the lack of significant survival separation in some predicted clusters should not be considered a shortcoming. Conversely, it suggests that the clustering may capture biologically meaningful heterogeneity within LGGs, which is crucial for further disease stratification and therapeutic development.

Many of the putative biomarkers identified have been previously reported in glioma studies, and their presence in the literature reinforces the trustworthiness of the findings, further validating their established roles in glioma biology. On the other hand, newly discovered biological features, such as *TMEM106A*, *TTBK1*, *ADAM33*, and *ARTN*, which play an important role in other cancers, requires further biological validation.

To deeper capture glioma heterogeneity, consensus clustering was performed integrating the results of multiple multi-view clustering methods. The consensus clustering with three clusters achieved the best alignment with known glioma types according to supervised metrics, demonstrating an improvement to capture the known molecular differences compared to the single multi-view methods and validating the biological relevance of the identified groups. Although unsupervised metrics were not superior to those of the best individual methods, their values are moderately high, indicating the presence of well-defined clusters. Despite the two-method consensus clustering with three clusters (based on CIMLR and intNMF) achieved better overall performance, the three-method approach emerges as a promising approach for exploring glioma subtyping. By synthesizing complementary insights from different clustering techniques, it offers a more integrative and balanced perspective. The identification of 5 optimal patient clusters may reflect deeper and more biologically meaningful differences, providing a richer framework for understanding glioma heterogeneity.

Future directions include exploring different consensus clustering techniques, as well as integrating additional omics layers, which may enhance clustering resolution and improve prognostic utility. The identification of more than three meaningful clusters also suggests that current glioma classifications or available omics datasets may be limiting; expanding both could offer more comprehensive insights and further refine glioma patient stratification.

Acknowledgements. The authors acknowledges Fundação para a Ciência e a Tecnologia I.P. for its financial support via CEECINST/00042/2021, UID/00297/2025 (https://doi.org/10.54499/UID/00297/2025) and UID/PRR/00297/2025 (https://doi.org/10.54499/UID/PRR/00297/2025) (Centro de Matemática e Aplicações – NOVA Math)", UID/00667/2025 (https://doi.org/10.54499/UID/00667/2025) (UNIDEMI), and the research project PTDC/CCI-BIO/4180/2020 "MONET – Multi-omic networks in gliomas" (https://doi.org/10.54499/PTDC/CCI-BIO/4180/2020).

Appendices

A Data Visualization

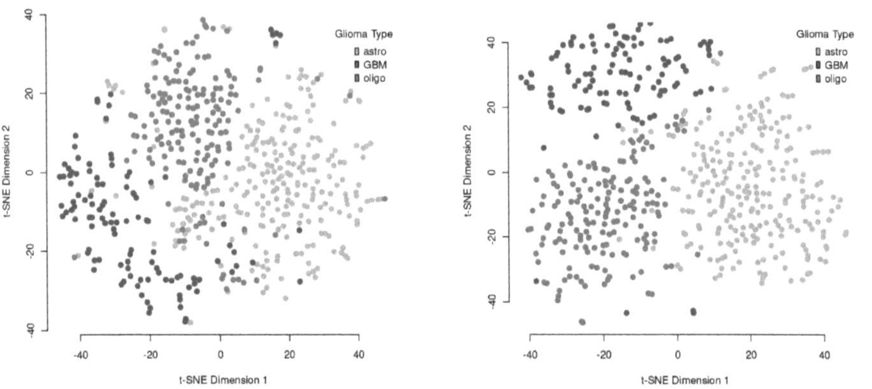

(a) (b)

Fig. 6. t-SNE 2D projection of **(a)** transcriptomics and **(b)** methylomics, where a clear group structure can be observed, particularly for methylomics.

B Multi-view Clustering Results

This section includes the results obtained from intNMF and moCluster multi-view clustering. Both methods were applied by considering three clusters to allow comparison, and an optimal number of clusters, which is different to each method. moCluster was applied following CPCA-based selection of latent components, and sparsity was subsequently introduced. Across different sparsity levels, the results remained consistent with the non-sparse solution. Sparse representations improved clustering performance and produced more stable patient groupings, therefore, our analyses focus on K-means clustering using a sparsity level of 0.50.

The confusion matrix showing a comparison between the predicted and true glioma patient labels is reported in Table 5.

When considering three clusters, both intNMF and moCluster, yield a clustering structure that does not clearly reflect the established diagnostic labels. Specifically, both methods tend to group a substantial number of astrocytoma and oligodendroglioma cases (into cluster 2 for intNMF and cluster 1 for moCluster), while GBM cases are predominantly grouped into a separate cluster (cluster 3). The remaining cluster in each method contains fewer patients, primarily consisting of astrocytoma and oligodendroglioma cases.

Table 5. Confusion matrices for intNMF, and moCluster, showing the correspondence between the clusters identified by each method (rows) and the true glioma types (columns). Each clustering method corresponds to a block of rows, separated by horizontal lines. The number of rows in each block varies according to the number of clusters identified by the respective method.

	Cluster	Astrocytoma	GBM	Oligodendroglioma	Total
intNMF (3 clusters)	1	97	19	47	163
	2	137	0	117	254
	3	15	93	2	110
intNMF (4 clusters)	1	2	102	1	105
	2	163	0	7	170
	3	4	0	120	124
	4	80	10	38	128
moCluster (3 clusters)	1	212	1	141	354
	2	27	2	23	52
	3	10	109	2	121
moCluster (5 clusters)	1	25	1	18	44
	2	48	1	29	78
	3	7	108	2	117
	4	161	2	14	177
	5	8	0	103	111

Considering the estimated optimal number of clusters, all clustering methods show a similar overall behavior. Specifically, each method identifies three main groups predominantly composed of patients with the same glioma type. This reinforces the alignment of the modern classification with molecular characteristics, supporting the validity of the current diagnostic guidelines. Furthermore, it demonstrates the capability of intNMF and moCluster to capture these molecular similarities. The remaining clusters (cluster 4 for intNMF, and clusters 1 and 2 for moCluster) comprise a subgroup of astrocytomas and oligodendrogliomas.

C Survival Analysis

This section contains the survival analysis results for the clusters obtained by intNMF and moCluster methods. When three clusters are considered, the intNMF is the only method leading to all pairwise survival curves with statistical difference (Fig. 7a), suggesting that besides elucidating tumor biology and stratification, the identified clusters may have clinical predictive value. All results of the statistical significance tests can be found in Table 6.

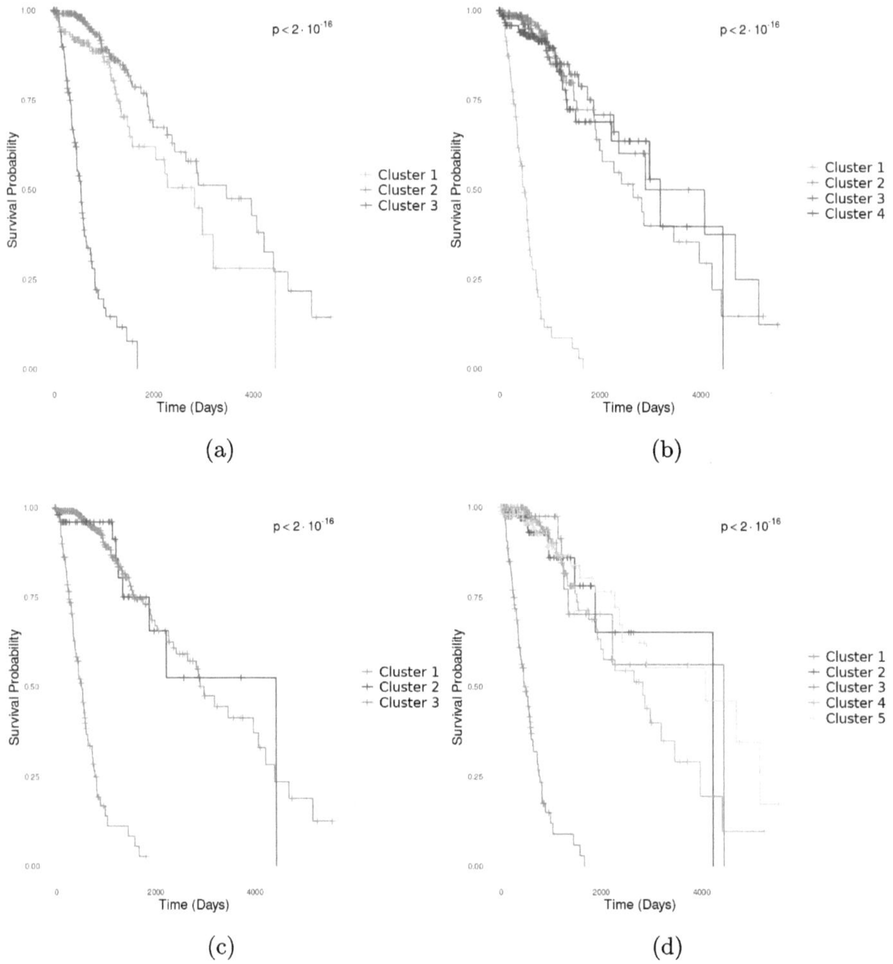

Fig. 7. Kaplan-Meier survival curves for **(a)** intNMF with 3 clusters, **(b)** intNMF with 4 clusters, **(c)** moCluster with 3 clusters, and **(d)** moCluster with 5 clusters. The events are represented with a vertical line in each curve and the *p*-values were calculated using the log-rank test. The complete results of pairwise log-rank tests are available in Table 6.

Table 6. P-values for log-rank test for each survival curve of the clustering methods (CC3, Consensus Clustering with 3 clusters; CC5, Consensus Clustering with 5 clusters).

CIMLR3	Cluster 1	Cluster 2
Cluster 2	9.490×10^{-25}	
Cluster 3	0.287	1.241×10^{-24}

CIMLR4	Cluster 1	Cluster 2	Cluster 3
Cluster 2	0.740		
Cluster 3	0.677	0.677	7.490×10^{-14}
Cluster 4	1.324×10^{-29}	1.752×10^{-36}	7.490×10^{-14}

intNMF3	Cluster 1	Cluster 2
Cluster 2	0.016	
Cluster 3	2.152×10^{-22}	4.696×10^{-46}

intNMF4	Cluster 1	Cluster 2	Cluster 3
Cluster 2	9.261×10^{-39}		
Cluster 3	2.707×10^{-29}	0.670	
Cluster 4	5.708×10^{-26}	0.869	0.670

intNMF4	Cluster 1	Cluster 2	Cluster 3	Cluster 4
Cluster 2	5.805×10^{-16}			
Cluster 3	9.332×10^{-38}	1.559×10^{-02}		
Cluster 4	0.641	3.963×10^{-12}	1.281×10^{-27}	
Cluster 5	0.117	1.017×10^{-04}	3.091×10^{-13}	0.050

intNMF4	Cluster 1	Cluster 2	Cluster 3	Cluster 4	Cluster 5
Cluster 2	3.750×10^{-37}				
Cluster 3	1.846×10^{-03}	6.777×10^{-08}			
Cluster 4	7.514×10^{-02}	5.465×10^{-16}	8.649×10^{-05}		
Cluster 5	5.467×10^{-13}	6.175×10^{-03}	7.844×10^{-02}	8.442×10^{-07}	
Cluster 6	0.399	1.994×10^{-19}	2.916×10^{-02}	2.547×10^{-02}	1.620×10^{-06}

moCluster3	Cluster 1	Cluster 2
Cluster 2	0.928	
Cluster 3	6.275×10^{-62}	4.200×10^{-13}

moCluster5	Cluster 1	Cluster 2	Cluster 3	Cluster 4
Cluster 2	0.878			
Cluster 3	3.483×10^{-12}	1.318×10^{-18}		
Cluster 4	0.878	0.878	4.843×10^{-41}	
Cluster 5	0.878	0.878	6.983×10^{-26}	0.434

CC3	Cluster 1	Cluster 2
Cluster 2	0.474	
Cluster 3	8.619×10^{-28}	5.526×10^{-29}

CC5	Cluster 1	Cluster 2	Cluster 3	Cluster 4
Cluster 2	0.556			
Cluster 3	5.819×10^{-44}	5.819×10^{-44}		
Cluster 4	0.472	0.798	9.882×10^{-08}	
Cluster 5	0.162	0.333	0.471	0.556

References

1. Brière, G., Darbo, É., Thébault, P., Uricaru, R.: Consensus clustering applied to multi-omics disease subtyping. BMC Bioinform. **22**(1), 361 (2021). https://doi.org/10.1186/s12859-021-04279-1
2. Bustos, M.A., et al: Cell-free plasma micrornas that identify patients with glioblastoma. Lab. Invest. **102**(7), 711–721 (2022). https://doi.org/10.1038/s41374-021-00720-4. https://www.sciencedirect.com/science/article/pii/S0023683722002069
3. Cai, Z., Poulos, R.C., Liu, J., Zhong, Q.: Machine learning for multi-omics data integration in cancer. iScience **25**(2), 103798 (2022). https://doi.org/10.1016/j.isci.2022.103798
4. Cantini, L., Zakeri, P., Hernandez, C., et al.: Benchmarking joint multi-omics dimensionality reduction approaches for the study of cancer. Nat. Commun. **12**, 124 (2021). https://doi.org/10.1038/s41467-020-20430-7
5. Chalise, P., Fridley, B.L.: Integrative clustering of multi-level 'omic data based on non-negative matrix factorization algorithm. PLoS ONE (2017). https://doi.org/10.1371/journal.pone.0176278
6. Chauvel, C., Novoloaca, A., Veyre, P., Reynier, F., Becker, J.: Evaluation of integrative clustering methods for the analysis of multi-omics data. Briefings Bioinform. **21**(2), 541–552 (2019). https://doi.org/10.1093/bib/bbz015
7. Fred, A.: Finding consistent clusters in data partitions. In: Kittler, J., Roli, F. (eds.) Multiple Classifier Systems, pp. 309–318. Springer, Heidelberg (2001)
8. Fridley, B., Wang, X. (eds.): Statistical Genomics. Humana, New York, NY (2023). https://doi.org/10.1007/978-1-0716-2986-4. ISBN: 978-1-0716-2986-4
9. Ghaemi, R., Sulaiman, M.N., Ibrahim, H.: A survey: clustering ensembles techniques, vol. 50 (2009)
10. Golalipour, K., Akbari, E., Hamidi, S.S., Lee, M., Enayatifar, R.: From clustering to clustering ensemble selection: a review. Eng. Appl. Artif. Intell. **104**, 104388 (2021). https://doi.org/10.1016/j.engappai.2021.104388. https://www.sciencedirect.com/science/article/pii/S0952197621002360
11. Herrera-Quiterio, G.A., Encarnación-Guevara, S.: The transmembrane proteins (tmem) and their role in cell proliferation, migration, invasion, and epithelial-mesenchymal transition in cancer. Front. Oncol. **13** (2023). https://doi.org/10.3389/fonc.2023.1244740. https://www.frontiersin.org/journals/oncology/articles/10.3389/fonc.2023.1244740

12. Hezam, K., Jiang, J., Sun, F., Zhang, X., Zhang, J.: Artemin promotes oncogenicity, metastasis and drug resistance in cancer cells. Rev. Neurosci. **29**(1), 93–98 (2018). https://doi.org/10.1515/revneuro-2017-0029
13. Ji, J., et al.: Long noncoding RNA SChLAP1 forms a growth-promoting complex with HNRNPL in human glioblastoma through stabilization of ACTN4 and activation of NF-KB signaling. Clin. Cancer Res. **25**(22), 6868–6881 (2019). https://doi.org/10.1158/1078-0432.CCR-19-0747
14. Kaufman, L., Rousseeuw, P.: Partitioning Around Medoids (Program PAM), chap. 2, pp. 68–125. Wiley (1990). https://doi.org/10.1002/9780470316801.ch2. https://onlinelibrary.wiley.com/doi/abs/10.1002/9780470316801.ch2
15. Kim, K.E., et al: Expression of ADAM33 is a novel regulatory mechanism in IL-18-secreted process in gastric cancer1. J. Immunol. **182**(6), 3548–3555 (2009). https://doi.org/10.4049/jimmunol.0801695
16. Ko, E.A., Zhou, T.: GPCR genes as a predictor of glioma severity and clinical outcome. J. Int. Med. Res. **50**(7), 03000605221113911 (2022). https://doi.org/10.1177/03000605221113911, pMID: 35903880
17. Korbecki, J., Kojder, K., Jeżewski, D., Simińska, D., Tomasiak, P., et al: Reduced expression of very-long-chain Acyl-CoA synthetases slc27a4 and slc27a6 in the glioblastoma tumor compared to the peritumoral area. Brain Sci. **13**(5) (2023). https://doi.org/10.3390/brainsci13050771. https://www.mdpi.com/2076-3425/13/5/771
18. Li, X., et al: Prognostic model and nomogram construction and validation with an autophagy-related gene signature in low-grade gliomas. Front. Genet. **13** (2022). https://doi.org/10.3389/fgene.2022.905751. https://www.frontiersin.org/journals/genetics/articles/10.3389/fgene.2022.905751
19. Louis, D.N., et al.: The 2021 who classification of tumors of the central nervous system: a summary. Neuro Oncol. **23**(8), 1231–1251 (2021). https://doi.org/10.1093/neuonc/noab106
20. Lourenço, A., Rota Bulò, S., Fred, A., Pelillo, M.: Consensus clustering with robust evidence accumulation. In: Heyden, A., Kahl, F., Olsson, C., Oskarsson, M., Tai, X.C. (eds.) Energy Minimization Methods in Computer Vision and Pattern Recognition, pp. 307–320. Springer, Heidelberg (2013)
21. Manica, G., Ribeiro, C., Oliveira, M., et al.: Down regulation of ADAM33 as a predictive biomarker of aggressive breast cancer. Sci. Rep. **7**, 44414 (2017). https://doi.org/10.1038/srep44414
22. Mendonça, M.L., et al.: Updating TCGA glioma classification through integration of molecular data following the latest who guidelines. Sci. Data **12**, 935 (2025). https://doi.org/10.1038/s41597-025-05117-2
23. Meng, C., Helm, D., Frejno, M., Kuster, B.: mocluster: identifying joint patterns across multiple omics data sets. J. Proteome Res. **15**(3), 755–765 (2016). https://doi.org/10.1021/acs.jproteome.5b00824
24. Mo, Q., et al.: Pattern discovery and cancer gene identification in integrated cancer genomic data. Proc. Natl. Acad. Sci. U.S.A. **110**(11), 4245–4250 (2013). https://doi.org/10.1073/pnas.1208949110
25. Pierre-Jean, M., Deleuze, J.F., Le Floch, E., Mauger, F.: Clustering and variable selection evaluation of 13 unsupervised methods for multi-omics data integration. Briefings Bioinform. **21**(6), 2011–2030 (2019). https://doi.org/10.1093/bib/bbz138
26. Purushothaman, K., Sivasankar, E., Krishnamoorthy, M., et al.: Computational identification of potential tau tubulin kinase 1 (TTBK1) inhibitors: a structural analog approach. In Silico Pharmacol. **12**, 66 (2024). https://doi.org/10.1007/s40203-024-00242-z

27. Qiao, Q., Wang, Y., Zhang, R., Pang, Q.: Autophagy related DNA methylation signature predict clinical prognosis and immune microenvironment in low-grade glioma. Transl. Cancer Res. **11**(7), 2157–2174 (2022). https://doi.org/10.21037/tcr-22-310
28. Ramazzotti, D., Lal, A., Wang, B., et al.: Multi-omic tumor data reveal diversity of molecular mechanisms that correlate with survival. Nat. Commun. **9**, 4453 (2018). https://doi.org/10.1038/s41467-018-06921-8
29. Shen, R., Olshen, A.B., Ladanyi, M.: Integrative clustering of multiple genomic data types using a joint latent variable model with application to breast and lung cancer subtype analysis. Bioinformatics **25**(22), 2906–2912 (2009). https://doi.org/10.1093/bioinformatics/btp543
30. Sun, S., Yang, C., Wang, K., et al.: Molecular and clinical characterization of PTRF in glioma via 1,022 samples. BMC Cancer **23**, 551 (2023). https://doi.org/10.1186/s12885-023-11001-2
31. Vega-Pons, S., Ruiz-Shulcloper, J.: A survey of clustering ensemble algorithms. IJPRAI **25**, 337–372 (2011). https://doi.org/10.1142/S0218001411008683
32. Vieira, F.G., Bispo, R., Lopes, M.B.: Integration of multi-omics data for the classification of glioma types and identification of novel biomarkers. Bioinform. Biol. Insights **18**, 11779322241249563 (2024). https://doi.org/10.1177/11779322241249563, pMID: 38737722
33. Wang, B., et al.: Similarity network fusion for aggregating data types on a genomic scale. Nat. Methods **11**, 333–337 (2014). https://doi.org/10.1038/nmeth.2810
34. Wang, X., Wang, X., Li, J., et al.: PDPN contributes to constructing immunosuppressive microenvironment in IDH wildtype glioma. Cancer Gene Ther. **30**, 345–357 (2023). https://doi.org/10.1038/s41417-022-00550-6
35. Wesseling, P., Capper, D.: Who 2016 classification of gliomas. Neuropathol. Appl. Neurobiol. **44**(2), 139–150 (2018). https://doi.org/10.1111/nan.12432
36. Xanthopoulos, P.: A review on consensus clustering methods. In: Optimization in Science and Engineering: In Honor of the 60th Birthday of Panos M. Pardalos (2014). https://api.semanticscholar.org/CorpusID:58626921
37. Yan, C., Su, L., Qi, X., Yang, Y., Wu, J.: Oncogenic involvement of NF-kB signaling pathway in glioma. Cancer Res. **80**(16_Suppl.), 4735 (2020). https://doi.org/10.1158/1538-7445.AM2020-4735
38. Yang, L., Yang, Y., Huang, L., Cui, X., Liu, Y.: From single- to multi-omics: future research trends in medicinal plants. Briefings Bioinform. **24**(1), bbac485 (2023). https://doi.org/10.1093/bib/bbac485
39. Zhang, Z., Xiao, Y., Zhao, S., et al.: FAM109B plays a tumorigenic role in low-grade gliomas and is associated with tumor-associated macrophages (TAMs). J. Transl. Med. **22**, 833 (2024). https://doi.org/10.1186/s12967-024-05641-6
40. Zhao, B., Xuan, R., Yang, G., et al.: A novel golgi related genes based correlation prognostic index can better predict the prognosis of glioma and responses to immunotherapy. Res. Square Preprint (2024). https://doi.org/10.21203/rs.3.rs-3961611/v1, version 1

Author Index

P. T. Monteiro (Ed.): CMSB 2026, LNBI 16678, p. 373, 2027.
https://doi.org/10.1007/978-3-032-30870-2

MIX
Papier aus verantwortungsvollen Quellen
Paper from responsible sources
FSC® C105338

If you have any concerns about our products,
you can contact us on
ProductSafety@springernature.com

In case Publisher is established outside the EU,
the EU authorized representative is:
Springer Nature Customer Service Center GmbH
Europaplatz 3, 69115 Heidelberg, Germany

Printed by Libri Plureos GmbH
in Hamburg, Germany